China, Hong Kong and the World Economy

Also by Lok Sang Ho

EXCHANGE RATE REGIMES AND MACROECONOMIC STABILITY
(*edited with Chi-wa Yuen*)

PRINCIPLES OF PUBLIC POLICY PRACTICE

HAPPINESS AND PUBLIC POLICY: Theory, Case Studies and Implications
(*edited with Yew-kwang Ng*)

Also by Robert Ash

CHINA'S ECONOMIC REFORM: A Study with Documents
(*with Christopher Howe and Y.Y. Kueh*)

CHINA'S INTEGRATION IN ASIA: Economic Security and Strategic Issues (*editor*)

CHINA'S ACCESSION TO THE WORLD TRADE ORGANIZATION: National and
International Perspectives (*edited with Heike Holbig*)

HONG KONG IN TRANSITION: One Country, Two Systems
(*edited with Peter Ferdinand, Brian Hook and Robin Porter*)

China, Hong Kong and the World Economy

Studies on Globalization

Festschrift in Honour of Professor Y.Y. Kueh

Edited by

Lok Sang Ho

and

Robert Ash

First published 2006 by
PALGRAVE MACMILLAN
Houndmills, Basingstoke, Hampshire RG21 6XS and
175 Fifth Avenue, New York, N.Y. 10010
Companies and representatives throughout the world

PALGRAVE MACMILLAN is the global academic imprint of the Palgrave
Macmillan division of St. Martin's Press, LLC and of Palgrave Macmillan Ltd.
Macmillan® is a registered trademark in the United States, United Kingdom
and other countries. Palgrave is a registered trademark in the European
Union and other countries.

ISBN 13: 978–1–4039–8742–6
ISBN 10: 1–4039–8742–4

This book is printed on paper suitable for recycling and made from fully
managed and sustained forest sources.

A catalogue record for this book is available from the British Library.

Library of Congress Cataloging-in-Publication Data
China, Hong Kong and the World Economy : Studies on Globalization /
edited by Lok Sang Ho and Robert Ash.
    p. cm.
  Festschrift in honour of Professor Y.Y. Kueh.
  Includes bibliographical references and index.
  ISBN 1–4039–8742–4 (hardback)
    1. China–Economic policy–2000- 2. China–Foreign economic relations.
3. Hong Kong (China)–Economic policy. 4. Hong Kong (China)–Foreign
economic relations. 5. Globalization. I. Ho, Lok-sang. II. Ash, Robert F.
HC427.95.C438 2006
337.51–dc22   2005056586

10   9   8   7   6   5   4   3   2   1
15 14 13 12 11 10 09 08 07 06

Printed and bound in Great Britain by
Antony Rowe Ltd, Chippenham and Eastbourne

Contents

Acknowledgements   vii

Foreword by Joseph C.H. Chai   viii

Foreword by Vincent Hoi Chuen Cheng   x

Notes on the Contributors   xi

List of Abbreviations   xv

1   Introduction   1
  Lok Sang Ho and Robert Ash

Part I   China and Globalization

2   China and the Global Economy: Challenges, Opportunities, Responsibilities   17
  Joseph E. Stiglitz

3   Unilateral and Regional Trade Liberalization: China's World Trade Organization Accession and Free Trade Agreement with the Association of South East Asian Nations   32
  Mesut Saygili and Kar-yiu Wong

4   The Economic Impact of China's Emergence as a Major Trading Nation   65
  Wing Thye Woo

5   Effects of Real Exchange Rate Volatility and Misalignment on Commodity Exports: The Case of China   87
  Jan P. Voon, Guangzhong Li and Jimmy Ran

6   A Sustainable Currency Regime for Hong Kong and the Mainland   101
  Lok Sang Ho

Part II   Hong Kong as China's City and as a Global City

7   Hong Kong as a Financial Centre of China and the World   121
  Y.C. Jao

8   The Evolving Role of Hong Kong as China's Middleman   152
  Yun-wing Sung

9   Market Integration between Hong Kong and the Chinese Mainland   170
  C. Simon Fan, Na Li and Xiangdong Wei

10 Economic Integration between Hong Kong and Mainland China: 186
Did Trade Hurt Hong Kong's Unskilled Workers?
Kui-yin Cheung and C. Simon Fan

11 Macroeconomic Instability in Hong Kong: Internal and 200
External Factors
Yue Ma and Raymond C.W. Ng

**Part III Foreign Direct Investment, Technology Transfer
and Economic Restructuring**

12 Taiwan's Scientific and Technological Development: A Newly- 221
industralizing Economy Experience of Institutional Evolution
Christopher Howe

13 Spillover Effects of Foreign Direct Investment and Technology 239
Transfer in China: Before and after its Accession to the
World Trade Organization
Ping Lin

14 The Impact of Trade Policy on Total Factor Productivity, 254
Efficiency and Technology: The Case of Chinese Provinces
in the 1990s
Yu Chen

**Part IV Trade, Investment and Implications for
Key Economic Sectors**

15 Investment, Investment Efficiency and Economic Growth 273
in China
Jun Zhang

16 Recent Developments in China's Agriculture and Prospects for 297
Future Agricultural Trade: Observations from the Grain Sector
Robert Ash

17 Environmental Impact on the Manufacturing Sector of China's 317
Accession to the World Trade Organization
Joseph C.H. Chai

Part V Corporate Governance and Management

18 The Supervisory Board in Chinese Corporate Governance 329
On Kit Tam and Helen Wei Hu

19 Managerial Autonomy and Firm Performance in China's 350
Listed Firms
Eric C. Chang and Sonia M.L. Wong

Y.Y. Kueh (Yak Yeow Kueh) Bibliography 371

Name Index 375

Subject Index 380

Acknowledgements

The Editors thank the Chinese University of Hong Kong, which sponsored the lecture by Professor Joseph Stiglitz in March 2005, and which gave us permission to publish Professor Stiglitz's contribution. Professor Stiglitz has kindly gone over the transcribed speech and made amendments.

Foreword

This Festschrift is dedicated to Professor Y.Y. Kueh (Kueh Yak Yeow) to mark his retirement after four decades of highly devoted university teaching and research. The Festschrift carries the same title as the course which Professor Kueh has taught for many years. As a teacher, Professor Kueh has nurtured two or three generations of prominent scholars and highly successful professionals and leaders in the public and banking and industry sectors. I am honoured to write this Preface on behalf of colleagues, associates, and his former students who have contributed to this congratulatory volume.

Y.Y. Kueh and I have a great deal in common and have shared many experiences in our lives. We both come from one of the least developed corners of the world, Sarawak, whose only claims to fame have been the head-hunting tradition of the indigenous Dayak tribes, and the Sarawak Museum which keeps many of the heads hunted. We both attended the same secondary school in Sarawak in the 1950s. We both pursued our undergraduate studies in Hong Kong; and in the 1960s, equipped with a scholarship, we both undertook our postgraduate studies in what was then West Germany. We went to Harvard one shortly after the other on post-doctoral studies. We even pursued the same area of study – economics – and, being of Chinese origin and concerned with economic development, we both have naturally focused our research on the economy of the Chinese mainland.

However, our shared experience ends when it comes to scholarly achievements, for Y.Y. Kueh has been a major figure in the tribe of China researchers and among academics whose work has revolved around China's post-1978 economic reforms and the earlier periods. Y.Y. Kueh is a prolific writer, a meticulous researcher and a deep thinker with a rare original flair. His brilliant insights have enabled him to undertake pivotal research, establish new baselines for further research, and open up fresh perspectives.

Kueh is also a gifted and conscientious editor. Some of the special issues of *The China Quarterly* edited by him have become academic best sellers and major points of reference for work on contemporary Chinese economics. In particular, his pioneering work on the great Chinese famine of 1959–61 is a major contribution to our knowledge and understanding of the Chinese economy under Mao Zedong. One reviewer fittingly rated this book about agricultural instability in China as a masterpiece of economic research, but he himself regards this, nevertheless, as a sideline.

Kueh's interest in the Chinese economy is wide ranging. He follows the School of Walter Eucken, the German economist inspired by Edmund Husserl (the nineteenth-century German founder of the philosophy of phenomenology), and is interested in anything 'phenomenal'. He has virtually covered every aspect of the contemporary Chinese economy, including economic planning and reforms (his specialty by training), industry, finance, agriculture and foreign trade and investment. Being based in Hong Kong, especially after the handover to Chinese sovereignty, which signals yet another unique phenomenon of regional economic integration of global significance, Kueh has extended his research to the new frontier as well.

On a more personal note, I should like to add that Kueh has always been a terrific friend, not only to me, but to my family as well. He truly values his friends and students. They, in turn, know that he would never let them down and hold him in high esteem. We all wish him a happy and relaxed life in retirement.

JOSEPH C.H. CHAI

Foreword

It is an honour and a pleasure for me to write a short message for this new book, *China, Hong Kong and the World Economy: Studies on Globalization* to mark the retirement of Professor Y.Y. Kueh. Professor Kueh is one of the pioneers in using scientific data to research the Chinese economy. He has written profusely on China and general economic issues and the works he has published have greatly helped both the academic and business world in understanding the immense complexity and changes in the Chinese economy. The experience of China in the last 50 years is a history of both great human errors and astonishing achievements. The rise and fall of economic central planning, and the success and problems of transforming the Chinese economy into a socialist market economy, offer great insight for governments and academia around the world and generate new policy ideas on economic growth. One hopes the world will be better as a result of the Chinese experience.

I had the great fortune of having been a student of Professor Kueh in the 1970s when I was studying economics at the New Asia College of the Chinese University of Hong Kong. I attended his classes which stimulated my strong interest in the Chinese economy and the comparison between central planning and market-driven economic development. I have benefited enormously from his teaching as well as his care for his students.

I wish him all the best in his retirement. However, I also sincerely wish that he could continue his academic research. We would all benefit from his work.

VINCENT HOI CHUEN CHENG
Chairman (Asia-Pacific)
The Hongkong and Shanghai Banking Corporation Limited

Notes on the Contributors

Robert Ash is Professor of Economics with reference to China and Taiwan in the Departments of Economics, and Financial Management Studies, at the School of Oriental and African Studies (SOAS), University of London. He is also Director of the Taiwan Studies Programme at SOAS, as well as being an Assistant Dean of the Faculty of Law and Social Sciences at the School. He was previously Director of the Contemporary China Institute at SOAS and Coordinator of the EU–China Academic Network.

Joseph C.H. Chai has recently retired from the University of Queensland, where he spent most of his academic career focusing on teaching and research into the Chinese economy. His books include, among others, *Financial Reform and Economic Development in China* (Advances in Chinese Economic Studies Series, with James Laurenceson, Edward Elgar 2003), *Economic History of Modern China* (with Sukhan Jackson and Howard White, Brunner Routledge 2001), *China's Economic Growth and Transition: Macroeconomic, Environmental and Social/Regional Dimensions* (edited with by C.A. Tisdell, Nova Science 1997).

Eric C. Chang is the Director and Chair of Finance of the School of Business at the University of Hong Kong. He received his PhD in Finance from Purdue University in 1982. Professor Chang is known for his research in derivative securities, international finance, capital asset pricing, mutual fund management and performance evaluation. He has published more than 30 articles in various leading journals.

Yu Chen has a PhD in Economics from the University of Auvergne-Clermont, Clermont Ferrand, France. She is Assistant Professor in Economics at the Faculty of Social Sciences and Humanities, University of Macau. Her research interests include the Chinese economy, international trade, foreign direct investment, productivity, economics of transition and institutions.

Kui-yin Cheung is an Associate Professor in the Department of Economics at Lingnan University, Hong Kong. He obtained his PhD in economics from the University of Washington, Seattle, USA. His research interests include applied econometrics and economic issues in Hong Kong and China. He is the co-author of several books and has published various articles locally and overseas.

C. Simon Fan is an Associate Professor of Economics at Lingnan University, Hong Kong. Holding a PhD from Brown University, his primary research areas are development economics and population/labour economics. His publications have appeared in *Economica, Economic Theory, Journal of Comparative Economics, Journal of Development Economics, Journal of Economic Behavior and Organization, Labour Economics, Oxford Economic Papers, Southern Economic Journal*, and other journals and scholarly books.

Lok Sang Ho is Professor of Economics at Lingnan University and Honorary Research Fellow of the Hong Kong Institute of Asia Pacific Studies, the Chinese University of Hong Kong. The Chinese economy is among his many research interests, and this work is mainly focused on monetary and fiscal policies. He is the author of *Principles of Public Policy Practice*, and joint editor (with Chi-wa Yuen) of *Exchange Rate Regimes and Macroeconomic Stability*, both published by Kluwer Academic Publishers, among other books and journal articles.

Christopher Howe is currently Research Professor, Chinese Business Management, School of Oriental and African Studies, London and Fellow of the British Academy and Chair of the Academy's China Panel. He is the author of various books and articles on China, Japan and East Asia. Publications include *The Origins of Japanese Trade Supremacy: Development and Technology in Asia from 1540 to the Pacific War* (Chicago University Press 1999) and, with Y.Y. Kueh, *China's Economic Reform: A Study with Documents* (Routledge).

Helen Wei Hu is a PhD candidate in the Department of Management, Faculty of Business and Economics, Monash University, Australia. She is a graduate of Tongji University, China and the University of London.

Y.C. Jao is the Honorary Professor in School of Economics and Finance in the University of Hong Kong where he has served for more than 30 years. He is the author of many books, including *Hong Kong as an International Financial Centre*, Hong Kong (City University Press 1997), and *The Asian Financial Crises and the Ordeal of Hong Kong*, (Westport CT and London, Quorum Books 2001).

Guangzhong Li is based at Zhongshan University, Guangzhou. His research interests include exchange rate economics and applied econometrics. Guangzhong is now working on exchange rate dynamics and the roles of financial and economic variables in predicting nominal exchange rates.

Na Li got her MPhil degree in Economics from the Department of Economics, Lingnan University.

Ping Lin is Professor of Economics at Lingnan University of Hong Kong. He is also a research fellow at the Centre for Public Policy Studies at Lingnan University. His research interests are centred on industrial organization, competition laws/policy in East Asia, the economics of innovation, foreign direct investment and technology transfer. His publications have appeared in the *Journal of Industrial Economics, International Journal of Industrial Organization, Review of Industrial Organization, European Economic Review, Journal of Economic Theory, Canadian Journal of Economics, Oxford Economic Papers*, and other academic journals.

Yue Ma obtained his BSc in optimal control theory from Xiamen University in China and his PhD in economics and econometrics from Manchester University. His research interests include economic modelling of exchange rate and banking. He is Professor of Economics at Lingnan University, Hong Kong, and also a Research Fellow of the Centre for Macroeconomics Studies, Xiamen University, China.

Raymond C.W. Ng attained his doctorate degree in economics at the University of Lancaster, England, in 1994. He is currently Senior Lecturer at the College of International Education, Hong Kong Baptist University. His areas of research interest include primarily open-economy macroeconomics and the economic development of Hong Kong.

Jimmy Ran has a PhD from West Virginia University, USA. His research areas include international finance, trade, monetary and macroeconomics, and economic development. He has been published in the *Southern Economic Journal, Applied Economics, Pacific Economic Review, Journal of Economic Research*, and is also the author of various book chapters. He has served as a referee for those journals. He is currently Associate Professor in Lingnan University, Hong Kong.

Mesut Saygili is a PhD candidate at the University of Washington. He received a master's degree from Middle East Technical University, Turkey in 1999 and another one from the University of Washington in 2002. He worked for the Under-secretary for Foreign Trade in Turkey in 1996 and is currently an on-leave researcher in the Central Bank of Turkey. His fields of research are international economics, econometrics and macroeconomics.

Joseph E. Stiglitz is one of the three 2001 Nobel Laureates in Economic Science. A former Chief Economist at the World Bank, he is currently University Professor of Economics at Columbia University.

Yun-Wing Sung is well known for his work on the relationship between Hong Kong Special Administration Region (SAR) and China. He is currently head of the Economics Department at the Chinese University. He is an editor of, and a contributor to, *The China-Hong Kong Connection: The Key to China's Open Door Policy* (Cambridge University Press).

On Kit Tam is Associate Dean (International) Faculty of Business and Economics, and Director, China Research Center, Monash Asia Institute, Monash University. He has published on China's economic and financial reform and corporate governance development.

Jan P. Voon is an Associate Professor at the Department of Economics, Lingnan University, Hong Kong. He specializes in Agricultural Economics, Public Sector Economics, Cost-Benefit Analysis, and the Chinese Economy. He has published more than 30 papers in different refereed economic journals.

Xiangdong Wei is currently a Professor in the Department of Economics, Lingnan University, Hong Kong. He is also an Honorary Research Fellow at the Business School, University of Birmingham, UK. His main areas of research are in labour economics, international trade and finance, and the Chinese and Hong Kong economies. He has published papers in internationally well-known journals such as *Journal of International Economics, Journal of Comparative Economics, Industrial and Labor Relations Review, Applied Economics, Southern Economic Journal*, and others.

Kar-yiu Wong is a Professor of Economics at the University of Washington. He received his PhD from Columbia University in 1983, specializing in international trade, commercial policy, economic growth, and Asian economies. He is the founding President of the Asia-Pacific Economic Association and the founding Director of the Research Center for International Economics. He has organized more than 30 conferences in the past ten years on themes related to international economics and Asian economies.

Sonia M.L. Wong is an Assistant Professor at the Department of Finance and Insurance of the Lingnan University. Her research focuses on China's financial sector reforms. She has published papers on the country's foreign exchange and banking reforms as well as the corporate governance of China's listed enterprises.

Wing Thye Woo is Professor of Economics, University of California, Davis, and Director of the East Asia Program at the Earth Institute of Columbia University. He is currently Editor of Asian Economic Papers and Coordinator of the Asian Economic Panel. He has been an adviser to a number of governments, including China, Indonesia, Malaysia and the US.

Jun Zhang is Professor of Economics at Department of Economics and Director for China Centre for Economic Studies (CCES) at Fudan University, Shanghai, China. He is also Adjunct Professor for Eexcutive MBA programmes at China Europe International Business School (CEIBS) and ASM–Aetna School of Management at Shanghai Jiaotong University.

List of Abbreviations

ADF	Augmented Dickey-Fuller
AFC	Asian Financial Crisis
AI	Authorized Institutions
ANOVA	analysis of variance
ASEAN	Association of South East Asian Nations
AUM	assets under management
BIS	Bank for International Settlements
BOD	Board of Directors
C&I	construction and installation works
CAR	capital adequacy ratio
CBA	currency board arrangement
CBRC	China Banking Regulatory Commission
CBS	Currency Board System
CCL	Computer and Communications Laboratory
CCP	Chinese Communist Party
CEO	Chief Executive Officer
CEPA	Closer Economic Partnership Arrangement
CG	corporate governance
CGE	computable general equilibrium
CM(BOD)	Chairman of the Board of Directors
CM(SUP)	Chairman of the Supervisory Board
CMU	Central Moneymarkets Unit
COD	Chemical Oxygen Demand
CPI	consumer price index
CSD	Census and Statistics Department
DAR	debt-to-assets ratio
DBDM	dual-board diagnostic model
DEA	Data Envelopment Analysis
DEAP	Data Envelopment Analysis (Computer) Program
DER	debt-to-equity ratio
DFC	domestic financial centre
DPP	Democratic Progressive Party
DTC	deposit-taking company
DVD	digital versatile disc
DvP	Delivery versus Payment
E&I	equipment and instruments purchase
EC	European Commission
ECM	error correction model
EEFSU	Eastern Europe and the former Soviet Union

EPS	earnings per share
ERSO	Electronics and Semi-Conductors Laboratory
EU	European Union
FAO	Food and Agriculture Organization
FDI	foreign direct investment
FEER	Fundamental Equilibrium Exchange Rate
FFE	foreign-funded enterprises
FIEs	foreign-invested enterprises
FTA	free trade agreement
FTAA	Free Trade Area of the Americas
GARCH	Generalized Autoregressive Conditional Heteroskedesticity
GATT	General Agreement on Tariffs and Trade
GDP	gross domestic product
GFC	global financial centre
GNP	gross national product
GOS	growth of sales
GTAP	Global Trade Analysis Project
HIBOR	Hong Kong interbank offer rate
HKD/HK$	Hong Kong dollar
HKEX	Hong Kong Exchanges and Clearing Ltd
HKMA	Hong Kong Monetary Authority
IBC	international banking centre
IC	integrated circuit
ICOR	incremental capital-output ratio
IEDB	International Economic Data Bank
IFCs	international financial centres
IIP	international investment position
IMF	International Monetary Fund
IP	intellectual property
IPR	intellectual property rights
IT	information technology
ITRI	Industrial Technology Research Institute
IPO	initial public offering
JBIC	Japan Bank for International Cooperation
K/L	capital over labour
KMT	Kuomintang (Nationalist Party)
LO	local office
LOP	Law of one price
M&A	mergers and acquisitions
MDBs	multilateral development banks
MFA	Multi-Fibre Agreement
MFN	most-favoured nation
MNCs	multinational corporations
MOEA	Ministry of Economic Affairs

MPF	Mandatory Provident Fund
MY	marketing year
NASDAQ	National Association of Securities Dealers Automated Quotations
NBFIs	non-bank financial institutions
NFC	national financial centre
NICs	newly-industrializing countries
NIEs	newly-industrializing economies
NPL	non-performing loan
NSC	National Science Council (Taiwan)
NTBs	non-tariff barriers
OBM	own-brand manufacturing
ODM	original design manufacturing
OECD	Organisation for Economic Co-operation and Development
OEM	original equipment manufacturing
OFC	offshore financial centre
OLBI	Open Lab Business Incubator
OLS	ordinary least squares
OTC	over-the-counter
P&G	Procter & Gamble
PBC	People's Bank of China
PNTR	Permanent Normal Trade Relations
PP	Phillips-Perron statistics
PPP	purchasing power parity
PRC	People's Republic of China
PvP	Payment versus Payment
QDIs	Qualified Debt Instruments
R & D	research and development
REIT	real estate investment trust
RER	real exchange rate
RERM	real exchange rate misalignment
RERV	real exchange rate volatility
RFC	regional financial centre
RHQ	regional headquarters
RLB	restricted licence bank
RMB	renminbi
RO	regional office
ROA	return on assets
ROE	return on equity
ROS	return on sales
ROW	rest of the world
RPI	retail price index
RTGS	Real Time Gross Settlement
SAIC	State Administration for Industry and Commerce
SAR	Special Administrative Region

SARS	Severe Acute Respiratory Syndrome
SC	Schwarz Criterion
SEPA	State Environmental Protection Agency
SFC	Securities and Futures Commission
SHSE	Shanghai Stock Exchange
SITC	Standard International Trade Classification
SMEs	small and medium-sized enterprises
SOB	state-owned bank
SOE	state-owned enterprise
SSES	Shanghai Stock Exchange Survey
STF	Shanghai Toothpaste Factory
SUR	Seemingly Unrelated Regression
SZSE	Shenzhen Stock Exchange
TAs	trade associations
TBs	tariff barriers
TEEMA	Taiwan Electronic and Electrical Manufacturers' Association
TFP	total factor productivity
TNC	trans-national corporation
TRIMs	Trade Related Investment Measures
TRQs	tariff-rate quotas
TSMC	Taiwan Semi-Conductor Manufacturing Company
TVE	township and village enterprise
UIP	uncovered interest parity
UMC	United Microelectronics Corporation
USD/US$	US dollar
USDA	United States Department of Agriculture
VAR	vector auto-regressive
WCU	World Currency Unit
WFE	World Federation of Exchanges
WIND	Wind Information Company Limited
WTO	World Trade Organization
XHNA	Xinhua News Agency

1
Introduction

Lok Sang Ho and Robert Ash

1979 is a watershed in modern economic history

Throughout the Mao Zedong era and in its immediate aftermath, Hong Kong served as a gateway to China and provided it with a window on the outside world. But in 1979 a profound change occurred, as China committed itself to an 'open door' strategy. Indeed, with hindsight, 1979 emerges as one of the most important years in human history as it was when the first communist country (and the world's most populous country) opened up its doors to the world. It is no exaggeration to suggest that from 1979 human history has begun to follow a wholly new course.

It is said that globalization is an ongoing process that has been under way for centuries. Traditionally, China's geo-strategic and economic interests lay beyond its land borders in Central Asia and the great landmass to the west. For hundreds of years, China had conducted trade with the western nations along the fabled Silk Road. In the early fifteenth century, the voyages of a Muslim eunuch at the Ming Dynasty court, named Zheng He, lent China's geo-strategic aspirations a maritime dimension. Between 1405 and 1433, he undertook seven epic voyages that took him to the South Pacific and Indian Oceans, Aden in the Gulf and even the shores of East Africa.

These historical expressions of territorial and maritime ventures are truly remarkable. But from the perspective of global political and economic history, 1979 will be remembered as the year of the birth of modern globalization. In this very year the communist bloc, with well over one-quarter of the world's population, began to establish a market-based economy. Access began to open up to huge pools of formerly inaccessible – and unproductive – labour. In international terms, the lack of physical mobility of this reservoir of cheap labour forced capital to 'migrate'. As a result, 'production fragmentation' emerged as an important aspect of globalization. As Joseph Stiglitz points out in Chapter 2 in this volume, China's opening-up to the world was akin to suddenly adding an extra 500 million unskilled workers to the labour forces of the US and Europe. For corporations that took advantage of this development, the effect was to exert downward pressure on wages while raising corporate profits and stock prices. With hindsight, the idea of 'China as an economic giant'[1] was also born in 1979. Starting in this year, the global profile of trade, the prices of raw materials (cotton, coal, petroleum, copper, steel, among others), the prices of consumer goods from apparel to appliances, the flows of world capital and labour, and even the flows of ideas and technical know-how all embarked on a new course of development, propelled to a large degree by events unfolding in China. Finally, as these developments unfolded, China's successful pursuit of high and sustained growth seemed to have generated a 'Chinese model of development', to be added to other established 'models', such as those of Japan, Hong Kong, or the newly-industrializing economies (NIEs).

Zero sum versus positive sum and distributional issues

Few would deny that the emergence of China as a global economic giant has had a positive impact on the global economy. Many have, however, also highlighted the major challenge this poses for the world as well as for individual countries. For example, according to Lester Brown of the Earth Policy Institute, China has now surpassed the United States as the world's leading consumer of key commodities (Brown, 2005). China's consumption of grain, meat, coal, and steel has already overtaken that of the US.[2] China's consumption of chemical fertilizers is now double that of the US. Its GDP in 2005 is fourth in the world, being exceeded only by those of Germany, Japan and the US. In 2003, the value of its merchandise trade was almost identical to that of Japan, and was surpassed only by Germany and the US. China's rapid economic growth is already having an impact on the Earth's resources and the environment; and people are worried about the consequences if such growth is sustained for much longer. China's booming economy has already exerted upward pressure on commodity prices. Meanwhile, on the other hand, its industries are out-competing many traditional producers and provide a range of cheap products from electronic goods to furniture.

In the past, many nations have responded to such competitive challenges through recourse to protectionist measures designed to shelter their domestic economies and soften the pain of adjustment. Alternatively they could take up the challenge posed while seizing the opportunities emerging in the process. As a matter of fact, the emerging opportunities for trade, investment, and collaborative development of technology and markets are vast. On the other hand, adjustment will often be painful, and sometimes very painful. But governments can reduce the pain through retraining programmes and more effective social safety provision. However, both Joseph Stiglitz (Chapter 2) and Wing Thye Woo (Chapter 4) express disappointment that national governments have expended more effort on promoting the cause of protectionism than on helping the 'natural' evolution of their economies.

Stiglitz (Chapter 2) eloquently shows that while China has had a huge impact on the global economy, its effect on the developing world has been even more profound. China's impact on the region and Association of South East Asian Nations (ASEAN) economies is explored by Mesut Saygili and Kar-yiu Wong (Chapter 3). They point out that in November 2002 – just one year after its accession to the World Trade Organization (WTO) – China signed a framework free trade agreement (FTA) with ASEAN. From a historical perspective, this might be interpreted as a natural development since well before the FTA was reached, intra-regional trade within South East Asia had risen rapidly (incidentally, mirroring a similar trend that was under way in Europe). Such developments have gradually reduced the weight of the United States whether as a trading partner, a destination for foreign direct investment (FDI), or a source of capital. Of course, the United States remains the dominant trading nation and still exerts the greatest influence on the world economy. Many would argue that from a global perspective, the relative decline in its dominance is a healthy development. Any diversification of growth hubs throughout the world points to declining global dependence on the US. This is a development that does not have necessarily negative implications even for the United States itself. Although its dominance has weakened, the US has benefited by gaining more room to adjust its monetary and fiscal policies to meet the needs of the domestic economy at the time, without fear of unduly influencing other nations.

The contribution by Saygili and Wong (Chapter 3) reinforces Stiglitz's argument that we live in a positive sum world. Using a 2-differentiated product, multifactor, three-country model, they find that ASEAN is likely to benefit significantly from China's accession to the WTO, as well as through the further surge in intra-regional trade following the free trade area agreement. The calibration of their model also suggests that labour in ASEAN will benefit from these developments, as a more efficient utilization of capital in the region raises labour productivity. The demonstration of this possibility is interesting in its own right. The force of the 'positive sum' logic is not in doubt, and neither is the fact that the 'pie' is growing; but how this pie is ultimately divided will depend on the relative bargaining powers of the parties concerned, which in turn will reflect the relationship between labour supply and demand. Cheung and Fan (Chapter 10) suggest that the interests of unskilled workers have been damaged by the opening-up of China, and this finding is consistent with Stiglitz's conjecture for the United States. For most of its own population – both urban and rural – China's rapid economic growth since 1979 has no doubt been a blessing. The extent of poverty reduction during this period is remarkable and without precedent in human history. In particular, huge numbers of previously rural underemployed (especially farmers) have migrated to the cities in search – often successfully – of work. The scale of the flows of migrant labour into, and out of, China's major cities is breathtaking, especially during the period of the Spring Festival. Because China typically exports the goods produced by this army of cheap labour, the sudden availability of a huge pool of labour is akin to 'adding hundreds of millions of workers to the workforce of Europe and America'. As a result the incomes of low-skilled workers throughout the world stagnate or decline, while those of higher-skilled workers and capitalists rise.

Thus since 1979 income inequality in the industrial world has worsened and the real incomes of the poor have stagnated. However, in China huge numbers of the poor began to find themselves able to make ends meet and were able to aspire to a 'good life'. Even so, poverty remains a very serious problem for many in China. According to an internal report circulating in 2003,[3] 14.59 million rural residents had a yearly income below 500 yuan; 90.33 million below 1,000 yuan; and 310.79 million had a yearly income between 1,000 and 2,000 yuan. Yet despite the serious scale of rural poverty, capital flight of 240 billion yuan a year was recorded as taking place from the rural sector. It is for this reason that a major agricultural tax relief initiative was launched in 2004 and agricultural prices were raised. In Chapter 16, Ash comments on the 2004 policy initiatives and investigates their rationale against the background of economic and welfare trends in the farm sector, as well as considering their implications for trade in cereals and grain, and for China's long-held adherence to the imperative of food self-sufficiency.

The efforts to raise farmers' incomes resulted in a yearly growth of 6.8 per cent for 2004, an impressive achievement after stagnant growth from 1997 to 2000 and the around 4 per cent growth during the 2001–3 period.[4] Whether these improvements can be sustained remains to be seen. There is an interesting contrast here with the United States, where policies in recent years have made income disparity worse, and are likely to fuel calls for the introduction of protectionist policies.

The unique and evolving roles of Hong Kong

The title of this volume is *China, Hong Kong and the World Economy: Studies on Globalization*. Hong Kong's own success had been an inspiration and a model for the Mainland, where many centres for the study of Hong Kong were set up during the 1980s. Hong Kong had also been China's main source of foreign capital and foreign direct investment. In 1989, ten years after China's opening-up, Hong Kong and Macau accounted for some two-thirds of all FDI. The opening of China was a boon to the Hong Kong economy; at the same time, the strength of Hong Kong's economy helped drive economic growth in the Mainland. As Tung Chee-hwa, the first Chief Executive of the Hong Kong Special Administrative Region (SAR), put it:

'If China prospers, Hong Kong will prosper; when Hong Kong prospers, China will do so too.' Hong Kong's unique role in helping transform the Mainland economy, and the parallel role of the Mainland *vis-à-vis* the Hong Kong economy, deserve careful study.

China's opening-up to the world was viewed in some quarters as the beginning of the end for Hong Kong in its role as a vibrant international commercial and financial hub. Hong Kong was home to the world's eighth-largest stock market, 500 banks from 43 nations, and the busiest container port on earth.[5] This prediction had superficial appeal, and for a short while it even appeared to be vindicated. Before the Mainland's opening-up, Hong Kong served as China's only window to the world, and its role as a 'middle-man' was a vital one for China. As China becomes more integrated into the world, while Hong Kong SAR increasingly integrates with the mainland (Fan, Li and Wei Chapter 9), this role will diminish. Fan, Li and Wei looked at panel price data on Hong Kong and four mainland cities, and found evidence for a significant degree of integration. Yet Hong Kong will not be just 'another mainland city', governed by corruption and political connections rather than the even-handed rule of law. Hong Kong's institutions, culture, values, work ethic, style of life and close links with the rest of the world are too deeply entrenched to disappear overnight. It is also unthinkable that any other Chinese city could readily establish and recreate these institutions and values. Given sufficient money, any city could install the best infrastructure within a short time. But making available the 'software' – values, culture, work habit and style, work ethic, institutions, people's market sense – will take a long time. For Hong Kong, the availability of such 'software' will continue to be its relative strength for many years to come. As Yun-wing Sung demonstrates in Chapter 8, the notion that Hong Kong's middleman role is doomed after China has fully opened up and integrated with the world economy is misguided and so far has not stood up to empirical testing.

This positive prognosis notwithstanding, Hong Kong did face serious problems after the transfer of sovereignty. For the first time since statistics were made available, in 1998 Hong Kong recorded negative economic growth, by as much as 5 per cent. Officially, the contraction was attributed to the Asian Financial Crisis (AFC). Yet the AFC did not cause the collapse of even a single licensed bank, whereas Hong Kong had seen truly serious financial crises in the 1960s and 1980s, and during the 1970s had seen two major oil crises. If the AFC was not the true cause of the economic crisis, was it possible that *Fortune* magazine's prediction was being realized? In fact, the suddenness of the economic decline threw doubt on that thesis. If it had been valid, any hope for Hong Kong's substantial recovery would have been dashed.[6] The rapid rebound of the Hong Kong economy from 2003, which has continued to the present day, clearly proved the thesis wrong. In short, the cause of Hong Kong's temporary demise must be sought elsewhere.[7]

Underscoring the perception of Hong Kong as 'a vibrant international commercial and financial hub', Y.C. Jao (Chapter 7) demonstrates the important functions that Hong Kong continues to perform for China, for the region, and for the world. As a financial centre, it continues to score high marks for providing institutions that inspire confidence and people who are attuned to the value of those institutions. As China puts in place its own financial institutional framework – partly by learning from Hong Kong and partly through indigenous efforts – it will find it attractive and necessary to continue to tap Hong Kong's talents.[8]

Just as Hong Kong's temporary problems should not be interpreted as reflecting fundamental problems inherent in its economic structure, so its recovery from 2003 should not be excessively attributed to the Closer Economic Partnership Arrangements (CEPA), which were announced in the summer of 2003, immediately after the Severe Acute Respiratory Syndrome (SARS) epidemic. At a seminar organized by *Mingpao* and Commercial Radio Hong Kong, John Tsang, Hong Kong's Secretary for Industry, Commerce and Technology announced that some 720 Hong Kong-registered enterprises had successfully obtained a certificate of service provider in Hong Kong and thereby become fully qualified to enter the Mainland market under the terms of CEPA. At the same time, about a billion dollars of new investment in Hong Kong was secured under the terms of CEPA in such industries as logistics, retail, transport, advertising, tourism and telecommunications. In 2005, there were even signs that some manufacturers were returning to Hong Kong after the reintroduction of textile quotas imposed by the United States. Overall, however, the direct economic benefits of CEPA, in terms of actual new investment in the SAR facilitated by it, appear to have been small. Similarly, a scheme launched after SARS that allows investors to obtain Hong Kong residency also appears to have had a relatively small direct impact on the local economy. In the first 20 months of operation it attracted 856 applications and a capital inflow estimated at over 4 billion Hong Kong dollars, but this was really insignificant for an economy with a GDP well in excess of 12 trillion dollars. For some time many people thought that individualized travel from several major Mainland provinces and cities[9] had contributed significantly to the recovery of Hong Kong's housing market. But reports of visitors from the Mainland snapping up several units during a single visit turned out to be invented, leaving the relevant brokerage company to be reprimanded. All this suggests that Hong Kong's remarkable recovery after 2003, though certainly helped by Beijing's favourable policies such as CEPA and individualized travel, probably did not depend on such policies as much as is often thought.

Hong Kong dollars and the RMB

Hong Kong distinguished itself from the mainland not only in its legal institutions, values, and work ethic, but also in providing a currency that was totally and freely convertible. Hong Kong imposes no foreign exchange control of any kind. In contrast, the Mainland still maintains a tight grip on the inward and outward flow of capital, even though a significant degree of liberalization has taken place in recent years (especially since 1994). Since 17 October 1983, the Hong Kong dollar has been officially tied to the US dollar at the rate of HK$7.8 to US$1 under a currency board system, whereas no official announcement was ever forthcoming to the effect that the RMB was tied to the US dollar. Officially, from 1994, when the government set up a nationwide inter-bank foreign exchange market and required all foreign exchange transactions to go through the banking system, the RMB was under some form of managed float. Initially exchanging at 8.7 yuan to the dollar, the RMB appreciated to slightly below 8.3 yuan to the dollar by 1997,[10] where it stayed until 21 July 2005, when the People's Bank of China announced a small (2 per cent) appreciation of the yuan against the US dollar and stated that henceforth the RMB would be on a managed float 'with reference to a basket of currencies'. The subject of under-valuation of the RMB and its subsequent revaluation in July 2005 was taken up by Voon, Li, and Ran (Chapter 5), who not only estimated the extent of under-valuation of the RMB against various currencies, but also suggested that the damage of revaluing the RMB on China's exports was probably overblown.

During the almost decade-old implicit and unannounced link to the US dollar, the exchange rate between the Hong Kong dollar (HKD) and the RMB was almost fixed, since the HKD was also linked to the US dollar. This de facto integration of the two currencies was favourable to trade and capital flows. From 7 p.m. on 21 July 2005, however, this implicit integration disappeared, leaving the HKD–RMB exchange rate to fluctuate. Logically, there is no reason why the Hong Kong dollar should not also be tied to some currency basket, which would certainly facilitate greater macroeconomic stability. In a paper published in 1990, Ho advocated a basket link, in fact stabilizing the Hong Kong dollar's effective exchange rate index. Thereafter, his work gradually led him to recommend a link to an indexed unit of account – the 'World Currency Unit' – that would represent a unit of stable purchasing power against global output. Ho (Chapter 6) recommends that the Mainland and Hong Kong currencies both be tied to this unit, thereby indirectly linking their currencies and effecting a stable exchange rate between the RMB and the HKD.

The idea of 'anchoring' currencies so that they represent stable purchasing power dates back to 1911, when Irving Fisher published his book, *The Purchasing Power of Money*. More recently, Robert Shiller of Yale University championed the cause of an indexed unit of account, and Ho (2000) was the first to spell out how an indexed unit of account representing stable global purchasing power could be set up.

Official orthodoxy insists that the HKD–USD link has worked well and that Hong Kong is different from the Mainland and does not need to shift to a basket link such as the RMB. But since there is no reason to expect synchronicity between Hong Kong's business cycle and that of the United States, the monetary policy suitable for the US might not also be suitable for Hong Kong (Yue Ma and Raymond Ng, Chapter 11). Indeed, the shrinking weight of the US in Hong Kong's foreign trade over the years and the increasing weight of the Mainland and intra-regional trade will make the USD–HKD link increasingly out-dated over time. Ma and Ng, using the vector auto-regressive framework, find that interest rates have dominated other variables in driving Hong Kong's macroeconomy. But under the USD–HKD link interest rates are not under Hong Kong's control. Over the years, Hong Kong has experienced episodes of overheatedness and excessive contraction, depending on the movements of US interest rates and the USD in the foreign exchange markets.

Technology, investment and efficiency

Anyone who has studied China's economic development is bound to have wondered whether China's 'hypergrowth' – average GDP growth of close to 10 per cent per year since its opening-up – can be sustained.[11] Paradoxically, China's very inefficiency points to excellent prospects for high growth through the considerable potential for efficiency improvements. From this perspective, the prospect for continued high growth will also be enhanced if investment has not yet been pushed to the limits, if the opportunities for technological improvement are still plentiful, or if current institutions are still far from optimal. Taking up the issue raised by Young (1994) and by Krugman (1994), who argue that the rapid Asian economic miracle witnessed to date had been associated more with adding more input than with enhancing the productivity of input, Zhang Jun (Chapter 15) offers the interesting finding that in contrast to the experience of the newly-industrializing economies, China's investment to GDP ratio, though high, has not risen in real terms over the years, suggesting a 'higher quality' growth. In particular, rural industrialization and the proliferation of small firms in the non-state sector raised productivity and stimulated growth. Adding to this result, Lin (Chapter 13) presents evidence of significant positive 'spillover effects' of FDI to Chinese firms during China's two-decade implementation of its 'swap the market for technology' policy. While a case study of digital versatile disc (DVD) patent royalty payments suggests that the magnitude of spillover effects may have been overestimated, China's accession to the WTO will be favourable for technology transfer to China. Its more open market, better business opportunities, improved intellectual property rights system and, perhaps more importantly, increased competition among foreign investors may induce them to bring in more and more advanced technology. Chen (Chapter 14) found trade a positive factor for productivity growth, which hovered around 3.9 per cent during the 1990s and accounted for some 37 per cent of the growth during this period. Both Lin's and Chen's results also suggest that China's economic growth is of high quality and is likely to be sustained. Further evidence on these points is that, according the 'Indicators of Technology-Based Competitiveness', conducted by Georgia Tech's Technology Policy and Assessment Center, during the decade to 2003, China more than doubled its score on 'technological standing', a key benchmark in gauging current global competitiveness. From a score of 20.7 in 1993, China's rating rose to 49.3 in 2003.[12]

Across the Taiwan Strait, Taiwan has been a dominant global player in the production of a range of hi-tech products from notebook computers to network cards (Howe, Chapter 12), and has today emerged as a primary source of FDI on the Mainland. The close collaboration between Taiwan and the Mainland has transformed what was already a formidable international technological force into one that will be very hard to beat. Moreover, Howe points out that some of the traditional leaders in technology (especially the United States) are reducing their spending on technology development or experiencing slow-downs in innovation and development as a result of excessive bureaucracy. As China (including Taiwan) surges ahead, the technological gap between China and traditional leaders, such as the US, Japan and Germany, is closing fast.

Environmental concerns

It is commonly believed that environmental decline is a likely, if not inevitable, cost of economic growth. China's hypergrowth underlines the seriousness of this threat, both for China itself and the rest of the world. However, positing a straightforward correction between environmental degradation and economic growth is simplistic. As Chai (Chapter 17) explains, China's entry to the WTO may actually have a positive environmental impact. His analysis draws attention to the existence of two positive effects – the 'composition' and the 'technical' effects – and shows that these promise to more than offset the negative 'scale effect', so that the net impact on the environment is positive.

Of course, economic growth is bound to consume resources. Guangdong, for example, faces an estimated yearly water shortage of 7.1 billion cubic metres (*Mingpao*, 15 February 2005), despite being the principal supplier of fresh water to Hong Kong.[13] China's rapid economic growth has undoubtedly contributed to increases in the prices of many raw materials (see above). However, China is also transforming itself into a more service-oriented economy that may be less taxing on the environment (the composition effect); and as economic growth continues, China is also better positioned to afford pollution abatement measures and infrastructures (the technical effect). The introduction of appropriate institutions (environmental protection laws and emission trading markets) will further facilitate these changes, and the prognosis is not altogether gloomy. Moreover, as Stiglitz suggests, if a 'heavyweight' country such as China commits to environmental protection, the demonstration effect on other countries is likely to be considerable.

Corporate governance and firm level performance

Globalization is not just a physical phenomenon about the movement of goods, capital and people: it is also a revolution in people's mindset, and involves changing to new ways of doing business, and of conducting peoples' lives, that are regarded as standard practice. For example, child labour and sweatshops are both considered uncivilized and unbecoming of modern states. Article 103 of the Company Law of China (1994) stipulates that all joint stock limited companies are to have a supervisory board. Both supervisors and directors are to be elected, appointed, or replaced by shareholders' general meetings. Yet, as Tam and Hu (Chapter 18) have found, having such formal structures set up is one thing, but making sure that they function as intended is quite another, and is much more difficult. As of now, investor protection in China is still weak; ownership concentration and insider dealing continue to limit the effectiveness of such supervisory boards. Complementing this result, Chang and Wong (Chapter 19) found that, for state-owned enterprises especially, a more independent management, one that is less influenced by state shareholders and the local Communist Party committees, will have favourable effects on firm performance, suggesting that the managers' objectives might be more in line with the profit-maximization objective. Fully privatizing listed firms and providing better protection for minority shareholders through reforms in corporate governance and legal systems are the ultimate keys to improving the performance of China's listed firms.

The future

China's economic prowess is no longer in doubt, and neither is the likelihood – even certainty – that China will continue, probably even more strongly, to assert its independence in its domestic policies (including monetary policy and especially exchange rate policy) and insist on its legitimate rights in international negotiations. At the same time, the process of opening-up will continue, as will that of liberalization (albeit proceeding at China's own pace). In many ways, the international community has been seduced by China's 'hypergrowth'; yet, through the eyes of the Chinese government, rapid growth is secondary to stability (*wending*). As a characteristic six-character phrase has it, *wending yadao yice* (stability dominates everything). So it is that 'caution' and 'sustainability' are the two buzzwords in China. Over the long run, at least from the experience of the People's Republic of China over the last three decades, caution and sustainability may maximize growth as a byproduct.

China's rapid rise has had many repercussions. To the industrial world, China has become a prime destination of FDI and a major trading partner, even though domestic politics has always focused on potential job losses, as outsourcing proceeds at a headlong pace and cheap imports flood the market. To the developing world, China's rapid rise has been a catalyst for action: in Asia, for example, Vietnam and India have followed in China's footsteps, and India is now emerging as a formidable competitor in its own right. North Korea is likely to be next in line to open up its economy and introduce similar reforms. We live indeed in interesting times.

Many countries see China as a model and a threat. But might it not be that China is doing no more than following current globalizing trends and taking advantage of the opportunities, as they present themselves, in the process of globalization? China – and Hong Kong SAR too – is positioning itself for the opportunities and bracing itself for the challenges. The rest of the world must do the same. When problems arise, they have to be overcome. Such a truism contains an eternal truth, and yet much of the world seems to be trying to ignore such problems in the hope that they will not materialize.

In tackling these problems, both a unilateral approach and a multilateral approach will be needed. Stiglitz makes the point that countries must re-examine their policies on social security provision and worker retraining, and be prepared to formulate new redistribution measures. If the labour market proves to be too rigid for adjustment, labour market institutions may have to be reformed. In addition, however, there is room for a multilateral approach – indeed, a 'globalist approach' – to tackle the problems arising out of globalization.

Addressing global issues through a globalist approach – sometimes dubbed 'globalism' – offers an appropriate way forward in dealing with environmental issues, trade issues, exchange rate issues, health issues, and (most of all) the problem of poverty. Ho's proposal of a World Currency Unit to anchor the RMB and other Asian currencies is an example of the globalist approach and promises to address a key issue that has perplexed the world since gold was dropped as a standard for the world's moneys. The Kyoto Protocol is another example of globalism. So is advocacy of a global minimum wage standard in order to address the global poverty problem. Although – or because of – all these being highly controversial issues, they deserve to be at the centre of the agenda for meetings of world leaders.

Resolving these issues in a way that satisfies the demands of social equity and profit-maximizing economic efficiency is a hugely complex task. Take the following simple example. In the early 1980s, a female worker operating a sewing machine would have earned about HKD 1,000 a month.

Today a woman operating a much faster machine in a factory in the Pearl River Delta earns a monthly wage of around RMB 800. Today's lower wage does not reflect lower productivity; indeed, productivity is now much higher than 20 years ago. Instead, it reflects the simple working of the forces of supply and demand. Because there is such an enormous supply of workers willing to accept a low wage in today's globalized world, wages have fallen to subsistence level. As a result, the existence of such a large number of working poor who lack the purchasing power to obtain even basic manufactured goods has generated a vicious circle. These goods command such a low price and face such weak demand that producers' margins are eroded and they cannot afford to pay higher wages.

If those (and there are many) struggling manufacturers are to avoid bankruptcy and all that it entails, perhaps the 'global minimum wage' should be regarded as no more than a guideline. Perhaps the multinational corporations that are currently highly profitable will voluntarily abide by the global minimum wage *guideline* and pay wages that provide their workers with a surplus with which to buy more consumer goods. Perhaps a corporate social responsibility label can endorse products that are produced in observance of the guideline. Perhaps the higher earnings of these workers can trickle down to help smaller enterprises that are struggling to survive. For the time being, there is no way of knowing how, or to what extent, the global approach will help resolve the many global issues that confront us. Only this approach, however, is likely to take us forward.

Notes

1 This is the title of another course introduced and taught by Y.Y. Kueh at Lingnan University for many years.
2 China accounted for almost half the rise in global steel production in 2004 (World Watch Institute, *Vital Signs, 2005–2006*).
3 Li Gu-cheng, *Oriental Daily*, 16 December 2003, citing Wang Yuzhao, President of the China Poverty Relief Fund.
4 *China Daily*, 1 February 2005(Hong Kong edition).
5 Louis Kraar, *Fortune* magazine, June 1995. As of July 2005 Hong Kong's stock market capitalization was a shade smaller than Spain's and ranks 9th in the world. The Hong Kong Stock Exchange ranks 4th by equity funds raised in 2005 (to July). Source: Hong Kong Stock Exchange.
6 Hong Kong's sudden return to life and 'vibrancy' from August 2003 caught almost everyone off guard. Housing prices, which had fallen by over 65% from a peak in 1997, rebounded strongly in a sustained fashion, while commercial properties rebounded even more strongly, by over 60% from the trough of mid-2003. In contrast, 10 years after the collapse of the bubble, Japan's housing prices remained depressed.
7 The interested reader may refer to Ho and Wong (2005).
8 From time to time job fairs are held in Hong Kong at which Mainland enterprises attempt to fill their positions with talent from the SAR. According to Chen Liang-yu, City Party Secretary of Shanghai, 1,278 Hong Kongers were working in Shanghai on a professional hiring scheme, while more than 10% of Shanghai's

   enterprises expressed their intention to hire Hong Kong talents (*Mingpao*, 11 August 2004).
9 At year-end 2004 these included Guangdong, Beijing, Shanghai, Fujian, Jiangsu and Zhejiang. Individualized travel is expected to expand further to cover other provinces and cities.
10 Speech by Su Ning, Deputy Governor of the People's Bank of China at the Conference of Montreal, Canada, 9 June 2004.
11 'Hypergrowth' was a term coined by Edward K.Y. Chen (1979).
12 http://gtresearchnews.gatech.edu/newsrelease/techexports.htm.
13 Hong Kong has its own reservoirs which have become increasingly unable to meet its growing needs. For years it was contractually obliged to buy water from Guangdong. During years when rain was copious, Hong Kong continued to import water from the Mainland, even though imported supplies were dumped into the open sea. The rigid contract took years to be renegotiated on a more rational basis.

References

Brown, Lester (2005), *China Replacing the United States as World's Leading Consumer*, Earth Policy Institute, Washington, DC, 16 February.

Chen, Edward K.Y. (1979), *Hypergrowth in Asian Economies: A Comparative Study of Hong Kong, Japan, Korea, Singapore and Taiwan*, New York: Holmes & Meier.

Fisher, Irving (1911), *The Purchasing Power of Money*, New York: Macmillan.

Ho, Lok Sang (2000), 'The World Currency Unit and the Global Indexed Bond', *The World Economy*, 23, 7, 939–50.

Ho, Lok Sang and Gary Wong (2005), 'Privatization of Public Housing: Did it Cause the 1998 Recession in Hong Kong?' *Contemporary Economic Policy* (forthcoming).

Krugman, Paul (1994), 'The Myth of Asia's Miracle', *Foreign Affairs*, 62–78.

Shiller, Robert (2003), *The New Financial Order: Risk in the 21st century*, Princeton, NJ: Princeton University Press.

Young, Alwyn (1994), 'Lessons for the East Asian NICs: A Contrarian View', *European Economic Review*, 38, 964–73.

Part I
China and Globalization

2

China and the Global Economy: Challenges, Opportunities, Responsibilities[1]

Joseph E. Stiglitz

China's rapid economic growth has had great impact on the global economy, but this is not a 'zero-sum' game as some worry. Rather, China's success can contribute to a more prosperous and stable global economy. China's accession to the WTO creates opportunities which include access to international markets, capital and technology. But globalization and China's move towards a market economy also entail a need for changes, such as enhancing the social safety net, promoting domestic demand, and changing the role of banks and financial institutions.

As China assumes increasing importance in the global economy, it will have to take on new responsibilities. China will have to play a central role in reforming the global financial and trading systems. China, already an important role model for the developing world, will have to work hard to ensure that the evolving global finance and trading systems are fair to these countries and help promote their development. And China will also have to assume new responsibilities towards the global environment – she will have to adopt stronger measures for protecting the environment and conserving scarce natural resources.

Introduction: we live in a positive-sum world

I would like first to describe the new landscape in the global economy. Then I will talk about several aspects of policies related to enhancing China's growth, and to its entry into the global economy. I will conclude with a brief discussion of one of the central problems facing the international community – the global environment – and China's growing responsibilities.

---

[1]This is edited from the Nobel Lecture Series lecture on China and the Global Economy delivered by Professor Stiglitz at the Chinese University of Hong Kong on 16 March 2005.

I want to begin by talking about some aspects of the current global economy. It's important to understand these, to appreciate some of the major changes that are occurring.

China has succeeded in generating rapid growth in the last four years, even when other parts of the world only had moderate growth. It has become one of the engines of growth for much of the rest of the world, and especially for Asia. The impact of China on the world economy has been enormous. For instance, when I was in Athens last summer, talking to a group in the shipping industry, people were jubilant about China's growth because as a result of China's demand for steel and other commodity imports, shipping prices had increased six fold. They had never had such an era of prosperity. They were hoping I would tell them that this would continue.

China has had large impacts on many other prices as well. Oil prices today are over 50 dollars a barrel and China no doubt plays a major role in that. It is not so much that supply has been reduced. In fact, supply has remained more or less steady. But China has increased its demand, resulting in an imbalance that has led to record prices.

There is a basic premise that is very important to understand. It is that we live in a *positive-sum world* where China's growth and success can contribute to a more prosperous and stable global economy. I emphasize this because in many parts of the world, there is a zero-sum mentality: it is simply assumed that China is growing at the expense of other countries. That's the mentality that arises when many people in the United States or in Europe see their jobs disappear. They see jobs being created in China while their jobs are being lost. They have regrettably come to the conclusion that it's a zero-sum world. But their jobs are being lost in part because there is bad macroeconomic management in the United States, Europe and elsewhere. It's not a problem created by China. If these countries' macroeconomic policies were well designed and implemented, then China's economic growth would unambiguously contribute to their well-being. While I emphasize the positive-sum nature of China's growth, I want to emphasize that there is nevertheless going to be very serious strain on the advanced industrial countries, and on many of the developing countries as well.

The challenge for the US and other nations

China's development and integration in the global economy is putting particular strain on unskilled workers in the United States and in other advanced industrial countries. Consider what would happen if the US and Europe added an extra five hundred million unskilled workers to their labour forces. That would put enormous downward pressure on wages. If you have minimum wage law to prevent this adjustment, you'll have high levels of unemployment. One or the other would inevitably occur.

There is a long-standing economic theory that trading goods is a substitute for movements in factors. In fact, my teacher Paul Samuelson proved a theorem called the Factor Price Equalization Theorem, which says that when there is free trade, then factor prices will get equalized. That's a really scary thought to a lot of people in America, because it means wages of unskilled workers in America would be the same as those in China. There's another economic theorem called the Stolper–Samuelson Theorem. It says that even when factor prices are not fully equalized, there's a tendency to move in that direction.

This is now standard and accepted theory. Yet these predictions have not come true – so far. Economists have been a little bit puzzled over why there hasn't been more wage equalization than there has been. There are a number of reasons. One of them is that an assumption in the standard theory, that the technology is the same in all the countries, is not true. Technologies in the advanced industries are not the same as technologies in the less developed countries.

Globalization has meant, however, that technologies now do move quickly around the world. Multinational companies have been very effective in transferring technologies from one country to another.

Strains on the American and European economies

We used to emphasize 50 years ago that the distinction between developed and less developed countries was a disparity of capital. The objective of the World Bank was to close that disparity. But disparities of knowledge and technology are now equally recognized. These disparities have become enormously reduced in the last 10 to 20 years, because of globalization. This means that the predictions of the standard theory are more likely to be evidenced in the future, as China and India are integrated into the global economies. Consistent with this, while the US GDP overall has grown over the last five years, the real income of the median (typical) American household has actually fallen by 1500 dollars.

The resulting downward pressures on wages and increasing inequalities will impose enormous strains on advanced industrial countries; and all the more so because the increased pace of change provides little time for the developed countries to adjust. The advanced industrial countries obviously will have to undertake policies to help their workers adjust. If they don't, there will be enormous protectionist pressures.

Yet the kinds of policies that the United States has embarked on in the last five years are precisely the wrong policies, because those policies are increasing the already growing inequalities and reducing the role of the government in helping adjustment. If our diagnosis is correct, the US should be trying to increase the progressivity of the tax system and the quality of the safety net. Yet both the quality of the safety net and the progressivity of the tax system have been reduced: The US has become less well prepared for these strains rather than more prepared.

Strains on the global economy

Another important aspect of the current global economy is that America's fiscal and trade deficits are imposing enormous drains on global savings. The US is using up a very large fraction of total global savings. It's an irony that the world's largest economy (the US), is borrowing from countries, most of which are much poorer, at a rate of more than 2 billion dollars a day. Some of these imbalances are giving rise to exchange rate instability.

The trade deficit largely is a result of the fiscal deficit, but the Bush Administration clearly does not want to take the blame. Just as Reagan sought to blame its deficits on Japan, Bush seeks to blame its deficits on China, and on its foreign exchange policy. This debate over who is to blame for the deficits – and what is the right foreign exchange policy – has become one of the central issues in international economic policy.

The new geopolitics following China's accession to the WTO

I want to turn now to what I might call the new geopolitics of trade and finance.

China's entry into the WTO is extremely important both for China and for the world. Let me first talk about the implications for China, and then turn to the new role in global political leadership that China must play. One of the things that WTO accession does is give China greater access to the world's markets. I described earlier some of the strains that will take place in the world economy as a result of China's integration into that economy. The increase in income inequality and the rise in unemployment almost surely will give rise to protectionism, or at least to protectionist sentiment.

The good news is that the Uruguay Round created the beginning of an international rule of law; and even if the 'rule of law' is unfair, some rule of law is better than no rule of law. Without a rule of law, only economic power matters. With a rule of law, America's ability to respond to the strains imposed by China (and India) through increased protectionism is restrained. We have already seen this in the steel sector, where following the East Asia crisis, there were marked increases in imports. The US domestic steel industry tried to deal with the problem by imposing tariffs on steel. In 2003, the WTO ruled that the US' steps were not allowed under WTO rules.

China's entry into the WTO is important for another reason. It puts new demands on China, and China will have to learn how to respond to these demands if it's going to maintain robust growth with equity.

Managing China's integration into the global economy

The foremost examples of sectors in which adjustments will have to occur are: agriculture and financial services. The agriculture problem today is a reflection of, among other things, the inequity and unfairness of the last round of WTO trade negotiations. The Uruguay Round left in place a legacy of large agricultural subsidies. After the Uruguay Round was completed in 1994, there was an understanding that these agricultural subsidies should be cut back. But there was some fine print in the agreement that most of the developing countries did not fully appreciate that talked about non-trade distorting subsidies. A non-trade distorting subsidy is supposedly a subsidy that does not distort trade. But almost all subsidies – and not just export subsidies – do in fact distort trade. A production subsidy increases output, and unless consumption is increased commensurately, that means exports will increase. Today, the US claims that most of its subsidies are not trade distorting. But the US has not come up with such a list, though trade official shave *claimed* to come up with one. Thus, the United States, rather than cutting back its subsidies in the way that was promised, actually doubled the subsidies to a hundred and ninety billion dollars over 10 years. The US claimed that these were all legal within the WTO framework because they were all non-trade distorting. Brazil got sufficiently annoyed that it went to the WTO and challenged the cotton subsidies. With subsidies of 4 billion dollars a year going to 25 thousand farmers in the US, the price of cotton fell dramatically, and some 10 million Sub-Saharan farmers became worse off. The same is true of a whole range of agricultural goods. The WTO came down on the side of Brazil; and though the US is appealing, it is clear that Brazil *should* prevail.

China now has to compete against these agricultural subsidies provided by the United States and the EU. China recognizes that one of its major problems is the disparity of income between the rural and urban sectors, and that accession to the WTO will place downward pressure on the one part of the society that has already been lagging behind. And therefore it's going to exacerbate the problems of the poorest part of the Chinese society. So it's essential to do something about agriculture so as to maintain growth with equity. Mechanisms for finding assistance within the WTO framework will need to be explored. There would be a high cost to direct subsidies to undo the damage; for the money spent on agricultural subsidies could have been spent on growth promoting investments, or even in strengthening more broadly social services, like education and health. One of the reasons for not appreciating the exchange rate (as the US is pressuring China to do) is that doing so would lead to lower prices for agricultural goods imported into China, hurting those in the rural sector even more.

A well functioning financial sector is important, because it is the brain of the economy. Therefore, it represents perhaps even more difficult policy challenges than agriculture. The problem is two-fold. First, the financial sector in China is not efficient. In a market economy, banks perform the role of allocating investment. A loan applicant goes to the bank, and the lender decides whether to give you access to credit. But in a pre-market or socialist economy, such as in China, banks do not perform that role. Instead, central government planners make the decisions about which projects will be undertaken. All the bank does is act as a treasurer and write cheques. It isn't doing the job of screening, monitoring or selecting projects and therefore, doesn't perform the classic role of a bank in a market economy. So an essential part of the transition to a market economy is the transformation of these institutions. This takes time and can be an arduous process. What makes it more difficult is that there is a legacy of liabilities that banks took upon themselves at a time when they were not assigned the task of monitoring or selecting on the basis of creditworthiness. So it is quite a challenge to prepare the financial system of China to compete with foreign banks and to create a level playing field. It is important for the government to help banks restructure their inherited assets and liabilities, so that, going forward, they can have a fresh start.

Some have suggested that while the WTO has presented a problem – competition from international banks will overwhelm China's domestic banks unless something is done – they also present the answer. Simply let the international banks take over. But typically, foreign banks do not provide broad-based finance to the economy. Many economies – such as Argentina and Mexico - have found that foreign banks are more likely and more anxious to lend to the likes of Coca Cola and IBM and large national firms. But they are not well equipped to screen or monitor small- and medium-sized domestic enterprises. So one of the consequences of financial market liberalisation – the entry of international banking institutions – is that credit dries up for smaller businesses. Thus, financial market liberalisation frequently has a negative rather than positive effect for many enterprises.

This particular concern played an important role in American economic history. In the 19th century, the US government did not allow banks to operate in more than one state. There was a fear that if national banks were created, all the money would flow out of the Midwest and the newly developing parts of the country to the more established money centres, such as New York. This restriction was only eliminated in 1995. But then, only a few years later, globalization (in the form of a financial services agreement within the WTO) required that everybody open up their banks.

How should a country like China respond to this concern about capital flows? One way is by enacting a general version of a community re-investment act. For example, a US law requires that banks lend a certain fraction of their portfolio in under-served communities - parts of the country where there's an insufficient supply of capital. The notion is that all banks – whether Chinese or foreign – would have to lend a certain percentage of its loan portfolio to small and medium sized enterprises, and this would help alleviate concerns about less capital for smaller businesses.

There are a number of other things that have to be done to strengthen domestic financial markets to help Chinese firms meet the new competition and to ensure that the adverse effects of liberalization are mitigated. These include creating broad base mortgage markets, facilitating consumer loans, and strengthening the domestic insurance industry. Foreign banks should be required to open up branches in underserved parts of the country – not just to provide banking services in those cities where there is already an ample supply. These reforms can be an important stimulus of future growth and help shift China away from reliance on exports so domestic demand would play a more important role.

In short, the opening up of the financial services sector under the WTO framework could be an enormous opportunity for China, but unless it responds in a fairly comprehensive way, it could also impose an enormous cost on the Chinese economy.

New opportunities

China's integration into the global economy has already provided China with access to new markets and to global technology. China has benefited enormously also from foreign direct investment. But the rules of the game provide not only greater access into China, but also reciprocal access for China. This is important because China's growth has been based on access to international markets, capital inflows and technology. One way of ensuring continued access to markets, resources and technology is by making investment elsewhere in the world.

China is now making some overtures in this direction: for instance, through China's investment in energy. One way of thinking about this issue is the following. Market economies are marked by risk. The market for one's exports may suddenly disappear (as many textile exporters outside of China are discovering – they simply can't compete with China), or the price of inputs, like oil, may soar. China was not blessed with a large endowment of gas or oil. A country with gas or oil will be less affected by an increase in the price of energy; with enough oil, the country will even be better off. But globalization has changed risk in a fundamental way, because a nation can now hedge risk. For instance, China is an importer of oil and natural resources. With its enormous accumulated foreign exchange reserves, China can hedge some of those risks by making appropriate investments in gas and oil reserves or stocks. It can also use some of its wealth to gain access to technology and to obtain distribution channels for its products.

China's role in reforming the international reserve system

China's huge savings has now put it in a critical position in the workings of the global financial system. The global financial system is supposed to help stabilize the economy, but in fact it has not been working well. There have been an enormous number of financial crises over the last 30 years. More than 130 countries have experienced various crises around the world.

Moreover, global financial markets are very peculiar. Standard theory says that the developed countries, should bear the risk of global investment but that is not often the way it works. More frequently, less-developed countries bear the risk.

A well functioning global financial system moves risk from the poor to the rich while money flows from the rich to the poor. In fact, just the opposite is currently happening, with the United States borrowing $2 billion a day.

While a full diagnosis of what is wrong with the global financial system is beyond the scope of this lecture, I want to draw attention to one aspect – the global reserve system. Much of what is wrong with the global financial system can be related to the global reserve system – the system in which countries hold dollars (or gold, or some other safe asset) as a reserve, as backing for their currency and as a backstop against a 'rainy day.' Countries hold reserves because of enormous utility associated with it. Exchange rates, interest rates, demand for goods and property prices are going up and down all the time. Reserves provide a buffer against these kinds of volatility.

As China's reserves have increased – to more than $700 billion – China has become a central player in the global reserve system. How it manages its reserves can have enormous effects on exchange rates and global financial stability.

There is a growing dissatisfaction with the global reserve system in the developing countries in Asia, particularly. Countries are told that, if they wish to avoid the kinds of crises that East Asia experienced in the late 1990s, they have to maintain reserves at least equal to short–term, foreign-denominated liabilities. Think about what this means from the perspective of a less-developed country. It must put aside large amounts of money in reserves. A less-developed country typically holds those reserves in the form of US treasury bills. Holding a US treasury bill means that the poor developing country is lending money to the United States. The less developed country lends money to the United States at an interest rate of roughly two and a half percent now, though it *was* one percent and it may go up to three, or three-and-a-half percent. Meanwhile these countries are also often borrowing large sums from the United States. But an American bank does not lend at 2%. Instead it charges something like 18%. If a firm borrows an extra $100 million from an American bank, the government must put aside in reserves $100 million – money that could have been invested so much better in its own country. There is, in fact, no net flow of funds: the country is simultaneously borrowing and lending $100 million to the US. But it borrows at 18% interest, and lends at 2, 3, or 4%. That's not a good deal for the developing country, but it is a good deal for the United States. We can think of the poor developing country as giving foreign aid to the United States. The United States had benefited from this system, but it has not worked well for developing countries. And with the magnitude of reserves held by the developing world growing into the trillions, the costs to the developing countries have increased commensurately.

During the winter of 2004–05, I travelled in a number of Southeast Asian countries. I met government officials who were unhappy with how their countries were treated during and after the Asian Financial Crisis of 1997. Their interests were not given sufficient weight during the Asian Financial Crisis. Particularly vexing was the US and IMF response to Japan's generous offer of a hundred billion dollars to help create the Asian Monetary Fund. Though the money would have been of enormous benefit to the countries in the region facing recessions, the US opposed it because of concern that the new fund would diminish American influence in Asia. The US decided to put America's interest over the well-being of East Asian countries and shot down the notion of the Asian Monetary Fund. And the result is the economic downturn in many of these Asian countries was much deeper and longer lasting that what otherwise would have been necessary.

In the US nobody remembers these little facts of history, but in the countries concerned people remember this and other aspects of the crisis with bitterness.

Thailand, Indonesia, Malaysia are recovering today. There is confidence in the future for their economies. But as they now reflect on past events and look into the future, they observe that they are now the world's savers, far more so than the US. Meanwhile, the US defends its profligate ways, its spending beyond its enormous means, boasting that it is the world's consumer of last resort. It argues that it has helped stimulate global demand for goods by consuming great amounts for many years. Therefore the world should thank them for that important favour.

But the game has changed. Now other countries may also be willing to become a consumer of last resort, if given the opportunity. They are wondering why they are giving money to the richest country in the world at low interest rates. Why not spend the money inside their own region, helping themselves and their neighbours grow?

Central banks around the world, and especially in Asia, have made an important discovery: they don't need dollars to back their currencies. What is important is a reserve of liquid assets. The basic principle of portfolio diversification would call for the diversification of the reserve assets. There has been indeed such a tendency. Recently, the Bank for International Settlements released data showing that there has been enormous movement out of dollars into other reserve currencies over the last three years. This trend is likely to continue. The increased perceived risk associated with the US dollar is likely to cause further diversification out of the dollar.

I am rather doubtful whether the current system can continue. Why? A reserve currency needs to be a good store of value, which is why inflation has always been viewed so negatively by central bankers. What we have come to recognize is that exchange rate fluctuations can be as bad as inflation. If for instance, for somebody in Europe the value of the dollar has gone down 50% in the last three years, from their perspective that's equivalent in effect to 50% inflation. In other words, their purchasing power in terms of what they can get in their own country, of the money they put in dollars is diminished. Increasingly, we see a negative dynamic: as confidence is eroded, investors move out of a currency, thereby weakening the currency further. Therefore the dollar is increasingly being perceived as not a good store of value.

Much of the problem is inherent in the structure of the current reserve system. Reserve currency countries remain increasingly in debt as other countries hold their currency. The ease of selling debt entices borrowing, but eventually the debt gets so large that a country's credibility is questioned.

This is a problem that has long been recognized. Keynes, for instance, wrote about it. But like many of the world's recognized problems, it is consistently ignored, because the problems only appear episodically. It is hard in the midst of a crisis to undertake deep systemic reforms; and once the crisis is past, the incentives for systemic reforms are also passed. Today, the optimists look at the recent turmoil as simply a passing phenomenon. Most people say how could the dollar be attacked? But some three decades ago – too far in the past for most of the young traders making money in the world's financial markets to remember – there was an attack on the Dollar. It can happen again.

Some optimists are similarly not worried by America's huge (trade and fiscal) deficits and China's burgeoning reserves. A theory of mutual interdependence has been put forward: America needs China to finance its huge deficits; but China needs America to purchase its goods. But there is a fundamental fallacy in this reasoning. China is, in effect, providing vendor finance; it is financing the purchase of its own goods. It could provide finance to help its own people increase their own consumption; it could provide finance to help its backward regions invest and grow more. It does not really need the US to buy its goods. But while China does not really need the US, it is not obvious that the US will easily find an alternative source of finance.

The bottom line is that countries are beginning to look for alternatives to the current global reserves system. There are now alternatives to the dollar. The euro is one alternative; if China should decide to liberalize its capital markets, the RMB could itself be another. But moving to a two-currency (or multiple currency) reserve system will not solve the problem. The problems of the global reserve system are deeper, and more fundamental reform is needed.

I've written about some of these alternatives, as has George Soros. China will have to play a central role in developing these systems. I emphasize this because unless a new system is created, instability in the global financial system will continue.

Within Asia, there is recognition that there needs to be more Asian cooperation, and in the last few years, there have been several important initiatives, including the so-called Chiang Mai initiative of May 2000, involving
swapping of reserves. It should be seen as a partial movement away from
the dollar reserve system. The Asian bond fund initiative is another laud-
able attempt. The countries of the region are determined not to let these
initiatives be sabotaged in the way the US and the IMF did for the Asian
Monetary Fund.

It is in China's interest – and within China's ability, given the magnitude
of its reserves – to help in the search for alternatives, and to help create
such a new global system. (In my forthcoming book, *Making Globalization
Work,* I describe more fully how such an alternative would work.)

China's new role in global leadership

Not long ago China was one of the least developed countries. Today
China is effectively becoming a middle-income country. As China's
economy has grown, so too has its potential role of leadership. It can
have an enormous impact on the developing world – including helping
reshape the global economic architecture in ways which are fairer to the
developing countries.

First, China is an important role model. Its experience proves that a
country can do better without Washington Consensus policies, both in
terms of growth and poverty and other indicators of human well-being.
There is, of course, a very active debate around the world about alternative
strategies of growth. But the evidence is overwhelming on one side.

China's economic policies are remarkably different from the set of pre-
scriptions that have been followed in East Asia. China should market that
model because other countries can learn from it and enhance their own
chances of success. Although not all policies that were successful in China
can be directly applied to other developing countries, China's enormous
success should at least form the basis of a discussion.

Second, China has an important role in helping other developing countries
get a fair trade agreement in future WTO development rounds. Developing
countries are at a marked disadvantage in negotiating fair trade agreements.
Trade negotiations cover dozens of issues, and the US and EU have dozens of
negotiators for each problem. If, for instance, the US needs more negotiators,
the pharmaceutical industry lends lobbyists. Most African countries will have
one person at most, or even several countries will share one negotiator on all
issues. The lone negotiatior can't be equally well informed about all the issues.
And many of the issues are highly technical. Therefore, developing countries
are at a stark disadvantage. China (with Brazil and India) is in a unique
position to mount an effective counter balance to the industrial countries
and help get a fair trade agreement.

With the failure of negotiations, the US has become engaged in a whole round of bilateral trade agreements. These agreements are generally good for the US but less so for the country it negotiates with. The US-Morocco free trade agreement of January 2006 is a perfect example. The outcome – that Moroccans have less access to generic drugs than people in the US, for example – reflects the balance of power. China can play an important role in international bargaining by offering other developing countries trade agreements on fair terms.

It is important for China to take a different approach than I think the US has taken toward these issues. The US position is: how can we use our economic muscle to exploit, to get out of these countries as much as we can. China must choose a different course.

The dynamics of America's trade negotiations are quite astounding. While improving relations is the ostensible reason for trade agreements, once a trade negotiator is bargaining, the memory of any motivation to improve relations disappears after a minute. The result – seen in Morocco – is street protests and rebuttals. So rather than making friends, the United States makes enemies.

China must recognize that when negotiating agreements with developing countries it needs to consider a broader interest than 'how can I exploit these weak developing countries.' In the long run, China will benefit – and so too will the world – if it approaches trade negotiations asking: 'What kind of an agreement is *fair* and will promote the development of the poorest countries of the world?'

Fair trade agreements are not a handout, but a 'hand-up'; they help a country increase its income by selling more. China should approach trade agreement negotiations with developing countries with a sense of helping some of the least developed countries in the world.

Trade theory says that the greatest gains from trade occur in North-South agreement – between advanced countries and less developed countries because there is greater disparity in resources, which gives more room for gains from trade. In practice this turns out not to be the case. Developing nations are gaining more from South-South agreements than from North-South ones. The reason is very simple: these are fairer agreements. By contrast, in the Uruguay Round, the last round of multilateral trade talks, resulted in the poorest 47 countries of the world becoming actually worse off by 1 to 2 percent of GDP. So they actually didn't get any gain; they were actually hurt. On this front, China can make a difference.

Environmental concerns and sustainable development

China's growth in the coming years will require huge amounts of resources, with global effects. At the initial stages of growth, countries don't use a lot of resources, for they are just barely surviving. At a later stage of economic development, a new economy emerges, when ideas are consumed and produced more than goods. Between these stages are periods when countries consume a lot of things like automobiles, roads, houses – and that's the stage that China has entered. This stage will entail the utilization of enormous physical resources. It will put enormous demand on the global environment. The implication is that if growth is to be sustainable, measures for conservation must be undertaken. And some of these measures can simultaneously help other developing countries.

There is increasing evidence of the effects of global warming: the melting of the polar ice cap, glacial retreat in the Himalayas, and similarly in the US. As we know, the Kyoto Protocol (effective February 2005) basically treated developing countries separately from industrial countries. They were not put under any specific obligations. One of the objections of the United States was that the developing countries were not participating. Therefore, it argued, it was a not a global agreement and could not solve the problem. Europe should be commended on this front for making a commitment to reduce greenhouse gas emission notwithstanding these concerns. Europe decided that it's more important to start doing something about global warming than to wait for a global agreement that was acceptable to all.

I think it would be an act of global citizenship for China to follow the EU in unilaterally committing to reduce greenhouse gases.

Obviously China is not going to be willing to sacrifice its growth under the Kyoto framework, which was that countries have to reduce their emission to below the 1990 level. That would require a very low growth rate, or unattainable increases in energy (emissions) efficiency. It is understandable both why China is not willing to sacrifice growth or to accept that the notion that Americans should be allowed to pollute on a per capita basis far more than what others (including those in China) are allowed.

We need an agreement that is both feasible and workable, and philosophically well-grounded, that is, which is consistent with some generally accepted principles of global social justice. China can, for instance, make a commitment to reduce greenhouse gases on a per-unit of GDP basis. To put it another way, China could make a commitment for greater efficiency. It would begin to make contributions to the reduction of greenhouse gases, using its inventory of tools from taxes to regulations. (Many of these policies would be good for its economy as well as for the global environment.) In this way, China would provide a role model for other developing countries and begin the process of global engagement on an issue of paramount importance.

China can both begin to address the problem of global warming and help other countries by engaging in an enhanced emissions trading scheme with other developing countries. One of the notions in the Kyoto provision was that participating countries should try to reduce carbon dioxide emission and other greenhouse gas emissions in an efficient way; by, for instance, finding countries that reduce emission at a low cost, compensating them, and 'buying' their reduction emission. China can start this kind of voluntary system by trading emissions with other developing countries and providing them with incentives and assistance, such as equipment to reduce their emissions. At the same time, China can provide financial assistance to promote economic growth in a sustainable way.

The issue of carbon sequestration was raised in Kyoto. (Carbon sequestration addresses the problem of reducing the concentration of greenhouse gases in the atmosphere, by having carbon absorbed by trees instead of reducing emissions. This will reduce the amount of carbon dioxide in the atmosphere and thus the degree of global warming. This idea was recognized in Kyoto, but the negotiators made one mistake. They tried to promote sequestration by creating forests without recognizing the need to avoid deforestation. If you have a forest and you burn it, that adds carbon dioxide to the atmosphere. So the current framework says if you have a forest, you are better off cutting it down and replanting than simply maintaining it. You can be compensated for planting, but under the present system you can't be compensated for avoiding deforestation.

This is a big issue, both for many tropical countries and for the globe. The current rate of deforestation going on in is enormous. The amount of carbon dioxide thrown into the atmosphere as a result of deforestation is comparable to the amount of carbon dioxide added by the United States, which is the largest polluter in the world. The effects of deforestation in Brazil and Indonesia are offsetting most of what Europe and the other participants in the Kyoto protocol are doing. At the same time, if the tropical countries were compensated for the 'environmental services' they provide for the world, the amount they received would be enormous – greater than what they are today receiving in development assistance.

Much of the deforestation which occurs is related to illegal and/or 'corrupt' logging, where developing countries receive but a fraction of the true value of their lumber. What we need is a system which recognizes avoiding deforestation, supports schemes for lumber certification, and ensures that developing countries get full and fair values for preserving their resources. (Certified lumber is timber that has been cut legally.) This plan would simultaneously solve a development problem, a poverty problem and an environmental problem. Much of the lumber from Indonesia and Papua New Guinea, including the illegal logging, is destined for China. China could play a big role in creating this scheme. China would make an enormous difference if it allowed the importation of certified lumber and supported the coalition of rainforest countries' demand for compensation for avoided deforestation.

Redefining China's role in the global economy

China is no longer a small player in the global economy. China's growth will impose strains on the global economic system. In the long run, if well managed, the world will benefit from China's prosperity. China will need to put more emphasis on managing domestic demand growth and continued emphasis on improvements in productivity and technology. China will need to be aware that globalization has been accompanied by increasing inequality and economic insecurity in many countries – both developed and less developed. Explicit measures to combat these will be needed.

Globalization has put strains on both developed and less developed countries. It will put strains on China. As its role in the global economy expands, China will have to assume increase its responsibilities – responsibilities for improving the rules of the game, enacting reforms in the global financial system that enhance stability and fairness, and bringing about reforms in the global trading system that are fair and that truly promote the well-being of developing countries.

China will also need to do its bit to improve the global environment: conserving natural resources, and helping create global agreements for reducing emissions (for instance through the new rainforest initiative). China will have to take on increasing responsibility for advancing the well-being of other developing countries, by promoting development-oriented trade and investment, by direct assistance, and by providing a role model. If China does live up to these responsibilities, I believe that everyone in the world will benefit. And by doing good, China will do well for itself.

3

Unilateral and Regional Trade Liberalization: China's World Trade Organization Accession and Free Trade Agreement with the Association of South East Asian Nations*

Mesut Saygili and Kar-yiu Wong

Introduction

The post-war economy of the world is characterized by a reduction of many of the government restrictions on the movements of goods and capital across countries. Through several rounds of multilateral trade negotiations, regional cooperation, and the unilateral trade liberalization of many countries, the world has seen a rapid dismantling of trade barriers and a resulting surge in international trade volumes, capital flows and national income levels.

The rise of the Chinese economy after the decision of the government at the end of the 1970s to liberalize many of its internal and external economic policies has created a series of shocks to the world economy. Because of the size of its economy and because of its impressive and nearly uninterrupted growth, China has affected other economies in many ways and generated a lot of discussion and concerns about the size and nature of some of these impacts. Therefore the rise of the economy and its liberalizing policies were met with mixed reactions from different countries and different individuals.

Recently two economic events concerning foreign trade liberalization of China have drawn particular attention from the government planners and economists of many countries. The first event is China's accession to the

*This project is supported in part by a grant from the International Centre for the Study of East Asian Development, Japan. The content originally was presented in a workshop at Claremont McKenna College, California, 25 February 2005, and at a conference at Xi'an Jiaotong University, Xi'an, China, 25–26 June 2005. Thanks are due to the discussants and participants of the workshop and conference for valuable comments.

World Trade Organization (WTO) in November 2001.[1] In order to gain accession into this organization, China promised to make changes in many of its trade and FDI policies. In particular, it agreed greatly to lower its tariffs, reduce its restrictions on the inflow of capital into some sectors, and change many of its corporate taxes on foreign investors.

The second event is that China and ASEAN signed a framework free trade agreement (FTA) in November 2002. They agreed to form a free trade area in ten years.[2] China and ASEAN have promised to remove nearly all the restrictions on the movement of goods between them. Japan and South Korea also expressed great interest in taking similar steps (i.e., forming free trade areas with ASEAN).

Based on the performance of the Chinese economy in the past 24 years, it is widely expected that China's accession to the WTO and the establishment of a China–ASEAN FTA will bring big changes to the economies of many other countries. These changes will probably benefit some countries and people, but will probably hurt the welfare of others.

Concerns about possible adverse effects of these two events have been growing. For example, when China becomes a member of the WTO, trade liberalization should greatly improve the competitiveness of Chinese products in world markets, and its economy will therefore become much more attractive to foreign direct investment. The concern is that the success of the Chinese trade performance could be at the expense of the ASEAN economies, because ASEAN products could lose market shares in third countries such as the United States, and because China could attract foreign capital which was originally supposed to be sent to ASEAN.

To examine and analyse some of these worries, Wong (2004) investigates some of the features of trade between China and some of the ASEAN member nations.[3] He does not find evidence to support the worry that ASEAN products will lose out to Chinese products in other countries. Instead, he argues that the existence of significant intra-industry trade could bring sound potential gains to all the countries concerned. Wong (2003) builds a theoretical three-country model to analyse the impacts of trade liberalization by China on the welfare of China, ASEAN and the rest of the world. He derives conditions under which the ASEAN could gain from China's accession to the WTO.

This chapter is another attempt to investigate the impacts of trade liberalization by China. Contrary to the previous work of Wong, it will examine not only China's accession to the WTO, but also the formation of a China–ASEAN free trade area. How these two forms of trade liberalization by China may affect international trade, international capital movement, commodity and factor prices, and welfare will be analysed.

This study constructs a two-good, multivariety, and three-country model. The 'countries' are conveniently called China, ASEAN and ROW (the rest of the world), while the two goods are manufacturing and agriculture. ROW consists of eight countries/economies: the USA, Japan, Australia, Canada, France, Italy, Germany and Hong Kong. We allow differentiation of products and the existence of internal economies of scale. Thus our model is suitable for analysing both inter-industry trade and intra-industry trade among the countries. Another feature of the present model is that capital movement is allowed. We will investigate the impacts of trade liberalization on the movement of goods and capital movement.

We start with a theoretical model. The model is very extensive and capable of capturing many of the issues of interest. The cost of building such a model is that it is so complicated that analysing the possible impacts of a shock, such as a reduction in tariff rates, is very difficult. Therefore, in the second half of this chapter, we solve the system numerically. We consider various cases and equilibria, depending on the assumed government policy parameters, which change after each stage of liberalization. We will investigate the following cases:

(a) the benchmark (this is the case before China's accession to the WTO);
(b) Scenario 1: this is the case in which China is a member of the WTO but before the China–ASEAN FTA;
(c) Scenario 2: this is the case in which China is a member of the WTO, and China and ASEAN draw up an FTA (however, the China-ASEAN FTA does not include liberalization in capital movement).

The rest of the chapter is organized as follows. The second section describes the three-country model; the third section presents the benchmark and some of the assumptions used in the simulation; the fourth section analyses the case in which China is a member of the WTO; the fifth section investigates Scenario 2, with China and ASEAN drawing up an FTA (and also with China being a member of the WTO); and finally there is the conclusion.

A three-country model

The model used here consists of two sectors with differentiated products, three (groups of) countries, and four factors (labour and three types of capital). The two sectors are manufacturing (m) and agriculture (a).[4] In each sector, there is a large number of monopolistically competitive firms, each of which employs labour and capital to produce a variety of the product. Free entry and exit ensures zero product of each firm in the long run.

The three countries or groups of countries/regions are China (c), ASEAN (a), and ROW (r). ASEAN is really a grouping of separate countries, but in this model, they are combined together and treated as a single country. ROW, or the rest of the world, consists of the USA, Japan, Australia, Canada, France, Italy, Germany and Hong Kong. These eight countries/regions are the most important trading partners of China and ASEAN.

Labour is a homogeneous factor, which is perfectly mobile within a country but immobile between countries. Each country possesses a special type of capital. Capital may move between countries.

There have been many similar models of differentiated products and monopolistic competition in the literature, but the present one will allow us to consider inter-industry trade, intra-industry trade and capital movement in a simple model.[5]

In country i, $i = c$, a and r, there are n_i^m types of manufactured goods and n_i^a types of agricultural goods produced by monopolistically competitive firms, where n_i^m and n_i^a are determined endogenously. Country i is endowed with L_i units of labour and K_i units of capital of its own type. Both factors can move perfectly and costlessly within their own country, but only capital can move internationally.[6]

Trade in commodities and capital movements exist among the countries. Before the China–ASEAN FTA is ratified, all countries have positive tariffs on the goods imported from other countries. For simplicity, it is assumed that no capital flows from China or ASEAN to the ROW. This assumption is justified by the fact that the actual capital flow from China and ASEAN to the rest of the world is insignificant and it is used to simplify the analysis.

In order to allow for cross-hauling of capital between China and ASEAN, we take the Armington assumption for capital, and distinguish three different types of capital: capital from China, capital from ASEAN, and capital from the ROW. Firms in China and ASEAN require all three types of capital in their production while firms in the ROW use capital from the ROW only. This implies that capital moves between China and ASEAN, from ROW to China and ASEAN, but not from China and ASEAN to ROW.[7]

Currently, country i imposes a non-prohibitive tariff of *ad valorem* rate of t_{ij}^h on the goods in sector h imported from country j, and an income tax rate of τ_{ij} on the capital from country j, i, $j = c$, a, r, $i \neq j$, and $h = m$, a. In equilibrium, the price of variety s of good h from country j in country I, q_{ij}^{hs}, is related to the corresponding price in country j, p_j^{hs} by

$$q_{tj}^{hs} = p_j^{hs}(1 + t_{ij}) \tag{3.1}$$

In other words, q_{ij}^{hs} is the price of variety s of good h from country j which the consumers and producers in country i are facing. Similarly, if capital flows from country i to country j are in equilibrium, the rental rate of capital in country I, r_{ii}, is equal to the after-tax rental rate in country j, r_{ji} $(1 - \tau_{ji})$, for $i = c$, a, r, $j = c$, a, and $I \neq j$:

$$r_{ii} = r_{ji}(1 - \tau_{ji}) \tag{3.2}$$

Goods shipped from country j to country i are subject to a per unit transport cost of, $(1 - g_{ji})$, where $0 < g_{ji} < 1$, meaning that if one unit of a good leaves country j, $(1 - g_{ji})$ is used to pay for the transport cost so that only g_{ji} units arrive.[8] Capital movement from one country to another is costless.

Preferences and technologies

We first describe the preferences and technology in China, as the other two countries have similar features. There is a large number of households with identical and homothetic preferences. The aggregate utility of the country can be represented by

$$U_c = (D_c^m)^{\theta_c} (D_c^a)^{1-\theta_c} \tag{3.3}$$

where D_i^h is a sub-utility defined as

$$D_c^h = \left[\sum_{s=1}^{n_c^h} (c_c^{hs})^{\xi_c^h} + \sum_{s=1}^{n_a^h} (c_c^{hs})^{\xi_c^h} + \sum_{s=1}^{n_r^h} (c_c^{hs})^{\xi_c^h} \right]^{1/\xi_c^h} \tag{3.4}$$

where c_{ci}^{hs} is China's consumption of type s of good h from country i, $i = a, r$. Note that $\sigma_c^h = (1 - \xi_c^h)/1$ is the elasticity of substitution of sector h in China. Because of the presence of transport costs, China actually imports m_{ci}^{hs} units of type s of good h from country i, but of each unit $(1 - g_{ci})$ is spent on the transport costs and only g_{ci} arrives for consumption. Thus

$$c_{ci}^{hs} = m_{ci}^{hs} g_{ci} \tag{3.5}$$

Let us now turn to the production side of the Chinese economy. Firms use labour and effective capital, $\bar{K}$, to produce each type of the goods. Technologies are identical for all firms in all countries. To produce type s of good j, a firm uses the production function given by

$$\alpha_c^h + \beta_c^h X_c^{hs} = \min \left(\frac{1}{\gamma_c^h} L_c^{hs}, \frac{1}{\delta_c^h} \tilde{K}_c^{hs} \right) \tag{3.6}$$

where L_c^{hs} and $\tilde{K}_c^{hs}$ are the labour and effective capital inputs, respectively, and α_c^h, β_c^h, γ_c^h and δ_c^h are positive parameters. Equation (3.6) shows that there is no factor substitution between labour and effective capital in the production process. The left-hand side of the function indicates the presence of economies of scale. Another feature of the production function is that all firms in each sector face the production function given by (3.6). The effective capital used by the firm producing variety s of good h in China, $\tilde{K}_c^{hs}$, is an index determined by a combination of the amounts of capital from different countries, and is given by

$$\tilde{K}_c^{hs} = (K_{cc}^{hs})^{\phi_c} (K_{ca}^{hs})^{\mu_c} (K_{cr}^{hs})^{1-\phi_c-\mu_c} \tag{3.7}$$

The way the effective capital is defined is based on the Armington assumption (Armington, 1969) that capitals from different countries are not the same, and that all three different types of capital are essential in the production process (except in ROW). The effective capital of sector h for variety s of ASEAN can be defined in a similar way as

$$\tilde{K}_a^{hs} = (K_{ac}^{hs})^{\phi_a} (K_{aa}^{hs})^{\mu_a} (K_{ar}^{hs})^{1-\phi_a-\mu_a} \tag{3.8}$$

We assume that there is no capital movement from China and ASEAN to ROW. Thus the effective capital of sector h of ROW can be defined as

$$\tilde{K}_r^{hs} = K_{rr}^{hs} \tag{3.9}$$

Note that in terms of preferences and technologies, all the varieties in the same sector are symmetrical. This implies that firms will choose to produce the same output of each variety and the consumers will choose to consume the same quantity of each variety of the same good. Thus for an equilibrium, we can define $c_i^h = c_i^{hs}$, $m_{ij}^h = m_{ij}^{hs}$, $X_i^h = X_i^{hs}$, $p_i^h = p_i^{hs}$, and, $q_{ij}^h = q_{ij}^{hs}$, for $i, j = c, a, r$; $h = m, a$, and all varieties of s.

Utility and profit maximization

The national income of China is equal to

$$Y_c = w_c L_c + r_c \bar{K}_c + T_c \tag{3.10}$$

where T_c is international transfer China receives. In the present model, it is equal to the total tax revenue the government receives through tariffs and income taxes on capital from other countries: that is,

$$T_c = \sum_j [t_{cj}^m p_j^m n_j^m m_{cj}^m + t_{cj}^a p_j^a n_j^a m_{cj}^a + \tau_{cj} r_{cj} K_{cj}] \tag{3.11}$$

where p_j^h is the market price of good h in country j, and r_{ij} is the rental rate of the capital from country j in country i.[9] The tax rates and the tax revenue will be taken as given by all households. The tax revenue is distributed as a lump sum to all households.

A representative household will choose an optimal basket of goods for consumption, taking the prices and income as given, to maximize its utility. The representative household will have an income equal to the national income, and with homothetic and identical preferences among households, the consumption of the representative household is the same as that of the economy. The maximization problem can be conceptually broken down in two stages. In the first stage, the economy chooses the two sub-utility indices to maximize the utility function as given by (3.3), taking the national income in (3.10) as given. In the second stage, the economy will choose the optimal consumption basket of each type of goods in order to maximize the corresponding sub-utility index as given by (3.4).

In the first stage, the first-order conditions give

$$\theta_c Y_c = n_c^m p_c^m c_c^m + n_a^m q_{ca}^m m_{ca}^m + n_r^m q_{cr}^m m_{cr}^m \tag{3.12}$$

$$(1 - \theta_c) Y_c = n_c^a p_c^a c_c^a + n_a^a q_{ca}^a m_{ca}^a + n_r^a q_{cr}^a m_{cr}^a \tag{3.13}$$

where the symmetry between the varieties of the same product in each country has been used. The right-hand sides of equations (3.12) and (3.13) represent expenditure on the two groups of goods, manufacturing and agriculture.

In stage 2, the representative household will maximize the sub-utility of each group of goods by choosing the right basket of that group of goods, taking either equation (3.12) or (3.13) as given. The first-order conditions yield

$$m_{ca}^h = c_c^h \left(\frac{p_c^h}{q_{ca}^h} \right)^{\sigma_c^h} g_{ca}^{\sigma_c^h - 1} \tag{3.14}$$

$$m_{cr}^h = c_c^h \left(\frac{p_c^h}{q_{cr}^h} \right)^{\sigma_c^h} g_{cr}^{\sigma_c^h - 1} \tag{3.15}$$

where $h = m, a$. Substitute equations (3.14) and (3.15) into equations (3.12) and (3.13) to get the consumption demands for the goods:

$$c_c^h = \frac{\zeta_c^h Y_c}{\tilde{p}_c^h} \tag{3.16}$$

$$m_{ci}^h = \frac{\zeta_c^h}{\tilde{p}_c^h} \left(\frac{p_c^h}{q_{ci}^h} \right)^{\sigma_c^h} g_{ci}^{\sigma_c^h - 1} \tag{3.17}$$

where $i = a, r, h = m, a, \zeta_c^m = \theta_c, \zeta_c^a = 1 - \theta_c$, and

$$\tilde{p}_c^h = p_c^h \left[n_c^h + n_a^h (p_c^h g_{ca}/q_{ca}^h)^{\sigma_c^h - 1} + n_r^h (p_c^h g_{cr}/q_{cr}^h)^{\sigma_c^h - 1} \right] \tag{3.18}$$

Variable $\tilde{p}_c^h / n_c^h$ can be interpreted as the effective price of a variety of the local good h in China. Using equations (3.16) and (3.17), we can see that the consumption demands are functions of commodity prices and the number of varieties of each good, with some exogenous variables given.

We now turn to the maximization problem of a representative firm. The problem can also be solved in two hypothetical stages. In the first stage, the firm chooses the optimal inputs of labour and effective capital, taking all factor prices as given. In the second stage, the firms choose different types of capital to produce the optimal effective capital.

To analyse the firm's maximization problem, note that the cost of capital for the production of type s of good h is given by

$$R_c^h = r_{cc} K_{cc}^h + r_{ca} K_{ca}^h + r_{cu} K_{cr}^h \tag{3.19}$$

where $h = m$, a, and the symmetry among the varieties of each good has been used. In the second stage, a firm will choose optimal inputs of capital by minimizing the cost of capital as given by (3.19), taking the effective capital, $\tilde{K}_c^h$, its dependant on different types of capital as given by (3.7), and the rental rates of capital as given. The different types of cost-minimizing capital for the production of each type of good h are given by

$$\tilde{K}_{cc}^h = \left(\frac{r_{cc}}{\phi_c}\right)^{\phi_c - 1} \left(\frac{r_{ca}}{\mu_c}\right)^{\mu_c} \left(\frac{r_{cr}}{1 - \phi_c - \mu_c}\right)^{1 - \phi_c - \mu_c} \tilde{K}_c^h \qquad (3.20)$$

$$\tilde{K}_{ca}^h = \left(\frac{r_{cc}}{\phi_c}\right)^{\phi_c} \left(\frac{r_{ca}}{\mu_c}\right)^{\mu_c - 1} \left(\frac{r_{cr}}{1 - \phi_c - \mu_c}\right)^{1 - \phi_c - \mu_c} \tilde{K}_c^h \qquad (3.21)$$

$$\tilde{K}_{cu}^h = \left(\frac{r_{cc}}{\phi_c}\right)^{\phi_c} \left(\frac{r_{ca}}{\mu_c}\right)^{\mu_c} \left(\frac{r_{cr}}{1 - \phi_c - \mu_c}\right)^{1 - \phi_c - \mu_c} \tilde{K}_c^h \qquad (3.22)$$

Equations (3.20) to (3.22) are combined to give the cost-minimising cost of capital in sector h:

$$R_c^h = R_c^h \left(r_{cc}, r_{ca}, r_{cr}, \tilde{K}_c^h\right) = \tilde{r}_c \tilde{K}_c^h \qquad (3.23)$$

where

$$\tilde{r}_c = \left(\frac{r_{cc}}{\phi_c}\right)^{\phi_c} \left(\frac{r_{ca}}{\mu_c}\right)^{\mu_c} \left(\frac{r_{cr}}{1 - \phi_c - \mu_c}\right)^{1 - \phi_c - \mu_c} \qquad (3.24)$$

which can be interpreted as the rental rate of the effective capital.

In the first stage of profit maximization, the firm producing each type of good h maximizes the following profit function, taking factor prices and the production function (3.6) as given, by choosing the labour and effective capital inputs:

$$\pi_c^h = p_c^h X_c^h - w_c L_c^h - \tilde{r}_c \tilde{K}_c^h \qquad (3.25)$$

Substitute the production function in (3.6) into (3.25) to give

$$\pi_c^h = p_c^h X_c^h - (w_c \gamma_c^h + \tilde{r}_c \delta_c^h)(\alpha_c^h + \beta_c^h X_c^h) \qquad (3.26)$$

The first-order condition of the profit-maximizing problem thus gives

$$p_c^h = (\gamma_c^h w_c + \delta_c^h \tilde{r}_c)\beta_c^h \sigma_c/(\sigma_c - 1) \qquad (3.27)$$

Equation (3.27) gives the relations between commodity prices and factor prices.

Free entry and exit under monopolistic competition implies that firms earn zero profit in the long run. Setting $\pi_c^h = 0$ and rearranging terms, we have

$$X_c^h = \frac{(w_c \gamma_c^h + \tilde{r}_c \delta_c^h)(\alpha_c^h + \beta_c^h X_c^{hs})}{p_c^h} \tag{3.28}$$

Making use of the price in (3.27) and the effective capital in (3.23), equation (3.28) reduces to

$$X_c^h = \frac{\alpha_c^h(\sigma_c^h - 1)}{\beta_c^h} \tag{3.29}$$

Equation (3.29) shows that the equilibrium output of each type of good depends only on the values of the relevant parameters. The equation applies to ASEAN and the ROW as well.

Equation (3.29) has a very useful implication: because the production of each variety depends only on the relevant parameters and not on government policies, and because of the link between the output and inputs as given by the production function, the corresponding amounts of labour and effective capital employed by each firm will be independent of the policies of the governments. The labour and effective capital employment of each sector will then be determined by the number of varieties of the sector.

Market equilibrium

The equilibrium of the labour market in country i, $i = c, a, r$, is

$$\bar{L}_i = \sigma_i \left(\alpha_i^m n_i^m \gamma_i^m + \alpha_i^a n_i^a \gamma_i^a \right) \tag{3.30}$$

The right-hand side of equation (3.30) is the total demand for labour, where the symmetry between all types of goods in the same sector has been used. The equilibrium of the Chinese capital market is described by the following equation:

$$\bar{K}_c = n_c^a \tilde{K}_{cc}^a + n_c^m \tilde{K}_{cc}^m + n_a^a \tilde{K}_{ac}^a + n_a^m \tilde{K}_{ac}^m \tag{3.31}$$

In equation (3.31), the left-hand side equals the given endowed capital while the right-hand side represents the demand for China capital in the two sectors of China and ASEAN.[10] Similarly, the equilibrium of the capital market in ASEAN is described by

$$\bar{K}_a = n_c^a \tilde{K}_{ca}^a + n_c^m \tilde{K}_{ca}^m + n_a^a \tilde{K}_{aa}^a + n_a^m \tilde{K}_{aa}^m \tag{3.32}$$

while that of the ROW capital market is

$$\bar{K}_r = n_r^a \tilde{K}_r^a + n_r^m \tilde{K}_r^m + n_c^a \tilde{K}_{cr}^a + n_c^m \tilde{K}_{cr}^m + n_a^a \tilde{K}_{ar}^a + n_a^m \tilde{K}_{ar}^a \tag{3.33}$$

The equilibrium of the market of type s of good h in China is given by

$$X_c^h = c_c^h + m_{ac}^h + m_{rc}^h \tag{3.34}$$

Similar equations for ASEAN and ROW can be stated.[11]

Simulation and the benchmark

Solving the system

The present three-country model can be described by the following reduced-form equations:

$$X_c^h = c_c^h + m_{ac}^h + m_{rc}^h \tag{3.35}$$

$$X_a^h = c_a^h + m_{ca}^h + m_{ra}^h \tag{3.36}$$

$$X_r^h = c_r^h + m_{cr}^h + m_{ae}^h \tag{3.37}$$

$$\bar{K}_c = n_c^a \tilde{K}_{cc}^a + n_c^m \tilde{K}_{cc}^m + n_a^a \tilde{K}_{ac}^a + n_a^m \tilde{K}_{ac}^m \tag{3.38}$$

$$\bar{K}_a = n_c^a \tilde{K}_{ca}^a + n_c^m \tilde{K}_{ca}^m + n_a^a \tilde{K}_{aa}^a + n_a^m \tilde{K}_{aa}^m \tag{3.39}$$

$$\bar{L}_i = \sigma_i \left(\alpha_i^m n_i^m \gamma_i^m + \alpha_i^a n_i^a \gamma^a \right) \tag{3.40}$$

Each of (3.35) to (3.37) in fact contains two equations, and (3.40) contains three equations. Together with (3.38) and (3.39), there are eleven equations. Note also that the equilibrium condition for the ROW capital market is regarded as redundant and is thus not included in the system of equations because of Walras's Law. All the demands can be expressed as functions of factor prices, commodity prices and tax rates, when given the exogenous variables and policy parameters, but commodity prices can in turn be expressed in terms of factor prices. Therefore equations (3.35) to (3.40) can all be expressed in terms of factor prices and the numbers of varieties. There are three wage rates and seven rental rates in the three countries. Equation (3.2), four of them, can be used to provide the links among the rental rates, and can be used to eliminate four rental rates. There are six unknown numbers of varieties in the countries. Thus there are twelve unknowns left, but one of them is chosen as the *numéraire* (having a value of one). When given the exogenous variables and policy parameters, the eleven equations are then solved for the eleven unknown variables. Once these variables are known, other endogenous variables can be solved using the equations described in the previous section.

The present study considers three sets of policy parameters and the corresponding three-country equilibria. A change in the policy parameters is due to (1) China's accession to the WTO in 2001; and (2) the formation of a free trade area between China and ASEAN. Thus this chapter focuses on the equilibria in the following situations:

(a) the benchmark, pre-WTO and pre-FTA;
(b) Scenario 1, after China's WTO accession;
(c) Scenario 2, after China's WTO accession and an ASEAN–China FTA.

The benchmark is the one before China's accession to the WTO and before the China-ASEAN FTA. China's accession to the WTO leads to unilateral trade liberalization (Scenario 1). It involves a reduction of the tariffs on goods from other countries and a change in its corporate tax policies. The formation of the China–ASEAN FTA implies a mutual reduction of the tariffs (down to zero) by these countries on the goods from other member countries of the FTA (Scenario 2). We will solve for the equilibrium of the system under each of these situations. A comparison between the benchmark and Scenario 1 shows the impacts of unilateral trade liberalization while a comparison between Scenario 1 and Scenario 2 will show the effects of regional trade liberalization on the member countries and non-member countries.

To solve for an equilibrium, we use actual observed data as much as possible. The tariff rates and corporate tax rates in each of the situations are based on the announced policies of the countries. Some figures, such as factor endowments and national income, come from government publications or are estimates made by others. The preference and technology parameters, including transport costs, are our estimates or assumptions. More details about the data sources, the assumptions, and the values of the parameters are given in Tables 3.1–6.

Table 3.1 presents the endowments of the countries. The labour endowment, or the effective labour, of a country depends on the quantity of physical labour and human capital. We use the approach suggested in Duffy and Papageorgiou (2000) to define the effective labour of a country, with human capital in different countries carefully considered. The table shows that China has the most workers, but ROW has the most effective labour, mainly because ROW has a substantial amount of human capital. ROW also has the highest physical capital. The capital–labour ratio is the highest in ROW but the lowest in China.

Table 3.2 presents the tariff rates imposed by the countries in different situations. We allow the possibility that each country imposes different tariff rates on different goods from the same country. When China joins the WTO (from the benchmark to Scenario 1), it reduces its tariff on manufacturing products from 11.3 per cent to 9.1 per cent, and that on agricultural products from 19.2 per cent to 15.8 per cent. ASEAN and ROW maintain the same tariff policies as before. When China and ASEAN form an FTA, with China's membership of the WTO (from Scenario 1 to Scenario 2) they remove the tariffs on the goods from each other.

Table 3.1 Endowments of the countries (1996–2000 average)

	China	ASEAN	ROW[f]
Labour, E_i[a]	754	255	363
Human capital, H_i[b]	5.21	5.07	10.33
Effective labour Coefficient, X_i[c]	0.18	0.19	0.68
Effective labour, $L_i = H_i^{Xi} E_i$[d]	1,014	347	1,497
Physical capital, K_i	674	464	5,107
K_i / L_i[e]	0.66	1.34	3.1

Notes and Sources:

[a] These are the labour force figures of the countries in 2002. For Malaysia (2001), Vietnam (2000) and Cambodia (2000), the labour force figures are based on the corresponding figures in the years indicated and the assumption that the growth rates of the labour force were the same as their population growth rates. Brunei and Laos did not have any labour force figures. These countries' labour force for the year 2002 are estimated from their population figure by assuming that they have the same labour participation rate as the remaining ASEAN countries. Data for the ASEAN countries and China are from the Asian Development Bank website (www.adb.org/statistics). Population data for Brunei, USA, France and Canada are taken from the World Bank website (http://www.worldbank.org/data/countrydata/countrydata.html). However, the labour force data for all ROW countries is taken from International Labour Organization website (http://laborsta.ilo.org/). Figures are in millions of labour units.

[b] Human capital (average number of years of education) figures are for the year 1987 and they are taken from Chris Papageorgiou's website, http://www.bus.lsu.edu/economics/faculty/cpapageorgiou/personal/welcome.html). This data set was used in Duffy and Papageorgiou (2000). Figures are in terms of average number of years of education units.

[c] Duffy and Papageorgiou (2000) provided estimates of X_i for 82 countries. Following that article, X_i estimate for low K/L countries is used for China. Their data samples include some ASEAN countries in both low and low-middle K/L groups. We used the average of those for the whole ASEAN countries. High K/L countries' X_i estimate is used for the all ROW countries except Japan. The parameter estimate for Japan is zero.

[d] Effective labour is the combination of population and human capital. Following Duffy and Papageorgiou (2000) effective capital is defined as $L_i - H_i^{Xi} E_i$. Figures are in millions of effective labour units.

[e] Capital stock estimates for a group of countries are given in Duffy and Papageorgiou (2000) for years up to 1987 (http://www.bus.lsu.edu/economics/faculty/cpapageorgiou/personal/welcome.html). The figures are extended to year 2000 by using World Penn Tables real USD investment data (http://pwt.econ.upenn.edu/php_site/pwt61_form.php). Capital is assumed to depreciate by 6 per cent every year following the method described in Duffy and Papageorgiou (2000). There are few data regarding capital stock in the ASEAN economies available. The capital stock for the whole ASEAN is estimated by assuming that the K/L ratio of the countries with no data (Brunei, Vietnam, Cambodia, Laos and Myanmar) is the same as the average K/L ratio of the ones with data (Indonesia, Malaysia, Singapore, Thailand and the Philippines). Figures are in USD ten billion units.

[f] ROW includes the USA, Japan, Australia, Canada, Italy, France, Germany and Hong Kong.

The corporate tax rates of the countries are given in Table 3.3. As China joins the WTO, due to harmonization of the tax systems, China actually raises its effective tax rates from 15 per cent to 33 per cent.

Table 3.2 Tariffs of the countries in different scenarios (%)

(a) benchmark

Country j	China		ASEAN		ROW	
	t_{cj}^m	t_{cj}^a	t_{aj}^m	t_{aj}^a	t_{rj}^m	t_{rj}^a
China	–	–	7.8	11.4	3.6	5.5
ASEAN	11.3	19.2	–	–	3.6	5.5
ROW	11.3	19.2	7.8	11.4	–	–

(b) post-WTO

Country j	China		ASEAN		ROW	
	t_{cj}^m	t_{cj}^a	t_{aj}^m	t_{aj}^a	t_{rj}^m	t_{rj}^a
China	–	–	7.8	11.4	3.6	5.5
ASEAN	9.1	15.8	–	–	3.6	5.5
ROW	9.1	15.8	7.8	11.4	–	–

(c) post-FTA

Country j	China		ASEAN		ROW	
	t_{cj}^m	t_{cj}^a	t_{aj}^m	t_{aj}^a	t_{rj}^m	t_{rj}^a
China	–	–	0	0	3.6	5.5
ASEAN	0	0	–	–	3.6	5.5
ROW	9.1	15.8	7.8	11.4	–	–

Notes and Sources:

1 Benchmark tariffs for agriculture and non-agriculture products were taken from the WTO website for the year 2002 except for Malaysia (2001), Thailand (2001), Brunei (2001) and Philippines (2003: see http://stat.wto.org/). The parameter for ASEAN is the GDP weighted average of individual member countries. ASEAN countries' GDPs are taken from the Asian Development Bank website for the year 2002 (http://www.adb.org/statistics). The ASEAN figure does not include Myanmar and Laos due to lack of data.

2 Post-WTO data represent the maximum tariff commitment of China in both agriculture and others.

3 ROW includes the USA, Japan, Australia, Canada, France, Italy, Germany and Hong Kong. Figures for ROW are GDP-weighted averages of individual figures.

Tables 3.4–6 present the assumed transport costs, preference parameters and technology parameters of the countries used in the simulation. These parameters are used in all the simulation exercises below.

Table 3.3 Corporate taxes of the countries in different scenarios (%)

(a) benchmark

Country k	China[a] τ_{ck}	ASEAN[b] τ_{ak}	ROW[c] τ_{rk}
China	–	28.7	38.3
ASEAN	15	–	38.3
ROW	15	28.7	–

(b) post-WTO

Country k	China[a] τ_{ck}	ASEAN[b] τ_{ak}	ROW[c] τ_{rk}
China	–	28.7	38.3
ASEAN	33	–	38.3
ROW	33	28.7	–

(c) post-FTA

Country k	China[a] τ_{ck}	ASEAN[b] τ_{ak}	ROW[c] τ_{rk}
China	–	28.7	38.3
ASEAN	33	–	38.3
ROW	33	28.7	–

Notes and Sources:
[a] Following the reports by PricewaterhouseCoopers (http://www.pwccn.com/home/eng/index.html), instead of the statutory rate, preferential corporate tax rates for the special zones are used. However, the same reports also claim that preferential treatments of the foreign companies will end due to WTO harmonization.
[b] GDP-weighted average of six ASEAN members (Indonesia, Malaysia, Singapore, Thailand, Vietnam and the Philippines).
[c] ROW includes the USA, Japan, Australia, Canada, France, Italy, Germany and Hong Kong. Figures for ROW are GDP-weighted averages of individual figures.
[d] Corporate tax rates are taken from the KPMG website (http://www.kpmg.co.uk/pubs/taxrates_04.pdf) for the year 2004.

The benchmark

To have a better understanding of the present model, we first present and analyse the benchmark. This is the situation before China becomes a member of the WTO and before China and ASEAN form a free trade area.

We substitute the values of the parameters described in Tables 3.1–6, including the post-WTO policy parameters, into the system of equations described in (3.35) to (3.40), and solve the system of equations using *Mathematica*. The results of the eleven unknown factor prices and number

Table 3.4   Transportation costs[a]

Country *j*	China[b] g_{cj}	ASEAN[c] g_{aj}	ROW[d] g_{rj}
China	–	0.90	0.87
ASEAN	0.90	–	0.83
ROW	0.85	0.83	–

Notes and Sources:

1 Variable g_{ij} is defined in such a way that it represents the fraction of a good left for consumption after paying for the transportation cost. So the transportation cost is $1 - g_{ij}$.

2 Transportation costs between countries are computed by using distance between capital cities as a proxy (http://www.wcrl.ars.usda.gov/cec/java/lat-long.htm). Following Frankel (1997), estimation of transportation cost between China and USA is 16 per cent. Transportation costs between ASEAN economies, USA and China are calculated by applying the formula:

$$Tcost\ (I,\ j) = 0.05 + \frac{Distance\ (i,j)}{Distance\ (China,\ USA)} * 0.11$$

This formula assumes that transportation cost consists of two components: a fixed cost and a part that is a function of distance. If the distance between two countries is the same as the distance between China and USA, the formula gives 16 per cent transportation costs. If the distance is greater, then the transportation cost increases less than proportionately due to the fixed cost term. Note also that Jakarta, Indonesia is chosen as a representative of all the ASEAN economies due to its size in terms of population and GDP. Considering that ASEAN economies are very localized compared to the countries/economies of ROW, this assumption did not change the result very much.

3 ROW includes the USA, Japan, Australia, Canada, France, Italy, Germany and Hong Kong. Figures for ROW are GDP-weighted averages of individual figures.

Table 3.5   Preference parameters

	China[a]	ASEAN[b]	ROW[c]
θ_i	0.53	0.27	0.27
ξ_i^m	5/6	5/6	5/6
σ_i^m	6	6	6
ξ_i^a	5/6	5/6	5/6
σ_i^a	6	6	6

Notes and Sources:

1 Variable θ_i is calculated by using the share of industry and agriculture + services in total domestic expenditure. All the figures are for the year 2003. Expenditure shares were taken from the *CIA Factbook Online* database (http://www.cia.gov/cia/publications/factbook/fields/2012.html). The parameter for ASEAN is the GDP-weighted average of individual members. ASEAN member country GDPs are taken from Asian Development Bank website for the year 2002 (except Myanmar, where the figures are for 2001: see http://www.adb.org/statistics). ASEAN data excludes Brunei due to lack of data.

2 $\sigma_i^h = 1/(1 - \xi_i^h)$.

Table 3.6   Technology parameters

(a) Industry *m*

Country *i*	China[a]	ASEAN[b]	ROW[c]
α_i^m	2	2	2
β_i^m	1	1	1
γ_i^m	0.20	0.30	0.48
δ_i^m	0.33	1.22	2.37
ϕ_i^m	0.90	0.914	1
μ_i^m	0.007	0.0002	0

(b) Industry *a*

Country *i*	China[a]	ASEAN[b]	ROW[c]
α_i^a	2	2	2
β_i^a	1	1	1
γ_i^a	0.80	0.70	0.52
δ_i^a	0.17	0.41	1.51
ϕ_i^m	0.90	0.914	1
μ_i^m	0.007	0.00017	0

Notes and Sources:

Industry *m* (manufacturing)   Industry *a* (agriculture)

1 The values of α_i^h and β_i^h are taken from Amiti (1998).

2 The values of parameters γ_i^h are obtained from the ratio of labour shares in the two industries and the ratio of production shares as follows:

$$\frac{L_i^a L_i}{L_i^m L_i} \cdot \frac{n_i^m X_i^m/(n_i^a X_i^a + n_i^m X_i^m)}{n_i^a X_i^a/(n_i^a X_i^a + n_i^m X_i^m)} = \frac{\gamma_i^a}{\gamma_i^m}$$

This ratio gives us the ratio of the labour intensity parameter if α_i^j, β_i^j δ_i^j and the prices of capital and labour-intensive goods are the same in both industries. After calculating this ratio, individual parameters for γ_i^j are solved for each country and each industry by using the fact that. $\gamma_i^a + \gamma_i^m = 1$.

3 In order to estimate δ_i^j for these countries the distribution of the employment of effective capital need to be calculated. Unfortunately these data are not available and we need to use some estimates. Sectoral distribution of FDI flows to ASEAN countries is available in the ASEAN secretariat website (http://www.aseansec.org) for the 1999–2003 period. For this period, the FDI shares of agriculture + services and industry are 48 per cent and 52 per cent respectively. The assumptions that parameters in the effective capital function are identical for different sectors ($\phi_i^a = \phi_i^m$ and $\mu_i^a = \mu_i^m$), free flow of capital within the country, and identical corporate income taxes on foreign direct investments on different sectors simplify the estimation. These assumptions help us conclude that a sector's share in total FDI will be equal to its share in total effective capital (including domestic capital). From the full employment condition, we can show that

$$\frac{1}{\gamma^j} L^j = \frac{1}{\delta^j} \bar{K}^j$$

Rearranging this term gives $\delta^j = \gamma^j \bar{K}^j/L^j$. Given the values for these parameters, we could calculate this parameter. Due to lack of data, Chinese data are assumed to have the same distribution of FDI in different sectors. The same parameters for the USA are calculated by using the distribution of fixed capital stock data (2002) provided by the US Department of Commerce (http://www.bea.doc.gov). In the calculations, the fixed capital stock is classified as 'agriculture+services' and industry categories. The shares of these sectors in the total capita stock (excluding real estate) are computed.

Notes and Sources: continued

4 The total expenditure shares of domestic and foreign capital are calculated by using domestic and FDI stock estimates for the average in the 2000–2 period. The ratio of value of FDI stock to the domestic capital stock gives us the parameter for the foreign capital. In order to distinguish further the composition of FDI as Chinese (or ASEAN) or USA we calculate the share of Chinese direct investment in ASEAN in the total value of FDI in ASEAN. This figure is 0.2 per cent for the 1995–2003 period. FDI and fixed capital investment figures are taken from the Asian Development Bank website (http://www.adb.org/statistics). Investment and FDI figures are added successively in order to calculate the stock of capital. A 6 per cent depreciation rate is considered following Duffy and Papageorgiou (2000). Some FDI data from the ASEAN Secretariat website (http://www.aseansec.org/home.htm) are also used in order to find the share of Chinese FDI in the total FDI to ASEAN.

5 ROW countries are the source of roughly 70 per cent of the FDI to China and ASEAN. We assumed that all of the FDI flows were coming from these countries.

6 Capital stock estimate for a group of countries is given in Duffy and Papageorgiou (2000) up to year 1987 (http://www.bus.lsu.edu/economics/faculty/cpapageorgiou/personal/ welcome.html). These data are extended to year 2000 by using World Penn Tables real USD investment data (http://pwt.econ.upenn.edu/php_site/pwt61_form.php). Capital is assumed to depreciate by 6 per cent every year following the method described in Duffy and Papageorgiou (2000). There are few data regarding capital stock of the ASEAN economies. Capital stock for the whole of ASEAN is estimated by assuming that the *K/L* ratios of the countries with no data (Brunei, Vietnam, Cambodia, Laos and Myanmar) are the same as the average *K/L* ratio of the ones with data (Indonesia, Malaysia, Singapore, Thailand and the Philippines). Figures are in USD 10 billion units.

of varieties of the two goods in the three countries are used to determine other endogenous variables.

Our analysis will focus on the trade and FDI relations among the countries and their welfare. Table 3.7 presents the flow of goods between any two pairs of countries. The export and import of each of the two types of goods of each country are presented in each of the three panels. Panel (a) shows that China is a significant exporter (in both gross and net terms) of manufacturing, most of which goes to ROW. China also exports agriculture, but the table shows that China imports much more agriculture than it exports. As a result, China is a net exporter of manufacturing but a net importer of agriculture. Most of China's foreign trade is with ROW. Another interesting feature is that while China has a trade surplus with ROW, it does have a small trade deficit with ASEAN.

ASEAN has smaller trade volumes with other countries. It has a trade surplus of 54.0 in manufacturing with other countries but a trade deficit in agriculture. It has about the same sizes of export to China and to ROW, but it imports more manufacturing from China and more agriculture from ROW. As a result, ASEAN has a trade deficit in manufacturing with China, but a trade deficit in agriculture with ROW.

ROW is a big trading partner for China and ASEAN. Because of its size, it has much bigger volumes of trade. It is a net importer of manufacturing from the other two countries, but a net exporter of agriculture. This model captures the fact that ROW runs a big trade deficit in terms of manufacturing and is a big exporter of agriculture.

Table 3.7   Foreign trade among the countries in the benchmark

(a) China

	Export to		Import from		Balance		
	in M	in A	in M	in A	in M	in A	Total
ASEAN	251	175	170	268	81	−93	−12
ROW	1,288	479	171	1,082	1,117	−602	514
Total	1,538	654	340	1,350	1,198	−696	502

(b) ASEAN

	Export to		Import from		Balance		
	in M	in A	in M	in A	in M	in A	Total
China	169.7	268.1	250.8	174.9	−81.0	93.2	12.2
ROW	167.9	296.2	32.9	436.3	135.0	−140.0	−5.1
Total	337.6	564.4	283.6	611.2	54.0	−46.9	7.1

(c) ROW

	Export to		Import from		Balance		
	in M	in A	in M	in A	in M	in A	Total
China	170.7	1,081.5	1,287.5	479.1	−1,116.8	602.4	−514.4
ASEAN	32.9	436.3	167.9	296.2	−135.0	140.0	5.1
Total	203.6	1,517.8	1,455.4	775.4	−1,251.8	742.4	−509.4

Notes:
M = manufacturing; A = agriculture.
Balance = export − import (Numbers shown may not be exactly the same as the differences because of rounding.)

Table 3.8 shows the capital flows among the three countries. In panel (a), one can see that China is a big recipient of foreign capital, mostly from ROW, both in manufacturing and in agriculture sectors. China and ASEAN have mutual flows of capital, even in the same industry. However, the outflow of capital from China is insignificant. So between China and ASEAN, capital flows mainly from ASEAN to China. Panel (b) shows a similar picture for ASEAN: it is a major recipient of capital from ROW. ASEAN sends considerable amounts of capital (manufacturing and agriculture) to China, but none to ROW. On the whole ASEAN is an important destination country for FDI from ROW.

ROW is clearly the most important source of FDI. Recall that the present model assumes that no capital flows from other countries to ROW. Because of its size, ROW is naturally a major source of FDI for China and ASEAN.

Table 3.8   Capital flows in the benchmark

(a) China

	Capital outflow		Capital inflow		Balance		
	in M	in A	in M	in A	in M	in A	Total
ASEAN	0.00068	0.00615	19	6	19	6	25
ROW	0.0	0.0	355	112	355	112	467
Total	0.00068	0.00615	373	118	373	118	492

(b) ASEAN

	Capital outflow		Capital inflow		Balance		
	in M	in A	in M	in A	in M	in A	Total
China	18.6	5.9	0.00631	0.00615	−18.6	−5.9	−24.5
ROW	0.0	0.0	21.4	20.8	21.4	20.8	42.2
Total	18.6	5.9	21.4	20.8	2.7	14.9	17.7

(c) ROW

	Capital outflow		Capital inflow		Balance		
	in M	in A	in M	in A	in M	in A	Total
China	354.7	112.5	0.0	0.0	−354.7	−112.5	−467.2
ASEAN	21.4	20.8	0.0	0.0	−21.4	−20.8	−42.2
Total	376.0	133.3	0.0	0.0	−376.0	−133.3	−509.4

Notes:
M = manufacturing; A = agriculture.
Balance = capital inflow – capital outflow (Numbers shown may not be exactly the same as the differences because of rounding.)

Table 3.9   Indices of intra-industry trade and intra-industry capital flows

	Intra-industry trade			Intra-industry *K* flows
	C–A	C–R	A–R	C–A
Manufacturing	0.8074	0.2341	0.3275	0.0007
Agriculture	0.7897	0.6140	0.8088	0.0021
Total	0.7872	0.5189	0.7015	0.0004

Notes:
C–A = China–ASEAN; C–R = China–ROW; A–R = ASEAN–ROW.
K = capital flow.
For the formulae of the indices of intra-industry trade and intra-industry capital flow, see the text.

In addition to the directions of movements of goods and capital, the possibility of intra-industry flows is equally important. Table 3.9 presents the indices of intra-industry trade and capital flows. For each sector, the index of intra-industry trade or capital flows between two countries, I_i, is defined as

$$I_i = 1 - \frac{|E_i - M_i|}{E_i + M_i} \tag{3.41}$$

where E_i is the export of sector i or capital inflow of one of the countries and M_i is the import of sector i or capital outflow, $i = m, a$. To show the overall degree of intra-industry trade and capital flow, the aggregate index of intra-industry trade or capital flow between two countries can be defined as

$$AI = \frac{(\Sigma_i E_i + \Sigma_i M_i) - \Sigma_i |E_i - M_i|}{(\Sigma_i E_i + \Sigma_i M_i) - (\Sigma_i E_i - \Sigma_i M_i)} \tag{3.42}$$

Note that the formula given in (3.42) includes an adjustment for the existence of trade imbalance.

The indices of intra-industry trade and capital flows for different pairs of countries in the benchmark are presented in Table 3.9. In terms of trade, China and ASEAN have a high degree of intra-industry trade in both manufacturing and agriculture sectors. This phenomenon is probably because of similar factor endowments of China and ASEAN. Trade between China and ROW is more of an inter-industry kind. The degree of intra-industry trade in manufacturing between ASEAN and ROW is also small, but the index for trade in agriculture between ASEAN and ROW is very high. The last row of Table 3.9 represents the aggregate indices of intra-industry trade, and it shows that China and ASEAN have a high degree of intra-industry trade. The latter point is an important one, which has not received much attention in the literature.

The last column of Table 3.9 presents the indices of intra-industry capital flow between China and ASEAN.[12] The table shows that the degree of intra-industry capital flow between China and ASEAN in either sector is positive but very small. That is because China receives considerable amount of capital from ASEAN but is not a major source of FDI. Note that because it is assumed that ROW receives no capital from China or ASEAN, the index of intra-industry capital flows between ROW and China or ASEAN is zero.

Scenario 1: China's World Trade Organization accession

In this section, we try to measure the impacts of China's WTO accession on foreign trade, capital movement and welfare. As China becomes a new member country of the WTO, it is committed to liberalizing its trade and FDI policies. Three major policy changes made by China can be summarized as follows: (1) China reduces its tariff rate on imported manufacturing from 11.3 per cent to 9.1 per cent and that on agriculture from 19.2 per cent to 15.8 per cent; (2) China opens some domestic sectors to foreign direct investment; and (3) for the purpose of accounting harmonization, China eliminates certain advantages granted to foreign firms, resulting in an increase in the effective taxes on foreign capital from 15 per cent to 33 per cent in China. The changes in China's trade and FDI policies are summarized by Tables 3.2 and 3.3. Note that all other countries do not have any obligation to make corresponding changes in their trade and FDI policies.

In order to find the impacts of this unilateral trade liberalization by China, we solve the equilibrium represented by equations (3.35) to (3.40), using the new policy parameters given in Table 3.2. The values of the endogenous variables in the system of equations are then used to determine all other endogenous variables of the model.

Tables 3.10 and 3.11 present the changes in the flows of commodities and capital among the three countries. Table 3.10 indicates that China's unilateral trade liberalization does lead to a substantial increase in its imports. In particular, there is an increase in China's import of manufacturing and agriculture from ASEAN and ROW. The increase in manufacturing imports from ROW is even more significant, at 55 per cent. Such an increase in imports causes a drop in domestic production of these products, leading to a shift of the resources from the import-competing sectors to the exportable sectors. As a result, China experiences a simultaneous rise in export of both manufacturing and agriculture. The jump in the export of agriculture is even more impressive than that of manufacturing: 28 per cent versus 7 per cent.

Not surprisingly, ASEAN benefits, at least in terms of trade with China, as a result of China's unilateral trade liberalization: its exports of manufacturing and agriculture to China jump by 27 per cent and 18 per cent, respectively. At the same time, its imports from China also rise, especially in agriculture. On the whole, ASEAN sees a substantial increase in trade with China as the latter joins the WTO.

ROW also experiences an expansion of trade as China becomes a member of the WTO, especially in terms of export of manufacturing to China. The main reason probably is that there is a bigger gap between China's capital–labour ratio and ROW's capital–labour ratio than between China's ratio and ASEAN's ratio. In other words, ROW, being the most capital-abundant country (group of countries), will be able significantly to improve its exports, especially its export of manufacturing, to China.

More interesting is that China's unilateral action encourages flows of commodities in all directions. This suggests that a country's trade liberal-

Table 3.10 Foreign trade among the countries after China's WTO Accession

(a) China

	Export to		Import from		Balance		
	in M	in A	in M	in A	in M	in A	Total
ASEAN	282 (12)	222 (27)	216 (27)	317 (18)	66	−95	−29
ROW	1,371 (7)	615 (28)	265 (55)	1,261 (17)	1,106	−647	460
Total	1,653 (7)	837 (28)	481 (41)	1,579 (17)	1,172	−742	431

(b) ASEAN

	Export to		Import from		Balance		
	in M	in A	in M	in A	in M	in A	Total
China	216 (27)	317 (18)	282 (12)	222 (27)	−66	95	29
ROW	185 (10)	342 (15)	47 (42)	491 (13)	138	−150	−12
Total	400 (19)	659 (17)	328 (16)	714 (17)	72	−55	17

(c) ROW

	Export to		Import from		Balance		
	in M	in A	in M	in A	in M	in A	Total
China	265 (55)	1,261 (17)	1,371 (7)	615 (28)	−1,106	647	−460
ASEAN	47 (42)	491 (13)	185 (10)	342 (15)	−138	150	12
Total	311 (53)	1,753 (16)	1,556 (7)	956 (23)	−1,244	796	−448

Notes:
M = manufacturing; A = agriculture.
Balance = export − import (Numbers shown may not be exactly the same as the differences because of rounding.)
Numbers in parentheses represent the percentage changes from the corresponding values in the benchmark.

ization could lead not only to a more efficient allocation of its domestic resources, but also to a more efficient allocation of resources in the rest of the world. As a result, the world's volume of trade increases.

One lesson suggested by our results is that while it is true that China's WTO accession could improve the competitiveness of China's products in the rest of the world, other countries could expect to export more to China. After all, China is not only a producer but also a consumer.

The impacts of China's WTO accession on international capital movements are presented in Table 3.11. As noted above, this policy includes changes in China's corporate taxation policy (i.e., China raises its effective tax rate on foreign investment income from 15 per cent to 33 per cent). Such a policy obviously has negative impacts on FDI in China, as

Table 3.11 Capital flows among the countries after China's WTO accession

(a) China

	Export to		Import from		Balance		
	in M	in A	in M	in A	in M	in A	Total
ASEAN	0.0067 (890)	0.0062 (0.5)	14 (–23)	5 (–21)	14	5	19
ROW	0	0	302 (–15)	99 (–12)	302	99	401
Total	0.0067 (890)	0.0062 (0.5)	316 (–15)	104 (–12)	316	104	420

(b) ASEAN

	Export to		Import from		Balance		
	in M	in A	in M	in A	in M	in A	Total
China	14 (–23)	5 (–21)	0.0067 (6)	0.0062 (0)	–14.3	–4.7	–18.9
ROW	0 (0)	0 (0)	24.7 (16)	22.8 (9)	24.7	22.8	47.5
Total	14 (–23)	5 (–21)	24.7 (16)	22.8 (9)	10.5	18.1	28.5

(c) ROW

	Export to		Import from		Balance		
	in M	in A	in M	in A	in M	in A	Total
China	302 (–15)	99 (–12)	0 (0)	0 (0)	–302	–99	–401
ASEAN	25 (16)	23 (9)	0 (0)	0 (0)	–25	–23	–47
Total	326 (13)	122 (9)	0 (0)	0 (0)	–326	–122	–448

Notes:
M = manufacturing; A = agriculture.
Balance = capital inflow – capital outflow.
Numbers in parentheses represent the percentage changes from the corresponding values in the benchmark.

confirmed by Table 3.11: the flows of foreign capital in both sectors to China drop substantially. There is an increase in the outflow of capital from both sectors in China. An interesting point is that while the percentage increase in the amount of capital outflow from China is huge, the absolute amount is in fact negligible because the amount of capital outflow was small to begin with.

Probably the more important result of China's WTO accession is that ROW increases its investment in ASEAN significantly while lowering its investment in China. This investment diversion effect is contrary to what some people have been worrying about. The reason for this result is that China actually tries to take back the incentives it provided to foreign investors before its accession to the WTO. Thus instead of losing foreign

Table 3.12 Indices of intra-industry trade and capital movement after China's WTO accession

	Intra-industry trade			Intra-industry *K* flows
	C–A	C–R	A–R	C–A
Manufacturing	0.8674 (7)	0.3238 (38)	0.4028 (23)	0.0009 (39)
Agriculture	0.8241 (4)	0.6553 (7)	0.8203 (1)	0.0026 (27)
Total	0.8218 (4)	0.5763 (11)	0.7217 (3)	0.0007 (72)

Notes:
C–A = China–ASEAN; C–R = China–ROW; A–R = ASEAN–ROW.
For the formulae of the indices of intra-industry trade and intra-industry capital flow, see the text.
Numbers in parentheses represent percentage changes in values from the corresponding ones before China's WTO accession.

investment, as some people have suggested, ASEAN actually gains more investment from ROW.

We now examine how intra-industry trade and capital flows may be affected. Table 3.12 presents the relevant indices, which are computed using equations (3.41) and (3.42). In order to show the degrees of impacts, the table also gives the percentage changes from the corresponding values in the benchmark. One interesting phenomenon is that all the indices go up, meaning that the intra-industry trade and capital flows between any pair of countries are enhanced. While intra-industry trade between China and ASEAN, and that between ASEAN and ROW, increase moderately, that between China and ROW displays a much bigger impact. In general, intra-industry trade in manufacturing is much greater than that in agriculture (not surprisingly).

Table 3.12 also shows the indices of intra-industry capital flows. The degree of intra-industry capital flows between China and ASEAN is small, since capital flows mostly from ASEAN and China. China is still not yet an important source of FDI. Although the indices of intra-industry capital flows between China and ROW are small, they show substantial percentage increases.

The welfare impacts of China's WTO accession are given in Table 3.13, which presents the values of GNP (including tax revenues) at domestic prices and welfare of the countries in different scenarios.[13] The welfare of each country is the utility of the representative household defined by equation (3.3). Table 3.13 shows that China's WTO accession leads to small changes in the countries' welfare; in particular, it benefits ASEAN but hurts China, while the utility of ROW remains about the same as before.

Perhaps the more interesting result is that China may be hurt by its accession to the WTO. Two questions immediately arise: how could this happen, and what are the implications, if any?

Table 3.13   Welfare impacts of various policies

	China		ASEAN		ROW	
	GNP_c	U_c	GNP_a	U_a	GNP_r	U_r
Benchmark	6,668	2,661	1,448	682	7,814	3,945
Post-WTO	7,520	2,652	1,676	687	8,983	3,944
change, %[a]	(12.8)	(–0.3)	(15.7)	(0.7)	(15.0)	(0.0)
Post-FTA	7,553	2,647	1,758	711	8,998	3,930
change, %[b]	(0.4)	(–0.2)	(4.9)	(3.5)	(0.2)	(–0.4)

[a] Percentage change from the corresponding ones in the benchmark.
[b] Percentage change from the corresponding ones in the post-WTO case.
Note: The welfare of each country is equal to the utility of the representative given by
  equation (3.3).

To identify the factors of a drop in welfare in the present model is not easy because the endogenous variables in general are inter-related. However, we can still work out the thinking behind this result. First, we note from Table 3.13 that after becoming a member of the WTO, China's national income increases by 12.8 per cent. This means that the gain in income from efficient resource allocation could cover the negative impact of a loss in tariff and corporate tax revenues. Second, Table 3.14 shows that China's WTO accession leads to jumps in the prices of all commodities. What is more, agricultural products become much more expensive than the manufacturing products do. For China, that is a bad news in terms of welfare because China is a net importer of agricultural products. Thus China experiences a deterioration in its terms of trade. Table 3.15 shows the numbers of varieties of the products produced by the countries. The last column gives the total number of varieties, which is an approximate indication of what the consumers enjoy.[14] The table shows that the con-

Table 3.14   Terms of trade

	China		ASEAN		ROW	
	p_c^m	p_c^a	p_a^m	p_a^a	p_r^m	p_r^a
Benchmark	3.98	3.09	3.61	2.80	3.89	2.94
Post-WTO	4.43	3.53	4.05	3.26	4.34	3.43
change, %[a]	(11.3)	(14.5)	(12.3)	(16.6)	(11.6)	(16.6)
Post-FTA	4.44	3.56	4.20	3.43	4.34	3.43
change, %[b]	(0.2)	(0.8)	(3.6)	(5.2)	(0.1)	(0.2)

[a] Percentage change from the corresponding ones in the benchmark.
[b] Percentage change from the corresponding ones in the post-WTO case.

Table 3.15   Number of varieties under various policies

	China		ASEAN		ROW		
	n_c^m	n_c^a	n_a^m	n_a^a	n_e^m	n_r^a	Total
Benchmark	122.0	75.1	12.4	36.0	21.4	220.2	487.1
Post-WTO	119.1	75.9	13.0	35.7	26.6	215.3	485.6
change, %[a]	(–2.4)	(1.0)	(5.1)	(–0.7)	(24.5)	(–2.2)	(–0.3)
Post-FTA	119.1	75.9	13.1	35.7	8,998	3,930	3,930
change, %[b]	(0.0)	(0.0)	(0.9)	(–0.1)	(–0.6)	(0.1)	(0.0)

[a] Percentage change from the corresponding ones in the benchmark.
[b] Percentage change from the corresponding ones in the post-WTO case.

sumers in the countries are facing a slightly smaller number of varieties, and this tends to hurt them.

What Tables 3.13–3.15 suggest is that China could be hurt by a deterioration of its terms of trade, despite a rise in its national income, as it joins the WTO. This result seems to be striking, since China chooses to be a member of this international organization voluntarily. While the present result is only suggestive and more analysis will be needed for a more definitive conclusion, we do note that the present policy involves both economic and political consideration for China. The present model can at best examine the economic impacts of the policy, however, so to examine the rationality of the present policy, one needs to investigate any possible political impacts.

Lastly, let us examine the impacts of the policy on income distribution in various countries. Table 3.16 gives the domestic wage–rental ratio of the countries (i.e., w_i/r_{ii} for $i = c$, a and r).[15] All these ratios increase as China becomes a new member of the WTO, implying that workers benefit relatively compared to capitalists. The intuition behind this result is that as China raises the effective tax rates on foreign investment, the international movement of all types of capital among the countries will substantially improve the productivity of the workers.

Table 3.16   Income distribution under various policies

	China	ASEAN	ROW
Benchmark	0.157	1.538	1.808
Post-WTO	0.175	1.659	2.589
Post-FTA	0.178	1.713	2.599

Note: The numbers represent the domestic wage–rental ratios, (i.e., w_i / r_{ii} for $i = c$, a and r).

Scenario 2: China–ASEAN FTA

We now turn to the next scenario: China and ASEAN form a free trade area. The economic integration requires that both countries remove tariffs on goods from each other, while the tariffs on the goods from non-member countries remain unchanged. The corporate tax rates imposed by the member countries are assumed to stay as before. The new tariff and tax rates of the countries assumed in this scenario are listed in Tables 3.2 and 3.3. Using these new policy parameters but keeping other exogenous variable parameters unchanged, the system of equations (3.35) to (3.40) is again solved for the eleven unknowns. Other endogenous variables are then determined.

Table 3.17   Foreign trade among countries ofter the China–ASEAN FTA

(a) China

	Export to		Import from		Balance		
	in M	in A	in M	in A	in M	in A	Total
ASEAN	360 (28)	403 (81)	303 (41)	567 (79)	57	−164	−107
ROW	1,389 (1)	605 (−2)	258 (−2)	1,198 (−5)	1,131	38	1,169
Total	1,750 (6)	1,008 (20)	562 (17)	1,765 (12)	1,188	−127	1,062

(b) ASEAN

	Export to		Import from		Balance		
	in M	in A	in M	in A	in M	in A	Total
China	303 (41)	567 (79)	360 (28)	403 (81)	−57	164	107
ROW	160 (−14)	271 (−21)	38 (−19)	481 (−2)	122	−210	−88
Total	463 (16)	838 (27)	398 (21)	884 (24)	64	−46	19

(c) ROW

	Export to		Import from		Balance		
	in M	in A	in M	in A	in M	in A	Total
China	258 (−2)	1,198 (−5)	1,389 (1)	605 (−2)	−1,131	593	−538
ASEAN	38 (−19)	481 (−2)	160 (−14)	271 (−21)	−122	210	88
Total	296 (−5)	1,679 (−4)	1,549 (−0)	876 (−8)	−1,253	803	−450

Notes:
M = manufacturing; A = agriculture.
Balance = export − import (Numbers shown may not be exactly the same as the differences because of rounding.)
Numbers in parentheses represent the percentage changes from the corresponding values in the post-WTO scenario.

We first examine the impacts of this FTA on the flows of commodities and capital in the world. Table 3.17 presents the new trade volumes of the countries after the formation of this FTA. It is clear from the table that the China–ASEAN FTA has a huge impact on their mutual trade, apparently at the expense of their trade with ROW. For example, China's exports of manufacturing and agriculture to ASEAN increase by 28 per cent and 81 per cent, respectively, while China's corresponding imports from ASEAN rise by 41 per cent and 79 per cent, respectively. These jumps come mainly from their trade with ROW. The table shows that ROW's trade with China and ASEAN drop substantially. For example, its total exports to China and ASEAN of manufacturing and agriculture decrease by 5 and 4 per cent, respectively, while its imports of manufacturing and agriculture from the

Table 3.18 Capital flows among the countries after the China–ASEAN FTA

(a) China

	Capital outflow		Capital inflow		Balance		
	in M	in A	in M	in A	in M	in A	Total
ASEAN	0.0070 (4)	0.0063 (3)	14 (–3)	5 (–3)	14	5	19
ROW	0	0	302 (0)	99 (0)	302	99	401
Total	0.0070 (4)	0.0063 (03)	316 (0)	104 (0)	316	104	420

(b) ASEAN

	Capital outflow		Capital inflow		Balance		
	in M	in A	in M	in A	in M	in A	Total
China	14 (–3)	5 (–3)	0.0070 (4)	0.0063 (3)	–14	–5	–18
ROW	0 (0)	0 (0)	26 (4)	23 (3)	26	23	49
Total	14 (–3)	5 (–3)	26 (4)	23 (3)	12	19	31

(c) ROW

	Capital outflow		Capital inflow		Balance		
	in M	in A	in M	in A	in M	in A	Total
China	302 (–0)	99 (–0)	0 (0)	0 (0)	–302	–99	–401
ASEAN	26 (4)	23 (3)	0 (0)	0 (0)	–26	–23	–49
Total	327 (0)	122 (1)	0 (0)	0 (0)	–327	–122	–450

Notes:
M = manufacturing; A = agriculture.
Balance = capital inflow – capital outflow (Numbers shown may not be exactly the same as the differences because of rounding.)
Numbers in parentheses represent the percentage changes from the corresponding values in the post-WTO scenario.

two countries drop slightly, by an imperceptible amount and 8 per cent, respectively.

Such trade diversion is not surprising, as the reduction of trade restrictions tends to encourage trade between the two countries. However, the substantial increase in the intra-regional trade implies that much trade between China and ASEAN has been created. As a result, China's total exports and imports all expand, and so do the total exports of ASEAN.

The impacts of the FTA on capital movement are much lower than those on trade (see Table 3.18). For example, China will expect a drop in the FDI in the manufacturing and agriculture sectors from ASEAN by about 3 per cent. Note that China remains a huge recipient of FDI.

Another way to see how the countries get more inter-dependent as a result of the China–ASEAN FTA is to examine how intra-industry trade and capital may be affected. Table 3.19 presents the new indices of intra-industry trade and capital movement. For example, the indices of intra-industry trade between China and ASEAN in manufacturing and agriculture both increase.[16] This shows that the FTA will encourage intra-industry trade between China and ASEAN. The degree of intra-industry trade between China and ROW goes up slightly, but that between ASEAN and ROW falls, in terms of both manufacturing and agriculture, and also the aggregate. The degree of intra-industry capital movement between China and ASEAN also rises, although it is small to begin with.[17]

Table 3.13 presents the welfare impacts of the China–ASEAN FTA. It shows that the welfare levels of China and ROW drop slightly, while ASEAN turns out to be a big winner: China's welfare falls by 0.2 per cent and ROW's by 0.4 per cent, while ASEAN's goes up by 3.5 per cent. To examine why the welfare of the countries changes in such ways, we first examine the national income levels of the countries. The interesting thing

Table 3.19 Indices of intra-industry trade and capital movement with the China–ASEAN FTA

	Intra-industry trade		Intra-industry K flows	
	C–A	C–R	A–R	C–A
Manufacturing	0.9137 (5)	0.3136 (–3)	0.3839 (–5)	0.0010 (7)
Agriculture	0.8307 (1)	0.6711 (2)	0.7208 (–12)	0.0028 (7)
Total	0.8113 (–1)	0.5929 (3)	0.5954 (–17)	0.0007 (6)

Notes:
C–A = China–ASEAN; C–R = China–ROW; A–R = ASEAN–ROW.
K = capital.
For the formulae of the indices of intra-industry trade and intra-industry capital flow, see the text.
Numbers in parentheses represent percentage changes in values from the corresponding ones in the post-WTO scenario.

is that all three countries get a higher national income level after the FTA, although the increase in ASEAN's national income is more substantial at 4.9 per cent.

Table 3.14 shows the terms of trade of the countries. While all domestic prices of the commodities increase, those of manufacturing and agriculture in ASEAN rise significantly. As a result, both China and ROW experience deterioration in their terms of trade (i.e., goods from ASEAN become more expensive to China and ROW). This turns out to be a significant negative factor for their welfare.

Table 3.15 presents the changes in the numbers of varieties in the countries. It is shown that the numbers remain fairly constant, especially the total number of varieties of the two goods. In the present exercise, we discover that the terms-of-trade effect is significant for the changes in welfare of countries.

Lastly, let us examine the impacts of the regional integration on income distribution in the three countries. Table 3.16 gives the wage–rental ratio, w_i / r_{ii} of country i, after the formation of the China–ASEAN FTA, which can be compared with the previous values. The table shows that the FTA raises the wage–rental ratios of the countries. In other words, workers in all countries can benefit relatively to the capitalists from such regional trade liberalization. One possible explanation for the change in the wage–rental ratio is that both unilateral and regional trade liberalization allow capital to be used more efficiently, thereby substantially improving the productivity of the workers.

Concluding remarks

Trade liberalization is a main feature of post-war world trade. Sometimes countries choose to liberalize trade and capital movement unilaterally, expecting to get healthy rewards in return. Multilateral trade liberalization happens when a large group of countries removes trade restrictions simultaneously. In addition to multilateralism, some countries form preferential trading clubs (such as free trade areas), imposing lower tariffs on the goods flowing within the club but keeping different tariffs on goods from non-member countries. Asia is relatively a late comer in terms of forming free trade areas, but once ASEAN decided to convert itself into a free trade area in 1992, many other countries in Asia caught the bug and have been negotiating with other countries to expand their list of FTA partners. These several channels of trade liberalization have brought unavoidable impacts to many countries.

The present chapter constructs a two-differentiated-product, three-country, four-factor model to investigate the effects of unilateral and regional trade liberalization. Using observed or assumed values of the countries' factor endowments, preference parameters and technology parameters, this chapter simulates several equilibria, based on the trade policies of the countries. The equilibria provide a convenient way of performing several comparative-static exercises in order to investigate how unilateral and regional trade liberalization may affect trade, capital movement, income distribution and welfare among the three countries in the present model.

This model has two major features: the presence of international capital movements and the existence of differentiated products. The former feature is used to capture the rising importance of international capital movements and their roles in welfare and income distribution. The latter feature is used to bring out the importance of increasing returns and trade between China and ASEAN. What is more, this feature allows us to examine the effects of trade liberalization on intra-industry trade which, we argue, is an important factor of the welfare of the countries.

One important objective of the exercises in the present chapter is to analyse whether China's WTO accession and the China–ASEAN FTA could hurt some neighbouring countries. The results obtained in the present project do not support the concerns that neighbouring countries may be hurt by a more open Chinese economy. For example, we showed that neighbouring economies may be able to benefit from China's unilateral trade liberalization. This result relies heavily on the existence of economies of scale and intra-industrial trade between China and ASEAN. Other countries, including Japan and the United States, may not have to worry about detrimental effects, either (see Table 3.13).

One result seems to be very interesting: China may experience a drop in its welfare when it liberalizes trade as a condition for its accession to the WTO, or when it forms a free trade area with ASEAN. We provided some reasons to explain why this is possible. Although we noted that this result is only preliminary, and although more research should be done to draw any definitive conclusions, this result does suggest that China may be expecting impacts beyond purely economic ones when it liberalizes its foreign trade.

While we have tried our best to rely on observed data to guess the values of some of the parameters, the results obtained here are simply a 'best guess' at the impacts of trade liberalization. Further work should be done, including the construction of a more complicated model.

Notes

1 China formally became a member of the WTO on 11 December 2001.
2 ASEAN decided back in 1992 to convert itself into a free trade area.
3 Wong (2004) investigates the trade between China and the following five ASEAN members: Singapore, Thailand, Malaysia, Indonesia and the Philippines.
4 Agriculture includes the service sector.
5 See Wong (1995, ch. 6) for a survey and some discussion about trade and capital movement under monopolistic competition. Amiti's model (Amiti, 1998)

is close to ours but the present one considers four factors and allows international capital movement.

6 The assumption of perfect and costless factor movements within a country is consistent with similar assumptions for this type of model. Because of this assumption, the present model is not suitable for analysing price disparities among different regions in the same country.

7 The assumption of no capital from China and ASEAN to ROW simplifies the analysis and is consistent with the fact that ROW receives an insignificant amount of capital from China and ASEAN.

8 For simplicity, we assume the same transport cost is needed for both types of goods shipped from country j to country i.

9 Note that when some of the capital flows to ASEAN, in equilibrium the domestic rental rate is equal to the after-tax rental rate of Chinese capital in ASEAN.

10 Recall that firms in ROW do not use capital from China or ASEAN.

11 The equilibrium condition of the capital market of ROW can be regarded as redundant because of Walras's Law.

12 The present chapter explains the co-existence of intra-industry trade and intra-industry capital flows by assuming monopolistic competition and regarding capital from different countries as different types of capital. Chan and Wong (2004) provide an alternative approach to intra-industry trade and intra-industry capital flows by focusing on the competition between oligopolistic firms.

13 The GNP of a country is defined in equation (3.10) while welfare is defined by equation (3.3).

14 The total is the sum of all the varieties of both products. However, the sum of varieties is not an exact indication of what the consumers enjoy because with trade restrictions and/or transport costs, consumers do not treat domestic varieties and foreign varieties equally.

15 This ratio, the ratio of domestic wage rate to local rental rate of capital at domestic price, is a comparison of the income levels of workers and capital-owners. Recall that the assumption of perfect and costless factor mobility within a country implies one price of each factor.

16 The aggregate index of intra-industry trade between China and ASEAN drops slightly. Note that because of the adjustment for trade balance, the aggregate index is not a weighted average of the indices of intra-industry trade of the sectors.

17 Again, intra-industry capital movement between either China or ASEAN and ROW is zero because of zero capital movement from China or ASEAN to ROW.

References

Amiti, Mary (1998), 'Inter-industry Trade in Manufactures: Does Country Size Matter?', *Journal of International Economics*, 44, 231–55.

Armington, P.S. (1969), 'A Theory of Demand for Products Distinguished by Place of Origin', *IMF Staff Papers* 16, 159–77.

Chan, Hsiu-Yi and Kar-yiu Wong (2004), 'Intraindustry Trade, Intraindustry Investment, and International Rivalry', *mimeo*, University of Washington.

Duffy, J. and C. Papageorgiou (2000), 'A Cross-Country Empirical Investigation of the Aggregate Production Function Specification', *Journal of Economic Growth*, 5 (1), 87–120.

Frankel, Jeffrey (1997), *Regional Trading Blocs*, Washington, DC: Institute for International Economics.

Wong, Kar-yiu (1995), *International Trade in Goods and Factor Mobility*, Cambridge, MA: MIT Press.

Wong, Kar-yiu (2003), 'The Impacts of China's WTO Accession on the Southeast Asian Economies: A Theoretical Analysis', *China Economic Review*, 14, 208–26.

Wong, Kar-yiu (2004), 'Trade Liberalization and Trade Relations: China's WTO Accession', *mimeo*, University of Washington.

4
The Economic Impact of China's Emergence as a Major Trading Nation*

Wing Thye Woo

Introduction

The key to understanding the international impact of China's emergence as a major economic power, as marked by its accession to the World Trade Organization (WTO), is that the global division of labour at the end of the last millennium was a highly unnatural one. It was unnatural because the self-imposed isolation of China in the 1949–79 period and its slow integration into the international economy in the 1980–91 period kept over one-fifth of the human race from meaningful participation in the world trade and investment systems. This is why China's accelerated integration into the world economy beginning in the mid-1990s has led to a significant relocation of labour-intensive industries to China. In mid-2003, the electronic and electrical firms in Penang, Malaysia, employed 17 per cent fewer workers than in 2000. On the other side of the Pacific, 500 of Mexico's 3,700 *maquiladoras* (foreign-owned export-oriented firms) have closed since 2001, and the surviving *maquiladoras* have reduced their employment by almost a third.

Foreign direct investment (FDI) into China increased from US$44.2 billion in 1997 to US$52.7 billion in 2002. This caused China's share of total FDI into the developing world during this period to rise from 22.9 per cent to 32.5 per cent, and its share of total FDI into Asia to soar from 40.6 per cent to 55.5 per cent.

The gorilla awakes

Developments like the above are the reason why the Prime Minister of Singapore, Goh Chok Tong, informed his fellow citizens during his National Day address in 2001 that:

*Reprinted with permission from: China's Growth as a Regional Economic Power: Impacts and Implications, Hearing before the US–China Economic and Security Review Commission, One Hundred and Eighth Congress, First Session, December 4, 2003, Washington: US Government Printing Office, 2003.

China poses a big economic challenge. Some economists describe China as an *800-pound trading gorilla*. A Hong Kong newspaper added that this gorilla was *very hungry*.

Even India is being flooded with cheap but good quality Chinese goods. Some Indian manufacturers are finding it hard to compete. So they have done the next best thing. They stick 'Made in China' labels on their products to boost sales ...

Our biggest challenge is therefore to secure a niche for ourselves as China swamps the world with her high quality but cheaper products. China's economy is potentially ten times the size of Japan's. Just ask yourself: how does Singapore compete against ten post-war Japans, all industrializing and exporting to the world at the same time?

I do not mean that China will overpower every other economy, and grow at the expense of everybody else. As China develops and exports more, its imports will grow too. There will be many opportunities to invest in China. We must grasp those opportunities.

Goh is certainly correct in pointing out that China cannot just be an exporter without also being an importer too. But the crucial issue is whether the composition of goods that China would import would require a complete overhaul of the production structures of East and South East Asia. Would China's WTO accession cause Indonesia, Malaysia, the Philippines and Thailand (the ASEAN-4) to de-industrialize and return to their role of the 1950s and 1960s as primary commodity exporters? Or would there be sufficient lucrative niches within the manufacturing production chains that the ASEAN-4 could specialize in?

The second scenario is certainly a possibility, particularly for Singapore, Taiwan and South Korea. In the opinion of Stanley Fischer, the former deputy managing director of the IMF: 'there is little cause for fear ... a big dynamic economy in the neighborhood is a benefit, not a curse, for those around it – look at Canada or Mexico ... Or, one might add, look at Asia after Japan emerged as an economic power from the 1970s onward' ('Don't fear China threat', *The Straits Times*, 4 September 2001).

Boom or doom? And for whom? These are the two questions that I would like to address in this chapter. In order to answer these questions about the international impact of China's rise as a major economic power, we have to first understand why China has been so arduous in its pursuit of WTO membership. Since WTO membership for China mainly requires it to implement drastic reductions in its trade barriers across the board in a relatively short period of time, one might question why WTO membership is necessary when China can achieve the same results by undertaking unilateral cuts in effective tariff rates by the amount that it chooses and within a time period that it determines. Why did China pursue protracted negotiations to get an arrangement where the lowering of trade barriers is externally supervised, and which leaves China open to international sanctions if the trade liberalization does not meet the externally imposed criteria, when unilateral trade deregulation is an option?

The answer to this riddle is that the fundamental reason for China's enthusiasm for WTO membership is that WTO membership will greatly enhance China's economic security. The United States enacted the Permanent Normal Trade Relations (PNTR) Act on 10 October 2000, and this ended the need for annual approval from the US Congress for most-favoured nation (MFN) status in order for its exports to compete in the US markets on equal terms against the exports from WTO countries. However, the important point to note is not the passage of PNTR itself, but the realistic situation that whatever laws are passed by Congress can also be repealed by Congress later without violating any international law. So, until China is a WTO member, which gives China unconditional, *permanent*, multilateral rights to trade with other WTO members, the threat of PNTR being repealed renders China's exports vulnerable to changing passions in the US political arena. Examples of recent events which could provoke such changes of heart include accidents such as military aircraft collisions in the South China Sea, and the Chinese burning of the US consulate in Chengdu following the unintended US bombing of the Chinese embassy in Belgrade. The importance to China of maintaining high export growth and of maintaining the competitiveness of its exports to the US market is hard to overstate.

The United States is China's biggest export market and, until the recent restrictions on steel imports, had been perceived as ideologically committed to free trade and consequently less prone to protectionism than Europe and Japan. Clearly, in order for exports to provide a sustainable growth engine, China must secure assured access to its biggest market, and, only WTO membership can prevent the United States from being able (unilaterally) to switch off one of China's most important growth engines by simply suspending the PNTR Act, and raising tariffs on China's exports. (The reader interested in the legal protocol under which China joined WTO should consult Qin, 2003.)

China's economic linkages to the world

China's enhanced economic security has important implications for its neighbours because the international movement of goods is only one of China's two economic links to the world; the international movement of capital is the other. The important but oft-neglected point in analysing China's WTO membership is that the removal of uncertainty about China's access to the US market increases China's reliability as a supplier. This means that producers of labour-intensive goods destined for sale in high-income economies can now reduce management costs by reducing the geographical diversification of its production facilities. More of the production can now be carried out in China because its labour costs are lower than in the ASEAN-4.

Analytically, the removal of the MFN threat when China officially became a WTO member at the end of 2001 is equivalent to a reduction in the risk premium demanded by investors in China's export-oriented industries. The complete picture of China's WTO membership is more than a reduction in China's effective tariffs; it also includes a reduction in the risk premium for investment in export-oriented production inside China. The effect of the tariff reduction is to reallocate the composition of China's output from importables to exportables and non-tradables; and the effect of the risk premium is to reconfigure the global distribution of FDI in China's favour.

There is indeed evidence of the FDI diversion effect created by China's WTO membership. The Japan Bank for International Cooperation (JBIC) conducts an annual survey of Japanese trans-national corporations (TNCs) to find out which are expected to be the top 10 locations for manufacturing FDI over the next three years. Table 4.1 contains the results from the surveys undertaken in 1996, 2000 and 2001. Some 68 per cent of Japanese TNCs listed China as one of the top 10 locations in 1996, and 65 per cent did so in 2000. These responses made China the most frequently identified promising location for FDI in both years (i.e., China was ranked first in the list of 10 locations).

The evidence in favour of our FDI diversion hypothesis is captured in the 2001 survey. It became clear to the international community at the end of 2000 that China's accession to WTO was imminent. The upshot was that the proportion of Japanese TNCs in 2001 that identified China as one of the 10 most promising locations for manufacturing FDI jumped to 82 per cent from 65 per cent in 2000. Most telling of all, the 'identification gap' between China and the United States, which were ranked first and second respectively in 2000 and 2001, widened from 24 percentage points in 2000 to 50 percentage points in 2001.

The frequency with which the ASEAN-4 economies were identified as top 10 locations for FDI dropped between 1996 and 2000, and the most important reason for this change in TNCs' perception could be the Asian Financial Crisis. The frequency with which Thailand was identified fell from 36 per cent to 24 per cent, Indonesia from 34 per cent to 15 per cent, Malaysia from 20 per cent to 12 per cent, and the Philippines from 13 per cent to 8 per cent. In terms of ranking within the 10 most cited locations, Thailand slipped from second to third, Indonesia from third to fourth and the Philippines from eighth to tenth, while Malaysia improved from sixth to fifth.

As the Asian Financial Crisis was over by early 2000, the changes in the frequency of identification and ranking of the ASEAN-4 economies on the

Table 4.1 The 10 most promising destinations for manufacturing FDI by Japanese TNCs over the next three years

Rank	1996 survey	%*	2000 survey	%*	2001 survey	%*
1	China	68	China	65	China	82
2	Thailand	36	United States	41	United States	32
3	Indonesia	34	Thailand	24	Thailand	25
4	United States	32	Indonesia	15	Indonesia	14
5	Vietnam	27	Malaysia	12	India	13
6	Malaysia	20	Taiwan	11	Vietnam	12
7	India	18	India	10	Taiwan	11
8	Philippines	13	Vietnam	9	Rep. of Korea	8
9	Singapore	10	Rep. of Korea	9	Malaysia	8
10	United Kingdom and Taiwan	7	Philippines	8	Singapore	6

** The share of firms that consider the country as promising in total respondent firms (multiple responses).

Source: United Nations Conference on Trade and Development (2002).

list of profitable FDI locations between 2000 and 2001 could therefore justifiably be attributed to the WTO-created improvement in China's reliability as an international supplier. The frequencies with which Thailand and Indonesia were identified as desirable FDI locations are practically identical in 2000 and 2001, but the identification gaps between them and China increased significantly. The China–Thailand gap went up from 41 percentage points to 57 percentage points, and the China–Indonesia gap from 50 percentage points to 68 percentage points. The frequency with which Malaysia was cited declined from 12 per cent to 8 per cent, and the Philippines dropped out of the top 10 list. Malaysia's rank dropped from fifth to ninth, and the China–Malaysian identification gap soared from 53 percentage points to 74 percentage points. These differences in the survey results of 2000 and 2001 are certainly consistent with our hypothesis of WTO-induced diversion of FDI to China.

A recent news report makes clear that the drop in inward FDI in Malaysia has been substantial in 2002, and that the Malaysian government has no doubt that much of the drop is due to FDI diversion to China:

> Malaysia attracted approved manufacturing FDI of only RM 2.16 billion ... for the first six months of this year [2002]. This is a sharp drop from the RM 18.82 billion it pulled in for the whole of last year.
>
> ... 'Everybody is feeling the pinch because the amount of FDIs has shrunk and then, a lot of that is going to China,' Dr. Mahathir [Prime Minister] told a news conference later. ('Malaysia turns inward for growth', *The Straits Times*, 21 September 2002)

To appreciate fully the importance of this diversion of FDI, we should be cognizant of the possibility that FDI diversion could be more than just a simple relocation of the capital stock. FDI might also generate positive externalities. The East Asian experience suggests that FDI could facilitate technological transfers (i.e. generate technological spillovers) not only to domestic firms in the same industry but also to domestic firms in other industries; see Okabe (2002). Furthermore, FDI could also help solve the difficulties of access to the international markets in these goods. In short, a country gaining FDI could experience not only a bigger capital stock but also possibly a (maybe temporary) increase in its total factor productivity (TFP) growth rate; while a country losing FDI could experience a (maybe temporary) slowdown in TFP growth as well as a (maybe temporary) lower capital stock.

Table 4.2 presents the evidence in support of the link between FDI and technological diffusion by presenting the index values of overall technological capacity, column (3), for a number of the 59 countries ranked in the *World Competitiveness Report* issued by the World Economic Forum (2000). Also shown in Table 4.2 are the two determinants of the overall

Table 4.2 Indices of indigenous ability to innovate, technology transfer from abroad, and overall technological capacity

Index of indigenous ability to innovate		Index of ability to get technology transfer from abroad		Index of overall technological capacity	
USA	1	Singapore	1	USA	1
Finland	2	Ireland	2	Finland	2
Germany	3	Luxembourg	3	Singapore	3
Switzerland	4	Malaysia	7	Ireland	4
Japan	5	Taiwan	12	Germany	5
Singapore	14	South Korea	13	Switzerland	6
Taiwan	16	Hong Kong	17	Japan	7
South Korea	22	Philippines	19	Malaysia	18
Hong Kong	27	India	26	Taiwan	24
Malaysia	30	Thailand	36	Korea	25
China	34	Japan	39	Hong Kong	30
India	38	China	43	Philippines	32
Philippines	47	Indonesia	45	India	37
Thailand	50	*ASEAN-4 (average)*	*27*	Thailand	43
Indonesia	55			China	48
ASEAN-4 (average)	*46*			Indonesia	50
				Ecuador	58
				Bolivia	59
				ASEAN-4 (average)	*36*

Notes:
The Indigenous Innovation Index and Technology Transfer Index are the two components of the Overall Technology Index.
The Overall Technology Index is combined with the Startup Index (relative ease in establishing a new firm) to produce the Economic Creativity Index
The Growth Competitiveness Idex is constructed from the Economic Creativity Index, the Finance Index (relative efficiency of the financial system),
and the International Index (degree of integration into the international economy).
These are the index values in 2000.

Source: World Economic Forum (2000).

technological capacity: the indigenous ability to innovate in column (1), and the ability to obtain technology transfer from abroad in column (2). The overall technological capacity index is determined by averaging the other two indices, the indigenous innovation index and the technology transfer index.

The rankings of the overall technology index for Malaysia (18), the Philippines (32), and Thailand (43) are above China (48), and Indonesia (50) is only slightly below China in ranking. However, it is important to realize that the higher average rank of the ASEAN-4 in overall technology (36) comes from the higher technology transfer from abroad: the rank of Malaysia is 7, the Philippines is 19, Thailand is 36, China is 43, and Indonesia is 45. China's indigenous ability to innovate is ranked 34 which is substantially above the rank of the ASEAN-4 to innovate indigenously (46). The point is that the average ASEAN-4 economy depends critically on technological diffusion through FDI to raise its overall technological level higher than China's. FDI diversion from China's WTO membership is therefore likely to cause the future rank of Indonesia, Malaysia, the Philippines and Thailand in the overall technology index to fall, and the rank of China to rise.

Since Hong Kong, Japan, Singapore, South Korea, and Taiwan rank above China in both the ability to innovate indigenously and to obtain foreign technology, the diversion of FDI into China is unlikely to affect their levels of technological capacity. The fact is that these five East Asian economies are some of the sources of FDI into China and into the ASEAN-4 means that they are amongst the sources of the technological diffusion that is being discussed.

In summary, there are three levels of answer when thinking about the consequences of China's WTO membership for the ASEAN-4. The first level is the standard analysis of a unilateral cut in China's effective tariff rates. The result is a redirection of labour and capital away from China's importable goods sector and towards its exportable goods sector, causing China to import and export more. A more detailed examination might reveal that the additional Chinese imports will be capital-intensive goods from the developed economies, and the additional Chinese exports will be labour-intensive goods to developed and developing countries. We call this first-level answer the *naive analysis*.

The second-level answer recognizes that not only would there be tariff cuts as required by WTO membership but also that the removal of the market access threat to China would be likely to lower the risk premium required for investing in China. The expectation generated by the latter development is that there would be diversion of FDI to China, especially from its East and South East Asian neighbours. We call this second-level answer the *FDI diversion analysis*.

The third-level answer enriches the second-level answer by pointing out that FDI would not only increase the domestic capital stock, but some argue that it could also increase technological transfers to the whole economy and improve the access of more Chinese goods to foreign markets. We call this the *analysis of the diversion of FDI with technological spillovers*.

Quantifying the impact – the G-cubed (Asia-Pacific) model[1]

The G-cubed Asia Pacific (AP-GCUBED) model is ideal for such analysis having both a detailed country coverage of the region and rich links between countries through goods and asset markets. The AP-GCUBED model encompasses the United States, Japan, Australia, New Zealand, South Korea, the Rest of the OECD (ROECD), China, Indonesia, Malaysia, the Philippines, Taiwan, Thailand, Hong Kong, Singapore, India, OPEC, EEFSU (Eastern Europe and the former Soviet Union), and the Rest of the World (ROW). Each of the 18 countries in the AP-GCUBED model has six sectors: energy, mining, agriculture, durable manufacturing, non-durable manufacturing, and services.

Each core economy or region in the model consists of several economic agents: households, the government, the financial sector and the six production sectors. Inter-temporal budget constraints on households, governments and nations (the latter through accumulations of foreign debt) are imposed. To accommodate these constraints, forward-looking behaviour is incorporated in consumption and investment decisions. The investment process is assumed to be subject to rising marginal costs of installation. Aggregate consumption is chosen to maximize an inter-temporal utility function subject to the constraint that the present value of consumption be equal to human wealth plus initial financial assets. International trade imbalances are financed by flows of financial assets between countries (except where capital controls are in place).

As a result of this structure, the AP-GCUBED model contains rich dynamic behaviour, driven on the one hand, by asset accumulation and, on the other, by wage adjustment to a neoclassical steady state. It embodies a wide range of assumptions about individual behaviour and empirical regularities in a dynamic general equilibrium framework. The interdependencies are solved out using a computer algorithm that solves for the rational expectations equilibrium of the global economy. It is important to stress that the term 'general equilibrium' is used to signify that as many interactions as possible are captured, not that all economies are in a full market clearing equilibrium at each point in time. Although it is assumed that market forces eventually drive the world economy to a neoclassical steady-state growth equilibrium, unemployment does emerge for long periods due to wage stickiness, to an extent that differs between countries due to differences in labour-market institutions. The model has approximately 7,400 equations in its current form with 140 jumping or forward-looking variables, and 263 state variables. More technical details of the model are available from the author.

I will undertake four sets of simulations:

- baseline simulation;
- naive simulation
- reduction in risk premium simulation
- diversion of FDI with technological spillover simulation

The baseline simulation: this simulation generates the future values of all the endogenous variables based on the assumption that the existing policy regimes in the world will persist indefinitely into the future. The tariff rates used are based on the GTAP 4 database which contains estimates of the levels of tariff and non-tariff barriers. The baseline simulation, in short, assumes that the trade regimes in 2000 are continued forever (which includes China's exclusion from WTO).

Counterfactual simulation no. 1 – the naive simulation: the only changes are the reduction in China's trade barriers (both tariff and non-tariff barriers). We assume that trade barriers are reduced gradually over time by an equal amount (measured in percentage points) over the ten-year period of 2003 to 2012.

Counterfactual simulation no. 2 – a reduction in the risk premium demanded by FDI (the FDI diversion simulation): this simulation supplements the naive simulation with a 1 percentage point reduction in the risk premium demanded by foreign investors in China.

Counterfactual simulation no. 3 – FDI creates technological spillovers in the host economy (the FDI with technological spillover simulation): we supplement the simulation of the FDI diversion case with the five conditions outlined below:

1 A temporary decrease in the TFP growth *rate* of the manufactured durable goods industries located in Indonesia, Malaysia, the Philippines and Thailand. We assume an annual decline of 1 percentage point beginning in 2003 until the TFP level is 10 percentage points below the baseline TFP *level* in 2012.

2 A temporary decrease in the TFP growth rate of the manufactured non-durable goods industries located in Indonesia, Malaysia, the Philippines and Thailand. We assume an annual decline of 1 percentage point beginning in 2003 until the TFP level is 10 percentage points below the baseline TFP level in 2012.

3 A temporary increase in the TFP growth rate of the manufactured durable goods industries in China. We assume an annual increase of 1 percentage point beginning in 2003 until the TFP level is 10 percentage points above the baseline TFP level in 2012.

4 A temporary increase in the TFP growth rate of the manufactured non-durable goods industries in China. We assume an annual increase of 1 percentage point beginning in 2003 until the TFP level is 10 percentage points above the baseline TFP level in 2012.

5 A temporary increase in the TFP growth rate of the service industries in China. We assume an annual increase of 1 percentage point beginning in 2003 until the TFP level is 10 percentage points above the baseline TFP level in 2012.

The above conditions are assumptions about the stances of public policy and the steepness of the learning curves in the ASEAN-4 and China. It is assumed that it will take a decade for the ASEAN-4 to improve their scientific bases sufficiently to offset the slowdown in technological diffusion due to the lower FDI inflows. It is also assumed that it will also take a decade for the Chinese sectors to master fully the new technology contained in the diverted FDI. Again these are assumptions rather than predictions, but they give indicative estimates of the impacts of a range of plausible assumptions.

The results of the simulations

Naive simulation: Figure 4.1 reports the deviations from baseline GDP of 11 economies: the United States, Europe, Australia, New Zealand, Japan,

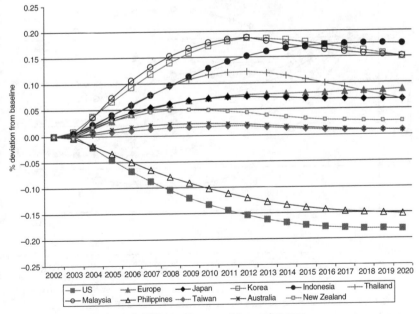

Figure 4.1 Change in real GDP in other countries: naive case

South Korea, Taiwan, Indonesia, Malaysia, the Philippines and Thailand. None of their GDP deviations are more than 0.2 per cent from the baseline, and this level is indistinguishable from measurement errors. Figure 4.2 shows the deviations of exports of 10 out of the 11 economies from the baseline to be less than 0.3 per cent. The largest export deviation is that of

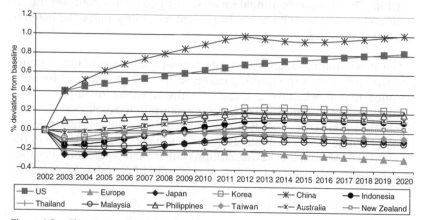

Figure 4.2   Change in exports: naive case

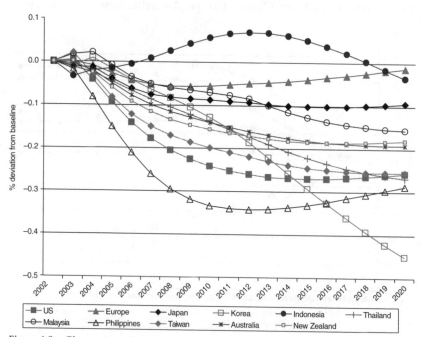

Figure 4.3   Change in real GDP in other countries: FDI diversion case

the United States which is 0.8 per cent above the baseline in 2020: possibly the reduction in Chinese protection of its import-competing industries led China to import more capital goods from the United States. In practical terms, however, China's WTO membership has no impact on these 11 economies.

Simulation of the FDI diversion case: Figure 4.3 reveals that while the deviations in GDP are negative for these 11 economies, their magnitudes are trivial. In 2020, the deviations of 10 economies are below 0.3 per cent, and Korea's deviation is almost –0.5 per cent. The export deviations exhibited in Figure 4.4 are almost the same as in Figure 4.2: US exports in 2002 are now 0.9 per cent above the baseline. On the whole, it is hard to say that any of the 11 economies is hurt in a non-trivial way.

Simulation of the case of FDI with technological spillovers: we consider this simulation to be the most realistic one. Figure 4.5 shows substantial long-run GDP losses by four South East Asian economies: 7 per cent for Thailand, 5 per cent for Malaysia and the Philippines, and 3 per cent for Indonesia. The GDP of the other seven countries shows minor long-run deviations from the baseline. Figure 4.6 reports that only the ASEAN-4 face significant export displacements. The United States, being primarily an exporter of capital goods and high value-added services, has the biggest positive deviation, which is about 0.9 per cent in 2020.

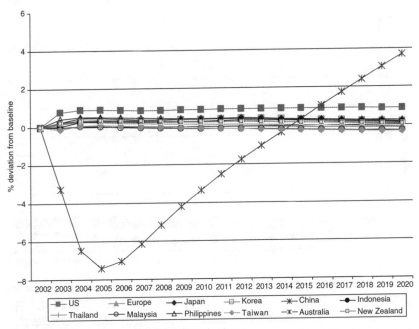

Figure 4.4 Change in exports: FDI diversion case

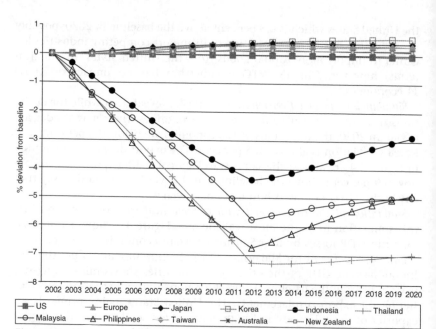

Figure 4.5   Change in real GDP in other economies: case of FDI with technological spillovers

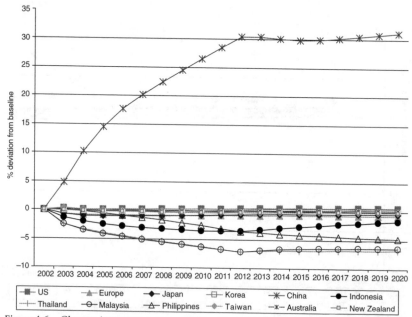

Figure 4.6   Change in exports: case of FDI with technological spillovers

The interested reader can find more details of the above simulations in McKibbin and Woo (2003a), and full details in McKibbin and Woo (2003b).

Economic impact on the ASEAN-4

Table 4.3 examines the export composition for the *FDI diversion scenario* and the *diversion of FDI with technological spillovers scenario* for China and the ASEAN-4. There are no substantial changes from the baseline for any ASEAN-4 country under FDI diversion. In the export compositions from the technological spillover simulation, we observe significant deviations from baseline in the ASEAN-4 countries. Table 4.3 shows the following information.

1 China's manufactured exports accounted for 27 percentage points of the 33 per cent increase in total exports above the baseline.
2 The manufacturing sectors in the ASEAN-4 show substantial long-run declines *vis-à-vis* their baselines. In Indonesia and the Philippines, the drop in manufactured exports exceed the drop in total exports; and in Malaysia and Thailand the decline in manufactured exports accounted for, respectively, 97 per cent and 91 per cent of the fall in total exports of 6.95 per cent and 8.09 per cent respectively.

This transfer of manufacturing jobs to China will not stop in the medium run because a vast amount of surplus agricultural labour remains to be tapped. Rightly, ASEAN is concerned about whether it would return to its previous role as a supplier of minerals and primary commodities. The likelihood of this development is greatly strengthened when one realizes that the other shoe is about to drop on ASEAN. India, which is still shallowly integrated into the world economy because of its strong economic nationalism and because it is home to another fifth of the world labour force, is now implementing significant economic deregulation in response to the sustained high growth in China; that is to say, the cap on FDI has been raised from 51 per cent to 76 per cent. One sobering scenario for ASEAN is that those manufacturing jobs that did not move to China would now migrate to India!

This gloom-and-doom projection for ASEAN is not inevitable, however. The final outcome actually rests largely in the hands of ASEAN leaders. When the ASEAN-4 are able to implement policies completely to offset the reduction in technological diffusion from the reduction in FDI, then we are back in the FDI diversion case. In the FDI diversion case, China's insertion of one-third more workers into the international division of labour leads to further division of labour (i.e., to even finer specialization in production activities) within the manufacturing sector worldwide rather than the displacement of the ASEAN-4 from manufacturing. The prerequisite for the

Table 4.3 Deviation of exports from baseline in 2020

	China	Indonesia	Malaysia	Philippines	Thailand
Simulation of FDI Diversion					
Deviation of total exports from baseline, in per cent	3.70	0.34	–0.04	0.12	–0.04
Contribution to deviation from baseline, in percentage points					
Energy	0.11	0.64	0.01	0.04	0.00
Mining	0.01	–0.02	0.00	0.01	0.00
Agriculture	–0.10	–0.02	0.08	0.04	0.12
Durable Manufacturing	1.44	–0.01	–0.08	0.02	–0.01
Non-durable Manufacturing	0.87	–0.14	0.01	0.02	–0.02
Services	1.36	–0.10	–0.06	–0.01	–0.13
Simulation of Diverted FDI with Technological Spillovers					
Deviation of total exports from baseline, in per cent	32.64	–3.20	–6.95	–5.22	–8.09
Contribution to deviation from baseline, in percentage points					
Energy	0.77	0.19	–0.02	0.02	0.00
Mining	0.16	0.00	0.00	–0.01	0.00
Agriculture	0.57	–0.20	–0.30	–0.11	–0.47
Durable Manufacturing	14.34	–0.07	–4.59 } 97% of –6.95	–3.05	–3.94 } 91% of –8.09
Non-durable Manufacturing	13.11	–3.28	–2.14	–2.36	–3.41
Services	3.69	0.15	0.10	0.28	–0.26

lengthening of the production chains in manufacturing to create niches in manufacturing activities for the ASEAN-4 is that they are technologically versatile. For the ASEAN-4 to have such versatility, their governments must invest in strengthening the scientific and technological capability of their citizens; see Yusof (2003) for a discussion of the Malaysian situation.

The ratcheting up of indigenous innovation in the ASEAN-4 requires, among many things, the institutionalization of synergistic relationships among the government, the business sector, and the universities. This national mobilization to promote indigenous innovation will have to over-turn many taboos. An illustration of such national taboos is the Malaysian redistribution policy to reduce income inequality across races, which results in the regulation that Malay Malaysians must own at least 30 per cent of a publicly listed firm; see Perkins and Woo (2000) for details. This means that a firm seeking listing must sell 30 per cent of its shares at a heavy discount. The upshot from this tax on firm growth is that, unlike Taiwanese firms, few Malaysian firms have expanded beyond import-competing enterprises to achieve economies of scale and become big exporters of manufactured goods. In the case of Malaysia, whether a zero-sum or a win–win outcome will emerge from its economic interaction with China will depend on whether the enlightened self-interest concept that 'a rising tide raises all ships' will prevail.

China has recently proposed the formation of a free trade area with South East Asia. This action should be recognized as a natural consequence of a fast-growing China that is anxious to undertake investments in the production of primary commodities and minerals so that its vertically-inte-grated conglomerates can better absorb large price shocks of raw materials should they appear. (This is also why China also recently attempted, unsuc-cessfully, to buy oil fields in Russia.) China's enthusiasm for a free trade area with ASEAN flows directly from the convergence of its economic inter-ests to those of the major developed countries: that is, the minimization of disruption from huge increases in the prices of raw commodities, the break-down of the international communication system, and the collapse of the open multilateral trading system. This last concern is particularly impor-tant because China cannot get rich by exporting only to its neighbours; it needs access to all the markets of the world to get rich. This means that any Chinese regional economic strategy is likely to be subordinate to the concern of helping to maintain an open multilateral trading system, and that if, and when, China becomes the leader of an Asian economic bloc, China is unlikely to shape it into a protectionist trade bloc, unless the European Union and the Free Trade Area of the Americas (FTAA) are already closed trade blocs.

South East Asia has welcomed the formation of an ASEAN–China free trade area because this will increase, first, its access to the increasingly important Chinese market; second, the possibility of lengthening the production chain to permit ASEAN to occupy some niches in the manufacturing process; and, third, the inflow of FDI from China to offset the loss to China of FDI from other countries. (The reader interested in the quantitative effects of the various combination of free trade areas within East and Southeast Asia should consult Cheong, 2003.)

Economic impact on the developed economies in East Asia, Western Europe and North America

For the developed economies, the integration of China yields net positive benefits from the more refined global division of labour. This is most clearly seen in how the industries in Hong Kong, Japan, Singapore, South Korea and Taiwan have preserved their competitiveness by shifting the labour-intensive manufacturing components of their production chains to China, and by expanding at home the higher value-added components of research and development, and of marketing and distribution; see, for example Abe (2003). The reason why my empirical work does not find much impact from China's emergence on the export and GDP levels of these five developed East Asian economies is because they were already in the stage of their product cycles where they were beginning to relocate their labour-intensive industries abroad. The emergence of low-wage China simply meant that more of these industries would be shifted to China instead of to the ASEAN-4.

Tain-Jy Chen (2003) has pointed out the possibility that the China challenge might be more difficult for Taiwan than for the other developed economies. Because the Taiwanese, unlike the Japanese and Koreans, incur minimal adjustment costs in fitting into the social and cultural life in mainland China, this means that the entire production chain, not just the manufacturing component, might move from Taiwan to China in the medium run.

The fact that the total value of the international trade of Western Europe and North America is not affected significantly by the rise of China is not surprising. These developed economies are now exporting a larger proportion of their capital-intensive goods and high value-added services to China and a lower proportion to the other Asian economies, and importing a bigger share of labour-intensive goods from China and a smaller share from the other Asian economies. This shift in the destination of Western European (North American) exports and in the sources of Western European (North American) imports is why there are noticeable changes in the composition of bilateral trade between Western Europe (North America) and individual Asian countries, but no noticeable change in the composition of overall trade between Western Europe (North America) and Asia.

Conclusion

Our analysis suggests that the full integration of China's huge labour force into the international division of labour could cause the ASEAN-4 to face the possibility of de-industrialization. However, this dismal outcome is by no means inevitable. This will happen only if the ASEAN-4 economies allow the drop in FDI inflow to lower the rate of technological diffusion to their economies. If the ASEAN-4 can prevent themselves from falling behind technologically, then they can also find lucrative niches in the lengthened production chains in manufacturing activities. This finding suggests that the ASEAN-4 must give the highest priority to deepening and widening their pools of human capital by speeding up the diffusion of new knowledge to their scientists and managers, and providing appropriate retraining programmes for the displaced workers.

The common challenge to the governments of the developed economies from the rise of China as a major manufacturer is how to upgrade the workers who have lost jobs in their manufacturing sectors. This challenge is no different from the structural adjustment that is needed to accommodate improvements in technological innovations. Just as one should not oppose technological progress in order to save obsolete industries, one should also not oppose free trade in order to save non-competitive industries. It is a failure of political will and of economic policy when governments in the developed economies impose protection instead of funding trade adjustment programmes to assist the workers in the trade-impacted sectors.

China taking its place in the international economic system will permit further specialization of tasks in the workplace, and this is a wealth-creating outcome. A country that can provide its workforce with the depth and range of scientific training required in the new workplace will be in line to receive some of the newly-created wealth. A country that is slow in building up its scientific and technological capability is one that does not understand the right remedy for the constant structural adjustment forced by globalization.

What has not yet been mentioned is that the fulfilment of the projected scenarios of China's impact on the global economy will necessitate China undertaking even bigger economic structural adjustments than any of its trade partners. My estimate is that the wide-ranging economic deregulation package that China agreed to implement for its WTO accession will cause at least one-fifth of its labour force to change jobs over the coming decade, and this could be a politically destabilizing process if not handled adeptly, and if external shocks were to slow down economic growth.

The tradeoff between stability and restructuring that is so starkly brought to the forefront by China's admission into WTO is really not a new tradeoff. What China's WTO membership has done is to accentuate an existing dilemma and not introduce a new one. The government has always realized that the soft budget constraint of the inefficient state-owned enterprise (SOE) sector is a constant threat to price stability, and the diversion of resources to keep this sector afloat is a drag on economic growth. But serious restructuring of SOEs means much more than facing higher urban unemployment; it also means confronting the politically powerful industrial–military complex and the industrial–bureaucratic complex. Economic rents now pose a bigger obstacle to restructuring than ideological sentimentality and, unlike the latter, they constitute a problem that the mere passing of time (i.e. the death of the remaining Stalinist sentimentalists) will not resolve. Because the greatest challenge to the deepening of economic reform and opening in China comes from the entrenched interests within the ruling structure, Woo (2001) has suggested that China's 'WTO accession could be seen as an attempt by reformers to lock economic policies on to a course for further marketization and internationalization that is costly to reverse'.

While the WTO benefits to China are likely to be immense, studies such as McKibbin and Woo (2003a) show that China's GDP in 2020 could be higher by as much as 20 per cent, whilst the WTO shocks could well stretch Chinese economic management to the limit. The granting of national treatment to foreign banks within the next three years will require China to re-capitalize the insolvent state-owned banks (SOBs) a second time since 1996, and to apply a financial tourniquet on the losses of the SOEs to attenuate the creation of non-performing loans. Because the reforms of the SOBs and SOEs are very expensive (in addition to being very difficult), they are likely to push China's fiscal position to the edge of unsustainability; see Sachs and Woo (2003). The outbreak of an AIDS pandemic, for example, could mean a large-scale public health programme that would bankrupt the government.

Developments external to China could also prevent the fulfilment of the scenarios projected by our analysis. External conflicts over North Korea, Taiwan, islands in the South China Sea, and Tibet could see a dramatic decline in FDI, and hence in the diffusion of technology, into China. Even a vastly less dramatic external event, such as the acceleration of economic deregulation in English-speaking India and its greater opening to inward FDI, could reduce the FDI flow into China, and China's exports of labour-intensive industrial products. In short, the realization of the potential for greater common prosperity created by China's integration into the world economy will require more than good economic management by China and its trade partners; good sense as well as good luck are also required by all parties.

Note

1 Full details of the model including a list of equations and parameters can be found online at: http://www.msgpl.com.au/msgpl/apgcubed46n/index.htm. The AP-GCUBED is based on the GCUBED model (described in McKibbin and Wilcoxen, 1998), which is in turn an expansion of the MSG2 model founded by

McKibbin and Sachs (1991). In AP-GCUBED, the behaviour of agents is modified to allow for short-run deviations from optimal behaviour either due to myopia or to restrictions on the ability of households and firms to borrow at the risk-free bond rate on government debt. Among other things, particularly in regard to treatment of asset markets, the model differs from traditional CGE models in allowing for short-run nominal wage rigidity (by different degrees in different countries) and therefore allows for significant periods of unemployment depending on the labour-market institutions in each country. The deviations from inter-temporal optimizing behaviour take the form of rules of thumb, which are chosen to generate the same steady-state behaviour as optimizing agents so that in the long run there is only a single inter-temporal optimizing equilibrium of the model. The AP-GCUBED model's assumptions hence differ from the market-clearing assumption in most CGE models.

References

Abe, Shigeyuki (2003), 'Is "China Fear" Warranted? Perspectives from Japan's Trade and Investment Relationships with China', *Asian Economic Papers*, 2(2), Spring/Summer, 106–31.

Chen, Tain-Jy (2003), 'Will Taiwan be Marginalised by China?', *Asian Economic Papers*, 2(2), Spring/Summer, 78–97.

Cheong, Inkyo (2003), 'Regionalism and Free Trade Agreements in East Asia', *Asian Economic Papers*, 2(2), Spring/Summer, 145–80.

McKibbin, W.J. and J. Sachs (1991), *Global Linkages: Macroeconomic Interdependence and Cooperation in the World Economy*, Washington, DC: Brookings Institution, June.

McKibbin, W.J. and P. Wilcoxen (1998), 'The Theoretical and Empirical Structure of the G-Cubed Model', *Economic Modelling* , 16(1) 123–48 (working paper version: http://www.msgpl.com.au/msgpl/download/struct.pdf).

McKibbin, W.J. and Wing Thye Woo (2003a), 'The Consequences of China's WTO Accession on its Neighbours', *Asian Economic Papers*, 2(2), Spring/Summer, 1–38.

McKibbin, W.J. and Wing Thye Woo (2003b), *The Global Economic Impact of China's WTO Accession*, Technical Working Paper, Paris: Trade Directorate, Organisation for Economic Co-operation and Development.

Okabe, Misa (2002), 'International R&D Spillovers and Trade Expansion', *ASEAN Economic Bulletin*, 19(2), August, 141–54.

Perkins, Dwight Heald and Wing Thye Woo (2000), 'Malaysia: Adjusting to Deep Integration with the World Economy', in Wing Thye Woo, Jeffrey D. Sachs and Klaus Schwab (eds), *The Asian Financial Crisis: Lessons for a Resilient Asia*, Cambridge, MA: MIT Press, 227–56.

Qin, Julia Ya (2003), '"WTO-Plus" Obligations and their Implications for the World Trade Organization Legal System: An Appraisal of the China Accession Protocol', *Journal of World Trade*, 37(3), 483–522.

Sachs, Jeffrey D., and Wing Thye Woo (2003), 'China's Growth after WTO Membership', *Journal of Chinese Economics and Business Studies*, 1(1), January, 1–33.

United Nations Conference on Trade and Development (2002), *World Investment Report 2002: Transnational Corporations and Export Competitiveness*, New York.

Wang, Zhi (2003), 'WTO Accession, the "Greater China" Free Trade Area, and Economic Integration across the Taiwan Strait', *China Economic Review*, 14, 316–41.

Woo, Wing Thye (2001), 'Recent Claims of China's Economic Exceptionalism: Reflections Inspired by WTO Accession', *China Economic Review*, 12(2/3), 107–36.

World Economic Forum (2000), *The Global Competitiveness Report 2000*, Oxford: Oxford University Press.

Yusof, Zainal Aznam (2003), 'Malaysia's Response to the China Challenge', *Asian Economic Papers*, 2(2), Spring/Summer, 46–73.

5
Effects of Real Exchange Rate Volatility and Misalignment on Commodity Exports: The Case of China

Jan P. Voon, Guangzhong Li and Jimmy Ran

Introduction

Exporters often face foreign exchange risk and uncertainty that may affect their exports. Foreign exchange risk is often measured by real exchange rate volatility (RERV). In developing countries characterized by fixed exchange rate regimes, exporters may also face the consequences of governments' economic and exchange rate policy mismanagements or regulations, which can give rise to real exchange rate misalignment (RERM). In the case of China, where the RMB:USD exchange rate had been fixed until 21 July 2005, RERM is believed to have occurred from time to time. This may pose another source of risk or uncertainty to the exporters.[1] This chapter examines Chinese exporters' behaviour through a conceptual and empirical investigation of RERV as well as RERM.[2]

Changes in volatility and misalignments influence the amount of exports. The existing literature has shown that risk/uncertainty–export link may be shaped by various factors (Darby *et al.*, 1999; Lee and Shin, 2000). Past efforts have been devoted mainly to assessing the real effects of RERV (e.g., Cushman, 1983; Koray and Lastrapes, 1989; Gagnon, 1993; Arize, 1995; Lee, 1999; Bacchetta and Wincoop, 2000; Chou, 2000; Sauer and Bohara, 2001; Servén, 2003). Little research has hitherto been directed to measuring the effects of RERM on exports. In the case of China, Zhang (2001) examined the RERM *per se* but not its effects on China's exports. Chou (2000) examined the RERV, but not the effects of RERM, on China's exports.

In this chapter, we first develop a theoretical model for measuring both RERV and RERM effects on a country's exports under a pegged exchange rate regime. Our model suggests that the effects of RERV and RERM on exports can indeed be significant depending on the magnitude of industry's aversion to risk as well as on the differences in importing country's characteristics. We manage to segregate the impacts of RERM on exports. For example, if industry is significantly risk-averse, increasing RER misalignment can increase exports provided that the negative effect of increasing risk on exports is smaller than the positive effect of increasing currency undervaluation on exports. Since one cannot readily observe an industry's attitude to risk, an empirical analysis is therefore warranted. This is accomplished here by using the export data disaggregated by industry and the Seemingly Unrelated Regression (SUR) methodology. Our empirical analysis shows that Chinese exporters, on average, tend to be risk-averse.

Our analysis has an important implication for China. China revalued its RMB exchange rate by 2.1 per cent against the US dollar on 21 July 2005. This would reduce the current RMB undervaluation *vis-à-vis* the US dollar,[3] and if the industry exporters are significantly risk-averse, the adverse impacts on its exports due to the RMB appreciation may be offset by the favourable impacts on its exports due to a concomitant decrease in real exchange rate volatility.

The rest of the chapter is organized as follows. The theoretical model is developed in the next section. The empirical model and the explanations of how the independent variables (for instance, the RERV and the RERM) are constructed and tested are provided in the third section. The fourth section describes the data used for the analysis, and discusses the test results as well as the results arising from the regression. The final section concludes the study.

The theoretical model

We evaluate in this section how exports of a country can be affected by both RERV and RERM.[4] We extend Bleaney and Fielding (2002) and Barkoulas, Baum and Caglayan (2002) in two ways: (1) incorporating real exchange rate misalignment variable in the model, and (2) using the stochastic maximization process. We treat price of exports (denominated in importing country's currency) as an endogenous variable, which will be affected by optimal decision of importing country. The importing country is assumed to maximize a utility function as follows:[5]

$$Z = [-\lambda (p_t - p_{t-1})^2 - (1 - \lambda)(y_t - y_t^* - k)^2] \qquad \lambda > 0, k > 0 \qquad (5.1)$$

where $p_t - p_{t-1}$ denotes inflation, y_t is output and y_t^* is equilibrium output. Because k (a country characteristic) is positive, this utility function is characterized by inflationary bias. The government maximizes equation (5.1) subject to an open economy expectations-augmented Phillips curve equation, which is represented as:

$$y = y^* + a (p_t - p_t^e) - c (q_t - q_t^*) \qquad a > 0, c > 0 \qquad (5.2)$$

where q_t^* is long-run equilibrium real exchange rate (RER), which can be interpreted as a fundamental value, and q_t is the RER of the importing country's currency which, in the case of China, may be expressed as RMB/importing country's currency. q_t may be expressed as:

$$q_t = q_t^* + M_t + \varepsilon_t \qquad \varepsilon_t \mid \Psi_t \sim N\,(0,\, \sigma_t^2) \tag{5.3}$$

where M_t represents RERM, ε has a normal distribution with mean zero and variance σ_t^2, which can also represent volatility of RER, and Ψ_t is the information set at time t. Since there is a random variable ε in the utility function, government has to choose price p_t to maximize the expectation of its utility function (which is derived by substituting equations (5.2) and (5.3) into (5.1); that is:

$$Max\ E(Z) = E\{-\lambda(p_t - p_{t-1})^2 - (1 - \lambda)[a(p_t - p_t^e) - c(M_t + \varepsilon_t) - k]^2\} \tag{5.4}$$

Differentiating with respect to p_t, and setting the differential equal to zero, we obtain:

$$\lambda\, p_t + (1 - \lambda)a^2\, p_t = \lambda\, p_{t-1} + (1 - \lambda)a^2\, p_t^e + a(1 - \lambda)(cM_t + k) \tag{5.5}$$

Under rational expectation, the economic agents choose p_t^e by taking expectations of equation (5.5), which yields:

$$P_t = p_{t-1} + abcM_t + abk$$
$$\text{where } b = \frac{1 - \lambda}{\lambda} \tag{5.6}$$

Once the importing country determines the p_t, the exporter will decide on the exports. The optimal problem faced by risk-averse exporters can be written as:

$$\underset{EX}{MaxU_t} = E[\pi(EX_t)] - \frac{1}{2}\gamma \text{var}\,[\pi(EX_t)]$$
$$\text{Where } \pi_t = q_t\, p_t\, EX_t - (dEX_t + EX_t^2) \tag{5.7}$$

In equation (5.7), γ denotes the coefficient of risk-aversion. Following Barkoulas, Baum and Caglayan (2002), the exporter incurs a non-stochastic quadratic cost of production $dEX_t + (1/2)EX_t^2$, where $d > 0$ and EX denotes the quantity exported. Substituting equation (5.6) into (5.7), we derive the following:

$$\begin{aligned} E[\pi(EX_t)] &= E(q_t\, p_t\, EX_t - dEX_t - \frac{1}{2}EX_t^2) \\ &= [(q_t^* + M_t)(p_{t-1} + abcM_t + abk)]EX_t - dEX_t - \frac{1}{2}EX_t^2 \end{aligned}$$

$$\text{var}[\pi(EX)] = EX^2\,(p_{t-1} + abcM_t + abk)^2\, \sigma_t^2 \tag{5.8}$$

By solving the optimal problem, we derive the export volume:

$$EX_t = \frac{(q_t^* + M_t)(p_{t-1} + abcM_t + abk)] - d}{1 + \gamma(p_{t-1} + abcM_t + abk)^2\,\sigma_t^2} \tag{5.9}$$

Case 1: risk-neutrality

If the exporter is risk-neutral ($\gamma = 0$), it is clear that as misalignment increases, the volume of export increases. The effect of volatility on export will not be significant.

Proof: If $\gamma = 0$, $EX_t = [(q_t^* + M_t)(p_{t-1} + abcM_t + abk)] - d$ and

$$\frac{\partial EX}{\partial M} = (p_{t-1} + abcM_t + abk) + abc(q_t^* + M_t) > 0$$

Case 2: risk-loving

If the exporter is predisposed to risk ($\gamma < 0$), increased misalignment and/or volatility will cause exports to rise. To demonstrate this, we let $p_t = p_{t-1} + abcM_t + abk$ (as in equation (5.6) and $E(q_t) = q_t^* + M_t$ (as in equation 5.3).

Proof: $\dfrac{\partial EX}{\partial M} = \dfrac{p_t + abcE(q_t)}{1 + \gamma p_t^2 \sigma_t^2} - \dfrac{2\gamma abcp_t[E(q_t)p_t - d]\sigma^2}{[1 + \gamma p_t^2 \sigma_t^2]^2} > 0$

$$\frac{\partial EX}{\partial \sigma^2} = \frac{2\gamma p_t^2[E(q_t)p_t - d]}{[1 + \gamma p_t^2 \sigma_t^2]^2} > 0$$

Case 3: risk-aversion

When the exporter is risk-averse ($\gamma > 0$), the effect of volatility on export will be negative, but the effect of misalignment on export is conditional upon:

(a) if $p_t^2 + 2abcd - abcE(q_t)\,p_t < 0$ and $0 < \gamma < \dfrac{p_t + abcE(q_t)}{[abcE(q_t)p_t - p_t^2 - 2abcd]}$, then

$$\frac{\partial EX}{\partial M} > 0$$

(b) if $p_t^2 + 2abcd - abcE(q_t)\,p_t > 0$ and $\gamma > \dfrac{p_t + abcE(q_t)}{[abcE(q_t)p_t - p_t^2 - 2abcd]}$, then

$$\frac{\partial EX}{\partial M} < 0$$

There are two perceived effects of M_t on exports. First, increasing M_t implies that the exchange rate becomes increasingly undervalued, which tends to raise exports. Second, increasing M_t also implies that the exchange rate becomes more and more distorted, which tend to depress exports. If q_t is relatively large (RER is relatively weak *vis-à-vis* the foreign currency) and, at the same time, if γ is relatively small (the exporter is relatively less risk-averse as in case 3a), the positive effect on exports induced by increasing undervaluation can exceed the negative effect on exports wrought by increasing distortion, hence contributing to a net positive impact on exports. Conversely, if q_t is relatively small (RER is relatively strong) and γ is relatively large (the exporter is relatively risk-averse as in case 3b), the positive effect on exports induced by increasing undervaluation will be smaller than the negative effect on exports wrought by increasing distortion, thereby contributing to a negative net effect on exports.[6] Therefore, whether or not export increases or decreases as M_t increases is largely an empirical question (since we cannot readily observe an industry's level of risk-aversion).

Equation (5.9) shows that changes in M_t or σ^2 can increase or decrease exports, depending on the value of γ as well as country characteristics. However, the effect of M_t on exports also depends on the relative strength or weakness of the domestic currency at the time when M_t changes. In what follows, we establish empirically the relationship between exports and the two variables, σ_t^2 and M_t, by controlling for the effects of country characteristics as well as the relative strength or weakness of the domestic currency at time t (these are constant across industries exporting to the same country). Other variables that can affect exports will also be used as the independent variables. We use an import-demand rather than export-supply function for our empirical analysis mainly because the cost data are not readily available. Another advantage is that our approach appears to be consistent with the literature and, hence, a comparison of our results with those from previous studies can be made accordingly.

The empirical model

Our estimated regression equations may be represented by:

$$\ln EX_{ij,t} = c_i + \alpha_i \ln Y_{j,t} + \beta_i \ln q_{j,t} + \delta_i \ln V_{j,t} + \theta_i \ln M_{j,t} + \varepsilon \qquad (5.10)$$

where $EX_{ij,t}$ is the export of industry i to country j in year t, c_i is the constant term, $Y_{j,t}$ is the importing country i's real GDP in year t, $q_{j,t}$ is the RER between China and country j in year t, $V_{j,t}$ is the RERV between China and country j in year t, $M_{j,t}$ is the RERM of China against country j in year t, and ε is the error component.

If q_t (in terms of RMB RER per foreign currency unit) increases, or Chinese RMB RER depreciates, the demand for exports would rise, so β_i is expected to be positive; α_i is also expected to be positive since Chinese exports would rise with foreign income; δ_i and θ_i, however, could be positive or negative depending on size of the coefficient of risk-aversion.

In our empirical analysis, the independent variables Y, q, V and M are derived as follows. Y is obtained by deflating the GDP of each importing country by its GDP deflator; q is represented by the conventional relationship: $q = ep_f/p_d$, where e is the Chinese RMB nominal price per unit of a foreign currency, p_f is the foreign consumer price index (CPI), and p_d is China's retail price index (RPI), which is a close proxy to the CPI data.[7] According to our specification of the process of RER (equation 5.3) and following Greene (2003), the variable V is generated by the GARCH (1,1) procedure:

$$RER_t = \alpha + \beta \, RER_{t-1} + \varepsilon_t$$
$$\sigma_t^2 = a_0 + a_1 \varepsilon_{t-1}^2 + a_2 \sigma_{t-1}^2$$

The derivation of the RERM variable, M, may be elaborated as follows. In theory, RERM can be represented by $M_t = q_t - q_t^*$ (as in Edwards, 1988; Darby *et al.*, 1999; Hinke and Montiel, 1999), where q_t is the actual RER at time t and q_t^* is the long-run equilibrium RER. Using the purchasing power parity (PPP) measure of misalignment, the long-run equilibrium RER can be expressed as: $q_t^* = e_0 \, (p_{f0}/p_{d0})$, where the subscript 0 denotes the base period. The estimation of q_t^* involves the identification of a base period, during which PPP holds and uses the subsequent movements of relative prices to estimate the base period's exchange rate to obtain the new estimate of q_t^*. It is not easy to identify an appropriate base year, and one way to overcome this is to use the long-run average of past relative exchange rates and prices as the benchmark for estimating the long-run equilibrium RER (see Chou and Shih, 1998). The Balassa–Samuelson effect provides a theoretical justification for observing a persistent long-term trend in the equilibrium RER (cited in Hinke and Montiel, 1999). In this study, we have chosen 1981–94 as the base period, to be consistent with Chou and Shih (1998).

Our derivations of q_t^* and M_t are in line with Hinke and Montiel's (1999) measures of long-run equilibrium RER and RERM. However, in practice, the derived M data series cannot be applied directly to our regression equation (5.10) above because two of our specified independent variables, q_t and M_t, are directly correlated.[8] To overcome this dilemma, we transform M_t into the absolute form, where $M_t = |q_t - q_t^*|$.[9] There are several advantages with this. First, the absolute form of M_t will not detract from the conventional definition of RERM, which has been expressed as the gap between the actual RER and some notion of a sustainable 'equilibrium' RER. Second, the absolute measures enable us to gauge the magnitude of the distortion from its fundamental value rather than the direction of change. Third, the absolute values of M_t permit the use of the log functional form, which is commonly used for regression analysis and is also convenient for comparison with the existing literature.

Prior to estimating M_t, it is crucial to test the validity of the long-run PPP. Similar to Chou and Shih (1998), for empirical purposes, we express the nominal exchange rates as $e_t = a_0 + a_1 (p_d/p_f)_t + \varepsilon_t$ where the lower case letters denote logarithms and ε is the error term capturing deviations from the PPP. If e_t and p_d/p_f are found to be cointegrated, these variables then have a long-run relationship. The cointegration analysis begins with testing for the order of integration of the log of the nominal exchange rate and the relative price series. To achieve this, we perform the Augmented Dickey–Fuller (ADF) test. The cointegration relationship between the nominal exchange rate and the relative price is then tested via two steps using the Johansen procedure.

The data and results

We investigate, by using the panel data, China's industry exports to the G7 countries (Canada, the UK, Germany, France, Italy, Japan and the US). The annual SITC data on the Chinese industry exports to these countries were obtained from the International Economic Data Bank (IEDB), Canberra. The export data correspond to the total dollar value exported, so we need to divide the export value by the relevant unit price in order to derive the export volume. We obtained the unit export prices from Datastream. For the variable Y, we collected the annual nominal GDP data and the GDP deflators from Datastream. For q_t, we obtained the different exchange rates data from Datastream, and the Chinese retail price indices (RPIs) for 1978–98 from the *China Statistical Yearbook*. For V, we used 1970–98 monthly data to estimate the GARCH (1,1) model and construct the annual RERV by taking the average of the monthly volatility generated by the model. Finally, the M_t data series are derived using the process developed above.

The results of the unit root tests for the nominal exchange rates and the relative prices are presented in Table 5.1. The results indicate that the log nominal exchange rates and the log relative price series are all $I (1)$, which denotes integration of order one. The results obtained by using the Johansen procedure in testing for cointegration on the same combinations of sample and exchange rates are reported in Table 5.2. Both 'max' and 'trace' statistics are reported, and they are compared with the critical values at the significance levels of 1 and 5 per cent to check how many cointegrating vectors are significant. Starting with the 'max' test and/or 'trace' test results, the null hypothesis $r = 0$ (no cointegration) is rejected in favour of $r = 1$ in Canada, Germany, France, Italy, Japan and the US. It thus supports long-run PPP relationships for these countries. We exclude the UK from our subsequent analysis because long-run PPP relationships do not hold for this country. Canada is subsequently excluded from the regression analysis because of the absence of China's continuous industry, specifically SITC-3, export data to this country.

Table 5.1 Unit root test for nominal exchange rate and relative price

Nominal exchange rates	ADF	PP	Relative prices	ADF	PP
$\log(e_{Can})$	−0.59	−0.57	$\log(p_d/p_{Can})$	0.20	0.12
$\Delta\log(e_{Can})$	−7.24	−15.87	$\Delta\log(p_d/p_{Can})$	−7.32	−15.76
$\log(e_{Ger})$	−0.47	−0.45	$\log(p_d/p_{Ger})$	0.28	0.24
$\Delta\log(e_{Ger})$	−6.03	−14.92	$\Delta\log(p_d/p_{Ger})$	−7.75	−16.84
$\log(e_{Fra})$	−0.26	−0.23	$\log(p_d/p_{Fra})$	0.13	0.03
$\Delta\log(e_{Fra})$	−5.97	−14.96	$\Delta\log(p_d/p_{Fra})$	−7.16	−15.66
$\log(e_{UK})$	−0.43	−0.34	$\log(p_d/p_{UK})$	−0.54	−0.73
$\Delta\log(e_{UK})$	−6.79	−15.26	$\Delta\log(p_d/p_{UK})$	−7.64	−15.88
$\log(e_{Ita})$	−0.48	−0.45	$\log(p_d/p_{Aus})$	−2.09	−2.23
$\Delta\log(e_{Ita})$	−6.06	−14.44	$\Delta\log(p_d/p_{Aus})$	−6.87	−15.62
$\log(e_{US})$	−0.45	−0.43	$\log(p_d/p_{US})$	0.11	0.003
$\Delta\log(e_{US})$	−6.84	−15.80	$\Delta\log(p_d/p_{US})$	−7.72	−15.90
$\log(e_{Jap})$	−0.52	−0.62	$\log(p_d/p_{Jap})$	0.50	0.38
$\Delta\log(e_{Jap})$	−6.21	−14.51	$\Delta\log(p_d/p_{Jap})$	−8.03	−15.72

Notes:
ADF denotes the Augmented Dickey–Fuller test statistics. The critical values for 5% (1%) are −2.873 (−3.458).
PP represents Phillips–Perron statistics. The critical values for 5% (1%) are −2.873 (−3.458).

Table 5.2 Results of cointegration tests

Exchange rate	Maximum Eigenvalue		Trace statistics		Lag*
	$H0: r=0$ $Ha: r=1$	$r \le 1$ $r=2$	$H: r=0$ $H: r \ge 1$	$r \le 1$ $r \ge 2$	
	9.99	4.10	14.09	4.10	2
Canada	13.40	7.45	21.15	7.45	2
Germany	18.19	3.07	21.26	3.07	2
France	18.44	4.10	22.54	4.10	2
UK	11.86	5.24	17.10	4.47	2
Italy	19.48	4.48	23.96	4.48	2
Japan	21.57	3.53	25.11	3.53	2
US	15.01	7.78	22.79	7.78	2
Critical values					
5%	15.67	9.24	19.96	9.24	
1%	20.20	12.97	24.60	12.97	

Notes:
r denotes the number of cointegrating vectors: the critical values are for 5% level of significance.
* denotes that the lag order of VAR is chosen by the criterion of Akaike Information Criterion (AIC) and Schwarz Criterion (SC).

Table 5.3   The seemingly unrelated regression results

	lnY	t	*Lnq*	t	*lnV*	t	*lnM*	t
France								
SITC0	1.76	2.97	0.47	1.86	−0.15	−2.06	−0.14	−3.60
SITC1	9.28	5.92	−0.43	−0.64	−0.16	−0.85	−0.01	−0.10
SITC2	0.72	0.75	0.61	1.48	−0.50	−4.24	−0.23	−3.82
SITC3	6.47	3.17	1.40	1.60	−0.29	−1.15	−0.23	−1.73
SITC4	−5.85	−1.71	−0.81	−0.55	0.18	0.43	−0.61	−2.77
SITC5	5.06	7.58	0.51	1.78	−0.28	−3.41	−0.17	−4.01
SITC6	3.08	3.91	0.64	1.90	−0.43	−4.45	−0.16	−3.09
SITC7	18.57	7.49	0.87	0.82	−0.73	−2.41	−0.24	−1.51
SITC8	8.77	5.98	0.74	1.17	−0.54	−3.03	−0.11	−1.20
SITC9	9.87	1.17	1.16	0.32	−1.59	−1.54	0.06	0.11
Germany								
SITC0	1.16	2.91	0.31	1.18	−0.01	−0.11	−0.15	−3.54
SITC1	1.46	0.63	0.76	0.50	0.44	1.15	−0.40	−1.60
SITC2	−0.53	−1.54	0.41	1.81	0.04	0.67	−0.11	−2.86
SITC3	9.75	3.10	−4.06	−1.97	0.64	1.22	0.31	0.89
SITC4	3.39	2.10	0.01	0.01	−0.34	−1.25	−0.06	−0.33
SITC5	3.27	3.90	0.51	0.92	0.00	0.02	−0.16	−1.78
SITC6	2.67	4.53	0.45	1.17	−0.13	−1.30	−0.20	−3.15
SITC7	10.46	4.31	1.44	0.91	−0.32	−0.81	−0.34	−1.29
SITC8	4.52	6.48	0.50	1.10	−0.19	−1.64	−0.20	−2.66
SITC9	1.91	0.44	1.76	0.62	−0.30	−0.41	−0.14	−0.29
Italy								
SITC0	1.52	1.67	−0.43	−1.11	0.35	4.13	0.04	0.57
SITC1	16.07	6.56	0.26	0.26	−0.22	−0.96	−0.21	−1.25
SITC2	−0.54	−0.58	0.64	1.66	−0.18	−2.09	−0.14	−2.28
SITC3	−3.16	−0.30	4.96	1.12	−0.66	−0.67	0.05	0.07
SITC4	−12.08	−2.36	3.33	1.55	0.03	0.06	−0.06	−0.17
SITC5	11.63	12.74	−0.40	−1.05	−0.14	−1.59	0.02	0.27
SITC6	5.21	8.60	0.10	0.38	−0.14	−2.57	−0.09	−2.06
SITC7	18.14	12.38	−1.39	−2.26	0.05	0.38	0.07	0.69
SITC8	7.94	10.93	−0.28	−0.90	−0.08	−1.20	−0.08	−1.58
SITC9	0.82	0.17	2.28	1.11	−0.77	−1.68	−0.41	−1.21
Japan								
SITC0	2.85	4.05	0.37	1.46	0.02	0.23	0.03	0.59
SITC1	2.10	1.89	0.04	0.10	0.15	1.09	0.03	0.47
SITC2	0.53	1.01	0.35	1.85	−0.01	−0.16	−0.08	−2.35
SITC3	1.63	1.89	0.40	1.27	−0.37	−3.41	−0.09	−1.58
SITC4	1.08	1.05	0.78	2.08	−0.42	−3.24	−0.03	−0.44
SITC5	4.59	6.69	−0.18	−0.73	−0.05	−0.56	−0.05	−1.18
SITC6	2.87	3.30	−0.30	−0.95	0.13	1.17	0.08	1.39
SITC7	13.42	6.42	−0.90	−1.19	0.16	0.62	0.17	1.21
SITC8	6.32	4.65	−0.31	−0.63	0.02	0.10	0.17	1.86
SITC9	0.24	0.07	1.37	1.08	−0.99	−2.27	−0.21	−0.90

Table 5.3   The seemingly unrelated regression results – *continued*

	lnY	t	*Lnq*	t	*lnV*	t	*lnM*	t
USA								
SITC0	1.99	3.68	1.15	4.73	0.61	0.86	–0.02	–0.54
SITC1	0.02	0.02	2.28	5.46	3.41	2.82	–0.05	–0.70
SITC2	1.75	2.03	0.08	0.20	0.91	0.81	0.03	0.48
SITC3	–9.31	–1.47	7.45	2.61	7.02	0.85	–0.14	–0.28
SITC4	5.94	3.01	–1.96	–2.21	1.62	0.63	–0.14	–0.87
SITC5	3.64	6.24	0.68	2.59	1.38	1.81	0.10	2.20
SITC6	2.48	2.91	0.92	2.39	1.68	1.51	0.03	0.40
SITC7	6.64	3.06	3.16	3.22	1.81	0.64	0.25	1.39
SITC8	2.96	2.12	1.52	2.41	1.54	0.84	0.19	1.64
SITC9	–8.92	–2.02	3.38	1.70	–2.06	–0.36	0.35	0.97

Our regression results are presented in Table 5.3. Our coefficient estimates are generally significant and exhibit the correct signs. The estimated GDP coefficients are reported to be significantly positive, as expected. Chinese exports appear in general to be income elastic, especially for the manufacturing industries (SITC 5-8).

A large majority of the estimated RER coefficients (β) is significant and exhibits the right sign. However, Chinese exports to Japan and the European countries do not appear to be responsive to movements in RMB real exchange rate. This implies that in the event of a RMB revaluation, China's exports to Japan and the European countries under study would be less adversely affected than its exports to the US.

The sign of the RERV coefficients (δ) can be positive or negative, consistent with our theoretical propositions. However, the estimated RERV coefficients are predominantly negative, except perhaps in the case of USA, where the RERV coefficients exhibited positive (but largely insignificant) signs. This implies that Chinese industry exporters are generally averse to RER volatility, especially for Japan and the European countries. Our results also show that most of the reported RERM coefficients (θ) are negative. This is particularly the case with the European countries, which is consistent with the results reported in previous studies (Sekkat and Varoudakis, 2000; Bleaney and Greenaway, 2001). Analysing this in the light of the theory proposed earlier, we deduce that Chinese exporters to these countries are reasonably risk-averse, as reflected by the coefficients of both the RERV and the RERM. Hence, RMB real exchange rate misalignment appears to be a distortion that exerts negative net influences on Chinese exports.

Compared with Darby *et al.* (1999), which showed empirically that volatility seemed to be more important than misalignment when assessing their impacts on investments, we demonstrated that misalignment appears to be at least as important as volatility when assessing their impacts on exports. This is the case because China has adopted a pegged exchange rate regime under which the RER tends to deviate from the PPP RER, in contrast to those countries investigated by Darby *et al.* (1999) for which a flexible regime has been instituted.

Conclusions

Both the theoretical and the empirical models have been developed for assessing the impacts of the RER, the RERV, and the RERM on China's industry exports. These three variables are crucial for management of real exchange rate policy in any country. Our general theoretical model shows that the RERM effects on exports can be positive or negative, depending on the magnitude of exporters' risk-aversion and country characteristics. If industry is risk-neutral or predisposed to risk, the effects of increased RERM on exports will be positive. If industry is risk-averse, the effects could be positive or negative, depending on industries' level of risk-aversion as well as relative strength of the domestic currency prevailing at time *t*. In the case of China, the net impacts of RER misalignments on exports are negative: the positive effect of increasing RMB undervaluation on exports appears to be smaller than the negative effect of increasing risk or distortion effect on exports.

The results of our empirical analysis seem to support the theory. In the case of Chinese commodity exports, particularly exports to the European countries and Japan, the exporters appeared to be risk-averse. There are some instances in this paper where the exporters are predisposed to both the RERV and the RERM, but there is not a reported case where Chinese exporters are significantly averse to RERV but predisposed to RERM and *vice versa*. It is also of interest that in the case of China (and possibly some other countries characterized by fixed exchange rate regimes), RER misalignments seem to be as important a variable as RER volatility. Hence, excluding RERM could indeed induce a missing-variable bias into the empirical analysis of China's exports.

Our results also imply that China may not be substantially disadvantaged as a result of its RER revaluation,[10] in contrast to conventional wisdom. As we observe from Figure 5.1, China's RMB has been very much undervalued, particularly in recent years. The attempt by the central government to revalue its RMB exchange rate by re-pegging the RMB to a basket of currencies helped to bring the undervalued real exchange rate closer to the equilibrium RER, which implies a lower level of distortion. Hence, the adverse impact on China's exports due to the real exchange rate appreciation (represented by β in equation 5.10) could be offset to some extent by the positive impact on its exports as a result of a reduction in RMB real exchange rate misalignment.

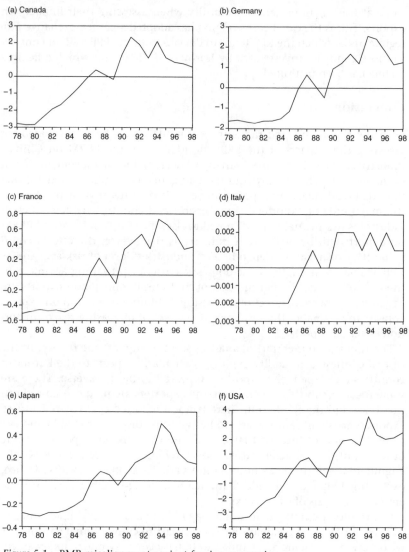

Figure 5.1   RMB misalignment against foreign currencies

Notes

1 By uncertainty, we refer not to the usual role of recurring random phenomena
   or variances, but to unanticipated events where probabilities cannot be
   quantified, as defined by Knight (1921) cited in Just (2001). RER, and hence
   RERM, is viewed as an uncertain variable in China because the RMB exchange
   rate is controlled to a large extent by the central government, and it is uncertain

as to how and when the Chinese government changes its RMB exchange rate. If the RER deviates substantially from its long-run equilibrium as a result of regulation or policy distortion, economic agents tend to be cautious when it comes to decision-making (e.g., investment, export, etc.).

2   Darby *et al.* (1999) identified RERM as an uncertainty variable on investments. Our chapter focuses on the impact of RERM on exports.

3   Attempts have also been made here to estimate the degrees of RMB misalignments against the foreign currencies over the last two decades or so. The results are illustrated in Figure 5.1.

4   Darby *et al.* (1999) performed a similar study of their impacts on investments rather than on exports. They concluded that it is not possible, from theory, to say that suppressing exchange rate volatility will automatically increase investment; there are situations where that will happen and situations where it will not.

5   Conversely, this can be seen as minimizing a loss function equal to the negative of this 'utility function'.

6   This is consistent with Darby *et al.* (1999), which asserted that persistent RER misalignment may not always depress investments.

7   Chinese CPI data were not available before 1985.

8   The multicollinearity problem will not be so obvious if one uses the M_t data that are derived using the other two alternative measures of misalignment, namely the black market premium methodology and the model-based methodology (Hinke and Montiel, 1999). However, there would be problems with data availability as well as potential empirical inaccuracies arising from the use of a large number of regressions and secondary estimates in order to estimate the long-run equilibrium RER over the sample period.

9   The correlation before the transformation is as high as 95 per cent for some countries and this effectively drops down to as low as 20 per cent after the transformation.

10 China could be under pressure to revalue its RMB exchange rate since US Treasury leader John Snow carried to China complaints from US manufacturers that the RMB was too cheap at its previous peg of about 8.28 to the greenback, giving Chinese exporters an unfair advantage that is worsening US unemployment and exports.

References

Arize, A.C. (1995), 'The Effects of Exchange-Rate Volatility on US Exports: An Empirical Investigation', *Southern Economic Journal*, 62 (1), 34–44.

Bacchetta, P. and E.V. Wincoop (2000), 'Does Exchange-Rate Stability Increase Trade and Welfare?', *Quarterly Journal of Economics*, 1093–109.

Barkoulas, John T., Christopher F. Baum and Mustafa Caglayan (2002), 'Exchange Rate Effects on the Volume and Variability of Trade Flows', *Journal of International Money and Finance*, 21, 481–96.

Bleaney, M. and D. Fielding (2002), 'Exchange Rate Regimes, Inflation and Output Volatility in Developing Countries', *Journal of Development Economics*, 68, 233–45.

Bleaney, M. and D. Greenaway (2001), 'The Impacts of Terms of Trade and Real Exchange Rate Volatility on Investment and Growth in Sub-Sahara Africa', *Journal of Development Economics*, 65, 491–500.

Chou, W.L. (2000), 'Exchange Rate Variability and China's Exports', *Journal of Comparative Economics*, 28, 61–79.

Chou, W.L. and Y.C. Shih (1998), 'The Equilibrium Exchange Rate of the Chinese Renminbi', *Journal of Comparative Economics*, 26, 165–74.

Cushman, D.O. (1983), The Effects of Real Exchange Rate Risk on International Trade', *Journal of International Economics*, 15 (2), 45–63.

Darby, J., A.H. Hallett, J. Ireland and L. Piscitelli (1999), 'The Impact of Exchange Rate Uncertainty on the Level of Investment', *The Economic Journal*, 109 (March), C55–C67.

Dellas, H. and B. Zilberfarb (1993), 'Real Exchange Rate Volatility and International Trade: A Reexamination of the Theory', *Southern Economic Journal*, 59 (4), 641–7.

Edwards, S. (1988), 'Exchange Rate Misalignment in Developing Countries', Baltimore, MD: The Johns Hopkins University Press.

Gagnon, J.E. (1993), 'Exchange Rate Variability and the Level of International Trade', *Journal of International Economics*, 34, 269–87.

Greene, W.H. (2003), *Econometrics Analysis*, 5th edn New York: McGraw-Hill.

Hinke, L.E. and P.J. Montiel (1999), *Exchange Rate Misalignment: Concepts and Measurement for Developing Countries*, New York: Oxford University Press.

Just, R.E. (2001), Addressing the Changing Nature of Uncertainty in Agriculture', *American Journal of Agricultural Economics*, 83 (5), 1131–53.

Knight, F. (1921), 'Risk, Uncertainty and Profit', Chicago, IL: University of Chicago Press.

Koray, F. and W.D. Lastrapes (1989), 'Real Exchange Rate Volatility and US Bilateral Trade: A VAR Approach', *The Review of Economics and Statistics*, 68, 311–15.

Lee, J. (1999), 'The Effect of Exchange Rate Volatility on Trade in Durables', *Review of International Economics*, 7 (2), 189–201.

Lee, J. and K. Shin (2000), 'The Role of a Variable Input in the Relationship between Investment and Uncertainty', *American Economic Review*, 90, 667–80.

Sauer, C. and A.K. Bohara (2001), 'Exchange Rate Volatility and Exports: Regional Differences between Developing and Industrialized Countries', *Review of International Economics*, 9 (1), 133–52.

Sekkat K. and A. Varoudakis (2000), 'Exchange Rate Management and Manufactured Exports in Sub-Sahara Africa', *Journal of Development Economics*, 61, 237–53.

Servén, L. (2003), 'Real-Exchange-Rate Uncertainty and Private Investment in LDCs', *Review of Economics and Statistics*, 85 (10), 212–18.

Zhang, Z. (2001), 'Real Exchange Rate Misalignment in China: An Empirical Investigation', *Journal of Comparative Economics*, 29, 80–94.

6
A Sustainable Currency Regime for Hong Kong and the Mainland

Lok Sang Ho*

Introduction

Joseph Stiglitz observed during a recent public lecture in Hong Kong that the world is badly in need of a new reserve asset.[1] This chapter follows up this idea and argues that China is in a unique position to contribute to the world by coming up with a new exchange rate arrangement involving just such a new reserve asset.

China has been very pragmatic and very innovative on the exchange rate management front. China came up with the idea of 'foreign exchange certificates' in 1980, shortly after Deng Xiaoping declared an open-door policy in 1978, and began to allow its citizens to set up foreign currency accounts from 1984. Foreigners visiting China would trade their foreign currencies for these certificates which were accepted in specific stores where they could buy goods otherwise beyond the reach of most citizens. Foreign exchange certificates were much sought after by ordinary people who would pay a premium to get them. In 1985 China further set up its first Foreign Exchange Adjustment Centre in Shenzhen to allow eligible enterprises to trade surplus foreign exchange for RMB and vice versa. Soon after this, similar centres were set up in many major cities including Shanghai, Guangzhou, Dalian, Xiamen and Zhuhai. The convertibility of a currency in practice is never a black or white matter: the Renminbi had been moving towards convertibility over the years, in more timid and smaller steps at first, then bolder and larger steps toward the late 1980s and early 1990s.[2]

Shortly after China's even bolder measures to liberalize the RMB in 1994, the 1997–8 Asian Financial Crisis (AFC) dealt a serious blow to many Asian

---

*The author acknowledges with thanks the able research assistance of Gary Wong and the comments of William Branson, Bennett McCallum, Lawrence Krause, Ping Lin, Yue Ma, Robert Shiller, John Williamson and Henry Wan who attended various presentations at different stages of preparation of this study.

economies, from Indonesia and Malaysia to Thailand and Korea, and shook the confidence of those who had subscribed to foreign exchange liberalization. Malaysia brought back foreign exchange control. China, which was spared much of the damage wrought by the AFC, was believed to have avoided such damage only because it had maintained a tight grip over capital flows in and out of the country. After the AFC, China had even more reason to believe that liberalizing the RMB should not mean a free float. Against this background, the announcement on 21 July 2005 that the RMB would follow a managed float system making reference to a basket of currencies, and the tiny 2 per cent revaluation against the US dollar were not at all surprising. The caution exercised by the State Administration for Foreign Exchange (SAFE) must be considered prudent and wise.

There is some evidence that the problems faced by many Asian countries during the AFC as well as those faced by such Latin American countries as Brazil and Argentina in the late 1990s seem to have been related to the unprecedented and sustained strength of the US dollar (to which these currencies were linked to a bigger or smaller degree) over the 1995–2001 period, and particularly during 1995–7. Sometimes the problem is not an exchange rate problem *per se*. When the strength of the US dollar increases the perception of risk in the markets, domestic interest rates could become painfully high.

It is the thesis of this study that neither the fixed exchange rate (in a currency board setting or otherwise) nor a floating exchange rate regime will be adequate to eliminate the instability arising from the haphazard drift of the real exchange rate. The challenge is to work out a managed float system (Williamson, 2000, 2002) consistent with the broad macroeconomic goals of price stability and sustainable growth.

An important part of this search for an efficient managed adjustment mechanism lies in finding an instrument that can serve as a 'real monetary anchor' so that a currency tied to it can maintain a real exchange rate level consistent with the fundamentals of the economy.[3] In practice 'real values' always involve the ratios of nominal variables (e.g., the 'real money balance' is just a monetary aggregate divided by a price index). So an important part of a 'real anchor' design is an automatic adjustment mechanism such that in the face of a movement in some nominal variables, other nominal variables will adjust appropriately and automatically so as to preserve the real values of the key variables which have been adapted to the economic fundamentals. While the link to the real anchor should not be affected by random perturbations to the economic fundamentals, in the event of permanent changes in such fundamentals, a mechanism to effect smooth, panic-free adjustment in the real link will be necessary.

There has been much discussion about a basket link in the literature (Kawai, 2001; Bird and Rajan, 2002; Yano and Kosaka, 2003). Ho (1990) proposed re-pegging the Hong Kong dollar to the effective exchange rate index, which is a trade-weighted basket of 15 currencies, and suggested using the US dollar–HK dollar exchange rate as the instrument to effect stability in the effective exchange rate index. A currency basket link is superior to a single currency link in that it will reduce the fluctuation of the home currency *vis-à-vis* any single currency. Yet because of inflation a currency tied to a currency basket may still be subject to real exchange rate fluctuations and may also not command stable purchasing power. As argued by Irving Fisher (1913a), money with unstable purchasing power is like an elastic measuring rod, and cannot be a very good form of money.

The second section argues for the need to have real exchange rates set and maintained at levels that are attuned to the fundamentals of the economy and describes a mechanism, called a World Currency Unit (WCU) link, that can facilitate the achievement of this. The next section describes the nature of the reserve asset in a world with real exchange rate anchors, and the section after that looks at the question of what constitutes the appropriate exchange rate and argues for the desirability for 'real exchange rate targeting' for countries such as China which do not have a very deep financial market. The fifth section looks at the subject of credibility, and argues that a monetary regime using the real exchange rate as an instrument to achieve both internal and external balance is probably as credible as you can get. The final section then discusses the implications for a world where more and more countries have adopted such real links and where more and more financial assets are denominated in the WCU and become available as reserve assets.

The WCU link for macroeconomic and monetary stability

There is consensus among economists that an excessively high real exchange rate will cause serious harm to the economy, even though there always remains controversy whether in a particular case a currency is overvalued or not and by how much. Is the RMB in 2005 overvalued and, if so, by how much? Was the Argentine peso overvalued before the dramatic depreciation in 2001? The answer may vary from economist to economist.[4] But the fact that many economists attribute the Argentine peso crisis to an overvalued peso suggests that economists believe generally that overvaluation of a currency can cause serious problems (Schuler 2005). China has been worried about a significant revaluation of the RMB, believing that the sharp appreciation of the Japanese yen was at least in part responsible for the more-than-a-decade-old stagnation of the Japanese economy from 1991. The chronic and worsening unemployment problem of the United Kingdom ahead of the 1992 sterling crisis was believed to be related to sterling overvaluation and invited George Soros to attack the currency. His success was very sweet for the fund that he managed, but it turned out to be sweet too for the UK. A combination of lower interest rates and currency

depreciation revived the United Kingdom economy in just months following its abandonment of the link to the European monetary mechanism on
16 September 1992.[5]

Clearly, in the absence of changes in real fundamentals, the drifting of a
nominal anchor (the host currency such as the US dollar) may bring about
exchange rates that are inconsistent with full employment (internal
balance) and external balance.

It is therefore highly desirable to link a currency to a real anchor at an
appropriate level (i.e., neither too high, so as to cause deflation, nor too
low, so as to cause overheating).[6] Once the real economy has been found to
be comfortable with some real exchange rate and anchored to the currency
at that rate, why should we let the real monetary conditions drift away
from these comfortable values due to the movement of the host currency?

Following the hint given by Fisher (1913a, 1913b) and Coats (1994) Ho
(2000) proposed an indexed unit of account based on a basket of 'world
output' that he advocated as the basis for denominating financial instruments such as bonds. This unit of account can serve very well as an anchor
for currencies. This unit of account, called the World Currency Unit, is not
a basket of currencies. Instead, the WCU link may be said to be a 'link with
a composite good' ('a composite good standard'). By design, the WCU
basket consists of the GDPs (outputs) of the key economic zones *in some
base year 0*. The five economic zones include the United States, the Euro
zone, Japan, Canada and Australia.[7] For exposition purposes, we will use
WCU_0 to refer to the base year physical basket of output underlying each
World Currency Unit, and use $V_{0US\$,t}$ to refer to the nominal value of WCU_0
in US dollars at time t.

Let Q_{i0} be the GDP of country/zone i in base year 0, measured in the
domestic currency. Thus:

$$WCU_0 = \lambda \{Q_{10}, Q_{20}, Q_{30}, Q_{40}, Q_{50}\} \tag{6.1}$$

This says that a WCU_0 is some fraction λ of the basket of base year GDPs.

Valuation of this unit in the base year, $V_{0US\$0}$, is obtained by defining λ
such that:

$$\lambda \Sigma\, Q_{i0} \cdot e_{i0} = US\$100 \tag{6.2}$$

where $\Sigma\, Q_{i0} \cdot e_{i0}$ is the nominal value of the GDP in the base year in US
dollars, and e_{i0} is the exchange rate converting one unit of the currency of i
into US\$ in year 0; λ is a scaling factor that defines the size of the basket
and thus the real value of the unit; and i is any of the five major
economies.

$V_{0US\$t}$ is the nominal value of one WCU_0 in US dollars at t. Changes in
the valuation of the WCU output basket over time reflect the forces of

exchange rate movements as well as domestic inflation/deflation in each of the represented economic zones. If Q_{i0} measured in current (let us represent the current moment with t) domestic prices increases because of inflation (P_{it}/P_{i0} rising) and/or if currency i appreciates against the US dollar (e_{it} rising), other things being equal, the nominal value of the WCU basket in US dollars will increase, but the underlying basket of real output remains the same. It is in this sense that we say $V_{0US\$,t}$ represents constant purchasing power.

$$V_{0US\$t} = \lambda \Sigma\, Q_{i0} \cdot P_{it}/P_{i0} \cdot e_{it} \qquad (6.3)$$

The nominal value of $V_{0US\$,t}$ can be updated easily according to (6.3) from moment to moment, even though P_{it}/P_{i0} is normally updated on a monthly basis. In principle P_{it}/P_{i0} should be based on the implicit GDP deflator, but for practical purposes, considering that announcements of GDP deflators are subject to long lags and frequent revisions and that the CPI tracks GDP deflators fairly well, we would recommend using the CPI in estimating the nominal values of the WCU.

With full transparency of the valuation formula given in (6.3), once the base year has been chosen and the WCU output basket has been defined, at any time τ the Monetary Authority may link the domestic currency to WCU_0 so that $\alpha_\tau\, V_{0US\$\tau} = 1$ unit of the domestic currency. *By adjusting the magnitude of the 'link coefficient', α, the Monetary Authority can achieve any level of effective real exchange rate desired. As a result, transition to a WCU-based regime can be completely smooth in the sense that the exchange rate vis-à-vis the US dollar stays the same momentarily.* The exchange rate *vis-à-vis* the US dollar will rise or fall from then on depending on whether the nominal value of the WCU rises or falls.

The kind of system proposed here will not match Schuler's definition of a currency board (Schuler, 2005), but there are many parallels. According to this proposal, banks may issue notes against reserve assets held with the monetary authority, much like the current Hong Kong system, where note-issuing commercial banks deposit US$1 for every HK$7.8 that they issue in the form of banknotes, and the Hong Kong Monetary Authority undertakes to convert these Hong Kong dollar notes back to US dollars at the same rate.[8] Under a WCU-based link, convertibility is guaranteed not at a fixed rate against the US dollar, but at a fixed rate in terms of real purchasing power ('real money', not 'nominal money'), although redeemable in US dollars or other currencies. This way the convertibility undertaking is not fixed in nominal terms but is fixed in real terms.

If economic fundamentals have changed permanently and significantly enough there will be a need to change the 'link coefficient' α. But to avoid panic or speculation, it is proposed that all the money that has already been issued at the old α will not be affected by any change in α. Thus, if a unit of the local currency (called the peso here for convenience) was issued with α_τ times $V_{0US\$\tau}$ worth of US dollars (or any other acceptable currency) deposited with the monetary authority, convertibility or redemption at time t will be at α_τ times $V_{0US\$t}$ of US dollars.

New reserve assets and the international settlement vehicle

Today the US dollar is the predominant reserve asset among the world's central banks and the universally accepted international settlement vehicle. Many commodities, including petroleum, are quoted in US dollars. One result of this is that the United States benefits from seigniorage, which is 'a financial reward accruing to the reserve currency as a result of its being used as a world money' (Husted and Melvin, 2003). As a result the United States can issue debt to the world (often taken up by much less well-off countries, such as China and Korea) in US dollars and repay years later, often in much depreciated US dollars. Indeed, as the world's largest net debtor nation holding foreign assets in foreign currencies and with its own debt issued in US dollars, there is a built-in incentive for the US to depreciate its currency. Depreciation will actually reduce America's net indebtedness to the world.

Thus, as urged by Joseph Stiglitz in his 2005 speech (in this volume), the world needs a new international reserve asset. Debt-issuers need to be held responsible for repaying the amount owed in real terms. The proposed indexed unit of account, called the World Currency Unit, serves this purpose well. Because the WCU is a unit of global real purchasing power, debt denominated in the WCU requires the debt-issuer to repay, in dollars, yen, Euros or any other currency, an amount commensurate with the latest valuation of the debt issued. The debt-issuer will not be asked to repay more, and will also be protected from having to repay more, which used to happen when debt had been issued in a currency that subsequently appreciated unexpectedly. At the same time, the debt-issuer also will not be allowed to repay less than the amount borrowed in the first place.

When a sufficient number of debt-issuers do issue bonds denominated in WCUs, such 'global indexed bonds' will serve as an excellent reserve asset for the world's central banks (Ho, 2000). Before this occurs, however, it may be feared that central banks will have difficulty matching their liabilities with the right kind of assets. Without dismissing these concerns, however, it must be pointed out that the central banks' real liabilities are preserved, so that they are protected from the risk of seeing their real liabilities explode as a result of exchange rate fluctuations. Their challenge is simply to invest their assets in a way that can preserve real values. There is no presumption that this is inherently more difficult than upholding a currency board based on a single host currency. To the extent that the real exchange rate is gauged at a level consistent with economic fundamentals, the challenge of defending a WCU link is likely to be easier than that of defending a single currency link when the exchange rate has deviated grossly from what is required by the fundamentals. The Argentine peso crisis and the AFC appear to bear this out.

What constitutes the right exchange rate?

In the literature there is much discussion about what constitutes the appropriate exchange rate. Williamson and Miller (1987) and Williamson (1994) coined the term 'Fundamental Equilibrium Exchange Rate' (FEER), describing this as the 'rate estimated to be consistent with simultaneous internal and external balance' (Williamson and Miller, 1987, Figure 2.1), and proposed to 'target' exchange rates at this level. This approach makes eminent sense, as exchange rates often deviate from the FEER because of short-term random events that affect currency demand and supply and expectations. We will now explore how the FEER is determined by internal and external balance requirements, so we can 'target' it.

From the equilibrium condition $GDP = C + I + G + X{-}M$, we can write $Yd + T - B$ (disposable income plus net taxes minus government interest payment) $= C + I + G + X - M$. This transposes to $T - G - B = I - S - (M - X)$. Thus the intersection of GS ($\equiv T - G - B$, public sector savings) with PD ($\equiv I - S - (M - X)$, private sector savings deficiency) determines equilibrium aggregate demand. Figure 6.1 now shows how aggregate demand can

Figure 6.1 Achieving internal balance with full employment and budget balance

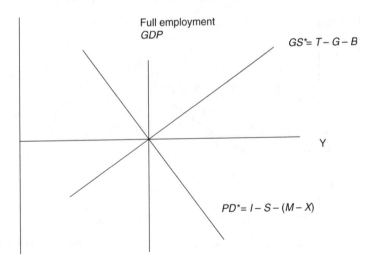

be achieved at the full employment output and at the same time achieve fiscal budget balance.

We can represent the full employment fiscal budget balance condition by writing $T(y_f) - G - B = 0$. This line is represented by GS^* in Figure 6.1. This will be described as the 'full employment budget balance fiscal position line'. Figure 6.1 further shows that there is a unique position of the $I - S - (M - X)$ line that will bring about a level of aggregate demand consistent with full employment. The monetary conditions underlying this PD^* will be referred to as the 'full employment compatible monetary conditions'. These conditions can be alternatively depicted as m^* in Figure 6.2.

In fact, m^* traces the combination of the real exchange rates and real interest rates such that equilibrium aggregate private sector demand is compatible with full employment. As we move down m^* the real interest rate falls boosting domestic demand, but the real effective exchange rate rises, reducing external demand and offsetting the domestic demand increase, so the composition of private sector demand changes without affecting the aggregate level.

To derive m^* we can express $I - S - (M - X)$ as a function f of real exchange rate e, real interest rate r, wealth w, and real GDP y. Thus we can write:

$$I - S - (M - X) = f(e, r, w, y) \tag{6.4}$$

By setting f at zero, we can write y as a function m of e, r and w. Taking w as given, *the function m (e, r|w) is an indicator of monetary conditions.*

Figure 6.2 Alternative (e,r) combinations compatible with full employment under alternative Forex market conditions (D=S provides for external balance)

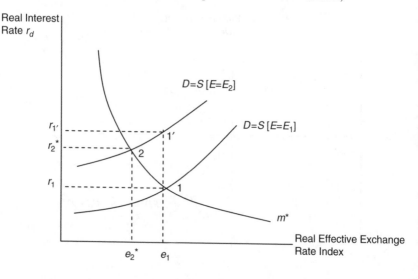

When m equals full employment GDP, the monetary conditions are consistent with full employment. m^* is one of many similarly shaped curves drawn in the (e, r) space but meets the additional condition that $m^* = y_f$.

The two upward sloping curves, $D = S[E = E_i]$ represent equilibrium in the foreign exchange market, where E is a shift parameter depicting short-term capital movement intentions. If capital outflow intentions are high, $D = S$ will be at a higher level, and a higher domestic interest rate will be needed for external balance. The real exchange rate has then to be lowered to maintain full employment (Point 2 rather than Point 1'). Increased external demand will then come in to replace the domestic demand that has been suppressed by the higher interest rates. The FEER thus will change with capital movements and is associated with a unique real interest rate (e.g., e^* with r^*).

The above analysis shows that to say that a currency is at FEER is not very meaningful, if real interest rates are too high. Schuler (2005) presented evidence that Argentina's exports were still growing ahead of the peso crisis. But if real interest rates had to be pushed very high to protect the currency from depreciating, then internal balance would still not be possible (point 1' in Figure 6.2).

To reiterate, the intersection of the $D = S$ line with m^* determines the fundamental equilibrium exchange rate (FEER) e^* and the real interest rate, *both of which* will be necessary to maintain internal and external balance at the same time. Given e^*, the rate at which the domestic currency should link to the WCU will be set at α_τ^*. Provided that fiscal policy maintains budget balance at full employment, setting α_τ at α_τ^* will bring about full employment, rendering the fiscal budget balanced. When price levels or nominal exchange rates for currencies comprising the WCU change, $V_{OUS\$t}$ changes, implying that given α_τ^* the nominal exchange rate of the domestic currency will change spontaneously to preserve full employment.

If the underlying economic fundamentals have changed permanently (e.g., when there is a permanent shift in the $I - S + X - M$ line, or when the relative productivities of different countries have changed), it may be necessary to adjust α upwards or downwards. Since the adjustment of α is in relation to the WCU, and since the real value of the WCU is constant, we can be sure that every marginal adjustment is an effective step in the right direction. In contrast, in the absence of such a real anchor link, a nominal depreciation could mean real appreciation and vice versa.

To see how the real convertibility guarantee arrests panic, suppose at time $\tau + k$, α is adjusted downwards, so the peso depreciates. Any new pesos issued as of $\tau + k$ will be designated as *vintage $\tau + k$. Pesos of vintage τ are now worth more than pesos of vintage $\tau + k$ and will be converted to the new pesos accordingly.* The same guarantee extends to all bank deposits prior to the time a devaluation is to take effect. With depositors' and cash holders' interests protected, bank runs will be averted.

A currency regime, in order to be sustainable (Bulir and Smidkova, 2005) and thus credible, needs to be adaptable and be compatible with full employment. If the currency regime produces an exchange rate that is not compatible with full employment and has no effective mechanism to adapt towards such a rate it cannot be sustainable and thus cannot be credible. In contrast, the system herein proposed, by allowing α to change as needed, is compatible with full employment and is therefore sustainable and credible.

Credibility

One may still ask if this system is sustainable in the face of shattered confidence. Given the Argentine experience in 2001–2 and the Asian experience in 1997–8, it does appear that if people firmly believe that the currency will collapse, nothing can be done. If we look at the Thai and the Indonesian experience carefully, however, we can only conclude that the collapse of confidence was a result of ineffective and misguided policies in the first place. Even in the case of Argentina, the collapse of confidence was the result of a string of misguided actions, and a lack of the necessary institutions to protect the interest of people who have legitimate claims to be protected.

If we look at the Thai experience, however, we find that the financial markets at first actually cheered the initial devaluation of the Thai baht. The Thai stock market jumped noticeably. But when interest rates were raised sharply higher around the region (the Philippine central bank raised the overnight lending rate to 24 per cent from 15 per cent on 3 July 1997), and austerity measures were announced on 5 August which further impressed upon investors that the region was headed for a dramatic economic slowdown, confidence began to crumble.

Under the proposal of a WCU link, full employment and economic stability are the explicit objectives of the central bank, and no attempt is made to defend an unrealistically high exchange rate. Interest rates will not be raised to defend the currency except for maintaining monetary conditions m^*. Holders of the domestic currency as well as bank deposits know that while the currency may devalue, their interests will be protected as the vintage of their monetary assets are specified and real convertibility at the original rate is guaranteed. The valuation of the currency will not be allowed to take on unrealistic values in the first place, unlike what may happen under a nominal tie to the US dollar. For all these reasons, and for the reason that the WCU itself represents purchasing power over a diversified portfolio of multiple-currency-denominated output, the risks involved in holding the local currency and assets of the local currency are reduced considerably. Because perceived risks are smaller, a collapse of confidence is less likely.

Over time there may be a need to add the GDPs of other countries to the basket. For example, in time the RMB will become fully convertible. If

China has relatively deep financial markets and its markets are predominantly free, then it may be appropriate to include China's GDP in the WCU basket. If financial markets are too shallow, short-term capital flows may cause gyrations in exchange rates.

When it becomes necessary to update the composition of the WCU basket, continuity of the series can be maintained by reconciling the valuation in the last period under the old basket and the valuation in the first period under the new basket. This procedure is routinely done with regard to the consumer price index and should be both transparent and automatic.

The credibility of the proposed system requires that the WCU be defined and that its nominal values be computed and updated round the clock by an authoritative international organization, such as the International Monetary Fund (IMF).

Conclusions and implications for the world

The idea of the WCU is, first and foremost, to promote accountability, transparency and efficiency. Issuers of bonds denominated in the WCU, whether official or private, will be held responsible for repaying debt in constant purchasing power plus the pledged real interest payments. Governments will not be able to inflate away or depreciate away their debts as they can now. There will be greater transparency about the real cost of borrowing and, if the entire world issues debt in the WCU, the world's capital market will become much more integrated. The world will have an alternative reserve asset to gold or the US dollar, and no country will collect seigniorage at the expense of others.

Each central bank that decides to tie its currency to the WCU will fix an appropriate exchange ratio to the WCU, namely α, and make appropriate adjustments as necessary, in addition to fixing an appropriate benchmark interest rate for its own currency. It is noteworthy that countries whose currencies are independently tied to the WCU are 'currency-integrated' for as long as their αs remain constant.

Figure 6.3 shows the changes in the nominal value of one $WCU_{1990US\$t}$, computed using IMF and OECD statistics, from 1983 to 2003. In revaluing the WCU basket, we use the consumer price indices of the different countries/zones, even though in principle GDP deflators would have been more appropriate. We do this because the GDP deflators are usually available only after a relatively long lag. Since the WCU is intended to be a unit of account ready to be used on a day-to-day basis, for practical reasons CPIs have to be used instead of GDP deflators in deriving the current values of the unit.

We may note that just before the AFC, the US dollar had an unprecedented appreciation against the WCU in the second quarter of 1997.

Figure 6.3 Value of the WCU with base year 1990 in US$, 1983–2003

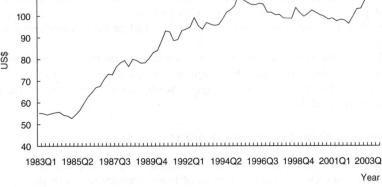

USD per WCU (2000 base year) 1983–2003

Figure 6.4 Real appreciation of US$ over two years (%)

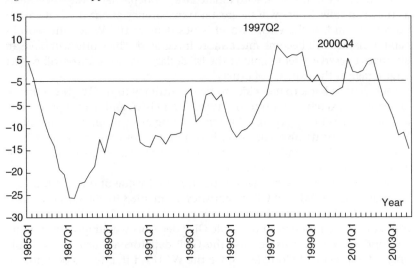

This no doubt caused serious strains in most of the countries whose currencies were tied to the US dollar, including both Asian and Latin American countries. Figure 6.4 shows the '2-year real exchange rate appreciation'

of the US dollar against the WCU (i.e., the percentage increase of the real value of US dollar over two years to time *t*). At the risk of over-simplification, the financial market turmoil of countries with currencies tied to the US dollar during the period 1995–2002 appears to be related to the strength of the US dollar.

Figure 6.4 shows that the US dollar by the second quarter of 1997 had appreciated almost by 8 per cent *vis-à-vis* the WCU over the preceding two years, and this strength greatly surpassed that of the first quarter in 1985, which was also a year of solid strength of the US dollar. This unprecedented strength of the US dollar no doubt produced much pressure on those economies whose currencies were tied to the dollar, and probably played an important role in the AFC itself.

To explore the possible advantages of a WCU link a simulation exercise was conducted. First, we estimated the relation between Hong Kong's total exports (HKTXI) on the one hand, and the real exchange rate (WCU/HKD) represented by HKRE and the GDP of OECD countries (represented by OGDP) on the other hand. We use the Johansen cointegration method. All variables are in natural logarithm form.

First, the Augmented Dickey–Fuller test indicates that the stationary properties of the three variables are $I(1)$ variables (see Table 6.1). Therefore, the Johansen procedure is then used to detect the existence of long-run relation, if any, between them. The results of the cointegration test (see Table 6.2) for the period from 1984 to 2004 showed that they are found to be cointegrated with $r = 1$. Table 6.3 reports the normalized cointegrating coefficients that can be interpreted as long-run coefficients. As can be seen, all coefficients carry the right signs and are statistically significant. According to the coefficients a 10 per cent appreciation in the real exchange rate will reduce real exports by 17 per cent. The error correction model (ECM) is shown in Table 6.4. The ECM term is negative and significant which also

Table 6.1 Augmented Dickey-Fuller test of unit root, 1984Q1 to 2004Q4

Variable name	Test on	No Trend	Trend	Conclusion
HKEX	Level	–1.7619	–1.4363	$I(1)$
	1st diff	–3.5693***	–4.3374***	
HKRE	Level	–1.5957	–1.8588	$I(1)$
	1st diff	–4.1429***	–4.1857***	
OGDP	Level	–1.0411	–2.4409	$I(1)$
	1st diff	–5.2889***	–5.3258***	

Notes:
The optimal lag period in ADF test is determined by the Akaike Information Criterion.
*** indicates 1% significant level.
95% critical value for the ADF tests that include constant and constant plus trend = –2.899 and –3.468 respectively

Table 6.2   Testing cointegration between HKEXI, HKRE and OGDP

Null hypothesis	Alternative hypothesis	Test statistics	5% critical value
Trace tests:		Trace Value	
$r = 0$	$r > 0$	30.86**	29.80
$r = 1$	$r > 1$	6.74	15.49
λ max tests:		λ max Value	
$r = 0$	$r = 1$	24.11**	21.13
$r = 1$	$r = 2$	5.80	14.26

Notes:
Lag length of the VAR is determined by Akaike's Information Criterion.
** denotes significance at 5% level and r indicates the number of cointegrating vectors.

Table 6.3   Normalized cointegrating coefficients

	HKRE	OGDP	Constant
Coefficients	−1.7306	1.8135	15.3521
(t-statistics)	(11.6816)***	(9.2648)***	

Notes:
*** denotes significance at 1% level.

Table 6.4   Error correction estimates: dependent variable: D(HKEXI)

	ECM (−1)	D(HKEXI) (−1)	D(HKRE) (−1)	D(OGDP) (−1)	Constant
Coefficient	−0.2078	0.1190	0.1078	1.3664	0.0157
(t-statistics)	(−4.9984)***	(1.2399)	(0.7568)	(1.5402)	(2.2242)**

Notes:
D denotes first differences.
ECM denotes error correction term.
** and *** denote significance at 5% and 1% level respectively.
Adj. $R^2 = 0.3433$.

re-confirms the fact that the series are cointegrated. The impact of linking with the WCU on exports is simulated by assuming that the Hong Kong dollar's value in US dollars follows those as implied by a WCU-link, and comparing with results from the benchmark of actual values. To do this, I re-estimate the cointegrating relation[9] from 1984 to 2000 only and then forecast the exports value from 2001 to 2004 assuming that the HK dollar is pegged to the WCU starting from year 2001 (i.e., the HKRE (WCU/HKD) is a constant value for the forecasted period). The predicted exports are as shown in Figure 6.5. As can be seen, the predicted export values are more stable

Figure 6.5   Hong Kong's total exports: linking to WCU as against linking to the US$

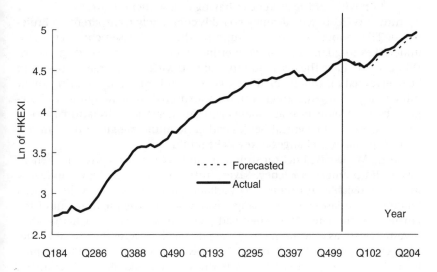

compared with the actual value. The standard deviation for the simulated exports and that for the actual exports are 0.1255 and 0.1451 respectively.

There are important benefits from the proposed WCU-based currency board arrangement. First, currencies on an adaptive WCU, or 'real monetary unit standard' as they are called, are flexible yet are truly anchored and stable. In the absence of a recognized permanent change in economic fundamentals, α will be kept stable. But adjustment in the nominal exchange rate *vis-à-vis* the US dollar will take place continuously and automatically as the US dollar appreciates or depreciates in the foreign exchange market. When the economic fundamentals have changed permanently, each adjustment of α is a real adjustment in the direction desired. In contrast, because the real value of the host currency under a traditional currency board is fluctuating all the time, changing the nominal peg need not imply a real adjustment in the right direction. Under a crawling peg that is not defined relative to a real anchor, a depreciation against the benchmark currency may be more than offset by changes in other key nominal variables.

Second, any two currencies on a WCU-based currency board are indirectly linked as long as their αs are unchanged. The RMB and the HKD will be integrated, as will any other currency similarly tied to the WCU. Integration of currencies is achieved without each currency losing its own identity. Regardless of the αs chosen, countries linked to the WCU will find that their currencies are linked to one another until such time as one or more countries re-adjust their αs. The increased stability of exchange rates will foster trade and promote efficiency-enhancing capital movements.

Thus the WCU mechanism provides much scope for de facto currency integration without the currencies having to lose their identities.

Third, a WCU-based currency board is completely transparent and rule-based. The monetary authority running the WCU-based currency board undertakes to guarantee full convertibility of liabilities issued in WCUs. While it does have the discretion to change α when the currency appears to be overvalued or undervalued relative to what is necessary to bring about full employment, adjustments in α are expected to be marginal and dictated by clear signs of inadequate aggregate demand or inflationary pressures.[10] Because the central bank's earlier liabilities are guaranteed in real terms,[11] panic over changes in α will be minimized.

Fourth, WCU-based debt instruments and WCU-based currencies benefit savers and promote efficiency. Savers in the past have had great difficulty finding a reliable instrument to harbour their savings. They have been haunted by inflation and exchange risks. Consider the predicament of the Japanese in the late 1980s: they had plenty of savings, but whether they invested overseas or at home they were doomed, because they would suffer huge exchange loss if they invested overseas and would suffer huge capital losses if they bought domestic assets whose prices had already been much inflated. Debt instruments denominated in the WCU offer a unique shelter against inflation and exchange losses. Households who keep their savings in a bank account also enjoy the same benefits if their currencies are tied to the WCU. On the other hand, investors who need to borrow will know the real cost of borrowing if the debt instrument is denominated in the WCU. This is quite unlike the case when WCU-based debt instruments do not exist. Under the latter case, they have to worry about whether the currency in which they borrow will appreciate significantly. When all investors know and read the cost of borrowing in like manner the capital market becomes more efficient. Projects that fail to bring in a high rate of return will not be funded.

Most important, the WCU-based currency board arrangement as proposed is sustainable because compatibility with full employment is an explicit objective in its operation. The parameter 'link coefficient' α will be adjusted so as to ensure that aggregate private demand is at a level compatible with full employment. This is certainly much more credible than currency boards that ignore the pain of surging unemployment. It is certainly easier to defend a WCU-based currency board with real exchange rates tuned in to the needs of the real economy than to defend a single currency link when the real exchange rate has grossly deviated from the fundamentals.

Appendix

Data sources

Hong Kong Census and Statistics Department, *Hong Kong Monthly Digest of Statistics*, various issues.

Hong Kong Census and Statistics Department, *Estimates of Gross Domestic Product, 1961–1999.*
International Monetary Fund, *International Financial Statistics,* various issues.
OECD, *Quarterly National Accounts database.*

List of variables and their descriptions

e	real effective exchange rate index
$e_{US\$}$	price of the local currency in US dollars, or US\$ exchange rate
$HKEXI$	Hong Kong Total Exports Volume Index, 2000=100
$HKRE$	WCU / HKD (the price of HKD in WCU)
$HKWC_t$	price of WCU in Hong Kong dollars at time t
$OGDP$	OECD GDP Volume Index, 2000=100
P	domestic price level, measured as consumer price index
R	local nominal prime rate
r	Real interest rate defined in WCU_0
RE_t	Real exchange rate defined relative to the WCU_0, $= P^* e_{US\$} / V_{0US\$t}$
WCU_0	World currency unit basket of GDPs in base year 0
$V_{0US\$t}$	Valuation of WCU_0 in US dollars at time t.

Notes

1 Joseph Stiglitz gave a public lecture on 'China's New Role in the World Economy' in March 2005.
2 See Ho (1989) for a full story of these and other changes in the 1980s and Ho (1998) for developments during the late 1990s.
3 A nominal anchor, such as a nominal link to a host currency, would imply an unintended real exchange rate change when price levels or the nominal exchange rate of the host currency changes.
4 Robert Mundell and Robert Barro had diametrically different views about the RMB, as reviewed in a seminar held at the Chinese University of Hong Kong in 2005. Schuler (2005), discussed diverse views and evidence about the possible overvaluation of the Argentine peso before its dramatic devaluation.
5 Unemployment stood at 10.3 per cent for the 16–59(female)/64(male) group in September 1992 and peaked in January 1993 at 10.9 per cent, from whence it kept falling for years to below 5 per cent by the end of 2003.
6 The asymmetry of the effects of overvaluation and undervaluation should be noted. When overvalued, domestic price and wage levels could fall to restore full employment, but with price and wage rigidity being the norm extended periods of high unemployment usually result. When undervalued, inflation normally readily occurs, and the results are usually less unpalatable.
7 These economic zones are representative in that they comprise the world's major industrial zones as well as major producers of primary goods, and their currencies are fully convertible.
8 In May 2005 The HK Monetary Authority introduced, with immediate effect, a strong-side Convertibility Undertaking to buy US dollars from licensed banks at 7.75, and announced the shifting of the existing weak-side Convertibility Undertaking from 7.80 to 7.85, to be phased in gradually and completed by 20 June.
9 The variables are found to be cointegrated and the normalized coefficients also carry with them significant and correct signs. The details of results are not reported here to save space but are available upon request.

10 This approach may prove superior to stabilizing a Monetary Conditions Index as discussed in http://www.bankofcanada.ca/en/mci2.htm, which is based on nominal exchange rates and nominal interest rates.
11 This does raise the question of whether central banks can take the risks inherent in making such guarantees. The objection will be reduced when borrowers, particularly governments, issue debt denominated in the WCU. When WCU-based assets are available central banks can hold them for reserve purposes.

References

Bird, Graham and Ramkishen Rajan (2002), 'Optimal Currency Baskets and the Third Currency Phenomenon: Exchange Rate Policy in Southeast Asia', *Journal of International Development*, November, 14 (8), 1053–73.
Bulir, Ales and Katerina Smidkova (2005), 'Exchange Rates in the New Accession Countries: What Have We Learnt from the Forerunners?', *IMF Working Paper*, WP/05/27 February, Washington, DC: IMF.
Coats, Warren L. Jr (1994), 'In Search of a Monetary Anchor: A New Monetary Standard', San Francisco: Institute for Contemporary Studies Press.
Fisher, Irving (1913a), *The Purchasing Power of Money*, 2nd edn, New York: Macmillan.
Fisher, Irving (1913b), 'A Compensated Dollar', *Quarterly Journal of Economics*, 27 (February) 213–35.
Ho, Lok Sang (1989), 'Whither China's Foreign Exchange Controls?', in Joseph Cheng (ed.), *China: Modernization in the 1980s* (Hong Kong: Chinese University of Hong Kong Press; New York: St. Martin's Press, 1989) 461–94.
Ho, Lok Sang (1990), 'A Proposal for an Adaptive Linked Exchange Rate System', *Hong Kong Economic Papers*, 20, 89–96.
Ho, Lok Sang (1998), 'China's Road to Exchange Rate Liberalisation', in Joseph Cheng (ed.), *China in the Post-Deng Era* (Hong Kong: Chinese University Press), 453–70.
Ho, Lok Sang (2000), 'Towards a New International Monetary Order: The World Currency and the Global Indexed Bond', *The World Economy*, 23 (7), 939–50.
Husted, Steven and Michael Melvin (2003), *International Economics*, 6th edn, Addison-Wesley.
Kawai, Masahiro (2001), 'Recommending a Currency Basket System for Emerging East Asia', in Lok-sang Ho and Chi-wa Yuen (eds), *Exchange Rate Regimes and Macroeconomic Stability*, Boston, MA: Kluwer Academic.
Schuler, Kurt (2005), 'Ignorance and Influence: U.S. Economists on Argentina's Depression of 1998–2002', *Economic Journal Watch*, August, 234–78.
Williamson, John (ed.) (1994), *Estimating Equilibrium Exchange Rates*, Washington, DC: Institute for International Economics.
Williamson, John (2000), *Exchange Rate Regimes for Emerging Markets: Reviving the Intermediate Option*, Washington, DC: Institute for International Economics.
Williamson, John (2002), 'The Evolution of Thought on Intermediate Exchange Rate Regimes', *Annals of the American Academy of Political and Social Science*, 579 (1), January, 73–86.
Williamson, John and Marcus Miller (1987), *Targets and Indicators: A Blueprint for the International Coordination of Economic Policy*, Washington, DC: Institute for International Economics.
Yano, Takashi and Hiroyuki Kosaka (2003), 'Trade Patterns and Exchange Rate Regimes: Testing the Asian Currency Basket Using an International Input-Output System', *Developing Economies*, 41 (1), March, 3–36.

Part II

Hong Kong as China's City and as a Global City

7
Hong Kong as a Financial Centre of China and the World

Y.C. Jao

Introduction

Since the 1970s, Hong Kong has emerged as one of the leading international financial centres (IFCs) of the world, especially the Asia-Pacific region. With economic and financial ties between the Mainland and Hong Kong strengthening considerably in recent years, Hong Kong has become more variegated and multifaceted as a financial hub. Despite shocks and disasters, such as the uncertainty and apprehension surrounding the transfer of sovereignty from the United Kingdom to the People's Republic of China (1982–97), the Asian Financial Crisis (1997–8), and the SARS epidemic (2003), Hong Kong's role as an IFC has not been permanently affected.

The purpose of this chapter is to analyse and explain Hong Kong's evolution into a financial centre for both China and the world. It is also meant as a personal tribute to Professor Y.Y. Kueh, an eminent authority on the contemporary Chinese economy, in whose honour this Festscrift is dedicated.

Some conceptual and historical issues: a brief review

Although Hong Kong is an IFC of some repute, its precise role and functions are not well understood. This section provides a brief literature review, to clear up some terminological, typological and historical issues. The first misconception, surprisingly prevalent, is that Hong Kong is an 'offshore financial centre' or 'offshore banking centre'. Even respected scholars (Dufey and Giddy, 1978; Johns, 1992), and international institutions, such as the Bank for International Settlements (BIS), commit this solecism.

To understand our argument, it would be useful to quote the definitions of 'offshore financial centre' and 'offshore banking centre' by two authorities. Roberts (1994a) states:

The term 'offshore financial centre' came into usage in the 1960s to describe a new phenomenon – the operations of financial centres which, though physically located within a country, have little connection with that country's financial system ... Offshore financial centres form a third tier in the hierarchy of international financial centres, performing a narrower and more passive range of financial functions than the global or the regional international financial centres. But unfortunately the distinctions are not clear-cut; for instance, by some yardsticks London and Switzerland are leading offshore financial centres because of their pre-eminent roles in the euromarket. Another possible source of confusion is the inconsistency in the terminology used in the literature on the subject: in this context, 'offshore financial centre' and 'offshore banking' are used interchangeably with 'international banking centre' and 'international banking'.

According to Johns (1992):

> Offshore banking is a qualitative rather than a geographically explicit locational term. It can apply either to: (1) banks that have located purposely in specific foreign jurisdiction, not necessarily island-based, whose legislative and tax frameworks and regulatory authorities are less restrictive in comparison with their home-based operational environment; or, to (2) specifically designated facilities or financial 'free' zones with their own separate customised legislative and tax regimes, available to domestic and/or foreign banks, which are exempted from all or specific regulatory controls and taxes on international banking activities that otherwise apply in the rest of the local economy.

From these definitions, Hong Kong is certainly not an offshore financial centre. The Hong Kong authorities have never set up an offshore centre or free zone with special regulatory or tax concessions which is completely insulated from the domestic economy. In fact, the authorities do not even distinguish between resident and non-resident, or domestic and foreign currency financial activities, on a substantive legal or administrative basis. Hewson (1982) recognizes this when, in an exhaustive study of offshore banking, he acknowledges that 'Hong Kong is not really an offshore centre in the sense that we have developed that term', even though 'there are important offshore activities conducted in Hong Kong' (p. 425). In other words, onshore and offshore activities are completely fused in Hong Kong.

Another relatively minor misconception is that Hong Kong is the third largest IFC in the world. Not surprisingly, this view used to be confined to Hong Kong and China, though some foreign observers also subscribe to it.[1] The exact basis for this ranking has never been clearly spelled out, though it has been vaguely suggested that the number of foreign banks and other financial institutions is the third largest, or the intensity of foreign bank activity is the third highest, next only to London and New York.

With the growing complexity of the modern financial system, people now realize that the number of foreign banks is not the only hallmark of an IFC. The rapid growth of financial markets, such as the stock market and the forex market, relative to the banking industry, also means that one has to consider a much wider spectrum of financial variables in ranking or comparing various cities as IFCs. There is also more awareness of the subtle difference between an IBC (international banking centre) and an IFC. Hence, hardly any knowledgeable person now considers Hong Kong as the third largest IFC in the world.

A more substantive issue is the dating of the emergence of Hong Kong as an IFC. The mainstream view, as represented by Jao (1979, 1980, 1997b), Hui (1992, 2004), Ho (1991), and Jones (1992) is that Hong Kong's emergence as an IFC did not occur until the 1970s. The advantages of this view are, first, it is backed by solid quantitative and factual evidence; second, it is also more in accordance with the trend of globalization among multinational corporations and financial institutions, which also accelerated around the 1970s; and third, it is supported by the policy shift on the part of the Hong Kong authorities from pure laissez faire to a more proactive stance towards creating an IFC.

An alternative view is represented by Reed (1981, 1983, 1989), Schenk (2001, 2002), and Meyer (2000). It asserts that Hong Kong's emergence as an IFC began much earlier than the 1970s. There are several drawbacks to this approach. First, the proponents of this view either cannot present solid statistical data to substantiate their case, or use flawed methodology in their argument. Second, they either cannot explain, or fail to take into account, many major historical events and paradoxes. No one would object to the view that the seeds of an IFC were sown much earlier than the 1970s, but they insisted that Hong Kong was already a major or dominant IFC well before the 1970s. For example, in his pioneering study of IFCs from 1900 to 1980, Reed (1981) asserted that Hong Kong was among the top ten international banking centres for every five-yearly interval except 1970 and 1980. Reed's analysis is based on nine variables which are all banking variables.[2] This analysis was later expanded into a 16-variable analysis for 1980 (Reed, 1983), on the basis of which Hong Kong is included among the third-tier centres in a four-tier hierarchy of IFCs. However, by ignoring other non-banking variables, such as forex, equity, debt and derivative market activities, Reed failed to take into account the subtle and not insignificant differences between an IBC and an IFC.

Schenk's work relied heavily on British government archives of the 1940s and 1950s which had recently been released. She showed how the British authorities – the Treasury, the Colonial Office, and the Bank of England –

attempted repeatedly to close down Hong Kong's free US dollar market and the gold market in order to protect the viability of the Empire-wide sterling system, but failed because of strenuous opposition from the Hong Kong government. However, she did not produce any quantitative evidence to show that Hong Kong was already a major IFC in the early post-1945 period. The mere existence of the free US dollar market and the gold market was inadequate.

Meyer (2000) treated Hong Kong as a global metropolis. An urban sociologist, Meyer went further than any other scholar in asserting that Hong Kong had been a business, trading and financial centre for Asia, dominating other financial centres such as Singapore and Tokyo, ever since the territory was ceded to Britain in 1842. However, Meyer talked vaguely about 'social networks of capital', but did not give any hard information on their contributions to Hong Kong's emergence as an IFC. Although the book covered the period 1840–1997, it totally ignored such key events in Hong Kong's modern financial history as the moratorium on banking licences in 1965–6, the loss of the Asian Dollar Market to Singapore in 1968, the conditional lifting of the banking moratorium in 1978–9, the reforms and liberalization of the banking sector and the securities markets (and so on) in the 1980s and early 1990s.

What kind of a financial centre is Hong Kong?

Financial centres may be classified according to their purpose, geographical reach and historical development. From the teleological standpoint, Hong Kong is a functional centre (i.e., one where financial activities and transactions really take place, and which generates substantial income and employment, both direct and indirect). Despite its low tax rates and narrow tax base, Hong Kong is not a tax haven, and therefore is not a paper centre (or brass-plate centre) which is used to book transactions in order to evade taxation, and which generates little or no income or employment. Hong Kong is also a centre where the onshore and offshore markets are completely integrated, as opposed to a segregated centre where these markets are clearly demarcated. Thus, once a financial institution is admitted into Hong Kong, it may engage freely in any financial transaction or activity, whether onshore or offshore, whether with residents or non-residents, or whether denominated in domestic or foreign currencies.

From the geographical perspective, IFCs can be further sub-divided into global financial centres (GFCs) and regional financial centres (RFCs).[3] By general agreement, there are only three GFCs in the world: London, New York and Tokyo (Roberts, 1994b). Hong Kong is not in the same league as the three GFCs. It is only an RFC or, more specifically, the second largest financial centre in the Asia-Pacific region.[4]

From the historical point of view, scholars have distinguished between the traditional centre, the financial entrepôt, and the offshore banking centre (Dufey and Giddy, 1978). The traditional centre serves as a net capital exporter to the world either by bank lending, or by capital-raising on the securities market. The financial entrepôt offers the services of its financial institutions and markets to both domestic and foreign residents. The offshore banking centre has already been explained. As will be shown later, Hong Kong now plays the role of net exporter of capital and financial entrepôt.

Finally, after the transfer of sovereignty in 1997, Hong Kong has also become China's offshore financial centre. Note however, that the term 'offshore financial centre' is used here from China's point of view. From Hong Kong's own point of view, the territory remains an integrated IFC.

Hong Kong as China's offshore financial centre

Hong Kong's reunification with China provides the political and legal basis for Hong Kong's role as an offshore financial centre (OFC) of China. It is true that, prior to 1 July 1997, Hong Kong also served as China's OFC, but this was in the de facto sense only. Since 1 July 1997, Hong Kong has been serving as China's OFC in the *de jure* sense as well.

The Basic Law of the Hong Kong Special Administrative Region stipulates that Hong Kong shall remain a free port pursuing free trade policy. It is a separate customs territory, and maintains its own independent monetary and fiscal systems. It also enjoys full autonomy in all other economic and financial affairs (Chapter V, Articles 105–135). These provisions are supplemented by seven principles governing monetary relations between China and Hong Kong as enunciated on 1 September 1996 by Chen Yuan, then Deputy Governor of the People's Bank of China, the central bank of China, at a Bank of England seminar held in London. These principles are so important that they are worth reproducing here for the public record.

First, the currencies and monetary systems of mainland China and Hong Kong will be mutually independent. To quote Chen:

> The Hong Kong dollar and the renminbi will circulate as legal tender in Hong Kong and mainland respectively. The Hong Kong dollar will be treated as a foreign currency in the mainland. Likewise, the renminbi will be treated as a foreign currency in Hong Kong … The two monetary systems are of equal importance to China in its reform and liberalization. One does not precede or be subsidiary to the other. They will operate in a mutually independent manner.

Second, the two monetary authorities in China and Hong Kong – that is, the People's Bank of China (PBC) and the Hong Kong Monetary Authority

(HKMA) – will be mutually independent but will cooperate closely with each other. The PBC will not set up any office in Hong Kong.

Third, financial institutions of China and Hong Kong setting up branches or offices in each other's territory will be regulated by the host authorities and treated respectively as foreign entities.

Fourth, the PBC will support currency stability in Hong Kong. Pursuant to its goal, the PBC and HKMA have signed a repurchase agreement in respect of US Treasury obligations. But Chen declared that 'under no circumstances will China draw on or resort to Hong Kong's Exchange Fund or other assets in any way and for any reason'.

Fifth, financial transactions between China and Hong Kong will be conducted in accordance with the rules and practices of international financial activities.

Sixth, mainland financial institutions in Hong Kong must abide by the laws of Hong Kong and will be supervised by the HKMA.

Seventh, Shanghai and Hong Kong will have complementary and mutually reinforcing relationships as financial centres.

These principles can be consolidated into one guiding principle, namely, 'one country, two currencies', which is the counterpart to the political principle of 'one country, two systems'. It totally rejects the notion that the Hong Kong dollar might be merged with the renminbi (RMB).

Chen's 'Seven Principles' could not have come at a more appropriate time. They serve to strengthen the Joint Declaration and the Basic Law by clarifying certain 'grey areas' hitherto undefined in both documents. They have also enhanced immeasurably confidence in the Hong Kong dollar during the transition to and beyond China's resumption of sovereignty.

We are, of course, more interested in how Hong Kong actually works as an OFC. In our view, the key point is that Hong Kong dollar is an independent and freely and fully convertible currency. Through this medium, China is able to convert its huge balance of payments surplus *vis-à-vis* Hong Kong into international reserve currencies. There has been so far no official estimate of exactly how much foreign exchange China earns from Hong Kong, though it is generally agreed that the amount must be quite substantial, and forms the *raison d'être* for Hong Kong's continued existence as an OFC. While China has liberalized its exchange rate controls on the current account since 1 December 1996, there is still a panoply of capital controls, and there is no timetable for the full convertibility of the RMB.

Banking and other financial services represent another area where there is a stark contrast between freedom in Hong Kong and the lack of it in China. In the first 30 years of the People's Republic, China practised an extreme form of 'financial repression', under which virtually all foreign banks and non-bank financial institutions (NBFIs) were driven out, domestic banks and NBFIs were nationalized with little or no compensation, and financial markets were all closed. After the economic reform and open-door policies were launched in 1979, foreign banks and NBFIs were gradually allowed to re-enter, though they were still barred from RMB business. It was not until its formal accession to the World Trade Organization (WTO) in 2001 that China pledged to grant national treatment to foreign banks and NBFIs by 2007.

Hong Kong as a free port has always implicitly accepted the principle of national treatment, which forms part of the principle of 'non-discrimination', one of the main pillars of the General Agreement on Tariffs and Trade (GATT) codified in 1947. As enshrined in Articles I and III of GATT, the most-favoured nation (MFN) clause requires that, subject to certain exceptions, imports from all sources should face identical barriers, while 'national treatment' requires that, once through the customs, foreign goods are subject to no taxes or regulations more onerous than those on equivalent domestic goods. Since then the concept has been extended to direct investment and the financial sector.

The US Department of the Treasury (1988) reconfirmed that Hong Kong had the best record of 'national treatment' in the Asia-Pacific region in 1986. The 1998 report contains complaints against 33 countries or regions, including China and Taiwan, for failing to accord full 'national treatment' to foreign banks and financial institutions, but none against Hong Kong. It says that 'U.S. financial institutions generally give authorities high marks for fairness and transparency and generally expressed the view that Hong Kong does not discriminate in terms of competitive opportunities' (p. 224).

A separate concept is 'reciprocity', which essentially means according foreign banks or other financial institutions the same treatment domestic banks or other financial institutions receive abroad. According to the HKMA, the 'reciprocity' required is the 'availability of some acceptable form of reciprocity to Hong Kong banks'. This means that absolute equality in mutual granting of banking licences is not required.[5] This has given rise to a situation whereby Hong Kong is underrepresented in some countries or territories which nevertheless have a large banking presence in Hong Kong.

China is a good example. As a result of Hong Kong's very liberal environment for banking and finance, China has been able, over the years, to build up a very substantial stake in Hong Kong's banking sector. As shown in Table 7.1, during the post-reunification era of 1 July 1997–30 September 2004, China on average accounted for 14.8 per cent of assets, 22.0 per cent of deposits from customers, and 16.9 per cent of loans and advances to customers in Hong Kong's banking sector. By contrast, Hong Kong-incorporated banks' share in China's banking sector was close to zero during the same period.

Hong Kong's financial sector (which includes the banking sector) is not only much freer, it is also much better supervised and regulated, particularly following a series of financial reforms since the mid-1980s (Jao, 2003a). By the time the 8 per cent minimum capital adequacy ratio (CAR)

Table 7.1   China's stake in Hong Kong's banking sector (HK$billion), end of year

	1997	1998	1999	2000	2001	2002	2003
Assets	957	1,004	957	1,050	987	1,016	1,079
% of sector total	11.4	13.8	14.1	15.1	16.0	16.9	16.6
Deposits from customers	591	681	676	745	724	754	784
% of sector total	22.1	23.0	21.3	21.3	21.6	22.7	22.0
Loans to customers	436	433	405	422	418	451	453
% of sector total	10.6	13.1	14.4	17.1	19.1	21.7	22.3

Source: Hong Kong Monetary Authority, *Annual Report*, 1997–2003.

was announced under the Basel Accord of 1988, Hong Kong was well-positioned to meet this international banking standard. Indeed, Hong Kong met this criterion in 1990, two years ahead of the target date of 1992. More remarkably, since 1997, despite the AFC of 1997–8, Hong Kong has maintained on average a CAR of about 17 per cent, more than double the internationally accepted minimum, and one of the highest in the world.[6] China, however, cannot meet the 8 per cent minimum CAR even now. Moreover, the Basel Committee on Banking Supervision has drafted a new Basel Accord (popularly known as Basel II) to replace the old one, now known as Basel I, by 2007. China has served notice that it cannot accept this new accord, because it is unable even to observe the laxer Basel I. Hong Kong's banking sector is now busily engaged in preparations for Basel II. Initial indications are that most banks can meet the much more sophisticated and rigorous risk control requirements, though many industry experts believe that smaller banks will come under greater pressure to merge with their bigger and stronger rivals.

A low CAR is not the only indicator of banking fragility. That China's banking sector is saddled with doubtful loans has been an open secret for many years. According to Liu Mingkang, newly appointed Chairman of the China Banking Regulatory Commission (CBRC), the average non-performing loan (NPL) ratio of the four big state-owned banks – Industrial and Commercial Bank of China, Bank of China, China Construction Bank, and Agricultural Bank of China – was 24.13 per cent at the end of March 2003.[7] A more recent analysis, citing CBRC, reports that the NPL ratio of the four state-owned banks fell from 31.1 per cent at the end of 2001 to 15.6 per cent in June 2004.[8] Hong Kong's NPL ratio is much more transparent and accurate. It was 4.03 per cent at the end of March 2003, but gradually fell to 3.17 at the end of 2003.[9]

Similarly, Hong Kong's supervision and regulation of the securities market is much sounder than China's. According to surveys of corporate governance

(CG) of 12 countries and territories in Asia (including Japan) in 2003, Hong Kong and China were ranked second and eighth respectively (Ho, 2004, pp. 366–9). To be sure, Hong Kong still has a long way to go before it can reach the CG standard of global financial centres such as London and New York. However, since its inception in 1989, the Securities and Futures Commission (SFC) has made numerous amendments to the Securities & Futures Ordinance (1 April 2003), both to strengthen the prudential supervision of the markets and to raise the CG standard of listed firms. Its latest consultation paper, for example, concerns the prevention of possible conflict-of-interest of an investment analyst when he or she recommends a particular stock.

In short, as long as significant differences exist between China and Hong Kong in terms of currency convertibility, capital mobility, access to banking and financial markets, and quality of prudential supervision and regulation, international investors and depositors will tend to place their funds offshore in Hong Kong.[10] This prevailing state of affairs is unlikely to change much in the immediate future, but while capital account liberalization is at least possible in the foreseeable future, China's banking fragility problem may take decades to solve, and will require reform of the whole state-owned sector.[11]

At the end of June 2003, China and Hong Kong signed the Closer Economic Partnership Arrangement (CEPA), which came into effect from January 2004. Under CEPA, Hong Kong-manufactured goods are exempt from tariffs or import duties for entry into China. In the field of banking, Hong Kong incorporated banks can enjoy the following benefits:

1 The asset requirement for them to set up branches in China is reduced from US$20 billion to US$6 billion. Though this has no impact on the bigger banks, smaller to medium banks are likely to benefit.
2 The criteria for qualifying China branches of such banks to conduct renminbi business are also relaxed.

Separately, in early 2004, China announced that Hong Kong banks were allowed to provide personal renminbi deposit, remittance, exchange and credit card services. However, the range of business is still very limited. The right to remit directly in renminbi is confined to those who already have a renminbi account in China. This is just another form of capital control. Nevertheless, 35 banks in Hong Kong began in February 2004 to offer such services, and by the end of 2004, total renminbi deposits were reported to exceed 10 billion yuan. The prospects of Hong Kong becoming an offshore renminbi centre were further boosted when in November 2004, China announced that, effective from 1 January 2005, the maximum amount of cash a resident may take out of China would be increased from 6,000 yuan to 20,000 yuan. While these developments are positive, it is still too early to judge their total effect on Hong Kong's financial sector as a whole.

The most visible manifestation of Hong Kong's importance as an OFC is its role as a fund-raising centre for Chinese entities. Table 7.2 shows the amount of funds raised on the Hong Kong stock market since 1993, when Chinese companies (state-owned or private sector-owned) were first listed in Hong Kong. H-shares are mainland Chinese firms directly listed on Hong Kong Exchanges and Clearing Ltd (HKEX), while Red Chips are companies with Chinese entities as the controlling shareholders but which are incorporated in Hong Kong. To be sure, Chinese companies can also raise capital on the Shanghai or Shenzhen stock market, but funds so raised are in inconvertible renminbi. For companies reaching the stage where expansion abroad becomes necessary, they must raise funds denominated in convertible currencies. In principle, they can also raise capital in New York, London and Singapore, but Hong Kong's remains the market of first choice. As Table 7.2 shows, the funds raised varied from year to year with considerable volatility but, during the 1993–2004 period, the cumulative total reached HK$857,363.70 million (US$110,200.98 million at the current exchange rate), a colossal amount by any standard.

If Hong Kong is an OFC of China, what is the role of Shanghai, the largest city in China? Although Shanghai was ahead of Hong Kong in the 1920s and 1930s as a financial centre of the Far East, it lost its status as an IFC as a result of the Second World War, civil war, and financial repression (Jones, 1992; Jao, 2003b). In 1990, Shanghai announced its intention of regaining its past glory as an IFC by setting up the New Pudong Area to attract banking and NBFIs. However, the two essential pre-conditions for the development of an IFC (namely, currency convertibility and free capital mobility) remain unsatisfied. By all the usual criteria of an IFC, Shanghai still has a long way to go (Jao, 2003b). Shanghai will therefore remain for a considerable time a national financial centre (NFC) or a domestic financial centre (DFC). While some competition is inevitable, the relationship between the two metropolises in the field of banking and finance is largely complementary for the time being. It is also pertinent to mention here that, due to political reasons, neither Mainland China nor Taiwan allows banks and other NBFIs from the other side to operate within its borders. Hong Kong, however, is the only Chinese city where banks and other NBFIs from both sides of the Taiwan Strait can co-exist and compete on an equal footing.

Hong Kong as a world international financial centre

In the early 1990s, when comparative international financial data were still inadequate, Hui (1992) argued that 'Hong Kong cannot be ranked higher than the fifth largest but should not be considered as lower than the ninth international financial centre.' Five years later, as 'hard' information had became more available, I used an extensive set of weighted quantitative

Table 7.2 Funds raised by H-shares and Red Chips on the Hong Kong Stock Exchange (end of year, HK$million)

	1993	1994	1995	1996	1997	1998	1999	2000	2001	2002	2003	2004
H-shares	8,141.52	9,879.81	2,991.35	7,871.66	33,084.23	3,552.52	4,263.69	52,394.87	6,832.08	18,046.20	48,266.54	58,841.93
Red Chips	15,079.23	13,226.54	6,673.61	19,009.11	80,984.81	17,374.85	55,581.59	293,658.67	19,081.27	52,722.23	4,893.23	24,912.16
Sub-total	23,220.75	23,106.35	9,664.96	26,880.77	114,069.04	20,927.37	59,845.28	346,053.54	25,913.35	70,768.43	53,159.77	83,754.09

Grand total HK$857,363.70 million (US$110,200.98 million)

Source: Hong Kong Exchanges and Clearing Ltd.

data to rank Hong Kong as an IFC. Overall, Hong Kong was ranked second largest IFC in the Asia-Pacific region, behind Tokyo but ahead of Singapore. For the world as a whole, Hong Kong's ranking was between the sixth and seventh largest IFC (Jao, 1997b).

Since then, East Asia has been hard hit by a series of human and natural disasters, including the AFC of 1997–8, and the SARS epidemic of 2003. Hong Kong has also suffered heavily from these two catastrophes. At the height of the SARS epidemic in the second quarter of 2003, a large part of the economy was paralysed, asset markets (stock market and real property markets) had fallen by between 50 and 65 per cent compared to their peaks in 1997, and the unemployment rate rose to a 30-year high of 8.7 per cent.

With the passing of the SARS epidemic in June 2003, the Hong Kong economy has rebounded sharply, helped also by China's relaxation of outward tourism and other measures such as CEPA (described above). Hong Kong's status as a world IFC has also received a shot in the arm. Below, is a review of data and events, and their impact on Hong Kong as an IFC in its own right, under several headings.

Foreign exchange market

The foreign market (forex) market is one of the most important and sensitive indicators of a city's status as an IFC. As is well known, a forex market does not have a fixed location or building in which to transact its business. It is a network of dealers in commercial or investment banks, connected by modern telecommunications. The volume of transactions there reflects not only the number and concentration of internationally active banks, but also openness to international trade, and the freedom of currency convertibility and capital mobility of the country/territory concerned. Thus, the lack of free currency convertibility and capital mobility is automatically reflected in the low volume of forex transactions.

Prior to 1986, there were no statistical data on forex markets. Some large multinational banks attempted to conduct their own surveys, but without success. In 1986, the BIS, popularly known as the 'Central Bank of Central Banks', began to organize and coordinate triennial central bank surveys of forex and derivatives market activity. At first, only a few countries participated. In the latest survey in April 2004, the number of participants increased to 52 countries and territories, including Hong Kong. The data so collected are the most authoritative and reliable so far available. Due to space constraints, we report only traditional forex trades such as spots, forwards and swaps, omitting other details such as currency pairs.

As shown in Table 7.3, Hong Kong's traditional forex turnover increased sharply from US$67 billion in 2001 to US$102 billion in 2004, or by 52.2 per cent. Hong Kong's world ranking also rose from seventh to sixth. However, recalling that in 1995, Hong Kong ranked fifth, the territory has not yet regained fully its former eminent position.

Table 7.3 Average daily forex market turnover (US$billion)

Ranking	April 2001			April 2004		
	Country/territory	Amount	Market share %	Country/territory	Amount	Market share %
1	United Kingdom	504	31.2	United Kingdom	753	31.3
2	United States	254	15.7	United States	461	19.2
3	Japan	147	9.1	Japan	199	8.3
4	Singapore	101	6.2	Singapore	125	5.2
5	Germany	88	5.5	Germany	118	4.9
6	Switzerland	71	4.4	Hong Kong	102	4.2
7	Hong Kong	67	4.1	Australia	81	3.4
8	Australia	52	3.2	Switzerland	79	3.3
9	France	48	3.0	France	64	2.7
10	Canada	42	2.8	Canada	54	2.2

Source: BIS, *Financial Central Bank Survey of Foreign Exchange and Derivatives Market Activity*, September 2004; Hong Kong Monetary Authority, *Quarterly Bulletin*, December 2004.

The BIS survey also includes over-the-counter (OTC) derivatives. As these are new products developed during the past two decades, their turnover reflects a country/territory's financial sophistication and innovativeness. Hong Kong's average daily turnover of OTC derivatives also grew sharply from US\$4 billion to US\$15 billion, or by 275 per cent during the same period. However, Hong Kong's OTC derivatives market is still too small compared to those of UK and US, whose comparative figures were US\$643 billion and US\$355 billion restively.

If the traditional forex and OTC derivatives turnover are combined, then Hong Kong's world ranking rose from eighth to seventh during 2001–4.

Equity market

Like the economy, Hong Kong's equity market came to life after the end of SARS in terms of prices and volumes. Table 7.4 shows that Hong Kong's market value (capitalization) rebounded sharply in 2004, and its world ranking also moved up from tenth in 2002 and 2003 to ninth in 2004, according to the World Federation of Exchanges (WFE). Note that the classification of stock exchanges lacks uniformity. Some are classified according to the country of origin, some according to the city where the exchange is located. The most controversial is the inclusion of Nasdaq, which is just a stock price index.[12] If Nasdaq were included in 'New York' as

Table 7.4   World's top eleven equity markets (end of month, US\$million)

Exchange	December 2004		December 2003		December 2002	
	Rank	Market value	Rank	Market value	Rank	Market value
New York	1	12,707,578.3	1	11,328,953.1	1	9,015,166.7
Tokyo	2	3,557,674.4	2	2,953,098.3	2	2,069,299.1
Nasdaq	3	3,532,912.0	3	2,844,192.6	3	1,994,494.0
London	4	2,815,928.0	4	2,425,822.0	4	1,785,198.8
Euronext	5	2,441,261.4	5	2,076,410.2	5	1,538,654.2
Germany	6	1,194,516.8	6	1,079,026.2	6	686,013.5
Toronto	7	1,177,517.9	7	910,230.6	7	579,788.9
Hong Kong	9	861,462.9	10	714,597.3	10	463,054.9
Switzerland	10	829,098.1	8	727,102.8	8	546,893.5
Spain	8	940,672.9	9	726,243.4	11	461,559.6
Italy	11	789,562.6	11	614,841.6	9	477,075.0

Notes:
Market value excludes investment funds.
Euronext: unified stock exchange formed in 2000 by the merger of stock exchanges of Paris, Amsterdam, Brussels and Lisbon.

Source: World Federation of Exchanges website.

one entity, Hong Kong's world ranking would be able to move up one more notch.

Another important and sensitive indicator is the new issue market (including initial public offerings and placements). As Table 7.5 shows, Hong Kong's world ranking, in terms of funds raised, rose from seventh in 2002 to fifth in 2003, and further to second in the first 9 months of 2004. Both industry practitioners and scholars agree that the main reason for this rapid growth stemmed from the seemingly insatiable demand by Chinese enterprises (both state- and private sector-owned) for capital funds denominated in a fully convertible currency. As already mentioned in the previous section, Hong Kong is the listing location of first choice. The mutually beneficial effects of such fund-raising are obvious: China gets the capital it needs for financing growth and modernization, while Hong Kong's position as an IFC receives a powerful long-term impetus for expansion.

Banking

Although the importance of banking (including both commercial banking and investment banking) as an intermediary has declined relative to the capital market, it is still the core of the financial sector in many countries, especially emerging economies where the capital market is less developed. As our focus now is Hong Kong's importance as an IFC, the key indicator is external, or cross-border loans and deposits. Table 7.6 presents comparative statistics on external loans and deposits, extracted from the BIS. In compiling this table, we first exclude tax havens which serve merely as 'paper centres' or 'brass-plate centres'.[13] We also exclude countries/territories

Table 7.5 World top ten new issue markets (end of month, US$billion)

	September 2004		December 2003		December 2002	
Rank	Exchange	Capital raised	Exchange	Capital raised	Exchange	Capital raised
1	New York	82.9	New York	81.6	New York	87.4
2	Hong Kong	28.4	Euronext	51.2	Euronext	36.0
3	London	23.9	London	30.2	London	34.4
4	Tokyo	18.7	Tokyo	29.0	Spain	21.4
5	Toronto	17.5	Hong Kong	27.5	Tokyo	15.7
6	Euronext	15.4	Australia	22.8	Toronto	14.5
7	Spain	15.0	Toronto	17.9	Hong Kong	14.2
8	Australia	15.0	Spain	17.8	Taiwan	13.2
9	Mumbai	11.8	Italy	14.4	Australia	12.3
10	Nasdaq	9.9	Taiwan	8.6	South Africa	9.8

Source: World Federation of Exchanges website.

Table 7.6 External loans and deposits of banks in reporting countries (US$billion) in all currencies *vis-à-vis* all sectors

	Dec. 2002	Dec. 2003	June 2004	Rank
Claims:				
UK	1,913.6	2,407.5	2,691.3	1
US	1,158.6	1,390.1	1,587.7	2
Germany	992.4	1,288.7	1,319.3	3
Switzerland	765.3	802.6	825.6	4
France	538.7	617.0	684.7	5
Japan	523.1	516.0	522.1	6
Netherlands	294.3	395.5	420.7	7
Belgium	234.4	339.4	374.1	8
Singapore	342.3	353.1	372.0	9
Hong Kong	291.6	323.6	349.9	10
Ireland	148.4	213.1	223.3	11
Italy	183.7	226.0	215.9	12
Spain	117.5	145.2	156.5	13
Liabilities:				
UK	2,309.8	2,864.7	3,134.4	1
USA	1,380.9	1,736.5	1,916.9	2
Germany	976.8	1,132.5	1,109.4	3
France	655.7	782.7	884.6	4
Switzerland	709.4	757.4	796.1	5
Japan	550.3	521.6	575.9	6
Netherlands	403.1	493.4	517.4	7
Belgium	324.0	429.4	468.7	8
Singapore	370.0	388.4	431.7	9
Spain	282.5	396.5	417.7	10
Italy	298.7	393.2	396.3	11
Ireland	228.9	310.8	337.3	12
Hong Kong	241.9	264.6	303.8	13

Source: *BIS Quarterly Review: International Banking and Financial Market Developments*, Dec. 2004.

whose external loans and deposits are much smaller than Hong Kong's. The idea is to limit the maximum number of major banking centres to 13.

As the table shows, Hong Kong's external banking claims (mostly loans) amounted to US$349.9 billion, while its external liabilities (mostly deposits) amounted to US$303.8 billion as at the end of June 2004. The world rankings were tenth and thirteenth respectively. In my book (Jao, 1997b), I estimated, on the basis of various external claims and liabilities, that Hong Kong in 1995–96 ranked on average as the fifth most important banking centre.[14] This recent setback appears related to the 1997–8 AFC and the SARS epidemic of 2003. Japan escaped the worst effects of both AFC and SARS, but it endured its own banking crisis of 1991–2003. The two global financial centres, New York and London, and other European centres were not affected at all by either AFC or SARS. Thus, Japan was overtaken by Germany, France and Switzerland, while Hong Kong and Singapore were overtaken by the Netherlands on the claims side, and Hong Kong was overtaken not only by the Netherlands and Belgium, but also by Spain, Italy and Ireland on the liabilities side.

However, between the end of 2002 and the end of June 2004, Hong Kong's external claims and liabilities grew by 20 per cent and 25.6 per cent respectively, so we can still speak of a recovery situation.

Whilst all international banks scaled back their operations in Hong Kong during the AFC and SARS, the retrenchment by Japanese banks was particularly savage. At the end of 1996, Japan had 86 authorized institutions under Hong Kong's three-tier banking system, the largest concentration of Japanese banks outside Tokyo, as shown in Table 7.7. As Japanese banks at that time used Hong Kong as a centre to lend to their clients all over the Asia-Pacific region, they collectively accounted for 44.5 per cent of the banking sector's assets, and 55.6 per cent of the banking sector's loans to customers. By the end of 2003, the number of Japanese authorized institutions had fallen from 92 to 22, or by 76.1 per cent. Their assets, deposits from customers, and loans to customers, as well as their market shares, had fallen by between 53.4 per cent and 93 per cent. Domestically, the supervisory authorities' pressures on the banks to improve their CAR forced Japanese banks to downsize, or even withdraw from abroad. The smaller and weaker banks were particularly vulnerable, and were the first to downsize or withdraw. Externally, the Japanese banks took a dim view, perhaps overpessimistically, of the economic prospects of East Asia and Hong Kong in the wake of AFC and SARS.

Table 7.7 Japanese banks' retrenchment in Hong Kong

	End of 1996	End of 2003	Change over 1996
No. of authorized institutions:			
Licensed banks	46	13	
Restricted licence banks	11	4	
Deposit-taking companies	35	5	
Total	92	22	−76.1%
Assets (HK$ billion)	3,516	624	−82.3%
Share of total banking sector	44.5%	9.6%	−78.4%
Deposits from customers (HK$ billion)	380	177	−53.4%
Share of total banking sector	15.5%	5%	−67.7%
Loans to customers (HK$ billion)	2,177	152	−93%
Share of total banking sector	55.6%	7.5%	−86.5%

Source: *HKMA Annual Report*, 1996–2003.

Although Table 7.6 shows that Hong Kong is behind Singapore on both the claims and the liabilities sides, Hong Kong's domestic banking sector is much larger than Singapore's. Singapore has larger external banking claims and liabilities because it hosts the Asian-dollar market.[15] An analogous relationship exists between the UK and the US. Compared to the US, the UK has a much smaller domestic banking sector, but it has much larger external banking claims and liabilities because it hosts the huge Euro-currency market.

Despite the banking sector's setbacks in quantitative terms, Hong Kong has received very good qualitative ratings from the World Economic Forum in respect of banking and finance.[16] As Table 7.8 shows, Hong Kong ranks fourth in respect of financial market sophistication, second in respect of soundness of banks, and first in respect of local equity market access, way ahead of Singapore, and also ahead of many other industrialized countries.

International investment position

It was not until the early 1990s that the Government's Census and Statistics Department (CSD) began work on balance of payments statistics, and the first balance of payment tables became available only from 1997. As a result of this work, for the first time hard information about Hong Kong's international investment position (IIP) also became available.

Table 7.9 presents Hong Kong's IIP for the period 2000–3. Hong Kong had net external assets for four consecutive years. Even during 2001–2, when both external assets and liabilities decreased, net assets still increased. In 2003, however, all three – assets, liabilities and net assets – showed

Table 7.8   Comparative qualitative indicators of banking and finance

Countries/ territories	Financial market sophistication	Soundness of banks	Local equity market access
United Kingdom	1	1	3
United States	2	6	5
Switzerland	3	3	11
Hong Kong	4	2	1
Australia	5	8	2
Canada	9	4	15
Germany	10	23	20
Singapore	14	18	14
France	20	24	7
Taiwan	27	61	12
Japan	33	77	10
China	63	65	67

Source: World Economic Forum, *The Global Competitiveness Report 2002–2003*.

Table 7.9   Hong Kong's international investment position (HK$billion, end of year)

	2000	Yearly change	2001	Yearly change	2002	Yearly change	2003	Yearly change
Assets	8,899.3	—	8,350.6	–6.2%	8,032.7	–3.8	9,124.9	+13.6%
Liabilities	7,169.7	—	6,282.7	–12.4%	5,355.4	–14.8	6,037.4	+12.7%
Net assets	1,729.5	—	2,068.0	+19.6%	2,677.4	+29.5	3,087.5	+15.3%

Source: Census and Statistics Department, *Balance of Payments Statistics*.

encouraging positive double-digit growth, confirming the resurgence of Hong Kong as an IFC.

Table 7.9 is also significant from the point of view of financial centre development. Prior to the availability of IIP data, Hong Kong was believed to be only a financial entrepôt (i.e., a centre which provides financial services and facilities to both residents and non-residents, and which serves as an intermediary between savers and investors, or between lenders and borrowers). Table 7.9 now demonstrates that Hong Kong is a capital exporter as well. The classic examples of capital-exporting financial centres are London (circa 1812–1919), New York (circa 1919–85), and Tokyo (circa 1970 to the present day). Now, both the UK and the US have become net debtors, while Hong Kong has become a new creditor to the world. Such are the vicissitudes of international finance.

Several things are clear from Table 7.9. First, despite various setbacks in recent years, Hong Kong remains one of the richest economies of the world. At the end of 2003, Hong Kong's net external assets amounted to HK$3,087.5 billion, or US$396.85 billion. This was a huge sum, which served to strengthen international confidence in Hong Kong as an IFC. Second, according to the CSD, Hong Kong's external assets and liabilities were equivalent to 748 per cent and 495 per cent respectively of GDP at the end of 2003. These data not only reflect the externally-oriented nature of Hong Kong's economy, but also its importance as a centre for investment flows, particularly in the Asia-Pacific region.

Regional headquarters

An IFC cannot exist on financial activities alone; it needs the nourishment and support of other non-financial activities. While banks and NBFIs support the development of other non-financial sectors through their financing, maturity transformation, insurance and other essential functions in a modern complex society, the non-financial sectors in their turn also stimulate the growth of the financial sector through their demand for all kinds of financial services and products. The positive interactions between the financial and real sectors constitute the main driving force for the emergence and growth of an IFC. Historically, many IFCs typically started their careers as sea ports. As domestic and external trade grew through the activities of its sea port, a city gradually became a commercial centre, transportation and communications centre, or tourism centre, say, finally developing into a city or metropolis assuming the role of an IFC. London, New York, Tokyo, Hong Kong and Singapore are examples. The ability of a city or metropolis to attract multinational corporations to set up regional headquarters (RHQs) therefore becomes another important hallmark of an IFC.

Hong Kong began its official survey of RHQs set up by overseas companies in the 1980s, first under the auspices of the government's Trade and Industry Department. Since 2000, these surveys have been taken over by the CSD. According to the definitions of the CSD:

(a) *a regional headquarters (RHQ)* is an office that has control over the operations of offices in the region (i.e., Hong Kong plus one or more other places), and manages the business without frequent referrals to its parent company outside Hong Kong;

(b) *a regional office (RO)* is an office that coordinates offices/operations in the region (i.e., Hong Kong plus one or more other places), and manages the business but with frequent referrals to its parent company outside Hong Kong or its regional headquarters;

(c) *a local office (LO)* is an office that solely takes charge of the business in Hong Kong on behalf of its parent company outside Hong Kong;

(d) *a parent company outside Hong Kong* is a company or an organization that has final management control over the operation of one or more offices in any region.

Table 7.10 provides summary statistics of overseas corporations' RHQ and ROs in Hong Kong. Note that the word 'region' means a geographical area much greater than, but also including, Hong Kong, such as Mainland China, Greater China, East Asia, South East Asia, Asia-Pacific and so on.

As may be easily seen from Table 7.10, except for 1998, the number of companies setting up RHQs increased steadily every year. The number of ROs dropped only in 2002. Their total sum rose from 2,514 in 1997 to 3,609 in 2004, with temporary declines only in 1998 and 2002.

Table 7.10 Overseas companies' RHQs and ROs in Hong Kong

	1997	1998	1999	2000	2001	2002	2003	2004
RHQs	903	819	840	855	944	948	966	1,098
ROs	1,611	1,630	1,650	2,146	2,293	2,171	2,241	2,511
Total	2,514	2,449	2,490	3,001	3,237	3,119	3,207	3,609

Source: Census and Statistics Department.

Some years ago, Michael Enright and his associates surveyed 8,000 major corporations in North America, Europe and Japan. The survey returned about 1,100 usable replies, forming the largest database of its kind. Hong Kong was found to be the dominant city of choice for RHQs in the Asia-Pacific region. Singapore was the favourite city for RHQs only in South East Asia. Other cities, such as Tokyo, Shanghai, Sydney, Kuala Lumpur and Taipei, lagged even more behind Hong Kong (Enright and Scott, 2000).

Other financial markets and industries

Under this heading, we can only very briefly review recent developments in other financial markets and industries, due to space limitations.

Hong Kong's fund management industry, though growing rapidly, is still dwarfed by those in the wealthy industrialized countries. In 2000, for example, Hong Kong had assets under management (AUM) of US$190 billion, but the comparative figures for London, New York, Tokyo and Paris were US$2,461 billion, US$2,363 billion, US$2,058 billion, and US$458 billion respectively. In the Asia-Pacific region (excluding Japan), Hong Kong was behind Australia but ahead of Singapore (Harrison and Wu, 2004; Harrison, 2002).

According to the SFC, AUM in Hong Kong doubled between 2002 and 2003, and the growth rate for 2003, 80.2 per cent, was particularly striking, showing the rapid recovery in the post-SARS era (see Table 7.11). The term 'fund management business' comprises asset management, advisory business, and other private banking activities. One notable trend in recent years has been the banking sector's move into wealth management, which partly explains the sharp jump in fund management activity in 2003. Another new factor was the launching of the Mandatory Provident Fund (MPF) in December 2000.

The international flavour of Hong Kong's fund management business is conveyed by the following facts: in 2003, funds sourced from overseas amounted to $1,860 billion, or 63 per cent of the total business; more than 80 international fund houses from the US, UK, Japan, Switzerland, France and other countries had operations here; 485 (or 37%) of the SFC licensed corporations were controlled by substantial overseas shareholders; and 50 per cent of the firms licensed to carry out asset management business had foreign controlling shareholders.

Table 7.11   Fund management business (HK$billion, year-end figures)

2000	Yearly change	2001	Yearly change	2002	Yearly change	2003	Yearly change
1,485	–	1,625	+9.4%	1,635	+0.62%	2,947	+80.2%

Source: SFC, Fund Management Survey 2003.

Prior to the 1990s, Hong Kong's debt market was virtually non-existent by international standards. The chronic fiscal surplus meant that what few bonds the government had issued had either been paid off or held to maturity. Other factors hindering the development of the bond market were the lack of a risk-free benchmark, the preference for equities and real estate by the investing public, the heavy reliance on bank finance by business firms, the lack of a bond rating agency, and the tax treatment of interest income from debt securities and so on (World Bank, 1995).

Since then, government agencies such as the HKMA's Exchange Fund, statutory bodies such as the Hong Kong Mortgage Corporation, the Airport Authority, and the Mass Transit Railway Corporation have issued a variety of fixed- and floating-rate instruments. They have been joined by foreign multilateral development banks (MDBs) as well as other overseas issuers. Tax treatment has also been improved, with securities issued by certain issuers totally exempt from profit tax. In the budget for 2003–04, the government announced that trading profits from Qualified Debt Instruments (QDIs) would be exempted totally from tax. The minimum maturity requirement for the current 50 per cent tax concession on QDI profits was also relaxed from five to three years. Faced by a structural fiscal deficit which emerged in 2002, the Hong Kong government, after much hesitation, launched a HK$20 billion bond issue in July 2004.

As shown in Table 7.12, the total amount of Hong Kong dollar debt instruments had increased moderately but steadily during the recent period 1997–2003. Foreign participation was considerable. In 2003, for example, MDBs and other overseas borrowers accounted for 37.5 per cent of the total outstanding amount. Moreover, many of the AI were of foreign parentage, though exact details about their composition are unknown. It seems safe to assume, however, that over half of the total amount in 2003 were issued by overseas entities. Securities issued by local corporation remained modest: in 2003, they accounted for 6 per cent of the total amount only. Moreover, the total outstanding amount, HK$557,764 million, was equivalent to only 45.7 per cent of Hong Kong's GDP in the same year, as against the average of 150 per cent in industrialized countries.

As with fund management, the insurance industry in Hong Kong is also strongly influenced by the ongoing trend of globalization. As shown in Table 7.13, of the 188 insurance companies operating in Hong Kong at the end of 2003, exactly half were incorporated overseas. All the top 20 reinsurers of the world had operations here, as shown in the figures in brackets in the table. Hong Kong probably has the largest concentrations of insurers in Asia outside Japan.

A recent study (Yeh, 2004) indicates that, while Hong Kong's GDP grew six-fold during the period 1982–99, the insurance gross premium expanded twelve times during the same period. However, compared to the industrialized countries, Hong Kong's insurance industry is still a laggard. In terms of

Table 7.12 Outstanding amount of Hong Kong dollar debt instruments (HK$million)

End of	Exchange fund	Statutory bodies	MDBs	Non-MDB overseas borrowers	AIs	Local corporations	Total
1997	101,650	2,295	26,150	10,032	188,387	26,183	354,698
1998	97,450	11,365	69,402	14,777	183,300	22,378	398,673
1999	101,874	21,572	61,287	43,767	177,915	37,331	443,745
2000	108,602	20,509	57,062	81,840	165,680	38,405	472,098
2001	113,750	36,227	51,104	102,897	150,960	38,880	493,818
2002	117,476	48,828	40,834	139,145	149,013	37,567	532,863
2003	120,152	56,780	27,855	181,522	137,988	33,466	557,764

Notes:

MDBs (multilateral development banks) refers to the Asian Development Bank, Council of Europe Social Development Fund, European Company for the Financing of Railroad Rolling Stock (Eurofima), European Investment Bank, European Bank for Reconstruction and Development, Inter-American Development Bank, International Bank for Reconstruction and Development, International Finance Corporation, African Development Bank, and Nordic Investment Bank. Income earned on debt securities issued by the MDBs is exempted from profits tax.

AI (Authorized Institutions) include licensed banks, restricted licence banks (RLBs), and deposit-taking companies (DTCs).

Source: HKMA Quarterly Bulletin, March 2004, No. 38, p. 33.

Table 7.13   Insurance companies by place of incorporation (end of 2003)

Place of incorporation	Number of authorized insurers	Type of business authorized		
		Pure long term	Pure general	Composite
Bahama Islands	1	–	1	–
Bermuda	14 *(1)*	8	4 *(1)*	2
Canada	3	3	–	–
China[a]	1	1	–	–
Denmark	1 *(1)*	–	1 *(1)*	–
Finland	1	–	1	–
France	5 *(1)*	–	5 *(1)*	–
Germany	5 *(3)*	–	2	3 *(3)*
Guernsey	1	1	–	–
India	2	–	2	–
Ireland	1	1	–	–
Isle of Man	5	5	–	–
Italy	1	–	–	1
Japan	6 *(1)*	–	6 *(1)*	–
Luxembourg	3	–	3	–
Netherlands	1	–	1	–
Philippines	1	–	1	–
Singapore	2	–	2	–
South Africa	1	1	–	–
Sweden	1 *(1)*	–	1 *(1)*	–
Switzerland	5 *(1)*	3	1	1 *(1)*
United Kingdom	14 *(1)*	6 *(1)*	6	2
United States of America	19 *(3)*	5 *(1)*	13 *(2)*	1
Non-Hong Kong	94 *(13)*	34 *(2)*	50 *(7)*	10 *(4)*
Hong Kong	94 *(10)*	12	73 *(9)*	9 *(1)*
Total	188 *(23)*	46 *(2)*	123 *(16)*	19 *(5)*

Figures in brackets denote the number of authorized insurers which are pure reinsurers.
[a] *Excluding insurers incorporated in Hong Kong.*

Source: Office of the Commissioner of Insurance (OCI) Annual Report.

insurance density and penetration, Hong Kong was only slightly above one-half of the OECD average.

As shown in Table 7.13, during 2000–3 the insurance industry grew substantially in terms of premium income, density and penetration. However, Hong Kong's insurance density and penetration in 2002 were still lower than the OECD average in 2000. Thus, Hong Kong's insurance density was HK\$14,991 (=US\$1,926.9), while the OECD average was US\$2,032.1, and Hong Kong's insurance penetration was 8.3 per cent in 2003, while the OECD average was 8.9 per cent in 2000.

Although Hong Kong was ahead of Singapore in 2000 in terms of insurance density and penetration, it was less successful than Singapore in attracting reinsurance and captive business (Yeh, 2004). Hong Kong needs to work harder to exploit opportunities created by China's opening of its vast insurance market, both for expansion into the Mainland, and to attract Chinese entities to enter the local market.

Market infrastructure

An IFC worthy of its name must possess a state-of-the-art technology to cope with increasingly voluminous and complex domestic and cross-border financial transactions efficiently and with minimum risk. It must also have modern market mechanisms to satisfy the demand for a variety of financial products and services by both residents and non-residents.

In 1996, Hong Kong launched its Real Time Gross Settlement (RTGS) for the Hong Kong dollar, the fourth RTGS in the world. One of the great achievements of RTGS is that it can eliminate settlement or payments risk, one specialized form of which is the Herstatt risk.[17] The RTGS also played a useful role in the defence of the Hong Kong dollar against currency speculators during the AFC (Jao, 2001, ch. 4).

Earlier, in 1990, the HKMA (or more precisely, its predecessor) introduced the Central Moneymarkets Unit (CMU) as one of the world's first paperless clearing, settlement and custodian systems for debt securities. A remarkable breakthrough was achieved in 2000, when the Hong Kong RTGS was linked to the US RTGS through Payment versus Payment (PvP) settlement for forex transactions, and both were in turn linked to CMU through Delivery versus Payment (DvP) settlement of securities. Linkage with the Euro RTGS was established in 2003, while joint cheque clearing between Hong Kong and Guangdong began in 2002. Since 1994, the CMU has also established links with the European Union's Euroclear and Clearstream, China's China Government Securities Trust and Clearing Company, Australia's AustraClear, South Korea's Korea Securities Depository, and so on. The long-term aim of the HKMA is to make Hong Kong a leading international centre of financial intermediation, which can provide 'universal, 24-hour access to multi-currency clearing and settlement services with RTGS, DvD and PvP capabilities'.[18]

In August 2003, the SFC introduced the guidelines for regulating real estate investment trusts (REITs). This initiative was an innovation in the right direction, for it paved the way for the listing of REITs, an important step in building up Hong Kong's market infrastructure.

Accordingly, in December 2004, the government-owned Housing Authority, which administers a low-cost housing estate, launched the initial public offering (IPO) of what it called 'Link REIT', which was basically a securitized package of car parks and shops that it owned. The public's response was overwhelming: the IPO was 120 times oversubscribed, with funds totalling HK$280 billion (US$35.9 billion) temporarily frozen.[19]

Had this IPO gone off successfully as planned, it would have brought benefits to all parties concerned, while Hong Kong's position as an IFC would have been given a tremendous boost, as the US$3 billion IPO would have been the largest of its kind in the world. Unfortunately, the IPO was stymied by politically-motivated litigation against it.[20] Although this sorry episode is not expected to affect Hong Kong's status as an IFC in the long run, it is an unpleasant reminder that domestic politics can be nasty and can catch us by surprise.

Conclusions

The purpose of this chapter has been to assess Hong Kong's status as a financial centre of China and the world. A major conclusion is that as long as Hong Kong distinguishes itself from other Chinese cities in respect of currency convertibility, capital mobility, economic freedom, rule of law, and the quality of prudential supervision and corporate governance, it will remain China's OFC. The term OFC is used advisedly from China's point of view after the 1997 transfer of sovereignty. From Hong Kong's own point of view, the territory remains an integrated financial centre, and an IFC in its own right. In my previous book on the same subject (Jao, 1997b), I concluded, on the basis of data available in 1995–96, that Hong Kong was between the sixth and seventh largest IFC in the world.[21]

Since then, Hong Kong has been hard hit by the AFC, the protracted Japanese banking crisis, and the SARS epidemic. Although recent data point to a resurgence of Hong Kong as an IFC, the financial sector, particularly the banking sector, has suffered. As a result, Hong Kong's world ranking has probably gone down one notch to between the seventh and eighth most significant world IFC. In the Asia-Pacific region, Hong Kong probably still retains the second spot, being behind Tokyo but ahead of Singapore (but the edge over Singapore is small).[22]

My previous book on Hong Kong as an IFC was written before the historic handover in 1997. The book was therefore much preoccupied with the post-1997 situation and China's commitment to the Joint Declaration and the Basic Law. It turned out that the transition to Chinese sovereignty took place quite smoothly. So far China has demonstrated its commitments to the principle of 'one country, two systems'. China has also shown its willingness to help Hong Kong in times of economic stress. However, other uncertainties and concerns remain.

Hong Kong is now in the midst of a difficult and complex metamorphosis into a knowledge-based economy, and events of the past seven years have exposed many structural problems. The widely held view in 1995–96, that East Asia, including Hong Kong, was the great 'growth pole' of the world, capable of self-perpetuating above-average performance, has now been exposed as a complacent myth after the devastating Asian Financial Crisis. At the time of writing, China's economy was still overheating, despite various 'macroeconomic adjustments' measures taken in early 2004. While the possibility of a hard landing which might set off a banking or financial crisis seems remote, it cannot be entirely ruled out. The health of China's economy and financial sector is obviously of great concern to Hong Kong.

Even more serious is the tense and potentially explosive relationship between China and Taiwan. The political gulf between the two sides of the Taiwan Strait remains as wide as ever. Any misstep or miscalculation on either side could degenerate into a military showdown, the consequences of which are too horrible even to contemplate. Hong Kong can only pray that both sides will exercise the utmost restraint in dealing with their differences.

In Jao (1997b), I cited Beirut and Shanghai as the two prime examples in the twentieth century of how an IFC could be ruined by war, civil strife and bad financial policies. This is a bitter lesson of history which both China and Hong Kong should take to heart.

Notes

1 For example, a French expert writes: 'Hong Kong est la troisième place financière du monde. Elle est de plus en plus considérée comme une alternative à Tokyo par les investisseurs étrangers désirant s'installer en Asie orientale. Les banques internationales y sont plus nombreuses qu'à Paris ou à Tokyo (560 banques, dont 360 succursales de banques étrangères' (Cini, 1993, p. 117). Translated this text reads 'Hong Kong is the third financial centre in the world. It is more and more considered as an alternative to Tokyo by overseas investors wishing to establish themselves in East Asia. The international banks are more numerous than in Paris or in Tokyo (560 banks, of which 360 are branches of overseas banks).'
2 The nine variable measures were (1) the number of large internationally active commercial banks headquartered in the centre; (2) the number of foreign financial centres with direct links to the local centre, when these links are provided by the local centres' internationally active banks; (3) the number of private banks (including investment and merchant banks) located in the centre; (4) the number of large internationally active foreign commercial banks with a banking office in the centre (representative offices are excluded); (5) the number of foreign financial centres with direct links to the local centre, when these links are provided by the foreign internationally active banks; (6) the total amount of foreign financial assets held in the centre; (7) the total amount of foreign financial liabilities residing in the centre; (8) the number of foreign financial centres with direct links to the local centre, when these links are provided by foreign internationally active banks (agency, branch, representative and subsidiary offices); and (9) the number of large internationally active foreign commercial banks with agencies, branches, or representative or subsidiary offices in the centre.
3 A 'region' in this context means a supra-national geographical area (say, one or two continents), not a sub-national one.

4 The term 'Asia-Pacific region' refers to countries or territories along the western edge of the Pacific Ocean, including China, Japan, Taiwan, Hong Kong, Korea, Brunei, Indonesia, Malaysia, the Philippines, Singapore, Thailand, Australia and New Zealand.

5 See Annex A, 'Criteria for Authorization', Hong Kong Monetary Authority 1994 Annual Report.

6 CAR is formally defined as the sum of paid-up capital and reserves to risk-adjusted assets. This definition will remain the same under Basel II, but 'risk' will be more strictly defined.

7 As reported in 'Bank tsar comes out fighting', *South China Morning Post*, 30 May 2003.

8 See 'Banking Reform in the Mainland', The Bank of East Asia, *Economic Analysis*, October 2004.

9 *Hong Kong Monetary Authority Quarterly Bulletin*, March 2004, p. 83.

10 We are talking here about 'portfolio investment', not 'foreign direct investment' (FDI). As far as FDI is concerned, China is still more attractive, given the sheer size of its domestic market.

11 China's foreign exchange reserves reached US$609.9 billion at the end of December 2004. Although on a per capita basis China's foreign reserves are still very small, their absolute size is big enough to make exchange control liberalization workable.

12 Recall that Nasdaq is the acronym of National Association of Securities Dealers Automated Quotations.

13 These excluded 'tax havens' are the Bahamas, the Cayman Islands, Jersey and Luxembourg. Those countries/territories, including tax havens, whose external loans and deposits are much smaller than Hong Kong's, such as Australia, Brazil, Denmark, etc., are also excluded.

14 At that time, I relied mainly on the IMF's *International Financial Statistics*. Unfortunately, since 1997, the IMF has ceased to publish such banking data.

15 In 1968, several American multinational banks intended to establish the Asian-dollar market in Hong Kong, which essentially was an extension of the Euro-dollar market to the Asian time-zone. The Hong Kong government at that time refused to abolish the interest withholding tax on foreign currency deposits, for short-term fiscal reasons. Singapore, however, was only too glad to accommodate the multinational banks. The Asian-dollar market therefore went to Singapore.

16 Hong Kong's overall competitiveness ranking was seventeenth, against Singapore's fourth, because of poor showing in respect of science and technology, innovativeness, and corporate governance.

17 Named after the German bank which collapsed in 1974 as a result of large forex loss. When Herstatt was shut (German time), dollar payments to American banks were not delivered. The exposed US banks were faced with a liquidity crisis, which came close to triggering a collapse of the US payments system (see Heffernan, 1996, p. 166).

18 For details, see HKMA, *Annual Report 2003*, and 'Development of Financial Infrastructure in Hong Kong', *HKMA Quarterly Bulletin*, 34, March 2003, pp. 40–5.

19 As reported in *Hong Kong Economic Journal Daily*, 10 December 2004.

20 Just before the Link REIT was about to be listed, two tenants of the Housing Authority's public housing estates, aided and abetted by some politicians, filed legal proceedings to stop it on the basis of an unsubstantiated claim that it rep-

resented a violation of the rights of tenants. After going through lower courts and a round of appeals, this allegation was finally defeated at the Court of Final Appeal.
21 The weights I used for ranking were: banking, 40 per cent; forex and derivatives market, 30 per cent; equity and debt markets, 25 per cent; others, 5 per cent. The top score was therefore one.
22 In 2004, the scores of Hong Kong and Singapore were 9.18 and 10.73 respectively.

References

Annells, D. (2002), 'Hong Kong as a Centre of Wealth Management', *Asia-Pacific Journal of Taxation*, 6 (2), Autumn, 67–72.

Chen, Y. (1995), 'Financial Relations between Hong Kong and the Mainland', in *Money and Banking in Hong Kong*, Hong Kong: Hong Kong Monetary Authority, pp. 47–55.

Chen, Y. (1996), 'Prospects for the Financial Relationship between Mainland China and Hong Kong after 1997', *Hong Kong Monetary Authority Quarterly Bulletin* (February), 38–43.

Cini, F. (1993), 'Métropole Régional ou Place Internationale?', in J.-P. Béja (ed.), *Hong Kong 1997: Fin de Siècle, Fin d'un Monde?*, Brussels: Espace. 117–52.

Dufey, G. and I.H. Giddy (1978), *The International Money Market*, Englewood Cliffs, NJ: Prentice Hall.

Enright, M. and E. Scott (2000), 'RHQ Special Issue', *Business Asia*, 11 December, 1–8.

Fell, R. (1992), *Crisis and Change: The Maturing of Hong Kong's Financial Markets*, Hong Kong: Longman.

Goldberg, M.A. (1996), 'The Development of a Network of Asia-Pacific Financial Centres', in D.K. Das (ed.), *Emerging Growth Pole: The Asia-Pacific Economy*, Singapore: Simon & Schuster, 380–404.

Harrison, M. (2002), 'Fund Management in Hong Kong and Singapore', *SFC Quarterly Bulletin*, 50 (Winter), 17–19.

Harrison, M. and Q. Wu (2004), 'Fund Management and Mutual Funds', in S.S.M. Ho, R.H. Scott and K.A. Wong (eds), *The Hong Kong Financial System: A New Era*, New York: Oxford University Press, ch. 4.

Heffernan, S. (1996), *Modern Banking in Theory and Practice*, New York: John Wiley.

Hewson, J.R. (1982), *Offshore Banking in Australia*, Canberra: Australian Government Publishing Services.

Ho, Simon S.M. (2004), 'Corporate Governance and Disclosures', in S.S.M. Ho, R.H. Scott and K.A. Wong (eds), *The Hong Kong Financial System: A New Age*, New York: Oxford University Press, ch. 15.

Ho, Y.K. (1991), 'Hong Kong as an International Financial Centre', in Y.K. Ho, R.H. Scott and K.A. Wong (eds), *The Hong Kong Financial System*, Hong Kong: Oxford University Press, 381–405.

Hui, G.W.L. (1992), 'Ranking Hong Kong as an international financial centre', *Hong Kong Economic Papers*, 22, 35–45.

Hui, G.W.L. (2004), 'A Quarter Century on: A Survey of Hong Kong as an International Financial Centre', in S.S.M. Ho, R.H. Scott and K.A. Wong (eds), *The Hong Kong Financial System: A New Age*, New York: Oxford University Press, ch. 17.

Jao, Y.C. (1979), 'The Rise of Hong Kong as a Financial Centre', *Asian Survey*, 19 (July), 674–94.

Jao, Y.C. (1980), 'Hong Kong as a Regional Financial Centre: Evolution and Prospects', in C.K. Leung, J.W. Cushman and Wang Gungwu (eds), *Hong Kong:*

Dilemmas of Growth, Canberra: Australian National University Press, pp. 161–94; reprinted in R. Roberts (1994c), 457–90.

Jao, Y.C. (1997a), 'Hong Kong as a Financial Centre for Greater China', in J.C.H. Chai, Y.Y. Kueh and C.A. Tisdell (eds), *China and the Asia Pacific Economy*, Commack, NY: Nova Science, ch. 6.

Jao, Y.C. (1997b), *Hong Kong as an International Financial Centre: Evolution, Prospects and Policies*, Hong Kong: City University of Hong Kong Press.

Jao, Y.C. (2001), *The Asian Financial Crisis and the Ordeal of Hong Kong*, Westport, CT and London: Quorum Books, Greenwood.

Jao, Y.C. (2003a), 'Financial Reform in Hong Kong', in M.J.B. Hall (ed.), *The International Handbook on Financial Reform*, Cheltenham: Edward Elgar, ch. 6, 113–33.

Jao, Y.C. (2003b), 'Shanghai and Hong Kong as International Financial Centres: Historical Perspective and Contemporary Analysis', paper presented to an international conference on 'Recent developments in Chinese finance', jointly sponsored by the University of Durham, East China Normal University and Shanghai Institute of International Finance, and held in Shanghai, 13–14 September 2003.

Johns, R.A. (1983), *Tax Havens and Offshore Finance*, London: Frances Pinter.

Johns, R.A. (1992), 'Offshore Banking', *The New Palgrave Dictionary of Money and Finance*, 3, 63–7.

Jones, J. (1992), 'International Financial Centres in Asia, the Middle East and Australia: A Historical Perspective', in Y. Cassis (ed.), *Finance and Financiers in European History, 1880–1960*, Cambridge: Cambridge University Press, 405–28.

McCarthy, I. (1979), 'Offshore Banking Centers: Benefits and Costs', *Finance and Development*, 16 (4), 45–8.

Meyer, D.R. (2000), *Hong Kong as a Global Metropolis*, Cambridge: Cambridge University Press.

Park, Y.S. (1982), 'The Economics of Offshore Financial Centers', *Columbia Journal of World Business*, 17 (4), winter, 1–5.

Reed, H.C. (1980), 'The Ascent of Tokyo as an International Financial Center', *Journal of International Business Studies*, 11 (3), winter, 19–35.

Reed, H.C. (1981), *The Preeminence of International Financial Centers*, New York: Praeger.

Reed, H.C. (1983), 'Appraising Corporate Investment Policy: A Financial Center Theory of Foreign Direct Investment', in C.P. Kindleberger and D.B. Audretsch (eds), *The Multinational Corporation in the 1980s*, Cambridge, MA: MIT Press, 219–44.

Reed, H.C. (1989), 'Financial Center Hegemony, Interest Rates and the Global Political Economy', in Y.S. Park and M. Essayyad (eds), *International Banking and Financial Centers*, Boston, MA: Kluwer Academic, 247–68.

Roberts, R. (ed.) (1994a), *International Financial Centres, Vol. 1, Concepts, Development and Dynamics*, Aldershot: Edward Elgar.

Roberts, R. (1994b), *International Financial Centres, Vol. 2, Global Financial Centres: London, New York, Tokyo*, Aldershot: Edward Elgar.

Roberts, R. (1994c), *International Financial Centres, Vol. 3, International Financial Centres of Europe, North America and Asia*, Aldershot: Edward Elgar.

Roberts, R. (1994d), *International Financial Centres, Vol. 4, Offshore Financial Centres*, Aldershot: Edward Elgar.

Schenk, Catherine R. (2001), *Hong Kong as an International Financial Centre: Emergence and Development 1945–65*, Routledge: London and New York.

Schenk, Catherine R. (2002), 'Banks and the Emergence of Hong Kong as an International Financial Center', *Journal of Financial Markets, Institutions and Money*, 12, 321–40.

US Treasury Department (1998), *National Treatment Study*, Washington, DC: Treasury Department.

World Bank (1995), *The Emerging Asian Bond Market: Hong Kong*, Washington, DC: The World Bank.

World Economic Forum (2003), *The Global Competitiveness Report 2002–2003*, New York: Oxford University Press.

Yam, Joseph (1995), 'Hong Kong as an International Financial Centre: Strategy Paper', *HKMA Quarterly Bulletin*, August, 32–48.

Yeh, J. (2004), 'The Insurance Industry', in S.S.M. Ho, R.H. Scott and K.A. Wong (eds), *The Hong Kong Financial System: A New Age*, New York: Oxford University Press, ch. 6.

8

The Evolving Role of Hong Kong as China's Middleman

Yun-Wing Sung

Introduction

While Hong Kong's historic role as a middleman for the Chinese Mainland rose to new prominence in the first 15 years of China's open-door era inaugurated in 1979, Hong Kong's shares of China's foreign investment and trade have declined since the mid-1990s. With China's full integration in the world economy, signalled by China's WTO entry in 2002, and the rapid development of rival hubs such as Shanghai and Shenzhen, it has often been argued that Hong Kong has no future as the Mainland's middleman.

In the early years of China's reform era, Hong Kong had a semi-monopoly position as a service hub for China due to the underdevelopment of China's service sector. China had neglected the development of its services sector in the pre-reform era because services were regarded as 'unproductive' in Marxist ideology. China did not allow significant foreign investment in services until Deng Xiaoping's 1992 southern tour in support of economic reforms. With the rapid development of China's service sector after the mid-1990s, Hong Kong lost its semi-monopoly position, and Hong Kong's share of Mainland's foreign trade and investment declined.

This chapter argues that the prognosis that Hong Kong has no future as China's middleman is misconstrued theoretically as well as empirically. In theory, the demand for middleman services rises as a command economy decentralizes. While the development of rival hubs such as Shanghai and Shenzhen has eroded Hong Kong's share of the China market, China's demand for middleman services has increased enormously with economic reforms. Moreover, economic development has caused the size of the Mainland economy to expand rapidly, again raising the demand for intermediation. In a nutshell, Hong Kong has come to have a smaller share of a bigger pie. It is, however, still possible for Hong Kong's slice of the cake to grow.

Empirically, the decline in Hong Kong's share of China's investment and trade has been overstated as part of Hong Kong's investment in China has been channelled via the tax haven economies (mostly Caribbean islands), and Hong Kong's China-related entrepôt trade has been increasingly diverted to offshore trade that does not touch Hong Kong, but is still handled by Hong Kong trading companies. The chapter corrects for such statistical biases.

The chapter is organized as follows. After this introduction, the next section discusses the theory of intermediation and its implications for the role of Hong Kong as China's middleman. The following two sections analyse Hong Kong's role in China's trade and foreign investment. The fifth section discusses the role of Hong Kong as a service hub, while the sixth section concludes.

The theory of intermediation

A naive view attributes Hong Kong's role as China's middleman to China's isolation in the Cold War era. This view is untenable. In theory, as well as in reality, an economy that is fully integrated with the world economy still demands intermediary services. Empirically, Hong Kong's Mainland-related trade and investment have increased by leaps and bounds since the inauguration of the open-door era in 1979.

Due to the transaction costs of establishing trade links, an exchange structure in which everyone is directly linked to everyone else (the Walrasian model) is generally inefficient; efficient structures minimize the number of trade links and necessarily involve intermediation (Townsend, 1978). Increasing the number of participants in a trading coalition decreases risks, but increases the number of links and raises transaction costs. A tradeoff is involved, and Townsend uses a core equilibrium concept to show how an equilibrium is generated.

Intermediation and decentralization

Since China's adoption of an open-door policy in 1979, it has become easier to trade directly with China. The transaction cost of establishing a direct trade link has fallen, as a result of which there should have been a rise in direct trade relative to indirect trade. However, China started to decentralize its foreign trade system in 1979, replacing vertical channels of command by horizontal links. The number of trading partners and trade links multiplied rapidly, creating a huge demand for intermediation. Part of the demand for intermediation was channelled to Hong Kong, because of its comparative advantage in trading.

The market composition of China's indirect trade via Hong Kong and the changing dependency over time of these markets on Hong Kong's entrepôt trade confirm the overwhelming importance of trade decentralization on intermediation (Sung, 1991, 141–3). Countries that have long histories of trading with China have found it worthwhile to pay for the fixed cost of establishing trade links, and they are less dependent on Hong Kong than new entrants. Political recognition and trade pacts also lower dependency on Hong Kong. However, the decentralization of China's trading system in 1979 and 1984 have increased the dependency of both old China hands and new entrants on Hong Kong's entrepôt trade.

Efficiency of large trading centres

In trading and transportation, there are significant economies of scale or scope, and also economies of agglomeration. Large trading and transportation hubs, such as Hong Kong, can provide trading and shipping services efficiently. Hong Kong has been the world's busiest container port for many years, boasting a record container throughput of nearly 22 million TEU in 2004. (One TEU = 20-foot container, representing a volume equal to 1,360 cubic feet.) Hong Kong is also the world's busiest hub for international air cargo.

In transportation, a successful shipping hub must have sufficient freight to attract shipping companies to make frequent calls. A large and busy port tends to be efficient because of economies of agglomeration: an increase in freight implies more frequent shipping, which will in turn attract more freight as the cargo can be shipped out speedily. This gives rise to the hub-and-spoke pattern in transportation: it is often more economical for feeder ports to transship through a major hub rather than relying on direct shipment.

In trade, Yamamura (1976, pp. 184–5) argues that significant economies of scale exist in the production of trading services, since the production of these services usually involves large fixed costs and small or declining marginal costs. In the production of market information, which is part and parcel of intermediation, he argues that considerable costs are involved, and the same market information is useful in many transactions. Moreover, trading firms can also consolidate small orders efficiently to use warehouse and shipping capacities to achieve economies of scale.

Traders tend to agglomerate in a city, suggesting that there are significant external economies involved. This implies that once a city acquires a comparative advantage in trade, the advantage feeds upon itself, and more trading firms will come to the city, making the city even more efficient in trade.

There are in fact external economies on both the demand and supply sides in trade. External economy on the demand side operates through search: an increase in the number of potential trading partners makes trade easier. External economies on the production side are also important in trade. Hicks (1969, pp. 47–9) observed that an increase in the number of merchants in the trading centre will permit specialization of labour, not only by lowering costs, but also by lowering risks. The larger the number of traders, the easier it is to acquire information, and the easier it is to arrange multilateral contracts or to develop specialized contracts such as insurance and hedging. Lucas (1985) stressed the importance of agglomeration, especially in service industries, because people in the same trade can interact and learn from one another. He called this the 'externality of human capital'.

The theory presented here predicts that a decline in travel and communication costs will lower the fixed costs of transactions, and thus the fraction of world trade handled through intermediation will decline. However, a decline in travel costs will shrink cost differentials between marketplaces and will lead some buyers to shift from small (local) marketplaces to larger (more distant) ones. For large trading centres, a decline in travel costs may not imply a fall in business. Despite the secular decline in transportation costs, Sung (1991, pp. 33–9) found that the share of world exports handled as re-exports by Hong Kong and Singapore has risen since 1962 and 1975 respectively.

Hong Kong's role in China's trade

Hong Kong's role as a middleman in the Mainland's trade takes the following forms:

1 Re-exports (entrepôt trade): Hong Kong companies buy goods outside Hong Kong for resale elsewhere, and the goods are imported into Hong Kong for re-exporting. The goods clear customs twice, the first time during importation and the second time during exportation.
2 Middleman in offshore trade: the goods do not go through Hong Kong customs. Hong Kong firms play a role in *merchanting* or *merchandising*:
   (a) merchanting – Hong Kong traders buy goods outside Hong Kong for export elsewhere, and such goods do not go through Hong Kong customs;
   (b) merchandising – Hong Kong traders arrange on behalf of buyers/ sellers outside Hong Kong the purchases/sales of goods without taking ownership of the goods involved; such goods do not go through Hong Kong customs.

Hong Kong has detailed statistics on its entrepôt trade since 1966. However, offshore trade does not go through Hong Kong customs, and its value can only be obtained through surveys. The Hong Kong Trade Development Council conducted such surveys for 1991, 1994 and 1997. Since 2000, the Census and Statistics Department of the Hong Kong government has conducted more detailed surveys every year. While complete statistics on offshore trade are only available for 2002–3, offshore trade in earlier years can be estimated with a reasonable degree of accuracy. The details of these estimations are given in the Appendix.

Offshore trade was small before 1991 because the Mainland's container ports were underdeveloped. Mainland cargo was carried to Hong Kong by land or barges for containerization and delivery overseas. The Mainland did not allow foreign investment in ports until Deng Xiaoping's historic 1992 southern tour in support of economic reforms. Since then, many container ports have been developed with the help of foreign capital, especially that of Hong Kong's premier conglomerate, Hutchison Whampoa. Since the mid-1990s, Shenzhen's burgeoning container ports have started to compete with Hong Kong. As shipping through Hong Kong involves significantly higher costs, some of the re-exports through Hong Kong have been diverted to offshore trade via Shenzhen ports.

It should be noted that Hong Kong faces stiffer competition in shipping than in trading because shipping requires container terminals and cargo areas which are relatively land-intensive. Trading activities (negotiation, arbitration, search, marketing, trade financing and documentation) are less land-intensive because trading firms can be housed in skyscrapers. While agglomeration increases efficiency, it also leads to rising costs, especially land costs. Unlike entrepôt trade, offshore trade does not require shipping through Hong Kong. Theory predicts that, with a rise in costs in Hong Kong, there will be diversion from entrepôt trade to offshore trade. In the same vein, trade-supporting services that are related directly to physical movement of cargo (e.g., shipping, trucking, warehousing) will decline relative to services not directly related to physical movement of cargo (e.g., search, negotiation, arbitration, trade financing, insurance, and documentation). This trend has been confirmed by a survey of Hong Kong companies (Hong Kong Trade Development Council, 1998).

Hong Kong's Mainland-related entrepôt trade and offshore trade

Figure 8.1 shows Hong Kong's Mainland-related entrepôt trade and offshore trade. It should be noted that 'Mainland related-trade' includes not only exports to the Mainland, but also Hong Kong's exports of Mainland goods to third economies. Mainland-related entrepôt trade grew extremely rapidly from US$1,265 million in 1979 to US$111,636 million in 1995, an average annual rate of over 32 per cent. The average annual rate of growth slowed to 6.6 per cent during 1995–7 because of competition from Shenzhen ports. The Asian Financial Crisis and the terrorist of attack of 11 September aggravated the situation, leading to negative growth or stagnation of Hong Kong's Mainland-related entrepôt trade during 1997–2001. However, Mainland-related entrepôt trade soared during 2001–4, growing at an average annual rate of 16.5 per cent. This is mainly due to the very rapid growth of the Mainland's trade (average annual rate of 31.3 per cent) after WTO entry. This

Figure 8.1   Hong Kong's Mainland-related entrepôt trade and offshore trade

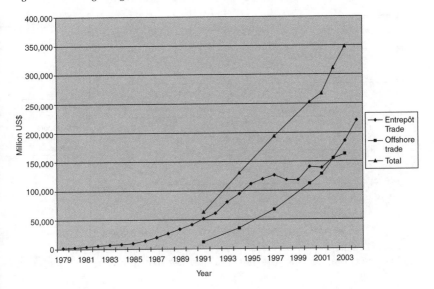

hypergrowth temporarily outstripped the capacity of Shenzhen ports. Through competition from Shenzhen ports, Hong Kong's Mainland-related entrepôt trade would stagnate if the Mainland's trade growth was moderate, but would exhibit healthy growth if it was spectacular.

Hong Kong's Mainland-related offshore trade grew much faster than its Mainland-related entrepôt trade. From 1997 to 2003, the average annual rate of the growth of the former was 16 per cent, compared to the latter's 6.5 per cent. Despite competition from Shenzhen ports, Hong Kong's Mainland-related offshore trade continued to exhibit healthy growth. By the early 2000s, Hong Kong's Mainland-related offshore trade had become nearly as large as its Mainland-related entrepôt trade.

Figure 8.2 shows the share of Mainland's trade handled by Hong Kong in the forms of entrepôt trade and offshore trade. The share handled as Hong Kong's entrepôt trade rose rapidly in the first 15 years of the reform era; it peaked in the mid-1990s at 41 per cent, and then declined to 22 per cent in 2003. The share handled as Hong Kong's offshore trade rose from 9 per cent in 1991 to a peak of 25 per cent in 2002, but declined to 19 per cent in 2003. The two shares combined peaked at 60 per cent in 1997, and declined to 41 per cent in 2003. Though the absolute value of Mainland's trade handled by Hong Kong has continued to grow quite rapidly, the share of Mainland's trade has fallen quite sharply due to the much more rapid growth of Mainland's trade.

Figure 8.2   Share of Mainland's trade handled by Hong Kong

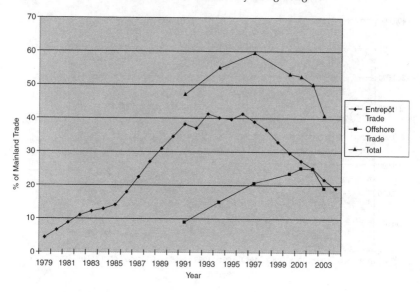

Gross margin of Hong Kong's Mainland-related trade

There have been two factors at work in the rapid growth of Hong Kong's Mainland-related offshore trade: namely, the expansion of Hong Kong's production base in South China, and the diversion to offshore trade from entrepôt trade. In terms of income and employment-creation for Hong Kong, the first factor is beneficial but the second factor is harmful because offshore trade bypasses the Hong Kong port.

Figure 8.3 shows the gross margin of Hong Kong's Mainland-related trade since 2000, the first year for which such data are available. The gross margin overstates total value-added slightly because leakages due to imported inputs used in the production of trading services are not deducted. However, such leakages are not large because services do not use a lot of imported inputs.[1]

While the value of Hong Kong's Mainland-related offshore trade was nearly as large as its Mainland-related entrepôt trade, the gross margin of offshore trade was much lower as it bypassed the port of Hong Kong. In 2003, the rates of gross margin for Hong Kong's Mainland-related entrepôt trade and offshore trade were 20.4 per cent and 8.6 per cent, respectively.

The rate of gross margin for Hong Kong's Mainland-related trade was quite high because such trade mainly involved trade between Hong Kong

Figure 8.3 Gross margin of Hong Kong's Mainland-related entrepôt trade and off-shore trade (US$ million)

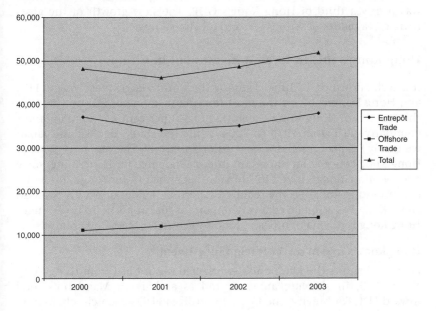

firms with their subsidiaries in South China. Hong Kong firms supply their factories in South China with raw materials imported from third countries, and the output is often re-exported through Hong Kong to third countries. Hong Kong is usually involved in many high value-adding activities in the production chain (e.g., order-taking, product design, sourcing of inputs, production management, financing, exporting, and marketing), while the labour-intensive and low value-adding processing is done in the Mainland (Sung, 2001, pp. 220–3).

From 2000 to 2003, while the growth of Mainland's trade handled by Hong Kong was rapid (an average annual rate of 11.4 per cent), the growth of the gross margin generated by such trade was slow (average annual rate of 2.5 per cent). This is partly due to the diversion from entrepôt trade to offshore trade. Moreover, from 2000 to 2003, the rate of gross margin of Hong Kong's Mainland-related entrepôt trade fell from 26.3 per cent to 20.4 per cent, while that of Hong Kong's offshore trade also fell, from 9.9 per cent to 8.6 per cent. This indicates that the Mainland has been able to perform more steps in the production chain, leaving less value-adding activities for Hong Kong.

International trade is the most important sector of the Hong Kong economy. In 2003, the gross margin of Hong Kong's Mainland-related trade was nearly a third of Hong Kong's GDP. The slow growth of the gross margin is a matter of serious concern for Hong Kong.

Hong Kong's role in foreign investment in China

It is well known that China is among the world's largest receivers of FDI, and Hong Kong is by far the most important source of FDI destined for the Mainland. Hong Kong accounted for 43 per cent of the Mainland's cumulative FDI from 1979 to 2004, while the shares of USA and Japan were only 8.5 per cent and 8.3 per cent respectively. The very large share of Hong Kong conceals an important intermediary role for Hong Kong, since many multinationals invest in China through their Hong Kong subsidiaries because Hong Kong has the required expertise. Besides direct investment, Hong Kong has also played a very important role in portfolio investment. Hong Kong is the major offshore funding centre for Mainland enterprises.

Hong Kong's role in direct foreign investment

Figure 8.4 shows the Mainland's contracted inward FDI from Hong Kong since 1979, in absolute amounts and as a share of Mainland's total inward FDI. For brevity, the figure for utilized FDI, which closely follows contracted FDI, is not shown. As expected, contracted FDI depends on expectations. It leads utilized FDI and is also more volatile.

Figure 8.4   Mainland's contracted FDI from Hong Kong

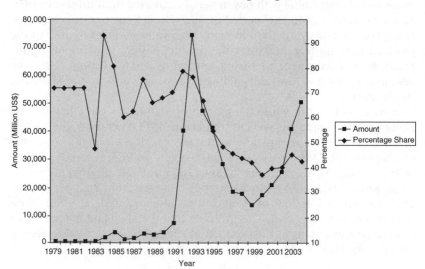

Hong Kong investors are very sensitive to Mainland's investment environment, and they were the first to rush into the China market after Deng Xiaoping's tour in support of economic reforms in early 1992. Hong Kong's investment in China soared, and Hong Kong's share of contracted and utilized FDI in China reached highs of 69 per cent and 68 per cent respectively in 1992. As other investors jumped on the China bandwagon, Hong Kong's shares declined after 1992.

Hong Kong's contracted FDI in China soared from US$3.8 billion in 1990 to a record of US$74 billion in 1993, but subsequently declined as the rise was too sharp to be sustainable. The Asian Financial Crisis aggravated the fall, and contracted FDI from Hong Kong fell to a low of US$ 13 billion in 1999. Since 2000 the Sino–US agreement signed in late 1999 on China's WTO entry has led to a sharp rebound in contracted FDI from Hong Kong, reaching a high of US$ 50 billion in 2004. The trend in utilized FDI was similar, but the fluctuations have been less pronounced.

Hong Kong's share of Mainland contracted FDI fell rapidly from 69 per cent in 1992 to a low of 27 per cent in 2000 in the aftermath of the Asian Financial Crisis, but recovered to reach 33 per cent in 2004. While the trend in utilized FDI lagged behind contracted FDI, the sharp decline in Hong Kong's share after 1992 appears to have stabilized at slightly over 30 per cent by 2003.

As mentioned above, many multinationals invest in the Mainland through Hong Kong subsidiaries, including Mainland enterprises that plan to take advantage of preferential treatment given to foreign investors. This implies that Hong Kong's direct investment in the Mainland is overstated. However, the fact that many multinationals invest in China via Hong Kong also implies that Hong Kong is an important intermediary in China's inward FDI.

While the Mainland's inward FDI from Hong Kong is overstated by the amount of non-Hong-Kong capital channelled via Hong Kong, it is understated by the amount of Hong Kong capital channelled to the Mainland via the tax haven economies in the Caribbean. When, in 1982, China announced its intention to take Hong Kong back in 1997, Hong Kong's large firms tried to insure against possible nationalization by registering in tax haven economies. By mid-1993, some 60 per cent of all listed companies in Hong Kong had moved their registration overseas (Sung, 2005, p. 26). As a result, tax haven economies accounted for 60 per cent of Hong Kong's outward FDI in 2000. A substantial amount of Hong Kong's investment in the Mainland is now likely to be channelled via the Caribbean. Many Taiwanese and Mainland companies that had channelled their investment to the Mainland via Hong Kong subsidiaries likewise shifted their registration from Hong Kong to offshore financial centres as insurance against possible intervention from the Mainland after the 1997 handover (Sung, 2005, p. 29). As a result, tax haven economies have become the second-largest investor in the Mainland in the late 1990s.

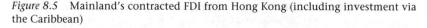

Figure 8.5 Mainland's contracted FDI from Hong Kong (including investment via the Caribbean)

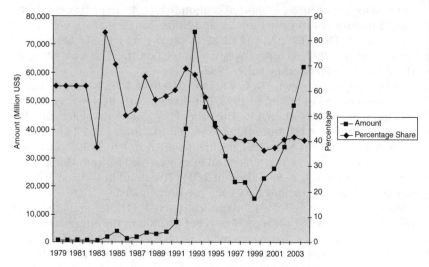

The decline of Hong Kong's share in the Mainland's inward FDI in recent years is overstated because Hong Kong firms (and also Hong Kong subsidiaries of Taiwanese and Mainland firms) are increasingly investing in the Mainland via the Caribbean. To correct for this bias, we assume in Figure 8.5 that half of the FDI from the Caribbean in the Mainland came from Hong Kong. While this guestimate is rough, it is not unreasonable as Hong Kong has consistently been the largest investor in the Mainland. Under this assumption, the decline of Hong Kong's share in Mainland's FDI is less pronounced, and Hong Kong's share in contracted and utilized FDI has stabilized at around 40 per cent in recent years. In a nutshell, Hong Kong's share of China's inward FDI is still very substantial.

Hong Kong's role in portfolio investment

Hong Kong has become the premier offshore centre for the funding of Chinese enterprises. In 1992, China approved the public listing of selective state enterprises in the Hong Kong stock market and their shares are popularly called H-shares. Besides tapping external funds, listing in Hong Kong also speeds up China's enterprise reforms, since listed firms have to follow international accounting standards.

Listed Hong Kong companies controlled by Mainland Chinese shareholders have been active in Hong Kong's stock market since the 1980s. A China-Affiliated Corporations Index, or Red Chips Index, was introduced by the Hang Seng Bank on 16 June 1997 in response to investor interests in Red Chips. By May 1997, H-shares and Red Chips had a market capitalization of US$ 56 billion, or 11 per cent of Hong Kong's stock market (Sung, 2005, p. 115).

By the end of 2004, 301 Mainland companies (H-shares, Red Chips, and other Mainland companies) were listed in Hong Kong with a total market capitalization of US$256 billion, which was 30 per cent of Hong Kong's total. Total funds raised by these companies in the previous 11 years amounted to US$102 billion (Hong Kong Trade and Development Council, 2005).

The role of Hong Kong in Mainland China's capital market goes far beyond being an important channel for raising capital. As the Mainland's capital markets are immature and highly distorted, Hong Kong provides the best market for pricing the risks of investment in the Mainland's listed enterprises. It is no accident that the vast majority of Mainland enterprises listed overseas are listed in Hong Kong. While a few are also listed in other overseas markets, more than 70 per cent of their trading is conducted in Hong Kong (Ma, 2005, p. 3).

Hong Kong as a service hub

Besides trade, transportation and financing, Hong Kong is also a hub for professional services and the regional headquarters of multinational companies. Hong Kong has a strong pool of professional service providers, such as accountants, lawyers and bankers who are familiar with the business environment of the Mainland.

While some prominent multinational companies have moved their regional headquarters from Hong Kong to Shanghai or other Mainland cities, the number of regional headquarters and representative offices of multinational companies in Hong Kong grew from 3,001 in mid-2000 to 3,609 in mid-2004. There was also a substantial growth in the number of persons engaged in these companies, from 135,000 in mid-2000 to 193,000 in mid-2004.[2]

The Mainland–Hong Kong CEPA (Closer Economic Partnership Arrangement), which is a Free Trade Area agreement between the Mainland and Hong Kong, gives Hong Kong service providers preferential access to the Mainland market. The agreement has strengthened the status of Hong Kong as China's premier service hub.

While Hong Kong is China's premier service hub, Shanghai is a serious rival. Shanghai has the advantage of location, since it is situated at the mouth of the Yangzi Delta, the largest and most prosperous region in China. But although Shanghai is set to become the domestic financial centre of China, it cannot compete with Hong Kong as a regional or international centre. Shanghai cannot become a serious contender as a regional or international financial centre unless the Renminbi can achieve convertibility on the capital account. Although China has achieved convertibility in merchandise trade, capital account convertibility will take much longer.

The development of infrastructure and services skills is a time-consuming and capital-intensive process. Moreover, the development of services is highly dependent on the existence of a clean, transparent, and even-handed regulatory environment. Though Shanghai is developing its financial institutions, a reputable legal framework and regulatory system takes time to evolve and mature. Given the corruption, inefficiency and immensity of China's bureaucracy, the development of an efficient international service and financial centre may prove difficult. In the context of China, a reputable legal and regulatory system needs political reforms, which are more time-consuming and risky than economic reforms.

Conclusion

The rapid development of services in the Mainland does not imply the demise of Hong Kong as China's premier service hub. While the shares of China's foreign trade and investment handled by Hong Kong have declined, the absolute volumes of Mainland-related trade and investment handled by Hong Kong are still growing. The demand for intermediation of the Mainland has increased enormously, partly because of rapid economic growth, and partly because of the continuing decentralization of the Chinese economy, which creates tremendous need for intermediation. Moreover, Hong Kong is very efficient in providing intermediary services due to economies of scale and agglomeration in such activities. Despite competition from rival hubs such as Shenzhen and Shanghai, Hong Kong still handles some 40 per cent of the Mainland's foreign trade and inward foreign direct investment.

Nevertheless, Hong Kong does face serious challenges from rival hubs. With rapid development of the service sector, the Mainland is able to undertake more steps in the production chain, leaving fewer value-adding services for Hong Kong. As Hong Kong's costs are much higher than those on the Mainland, Hong Kong has to concentrate on higher value activities that are least affected by high factor costs: for example, trading, business services and financial services. Such services are least affected by high land prices and wages because they are neither land-intensive nor labour-intensive. New York and London long ago lost their comparative advantage in manufacturing, but their positions in trading, business and finance remain formidable.

As Hong Kong is the Mainland's premier services hub, Hong Kong's exports of Mainland-related services are extremely large. Table 8.1 shows that Hong Kong's exports of Mainland-related services in 2003 were US$61.1 billion, or 37 per cent of Hong Kong's GDP. The gross margin of Hong Kong's Mainland-related entrepôt trade, which is not usually classified under export of services, is regarded as service exports in the table because the gross margin of entrepôt trade conceptually represents services

Table 8.1 Hong Kong's Mainland-related services exports, 2003 (US$billion)

| | | Services related to Mainland's trade | | | | | | | |
| | Gross margin of entrepôt trade | Offshore trade | | | Sub-total | Transportation | Tourism | Other services | Total |
		Merchanting	Merchandising	Sub-total					
	37.8	12.9	2.0	14.9	52.7	2.4	4.4	1.6	61.1
(i)	(24.1)	(8.2)	(1.2)	(9.4)	(33.5)	(1.5)	(2.7)	(1.0)	(38.7)
(ii)	(61.9)	(21.1)	(3.3)	(24.4)	(86.3)	(3.9)	(7.2)	(2.6)	(100)

(i) Per centage share to Hong Kong's GDP.
(ii) Per centage share to total.

Source: See text for estimation of services related to the Mainland's trade. Other data are taken from *Report on Hong Kong Trade in Services for 2003*, Hong Kong: Census and Statistics Department.

embodied in re-exports. The 2003 gross margin was US$37.8 billion, or 62 per cent of Hong Kong's exports of Mainland-related services. Services related to Mainland's trade (entrepôt trade and offshore trade) were US$52.7 billion, or 86 per cent of Hong Kong's exports of Mainland-related services.

Table 8.1 shows that Hong Kong's exports of Mainland-related services are mainly associated with flows of goods and people: for example, services related to Mainland's trade (86.3 per cent), transportation (3.9 per cent), and tourism (7.2 per cent). These three items added up to 97.4 per cent of the total. Other services (exports of pure services not related to flows of goods and people, e.g., finance, insurance, professional, business, and social services) were only US$1.6 billion, or 2.6 per cent of the total. This shows that the Mainland's markets for pure services are not yet very open. While Hong Kong's exports of services (including financing and business services) embodied in Mainland-related trade are large, exports of pure services, especially pure services not related to flows of goods and people, are small.

With entry to the WTO, China is committed to opening its service sectors in 2005–6. With preferential access for Hong Kong's service providers under the Mainland-Hong Kong CEPA, and Hong Kong's comparative advantage in services, liberalization of the Mainland's services will be highly advantageous for Hong Kong.

Appendix: estimating Hong Kong's offshore trade

Offshore trade includes *merchanting* and *merchandising*. Government surveys give data on the value of goods and gross margin in merchanting for 2000–3, but comparable data on merchandising are only available for 2002–3. For 2000–1, only the gross margin of the merchandising of the Mainland's imports is available. Table A8.1 shows the estimation of the value of goods and gross margin of merchandising. The estimation assumes that the commission rate of merchandising for 2001–2 is the same as the average for 2002–3. The estimation should be fairly robust since the commission rate does not appear to change a lot. Moreover, merchandising is small relative to merchanting. For instance, in 2003, a year for which hard data are available, the gross margin of merchandising was less than 9 per cent of that of merchanting. Adding the estimated data of merchandising to that of merchanting gives the data of offshore trade from 2000–1.

Table A8.2 shows Mainland's trade handled by Hong Kong as re-exports (entrepôt trade) and as offshore trade. The estimation of offshore trade from 2000 to 2003 is described above. For the years 1991, 1994 and 1997, data on *Hong Kong's offshore exports of Mainland goods* are available from surveys of the Hong Kong Trade Development Council. However, data on *Hong Kong's offshore imports for the Mainland* are not available. They are estimated here on the assumption that the ratio of offshore trade to entrepôt trade on the import side is the same as that on the export side. In other words, the ratio of *offshore imports* to *Hong Kong's re-exports to the Mainland* is the same as the ratio of *offshore exports* to *Hong Kong's re-exports of Mainland goods*.

Table A8.1 Hong Kong's offshore merchandising of Mainland-related trade (US$million)

	Mainland's exports			Mainland's imports			Mainland's trade	
	Gross margin	Value of goods[a]	Commission rate (%)	Gross margin	Value of goods[a]	Commission rate (%)	Gross margin	Value of goods
2000	348[b]	10,306	4.25[d]	175[c]	5,844	3.0[d]	613	16,149
2001	443[b]	10,424	4.25[d]	177[c]	5,906	3.0[d]	620	16,330
2002	694[c]	17,119	4.1[c]	288[c]	9,282	3.1[c]	982	26,401
2003	811[c]	18,252	4.4[c]	307[c]	10,575	2.9[c]	1,118	28,827

[a] Values of goods are obtained by dividing the gross margin by the commission rate.
[b] Taken to be 2.5 times (ratio for 2002–3) of the gross margin of the merchanting of the Mainland's imports.
[c] Data taken from Report.
[d] Average commission rate for 2002–3.

Source: Report on Hong Kong Trade in Services Statistics for 2003, Census and Statistics Department, Hong Kong

Table A8.2   The Mainland's trade handled by Hong Kong (US$million)

Year	As HK's re-exports	As HK's offshore trade	Total
1991	51,952[a]	12,122[b]	64,074
	(38.3)	(8.9)	(47.2)
1994	94,819[a]	35,611[b]	130,430
	(40.1)	(15.0)	(55.1)
1997	126,758[a]	67,006[b]	193,764
	(39.0)	(20.6)	(59.6)
2000	140,632[a]	111,422[c]	252,054
	(29.7)	(23.5)	(53.1)
2001	139,318[a]	128,433[c]	267,751
	(27.3)	(25.2)	(52.5)
2002	155,837	154,980[c]	310,817
	(25.1)	(25.0)	(50.1)
2003	185,149[a]	162,941[c]	348,090
	(21.8)	(19.1)	(40.9)
2004	220,177	–	–
	(19.1)	–	–

Figures in brackets represent percentage share to China's trade.
[a] Taken from Table 4.2 of Sung 2005:78
[b] Estimated from ratio of HK's offshore exports of Mainland origin to HK's re-exports of
  Mainland origin. See text for method of estimation. The ratios are taken from surveys of the
  Hong Kong Trade Development Council (HKTDC): That for 1991 is from HKTDC 1996:8, and
  those for 1994 & 1997 are from HKTDC 2002:8.
[c] Sum of off-shore merchandising (Table A8.1) and merchanting (see source in Table A8.1).

Notes

1   In the early 2000s, the leakage of Hong Kong's import/export trade sector was no
  more than 5 per cent (Sung, 2004, Table 3.5).
2   Census and Statistics Department, Hong Kong, 2000 and 2004, *Report on Annual
  Survey of Regional Offices Representing Overseas Companies in Hong Kong*, Hong
  Kong.

References

Hicks, John (1969), *A Theory of Economic History*, London: Oxford University Press.
Hong Kong Trade Development Council (1996), *Hong Kong's Trade and Trade Sup-
  porting Services*, Hong Kong, April.
Hong Kong Trade Development Council (1998), *The Rise in Offshore Trade and
  Offshore Investment*, Hong Kong, September.
Hong Kong Trade Development Council (2002), *Hong Kong's Trade and Trade
  Supporting Services: New Developments and Prospects*, Hong Kong, January.
Hong Kong Trade Development Council (2005), *Economic and Trade Information on
  Hong Kong*, Hong Kong, June (http://www.tdctrade.com/main/economic.htm).
Lucas, Robert (1985), 'The Mechanics of Economic Development', Marshall Lecture,
  Cambridge University, Cambridge.

Ma, Frederick (2005), 'Elements of Successful M&A in China', Speech by the Secretary for Financial Services and the Treasury, Mr Frederic Ma, at the Young Entrepreneurs' Organization Luncheon, Hong Kong, 9 April.

Sung, Yun-Wing (1991), *The China–Hong Kong Connection: The Key to China's Open-Door Policy*, Cambridge: Cambridge University Press.

Sung, Yun-Wing (2001), 'Export-Oriented Foreign Direct Investment in the People's Republic of China: Division of Value Added between Source and Host Economies', in Leonard K. Cheng and Henryk Kierzkowski (eds), *Global Production and Trade in East Asia*, Boston, MA: Kluwer Academic, 207–25.

Sung, Yun-Wing (2004), 'Hong Kong's Economic Integration with the Pearl River Delta: Quantifying the Benefits and Costs', mimeograph.

Sung, Yun-Wing (2005), *The Emergence of Greater China: The Economic Integration of Mainland China, Taiwan and Hong Kong*, Basingstoke and New York: Palgrave Macmillan.

Townsend, R.M. (1978), 'Intermediation with Costly Bilateral Exchange', *Review of Economic Studies*, 45, 417–25.

Yamamura, Kozo (1976), 'General Trading Companies in Japan: Their Origins and Growth', in Hugh Patrick (ed.), *Japanese Industrialization and its Social Consequences*, Berkeley, CA: University of California Press.

9
Market Integration between Hong Kong and the Chinese Mainland*

C. Simon Fan, Na Li and Xiangdong Wei

Introduction

Over the years, Hong Kong has developed close economic links with the Chinese Mainland, and has benefited greatly from China's open-door policy and economic reforms since 1979. The correlation between the cyclical components of Hong Kong's GDP and industrial production in China rose sharply in the late 1980s and has remained high during the 1990s. This is partly explained by the expansion of bilateral trade flows between Hong Kong and China. More recently, with Hong Kong's return to China in 1997 and the implementation of the Mainland and Hong Kong Closer Economic Partnership Arrangement (CEPA) in January 2004, the economies of Hong Kong and the Chinese Mainland are becoming even more closely related. The Mainland is now Hong Kong's largest trading partner, accounting for over 40 per cent of Hong Kong's total trade value. Reciprocally, Hong Kong has become the Mainland's third largest trading partner after Japan and the US in recent years.

There are many studies on the economic integration between Hong Kong and the Mainland, particularly in the areas of trade and investment. However, studies on how such economic links affect the market integration between these two sides are still rare. This chapter will provide a quantitative assessment of the degree of market integration between Hong Kong and the Chinese Mainland. Using a panel of 17 commodity prices from Hong Kong and four major Mainland cities (Beijing, Shanghai, Shenzhen and Guangzhou) for a period of almost 100 months, we estimate whether relative prices exhibited convergence between Hong Kong and the Mainland cities, and identify the speed of convergence in relative prices in the five cities. Such a study not only sheds light on how closely the economies of Hong Kong and

*The financial support from the Hong Kong Research Grant Council Competitive Earmarked Grant (LU3112/03H) and Lingnan University Direct Allocation Grant (DS03A1) is gratefully acknowledged.

the Mainland are integrated, but also provides evidence on the extent of market forces operating in the Mainland economies.

Furthermore, the test of price convergence between Hong Kong and the Mainland can also be viewed as another attempt to test the theory of PPP (purchasing power parity) or LOP (law of one price) in an already well-established field of study in international economics. In recent years, there has been a renewed interest in the study of PPP/LOP, fuelled by newly found datasets or methodologies. For example, Engel and Rogers (1994) examine the nature of the deviation from purchasing power parity, using price data for the US and Canada. They found that price deviation is much higher for two cities located in different countries than for two equidistant cities in the same countries, and that national borders are an additional contributor to cross-country price variability beyond transportation costs. Wei and Parsley (1995) used a dataset of 27 tradable goods prices in the US and Japan, and showed that a simple average of good-level real exchange rates tracks the normal exchange rate well, suggesting strong evidence of sticky prices. Fan and Wei (2005) utilize the recently developed econometric methods of panel unit root tests and non-linear mean-reversion to investigate the convergence to the law of one price in China. They find that prices did converge to the law of one price in China for an overwhelming majority of goods and services in a large dataset. Moreover, they discover that the patterns of price convergence in the transitional economy of China are similar to those obtained in the OECD countries.

Background information

The development of the market economy in China

Over the past two decades, China has successfully combined a market mechanism with its cardinal public ownership system, which ushered in an era of unprecedented progress. In particular, encouraged by Deng Xiaoping's exhortation during his famous tour of southern China in 1992, China experienced a major increase in foreign and domestic investment and began to work towards establishing a market-oriented economy. Today non-state economies account for about half of the country's GDP, and the market mechanism is playing a fundamental role in the economic life of China.

In order to extend the regulatory function of the market, the Chinese government has gradually reduced the categories of products under central planning, eliminated the restriction that enterprises were only allowed to engage in production but not in commercial operation, and abolished the practice of the state fixing commodity prices. As a result, Chinese firms have been subject to less and less government control in their decisions to purchase, produce and sell. Enterprises have been able to organize and establish wholesale markets and trading centres; the wholesale and retail commercial systems have been restructured; and the non-state sector has been encouraged to engage in commercial activities.

Through the reform, the unitary pattern in which the public economy monopolized commercial activities has been gradually broken up, and the commodity market has been established and has operated efficiently. Before 1978, some 791 types of product were under state plans in production and sales. Now, however, only five of them are still controlled by the government, while the rest are subject to the coordination of the market mechanism. Nowadays, department stores, supermarkets and chain stores are scattered everywhere in both rural and urban areas. In 1999, China had 1,800 chain stores, over 2,000 various flea markets, over 1,000 leasing enterprises, and over 1,000 auction firms. Moreover, electronic commercial business has developed rapidly and modern logistic firms have replaced traditional storage and transport enterprises. A great variety of food, clothing and other commodities satisfies the needs of consumers. Total market sales grew every year. In 1999, the rural market achieved 1,204.3 billion Yuans' sales of consumer goods, which is 11.4 times the figure in 1978; the urban market achieved 1,909.2 billion Yuans' sales of consumer goods, 37.8 times the figure in 1978.

The price reform was also carried out gradually and continuously. The government has classified prices into three general categories: the price fixed by the state, the price subjected to the state's 'guidance', and the market price. The control of grain prices was first loosened in 1979, and the government started to deregulate the prices of most commodities in 1985. In 1992, the number of categories of government-priced commodities was slashed from 737 to 89, which marked the formation of a market economy in China. By 1999, the pricing of 95 per cent of consumer goods and 80 per cent of investment goods were largely determined by the market. In 2001, China successfully acceded to the World Trade Organization, which demonstrates that a fully-fledged 'socialist market system' is taking shape in China as a result of its determination to become part of the global market economy.

Economic integration between the Chinese Mainland and Hong Kong

China's economic relationship with Hong Kong has been getting stronger year by year, especially after the Hong Kong's return to China in 1997. After the Second World War, the abundant supply of inexpensive labour supported the rapid growth of Hong Kong's manufacturing sector until the 1970s. By the late 1970s, however, Hong Kong's competitiveness had started to erode as land and labour costs rose. Thus, when China embarked on its economic reform in 1979, manufacturing industries started to relocate from Hong Kong to southern China, where labour and land costs were much lower. By the mid-1990s, according to private estimates, about 25,000 Hong Kong firms were operating plants, employing a total of 4.5 million workers, in southern China.

The substantial movement of manufacturing operations from Hong Kong into Mainland China led to drastic structural change in Hong Kong. Export-oriented Hong Kong firms in China, together with the sustained rapid increase in Chinese domestic firms' exports, boosted the development of supporting service industries in Hong Kong, most notably in trade and financial services. As a result, Mainland China and Hong Kong have become increasingly closely linked. For example, due to the expansion of bilateral trade flows between Hong Kong and China, the correlation between the cyclical components of Hong Kong's GDP and industrial production in China rose sharply in the late 1980s and has remained high during the 1990s.

One major force shaping Hong Kong is its economic integration with the Pearl River Delta area. The relocation of Hong Kong's manufacturing facilities to its northern border over the past 25 years has to a great extent tied Hong Kong's export performance to manufacturing activities undertaken in its immediate hinterland. Re-exports now account for nearly 90 per cent of Hong Kong's exports, the bulk of which either originate from or go to the Mainland. As such, the gradual shift in the Mainland's export gravity from the Pearl River Delta area to eastern and northern China in recent years is a cause for concern. In the first 10 months of 2001, Hong Kong's re-exports declined by 3.4 per cent, while the Mainland's exports rose by 6.1 per cent, reflecting this trend as well as an improvement in port facilities in Shenzhen.

With China's WTO accession in 2001, it is possible for Hong Kong and other overseas companies to be major stakeholders in Mainland entities across a wide range of sectors. They will have more and more access to the Mainland market as domestic entities enjoying national treatment. Accession will be a defining moment in terms of the Mainland's further integration with the world economy and for Hong Kong's pivotal role in that process. Hong Kong is the Mainland's most important trade partner, handling over 40 per cent of China's trade volume. Also, it is the Mainland's largest source of foreign direct investment. The economic fortunes of both China and Hong Kong will be influenced more and more by the performance of each other's economy, and both must continue to adjust to the rapidly changing environment in order to realize growth potential.

Price convergence and market integration between Hong Kong and the Chinese Mainland

In this section, we first describe the data. Then, we discuss the empirical approaches used for this study (i.e., the panel unit root tests developed by Levin, Lin and Chu, 2002). Finally, we present and analyse the empirical findings.

The data

The study used a panel dataset of monthly product prices from Hong Kong, Beijing, Shanghai, Shenzhen and Guangzhou for the period from January

1997 to September 2002. The price data for Chinese Mainland cities were collected from the China Price Information Centre (under the National Development and Reform Centre). These are actual price data for products ranging from agricultural products, industrial materials to services. For the corresponding Hong Kong data, we used monthly consumer price index (CPI) data published by the Hong Kong Census and Statistics Department. We selected only those price indices that are for very specific type of goods or services to match with the corresponding goods or services in Chinese Mainland (e.g., the price index for beef in Hong Kong is used to derive the price for beef in Hong Kong and then this is matched with price for beef in the Mainland). As the Hong Kong data are not actual price data but indices, we went to the actual market to obtain the Hong Kong spot price data in September 2002. Then, we converted all price indices into actual prices. We further converted all Hong Kong prices from Hong Kong dollars into Renminbi (Yuan) and also use the same measurement unit as the corresponding prices for the products in the Mainland.

For the purpose of studying price convergence, we need to choose prices for reasonably homogeneous products across these cities. For the products in the Mainland, they were all meant to be specific homogeneous products when collected by the government. However, the Hong Kong data were mostly for different categories of products, rather than specific products, so we only managed to match 17 products and services from these two data sources, which were all by and large quite specific and could be reasonably viewed as homogeneous. This list of 17 products and services and their simple descriptive statistics are shown in Table 9.1.

In Table 9.1, we further group these 17 products and services into three groups: tradable, semi-tradable and services. The tradable consists of 10 products: pork, beef, rice, eggs, sugar, edible oils, Chinese wines, beer, cigarettes and motor fuel. Semi-tradable goods, which include jewellery, electricity and hair dressing, are so classified as it may be debatable whether they can be traded or not. For example, Hong Kong imports electricity from Dayawan nuclear power station, which is within the Mainland. There are also electricity networks across different regions that belong to some large state-owned electricity suppliers within China. One could also argue that since so many Hong Kong residents go to Shenzhen for hair-cutting services regularly, haircuts may also be viewed as tradable, at least between Shenzhen and Hong Kong. Jewellery was listed under this category simply due to the fact that the Chinese Customs set limit on the quantity of jewellery a traveller can bring into China. The remaining four categories fall into the category of services; they are medical services (hospital in-patient fees per day), school tuition fees, taxi fares, and liquefied petroleum gas.

For the purpose of testing price convergence and market integration, the use of tradable goods may already be sufficient. We also include some apparently non-tradable goods or services in the dataset for the following two reasons. First, it is increasingly difficult to draw a clear line between

Table 9.1 Descriptive statistics of prices: 1

	Mean (Mainland)	Mean (Hong Kong and Mainland)
Tradable:		
Pork ($/Jin)	8.328	11.85
Beef ($/Jin)	8.399	14.22
Rice ($/Jin)	1.5	2.056
Eggs ($/Jin)	2.907	3.961
Sugar ($/Jin)	2.367	2.971
Edible oils ($/kg)	4.025	3.367
Motor fuel ($/litre)	3314.8	5013.7
Chinese wines ($/bottle)	17.712	22.517
Beer ($/tin)	3.802	4.912
Cigarettes ($/pack)	9.704	15.503
Semi-tradable:		
Jewellery ($/g)	111.333	101.7
Electricity ($/Joule)	58.363	68.539
Hair-dressing ($/one)	12	33.86
Service:		
Petroleum gas ($/bottle)	4.604	14.552
Taxi fares ($/km)	2.152	3.211
High school tuition fees ($/semester)	482.75	1485.1
Hospital fees ($/day)	21.732	26.95

Sample: 276 for Mainland China
345 for Hong Kong and Mainland

tradable and non-tradable commodities, especially under the close economic ties between Hong Kong and the Mainland. Second, the inclusion of some of the non-tradable goods may enable us to look at other aspects of convergence, such as living standards and institutional arrangements. In what follows, we test price convergence based on both individual products and these product groups, so the classification here should not greatly influence the results of our study.

The methodology

Panel unit root tests have been widely applied in the testing of PPP/LOP in recent years. This is due partly to the fact that they are more powerful than unit root tests for a single time series data and partly to the availability of panel data with a long time span. Specifically, the test of price convergence is typically carried out by estimating the following equation:

$$\Delta q_{i,k,t} = \alpha_{i,k} + \beta q_{i,k,t-1} + \sum_{n=1}^{N} \gamma_n \, \Delta q_{i,k,t-n} + \varepsilon_{i,k,t} \tag{9.1}$$

where $q_{i,k,t}$ is the log difference in the price of product i in city k, relative to the mean price of all cities for commodity i at time t, and Δ is the first difference operator. The length of lags, N, is used to account for possible serial correlation in the error term.

Central to the test of convergence is the estimated value of β. If $\beta \geq 0$, the price differential $q_{i,k,t}$ is non-stationary, implying persistent or explosive price divergence. A negative and statistically significant value of β implies price convergence, and its magnitude determines the speed of convergence. Specifically, the half-life of a shock to the price differential is computed as $-\ln(2)/\ln(1+\beta)$. If equation (9.1) is estimated based on annual data, an estimated value of β, say -0.5, suggests that the price differential is to be reduced by half in one year, other things being equal. The estimated value of $\alpha_{i,k}$ can be used to test the hypothesis of long-run price equalization. A value of $\alpha_{i,k}$ not significantly different from zero suggests that the price of product i in the benchmark city will eventually be equal to that in city k. By contrast, a value of $\alpha_{i,k}$ that is significantly positive suggests that the price of product i in the benchmark city will be persistently higher than that in city k.

The distribution of price differentials provides important information about how different price discrepancies across products and cities are. If price differentials (in percentage terms) are not much different across products, they are more likely to be explained by factors such as transportation costs. However, if price differentials differ significantly, the distribution will have a large standard deviation, suggesting a broader range of factors behind the differentials. For basic information on price deviation, the mean absolute value of price differentials can be used. The price differential $q_{i,k,t}$ is defined as the log difference in the price of commodity i at time t between city k and the mean price of all cities for commodity i at time t, namely,

$$q_{i,k,t} = \ln(p_{i,k,t}/p_{i,t})$$

At any given point of time, the standard deviation and the mean absolute value of $q_{i,k,t}$ across products and cities provide measures of price dispersion of that time.

This chapter is based on the econometric method developed by Levin, Lin and Chu (2002), who assume that each individual unit in the panel shares the same AR(1) coefficient, but allows for individual effects, time effects and possibly a time trend. Lags of the dependent variable may be introduced to allow for serial correlation in the errors. The test may be viewed as a pooled Augmented Dickey-Fuller test. Formally, the structure of Levin, Lin and Chu (2002) is summarized in the following equation:

$$\Delta Y_{i,t} = \alpha_u + \delta_i t + \theta_t + \beta Y_{i,t-1} + \xi_{i,t}, i = 1,2...N, t = 1,2...T \qquad (9.2)$$

It allows for fixed effects and unit-specific time trends in addition to common time effects. The unit-specific fixed effects are an important source of heterogeneity here since the coefficient of the lagged dependent variable is restricted to being homogeneous across all units of the panel. The Levin and Lin tests amount to testing for the null hypothesis $H_0 : \beta = 0$ against the alternative $H_A : \beta = 0$.

Empirical results and implications

This sub-section begins with a statistical analysis of the data, focusing on changes of price dispersion over time and the current level of the average price differential. It then tests the hypothesis of price convergence between Hong Kong and the Mainland using the panel unit root test of Levin, Lin and Chu (2002), and calculates the half-life of price convergence.

Before discussing our regression results, it is useful to look at some summary statistics of the price data. The distribution of price differentials provides important information about how different price discrepancies across products and cities are. If price differentials are not much different across products, they are more likely to be explained by factors such as transportation costs. However, if price differentials differ significantly, the distribution will have a large standard deviation, suggesting that a broader range of factors lies behind the differentials. In this study, we use Shenzhen as the benchmark city. This choice of benchmark city is entirely arbitrary, and should not affect the results at all.

Table 9.1 shows the descriptive statistics of prices commodity by commodity. The first column shows the mean prices of four mainland cities, while the second is purely for the mean price of Hong Kong. We can see at first glance that except for the category of edible oils and jewellery, for the remaining 15 categories the mean prices are always higher for Hong Kong relative to Mainland cities. Furthermore, the mean prices show that there indeed exist large price discrepancies between Hong Kong and the Mainland. However, it is far from sufficient to conclude that there is no convergence tendency in prices between the two regions. In order to give a structural description, we sort all the commodities into two categories in Table 9.2, tradable goods (including 10 commodities) and semi-tradable and services (the remaining seven).

In the upper panel of the table for tradable goods, the mean value and standard deviations for prices are similar for Beijing, Shenzhen, Shanghai and Guangzhou. It indicates that the prices of tradable goods were more likely to converge in China.

Let as now look at the results for services group in the lower panel of the table. For Shenzhen, Shanghai and Guangzhou, the most open cities in China, small discrepancies in mean values and standard deviations exist, but much lower values are found for Beijing. The reason for such a big gap may lie in the fact that in the category of high school tuition fees, Beijing's

Table 9.2   Descriptive statistics of prices: 2

	Beijing	Shenzhen	Shanghai	Guangzhou	Hong Kong
Tradable goods:					
Mean	335.6	336.9	339.7	337.4	1,197.4
Std Dev.	1,002.5	1,014.8	1,015.9	1,024.8	3,546
Obs	690	690	690	690	690
Semi-tradable and services:					
Mean	55.1	111.9	108.4	120.4	842.6
Std Dev.	83.8	211.7	213.6	211.2	1,924.5
Obs	483	483	483	483	483

Sample size: 690 for tradable goods
483 for semi-tradable and services

data were mainly collected from ordinary high schools, while the other cities' were from famous and expensive private schools. Hong Kong's mean value and standard deviation are very different from those of the four

Table 9.3   Variability of price differential, Hong Kong and Mainland China

	Mean	Abs (mean)	Std Dev.
Tradable:			
Pork	1.031899	6.769	9.245
Beef	1.080551	10.56	12.92
Rice	0.070894	1.15	1.398
Eggs	0.167246	2.046	2.572
Sugar	0.05337	1.256	1.647
Edible oils	0.658428	1.975	2.035
Motor fuel	427.9986	1969	3715.954
Chinese wines	−2.43051	15.41	16.23
Beer	0.383732	2.07	2.569
Cigarettes	1.685145	1.15	19.976
Semi–tradable:			
Jewellery	−1.09123	18.35	22.86
Electricity	−0.42215	20.87	26.375
Hair–dressing	7.215942	36.51	46.78
Service:			
Petroleum gas	1.73	19.89	23.07
Taxi fares	0.202754	1.915	2.374
High school tuition fees	216.5362	1788	2235
Hospital fees	0.260043	10.22	12.66

Sample size: 276 observations
Cross-section:4

mainland cities. It is not surprising, for Hong Kong has a much higher income level and living standards than the Mainland cities.

Next, we calculate the mean absolute values of price differentials with respect to the benchmark city and the corresponding standard deviations. Likewise, we first present the statistics for each of the 17 commodities.

Table 9.3 shows the price dispersion by pooling the data for Hong Kong and the Mainland cities, while Table 9.4 shows the price dispersion within the Mainland cities only. It is clear by comparison that, for all these 17 categories, both the mean absolute values of price differentials and standard deviations are to some extent bigger when Hong Kong is included than when it is not. Also note that with or without Hong Kong the corresponding figures are always much greater than that across US cities or countries in the euro zone.[1] Differences in income levels, the degree of factor mobility, and monetary and tax policies were probably the factors behind a larger price differential between Hong Kong and the Mainland, as well as amongst Chinese cities. Furthermore, we examine price dispersion

Table 9.4   Variability of price differential within the Mainland China

	Mean	Abs (mean)	Std Dev.
Tradable:			
Pork	0.201594	1.51	5.845
Beef	−0.49981	1.075	1.154
Rice	−0.17174	0.31	0.903
Eggs	−0.128	0.339	1.16
Sugar	−0.13029	0.782	0.979
Edible oils	1.097379	1.115	0.809
Motor fuel	4.373188	262.8	312.52
Chinese wines	−4.84251	10.22	11.574
Beer	0.141848	0.86	1.099
Cigarettes	0.311836	0.31	0.811
Semi-tradable:			
Electricity	−3.95478	9.866	12.319
Hair–dressing	2.33333	5	4.933
Jewellery	1.758454	5.46	6.386
Service:			
Taxi fares	−0.08261	0.369	0.3934
High school tuition fees	−45.41	173.2	210.4
Petroleum gas	−3.31617	3.316	0.685
Hospital fees	−1.39686	3.39	3.867

Sample size: 207
Observations
Cross-section: 3

Table 9.5   Comparison of tradable goods and non-tradable goods

	Mean	**Std Dev.**	**Observations**
Variability of price differential			
Tradables	1.06	31.09	3,381
Semi-tradable and services	183	2,361	2,277
Mean absolute price differential			
Tradable	20.78	23.12	3,381
Semi-tradable and services	1,486	1,835	2,277

by separating commodities into two groups: that is, tradables versus non-tradables (semi-tradables and services). Table 9.5 reveals that tradable goods have much smaller mean variability and mean absolute values in price differentials than non-tradable goods.

Table 9.6   Levin-Lin-Chu test for price differentials, Hong Kong and Mainland China

	coefficients	t-value	t-star	Significance	Half-life
Tradable:					
Pork	−0.78537	−13.26	−12.5	***	0.45
Beef	−0.23563	−5.357	−2.097	**	2.58
Rice	−0.76332	−11.305	−10.46	***	0.48
Eggs	−0.80313	−13.55	−12.74	***	0.43
Sugar	−0.66559	−11.623	−10.7	***	0.63
Edible oils	−0.15395	−5.049	−2.908	***	4.15
Motor fuel	−0.10861	−3.819	−1.078		
Chinese wines	−0.0883	−3.39	0.42358		
Beer	−0.11302	−4.056	−1.21		
Cigarettes	−0.66988	−11.739	−10.81	***	0.63
Semi-tradable:					
Electricity	−0.10522	−2.939	0.28129		
Hair-dressing	0.00992	0.622	2.81		
Jewellery	−0.06803	−2.889	−0.954		
Service:					
Taxi fares	−0.05759	−2.987	−0.634		
High school tuition fees	−0.05957	−3.177	−0.96327		
Petroleum gas	−0.05537	−2.882	−1.117		
Hospital fees	−0.09513	−4.621	−2.953	***	6.93
Overall	−0.04253	−9.192	−3.497	***	16.29

*** 1% significant

We now turn to the regression analysis. As discussed before, to test price convergence is equivalent to testing whether the price differential series are stationary or not. This requires us to carry out a unit root test for the price differential series, $q_{i,k,t} = \ln(p_{i,benchmark,t}/p_{i,k,t})$, where $p_{i,k,t}$ is the price of product i in city k at time t). Following Parsley and Wei (1996), we run a panel unit root test as it can significantly raise the power of the unit root test (see Levin, Lin and Chu, 2002).

First, we carry out the Levin–Lin–Chu test for the 17 categories separately. The results are presented in Tables 9.6 and 9.7. In Table 9.6, we include Hong Kong as one cross-sectional unit (there are in total four cross-sectional units here as Shengzhen is the benchmark city and has to be dropped). The results indicate that for seven out of ten tradable goods and one out of four services we can reject the null hypothesis of having a unit root, which implies that their prices converge. The estimated half-lives for

Table 9.7   Levin-Lin-Chu test for price differentials, within Mainland China

	coefficients	t-value	t-star	significance	Half-life
Tradable:					
Pork	−0.87435	−12.568	−12.13	***	0.33
Beef	−0.33091	−5.472	−2.315	***	1.72
Rice	−0.83641	−9.89	−9.5	***	0.38
Eggs	−0.96072	−13.745	−13.52	***	0.21
Sugar	−0.95772	−13.687	−13.59	***	0.22
Edible oils	−0.12407	−3.83	−1.84	**	5.23
Motor fuel	−0.14654	−3.945	−0.927		
Chinese wines	−0.09085	−2.948	0.424		
Beer	−0.12276	−3.644	−1.144		
Cigarettes	−0.14265	−3.924	−2.16	**	4.5
Semi-tradable:					
Electricity	−0.13541	−3.938	−1.638	**	4.76
Hair–dressing	−0.02835	−1.579	1.99		
Jewellery	−0.1126	−4.109	−1.285		
Service:					
Taxi fares	−0.06638	−3.02	−1.163		
High school tuition fees	−0.1226	−3.755	−1.2442	*	5.29
Petroleum gas	−0.05267	−2.585	−0.83		
Hospital fees	−0.1353	−4.284	−2.318	***	4.77
Overall	−0.08283	−10.683	−6.65312	***	8.37

* 10% significant
** 5% significant
*** 1% significant

these converged prices range from 0.43 month (eggs) to 6.93 months (hospital in-patient fees), with generally shorter half-lives for tradable goods. Furthermore, we also pool all the prices together and run an overall unit root test. The result shown at the bottom of Table 9.6 indicates that there is an overall price convergence at a significance level below 1 per cent. The overall half-life is 16.29 months. Table 9.7 simply repeats the work for the Mainland cities only. It emerges that for the Mainland cities alone the prices for an additional semi-tradable good (jewellery) and one service (high school tuition fees) converge, too. More importantly, the estimated half-lives for almost all converged prices are shorter in Table 9.7 than in Table 9.6 (edible oil is the only exceptional case), and the overall half-life is 8.37 months, which is about half of the length in Table 9.6.

The literature most related to our work is Ha and Fan (2002), who use panel data on the commodity prices of Hong Kong and four mainland cities. They found statistical evidence of price convergence between Hong Kong and the mainland cities, with the average half-life of price differentials estimated at 6.5 years. Similar to their study, we also investigate price convergence between four mainland cities (Shenzhen, Guangzhou, Shanghai and Beijing) and Hong Kong. Our work differs from Ha and Fan (2002) in that while Ha and Fan use annual price data, our dataset provides us with monthly information about the prices of homogeneous commodities. Based on the annual price data collected by the Economist Intelligence Unit, Ha and Fan (2002) found that the average half-life of price differentials is estimated to be around 3 years amongst Chinese cities, and 6.5 years when Hong Kong was included. The much longer half-life estimated from their study may be attributable to the fact that they used annual price data. The monthly price data used in the current study should be more closely matched with the actual time-span needed for price arbitrage, and therefore are subject to less of a measurement problem (see Taylor, 2001 for the discussion on the pitfalls of using low frequency data to study price convergence). Similarly, Parsley and Wei (1996), using quarterly data, found that the average half-life of price differentials among a group of 48 US cities was about 1–1.25 years for goods, and 5 years for services, which were also somewhat longer than the results here. Overall, our estimated results demonstrate that there is strong evidence to support price convergence both within Chinese cities and between Hong Kong and the Mainland.

Next, we repeat the test with an added city-specific fixed effect in the model. The inclusion of the fixed effect can better capture any city-specific heterogeneity in transaction costs, institutional settings and so on, and hence should result in even stronger support for price convergence. Indeed, the results in Table 9.8 (with Hong Kong in) and 9.9 (without Hong Kong) demonstrate that more product prices now converge.

Table 9.8 Levin-Lin-Chu test for price differentials, Hong Kong and the Mainland (fixed effects)

	coefficients	t-value	t-star	significance	Half-life
Tradable:					
Pork	−0.045	−2.471	−2.45	***	15.4
Beef	−0.00186	−.548	−0.544		
Rice	−0.02226	−1.175	−1.165		
Eggs	−0.01457	−1.078	−1.069	***	
Sugar	−0.02485	−1.685	−1.672	**	27.9
Edible oils	−0.00413	−1.168	−1.158		
Motor fuel	−0.00703	−1.412	−1.4	*	98.6
Chinese wines	−0.00706	−0.909	−0.902		
Beer	−0.01295	−0.913	−0.906		
Cigarettes	−0.02814	−4.562	−4.526	***	24.6
Semi-tradable:					
Electricity	−0.00718	−1.85	−1.835	**	96.5
Hair–dressing	−0.00134	−2.842	2.819	***	517.3
Jewellery	−0.0122	−2.144	−2.127	**	56.2
Service:					
Taxi fares	−0.00394	−1.458	−1.446	*	175.9
High school tuition fees	−0.01168	−2.371	−2.352	***	59.3
Petroleum gas	−0.00118	−1.353	−1.342	*	587.4
Hospital fees	−0.0255	−2.848	−2.819	***	27.2
Overall	−0.01797	−5.974	−5.974	***	38.57

* 10% significant
** 5% significant
*** 1% significant

Moreover, from the results with Hong Kong we see that for some of the tradable goods their prices are found to converge without the fixed effect but not so with the fixed effect. It is also the case that the speed of convergence based on the estimated half-life is now generally longer with the fixed effect (overall 38.57 months with Hong Kong prices) than without the fixed effect (only 16.29).

Conclusions

To summarize, there are a few noteworthy observations. First, we found statistical evidence of price convergence between Hong Kong and China, using panel monthly data of commodity prices in Beijing, Shanghai, Shenzhen, Guangzhou and Hong Kong for the period 1997–2002. Second, tradable goods are generally more likely to show price convergence than

Table 9.9   Levin-Lin-Chu test for price differentials, within the Mainland (fixed effects)

	coefficients	t-value	t-star	significance	Half-life
Tradable:					
Pork	−0.757	−11.094	−11.01	***	0.92
Beef	−0.111	−3.834	−3.803	***	6.24
Rice	−0.697	−6.505	−6.453	***	0.99
Eggs	−0.73	−8.304	−8.237	***	0.95
Sugar	−0.02119	−0.87	−0.86323		
Edible oils	−0.04726	−2.316	−2.297	**	14.67
Motor fuel	−0.13456	−3.5	−3.473	***	5.15
Chinese wines	−0.03121	−1.704	−1.69	**	22.2
Beer	−0.0146	−1.031	−1.02252		
Cigarettes	−0.08733	−2.709	−2.687	***	7.94
Semi-tradable:					
Electricity	−0.1212	−3.413	−2.134		
Hair–dressing	−0.03783	−1.532	−1.519	*	18.32
Jewellery	−0.00352	−1.817	−1.80256	**	196.9
Service:					
Taxi fares	−0.00798	−1.238	−1.2279		
High school tuition fees	−0.03134	−1.72	−1.706	**	22.12
Petroleum gas	−0.00596	−1.862	−1.847	**	116.3
Hospital fees	−0.07931	−3.654	−3.625	***	8.74
Overall	−0.06689	−9.575	−9.575	***	10.36

* 10% significant
** 5% significant
*** 1% significant

services, and the speed of price convergence for tradable goods is also generally faster than for services. It is also the case that the speed of price convergence based on estimated half-life is faster within Mainland cities than within Mainland cities and Hong Kong.

The current evidence suggests that there is already a high level of integration between the markets in Hong Kong and the Mainland. Looking into the future, one would have the confidence to say that the speed of price convergence might accelerate in future years, owing to the increased economic integration of Hong Kong and the Mainland, and a reduced income and productivity gap.

Note

1   The standard deviation of price differentials is 0.17 for the US cities and 0.11 for the European countries (Ha and Fan, 2002).

References

Engel, Charles and John Rogers (1994), 'How Wide Is the Border?', *American Economic Review*, 86, 1112–25.

Fan, C. Simon and Xiangdong Wei (2005), 'The Law of One Price: Evidence from the Transitional Economy of China', forthcoming in the *Review of Economics and Stattistics*.

Ha, Jiming and Kelvin Fan (2002), 'Price Convergence between Hong Kong and the Mainland', Hong Kong Monetary Authority, discussion paper, June.

Levin, Andrew, Chien-Fu Lin and Chia-Shang James Chu (2002), 'Unit Root Tests in Panel Data: Asymptotic and Finite-Sample Properties', *Journal of Econometrics*, 108 (1), 1–24.

Parsley, David and Shang-jin Wei (1996), 'Convergence to the Law of One Price without Trade Barriers or Currency Fluctuations', *Quarterly Journal of Economics*, 111, 1211–36.

Taylor, Alan (2001), 'Potential Pitfalls for the Purchasing-Power-Parity Puzzle? Sampling and Specification Biases in Mean-Reversion Tests of the Law of One Price', *Econometrica*, 69 (2), 473–98.

Wei, Shang-jin and David Parsley (1995), 'Purchasing Power Dis-Parity during the Floating Rate Period: Exchange Rate Volatility, Trade Barriers, and Other Culprits', *NBER Working Paper series*, No. 5032.

10
Economic Integration between Hong Kong and Mainland China: Did Trade Hurt Hong Kong's Unskilled Workers?

Kui-yin Cheung and C. Simon Fan

Introduction

From 1979 onwards, the economic linkage between Hong Kong and Mainland China has proceeded at a remarkable speed. Hong Kong has been the dominant supplier of FDI in China, contributing about 60 per cent of the inflow of investment capital. Meanwhile, the volume of trade between these two regions relative to Hong Kong's GDP has reached more than 100% of Hong Kong's GDP over the past two decades. The purpose of this chapter is an attempt to further our understanding about the impact of Hong Kong–Mainland economic integration on the income distribution of Hong Kong for the past 20 years. Specifically, we try to address the question of whether increasing trade between the Mainland and Hong Kong worsened the earnings gap between unskilled and skilled workers in Hong Kong.

This chapter will have significant policy implications for Hong Kong. Moreover, it tries to add to the literature on trade and inequality. The issue of trade and wages has received increasing attention in the recent economic literature. This concern is largely due to the fact that since the late 1970s, the wage inequality between unskilled and skilled workers in many developed countries has widened considerably. For example, in the United States, the wage premium of a college education compared with a high school education has increased by about 20 per cent (Borjas and Ramey, 1994). However, the importance of trade on wage inequality remains the subject of a fierce debate. On the one hand, some economists (e.g., Wood, 1995; Leamer, 1996) believe that wage inequality has risen because factor price equalization has been at work through increasing the volume of international trade between developed and developing countries. Because developed countries are abundant in skilled labour, while developing countries are abundant in unskilled labour, the Stolper–Samuelson theorem in the theory of international trade clearly predicts that unskilled (skilled) workers in developed countries will earn lower (higher) real wage rates from trading with developing countries. On the other hand, some economists (e.g.,

Richardson, 1995; Krugman, 1995) argue that the effects of trade on wage inequality may not be empirically significant. In particular, they point out that the trade volume between some advanced countries (e.g., the USA) and developing countries still constitutes only a small percentage of total spending in the advanced nations.

This chapter tries to contribute to the existing literature by empirically examining the effects of Hong Kong–Chinese Mainland trade on the earnings inequality in Hong Kong among different industries over the period 1982 to 2003. It is related to Cheung and Fan (2001, 2002) and Fan and Cheung (2004), and it extends our earlier work in two main respects.[1] First, the current empirical study uses much more recent data, and thus its empirical findings will have more relevant policy implications. Second, this study employs the econometric method of causality test, which leads to some interesting findings that complement our previous work.

In the remainder of this chapter, we first provide some useful background information in the second section. The third and fourth sections discuss the theoretical hypotheses and the data used in this chapter, respectively. In the fifth section, we use cointegration techniques to examine the long-run relationship between wage inequality in Hong Kong and Hong Kong–Mainland China trade. In particular, the empirical analysis shows that the relative wage gap between skilled workers and unskilled workers in Hong Kong among different industries increased significantly as the trade volume between Hong Kong and Mainland China rose. Quantitatively, we have estimated that the change in relative wage inequality between skilled and unskilled workers with respect to a 1 per cent change in the share of trade volume with China in the *manufacturing, financing, personal* and *transport service* sectors are 0.02, 0.019, 0.002 and 0.02 respectively. The final section summarizes the empirical findings.

Background information

Hong Kong has experienced a significant rise in income inequality over the last two decades. Some information on the changes of household income distribution in Hong Kong is presented in Table 10.1.

For example, from Table 10.1, we can see that in 2001, the 40% of households with the lowest incomes are estimated to receive about 11% of the national income, whereas the 20% of households with the highest incomes account for 56%. This pattern of inequality has changed little, with the exception of 1986, but the situation has tended to get more unequal when compared to 1981. The Gini coefficient has increased from 0.451 in 1981 to 0.525 in 2001. In particular, the wage gap between skilled and unskilled labour has been rising. The share of national income received by the highest quintile has gone from 10 times the income share received by the first quintile in 1981 to 17 times in 2001. The deteriorating income

Table 10.1 Changes in household income distribution in Hong Kong, 1981–2001

Income group	Income share (%)				
	1981	1986	1991	1996	2001
Lowest quintile	4.6	5.0	4.3	3.7	3.2
2nd quintile	9.8	9.8	9.0	8.2	7.8
3rd quintile	14.3	14.0	13.5	12.7	12.6
4th quintile	20.9	20.5	20.4	19.1	19.9
Highest quintile	50.4	50.7	52.8	56.3	55.5
Total	100.0	100.0	100.0	100.0	100.0
Gini coefficient	0.451	0.453	0.476	0.518	0.525
1st and 2nd quintile	14.4	14.8	13.3	11.9	11.0
Ratio of 5th quintile/ 1st quintile	10.96	10.14	12.28	15.22	17.34

Source: *Hong Kong Population Census*, various issues, Census and Statistical Department, Hong Kong.

distribution in Hong Kong has become a more and more important issue in Hong Kong. In fact, in his 2005 policy address, the former Chief Executive of Hong Kong, Tung Chee Hwa, highlighted the fact that helping the poor and reducing income inequality has become a key issue for the government of Hong Kong.

The increasing income inequality in Hong Kong appears to be in rough concordance with its increasing trade and integration with the Chinese Mainland. Indeed, the volume of trade between these two regions relative to Hong Kong's total trade has been unusually large. According to UN international statistics, Hong Kong–Mainland China bilateral trade has grown at an extraordinary rate. For example, the trade volume between the two regions was only US$9.14 billion in 1981 and ranked eleventh in the world's bilateral merchandise trade flows. In 1993, it reached US$148 billion, surpassing the US–Mexico bilateral trade and being ranked third in the world. In 2003, the volume of trade between Hong Kong and Chinese Mainland was about 43% of Hong Kong's total trade (see Table 10.2). As a matter of fact, the flows of goods and capital between southern China, Hong Kong and Taiwan have been so rapidly expanded that they are often referred to as 'Greater China' in the literature (e.g., Ash and Kueh, 1993).

The economic integration between Hong Kong and the Mainland has resulted in a restructuring of the Hong Kong economy over the past two decades. Between 1980 and 1987, manufacturing firms in Hong Kong relocated most of their production bases to Southern China. Consequently, a large number of local workers were laid off, and were displaced by Mainland workers, particularly in Guangdong. During this period, around 60,000 jobs were lost in the manufacturing sector every year. The decrease in employment in the manufacturing industries in Hong Kong has continued, and the size of the decrease has stabilized at the level of around 10,000 a year since 1998. Nowadays, the manufacturing sector employs barely over 147,000 workers, or 5.4% of the total workforce, which is in sharp contrast to the more than 990,000 workers, or 47% of the workforce, in the early 1980s.

The decline of the manufacturing sector was associated with the increasing importance of the services sector in Hong Kong economy. The employment share in financing, insurance, real estate and business services has increased by more than two-fold. Meanwhile, because the service sectors in Hong Kong are labour-intensive, their expansion has created a large number of jobs so that large-scale unemployment did not occur in Hong Kong during the 1980s and early 1990s.

While the relocation of businesses from Hong Kong to the Mainland resulted in declining output (from 24.3 per cent in 1984 to 4.1 per cent in 2003) and employment shares (from 45.7 per cent in 1984 to 5.4 per cent in 2003) of the manufacturing sector in Hong Kong, the productivity of this sector in fact has increased. For example, during the period from 1982 to 2003, the share of output decreased by 4.2 per cent per year, and the share of employment decreased by 4.5 per cent per year. Thus, there must have been a steady increase in the labour productivity of the manufacturing sector. This increased labour productivity has largely resulted from the upgraded skill level within the manufacturing industries as Hong Kong shifted its manufacturing production base to Southern China. In other words, while Hong Kong has lost its cost advantage in the course of its development, it has also considerably upgraded other aspects of its competitiveness, which in particular includes a better-educated workforce and the associated increased capacity of adopting more efficient production technologies.

Compared with the manufacturing industries, the service sector has become more intensive in its use of labour. For example, the number employed in finance, insurance, real estate and business services industries increased by 30 per cent for the period from 1984 to 2003. Its output share, however, has only increased by 21 percentage points. This implies that the labour productivity for the services sector (finance, transportation, wholesale and personal services) decreased by 9 percentage points during that period. Despite a fall in the labour productivity of the territory's services sector, the sector's relative productivity is still about 200 per cent higher than that in the manufacturing sector. The services will be increasingly intensive in their uses of skilled labour. For instance, the skill level required for working in the banking industry in Hong Kong has been raised significantly along with the growing sophistication of services offered as well as the wider use of computers.

For the production and the elementary jobs, the manufacturing sector, however, has suffered the largest decrease during the study period. This is due to the fact that Hong Kong's FDI in Mainland China has been concentrated mainly in labour-intensive manufacturing industries. The workers in Hong Kong are focused primarily on procuring contracts, designing, marketing and distribution of the finished products. This indirectly leads to an upgrading of skills within the manufacturing sector, despite the decrease in size in terms of both output and employment of the sector.

In the services sector, other than the finance industry, it is the personal services industry that has absorbed most of the production workers released from the manufacturing industries. Employment in the personal services industry has increased from 1.43 million to 2.52 million between 1992 and 2002, the largest increase (75.2%) among all industries. As a whole, we observe that there has been a steady decrease in the demand for unskilled workers in every sector.

Theoretical background

In the recent economic literature, the effects of trade on wage inequality are usually analysed in a Heckscher–Ohlin model with skilled and unskilled labour as the two factors of production. This framework is particularly useful in relation to the trade between two economies with large income disparities. The income disparity between Hong Kong and China over the last two decades has been very large, despite the fact that China has experienced very rapid economic growth since 1978. For example, in 1996, the average income in Mainland China was only US$678, which was only 2.8 per cent of the average income in Hong Kong. Even in the richest province of China, Guangdong, the average income was only US$1024.9, which was 4.7 per cent of the average income in Hong Kong in 1996.

In the Hong Kong–Mainland China context and under the Heckscher–Ohlin framework, clearly Mainland China has been abundant in unskilled labour, while Hong Kong has been abundant in skilled labour. The Stolper–Samuelson and factor price equalization theorems immediately imply that as the trade activities between Hong Kong and Mainland China increase, the wage gap between skilled and unskilled labour in Hong Kong will increase. The large income gap between Hong Kong and Mainland China suggests that this empirical study will provide a good test of the theories on North–South trade and the Stolper–Samuelson theorem.

Moreover, we note that the per capita income of Hong Kong has been significantly lower than most of its trading partners (such as the United States, Japan and Germany). So, the Stolper–Samuelson and factor price equalization theorems imply that Hong Kong's trade with these rich countries will decrease the wage gap in Hong Kong.[2] For example, in 1993, the per capita income of Hong Kong was US$13,890, which was significantly lower than that of the USA (US$22,956) and that of Japan (US$25,089).[3] Meanwhile, from the Hong Kong trade statistics, we found that the trade volume between other developing countries and Hong Kong was very small when compared to that between China and Hong Kong. Thus, we come up with the following hypothesis: *the relative wage between skilled and unskilled workers in Hong Kong increases as the share of the volume of Hong Kong's trade with Mainland China in Hong Kong's total trade volume rises.* In other words, the increase in Hong Kong–Mainland China trade hurts the unskilled workers in Hong Kong.

In addition, the closer economic linkage between Hong Kong and Mainland China since 1979 has led to structural changes in Hong Kong's economy.[4] It is reported that these structural changes have had a significant impact on wage inequality (e.g., Suen, 1995). Therefore, the share of output contribution of each sector to GDP at factor cost is included in our regression analysis. Further, we include the unemployment rate in Hong Kong as a proxy variable for economic environment in our regression analysis for two reasons: first, it is an important indicator of the business cycles in Hong Kong; second, it is well known that business cycles affect skilled and unskilled workers differently (e.g., Rosen, 1968; Ashenfelter and Ham, 1979).

Finally, we consider that an individual's human capital includes both his or her general human capital and specific human capital (Becker, 1993). So, an individual's skill can be largely specific to a certain industrial sector, and the skills in different sectors of production can be very different. For example, an engineer in the textile industry may find his or her skill much less useful or even useless if he or she works for an insurance company. The essence of the Stolper–Samuelson and factor price equalization theorems is that North–South trade increases the demand for skilled labour and decreases the demand for unskilled labour in the North, and hence affects the wage gap. Thus, we divide workers into four industrial sectors in our regression analysis.

In summary, the regression equation is

$$\left(\frac{W^i_{sk}}{W^i_{unsk}} \right)_t = \beta_0 + \beta_1 (TRSH_{t-1}) + \beta_2 (GDPSH_{i,t}) + \beta_3 (UNEMP_t) + \varepsilon_t \quad (10.1)$$

where $TRSH_{t-1}$ is the share of total trade between Hong Kong and Mainland China related to Hong Kong's total trade at time $t-1$; $GDPSH_{i,t}$ is the percentage contribution of industry i to GDP at factor cost at period t; and $UNEMP_t$ is the overall unemployment rate at period t.

Data description

In this chapter, the wage gap between skilled and unskilled labour is measured as the wage ratio between these two groups among four different

Table 10.2   Hong Kong-China trade, 1982–2003 (HK$billion)

Year	Total trade with China (2)	Total trade in Hong Kong (3)	% share (2)/(3)
1982	44.73	270.28	16.55
1983	61.23	336.14	18.21
1984	95.10	444.81	21.38
1985	120.18	466.57	25.76
1986	140.55	552.49	25.44
1987	205.40	755.98	27.17
1988	288.57	991.87	29.09
1989	343.44	1,133.29	30.30
1990	394.51	1,282.40	30.76
1991	501.08	1,544.87	32.44
1992	628.11	1,880.25	33.41
1993	740.09	2,118.85	34.93
1994	854.72	2,420.72	35.31
1995	987.08	2,835.25	34.81
1996	1,049.81	2,933.50	35.79
1997	1,116.12	3,071.04	36.34
1998	1,044.05	2,776.74	37.60
1999	1,057.15	2,741.72	38.56
2000	1,257.97	3,230.65	38.94
2001	1,228.10	3,049.18	40.28
2002	1,330.32	3,179.94	41.83
2003	1,528.20	3,548.20	43.07

Source: Hong Kong Annual Digest of Statistics, various issues, and *China Statistical Yearbook*, various issues.

sectors of production in Hong Kong. These sectors are: (1) manufacturing; (2) wholesale, retail and import/export trade, restaurants and hotels; (3) transportation services; and (4) financial services, insurance, real estate and business services. The wage indices of skilled and unskilled workers are obtained from the report on *Time Series of Real Wage Indices by Economic Sector by Occupational Group*, prepared by the Hong Kong Census and Statistics Department. The sample period is from 1982 to 2003.

The data on the unemployment rate in Hong Kong and Hong Kong–Mainland China trade are obtained from various issues of the *Hong Kong Annual Digest of Statistics*. Table 10.2 illustrates the increasing trade between Hong Kong and Mainland China.

From Table 10.2, we can see that Hong Kong–Mainland China trade, in terms of both the absolute trade volume and the share of the volume of Hong Kong's trade with Mainland China in Hong Kong's total trade volume, has been rising rapidly. Indeed, the rapid expansion of Mainland China's foreign trade since 1978 is one of the most remarkable features of the impact of its open-door policy. Meanwhile, Hong Kong has played a key role in the Mainland's expansion of international trade.

Cointegration analysis

A statistical diagnosis for the univariate trend properties of time series is a prerequisite in studying the nexus between trade and relative wages. The causal relation between them is not spurious provided that the variables are non-stationary in the level form but stationary in the first difference or second difference form. This feature is also required to examine the existence of a long-run stable relationship between these variables.

In order to determine the integrating orders of the time-series variables, the Phillips–Perron procedure is used to test each variable for a unit root in its level, and then in the first or second difference form. Table 10.3 presents the results of testing of the relative wages for various industries, the share of Hong Kong's trade with Mainland China, the share of output contributions of each sector to GDP and the unemployment rate. The second column of the table shows the test statistics for the regression that contains

Table 10.3   Phillips-Perron unit root tests on relative wages, total trade with China, sector-output contributions and unemployment rate

Variable	First difference form	
	(with constant term)	(with trend and constant term)
RWM	–5.812***	–5.941***
RWF	–4.749***	–4.616***
RWPER	–6.581***	–6.361**
RWTR	–5.159***	–5.092***
TRCSH	–4.093***	–4.081**
MGDP	–3.771**	–3.560*
FGDP	–4.350***	–4.764***
PERGDP	–3.953***	–4.804***
TRGDP	–4.603***	–4.471***
UNEMP	–3.566***	–5.347***

Notes:
RWM = relative wage rate in manufacturing sector; RWF = relative wage rate in financial sector; RWPER = relative wage rate in personal service sector; RWTR = relative wage rate in transport service sector; TRCSH = the share of Hong Kong's total trade with Mainland China to Hong Kong's total trade; MGDP = the share of contribution to GDP at factor cost for manufacturing sector; FGDP = the share of contribution to GDP at factor cost for financial sector; PERGDP = the share of contribution to GDP at factor cost for personal service sector; TRGDP = the share of contribution to GDP at factor cost for transport service sector; UNEMP = unemployment rate.
    The critical values are according to MacKinnon's statistics:
*** Statistically significant at the 1 per cent level.
** Statistically significant at the 5 per cent level.
* Statistically significant at the 10 per cent level.

both a constant and a time trend. Based on the critical values reported by MacKinnon (1991), the null hypothesis of a unit root for each variable in first difference was rejected at either the 1% or 5% level of significance. This indicates that all variables are characterized as integration of first differencing.

As a stochastic trend has been confirmed for each of the series, the observed time series possess trends which can be removed by first differencing. The question then is whether there exists some long-run equilibrium relationship between these variables. A linear combination may exist between two or more economic variables, which converge to a long-run equilibrium, even though the series by themselves (at level form) are non-stationary. In other words, when they are cointegrated, a linear combination of them may result in a stationary series.

In this chapter, the Johansen (1991) multivariate cointegrating testing approach based on maximum-likelihood estimation is employed to test for the null hypothesis of the existence of a long-run stable relationship between the relative wages of the skilled and unskilled workers, the share of Hong Kong–China trade, the share of output contributions, and the unemployment rate. The advantage of using the Johansen cointegrating test is that it provided a maximum-likelihood estimation procedure, which simultaneously regresses vector auto-regressions (error correction model or ECM) to estimate cointegrating vectors. In addition, this method is capable of identifying multiple cointegrating vectors, and it is also orthogonal to an arbitrary normalization.

Table 10.4 presents the results from the cointegrating tests for long-run relationship between trade, output contributions and unemployment rates on relative wages. According to the critical values reported by Johansen and Juselius (1990), both maximal-eigenvalue test statistics and trace test statistics provide the benchmark in examining the existence of a cointegrating relationship between the relative wages and trade, output contributions and unemployment variables for all industries.

Table 10.5 reports the estimated long-run parameters of relative wage of skilled and unskilled workers for the four industries in Hong Kong (i.e., manufacturing, M, finance, F, personal, P, and transport services, T).

For the manufacturing industries, we found that the increase in the share of total trade with China would raise the relative wage of skilled and unskilled workers. It is estimated that for a 1 per cent increase in the share of total trade with China, the relative wage ratio would increase by 0.02. However, the expansion of the share of industry's output contribution would decrease the wage ratio by 0.001, and thus decrease the wage inequality of the two groups. It is, however, not statistically significantly different from zero. The increase in the unemployment rate would raise the relative wage of manufacturing workers by 0.018. Both estimates of the trade share and unemployment rate are statistically significantly different from zero at the 1 per cent significance level.

Table 10.4 Johansen's cointegration tests for long-run relations between trade, output contributions, unemployment rate and relative wages

Null hypothesis	$r = 0$	$r \leq 1$	$r \leq 2$
Trace tests:			
RWM	110.59***	54.18**	17.35
RWF	84.06***	46.50**	21.33
RWPER	84.39***	42.12**	14.29
RWTR	71.11**	42.13**	15.12
Eigenvalues:			
RWM	0.948***	0.856**	0.588
RWF	0.862***	0.734**	0.405
RWPER	0.891***	0.768**	0.414
RWTR	0.782***	0.758**	0.396

*** Statistically significant at the 1 per cent level.
** Statistically significant at the 5 per cent level.

Table 10.5 The long-run parameters of the relative wage equations (W_{sk}^i / W_{unsk}^i) for the period 1982–2003

TRCSH	GDPSH	UNEMP	C	Trend	Log likelihood
Manufacturing sector:					
0.020***	–0.001***	0.018***	–0.909	–0.015	–11.43
(0.002)	(0.002)	(0.004)			
Finance sector:					
0.020***	0.018***	0.094***	–0.662	0.053	–41.23
(0.003)	(0.004)	(0.011)			
Personal service sector:					
0.002	0.057**	–0.062**	0.262	0.013	–3.82
(0.002)	(0.024)	(0.032)			
Transport sector:					
0.020***	0.002	0.086***	–0.767	0.043	–15.90
(0.004)	(0.022)	(0.014)			

Notes:
TRCSH = the share of Hong Kong's total trade with Mainland China to Hong Kong's total trade, GDPSH = the share of contribution to GDP at factor cost for the sector in question; UNEMP = unemployment rate, C = Intercept term, Trend = the time trend.
Figures in parentheses are t-statistics.
*** denotes statistically significantly at 1% level.
** denotes statistically significantly at 5% level.

Similar results are observed in the finance (F) and transport service (T) industries, which are statistically significant at the 1 per cent level. It is estimated that a 1 per cent increase in the share of total trade with China would increase the wage ratio of skilled and unskilled workers by 0.019 and 0.02, respectively. The estimate for the personal (P) sector is 0.002, though positive, but statistically insignificantly different from zero. All in all, our empirical findings confirm our hypothesis that the increase in the share of Hong Kong–China trade hurts unskilled labour in Hong Kong.

Furthermore, we would like to investigate if there is a one-way or mutual causation in this bivariate time series setting. The Granger causality test, which is the standard test in the literature, is used to determine whether lagged information on a variable, say X, has any statistically significant role in explaining Y. The pair-wise Granger causality test on long-run relations between Hong Kong trade share and relative wages of skilled and unskilled workers in each sector is shown in Table 10.6.

'The Hong Kong–China trade share does not Granger cause relative wages' is rejected at either the 5 or the 10 per cent significance level for all sectors. 'Relative wages do not Granger cause the Hong Kong–China trade share', however, cannot be rejected in all cases. These results indicate that there is a one-way causal effect from the Hong Kong–China trade share to relative wages, which reconfirms our hypothesis that the Hong Kong–China trade share causes the widening of the relative wages in all sectors.

The impacts of the share of output contribution to GDP on relative wages are somewhat mixed. It is positive in the finance, personal and transportation sectors but negative in the manufacturing sector. The negative effect on the manufacturing sector might have been due to the relatively unskilled labour-intensive nature of the manufacturing industry. As the manufacturing sector expands, it has a greater demand for unskilled workers than skilled workers, which reduces the wage gap between skilled

Table 10.6 Pairwise Granger causality tests on long-run relations between Hong Kong–China trade share and relative wages of skilled and unskilled workers in each sector

Sector	Lags	F-statistic	Probability
TRCSH does not Granger cause RWM	4	3.087	0.074
RWM does not Granger cause TRCSH		0.810	0.549
TRCSH does not Granger cause RWF	4	3.542	0.053
RWF does not Granger cause TRCSH		0.803	0.553
TRCSH does not Granger cause RWTR	3	2.543	0.105
RWTR does not Granger cause TRCSH		0.576	0.642
TRCSH does not Granger cause RWPER	4	4.476	0.029
RWPER does not Granger cause TRCSH		1.571	0.263

and unskilled workers. However, for the other three sectors, as the sector expands, they have a greater demand for skilled workers than unskilled workers, which increases the wage gap between skilled and unskilled workers. As discussed above, the skill level required in the services industries has been raised significantly, along with the growing sophistication of the services offered as well as the wider use of computers. Consequently the more labour the sector absorbed, the higher would be the demand for relatively skilled workers. Thus, as the service industries expanded, this increased the relative wage gap between skilled and unskilled labour.

Further, the regression analysis indicates that there is a positive, and statistically significant, correlation between the unemployment rate and the wage gap between skilled and unskilled labour in all sectors except in the personal service sector in Hong Kong. It is well known that in an economic downturn, the increase in unemployment for unskilled labour is significantly higher than that for skilled labour. In particular, the least productive unskilled workers often become unemployed in a recession. Thus, as the unemployment rate rises in a recession, the average wages of unskilled workers are negatively affected compared with those of skilled workers due to the fact that lower-paid unskilled workers may lose their jobs in the recession. In addition, in the past decade, the manufacturing industries in Hong Kong have emerged as being more skill-intensive with a decrease in size in terms of both output and employment.[5] So, with the increase in relative demand for skilled workers and for skill upgrading within the manufacturing industries, the increase in the unemployment rate has had a positive effect on the wage gap between skilled and unskilled labour. Moreover, as discussed above, a similar logic also applies to finance and transport sectors. The personal services sector, however, has absorbed most of the unskilled labour force in Hong Kong as the other three sectors upgraded their technology. As personal service activities became more unskilled labour-intensive, the increase in unemployment rates had a negative effect on the relative wage ratio between skilled and unskilled workers.

Summary

For the past 25 years, economic integration between Hong Kong and China has proceeded at a remarkable speed. This chapter is concerned about the impact of Hong Kong–Mainland economic integration on the income distribution of Hong Kong. Specifically, we have tried to address the question of whether the increasing trade between the Mainland and Hong Kong has worsened the earning gap between unskilled and skilled workers in Hong Kong.

We generated hypotheses within the context of the Heckscher–Ohlin model, and used cointegration techniques to test the hypotheses. Our empirical findings showed support for the hypothesis that the wage ratio between skilled workers and unskilled workers in Hong Kong increased significantly as the trade volume between Hong Kong and China rose. Quantitatively, between 1982 and 2003, we estimated that the elasticities of the change in relative wage inequality between skilled and unskilled workers with respect to a 1 per cent change in the share of trade volume with China in the *manufacturing, financing, personal* and *transport service* sectors are 2%, 1.9%, 0.2% and 2%, respectively. Thus, our findings add further evidence to the empirical literature on trade and inequality. Furthermore, based on the Granger causality test, we find that there is a one-way causal effect from the Hong Kong–China trade share to relative wages, which reconfirms our hypothesis that the Hong Kong–China trade share causes the widening of the relative wages in all sectors. In sum, our empirical study shows that the increasing trade between Hong Kong and the Chinese Mainland is an important factor that led to growing earnings inequality in Hong Kong. The findings support the Stolper–Samuelson theorem that unskilled workers in developed countries will earn lower real wage rates from trading with developing countries.

Notes

1 Further, it complements Cheung and Fan (2001), who directly study the impact of Hong Kong's investment in China on the income distribution of Hong Kong.
2 Wood (1997) shows that in Hong Kong, the greater openness to trade in the 1960s and 1970s led to a narrowing of the wage gap between skilled and unskilled workers.
3 *Statistical Yearbook*, Department of Economic and Social Affairs, Statistics Division, United Nations, NY, various issues.
4 Since China began to implement the 'reform and open door' policy in 1979, Hong Kong entrepreneurs have shifted most of their manufacturing activities from Hong Kong to the mainland of China in search of a higher profit rate. The relocation of manufacturing production from Hong Kong to Mainland China has had an adverse effect on the wages of less-skilled workers in Hong Kong.
5 The workers in manufacturing industries in Hong Kong are focused primarily on procuring contracts, and the designing, marketing and distributing of the finished products.

References

Ash, Robert F. and Y.Y. Kueh (1993), 'Economic Integration within Greater China: Trade and Investment Flows between China, Hong Kong and Taiwan', *China Quarterly*, 136, 711–45.
Ashenfelter, Orley and J. Ham (1979), 'Education, Unemployment, and Earnings', *Journal of Political Economy*, 87 (5), S99–116.
Becker, Gary (1993) *Human Capital: A Theoretical and Empirical Analysis, with Special Reference to Education*, 3rd edn, Chicago, IL: The University of Chicago Press.
Borjas, George and Valerie A. Ramey (1994), 'Time Series Evidence on the Sources of Trends in Wage Inequality', *American Economic Review, Paper and Proceedings*, 84 (2), 10–16.

Cheung, Kui-yin and Chengze Simon Fan (2001), 'Hong Kong Investment in China and Income Distribution of Hong Kong', *Journal of Economic Integration*, 16 (4), 525–43.

Cheung, Kui-yin and Chengze Simon Fan (2002), 'Does Trade Lead to Wage Inequality? A Cross-industry Analysis', *Journal of Asia Pacific Economy*, 7 (2), 147–59.

Fan, C. Simon and Kui-yin Cheung (2004), 'Trade and Wage Inequality: The Hong Kong Case', *Pacific Economic Review*, 9 (2), 131–42.

Johansen, S. (1991), 'Estimation and Hypothesis Testing of Cointegration Vectors in Gaussian Vector Autoregressive Models', *Econometrica*, 59, 1,551–80.

Johansen, S and K. Juselius (1990), 'Maximum Likelihood Estimation and Inference on Cointegration – with Application to the Demand for Money', *Oxford Bulletin of Economics and Statistics*, 52, 169–210.

Krugman, Paul (1995), 'Growing World Trade: Causes and Consequences', *Brookings Papers on Economic Activity*, 1, 327–62.

Leamer, Edward E. (1996), 'In Search of Stolper–Samuelson Effects on U.S. Wages', *National Bureau of Economic Research Working Paper* No. 5427.

MacKinnon, J.G. (1991), 'Critical Values for Cointegration Tests', in R.E. Engle and C.W.J. Granger (eds), *Long-run Economic Relationships: Readings in Cointegration*, Oxford: Oxford University Press.

Richardson, J.D. (1995), 'Income Inequality and Trade: How to Think, What to Conclude', *Journal of Economic Perspectives*, 9, 33–55.

Rosen, Sherwin (1968), 'Short-Run Employment Variation on Class-I Railroads in the U.S., 1947–1963', *Econometrica*, 36, 511–29.

Suen, Wing (1995), 'Impact of Sectoral Shifts on Hong Kong Workers', *The Journal of International Trade and Economic Development*, 4 (2), 135–52.

Wood, Adrian (1995), 'How Trade Hurt Unskilled Workers', *Journal of Economic Perspectives*, 9, 57–80.

Wood, Adrian (1997), 'Openness and Wage Inequality in Developing Countries: The Latin American Challenge to East Asian Wisdom', *World Bank Economic Review*, 11, 33–57.

11
Macroeconomic Instability in Hong Kong: Internal and External Factors*

Yue Ma and Raymond C.W. Ng

Introduction

Since the adoption of the linked exchange rate system in October 1983, tying the Hong Kong dollar to the US dollar, Hong Kong's economic performance has been quite volatile. The rate of inflation reached 10.1 per cent in 1989 and 12 per cent in 1991. It averaged 7.14 per cent in the second half of the 1980s, and 9.34 per cent in the first half of the 1990s (see Figure 11.1). The GDP growth rate varied even more sharply, from the intra-year high of 14 per cent in 1987 to an intra-year negative 7 per cent in 1998 (see Figure 11.2).

Inflation in an open economy like Hong Kong's is caused by a combination of external and domestically generated factors. These include foreign exchange volatility, 'imported inflation', and overheating domestic demand. In the case of Hong Kong, however, the US dollar peg, which basically eliminates exchange rate fluctuations *vis-à-vis* the US dollar, also seems to have played a crucial role in generating inflation. This is quite unexpected, because under the peg the government would presumably be expected to adopt a highly prudent fiscal policy regime and to accept passively the monetary conditions dictated by the US Federal Reserve. Under

*We are grateful to Professor Y.Y. Kueh, who inspired our interest in many important contemporary issues and problems in Greater China, including the one that we examine in this chapter. Without his inspiration and guidance, this project would not have been possible.

We also acknowledge the useful suggestions and comments from Professor Lok Sang Ho, Professor Robert Ash, and seminar participants of Lingnan University, Hong Kong, and the University of Macau. This chapter is based on a project supported by a Competitive Earmarked Research Grant (No. LU3110/03H) from the Hong Kong SAR Research Grant Council and a research grant from Lingnan University (No. RES-007/200), Hong Kong. Tang Wing Hin provided helpful research assistance. However, we are responsible for any remaining errors.

Figure 11.1   Annual inflation rate (%)

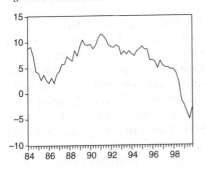

Figure 11.2   GDP growth rate (%)

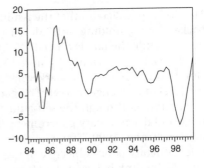

Figure 11.3   Hong Kong's interest rate

Figure 11.4   US interest rate

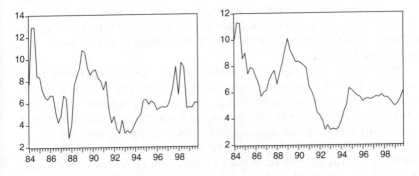

the link with the US dollar, changes in interest rates in Hong Kong must follow closely those of the United States in order to avoid undesirable capital outflows or inflows (see Figures 11.3 and 11.4). Serious economic instability might result from a lack of synchronization between the economic cycles in Hong Kong and the US. For instance, just when the interest rate needs to be raised to contain overheated investment and consumer expenditures, the Hong Kong Monetary Authority might be obliged to allow interest rates to fall, risking even higher inflation.

This chapter examines the extent to which the dollar peg may have helped to exacerbate macroeconomic volatilities in Hong Kong, by estimating an IS–LM open economy model for Hong Kong via a structural vector auto-regressive (VAR) process (Gali, 1992; Rogers, 1999). The econometric techniques of impulse response and variance decomposition analysis are applied to the VAR model to separate the major causes of inflation and instability.

Before we spell out the IS–LM model and conduct the empirical analysis we will first discuss the conditions required for maintaining macroeconomic stability under the dollar peg.

Conditions for macroeconomic stability under the dollar peg

The dollar peg dictates that the issuing of the Hong Kong currency is fully backed by the holding of US dollar reserves at the rate of HK$7.8 per US dollar. While the rate is officially fixed (for the issuing and redemption of the Hong Kong currency by note-issuing banks), the actual value of the Hong Kong dollar in the marketplace is nevertheless freely determined at the foreign exchange market. The parity between official and market rates is maintained through the self-adjusting mechanism of interest rate arbitrage and discretionary government intervention in the foreign exchange market (Tsang, 1999; Tsang and Ma, 2002). As a result, the primary and sole monetary policy objective of the Hong Kong Monetary Authority is to uphold the link between the Hong Kong dollar and the US dollar, while allowing exchange rates against other currencies to find their own levels. Depending on the strength or weakness of the US dollar, the effective exchange rate of the Hong Kong dollar may rise or decline, lending contractionary or expansionary pressures to the economy, as the case may be (see Figure 11.5).

Theoretically, macroeconomic stability for an economy operating under such a 'currency board arrangement' (CBA) may be restored automatically through domestic price readjustments. That is to say, in times of economic boom, domestic prices will adjust upward. Higher prices should, however, weaken the economy's price competitiveness, thereby discouraging exports and stimulating imports. This will in turn help to reduce demand pressures. Furthermore, the deteriorating trade balance will offset the initial expansion of the economy. However, as both the exchange rate and interest rate are not allowed to adjust under a CBA, price readjustments to restore macroeconomic stability may be bigger and could take longer than would otherwise be expected under a floating exchange rate regime, under which

Figure 11.5 Hong Kong's effective exchange rate

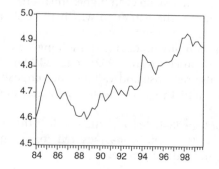

both the interest rate and exchange rate may adjust freely to help moderate any excessive price fluctuations. A pegged exchange rate regime therefore does not necessarily guarantee economic stability. More importantly, since inflation can be expectation-augmented, it may generate its own self-fulfilling momentum in the absence of an independent monetary policy with an inflation target under a floating exchange rate regime.

Viewed in this way, the success of a pegged exchange rate regime in a small, completely open economy like that of Hong Kong presupposes certain external and internal conditions. These include: (1) a synchronized business cycle with the country to whose currency the Hong Kong dollar is pegged (this is important, since under the pegged exchange rate regime the government concerned is deprived of any monetary policy flexibility to counter cyclical movements); (2) a stable world price system to hedge against excessive domestic price instability; (3) a sound domestic banking system to ensure efficient allocation of capital resources, including trade financing; and (4) a competitive domestic market to forestall major market distortions and resource misallocation that may arise through high inflation, independent of the pegged exchange rate regime or in spite of the sound banking system.

There is a large literature that addresses Hong Kong's economic instability. Ma, Meredith and Yiu (2002) and Tsang and Ma (2002) focus on the technical viability of the currency board system. Kueh (2001), and Kueh and Ng (2002) examine the implications of the Asian financial crisis and the role of the 'China factor' in relation to the dollar peg. Jao (1998) looks at the history of instability associated with the CBA. Siregar and Walker (2000) analyse the impact of monetary shocks on the real exchange rate. Chou and Lin (1994) address the external factors within the Hong Kong model for the LINK project coordinated by Lawrence Klein. In a separate Hong Kong model, Ma, Tsang and Tang (1998) explicitly build in the 'China factor' as an important explanatory variable. Ho and Wong (2005) attribute the prolonged economic depression since 1997 to shortcomings in the government's housing policy. Ng and Chen (1998) stress the importance of organizational reform in order to enhance the monetary management mechanism. Tsang and Ma (2002) find clear empirical evidence of 'currency substitution' (domestic for foreign currency and vice versa) as a possible explanation of instability, with important policy implications for the choice of the exchange rate regimes.

This chapter proposes a more comprehensive macroeconometric framework for assessing the relative importance of the various sources, external and internal, of economic instability in the Hong Kong economy.

An open economy theoretical model for Hong Kong

Following the work of Gali (1992) and Rogers (1999), we adopt an open economy IS–LM model with a short-run Phillips curve to identify the structural shocks. In particular, we modify the IS–LM framework by incorporating the restrictions of a CBA on the macroeconomic adjustments. We then estimate the model by a structural VAR process. The econometric techniques of impulse response and variance decomposition analysis will be applied to the VAR model. The intention is that the major causes of the macroeconomic instability and inflationary pressure in Hong Kong may be determined more accurately.

An IS–LM model of the Hong Kong economy

The following outlines a simplified version of the IS–LM model for an open economy under a linked exchange rate regime:

$$y_t = -\alpha_1(e_t + p_t - pim_t) - \alpha_2[R_t - E_t(\Delta p_{t+1})] + u_t^{IS} \tag{11.1}$$

$$m_t^d = p_t + \alpha_3 y_t - \alpha_4 r_t + \alpha_5 Rus_t + \alpha_6 \Delta e_t + u_t^{md} \tag{11.2}$$

$$m_t^s = m_t^d \tag{11.3}$$

$$R_t = Rus_t - E_t(\Delta e_{t+1}) + u_t^R \tag{11.4}$$

$$Rus_t = u_t^{Rus} \tag{11.5}$$

$$p_t = u_7 \, pim_t + \alpha_8[y_t - y^n] + u_t^p \tag{11.6}$$

$$pim_t = -\alpha_9 e_t + u_t^{pim} \tag{11.7}$$

$$e_t = u_t^e \tag{11.8}$$

where

α_i	= parameters
e_t	= log of nominal effective exchange rate index
$E_t(\Delta e_{t+1})$	= expected change of e_{t+1}
$E_t(\Delta p_{t+1})$	= expected change of p_{t+1}
m_t^d	= log of nominal demand for money
m_t^s	= log of nominal money supply
p_t	= log of consumer price index
pim_t	= log of import prices
R_t	= Hong Kong's nominal interest rate
Rus_t	= US nominal interest rate
u_t^j	= structural shocks
y_t	= log of real aggregate demand
y^n	= log of potential output

Equation (11.1) represents an open-economy IS equation. Real aggregate demand (y) is essentially determined by the real exchange rate ($e_t - p_t - pim_t$), the real interest rate [$R_t - E_t(\Delta p_{t+1})$], and structural shocks of demand (u_t^{IS}). Equation (11.2) is the demand for money equation. Money market equilibrium and the LM curve are given by equations (11.3) and (11.2), respectively. Demand for money (m_t^d) is determined positively by real aggregate demand (y) and negatively by the nominal domestic interest rate (R_t). The US interest rate (Rus_t) in Equation (11.2) is to model the currency substitution effect. A change in the US interest rate affects the opportunity cost of holding US dollars and therefore has an impact on demand for Hong Kong dollars. Similarly, the inclusion of the expected appreciation of exchange rate [$E_t(\Delta e_{t+1})$] is to capture the impact of the portfolio adjustment on the demand for money due to exchange rate variations. Equation (11.4) is the uncovered interest parity (UIP) condition. It shows the intrinsic interest rate arbitrage mechanism under the dollar peg. The UIP requires domestic interest rate (R_t) to follow the US interest rate (Rus_t) closely subject to a stochastic shock (u_t^R). Equations (11.5) and (11.8) indicate that the US interest rate and the Hong Kong exchange rate are determined exogenously and are subject to external shocks only. Equation (11.6) is a modified short-run Phillips curve. In the small open economy of Hong Kong, aggregate price level (p) is influenced by both import prices (pim_t) and excess domestic demand ($y_t - y^n$). Finally, as given in Equation (11.7), import prices (pim_t) are associated with the exchange rate and a structural shock.

Econometric techniques

Assuming adaptive expectations, the theoretical model can be estimated by a structural VAR process with a 7×1 vector $X_t = (Rus, R, e, pim, y, p, m)_t'$. In addition, there are seven independent structural shocks governing the economy with the ordering as $U_t = (u_t^{Rus}, u_t^R, u_t^e, u_t^{pim}, u_t^y, u_t^p, u_t^{md})'$. One of the advantages of estimating the model by a VAR process is that the dynamic adjustment of the economy is fully maintained with minimum theoretical restrictions (Rogers, 1999).

Having identified the structural shocks from the extended IS–LM model, we next investigate the major sources of macro-instability and inflationary pressure in Hong Kong under the dollar peg. In the traditional IS–LM model, it is usually assumed that the price level is sticky and is given. In our extended IS–LM model, we have relaxed this assumption and modelled the price mechanism in detail (cf. equations 11.6 and 11.7). As argued earlier, the peg has exposed Hong Kong to external monetary shocks. We examine whether such monetary shocks as variations in interest rate and money supply should have greater or more persistent impact on inflation and aggregate demand than shocks from changes in import prices or exchange rate. This can be done by applying the impulse response and variance decomposition analyses. The impulse response function may identify the direction and persistence of a shock. Variance decomposition analysis helps to assess the relative importance of the shocks at various time horizons by examining the proportion of the variance of forecast error of the variable that is explained by each of the shocks.

Data sources

The structural VAR model is estimated for the period of 1982Q1 to 1999Q4 by using quarterly data, with y defined as the log of real GDP in constant 1990 prices and m measured as the log of HK\$ money supply M2. (In Hong Kong, several measures of money supply are compiled: M1 = currency held by public + demand deposits; M2 = M1 + savings and time deposits with licensed banks + Negotiable Certificates of Deposits issued by licensed banks and held by the public.) The price variable p is defined as the log of consumer price index (A) (1990=100). We use seasonally adjusted series of y, m and p. In addition, e is measured as the log of trade-weighted effective exchange rate (1990=100), and pim is measured as log of the deflator for the imported goods and services weighted by their relative shares. Nominal interest rate R is measured as the nominal 3-month Hong Kong interbank offer rate (HIBOR) and Rus is defined as the US 3-month interbank interest rate. All variables except R and Rus are expressed in logarithms. The data for Hong Kong are collected from various issues of the *Monthly Digest of Statistics* published by the Hong Kong Census and Statistics Department. Rus is obtained from the website of the Federal Reserve Bank of the US.

Empirical evidence: a structural vector auto-aggressive approach

In this section, we first briefly discuss the econometric technique applied in this chapter and give some interpretations of the structural shocks in our Hong Kong model. We then present the empirical evidence for the model and discuss their policy implications.

Identification of shocks in the IS–LM model

Suppose the IS–LM model of the Hong Kong economy can be written as a structural VAR model as follows:

$$D(L)X_t = U_t \tag{11.9}$$

where $X_t = (Rus_t, R_t, e_t, pim_t, y_t, p_t, m_t)'$, which is defined in equations (11.1) to (11.8), $U_t = (u_t^{Rus}, u_t^R, u_t^e, u_t^{pim}, u_t^{IS}, u_t^p, u_t^{md})'$, $U_t \sim N(0, I_7)$, where I_7 is a 7×7 identity matrix, and $D(L) = \sum_{i=0}^{q} D_i L^i$ where, $D(L)$ is qth order matrix of polynomials with the lag operator L. D_o is the structural parameter matrix that captures the contemporaneous relationship of X_t. As most of the macroeconomic time series are non-stationary, it is necessary to re-parameterize equation (11.9) into the first-difference form:[1]

$$A_o\Delta X_t = \sum_{i=1}^{q-1} A_i\Delta X_{t-i} + A_q X_{t-q} + U_t \tag{11.10}$$

where $\Delta X_t = X_t - X_{t-1}$, $A_o = D_o$, $A_i = -\sum_{j=0}^{i} D_j$, $(i=1, 2, ..., q)$.

The reduced-form of (11.10) can be estimated by using Johansen's (1988) cointegration procedure as follows:

$$\Delta X_t = \sum_{i=1}^{q-1} \Gamma_i \Delta X_{t-i} + \Gamma_q X_{t-q} + V_t \tag{11.11}$$

where

$$\Gamma_i = A_0^{-1} A_i, \ (i=1, 2, \ ..... \ q), \tag{11.12}$$

and $V_t \sim N(0, \Omega)$ is the reduced-form residual and is assumed to be a linear transformation of the structural shocks:

$$V_t = A_0^{-1} U_t \tag{11.13}$$

If we can identify A_0 from the estimated (11.11), then we can recover all structural parameters A_i $(i = 1, 2, ..., q)$ and the structural shocks U_t by (11.12) and (11.13) respectively, given the fact that Γ_i $(i = 1, 2, ... q)$ are estimated from (11.11).

We use the following relationship to identify A_0:

$$A_0 \Omega A_0' = I_7 \tag{11.14}$$

There are $7 \times 7 = 49$ parameters in A_0 but there are only $7 \times [(7 +1)/2] = 28$ equations in (11.14), since Ω is a symmetric matrix. Therefore, we need to propose $49 - 28 = 21$ restrictions on A_0 to identify the whole matrix A_0.

To achieve this identification purpose, we impose zeros for the upper triangular of A_0:

$$A_0 = \begin{bmatrix} a_{11} & 0 & ... & 0 \\ a_{21} & a_{22} & ... & 0 \\ ... & ... & \diagdown & ... \\ a_{71} & a_{72} & ... & a_{77} \end{bmatrix} \tag{11.15}$$

which states that A_0 is a lower triangular matrix, so is A_0^{-1} (see Chiang, 1984, for example).

The econometric implications of (11.15) become clear if we rewrite (11.11) as follows:

$$\Delta X_t = \sum_{i=1}^{q-1} \Gamma_i \Delta X_{t-i} + \Gamma_q X_{t-q} + A_0^{-1} U_t \tag{11.16}$$

A low triangular A_0^{-1} implies that (11.16) is a recursive system in the sense that the structural shock u_t^k $(k = 1, 2, ... 7)$ enters the system (11.16) recursively, where $U_t = (u_t^1, u_t^2, ... u_t^7)' = (u_t^{Rus}, u_t^R, u_t^e, u_t^{pim}, u_t^y, u_t^p, u_t^{md})'$. In other words, equation k is only subject to shocks of u_t^1, u_t^2, ..., u_t^k, but it is immune from the shocks of u_t^{k+1}, u_t^{k+2}, ..., u_t^7.

The economic implications of (11.15) can be given intuitively as follows.

1 *Rus* is exogenous to the Hong Kong economy and depends upon factors outside the Hong Kong economic system, such as inflation and economic growth in the US. Hong Kong's interest rate, R, responds only to the US interest rate, *Rus*. R does not depend on Hong Kong's economic situation. This models the operation of its Currency Board System in Hong Kong. The CBS also implies that the effective exchange rate of Hong Kong is subject to the shocks from *Rus* and interest rate shocks from other countries due to the movements of the US dollar against other foreign currencies. These assumptions about *Rus*, R and e imply zero-restrictions in the first three rows of A_o in (11.15).
2 Import price *pim* depends on the exchange rate in equation (11.7) and domestic price p is modelled by a modified Phillips curve (11.6). The structures of (11.6) and (11.7) impose zeros for the fourth and fifth rows of A_o in (11.15).
3 Finally, equations (11.1) and (11.2) imply zeros in the last two rows of A_o in (11.15).

Estimation results

We use quarterly data ranging from 1982Q1 to 1999Q4 to estimate our reduced-form VAR of $X_t = (Rus_t, R_t, e_t, pim_t, y_t, p_t, m_t)'$, which are defined in equations (11.1) to (11.8). Augmented Dickey-Fuller (ADF) tests were first performed to investigate the stationarity of these seven time series. The results indicated that lagged values of all the time series were integrated of order one [I(1)] (see Table 11.1).

The Johansen (1988) cointegration procedure was then applied to the seven-variable VAR system in order to identify the number of cointegration

Table 11.1 Augmented Dickey-Fuller tests

Variable name	H_0: I(1) level	H_0: I(2) 1st difference	Conclusion
Rus	−2.074560	−4.336218***	I(1)
R	−2.275142	−6.198538***	I(1)
e	−1.574086	−4.039400***	I(1)
pim	−1.343665	−4.137328***	I(1)
y	−1.018612	−6.965631***	I(1)
p	−0.621755	−2.943723**	I(1)
Ms	−0.434725	−5.701037***	I(1)

**(***) denotes rejection of the null hypothesis at the 5%(1%) significance level.
The definition of the variables are given in Equations (11.1) to (11.8) in the main text.

Table 11.2 Johansen (1988) cointegration tests

Eigenvalue	Likelihood ratio	5 per cent critical value	1 per cent critical value	Hypothesized number of cointegrating vectors
0.676425	211.1277	109.99	119.80	None ***
0.509324	133.2733	82.49	90.45	At most 1 ***
0.428040	84.14735	59.46	66.52	At most 2 ***
0.266249	45.59806	39.89	45.58	At most 3 ***
0.236358	24.23664	24.31	29.75	At most 4
0.076796	5.630403	12.53	16.31	At most 5
0.001694	0.116956	3.84	6.51	At most 6

NB:
1 *** denotes rejection of the hypothesis at the 1% significance level.
2 Likelihood Ratio test indicates 4 cointegrating vectors at the 1% significance level.
3 Test assumption: no deterministic trend in the data.
4 Variable definitions are given in Equations (11.1) to (11.8) in the main text.

Un-normalized Cointegrating Coefficients:

Rus	R	e	pim	y	p	Ms
0.019736	0.013067	1.307892	–2.360004	6.581025	1.643693	–2.557951
–0.085234	0.092551	–0.569450	0.602642	–2.022876	–1.042576	1.048743
–0.068236	0.019216	0.578339	–1.913066	4.512603	–1.320334	–0.626520
–0.000706	–0.026131	0.619108	0.001927	–5.953487	–2.373745	2.696745

Sample: 1982Q1 1999Q4, 69 observations
Variables: Rus, R, e, pim, y, p, Ms (with 2 lags)

vectors in equation (11.11). Table 11.2 shows that there are four cointegration vectors among these seven variables. The first cointegrating vector is interpreted as the open economy IS curve of equation (11.1). The second cointegrating vector is a money demand function with currency substitution behaviour. The currency substitution behaviour is characterized by the significant appearance of the US interest rate in the money demand function. This evidence is consistent with the finding by Tsang and Ma (2002).

The third cointegrating vector is regarded as the uncovered interest parity condition of equation (11.4). Finally, the fourth cointegrating vector can be identified as the import price equation (11.7).

Having estimated the cointegration relationship and the reduced-form system (11.11), we apply the identification restrictions of (11.15) to recover the structural parameters and shocks in equation (11.10). This enables us to conduct impulse response[2] and variance decomposition analyses for the structural VAR.

Figure 11.6(a) Response of y (log GDP) to one standard deviation innovation

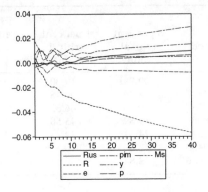

Figure 11.6(b) Response of p (log CPI) to one standard deviation innovation

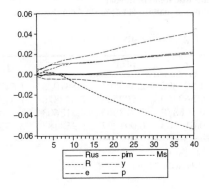

Figure 11.6(c) Response of Ms (log money supply) to one standard deviation innovation

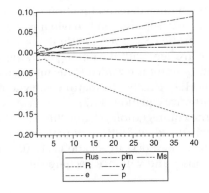

Figure 11.6 shows the impulse response of the real GDP, CPI and nominal money supply of the Hong Kong economy to various one-standard-deviation structural shocks. The structural shocks to the VAR model are temporary, but the response of the endogenous variables (such as real GDP, CPI and nominal money supply) may be transitional or permanent. It also can trace the source of the important shock, whether it is originated from demand shock (real GDP shock), price shock, or the monetary shock.

We find that all these structural shocks have permanent effects on the Hong Kong economy, although the size of the effect varies. Furthermore, these effects are increasing in size over time and are statistically significant according to the one-standard-error criterion introduced by Shapiro and Watson (1988). Therefore, the evidence indicates that our IS–LM model captures important external and internal factors that influence the Hong Kong economy. In addition, the findings indicate that the shock in the domestic interest rate has apparently had an accelerating impact on all three macro-variables.

Whilst the impulse response analysis provides the duration and magnitude of the impacts of the shocks on the economy, the variance decomposition analysis addresses the question of the relative importance of these shocks. Table 11.3 reports the decomposition of both the short-run and long-run variance of the forecast-errors for real GDP, CPI, nominal money supply (m) and Hong Kong interest rate (R) due to various structural disturbances. For example, Table 11.3(a) indicates the decomposition of the variance of real GDP over time if all the shocks occurred in Quarter 1. Specifically, the first row of Table 11.3(a) shows the decomposition of the variance of real GDP in the first quarter (i.e., the immediate impacts on real GDP after the shocks occurred). It suggests that nearly 79.9 per cent of the total variance of real GDP is due to its own shock which occurred in Quarter 1. Import price shock, US interest rate shock, effective exchange rate shock, and the Hong Kong interest rate shock contribute only 12.5, 5.1, 2.1 and 0.4 per cent, respectively, to the variance of real GDP in Quarter 1. The shocks of CPI and money supply do not contribute to the real GDP instantaneously, although they do make some contributions in the subsequent quarters.

The Hong Kong interest rate (R), import price (pim) and domestic demand (y) shocks are found to be the largest influential factors affecting the real GDP, CPI and money supply variables in the long run (i.e., over 40 quarters, or 10 years cf. Figure 11.7(a)). In the short run, shocks from the US interest rate have a bigger impact on the real GDP of Hong Kong than shocks from Hong Kong interest rates. In addition, US interest rate shocks also have a bigger impact on the money supply of Hong Kong than shocks from the effective exchange rate, the import price and the CPI. In the long run, the US interest rate (Rus) is confirmed to be the driving force for the Hong Kong interest rate (R), although Rus appears to have a relatively small effect on R in the short run.

Table 11.3 Variance decomposition of real GDP, CPI and money supply (in %)

Quarter	Rus	R	e	pim	y	p	Ms
(a) Variance decomposition of y (log GDP)							
1	5.059443	0.406330	2.112472	12.52434	79.89741	0.000000	0.000000
2	2.896267	4.381277	1.642363	24.15171	55.37009	0.001311	11.55698
3	2.138001	11.71339	2.433171	24.93141	40.94755	0.077047	17.75943
4	1.570838	27.24447	5.874587	20.52409	31.13780	0.198813	13.44940
8	0.685769	53.29487	3.439162	15.99620	18.44653	0.313196	7.824274
20	1.011005	70.44089	2.094005	15.49451	7.854869	0.332082	2.772636
40	1.751756	70.84373	1.526698	17.91363	5.985367	0.690238	1.288578
(b) Variance decomposition of p (log CPI)							
1	1.253277	2.850728	3.865566	20.49419	5.085460	66.45078	0.000000
2	1.408756	3.916780	8.320667	36.34818	4.134423	45.80257	0.068618
3	0.829990	4.115491	9.900667	33.86692	8.116466	43.13263	0.037832
4	0.661402	3.164353	8.960117	36.55116	9.660913	40.97782	0.024229
8	0.342892	1.364994	5.974029	42.72232	16.69954	32.87859	0.017633
20	0.169731	25.43485	3.962096	38.30213	15.06361	17.06193	0.005662
40	0.611890	44.51179	3.203713	31.94914	9.981310	9.740859	0.001294
(c) Variance decomposition of Ms (log nominal money supply)							
1	5.795056	40.71260	1.866964	0.244712	5.147364	0.834029	45.39927
2	2.744166	35.68402	0.902024	1.051595	14.14765	2.026589	43.44395
3	2.050901	36.88395	1.717256	1.984689	16.95284	3.234168	37.17620
4	1.591936	43.71975	2.496439	3.713226	16.51386	2.519769	29.44502
8	0.784071	56.50726	2.812822	11.80720	13.45434	0.811589	13.82271
20	0.923285	65.92649	2.276776	17.70526	8.878178	1.008586	3.281423
40	1.366908	67.62357	1.978558	19.60881	6.750474	1.589805	1.081871

Table 11.3 Variance decomposition of real GDP, CPI and money supply (in %) – *continued*

Quarter	Rus	R	e	pim	y	p	Ms
(d) Variance decomposition of R (3-month HIBOR)							
1	30.70174	69.29826	0.000000	0.000000	0.000000	0.000000	0.000000
2	39.79282	52.35701	1.212262	0.822742	5.087054	0.564301	0.163816
3	48.24098	42.20271	0.976789	0.916932	4.249792	2.763899	0.648901
4	49.22010	37.49772	0.858432	4.024394	4.104437	2.655226	1.639686
8	52.37011	27.69706	1.871976	6.583263	3.876035	2.318800	5.282756
20	41.18190	16.79896	8.659563	5.499059	3.738567	15.43669	8.685254
40	34.06765	12.14754	11.43300	5.489052	4.835042	22.52183	9.505890

The definitions of the variables are given in Equations (11.1) to (11.8) in the main text.

Figure 11.7(a)   Variance decomposition of y (log GDP)

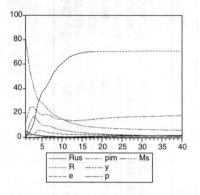

Figure 11.7(b)   Variance decomposition of p (log CPI)

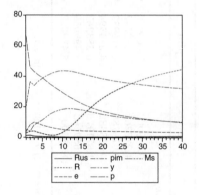

Figure 11.7(c)   Variance decomposition of Ms (log money supply)

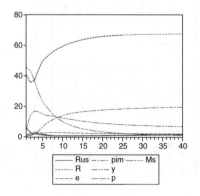

The variance decomposition of real GDP shows that the demand instability in the short run (i.e., one-quarter after the shock) is dominated by the demand shocks (80 per cent) itself. However, in the long run, the relative importance of the demand shocks is not as visible as the other shocks. The demand instability in the long run is contributed by the Hong Kong interest rate shocks (71 per cent), import price shocks (18 per cent), domestic demand shocks (6 per cent), and the combined shocks (5 per cent) of the US interest rate, effective exchange rate, nominal money supply, and CPI (in descending order of size).

The variance decomposition of the CPI also reveals that the largest contribution to the price instability in the long run is from the Hong Kong interest rate (R) (48 per cent), followed by import price shocks (30 per cent), domestic demand shocks (9 per cent), inflation shocks (8 per cent), and the combined shocks (5 per cent) of the effective exchange rate, US interest rate, and nominal money supply (in descending order of the sizes: cf. Figure 11.7(b) and Table 11.3). The variance decomposition of nominal money supply gives a similar picture (cf. Figure 11.7(c) and Table 11.3). The biggest contributing factor to monetary instability in the long run is the Hong Kong interest rate (R) (68 per cent).

The empirical findings suggest quite clearly that variation in domestic interest rate is the single most important source of volatility in Hong Kong's GDP growth, inflation and money supply, whilst the US interest rate has remained an indirect factor. The adoption of the dollar peg has thus effectively rendered Hong Kong's monetary conditions totally dependent on US monetary policy. This was particularly problematic for Hong Kong during the late 1980s and early 1990s. At that time, Hong Kong had high inflation coupled with strong GDP growth recovery from the 1989 trough (see Figures 11.1 and 11.2). However, as interest rates in Hong Kong had to be kept in line with that in the US to keep the dollar peg intact, any excessive aggregate demand could not be contained by adjusting the prevailing interest rate upwards. The upshot was that Hong Kong was subject to continuous overheating and persistent inflationary pressures. The real interest rates hovered around zero for many years after the dollar peg was adopted, until the trend was abruptly ended by the Asian Financial Crisis (see Figure 11.5). In other words, the first condition (i.e., a synchronized business cycle with the US) required for achieving macroeconomic stability in Hong Kong under the peg could not be fulfilled.

As for the other three conditions, the estimated results also suggest that they were not all fulfilled. The impulse response analysis reveals that shocks from foreign inflation, as well as from domestic output and domestic price, all have a permanent impact on domestic price. In addition, based on variance decomposition analysis, all three different types of shock account for a significant share in the variation of domestic price, particularly over the longer run.

Figure 11.8 Hong Kong's real interest rate

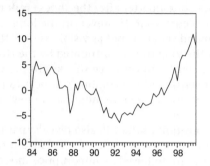

It should be noted that under the dollar peg, foreign inflation can be expected to be translated into domestic inflation with relative ease. Moreover, the fact that both domestic output and domestic price shocks also affect quite strongly the movements of domestic prices seems to suggest the existence of a certain market rigidity or imperfection. Without a competitive, flexible market to restore macroeconomic stability in response to various economic shocks, price adjustments are bound to be more volatile and prolonged than they would otherwise be. The point made warrants further research in order to identify the specific sources and mechanisms of such market rigidity.

However, shocks to the money supply variable have had almost no impact on Hong Kong's price volatilities. This confirms the validity of the third condition in the case of Hong Kong: that is, a sound banking system in Hong Kong provides a stable financial environment for both international and domestic economic activities.

Conclusions

Among all internal and external factors that affect macroeconomic stability in Hong Kong under the dollar peg, the Hong Kong interest rate turns out to be the most dominant. It directly affects GDP, price and money supply. By virtue of the peg, US interest rates also exert a direct and indirect impact on Hong Kong in the short run, but US interest rates play a smaller role than Hong Kong interest rates in determining Hong Kong's economic performance. Over the long run, however, the US interest rate appears to be the driving force of the adjustment in the Hong Kong interest rate.

International prices are another factor bearing on Hong Kong's domestic demand and price movements; and domestic demand in itself also contributes significantly to macroeconomic instability, although its influence is smaller than that of Hong Kong interest rate and import price. Last but not least, Hong Kong's sound banking system has helped to create a stable currency demand environment for its economy, in spite of significant 'currency substitution' activities conducted by residents.

Our findings provide a tenable framework for understanding the financial and monetary transmission mechanisms in Hong Kong. By extending the current linear VAR model to a non-linear VAR model (see, e.g, Ma and Kanas, 2000), or to a non-linear structural model (Ma, Meredith and Yiu, 2002), the methodology promises fruitful avenues of research into the Hong Kong's current target zone arrangement, in order to improve its exchange rate system.

Notes

1 If none of the variables in X_t is cointegrated with another one, then $A_q = 0$ and we are left with a standard structural VAR in the first-difference of X_t (Rogers, 1999). If some of the variables are cointegrated, then $A_q \neq 0$.
2 Early theoretical work can be found in Ma (1992), for example.

References

Chiang, A.C. (1984), *Fundamental Methods of Mathematical Economics*, 3rd edn, New York: McGraw-Hill.

Chou, W.L. and T.B. Lin (1994), 'Hong Kong Model', in S. Ichimura and Y. Matsumoto (eds), *Econometric Models of Asian-Pacific Countries*, Tokyo: Springer-Verlag.

Gali, J. (1992), 'How Well Does the IS–LM Model Fit Postwar US Data?', *Quarterly Journal of Economics*, 107, 709–38.

Ho, Lok Sang and Gary Wong (2005), 'Privatization of Public Housing: How it Led to a Deep Recession in Hong Kong', *Contemporary Economic Policy*, forthcoming.

Jao, Y.C. (1998), 'The Working of the Currency Board: The Experience of Hong Kong, 1935–97', *Pacific Economic Review*, 3 (3), 219–42.

Johansen, S. (1988), 'Statistical Analysis of Cointegration Vectors', *Journal of Economic Dynamics and Control*, 12, 231–54.

Kueh, Y.Y. (2001), 'The Greater China Growth Triangle in the Asian Financial Crisis', in Shahid Jusuf, Simon Evenett and Weiping Wu (eds), *Facets of Globalization: International and Local Dimensions of Development*, Washington, DC: The World Bank, 57–77.

Kueh, Y.Y. and Raymond C.W. Ng (2002), 'The Interplay of the "China Factor" and US Dollar Peg in the Hong Kong Economy', *China Quarterly* (London), 170, 387–412.

Ma, Y. (1992), 'Policy Measurement for the Dynamic Linear Model with Expectations Variables: A Multiplier Approach', *Computational Economics*, 5, 303–12.

Ma, Yue and A. Kanas (2000), 'Testing Nonlinear Relationship among Fundamentals and Exchange Rates in the ERM', *Journal of International Money and Finance*, 19, 135–52.

Ma, Yue, G. Meredith and M. Yiu (2002), 'A Currency Board Model of Hong Kong', Hong Kong Institute for Monetary Research Working Paper, No. 1/2002, www.hkimr.org.

Ma, Yue, Shu-ki Tsang and Shu-hung Tang (1998), 'The China Factor and the Hong Kong Economy', *International Review of Applied Economics*, 12 (1), 89–106.

Ng, Raymond C.W. and Edward K.Y. Chen (1998), 'The Role of Monetary Management under a Linked Exchange Rate Regime: The Case of Hong Kong', in C.H. Kwan, Donna Vandenbrink and Chia Siow Yue (eds), *Coping with Capital Flows in East Asia*, Singapore: Institute of Southeast Asian Studies, 136–70.

Rogers, J.H. (1999), 'Monetary Shocks and Real Exchange Rates', *Journal of International Economics*, 49 (2), 269–88.

Shapiro, M. and M. Watson (1988), 'Sources of Business Cycle Fluctuations', *NBER Macroeconomics Annual*, 3, 111–48.

Siregar, R.Y. and W.C. Walker (2000), 'Monetary Shocks and the Fundamental Determinants of the Real Exchange Rate under the Hong Kong Currency Board', *Asian Economic Journal*, 14, 1–21.

Tsang, Shu-ki (1999), 'Fixing the Exchange Rate through a Currency Board Arrangement: Efficiency Risk, Systemic Risk and Exit Cost', *Asian Economic Journal*, 13, 239–66.

Tsang, Shu-ki and Yue Ma (2002), 'Currency Substitution and Speculative Attacks on a Currency Board System', *Journal of International Money and Finance*, 21 (1), 53–78.

Part III

Foreign Direct Investment, Technology Transfer and Economic Restructuring

12
Taiwan's Scientific and Technological Development: A Newly-industrializing Economy Experience of Institutional Evolution

Christopher Howe

Introduction

We now have a generation of literature available that analyses the development of the first four Asian newly-industrializing economies (NIEs). In its early stages this focused on certain perceived commonalities between the four cases of Taiwan, Hong Kong, Singapore and South Korea. All, for example, were praised for 'open' rather than 'autarchic' trade orientation and all were seen to have made substantial use of market mechanisms. Later, Taiwan and Korea were differentiated as case studies in which 'industrial policy' modified markets. In both countries, political histories that left a legacy of governmental authority relatively independent of 'society' and vested interests were seen as having contributed to the success of these models.

In the 1990s a new debate emerged. This sought to understand the 'sources of growth'. Sceptical analysts suggested that extensive development based on high rates of investment and labour input would, eventually, exhaust itself, presenting policy-makers with new challenges. Finally, most recently, the Asian Financial Crisis and its aftermath generated a new flurry of writing, which attempted to understand the shorter- and longer-term implications of this episode.

The Asian background to the more recent of these waves of intellectual activity has been highlighted in the emergence of two significant trends. One has been the rise of the Chinese external economy and China's new-found place as a powerful magnet for FDI, and the other has been the long-term stagnation of the Japanese growth rate. The changing fortunes of China and Japan have both, in different but related ways, had major impacts on the economic evolution of the NIEs and other Asian economies. Intra-regional and inter-industry trade has grown rapidly. Such growth has been substantially based on flows of FDI and the linkages between this deepening regional division of labour and the market expansion for final goods, mainly in the US and EU.[1]

A basic thought underlying this brief commentary is that surely we have reached a point at which understanding of the NIEs requires us to focus ever more closely on *differences* between them and, in particular, to seek greater clarity about institutional and other variations. The common properties of the NIEs were real (if exaggerated) in the 1960s and 1970s but, in the last two decades, as development paths have clearly diverged, these have become less and less helpful to our understanding.

As a case in point, I should like in this chapter to discuss the Taiwanese experience of technological improvement. In the conclusion, I suggest some fundamental contrasts between Taiwan and the other NIEs.

Background to the Taiwanese case

I believe that Taiwan is a good case to consider at the present time. One reason for thinking this is that in Taiwan itself there is clear evidence that the limits of its most recent, highly successful phase of development are being reached. As a result, initiatives of various kinds are already being undertaken as the government seeks to support the private sector in finding ways ahead.[2]

Some of the concerns being raised within Taiwan, however, are widely shared in other economies. Indeed, there is growing global awareness of the importance of science and technology policy issues. The public and private sectors are both acutely aware of the dangers of being left behind in the race to exploit the economic potential of new discoveries and innovation and, in particular, to develop the human resources needed to achieve this. Three, rather different, manifestations of this crisis serve to illustrate this. In the United States, current budgets project an *absolute* diminution of resources for publicly financed scientific research. This shift represents the reversal of a trend stretching back to the Second World War and reflects a redistribution in favour of research and development (R & D) for 'homeland security'. The cuts now proposed include the abandonment of the Hubble telescope – a programme that took more than 30 years to develop and is widely regarded as one of the triumphs of American twentieth-century science – not only in a purely scientific sense, but also in terms of the success of the organizational funding network that made the scientific work possible.[3] Meanwhile, in Paris in the summer of 2004, hundreds of scientific workers took to the streets. Borrowing techniques developed by French farmers, public sector workers and others, they attacked, with some success, modest proposals to change the French system of innovation (widely acknowledged to be excessively bureaucratic and underperforming).[4] A few months later, in December 2004, a lengthy and historic attempt to reform the German federal government system collapsed because of the refusal of the States (*Länder*) to surrender powers over educational arrangements.

Why should these issues have bubbled to the surface at this time? Briefly, the following factors help provide an explanation. In the past 15 years, competitive pressures in world markets have intensified. This partly reflects global and localized forms of liberalization and integration. More importantly, however, it reflects organizational innovations by the most competitive companies in the forms of out-sourcing and the elaboration of Global Value Chains. These initiatives have been especially important in the production of standardized goods (e.g., laptops) and products in which a high proportion of the components can be standardized (e.g., vehicles). Underlying these new structures have been innovations in finance, communications and business relationships. In Asia, as argued above, these changes have been propelled by both the opening of China and the pressures on Japanese business to survive through re-structuring and re-locating. Thus, technical change has been both a cause and an effect of transformation in Asia, where rising firm and national capabilities are increasingly seen as keys to survival.

From a longer-term perspective, two further considerations arise. On the negative side, demographic trends in the advanced – and several Asian – economies highlight ageing workforces and rising dependency; and, in the case of Japan, they show the likelihood of absolute population decline. Within these scenarios rising productivity will be essential if social and political structures are to be given the chance to evolve in stable rather than chaotic ways.

On the positive side, however, it is clear that we are only in the early stages of revolutions in both electronics/information and the life sciences. Both of these fields hold huge potential for productivity and human welfare gains, if only such benefits can be realized through R & D and widespread diffusion of innovation.

Finally, it is important to relate the real to the financial world, a fundamental linkage emphasized by Schumpeter.[5] R & D and its industrial application requires financial support of many different kinds. Two recent developments are important here. One has been the 'dotcom' boom and bust, an episode that illustrated the potential that innovations have to bewitch and destabilize capital markets. Second, there is the problem of public sector deficits. It is noteworthy that for different reasons in each of them, such deficits have become large and intractable in the three economies – those of the US, Japan and Germany – that we identify as the core innovators in the world system. The net effect of these factors is that at precisely the time when the financial needs of innovation are great at every stage (i.e., from 'pure' research through to commercialization), provision of finance is a problem. In the case of public resources, this shortage is partly responsible for a re-thinking of the fundamental post-Second World War paradigm that defined basic knowledge as a public good, likely to be undersupplied in the absence of public subsidy.

A framework for Taiwan

In thinking about Taiwan's experience of innovation we need to summarize the elements that go into these activities, giving particular attention to those that fall within the scope of public policy. The most important of these would seem to be:

(a) human resource development in educational institutions and in the workplace;
(b) The nature of domestic and international markets for skilled manpower as they affect Taiwan;
(c) Public and private budgets and institutional arrangements for R & D;
(d) Market structures and firm behaviour that encourage or suppress innovation and risk taking;
(e) Intellectual property arrangements;
(f) Intangible cultural and historical factors that affect individual or collective behaviour.

Table 12.1   Basic factors in science and technology performance

	US	Japan
Human resource development	Mixture of public and private educational institutions; decentralized government controls; lifelong learning with certifiable qualifications available	Mainly public sector with centralized controls; importance of in-house 'on the job learning', with less emphasis on development of specialization
Markets for human resources	High mobility of all kinds and strong net inflows of international human resources	Limited inter-firm mobility and very limited attraction to international talent
R and D	Strong private sector but large public funds in support of 'pure ' research and defence	Heavy reliance on private sector expenditures, mainly for 'development' rather than 'research'
Market structures	Highly competitive markets with large and small firms active in innovation to compete	High tolerance of imperfectly competitive structures with large companies dominant in R and D (Schumpeterian model)
Intellectual Property arrangements	Highly protective of individual/private interests	Traditionally somewhat more biased towards the public interest
Cultural factors	Cult of youth	Cult of age

It is remarkable how these six categories can vary, even between highly innovative, advanced economies. Taking two very different types – Japan and the United States – six major contrasts are summarized in Table 12.1.

Of course this sketch contains elements of caricature and represents a stylized version of the two systems in the 1960s and 1970s. Further, it would be possible to argue that the models simply contrast arrangements in a technological frontier economy with those of a fast, successful follower. But this would be too simplistic. Embedded in the antitheses are real policy alternatives. Indeed, France, Germany and the UK all have systems with other significant points of differentiation. It is significant too that during the past decade the Japanese and US systems have, in interesting ways, begun to learn from each other.

There are major problems in analysing and explaining the results of science and technology policies. To measure performance we have conventional indicators including the R & D budget, supplies of high-level manpower, patent data and changing performance in science and engineering citation indices. But in looking at industrial case studies, aggregation of performance into simple indicators is a problem because industry characteristics vary so much. Raw materials, production processes, world market structures for products, ease of access to existing generic and commercial knowledge all demand consideration in evaluating a particular example.

Further, in looking at national aggregated case studies there is a tendency to search for models and paradigms of technology policy. But at this level of abstraction such searches all too easily miss the point that, driven by internal evolution and external factors (both systemic and random), the important point of a model may be its own change.

In an attempt to address these problems, this chapter looks at Taiwan's experience of technology development, focusing mainly on the electrical/electronics sector, but with reference too to the experience of other sectors. This is an obvious choice, since it is the dynamism of these industries that has been central to the expansion of East Asia's regional trade and FDI growth in the past decade.[6]

One measure of recent Taiwanese achievements in this sector is captured in estimates of Taiwan's world market shares for important information technology (IT) products (see Table 12.2).

Purchases by foreign brand-owning manufacturers are estimated to account for over 90 per cent of total hardware sales, the balance being Taiwan's own brand production. In 2001, for example, 76 per cent of foreign orders were from the US and 12 per cent from Japan, but with Japanese orders growing more rapidly.[7]

Underlying the extraordinary success of Taiwan as a supplier on OEM/ODM contracts has been the development of 'open standards' for IT equipment and components. This has facilitated what Stan Shih calls the 'super disintegration' of the industry, a phrase that captures the hugely expanded

Table 12.2   Taiwan's shares of world markets of important IT export products, 2003

Product	Market share by value	Market share by volume
Notebook PCs	58	64
Wireless local area networks	42	91
Integrated circuit foundry	71	n.a.
Motherboards	72	79
Recordable optical disks	77	79
Network cards	35	91

n.a. = not available

Source: Council for Economic Planning and Development, *Taiwan Statistical Data Book 2004*, p. 11.

opportunities for re-configuring patterns of out-sourcing of components and sub-systems. These re-configurations often occur with great speed and across national boundaries.[8]

These re-configurations, hugely important to Taiwan, are not only matters of geography and location; they are also critical to the changing power and profitability of firms within the relevant value chains. Max Boisot's concept of the 'paradox of value' is very helpful here. Boisot's argument is that products move through cycles in which the codification and abstraction of all the knowledge relevant to them make possible both increased value and diffusion; but that, ultimately, diffusion makes knowledge commonplace, thereby destroying the financial leverage that flows from narrower, proprietary control.[9] Thus, the more that participation in value chains reflects the expansion of commonplace knowledge, the lower the returns to it are likely to be. The major beneficiaries from commodity chain configurations are those who possess the skill assets to control new product conception and design, manufacture of key capital equipment and components, brands, complementary logistic and marketing strengths, and the capabilities needed to forge and develop new chains. For firms in value chains the goal must be to extend control from low to high return segments of the chain. For governments and the public sector, an overriding objective has to be to help firms evolve in this direction.

The other implication of Boisot's 'paradox' is that firms with seemingly secure positions in the chain may lose their advantages abruptly. This will happen if competitors acquire relevant knowledge, or are enabled to by-pass existing positions with product variants or exploitation of markets that can be served with new (sometimes 'inferior') technologies.[10] The significance of this risk factor varies according to the scale of resources committed to particular activities.[11]

Human resource development

High school and university numbers have grown rapidly since the 1950s. School participation is close to 100 per cent and educational participation for 18–21 year olds rose from 10 per cent in 1976 to 35 per cent by 2000. In the eight years from 1994/5 to 2003/4 alone, total university enrolment rose from 340,000 to 980,000. Within these totals the numbers in science and engineering disciplines have been very high, influenced by government direction.

Numbers of higher degree holders in science and technology are also impressive, and these are reflected in the high proportion of such staff in technology institutions, science parks and major companies, especially in the IT and in the IC fabrication and design sectors.

Taiwan's high level manpower supply has also been strongly influenced by the outflow and return of students to the US and, to a smaller extent, Europe. In the 1990s the number of returnees ranged between 3,000 and 6,000 per annum. A great advantage conferred by this reverse migration is not only the quality of education received by the returnees, but also the fact that many of them have benefited from post-educational experience in foreign companies and science parks. The phenomenon of reverse migration has not been accidental. It was encouraged on a personal basis by key individuals and later supported by a variety of policies.[12] These included remission of draft avoidance penalties and the creation of government science parks and corporate environments, both of which provided lifestyles and comforts that were not generally available in Taiwan, but were required by those acclimatised to living in the West.

At least as important as formal education has been the growing role of learning and personal development inside companies. In the early stages, Taiwan's foreign investors – especially Americans and Japanese – were important in this respect. The Japanese were especially important in imparting to Taiwanese the fundamentals of quality control, while an important route of American skill diffusion was through 'breakaway' employees who subsequently became sub-contractors.[13] In the past two decades the largest Taiwanese companies have also, increasingly, understood the importance of training, both directly 'in house' and indirectly through their business

Table 12.3 Distribution of students in higher education by main disciplines, 2003–4 (%)

Engineering	Natural sciences	Maths and computing	Medicine	Humanities	Social science and business
22.9	2.7	10.2	8.5	8.4	26.3

Source: Taiwan Statistical Data Book 2004, pp. 280–1.

networks. For the largest companies, whether foreign investors or Taiwanese, growth and diffusion of skills is not a charitable or public-spirited act; rather, it is a means by which they can out-source an ever-widening variety of tasks to enterprises. This can reduce their costs because the sub-contractors are flexible, specialized and acquire increasing economies of scale. By progressive enlargement of sub-contracting the main companies are also sharing financial and technological risks within the system. Where key components are volatile in price or problematic new processes are under experimentation, this may be an important, if less obvious, benefit of diffusing skill formation.

The fluidity of movement between companies and the 'Boss Island' phenomenon – the process whereby employees leave paid employment to establish their own businesses (often becoming sub-contractors to the original employer) – ensures that all skills, whether acquired through formal or other routes, are rapidly disseminated throughout the economy.

Direct government leadership and expenditure

A basic function of government has been the provision of a long-term framework for science and technology at three levels. At the highest level of abstraction are visions of the future; next come more specific, strategic objectives; and finally, there are remarkably detailed and specific plans. Before political reform the vision was provided by the KMT (Kuomintang) as part of its ongoing political development. In the multi-party era the position is more complex, although from statements and documents of all kinds it is hard to pinpoint any significant differences between the KMT and the DPP (Democratic Progressive Party) in terms of their visions for this field of policy. Both emphasize the central significance of knowledge and innovation to the security and prosperity of Taiwan. Both accept that government has a crucial, if evolving, role to lead and provide resources for this. The key organizations involved in the formation and implementation of science and technology policy are shown in Figure 12.1.

Within this framework the National Science Council (NSC), the Ministries and other governmental bodies are responsible to the Executive Yuan. The Academia Sinica is directly responsible to the Office of the President. The NSC and all governmental bodies sponsor research both 'in house' (in public sector labs and centres) externally (in universities and other private research centres and laboratories). The relative size of the main budgets for the public sector are shown in Table 12.4.

In practical terms the NSC is the key body since it provides leadership in preparing visions, which it then converts into strategic objectives and, subsequently, into detailed plans. In its pioneering White Paper of 1997, for example, the NSC set out three visionary goals. These were to transform Taiwan into:

Figure 12.1 Taiwan's public sector science and technology administration

Executive Yuan	Executive Yuan Science and Technology Advisory Group
National Science Council	Academia Sinica
Ministries of: Economic Affairs Education Transport and Communication Council of Agriculture	
Other organizations: Atomic Energy Council Department of Health Environmental Protection Administration	

(a) an Asia-Pacific research stronghold;
(b) an Asia-Pacific high technology manufacturing sector;
(c) a technologically advanced nation.[14]

Twelve strategies were proposed in order to achieve these goals. They included raising the R & D/GDP ratio from 2.5 per cent to 3 per cent by 2010; improving the integration of public and private sector research activities; developing science parks; technology targeting; enhancing public understanding of science and technology through education; and providing appropriate legal frameworks for science and technology development.[15]

The NSC also organizes regular national science and technology conferences, coordinates public sector activities, and dispenses thousands of grants.[16] Collaboration with the Ministry of Economic Affairs is particularly important. The distribution of the NSC budget for grants between the main

Table 12.4 Distribution of central government science and technology budget, by department, 2004 (percentage shares, excluding defence)

Department	% share
MOEA	36.8
NSC	34.3
Academia Sinica	9.8
Council of Agriculture	5.3
Department of Health	4.7
Ministry of Transport and Communications	1.1
Ministry of Education	1.1
Atomic Energy Council	1.1
EPA (Environmental Protection Administration)	0.1

Note: Total value of budget = $NT67.163 billion.

Source: National Science Council, *Indicators of Science and Technology (Charts) 2004*, p. 47.

Table 12.5   Distribution of NSC special topic grants by subject, 1991 and 1997
(expenditure, % shares)

Field	Percentage share, 1991	Percentage share, 1997
Natural sciences	25	27
Engineering and applied science	33	32
Biology, medicine and agriculture	34	24
Humanities, social science and science education	8	13
Other	0	4
Total	100	100

Source: National Science Council Review, 1990–91, p. 49; *National Science Council Review,* 1997, p. 8.

subject areas (shown for 1991 and 1997 in Table 12.5) is a useful indication of government research priorities.

The quite high success rates, by European and American standards, of grant applications submitted to the NSC suggest that they are probably subject to considerable preparation and preliminary screening. In 1996, for example, approximately two-thirds of applications were successful.

Looked at from an international perspective, the NSC's role and range of activities are unique. There are other organizations around the world with similar sounding titles, but none of these to my mind fulfils the range of roles of the Taiwan NSC or could be shown to have had such a direct and tangible influence on both policy and policy implementation. Current plans to merge the NSC to form a larger body will be discussed in the conclusion to this chapter.

Some of Taiwan's other governmental science and technology institutions are also of great interest, with only Korea providing serious points of comparison and similarity.[17] The most famous example is certainly the Industrial Technology Research Institute (ITRI). This is a publicly funded body charged with the function of enhancing private sector research and technology capabilities. It does this through a family of specialized laboratories, of which a particularly well known example is the laboratory for Electronics and Semi-Conductors (ERSO). Founded in 1973, ERSO has had to assist relatively small companies develop technological strengths, make appropriate alliances with foreign partners, and fulfil technology targets. As the private sector has matured, ERSO's role has changed; but small-scale and start-up companies remain of great importance to its mission. A key current project is its Open Lab Business Incubator (OLBI) programme. There are many OLBIs, but the biggest is in Hsinchu County. The programme offers small companies a range of technical and research services and, in addition, the OLBI is home to companies offering support in finance, accounting, staff recruitment and other specialized business services. Successfully 'incubated' high technology companies are, if they fulfil the strict criteria, able to move on to the full science park locations.

Science parks are another well established component of government activity. Based on the Stanford model, the Hsinchu Park started business in 1980. The Park has had two distinct functions. One is to provide a physical environment and infrastructure of the quality needed for high technology industries. Water quality and guarantees of uninterrupted electricity supplies are particularly important.[18] The Park's other function has been to attract returnee Taiwanese to set up new companies. In this respect the Parks have been very successful, with returnees responsible for a high proportion of the Park start-ups. In 2000, for example, it was reported that 115 of the Hsinchu Park's 297 companies were founded by returnees.

Admission to the Parks is not open. Strict criteria are applied in terms of past and planned growth, product character, commitment to R & D expenditures, and so on. In the event, the Hsinchu Park has proved to be particularly important for the development of the IC foundry industry. It has also been home to companies that have supplied extraordinarily high shares of the world's IT products, although many of these are of a quite standardized variety and can now hardly be classified as 'high' technology.[19]

The success of Hsinchu led to establishment of the Southern (Tainan) science park in 1995. By 2003, total sales by science park companies were US$25 billion. Of this 60 per cent were IC output, 18 per cent opto-electronic products, and 13 per cent computer equipment.[20]

The private sector

So far we have briefly reviewed the nature of direct government expenditures on technology development through the NSC, the Ministry of Economic Affairs, and the science park programmes. Some of these expenditures are designed to benefit the public sector and defence, but most of them link directly to the private sector.

Apart from direct expenditures in the form of grants and similar forms of funding, another important contribution by government to the private sector is the provision of high-level manpower from public sector institutions, sometimes in the form of ready-to-go 'spin off' companies. Two outstanding firms created in this way are the Taiwan Semi-Conductor Manufacturing Company (TSMC) and United Microelectronics Corporation (UMC). The TSMC was a direct continuation of an ITRI research project and was developed in alliance with Philips to provide semi-conductor fabrication for *local* IC design houses. The concept of a purely manufacturing facility that would require large capital investment and be wholly dependent on design houses and other customers for full capacity usage had been tried in the US, but the wholehearted Taiwanese utilization of the concept as a national strategy was still highly original. The subsequent history of the company, increasingly supported by a string of high-quality international customers, has demonstrated – to date at least – the viability of the model.[21]

The origins of the UMC were even more remarkable in that government supplied almost all the human, physical and technological resources needed for the start-up, and the Ministry of Economic Affairs even put together a small consortium to provide the initial financial capital. The UMC was also notable in that it was the first Taiwanese company in the Hsinchu science park.

It is possible to describe the Taiwanese science and technology arrangements as a 'system' and perhaps, therefore, as one of a family of 'national innovation systems'. However, one can only do this by focusing on the national strategic objectives and on the functions of the public institutions involved. These remained plausibly stable over the three decades from the late 1960s to the 1990s.

In the same period, however, the nature of the interaction of this public dimension with the private sector has changed almost beyond recognition. Thus, although objectives and the key institutions in Taiwan are still identifiable, the private sector and its capabilities have undergone continuous expansion and, as the world business environment has changed, the functions of the public side have also changed enormously. One indication of the private sector transformation is provided by the changing role of the Taiwan Electronic and Electrical Manufacturers' Association (TEEMA).

Taiwanese trade associations (TAs) often have quite long pedigrees. Industry associations were an indispensable element in the Japanese system of industrial policy but, in Taiwan, the Japanese set up TAs as a means of colonial *control* rather than of *development*. However, the Taiwanese members set about changing this by turning their TAs into lobbying organizations that protected Taiwanese commercial rights, and they pressed the colonial government to improve the physical infrastructure for business, especially transportation.

In the 1960s and 1970s TEEMA had an important role in helping to maximize the technological spillover from foreign-invested plants to local companies. It did this by encouraging the government to set high local content targets, and then by assisting Taiwanese companies to establish sub-contracting networks, programmes of training and marketing initiatives.[22]

As the private sector became stronger *vis-à-vis* foreign-invested plants, this function declined. The TEEMA then developed alternative ways to develop the industry's capabilities. One route by which this has been achieved is through encouraging industry participation in research consortia. These consortia are given highly specific technology objectives and usually involve an ITRI lab such as ERSO or CCL (Computer and Communications Laboratory). The most well known of these consortia is the Notebook PC Consortium.

The rise of desktop and smaller computing machines with potential mass markets represented an important opportunity for the Taiwanese IT industry which, by the 1990s, had acquired a wide variety of production know-how through OEM-type routes. The Notebook revolution offered the industry a chance to widen its scope and enter the higher-return elements of the value chain. However, Notebooks presented several technical challenges, including miniaturization, heat control and power supply problems. Following its establishment, the Consortium identified major issues and allocated responsibilities to solve them.

The overall evaluation of the Consortium remains controversial, but it is undeniable that it and other consortia have played an important role in both developing and diffusing skills among Taiwanese companies.[23]

The above sketch suggests that Taiwanese IT technology went through two major phases: one representing early start-up, the other relative maturity. There is, however, a better case for understanding this progression in terms of first, a three-stage approach determined mainly by domestic and foreign business linkages; and second, a four-stage approach, based on different types of technological learning. The three stages are shown in Figure 12.2.

Working their way through these three phases of business development are four types of technological change. These are summarized in Figure 12.3.

Figure 12.2   Main phases of business institutional development

Phase 1	Late 1960s–1970s	In this phase firms are generally small and levels of competence are low. The key to development are links with newly arrived foreign investors, themselves driven by stiff cost reduction objectives. Government (ITRI) and Trade Association support vital as many new small firms form.
Phase 11	1980s–1990s	Taiwanese technical and business strengths improve markedly. A number of large firms emerge with some world class competencies and highly developed small firm networks evolve. The Taiwanese electrical and electronics industry enjoys a 'Golden Age' based mainly on the OEM/sub-contracting mode. Government science and technology objectives clarified after the First National Science and Technology Conference (1978).
Phase 111	Late 1990s–present	Taiwanese firms benefit from an enhanced IP regime and a new willingness of Japanese firms to partner them, but new pressures threaten as OEM/ODM competitors arise and domestic firms struggle to find profitable positions in value chains. The dilemma posed by further business and technology linkages across the Taiwan Straits becomes acute and public/private interests begin to diverge.

Figure 12.3 Main phases of technological change

Phase 1	Spillovers from FDI plants give Taiwanese firms a small group production competencies in basic components and processes
Phase 11	Widening range of competencies as local content targets fulfilled, sub-contracting networks spread skills and experience gained in the 'Apple Clone' boom gives added confidence to Taiwanese producers.
Phase 111	OEM/ODM initiatives continue and golden age of 1990s unfolds
Phase 1V	ODM/OBM increasingly based on domestic R & D, on foreign R & D based in Taiwan, and on agreed transfers of key technologies (such as thin film transistor screens) from Japanese customer/partners

Two qualifications must be made here. First, the progression of these stages in terms of both business organization and technological competency suggests a movement within some kind of natural hierarchy. This is not quite so. The precise ways in which OEM-type contracts have imparted competencies to Taiwanese firms are still only partly understood. These learning channels have not been examined as satisfactorily as they have in the Korean case.[24] However, we may observe that many IT firms choose to remain in the OEM/ODM branches of work. In addition, the major IC fabrication companies stick closely to fabrication functions on the basis of designs supplied by customers, whose continuing loyalty could not be guaranteed by any other means. Meanwhile, in the IT sector ACER has experimented with a wide range of business modes. In Europe and smaller markets ACER has a comprehensive own-brand strategy; but in the US it supplies OEM/ODM computing units for high-volume customers, while simultaneously building up an own-brand reputation in peripherals.

This behaviour suggests many possibilities. One is that even when technical competence and business capabilities are high, close relationships with customers and world markets through OEM-type links remain highly valued. In these circumstances, OEM specialists still have many ways in which they can raise returns to their efforts other than following the independent, own-brand route. For example, creative logistics, marketing, co-design projects, testing services and – above all – rising capabilities to reconfigure value chains *within* the confines of OEM tasks can all facilitate higher returns.[25]

Second, we must revert to the point that full development of Taiwan's IT and IC fabrication trajectory was dependent on world-wide trends towards standardization, open architecture and the development of novel coding systems for ICs. These made possible Stan Shih's 'super disintegration' and allowed the dramatic growth of the IC fabrication companies to take place. However, Taiwan's ability to take advantage of this opportunity when it occurred was, to some extent, fortuitous. Later arrivals have found that the rewards in the manufacturing segments of the value chains have been rather thin.

Conclusions

Taiwan's arrangements for science and technology have evolved in a complex way. This reflects interaction between a changing global and regional (i.e., East Asian) business environment, and Taiwanese human resources and institutional creativity. Whether in terms of output and exports of high technology goods, or of indicators such as foreign patents and science/engineering citation indices, Taiwanese achievements are impressive. In the 1960s Taiwanese firms in electrical/electronics activities sector were small, isolated and had very limited technological competence. Today, the sector is a multi-layered system. Larger firms are fully able to 'dance with the enemy' (i.e., form alliances with MNCs: see Stan Shih) while smaller companies are networked into flexible, specialized, fast learning groups.[26]

Taiwan's achievements are by no means limited to the much publicized electronics sector. Remarkable developments, for example, have also taken place in programmes to upgrade 'older' industries, including textiles and footwear. In addition, through exceptional application of new research in the material sciences, Taiwan has become a global leader in industries such as bicycles and golf clubs. In the case of the cycle industry there have actually been two distinct achievements. One is that by sub-contracting and relocating, companies such as Giant have been able to secure own-brand status at the lower end of the market. The other is that by plunging into technology transfer in high technology transmission systems and carbon frames, they have also developed the strengths to maintain high-end production of own-brand super bikes in Taiwan. In golf, Taiwanese manufacturers have seized the initiative in producing 70 per cent of the world market in titanium and other highly sophisticated ceramic and fusion club heads, although in this sector Taiwanese producers basically remain in the grip of the big brand buyers.

Taiwan's science and technology policies and systems are, in fact, quite unlike those in any of the three other first-echelon East Asian NIEs, as they operated during most of the period between the 1950s and 1990s. In Singapore, for example, only limited efforts were made during this period to create new public institutions or to use universities for technology transfer, research and development. The Korean 'model' was also quite different in terms of its business and financial systems. In both of these cases, the scale of each economy was a big factor determining what was possible. Singapore was constrained by its mini-size status; Korea has had the advantages of a domestic market more than twice the size of Taiwan's.

In Hong Kong, the colonial laissez faire approach to education and economic policy generated an economy that has no significant international advantages in any form of domestic industrial production and is therefore now mainly specialized in trade, tourism, financial, managerial and other services.

Nevertheless, for all its past successes the Taiwanese scene today shows some clear evidence of stress and strain. On the positive side, the private sector is demonstrably and successfully taking over important public sector functions, not only in R & D and training, but even in the establishment of what are, in essence, private sector mini science parks. But problems lie ahead too, the most serious of which are likely to be the following.

1 Taiwanese companies are up against a variety of 'glass ceilings'. This is partly because the Taiwanese home market is small and costly to protect, making it difficult to develop new products or own-brands, or to experiment with new 'standards' that might eventually be adopted internationally. In addition, through their successful partnerships with MNCs (especially in the US), the Taiwanese are vulnerable to pressures from those MNCs not to enter the higher return segments of value chains.

2 The role of government and the universities has now reached the point at which even the 'forms' of the old system are clearly anachronistic. A fundamental re-think of the roles to be played by universities, in both training and R & D, is needed. In terms of training, student number expansion in recent years has led to a decline in resources per capita, to the extent that expenditure per student is now lower even than that in mainland China, and very far from standards in the US and most of Europe. Furthermore, if Taiwan is to progress into the higher reaches of product conception, design and development, the whole 'directed' mode of research has to change, both in universities and in the ITRI-led system. The need for change is clear. The danger is that changing arrangements could damage what is still good and valid in Taiwan, amongst which I would include the NSC and its traditionally high status.

3 We are now for the first time witnessing quite serious splits between the high technology private sector and the government. These are reflected not only in the disputes, threats and subterfuges surrounding the cross-straits diffusion of technology, but also in Annette Lu's comments to the 2005 National Science and Technology Conference. This divergence must be regarded as a worrying development. The harmonization of public/private interests has played a key role in past achievement; without it, future success cannot be guaranteed.

Notes

1 Ng and Yeats (2003).
2 An important recent survey of some of the issues is Berger and Lester (2005). Like its predecessors, this book is prescriptive. The conclusions on Taiwan are generally very sound and it will be interesting to see if this study is more influential with policy-makers than their earlier work on Hong Kong.

3 See Smith (1992). Funds for university research have been in decline for some years. The importance of this is discussed in Lester and Piore (2004).
4 Llerena, Matt and Schaffer (2003).
5 Schumpeter (1951).
6 Of the 19 products with an East Asian intra-regional export growth rate of *more than* 20 per cent per annum for 1985–2001, 13 were electrical/electronic commodities on the SITC-4 digit classification. See Ng and Yeats (2003), p. 39.
7 *Taipei Journal*, 12 April 2002.
8 Shih (2002); Fuller *et al* (2005).
9 Boisot (1999).
10 Christensen (1997).
11 In 1995 semiconductors produced 50 per cent of Hitachi's profits. Three years later they were responsible for 50 per cent of unprecedented losses: Whittaker (2003).
12 For example, Morris Chang of TSMC was persuaded to return to Taiwan from Texas Instruments by the immensely influential K.T. Li.
13 These points are discussed in Kawakami (1996).
14 National Science Council (1997).
15 The First Basic Law for Science and Technology was enacted in 1997. It had 32 articles setting out principles for science and technology development in Taiwan. The use of legal frameworks for technology is a practice that closely mirrors that of Japan. Details of the Law are in National Science Council (1999).
16 The first Conference was held in 1978. The most recent was in January 2005 and at this the Science and Technology Plan for 2005–8 was drawn up: *Taiwan Journal*, 21 January 2005.
17 Chung-hua Institution for Economic Research (1995).
18 The electricity problem bedevils science parks in China and, when the Californian electricity crisis unfolded, high technology firms were immediately in acute trouble. In Taiwan, the impact of earthquakes on the power supply remains an anxiety because the impact of natural disasters is harder to anticipate than simple planning failure (China) or private sector/regulation failure (California).
19 Based on the *National Science Council Review*, various years, briefing at the Hsinchu Park, issues of the NSC's *Science News*, and material in Chang and Yu (2001).
20 National Science Council (2004).
21 A valuable group of short company histories is included in John A. Mathews (1995). The contrast between the Korean and Taiwanese approaches to IC are discussed in Keller and Pauly (2003).
22 By the early 1970s the local content rule for black and white televisions, for example, was over 90 per cent: Kawakami (1996), p. 21.
23 See in particular the thoughtful comments in Poon (2002).
24 See Cyhn (2002).
25 See comments in Teece (2000).
26 Space precludes discussion of the way in which cross-straits and other transnational networks have evolved from Taiwanese ones.

References

Berger, Suzanne and Richard Lester (eds) (2005), *Global Taiwan. Building Competitive Strengths in a New International Economy*, Armonk, NY: M.E. Sharpe.

Boisot, Max H. (1999), *Knowledge Assets. Securing Competitive Advantage in the Information Economy*, Oxford: Oxford University Press.

Chang, Chun-Yen and Po-Lung Yu (2001), *Made by Taiwan. Booming in the Information Technology Era*, NJ: World Scientific, ch. 11.

Christensen, Clayton M. (1997), *The Innovator's Dilemma. When New Technologies Cause Great Firms to Fail*, Cambridge, MA: Harvard Business School Press.

Chung-hua Institution for Economic Research (1995), *Technology Support Institutions and Policy Priorities for Industrial Development in Taiwan*, Republic of China.

Cyhn, Jin W. (2002), *Technology Transfer and International Production. The Development of the Electronics Industry in Korea*, Cheltenham: Edward Elgar, esp. ch. 3.

Fuller, Douglas B. *et al.* (2005), 'Leading, Following, or Cooked Goose?', in Berger and Lester (2005), pp. 76–96.

Kawakami, Momoko (1996), *Development of Small and Medium-Sized Manufacturers in Taiwan's PC Industry*, Chung-hua Institution for Economic Research, Discussion Paper Series No. 9606.

Keller, William W. and Louis W. Pauly (2003), 'Crisis and Adaptation in Taiwan and South Korea. The Political Economy of Semi-Conductors', in W.W. Keller and Richard J. Samuels (eds), *Crisis and Innovation in Asian Technology*, Cambridge: Cambridge University Press, pp. 137–59.

Lester, Richard K. and Michael J. Piore (2004), *Innovation. The Missing Dimension*, Cambridge, MA: Harvard University Press.

Llerena, P., Mireille Matt and Véronique Schaffer (2003), 'The Evolution of French Research Policies and the Impacts on the Universities and Public Research Organisations', in Aldo Geuna *et al.* (eds), *Science and Innovation. Rethinking the Rationales for Funding and Governance*, Cheltenham: Edward Elgar.

Mathews, John A. (1995), *High-Technology Industrialisation in East Asia: The Case of the Semiconductor Industry in Taiwan and Korea*, Taipei: Chung-hua Institution for Economic Research, ch. 3.

Ng, Francis and Alexander Yeats (2003), *Major Trade Trends in East Asia*, Washington, DC: World Bank Policy Research Working Paper.

NSC (1997), *White Paper on Science and Technology. Vision for the Development of Science and Technology in 21st Century Taiwan*, Taipei.

NSC (1999), *Science Bulletin*, June p. 1.

NSC (2004), *Indicators of Science and Technology 2004*, Taipei, 118–19.

Poon, Teresa Shuk-Ching (2002), *Competition and Cooperation in Taiwan's Information Technology Industry. Inter-Firm Networks and Industrial Upgrading*. Westport, CT: Quorum Books, 98–103.

Schumpeter, Joseph A. (1951), *The Theory of Economic Development*, Cambridge, MA: Harvard University Press.

Shih, Stan (2002), *Growing Global. A Corporate Vision Masterclass*, New York: John Wiley, ch. 1.

Smith, Robert W. (1992), 'The Biggest Kind of Big Science: Astronomers and the Space Telescope', in *Big Science. The Growth of Large Scale Research*, Stanford, CA: Stanford University Press, 184–211.

Teece, David J. (2000), 'Firm Capabilities and Economic Development: The Implications for Newly Industrializing Economies', in Linsu Kim and Richard R. Nelson (eds), *Technology, Learning, and Innovation. Experiences of Newly Industrializing Countries*, Cambridge: Cambridge University Press.

Whittaker, D.H. (2003), 'Crisis and Innovation in Japan', in William W. Keller and Richard J. Samuels (eds), *Crisis and Innovation in Asian Technology*, Cambridge: Cambridge University Press, 65.

13
Spillover Effects of Foreign Direct Investment and Technology Transfer in China: Before and after its Accession to the World Trade Organization

Ping Lin

Introduction

China has been the world's largest foreign direct investment (FDI) recipient among developing countries since the early 1990s, and overtook the United States as the number one recipient of FDI in 2003. Without doubt, China has been benefiting enormously from such an inflow of foreign capital in terms of economic growth, employment, and technological progress. The trend of massive FDI inflow has continued since China acceded to the World Trade Organization (WTO) in late 2001. Will the nature and benefits of FDI to China stay as before? How does China's WTO membership impact on the process and magnitudes of FDI and technology transfer to China?

The purpose of this chapter is two-fold. First, we review the main channels via which the spillover effects of FDI and technology transfer take place to China, particularly under the government's 'swap the market for technology' policy, as well as some of the recent empirical studies that attempt to quantify the (horizontal and vertical) spillover effects of FDI on local industries in China. Second, given that China's entry to the WTO changed 'the rules of the game', particularly for Chinese firms, we discuss some major obstacles China may face in the future in terms of creating FDI spillover effects and attracting technology transfer. In particular, as the government can no longer force foreign investors to transfer technology to China in exchange for entry to its market, what will shape the incentives of foreign investors for technology transfer? In addition, with intellectual property right protection in China significantly improved, it is more costly for domestic industries to learn/imitate foreign technology and products. This will certainly significantly lower the level of the spillover effects from FDI. Furthermore, the dominant position of multinational corporations, supported by their technological and managerial superiority over local

239

firms, may potentially hurt the competition process in Chinese industries. To illustrate the major difficulties facing China, two detailed case studies are included: one covers the recent patent royalty disputes among leading multinational corporations and domestic DVD-player manufacturers, which indicates that the spillover effects of FDI in China will be much weaker since China joined the WTO, and the other is about the question of 'killing off' famous local brands by foreign investors in detergent and toothpaste markets, which highlights the competition concerns in the Chinese government in recent years about the abuse of market power by multinationals in China.

Foreign direct investment in China: an overview

Ever since its opening-up to the outside world in the late 1970s, foreign investors have been rushing in to China, attracted by its abundant labour force and its huge market size. The amount of FDI inflow to China has increased dramatically, from $3.38 billion (in nominal value) in 1980 to $53.51 billion in 2003. By the end of 2003, China had taken in over $500 billion in FDI (see Figure 13.1).

In the early 1980s, China's FDI policies were mainly characterised by the passing of new regulations to permit joint ventures between foreign investors and local partners and setting up Special Economic Zones. During this period, FDI inflow was low and remained roughly constant. Since 1986, China has started to further open up to FDI and has adopted more favourable policies to encourage FDI inflow. Foreign investors have been given preferential tax treatment, the freedom to import inputs, simpler business licensing procedures, and so on. In the 1990s, the Chinese government permitted wholly foreign-owned enterprises as a new entry mode of

Figure 13.1   Actual value of FDI in China (billion US dollars)

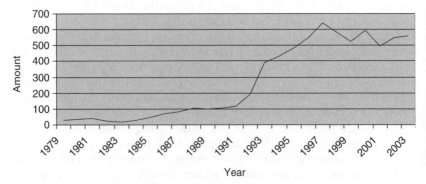

Source: *Statistical Yearbooks of China*, 1980–2004

FDI. During the past few years, wholly foreign-owned enterprises have become the most popular form of entry mode FDI to China, representing 65.14 per cent of new contracts in 2003. Most recently, the government has allowed, and in some cases even encouraged, foreign investors to merge with, or acquire, domestic firms. As a result, more and more new FDI projects are taking the form of merger or acquisition. In many cases, the target firms are either state-owned enterprises and/or other leading or promising companies.

The entry of foreign investors into Chinese sectors is broad and massive. Table 13.1 contains information about the presence of FDI in two-digit Chinese manufacturing industries. As can be seen, the sales revenues of foreign-invested enterprises (joint ventures and wholly foreign-owned companies) as a percentage of industrial totals have increased during recent years. In 2002, foreign-invested enterprises accounted for over 30 per cent

Table 13.1 Ratio of foreign-invested enterprises' sales to industry total (%)

Industrial sectors	1995	2002
Food processing	21.20	25.88
Food manufacturing	30.48	40.73
Beverage manufacturing	26.20	30.88
Tobacco processing	0.56	0.47
Textile industry	17.88	21.66
Garments and other fibre products	50.81	45.48
Leather, furs and related products	54.14	53.16
Timber processing	27.27	25.83
Furniture manufacturing	30.67	47.21
Papermaking and paper products	17.01	32.78
Printing and record medium	18.26	33.76
Cultural and sports goods	50.71	59.99
Petroleum processing and coking	1.41	9.87
Raw chemical materials and products	12.62	22.17
Pharmaceutical products	18.28	21.71
Chemical fibre	12.65	25.38
Rubber products	24.98	38.99
Plastic products	33.05	42.03
Non-metal mineral products	11.40	19.20
Ferrous metals	6.23	7.55
Non-ferrous metals	12.51	12.56
Metal products	26.64	37.16
Ordinary machinery	14.50	24.02
Special purpose equipment	8.95	20.25
Transport equipment	25.21	32.57
Electric equipment and machinery	24.17	33.57
Electronic and telecom equipment	60.80	73.92

Source: China Statistical Yearbooks.

of total sales in many Chinese industries. The ratios were over 50 per cent in such industries as leather and fur products, cultural and sport products, and as high as 73 per cent in the electronic and telecommunication equipment sector. The trend of rising foreign enterprises' presence highlights increased foreign competition in China's market, as well as the contribution of FDI to the Chinese economy.

'Swap the market for technology'

One of the primary goals of China's FDI policies is to promote technology transfer to China, especially from multinational companies (see, e.g., Long, 2005). Ever since China opened up to the outside world, the government has put in place various policy measures so as to foster technology transfer. For example, additional tax cuts were granted to joint ventures employing advanced technologies; permission was given to whole foreign-owned enterprises on the condition that they adopted advanced technology.[1] Such restrictions were removed in 2001 when China was preparing for entry to the WTO. Industries are classified into encouraged, allowed, restricted and prohibited by *The Guiding Catalogue of Foreign Investment* in 1995. The encouraged group includes investments in infrastructure or developing modern agriculture; those with new/advanced technology, saving energy and/or raw material, improving economic efficiency; those which are export-oriented; and those involving new technology/equipment making use of natural/regenerative resources and reducing pollution. The catalogue has been revised several times – most recently in 2002 after the People's Republic of China (PRC) entered the WTO – and has become increasingly less restrictive. According to the 2002 version, prohibited industries include certain financial services, air transportation, the media, and electricity transmission.

The Chinese government understands that FDI not only brings in advanced technology, but also generates spillover effects to the rest of the economy. FDI spillovers can take place either horizontally or vertically. Horizontal spillovers occur when FDI firms' presence benefits their competitors in the same industry via channels such as reverse engineering, labour turnover, and the demonstration effect (Blomstrom and Kokko, 1998; Aitken and Harrison, 1999). First, local firms can learn the designs of the new products and technology, through reverse engineering, for example, and then improve upon them to come up with new products or processes. Second, spillovers can take place via labour turnover when skilled workers move from FDI firms to local firms, or set up their own business. Formal and informal contacts between employees of FDI and local firms can also benefit local firms in terms of market information and technological know-how. Quite a number of lawsuits against unfair methods of competition in China in recent years are related to this type of labour mobility.[2] Third, FDI has a *demonstration effect*: the mere presence of foreign products in domestic markets can stimulate local firms' creative thinking and thus help to generate blueprints for new products and processes. Moreover, since the products or technologies that FDI firms bring in have already been 'tested' in foreign markets, similar products and technologies will probably work well for the host country as well.

On the other hand, vertical spillovers occur when FDI firms transfer technological know-how to their local suppliers through technology licensing and staff training (backward linkages) or when FDI firms' products raise their customers' productivity in the downstream sector.[3] A policy designed specifically to promote backward linkages of FDI is local content requirement, which requires a foreign investor to purchase a certain amount of intermediate input from local suppliers, as opposed to from international markets. For instance, during the 1990s China required that the local content rate of all cars made in China be at least 40 per cent and this had to increase to 60 per cent in a year and to 80 per cent two years after the project started operating (*China Daily*, 5 July 2004).

However, both horizontal and vertical effects of FDI can be negative. First, the entry of foreign investors (especially multinational corporations) increases competition, thereby eroding the market shares of domestic incumbents and causing their productivity to decline. This is particularly likely in developing countries where domestic firms are less efficient and thus unable to compete with foreign multinational corporations. In China, this 'crowding-out' effect of FDI also takes another form: foreign companies in China are able to hire away skilled workers from their local competitors because of their higher salaries and more promising career development path. In the automobile manufacturing industry, for example, there have been occasions when a group of R & D personnel of a domestic carmaker left to work for multinational firms (*China's Industrial Development Report*, 2004, p. 441).

In terms of vertical linkages, inward FDI can potentially hurt local suppliers if foreign investors choose to import the intermediate goods they use in production (for quality considerations, for instance), instead of sourcing them locally. For example, in the 1990s, China's machine tool and aircraft industries suffered significant decline partly because their downstream customers insisted on sourcing intermediate goods from overseas markets. Such displacement of pre-existing linkages, as emphasized in Rodriguez-Clare (1996) and Lin and Saggi (2005), is certainly detrimental to the host country.

Quantifying FDI spillover effects in China

Some scholars have recently empirically tested the spillovers effects of FDI on Chinese industries. Cheung and Lin (2004) studied the spillovers effects of FDI on innovation in China. Using provincial data from 1995 to 2000, they found positive effects of FDI on the number of domestic patent applications in China. In particular, the number of domestic patent applications in each province depends positively and significantly on the share of FDI to China that goes to each province. This finding is robust under both pooled time-series and cross-section data estimation and panel data analysis, as well as for different types of patent application (invention, utility model, and external design). The spillover effect is the strongest for minor innovations such as external design patent, highlighting a 'demonstration effect' of FDI. Using the 1995 Third Industrial Census of China, Chuang and Hsu (2004) also found evidence of positive spillover effects on domestic firms' productivity. Dividing the firms into a high-technology group and a low-technology group, the authors found that the effects are stronger for the latter group, supporting the technology-gap learning theory that domestic firms are less likely to be able to learn from foreign investors if they are technologically too far behind. Other recent studies include Hu and Jefferson (2002) who found positive evidence of horizontal spillover effects of FDI in China's electronic and textile industries.

The evidence of positive horizontal spillover effects of FDI as found in the recent literature is not surprising, given the fact that intellectual property right protection was weak prior to China's entry to the WTO in late 2001. It is well known that foreign technology and products have been routinely imitated or counterfeited by some Chinese firms during the past decade, although the situation is improving as China has been strengthening its intellectual property rights (IPR) system.

Empirical analysis of vertical effects of FDI in China is lacking. To our best knowledge, Liu and Lin (2004) is the only study that tests the backward linkages effect of FDI in China. Following the approach of Blalock and Gertler (2002) and Javorcik (2004), who study backward linkage effects of FDI in Indonesia and Lithuania respectively, Liu and Lin regress the value added of each industry against capital, labour, horizontal FDI and vertical FDI variables. Horizontal FDI is measured by the proportion of an industry's output produced by foreign-funded enterprises, as illustrated in Table 13.1, and backward FDI is the share of an industry's output purchased by downstream foreign-funded enterprises in the host country. They used the annual data for 28 two-digit industries published in China's *Statistical Yearbook* for the period from 1994 to 2003. While the pooled data ordinary least squares estimations show negative and significant backward linkages effects from FDI, the panel data estimations show that such effects are positive and significant (under both fixed effect and the random effect models). The horizontal effects of FDI are positive in both sets of estimations, which is consistent with the findings of Cheung and Lin (2004) obtained from analysis of provincial data.

World Trade Organization membership and technology transfer

Two important features of China's FDI policies and economic environment during the pre-WTO era are that FDI was mostly conditional on technology transfer and that China's intellectual property right protection system was weak. These two factors obviously have strong bearings on the effectiveness of China's FDI policies. It is important to bear in mind that these factors are the main driving forces behind any observations regarding the magnitudes of the spillover effects and technology transfer.

No more forced technology transfer

As mentioned earlier, FDI inflows to China during the past two decades have been under direct and tight control by the central and local governments. Industrial policies and various administrative regulations were designed to stipulate which industries foreign capital could enter and what entry modes could be adopted, as well as to place conditions on technology transfer. There have been reports over the past several years of some foreign companies being 'forced' to transfer technology to China in exchange for access to its enormous market.[4] A recent survey of some EU firms revealed that 46 per cent of the technology transfers to China by these EU firms were because of the government policies and regulations requiring local sources and/or technology transfer.[5]

With its accession to the WTO, China agreed to eliminate restrictive conditions on foreign investors. For example, in the bilateral agreement between China and the US, China agreed it would not make foreign investment or import approvals conditional on technology transfer or on conducting R & D in China. China also agreed that it would eliminate requirements mandating that the Chinese partners in a joint venture would gain ownership of trade secrets after a certain number of years.[6] Local-content requirements are not permitted under the WTO's Agreement on Trade Related Investment Measures (TRIMs). With the removal of the requirements, China lost an important channel of obtaining foreign technology, namely 'forced technology transfer'.

Some are worried that China's commitment to following the WTO rules and removal of 'forced technology transfer' in particular may hamper technology transfer to China. However, this need not be the case. China's entry to the WTO changes the 'rules of the game' and, subsequently, the incentive for voluntary technology transfer on the part of foreign investors. It may be argued that, under guidance from 'the invisible hand', technology transfer to China will continue, possibly on a larger scale.

First, without any doubt, the enforcement of the IPR laws in China has been greatly improved since it joined the WTO. The Chinese government has a stronger incentive to strengthen IPR law enforcement because, on the one hand, its credibility is at stake and on the other hand, violations are subject to the dispute settlement mechanism at the WTO. Improved law enforcement reduces the risk of transferring technology to China and hence encourages FDI with advanced technology.

Second, due to China's accession to the WTO and various trade and investment barriers being phased out and soon removed, foreign investors will enjoy a freer and wider range of business opportunities in China. This will certainly increase the benefits of transferring technology.

Third, there is also a competition-induced incentive at work. As more and more foreign investors enter the Chinese market, competition will be intensified, making them more tempted to bring state-of-the-art products and technology, so as to gain a better market position over competitors. In fact, technology transfer to China in the past has been motivated by normal business considerations, such as market expansion or responses to pressures from rival firms, in addition to being required by government regulations. According to the survey on EU firms by Bennett *et al.* (2000), when asked what were the reasons for technology transfer to China, 80 per cent of the companies cited market access, 57 per cent cited cost advantage, 48 per cent cited it being 'part of the company's globalization strategy', and 33 per cent cited response to competitors' moves (actual or potential).

The above-mentioned factors, especially the competition effect, will continue to be the main motivations for foreign technology transfer to China. It may be that the additional incentive for FDI and technology transfer induced by better IPR protection, more business opportunities and increased competition is so strong that China will receive more and better technology transfer after its accession to the WTO, compared to the case of 'forced technology transfer'.

End of free-riding

It is well known that China's overall environment for intellectual property right protection was not as good during the pre-WTO period (i.e., prior to 2002) as it has become afterwards. This implies that the spillover effects of FDI (horizontal and vertical) on domestic firms would have been weaker had intellectual property rights been better protected in China, and that the magnitudes of FDI spillovers in the future are likely to be lower. The case study about the DVD player market illustrates the point that some of the observed profits of domestic firms in China are in fact 'technology licensing fees' that should have been paid to foreign patent holders, and that the 'free lunch' aspect of using foreign technology has come to an end as China is now a member of the WTO.

At least two things can be learned from this case study in relation to the spillover effects of FDI. First, as China now must play under the WTO rules and continues to improve protection of intellectual property rights, Chinese firms currently operate in an environment that is totally different

Case Study: 'Overdue' DVD Patent Royalties

In 2002, China's DVD (digital versatile disc) player industry suffered a huge blow when the world's major DVD developers accused domestic DVD player makers in China of infringing their patented technologies, and demanded huge amounts of royalty payments.

A DVD player has more than 200 patents, most of which are owned by foreign manufacturers. Chinese DVD player makers buy key parts, in which the patented technologies are embedded, from abroad to make DVD players, and had undercut their foreign counterparts in the overseas market backed by cheap raw materials and labour. In 2001, China's DVD player makers contributed about 25 per cent to the world's total production and 40 per cent to the world total exports, selling around 10 million DVD machines in the overseas market (China Central TV *Economic News 30 Minutes*, 14 May 2002).

Domestic DVD producers in China apparently did not know that they ought to pay patent royalties to DVD developers until 1999 (nine years after China started producing DVDs) when Hitachi, Panasonic, Mitsubishi, Time Warner, Toshiba and JVC (the 6Cs) notified domestic DVD makers that they had to pay for using their patents. The 6Cs were then followed by another alliance of DVD developers – Philips, Pioneer and Sony (which is known as the 3Cs) – and Thomson, which is known as 1C. Caught by surprise and then accepting the infringement charges, over 100 Chinese DVD makers empowered the China Electronic Acoustic Equipment Association to negotiate with the DVD developers on the amount of the patent fee. After over two years of negotiations, out-of-court agreements were reached which entail about US$21.3 royalty payments for each DVD player made in China and sold in other countries. Starting in 1 January 2003, a royalty of between US$12 and US$13 has to be paid for each DVD player made and sold in China (*Beijing Evening News*, 18 July 2003; *China's Industrial Development Report* (2004), p. 272).

Representing about a 20 per cent increase in total DVD production costs, these patent fee charges had immediate and significant negative effects on the Chinese DVD industry: many DVD companies had to close down or switch to other business lines. For example, Bao An District in Shenzhen City, one of China's major DVD production bases, had over 140 DVD player producers in the late 1990s; but the figure declined to less than 40 in early 2004, primarily as a result of the patent fee charges. See Jing Hua Shi Bao (*Jinghua Times*), 30 June 2004.

Case Study: continued
   In the eyes of many DVD player manufacturers, the patent fee incident may not only be about IPR protection. China's DVD player industry began in the mid-1990s and boomed as more and more entrepreneurs entered and profited from making the trendy appliance. But the patent holders did not ask for payment until the late 1990s when the manufacturing companies had matured. This tactic is called by some 'feeding the fish before eating it' (*China Daily*, 2 February 2005).

from before. This implies that the degree of horizontal spillover will be lower in the post-WTO era. Second, evidence of positive spillover effects found for the pre-WTO period may have to be discounted if the 'free lunch' during that period is in fact not free but has to be paid for later in terms of declined market shares and even close-downs, as the DVD player manufacturers realized soon after China entered the WTO in late 2001.

It is important too that the DVD patent royalty incident should not be taken as an isolated event. Rather, it is an indication of a widespread pattern of industrial practice because Chinese firms may not fully have understood the implications of their decisions with regard to utilizing foreign capital and technology prior to China's entry to the WTO. Recently, foreign patent holders in such sectors as television manufacturing, motorcycles, pharmaceuticals, batteries and so on began to accuse some Chinese producers of infringing their patented production technology and to demand delayed patent fee payments as well (*China Youth Daily*, 5 February 2005).

'Dancing with the wolf': competition concerns of foreign direct investment

In recent years, the Chinese government has become increasingly aware of the detrimental effects of inward FDI on Chinese industries. One primary negative effect of FDI on domestic firms in China is that increased competition from foreign investors, especially the multinational corporations, has eroded their market shares significantly. In some cases, famous domestic brands are acquired or even killed by multinational companies, causing widespread reactions from Chinese firms and government. There is a growing concern that foreign enterprises may soon dominate all the country's industries, and that domestic firms will be driven out of business. The potentially negative consequences of foreign acquisitions for domestic brands are illustrated by the case of a leading domestic brand of toothpaste that is allegedly being 'killed off' by the foreign multinational that bought it.

A Case Study of Local Brand Acquisitions by Unilever and P&G

In early 2002 a bitter row erupted between Unilever, the consumer goods multinational, and the Shanghai Toothpaste Factory (STF), a well-known domestic company, over a brand agreement for Zhonghua toothpaste. Zhonghua had been the best-selling toothpaste brand in the PRC for decades. In 1993, Unilever and STF signed an agreement giving Unilever the sole right to manufacture, market and sell the Zhonghua brand in the PRC. The agreement had an unlimited term, subject to trademark renewal every 10 years. The key condition for renewal was that the total production volume in the last year of the agreement should be higher than that in the first year.

As the end of the first 10-year period approached, STF told Unilever that it wanted to end the agreement and take back the brand because it had 'suffered bad treatment at Unilever's hands' (*China Daily*, 16 January 2002). STF had already taken back another brand of toothpaste leased to Unilever – Maxam – in 2000. Unilever (China) Limited responded that, far from shelving the product, it had given it more attention than it deserved. The company claimed to have spent a considerable sum on developing the Zhonghua brand – on average, 53 per cent of its annual advertising and promotion budget in the oral category – and said that production of the toothpaste had risen to 40,000 tons in 2002 compared with 35,000 tonnes in 1993. Unilever had also invested in new packaging for the Zhonghua brand and had launched a promotional campaign in August 2001 to boost sales (*China Daily*, 16 January 2002).

STF disagreed. 'Unilever did not manage to push the sales higher till almost the end of the first decade. Nevertheless, we are determined to take back the Zhonghua brand. Zhonghua is a national brand name, with a long history, we must protect it', said a top manager (*China Management Daily*, 22 November 2001). Following the disputes, Unilever and STF agreed in 2003 to continue their cooperation by renewing the leasing contract of the Zhonghua brand name, on condition that the brand would be in a priority position in Unilever's product lines in China (*Southern Daily*, 22 September 2004). It is also reported that Unilever's decision to position Zhonghua as one of its leading brands, and its recent national campaign to promote the brand, is a damage control effort so as to change its negative image of 'local brand killer' among Chinese consumers (*Beijing Modern Commerce Daily*, 29 September 2004).[7]

Case Study: continued

Another multinational, Procter & Gamble (P&G), has also been accused of 'freezing' a local brand. In 1994, P&G set up a joint venture with the Beijing Second Daily Cosmetic Factory to produce and sell Panda detergent. The Beijing firm took 35 per cent of the share of the joint venture for its detergent brand, Panda, and the production facilities. Panda was among the three best-selling detergent brands in the PRC when the joint venture was launched, but today it is hard to find it in the shops. In September 2000, the Beijing firm bought back the brand, but by that time its position in the market had been reduced to almost nothing whereas P&G's own brand, Tide, had become a family name. In six years, production of Panda detergent had dropped from 60,000 to 4,000 tonnes (*China Daily*, 16 January 2002).

Parallel to such brand acquisitions which occured within existing joint ventures, foreign firms have also been active in merging with or acquiring domestic firms in recent years. For instance, L'Oréal, one of the world's leading beauty product companies, recently reached agreement to take over two leading domestic brands in China. It bought the Chinese cosmetic and skincare brand Mininurse in December 2003, followed by another deal in January 2004 to acquire Yue-Sai. In 2002, its first year as a WTO member, China overtook Japan to become the most active mergers and acquisitions (M&A) market in Asia. Foreign companies spent $13.9 billion from January to November 2002 purchasing Chinese firms, up by 180 per cent on the $4.9 billion spent in 2001 (*The US-China Business Council*, 2003). Foreign investors have been increasingly using M&A as a vehicle for strategic positioning in China's market (e.g., to gain immediate access to distribution channels, customers or control of domestic companies with great potential, etc.).

In response to the rapid emergence of FDI-related M&As, the Chinese government set up an M&A notification/evaluation system in March 2003, the first of its kind in the country, which spells out the criteria and procedures for foreign investors to report merger and acquisition transactions involving domestic firms. A distinct feature of this regulation is that it targets foreign investors only. This caused widespread concern among foreign investors (see Lin, 2005 for a detailed description and analysis of the regulation).

Alleged abuse of dominant position by the MNCs

Multinational corporations are also targeted in business practices other than mergers and acquisitions. In early June 2004, after a year-long investigation, the State Administration for Industry and Commerce (SAIC),

China's enforcement agency for its 1993 Law against Unfair Methods of Competition, released a report entitled *The Competition-restricting Behaviour of Multinational Companies in China and Countermeasures* (SAIC, 2004). This report, the first of its kind in the country, said that some multinational companies commanded obviously dominant positions in their industries and were using their advantage to curb competition. It accused several multinationals of attempting to limit competition through strategies such as predatory pricing, exclusive dealing, tied sales, and M&As. The report specifically mentioned Microsoft and Eastman Kodak, which both however denied any wrongdoing.[8]

In the case of Kodak, the SAIC drew attention to the agreement signed in 1998 between Kodak, the State Development and Planning Commission, the State Economic and Trade Commission, and the Ministry of Foreign Trade and Economic Cooperation, under which Kodak undertook to invest a total of $2 billion in acquiring all of the country's domestic imaging factories, except those of Lucky Film. For its part, the government agreed not to allow the establishment of any other joint venture in the imaging sector between 1998 and 2000. In response to the SAIC report, Kodak released a statement saying that the company had never done anything to circumvent the normal processes of market competition.

Some scholars argued that China should learn more about the potentially negative effects of the presence of multinational giants and take steps – such as passing anti-monopoly legislation and revising the 1993 Anti Unfair Competition Law – to prevent them from employing anti-competitive practices (*China Business Weekly*, 8 June 2004). Others are less worried about the presence of foreign companies in the PRC, arguing that the dominant market share of foreign firms as a whole, rather than of a single firm, does not necessarily imply monopoly in the PRC's markets (see, for example, Jiang, 2002). China now is at the last stage of bringing in its anti-monopoly law, the first version of which was drafted in early 1990s and has been revised many times since. While it is not likely that the law will target specific types of firm, the recent resentment of alleged abuses of market power by multinational corporations in China has certainly helped to speed up the legislation process.

The recent developments indicate that China's accession to the WTO in 2002 reshaped the rules of the game and the entire business and economic environment in which both domestic and foreign firms operate. The incentive for, and effects of, FDI and technology transfer to China are likely to change drastically as well.

Concluding remarks

China adopted its 'swap the market for technology' policy over two decades ago with the objective of bringing FDI with advanced technology

and stimulating technological progress by domestic firms via spillover channels of FDI. While there is empirical evidence of positive spillover effects from
FDI on Chinese firms during the 1990s, China has 'lost' two important channels for technological progress as the result of its accession to the WTO in late
2001. Technology transfer to China can no longer be forced by government
regulations, and Chinese firms must respect intellectual property rights (so
imitations of foreign technology become more costly). However, removal of
'forced technology transfer' need not slow down technology transfer in
China. Its more open market, better business opportunities, improved intellectual property rights system, and, perhaps more importantly, increased competition among foreign investors may induce them to bring in more and
more advanced technology. On the other hand, with the WTO rules in place,
Chinese companies, such as DVD player makers, must pay for using foreign
technology. This translates into weaker spillover effects of FDI. In sum, unlike
in the pre-WTO period, China is likely to witness a larger scale of technology
transfer but lower level of spillover effects of FDI in the future. One consequence of this is that market dominance of foreign investors, especially multinational companies in China's market, is likely to be reinforced, as the
Chinese government has now accepted.

Notes

1   See China Ministry of Commerce (1990).
2   See Chu (2001).
3   Lall (1980) notes that technology transfer from multinationals to local suppliers
    can take place in several ways. A multinational might (1) help prospective sup-
    pliers set up production capacities; (2) provide technical assistance/information
    to raise the quality of suppliers' products and/or to facilitate innovations; and
    (3) provide training and help in management and organization. See also Moran
    (1998, 2002).
4   See 'U.S. Commercial Technology Transfers to the PRC', 1999, a research report
    by the Bureau of Export Administration and the Office of Strategic Industries and
    Economic Security of the US.
5   See Bennett *et al.* (2000).
6   See the sector papers by the Washington Council on International Trade at
    http://www/wcit.org/Chinawto_sectorpapers.htm.
7   In addition to Zhonghua and Maxam, Unilever had also acquired four other local
    brands in China during the 1990s in the fields of detergent, tea production, and
    ice cream, most of which had either struggled or disappeared from the markets
    (*Beijing Modern Commerce Daily*, 29 September 2004).
8   *China Daily*, Hong Kong edition, 18 June 2004. Microsoft stated that the
    company's conduct in the PRC was in line with Chinese laws and regulations
    (*China Daily*, 2 June 2004).

References

Aitken, B.J. and A. Harrison (1999), 'Do Domestic Firms Benefit from Direct
    Foreign Investment? Evidence from Venezuela', *American Economic Review*, 89,
    605–18.

Bennett, D., X. Liu, D. Parker, F. Steward and K. Vaidya (2000), 'Technology Transfer to China: A Study of Strategy in 20 EU Industrial Countries', Birmingham: Aston Business School, Aston University.

Blalock, Garrick and Paul Gertler (2002), 'Technology Diffusion from Foreign Direct Investment through Supply Chain', Working Paper, Cornell University.

Blomstrom, M. and A. Kokko (1998), 'Multinational Corporations and Spillovers', *Journal of Economic Surveys*, 12 (3), 247–78.

Cheung, K.Y. and P. Lin (2004), 'The Spillover Effect of FDI on Innovation in China: Evidence from the Provincial Data', *China Economic Review*, 15, 25–44.

China Ministry of Commerce (1990), *Detailed Implementing Rules for the Law of the People's Republic of China on Wholly Foreign-Owned Enterprises*, www.mfcom.gov.cn.

China's Industrial Development Report (2004), Beijing: Economics and Management Press.

Chu, M.C. (2001), *Selected Litigation Cases of Anti-unfair Competition Disputes* (in Chinese), Shanghai: Sanlian Press.

Chuang, Y.C. and P.F. Hsu (2004), 'FDI, Trade, and Spillover Efficiency: Evidence from China's Manufacturing Sector', *Applied Economics*, 36 (10), 1103–15.

Hu, A. and G. Jefferson (2002), 'FDI Impact of Spillover: Evidence from China's Electronic and Textile Industries', *The World Economy*, 25 (8), 1063–76.

Javorcik, B.S. (2004), 'Does Foreign Direct Investment Increase the Productivity of Domestic Firms? In Search of Spillovers through Backward Linkages', *American Economic Review*, 94 (3), 605–27.

Jiang, X. (2002), 'FDI, Market Structure, and Competition Behaviour of Foreign Firms', *Economic Research Journal* (in Chinese), September, 31–8.

Lall, S. (1980), 'Vertical Inter-Firm Linkages in LDCs: An Empirical Study', *Oxford Bulletin of Economics and Statistics*, 42, 203–6.

Lin, P. (2005), 'Competition Policy in China: Interactions with Industrial and FDI Policies', in D. Brooks and S. Evernett (eds), *Competition Policy and Development in Asia*, Basingstoke: Palgrave.

Lin, P. and K. Saggi (2005), 'Multinationals, Exclusivity, and Backward Linkages', *Journal of International Economics*, forthcoming.

Liu, Z.M. and P. Lin (2004), 'Backward Linkages of Foreign Direct Investment: Evidence from China', mimeo, Lingnan University.

Long, G.Q. (2005), 'China's FDI Policies; Review and Evaluation', in T. Moran, E.M. Graham and M. Blomstrom (eds), *Does Foreign Direct Investment Promote Development?*, Washington, DC: Institute For International Economics, Centre for Global Development.

Moran, T. (1998), *Foreign Direct Investment and Development*, Washington, DC: Institute for International Economics.

Moran, T. (2002), *Capturing the benefits of foreign direct investment. Strategy and Tactics for the Doha Round*, Manila: Asian Development Bank.

Rodriguez-Clare, Andre (1996), 'Multinationals, Linkages, and Economic Development', *American Economic Review*, 86, 852–73.

SAIC (2004), *The Competition-restricting Behaviour of Multinational Companies in China and Countermeasures*, Beijing.

US–China Business Council (2003), *Foreign Investment in China*, available at http://uschina.org/statistics/2003foreigninvestment.html.

Washington Council on International Trade http://www/wcit.org/Chinawto_sector-papers.htm.

14
The Impact of Trade Policy on Total Factor Productivity, Efficiency and Technology: The Case of Chinese Provinces in the 1990s

Yu Chen

Introduction

Total factor productivity (TFP) growth is an important indicator of the improvement in an economy's ability to produce more output with a limited amount of input or to produce the same amount of output using less input. The question of whether GDP growth has been driven mainly by total factor productivity growth has been at the heart of the debate on the 'Asian Miracle': some argue that the high rate of economic growth of Hong Kong, Taiwan, Singapore and Korea was accompanied by high productivity growth (World Bank, 1993; Chen, 1997), while others conclude that the good performance of these economies was more a 'myth' than a 'miracle' and that their output grew because of high factor accumulation rather than because of TFP growth (Young, 1993, 1995; Krugman, 1994).

The same issue has been raised as regards the rapidly growing Chinese economy. It is generally observed that in centrally-planned economies, workers lack incentives to improve their efficiency and firms lack motivation to update their technology; therefore the economy's productivity grows very slowly. For more than two decades China has been growing at an impressive rate, which has stimulated many economists to look closer into this economy and to investigate the sources of its rapid growth. A number of previous studies have found positive productivity growth in China during the reform period, using aggregate data at the country level and the traditional growth accounting method (Borensztein and Ostry, 1996; Hu and Khan, 1997; World Bank, 1997; Maddison, 1998; Woo, 1998). In these studies the contribution of total factor productivity to GDP growth varies from 13 to 55 per cent, showing divergent appreciation of the role of total factor productivity in China's economic growth. This study intends to enrich this literature by proposing an estimation for a more recent period and using a non-parametric method, Data Envelopment Analysis (DEA), which has the advantage of relaxing some strict hypotheses required by the parametric method, such as perfect competition and profit maximization of the economic agents. These hypotheses would be too strong for a developing country or an economy in transition. In addition, we use the DEA method to decompose TFP growth into efficiency improvement and technological progress. As a preview, the empirical results show that in China, during 1992–99, total factor productivity grew, on average, 3.9 per cent per year, and that 37 per cent of the economic growth during this period could be attributed to TFP growth.

A second body of literature on the Chinese economy has drawn attention to China's international trade expansion, which has made China now one of the biggest traders on the world market. China opened up to foreign trade in the hope of importing new technology from abroad so as to upgrade the technological level at home, and brought in foreign competition to pressure home enterprises to improve efficiency. It would be interesting to see whether international trade achieved these objectives and contributed to TFP growth in China. A number of studies have shown a positive effect of trade volume on economic growth. However, I would like to focus on the *policy* component of trade. That is to say, the *observed* trade volume of an economy depends on both structural factors, notably geographical conditions, and trade *policy*. While geography can hardly be changed, trade policy can be changed according to the government's policy orientation. In this chapter, I would like to take out the *policy* component from the observed trade, and evaluate its impact on total factor productivity growth.

A third point to highlight here is that I shall attempt to decompose TFP growth into efficiency growth and technological growth with the help of the Malmquist index, which is explained below, and which evaluates the impact of trade policy on these two components, in order to see whether the impact was different: that is, whether trade policy was more effective in upgrading technology or improving efficiency.

The sections are organized as follows: the next section presents the DEA method that we employ to calculate TFP growth, efficiency improvement and technology progress, as well as the procedure by which we obtain the policy component of observed trade. The third section presents the empirical model and estimation results, while the last section concludes.

Methodological and conceptual issues

Measuring TFP growth

Over the years, various methods have been developed to measure TFP growth. Overviews of the alternative methods can be found in Grosskopf (1993), Chaffai (1997), and Coelli, Rao and Batteses (1998). Broadly speaking, these methods can be divided into parametric versus non-parametric approaches. Parametric models construct an average production, cost or profit relationship based on a specified functional form and an assumed distribution form of the residuals. Non-parametric models, on the contrary, do not impose a priori any functional form on the underlying technology or any distribution form on the residuals; results are obtained through programming models rather than econometric estimations; they define frontiers and state the technical efficiency of firms relative to the best-practice firm(s). The use of the parametric method usually requires some strict assumptions regarding the distribution form of the residuals, the behavioural manner of the firms and the competitiveness of the markets, while the non-parametric approach is independent of any specific functional form or distribution form of the residuals, and relaxes such strict assumptions as competitive markets and profit-maximizing behaviour of the firms. So a non-parametric approach might be more relevant when developing or transitional economies are being analysed, or when an economy has a large public sector. These are the main considerations that have made us try a non-parametric approach, the Malmquist TFP index using DEA, to analyse the Chinese case.

Also, an important feature of this approach is that it can distinguish between efficiency change and technological progress as sources of total factor productivity growth, the former referring to catching up to the production frontier and the latter to the shifting of the frontier. This distinction is important because between two periods (for example, if there is some degree of efficiency decline and more degree of technological progress, or some technological decline and more efficiency improvement) TFP may still grow as the result of the combined effect of efficiency and technological changes, but one cannot tell how efficiency and technology have changed respectively without the decomposition of TFP growth. This uncertainty about the changes of the components of TFP will rouse uncertainty in, or even mislead, policy-makers: for example, a 'residual' TFP growth may pass for a sign of the success of efficiency-enhancing policies, while in effect efficiency has declined, and it is technological progress that has driven TFP up.

The Malmquist TFP index

To outline briefly the definition of the Malmquist TFP index (for more details, please refer to Färe *et al.*, 1994; Coelli, Rao and Batteses, 1998). The Malmquist index is defined using distance functions, which allow a production technology to be described without the need to specify a behavioural objective such as cost minimization or profit maximization. One may define input-oriented distance functions and output-oriented distance functions. We consider here an output-oriented distance function, knowing that an input-oriented distance function can be defined in a similar way.

A production technology may be defined using the output set, $P(x)$, which represents the set of all output vectors, y, which can be produced using the input vector, x:

$$P(x) = \{y: x \text{ can produce } y\} \tag{14.1}$$

The output distance function is defined as:

$$d_0(x, y) = \min[\delta: (y/\delta) \in P(x)] \tag{14.2}$$

which will take a value less than, equal to or greater than one if the output vector, y, is located inside, upon or outside the possible production set, $P(x)$.

The Malmquist TFP index measures the TFP change between two data points by calculating the ratio of the distances of each data point relative to a common technology. Following Färe *et al.* (1994), the Malmquist (output-oriented) TFP index between period s (the base period) and period t is given by:

$$m_0(y_s, x_s, y_t, x_t) = \left[\frac{d_0^s (y_t, x_t)}{d_0^s (y_s, x_s)} \times \frac{d_0^t (y_t, x_t)}{d_0^t (y_s, x_s)} \right]^{1/2} \tag{14.3}$$

where the notion $d_0^s (y_t, x_t)$ represents the distance between the observation in period t and the technology in period s, represents the distance between the observation in period s, $d_0^s (y_s, x_s)$ and the technology in period s, and so on. A value of m_0 less than, equal or greater than one indicates decline, stagnation or increase in TFP.

An equivalent way of writing (14.3) is:

$$m_0(y_s, x_s, y_t, x_t) = \frac{d_0^t (y_t, x_t)}{d_0^s (y_s, x_s)} \left[\frac{d_0^s (y_t, x_t)}{d_0^t (y_t, x_t)} \times \frac{d_0^s (y_s, x_s)}{d_0^t (y_s, x_s)} \right]^{1/2} \tag{14.4}$$

where the ratio outside the square brackets measures technical efficiency change and the part inside the brackets measures technological change between the two periods.

As a graphic illustration, Figure 14.1 illustrates how economic growth can be decomposed into factor accumulation, efficiency improvement and technological progress. Points A_1 and A_2 represent respectively the observed production levels Y_1 and Y_2 for input levels X_1 and X_2 in periods 1 and 2; Y_1^f and Y_2^f are the maximum (or potential) production levels for the same input levels X_1 and X_2. The distance between the observed and potential production levels is an indicator of production inefficiency, measured by TE_1 and TE_2 for periods 1 and 2, respectively. Production growth can therefore be measured as:

$$\Delta Y = Y_2 - Y_1 = (Y_2^f - TE_2) - (Y_1^f - TE_1) = (Y_2^f - Y_{12}) + (Y_{12} - Y_1^f) \\ + (TE_1 - TE_2) \tag{14.5}$$

where $(Y_2^f - Y_{12})$ is attributable to technical progress, $(Y_{12} - Y_1^f)$ to input growth, and $(TE_1 - TE_2)$ to efficiency improvement. TFP growth is the combined outcome of technical progress and efficiency improvement.

Figure 14.1   Decomposition of production growth

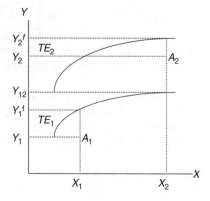

Measuring the policy component of trade

Trade openness is widely measured by the ratio of the sum of exports and imports over gross domestic production, $(X + M)/Y$. And trade policy is often measured with reference to policy instruments affecting trade: average level of tariffs, percentage of liberalized imports, level of export taxes, and so on. However, by definition, these policy measures are partial, as they capture only one or two aspects of the trade system. Also, such practices as according preferential policies to certain kinds of imports cannot be captured by these measures. Here, we measure trade policy by comparing the value of observed trade with a 'normal', or expected, trade value according to a series of structural factors, similar to Guillaumont (1994), Frankel and Romer (1999) and Wei (2000). The basic idea is to regress the observed trade volume on all the structural factors capable of influencing trade yet independent of trade policies, so that the residual is the indicator of trade policy, called 'revealed' trade policy. Such an indicator takes into account the combined outcome of multiple policy aspects affecting trade, without resorting to subjective weightings of these aspects. These aspects can include tariffs and other formal rules and regulations but, more than these, the 'revealed' trade policy may capture other policy aspects such as the exemption or reduction of import duty or other preferential policies. If the provincial governments cannot lay out the formal tariff level which is set nationally, they may have some (or many) discrepancies with regard to those preferential policies. The 'revealed' trade policy may also reflect the attitude of a provincial government towards trade, which can influence various administrative procedures concerning trade: for example, a more favourable attitude towards trade can encourage the simplification of the administrative procedures.

To obtain the 'revealed' trade policy indicator, the observed provincial trade ratio $(X + M)/Y$, is regressed on the following structural factors.

1 Country size: the larger a country or province, the less it is likely to be highly specialized.
2 Level of development: the higher the level of development of a country, the greater its capacity to specialize and to be competitive in the world market with respect to a wide range of products. With the increase of per capita product, demand for imports will increase.
3 Infrastructures: the higher the infrastructure level, the lower the transport costs, which is favourable for trade expansion.
4 Coastal dummy: coastal provinces have an advantageous geographical position for international trade compared to interior provinces.
5 Natural resources: abundant natural resources can contribute to export expansion.

Empirical results

Growth of total factor productivity and of its components in Chinese provinces

Data has been drawn from a panel covering 29 Chinese provinces for the period 1992–1999.[1] The 1990s may be regarded as a period when the Chinese economy was accelerating its efforts to open up to the outside world. This highlights the interest in investigating the effect of its opening-up on its TFP growth during this period, especially for the period after 1992, when the restricted policies towards trade and FDI in the years following the political events of 1989 were lessened and when Deng Xiaoping made his tour to South China and delivered a speech encouraging more economic liberalization and further opening-up to the outside world.[2]

For DEA programming,[3] we have one output and two inputs. The output is real GDP, which is nominal GDP deflated by the implicit GDP deflator. The inputs are labour and capital stock. Labour is the number of employed persons.[4] Capital stock is estimated with the assumption of perpetual inventory (see Appendix 1), as data about the capital stock are not available.

Growth of TFP and of its components in Chinese provinces in the 1990s

I obtain the Malmquist TFP growth index and the growth indices of its two components, efficiency and technology, for each of the 29 Chinese provinces during 1993–1999. Figure 14.2 illustrates the evolution of the annual means of these indices, with all provinces taken together.

As illustrated in Figure 14.2, on average, between 1992 and 1999, TFP grew at an annual rate of 3.9 per cent in China. This rate is compatible with those found in the above-mentioned studies on China's growth accounting. TFP grew most rapidly in 1993, attaining 8 per cent; it continued to grow throughout the whole period, though its growth rate declined. The TFP components, efficiency improvement and technological progress, grew at an annual rate of 1.6 per cent and 2.3 per cent, respectively. About

Figure 14.2   Growth of TFP, efficiency and technology, 29 Chinese provinces as a whole, 1993–1999

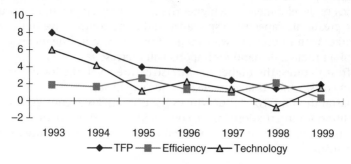

60 per cent of TFP growth during this period can be attributed to technological progress and 40 per cent to efficiency improvement.

By regrouping the 29 provinces into the eastern, central and western regions, we obtain Figures 14.3, 14.4 and 14.5. (See Appendix 2 for a list of which province is in which region.)

Figure 14.3   TFP growth, regional averages, 1993–1999

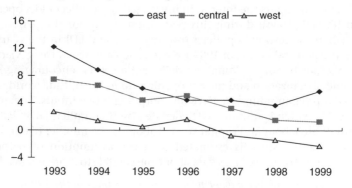

Figure 14.4   Efficiency growth, regional averages, 1993–1999

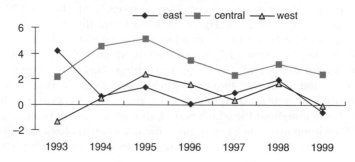

Figure 14.5   Technology growth, regional averages, 1993–1999

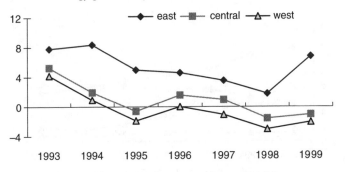

TFP kept growing in both the eastern and central regions between 1992 and 1999, faster in the former than in the latter except for 1996, while it grew at a lower rate during 1992–1996 and began to decline in 1997 in the western region. In terms of efficiency improvement, the central region performed better than the eastern region, this latter performing better than the western region. In terms of technological progress, the eastern region experienced far more rapid annual technological progress rates than the central and western regions (Table 14.1 shows the regional statistics). The decomposition of TFP growth into efficiency improvement and technological progress allows us to see that in the eastern region in the 1990s, the primary source of TFP growth was technological progress, while in the central region, the primary source of TFP growth was efficiency improvement in the same period. This finding may be supportive of the hypothesis of a 'leader–follower' development model or a 'flying geese' model among different regions of China: in the 1980s the eastern region, which was the first to take off economically, experienced important efficiency improvement, and then in the 1990s the dominant source of TFP growth shifted to technological progress, which it achieved with accelerated opening-up, while the central region was still at an earlier stage (compared to the eastern region) of economic reform and development in the 1990s, where

Table 14.1   TFP growth, efficiency improvement and technological progress in China's regions, averages for 1992–1999 (%)

	TFP	Efficiency	Technology
National	*3.9*	*1.6*	*2.3*
East	6.5	1.2	5.4
Central	4.2	3.3	0.9
West	0.3	0.7	–0.4

Figure 14.6   Growth of real GDP, capital, employment and TFP in China in the 1990s

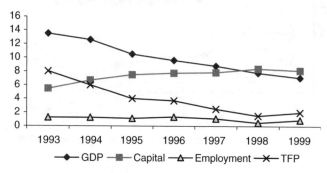

Source: GDP and employment: *China Statistical Yearbook 2000*; capital and TFP: author's estimation.

efficiency improvement played a dominant role in TFP growth. The western region, however, still lagged behind regarding all these aspects.

China's economic growth and TFP growth in the 1990s

Figure 14.6 shows the growth of real GDP, capital, employment and TFP in China between 1992 and 1999, and Figure 14.7 shows the contribution of TFP to economic growth. While the growth rate of capital kept increasing and that of employment fluctuated between 0.5 per cent and 1.33 per cent, those of TFP and real GDP kept declining,[5] except for 1999, when the TFP growth rate slightly accelerated. The tendency of the contribution of TFP growth to real GDP growth was also a decline, except for 1999 (Figure 14.7). On average, 37 per cent of economic growth in China during 1992–1999 can be attributed to TFP growth (Table 14.2). This provides an answer, for the 1990s, to the question of whether China's economic growth was uniquely drawn by factor accumulation. On the other hand, Figure 14.6 shows that the recent slowdown in the China's economic

Figure 14.7   Contribution of TFP to economic growth in China in the 1990s

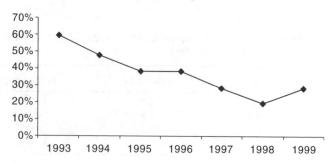

Table 14.2   Sources of economic growth in China, 1992–1999

	Contribution (%)
Real GDP growth	100
Factor accumulation	63
TFP growth, of which:	37
efficiency improvement	40
technological progress	60

growth rate was mainly due to the slowdown in the TFP growth rate (hence the necessity of investigating the explanatory variables of TFP growth).

'Revealed' trade policy

The ratio of observed international trade over GDP in each province, $(X + M)/Y$, is regressed by ordinary least squares on the following structural variables: country size, measured by the population and the area of a province; level of development, measured by per capita GDP; production of the sectors of natural resources (coal mining, oil, ferrous and non-ferrous metal extraction, timber and bamboo); infrastructure level; and a dummy for coastal provinces. The results are presented in Table 14.3. The variable of natural resources is not presented as it did not turn out to be significant in our estimation, implying that the endowment of natural resources did not play an important role in increasing the international trade of Chinese provinces.

We obtain the indicator of revealed trade policy by taking the residual of the above regression, named *TRAPOL*. By looking at the ranking of the provinces according to observed trade and that according to *TRAPOL*, we observe some position changes. Some provinces which did not have high ratios of observed trade over GDP actually had a more favourable policy

Table 14.3   'Revealed' trade policy in Chinese provinces, 1992–1999

Explanatory variable	Coefficient (t-student)
Population_1	–0.84 (–6.86)
Area	–0.20 (–3.55)
GDP_1	0.45 (7.18)
Infrastructure_1	0.46 (2.93)
Coastal dummy	0.89 (8.87)

Note:
The dependant variable is the ratio of observed trade over GDP. All variable except the coastal dummy are in logarithm. Population, GDP and infrastructure are lagged for one year (to avoid an eventual endogeneity problem). The standard deviations have been corrected by the method of White. R-squared = 0.69; number of observations is 232.

attitude towards international trade, as measured by *TRAPOL*, than some of the provinces which had high observed trade ratios; their lower observed trade ratios were due to their disadvantageous geographical positions. This is the case, for example, for the provinces of Jilin, Shanxi and Inner Mongolia, which ranked eleventh, fifteenth and nineteenth, respectively, according to the observed trade ratio, and which rose respectively to third, eighth and twelfth places in the ranking by *TRAPOL*.

Impact of trade policy on the growth of total factor productivity, efficiency and technology

This data being a panel of 29 Chinese provinces and covering eight years from 1992 to 1999, I estimate the impact of trade policy on the growth of total factor productivity, efficiency and technology by the following model:

$$gTFP \text{ (or } EFF \text{ or } TECH)_{it} = \beta_t TRAPOL_{it} + \beta_2 X_{it} + \alpha_i + \eta_t + \varepsilon_{it} \qquad (14.6)$$

where *gTFP* (or *gEFF* or *gTECH*) is the growth of total factor productivity (or the growth of efficiency or technology) as obtained above; *TRAPOL* is the above-defined indicator of trade policy, our variable of interest; X is a vector of control variables susceptible to influence the growth of TFP (or *EFF* or *TECH*), including the share of foreign direct investment in GDP (FDI), the share of government's budgetary expenditures in GDP (GOV), the share of foreign-funded enterprises in total exports (XFFE), the share of state-owned enterprises in total employment, and the ratio of capital over labour (K/L). The important role that foreign direct investment plays in helping to update the recipient country's technology has long been identified both theoretically and empirically, and thus should be an important control variable in our estimated equations. The share of foreign-funded enterprises in total exports is included under the consideration that a large share of foreign-funded enterprises (FFE) is engaged in the processing trade, which is mostly labour-intensive (International Trade Center, 1995), and which may have a different effect on total factor productivity and its components from ordinary trade. The ratio of capital to labour is an indicator measuring the degree of 'capital deepening' of an economy (Sun, Hone and Doucouliages, 1999); a higher capital–labour ratio represents a higher technological content embodied in the production process; an increase in this ratio is in general associated with the adoption of new technology, and therefore this ratio is expected to be associated positively with TFP growth and technological progress. Most state-owned enterprises (SOEs) face the problem of lack of incentives and soft budget constraints, so it is expected that the larger the share of SOEs in the economy, the slower the efficiency or productivity improvement; we reflect this hypothesis by including the part of state-owned enterprises in total employment. The ratio of total government expenditures to GDP is a proxy for the size of the

Table 14.4 Impact of trade policy on total factor productivity, technological progress and efficiency improvement in China's provinces, 1992–1999

	(1) TFP	(2) Technology	(3) Efficiency
TRAPOL	0.27 (2.18)	0.25 (2.74)	0.23 (2.03)
FDI	0.26 (1.79)	0.63 (7.71)	–0.04 (–0.40)
XFFE	–0.01 (–0.11)	–0.43 (–1.44)	0.02 (0.29)
K/L	0.007 (4.47)	0.015 (11.84)	–0.002 (–1.99)
SOE	–0.37 (–2.48)	–0.02 (–0.43)	–0.09 (–1.68)
GOV	–0.41 (–1.99)	–0.04 (–0.68)	–0.08 (–1.70)
BM-LP chi2	149.5	58.06	64.38
Hausman chi2	18.02	18.07	9.04
R^2	0.54	0.56	0.14

Notes:
The dependant variable of (1), (2) and (3) is respectively total factor productivity growth, technological progress, and efficiency improvement. The models (1) and (2) are with fixed effects, model (3) is with random effects. We have tested TRAPOL and FDI for exogeneity by their lagged value of one and two years. For model (1), the P-value of the overidentification test is 0.76, indicating that the instruments are good; the P-value of the Davidson–MacKinnon test is 0.60, indicating that one can accept the null hypothesis that the estimation without instrumentation is coherent. For (2), FDI is instrumented (by its lagged value), as the P-value of the overidentification test is 0.34 and that of the Davidson–MacKinnon test is 0.04, with no need to instrument TRAPOL. For (3) the P-value of the Davidson–MacKinnon test shows no need to instrument. R^2-within is reported for (1) and (2), R^2-overall for (3). Year 1993 is positive, years 1995 to 1999 are negative, and year 1994 is not significant. The number of observations = 203 for all the three models.

government in economic activities. Larger government may imply more administrative interference in the market, which may reduce efficiency (Levine and Renelt, 1992): α_i is supposed to capture the effects of non-observed characteristics, specific to each province, time-invariant and capable of affecting the dependant variable, such as geographical conditions in each province; η_t represents possible temporal effects that would affect the dependant variable for all the provinces in one year or another, such as important national political event or reform measures. The regression results are presented in Table 14.4.

Our variable of interest, *TRAPOL*, had significant and positive effects on the growth of total factor productivity, technological progress and efficiency improvement. That is to say, if a province has a more favourable policy attitude towards international trade, its TFP, efficiency and technology would tend to grow faster, all other things being equal. This is so even for inland provinces. For example, for the provinces of Jilin, Shanxi and Inner Mongolia, their relatively good position in the ranking by *TRAPOL* contributed to their relatively advanced positions in the rankings by TFP growth rate, efficiency improvement rate and technological progress rate,[6] despite their relatively low position in the ranking by observed trade volume. A favourable policy attitude towards trade may actually be translated into policy measures which encourage the transfer of foreign technology, a more welcome climate for foreign expertise, pressure on local firms to learn and apply more efficient managerial skills and techniques, more emphasis on improving the education level of the population in order to assimilate foreign technology, and so on, thus aiding local productivity growth.

Concerning other control variables, it is interesting to see that some of them have quite different effects on TFP growth, technological progress · and efficiency improvement. FDI has significant and positive impact on TFP growth, and this is mainly through its positive impact on technological progress. The share of foreign-funded firms, however, did not show significant effects on TFP growth, technological progress and efficiency improvement during this period. The impact of capital deepening is significant and positive on TFP growth, which is the net outcome of two opposite effects: a positive effect on technological progress and a negative effect on efficiency improvement. This implies that while a higher capital over labour ratio represents higher technology content in the production process, it could result in a loss of efficiency. Possibly when enterprises concentrate on increasing capital investment, less attention is paid to avoiding waste and improving the efficiency of utilization of capital. The share of state-owned enterprises in total employment had a negative impact on TFP growth, and this mainly through its negative effect on efficiency improvement, which confirms the usual finding in the literature of low efficiency of SOE. The share of government expenditure in GDP had a negative effect on TFP growth, also mainly through its negative effect on efficiency improvement, implying that in the continuing transition process of the Chinese economy to a market-oriented one, the Chinese government might still need to reduce its size and give more freedom to the market so that it may manage the function of resources allocation more efficiently.

Conclusion

This chapter has tried to estimate the impact of trade policy, instead of the observed trade volume, on TFP growth in China. Based on a panel covering 29 Chinese provinces and the recent period of 1992–9, and using a non-parametric method, DEA, to calculate the Malmquist indices of total factor productivity growth, efficiency improvement and technological progress, we find that in China's TFP, efficiency and technology grew, on average, at an annual rate of 3.9 per cent, 1.6 per cent and 2.3 per cent, respectively, and that 37 per cent of the economic growth during this period can be attributed to TFP growth. Measuring trade policy by the residual of a normalization equation which regresses the observed trade ratio on structural factors independent of trade policy, we find that trade policy had a positive impact on total factor productivity growth, and this through its positive effect both on technological progress and on efficiency improvement.

The empirical findings of this chapter provide, on the one hand, an answer to the debate on the sources of economic growth in China in the 1990s and, on the other, confirm the virtue of the policy of opening-up to the outside world. The finding on the positive impact of the revealed trade policy on TFP growth is especially encouraging for China's interior provinces. Despite the fact that inland provinces have disadvantageous geographical positions compared to coastal provinces, a more favourable policy attitude towards international trade, which can be translated into encouraging policy measures for the importation of foreign advanced technology and managerial skills and for the building of a propitious environment for developing trade and cooperation with foreign expertise, would encourage or pressure local enterprises to improve their productivity, all other things being equal.

Finally, our empirical findings also concern some other subjects. FDI contributed to TFP growth mainly through contributing to technological progress. Reform in the public sector, including both SOEs and the government, should still speed up in order to improve efficiency, which will accelerate TFP growth. While capital deepening can raise the technological level, our findings also draw attention to the fact that more efforts should be made to improve the utilization efficiency of the capital.

Appendix 1: Estimating capital stock

The perpetual inventory method is the most utilized for capital stock estimation, which defines the evolution of the fixed capital stock as:

$$K_t = (1 - \delta) K_{t-1} + I_t$$

where K_{t-1} and K_t are the capital stocks of periods $t-1$ and t, I_t is the investment in period t and δ is the depreciation rate of the capital stock. To apply this method, we need the data for I_t, δ and K_{t-1}. I_t is investment in fixed capital deflated by the investment deflator, obtained using the price indices of investment. The depreciation rate of capital stock is assumed to be 5 per cent (Wu, 1999). The capital stock of the first year is assumed to be equal to the sum of all past investments (Wu, 1999). Symbolically,

$$K(1) = \int_{-\infty}^{1} I(t)dt = \frac{I(0)e^{\theta}}{\theta}$$

where $I(t) = I(0)e^{\theta t}$, θ and $I(0)$ are estimated by linear regressions using the investment series (1992–9).

Appendix 2: List of regions and provinces

The eastern region includes: Beijing, Tianjin, Hebei, Liaoning, Shanghai, Jiangsu, Zhejiang, Fujian, Shandong, Guangdong, Guangxi and Hainan.

The central region includes: Shanxi, Inner Mongolia, Jilin, Heilongjiang, Anhui, Jiangxi, Henan, Hunan and Hubei.

The western region includes: Sichuan (including Chongqing), Guizhou, Yunnan, Shaanxi, Gansu, Qinghai, Ningxia and Xinjiang.

Notes

1   Tibet is not included in the estimation due to incomplete data.
2   The fact that the price indices for investment in fixed capital (necessary for the capital stock estimation) are available only for the period 1992–9 is another reason for why we cover only this period.
3   I employ the DEAP computer program developed by Coelli (1996).
4   The number of hours worked would be a better measure of labour input but I do not have such data.
5   These tendencies indicate important inefficient allocation or utilization, or waste, of physical capital in China, which was emphasized in Rawski (1999).
6   They are respectively at third, eighth and fifth places in TFP growth ranking, sixth, seventh and third in efficiency improvement ranking, and seventh, eighth and thirteenth in technological progress ranking.

References

Borensztein, E. and J.D. Ostry (1996), 'Accounting for China's Growth Performance', *American Economic Review*, Papers and Proceedings, 86 (2), May, 224–8.

Chaffai, M.E. (1997), 'Estimation de frontières d'efficience: un survol des développements récents de la littérature' (Estimation of Efficiency Frontiers: A Survey of Recent Developments in the Literature), *Revue d'Economie du Développement*, 3 (September).

Chen, K.Y. (1997), 'The TFP Debate: Determinants of Economic Growth in East Asia', *Asian Pacific Economic Literature*, 11 (1), 18–38.

Coelli, T.J. (1996), 'A Guide to DEAP Version 2.1: A Data Envelopment Analysis (Computer) Program', *CEPA Working Papers*, 8/96, University of New England, Australia.

Coelli, T.J., D.S.P. Rao and G.E. Batteses (1998), *An Introduction to Efficiency and Productivity Analysis*, London: Kluwer Academic.

Färe, R., S. Grosskopf, M. Norris and Z. Zhang (1994), 'Productivity Growth, Technical Progress, and Efficiency Change in Industrialized Countries', *American Economic Review*, 84 (1).

Frankel, J. and D. Romer (1999), 'Does Trade Cause Growth?', *American Economic Review*, 89 (3), 379–99.

Grosskopf, S. (1993), 'Efficiency and Productivity', in H.O. Fried, C.A.K. Lovell and S.S. Schmidt (eds), *The Measurement of Productive Efficiency: Techniques and Applications*, Oxford: Oxford University Press.

Guillaumont, P. (1994), 'Politique d'ouverture et croissance économique: les effets de la croissance et de l'instabilité des exportations' ['Policy of opening and economic growth: the effects of growth and of instability of exports'], *Revue d'Economie du développement*, (1), pp. 91–114.

Hu, Z. and M.S. Khan (1997), 'Why is China Growing So Fast?', *IMF Staff Papers*, 44 (1), March.

International Trade Center (1995), *Survey of China's Foreign Trade, An Analysis of China's Export and Import Data at the Enterprise Level*, Geneva: UNCTAD/WTO.

Krugman, P. (1994), 'Myth of Asia's Miracle', *Foreign Affairs*, 73, 62–78.

Levine, R. and D. Renelt (1992), 'A Sensitivity Analysis of Cross-country Growth Regressions', *American Economic Review*, 82 (4), 942–63.

Maddison, A. (1998), *The Chinese Economy: An Historical Perspective*, Paris: OECD.

Rawski, T.G. (1999), 'The Political Economy of China's Declining Growth', document, University of Pittsburgh.

Sun, H., P. Hone and H. Doucouliages (1999), 'Economic Openness and Technical Efficiency: A Case Study of Chinese Manufacturing Industries', *Economics of Transition*, 7 (3), 615–36.

Wei, S.J. (2000), 'Natural Openness and Good Government', *NBER Working Papers*, No. W7765, June.

Woo, W.T. (1998), 'Chinese Economic Growth: Sources and Prospects', in M. Fouquin and F. Lemoine (eds), *The Chinese Economy*, London: Economica.

World Bank (1993), *The East Asian Miracle: Economic Growth and Public Policy*, New York: Oxford University Press.

World Bank (1997), *China: 2020: Development Challenges in the New Century*, Washington DC.

Wu, Y.R. (1999), 'Productivity and Efficiency in China's Regional Economics', in Tsu-Tan Fu *et al.*, *Economic Efficiency and Productivity Growth in the Asian-Pacific Region*, Cheltenham: Edward Elgar.

Young, A. (1993), 'Lessons from the East Asian NICs: a Contrarian View', *NEBR Working Papers*, No. 4482.

Young, A. (1995), 'The Tyranny of Numbers: Confronting the Statistical Realities of the East Asian Experiences', *The Quarterly Journal of Economics*, 110 (8), 64–79.

Part IV

Trade, Investment and Implications for Key Economic Sectors

15
Investment, Investment Efficiency and Economic Growth in China*

Jun Zhang

Introduction

China has maintained rapid economic growth for more than 20 years since the economic reform programmes started in the early 1980s. This performance record is not only unique among all the transitional economies, but also superior to the Asia Miracle of the East Asian Newly-industrializing Economies (NIEs) between the 1960s and the 1980s.

However, despite the size difference, China's growth pattern is similar to that of the NIEs and may similarly be described in terms of the investment-growth model (Zhang, 2002). Although about 70 per cent of its population lives in rural areas, China's economic growth mainly depended on the rapid expansion of the manufacturing sector rather than on agriculture, except in the early 1980s. The value added of the industrial sector has accounted for 45 per cent of China's total GDP, while that of agriculture has represented only about 10 per cent (and is still declining). It is manufacturing rather than agriculture that has driven China's economic growth.

Due to the importance of the *manufacturing* industries, international trade has played a crucial role in China's economic growth during the post-reform era. This also parallels the experience of the NIEs. Despite a different pattern of FDI inflow between China and most of the NIEs, there is great similarity in their efforts regarding export promotion and trade expansion. FDI inflow has played an important part in China's export growth in the 1990s and since, with 80 per cent of China's exports being manufactured exports, more than half of which come from foreign-invested enterprises (FIEs) in China.

---

*An earlier version of this paper was initially prepared during my visit to Kyungpook National University in Korea (September–December, 2002). I would like to thank China's National Social Sciences Foundation (2002) for financial support. I am also indebted to the research assistant, Shi-yi Chen, for his help in data collection. All remaining errors are the responsibility of the author.

In the past two decades a great deal of economic literature on growth and industrialization has been produced which has helped to explain the nature and pattern of growth during the East Asian Miracle (e.g., Lau and Kim, 1992; Young, 1994; Kim and Lau, 1996). It is widely believed that the East Asian model is best characterized in terms of an investment-growth paradigm, captured in such indicators as high investment/GDP ratio, rising capital–output ratio, or incremental capital–output ratio (ICOR).[1] In this chapter let us observe and describe the pattern of *aggregate* investment in China, discuss its investment-growth nexus in the context of the East Asian NIEs, and examine investment efficiency during the high-growth period.

The chapter finds that investment did not grow faster than output during most of the reform period, and the investment/GDP ratio did not rise rapidly until recently. China has successfully utilized its unlimited supply of labour (mostly rural) through massive rural industrialization since it embarked on reform. The success of rural industrialization owes much to the proliferation of millions of rural and small enterprises, which have been market-orientated and have used appropriately simple and labour-intensive technology.

The chapter is organized as follows: in the next section we present an analysis of the proportion of investment to GDP in China during the past two decades, and describe the investment behaviour at an aggregate level, offering some comparisons with East Asian NIEs. In the third section we calculate the real investment/GDP ratio and ICOR in order to investigate whether China has overinvested during the period of high growth. The final section offers some concluding remarks.

China's investment pattern in the context of East Asia

Investment rates

Table 15.1 provides estimates of investment rates (investment as a proportion of GDP) in China between 1978 and 2000 in nominal terms and on the basis of three different definitions. Investment rate one is calculated by using data on investment defined as 'total social investment in fixed assets' (*quan shehui guding zichan touzi e*).[2] Investment rate two and investment rate three are calculated using estimates of 'gross value of capital formation' and 'gross fixed capital formation', respectively. The difference between the gross value of capital formation and gross fixed capital formation is given by the change in inventories, as explained in the standard national accounts.

On average during 1978–2000, investment rate one was about 30 per cent, while investment rate two was around 37 per cent. The difference between investment rate one and investment rate three narrowed over time. The investment rates of China today are definitely much higher than those of Japan and the US at similar stages of high growth. It is also far

Year	GDP	Total social investments in fixed assets	Investment rate 1	GDP measured by expenditure approach	Gross capital formation	Investment rate 2	Gross fixed capital formation	Investment rate 3
1978				3,605.6	1,377.9	38.2	1,073.9	29.78
1979	4,038.2			4,074	1,474.2	36.2	1,151.2	28.26
1980	4,517.8	910.9	20.16	4,551.3	1,590	34.9	1,318	28.96
1981	4,862.4	961	19.76	4,901.4	1,581	32.3	1,253	25.56
1982	5,294.7	1,230.4	23.24	5,489.2	1,760.2	32.1	1,493.2	27.2
1983	5,934.5	1,430.1	24.1	6,076.3	2,005	33	1,709	28.13
1984	7,171	1,832.9	25.56	7,164.4	2,468.6	34.5	2,125.6	29.67
1985	8,964.4	2,543.2	28.37	8,792.1	3,386	38.5	2,641	30.04
1986	10,202.2	3,120.6	30.59	10,132.8	3,846	38	3,098	30.57
1987	11,962.5	3,791.7	31.7	11,784.7	4,322	36.7	3,742	31.75
1988	14,928.3	4,753.8	31.84	14,704	5,495	37.4	4,624	31.45
1989	16,909.2	4,410.4	26.08	16,466	6,095	37	4,339	26.35
1990	18,547.9	4,517	24.35	18,319.5	6,444	35.2	4,732	25.83
1991	21,617.8	5,594.5	25.88	21,280.4	7,517	35.3	5,940	27.91
1992	26,638.1	8,080.1	30.33	25,863.7	9,636	37.3	8,317	32.16
1993	34,634.4	13,072.3	37.74	34,500.7	14,998	43.5	12,980	37.62
1994	46,759.4	17,042.1	36.45	46,690.7	19,260.6	41.3	16,856.3	36.1
1995	58,478.1	20,019.3	34.23	58,510.5	23,877	40.8	20,300.5	34.7
1996	67,884.6	22,913.5	33.75	68,330.4	26,867.2	39.3	23,336.1	34.15
1997	74,462.6	24,941.1	33.49	74,894.2	28,457.6	38	25,154.2	33.59
1998	78,345.2	28,406.2	36.26	79,003.3	29,545.9	37.4	27,630.8	34.97
1999	82,067.5	29,854.7	36.38	82,673.1	30,701.6	37.1	29,475.5	35.65
2000	89,403.6	32,917.7	36.82	89,112.5	32,255	36.2	32,623.8	36.61

Note: Investment rate 1 = total social investments in fixed assets/GDP*100%. Meanwhile we also give the GDP measurement by the expenditure approach in which investment is measured by the gross capital formation. Because gross capital formation consists of both gross fixed capital formation and inventory increase, we therefore calculate both the investment rate 2 and investment rate 3. The value unit is 100 million Chinese RMB yuan and the unit of the investment rates is %.

Source: China Statistical Yearbook (NBS, 2001).

higher than those of Hong Kong and Taiwan, whose investment rates between 1966 and 1998 were just 25.4 per cent and 23.7 per cent, respectively (Toh and Ng, 2002). China's investment rates are comparable to those of Singapore (in the 1970s–1980s), South Korea, Thailand and Malaysia. For example, the average investment rate in fixed assets of Singapore was 35.4 per cent between 1966 and 1998, which is the highest among the 'four little dragons (Hong Kong, Singapore, South Korea, Taiwan) in East Asia'.[3]

The ratio of inventory increase over GDP can be easily calculated by taking the difference between investment rates two and three in Table 15.1, which is illustrated in Figure 15.1. Between 1978 and 1995, this ratio was relatively stable and averaged about 8 per cent, which is much higher than in other market economies. Since the middle of the 1990s, however, China's inventory increase as a percentage of GDP has consistently declined.

Industrial share of GDP and structural change of the manufacturing sector

It is widely believed that China's success in transforming the centrally planned economy has been largely due to its success in promoting and expanding its industrial sector, and manufacturing in particular. In this sub-section we describe China's industrial transformation by examining the industrial share in Chinese GDP and investment growth in manufacturing industries during 1978–2000.

Figures 15.2 and 15.3 present both the industrial, and construction and installation shares in GDP from 1981 to 2000. The industrial share in China's GDP was around 45 per cent, which is quite similar to that achieved during the rapid phase of development in East Asia (especially in Korea and Singapore). The importance of the industrial sector in China's gross investment can also be shown by the expenditure breakdown of total

Figure 15.1   The ratio of inventory increase to GDP in China, 1978–2000

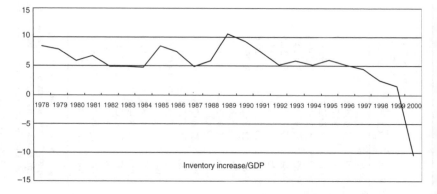

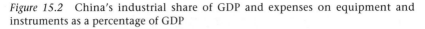

Figure 15.2 China's industrial share of GDP and expenses on equipment and instruments as a percentage of GDP

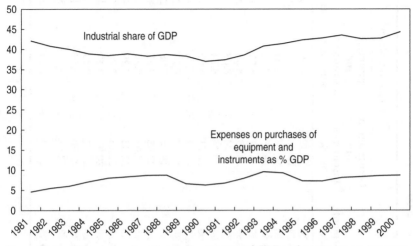

Figure 15.3 China's construction as percentage of GDP and expenses on construction and installation as percentage of total investment

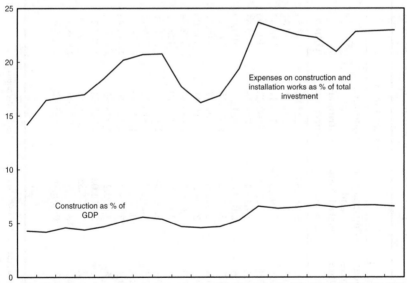

social fixed investment. As Table 15.2 shows, total social investment in fixed assets has derived mostly from expenditure on both construction and installation works (C&I), and equipment and instruments purchases (E&I: see also Figures 15.2 and 15.3).

Table 15.2 Composition of total social investment in fixed assets in China (1981–2000)

Year	Total social investments in fixed assets (100 million yuan)	Accounted for by: Construction and installation works	Equipment and instruments purchases	Others	Investment rate	Accounted for by: Construction and installation works	Equipment and instruments purchases	Others
1981	961.0	689.83	223.64	47.54	19.76	14.19	4.60	0.98
1982	1,230.4	871.12	291.41	67.87	23.24	16.45	5.50	1.28
1983	1,430.1	993.32	358.31	78.43	24.10	16.74	6.04	1.32
1984	1,832.9	1,217.58	509.23	106.06	25.56	16.98	7.10	1.48
1985	2,543.2	1,655.46	718.08	169.65	28.37	18.47	8.01	1.89
1986	3,120.6	2,059.66	851.95	208.99	30.59	20.19	8.35	2.05
1987	3,791.7	2,475.65	1,038.78	277.26	31.70	20.70	8.68	2.32
1988	4,753.8	3,099.66	1,305.37	348.77	31.84	20.76	8.74	2.34
1989	4,410.4	2,994.59	1,115.81	300.00	26.08	17.71	6.60	1.77
1990	4,517.0	3,008.72	1,165.54	342.74	24.35	16.22	6.28	1.85
1991	5,594.5	3,647.68	1,460.19	486.63	25.88	16.87	6.75	2.25
1992	8,080.1	5,163.37	2,125.14	791.58	30.33	19.38	7.98	2.97
1993	13,072.3	8,201.21	3,315.92	1,555.18	37.74	23.68	9.57	4.49
1994	17,042.1	10,786.52	4,328.26	1,928.08	36.45	23.07	9.26	4.12
1995	20,019.3	13,173.33	4,262.46	2,583.48	34.23	22.53	7.29	4.42
1996	22,913.5	15,109.29	4,925.98	2,878.28	33.75	22.26	7.26	4.24
1997	24,941.1	15,614.03	6,044.84	3,282.25	33.49	20.97	8.12	4.41
1998	28,406.2	17,874.53	6,528.53	4,003.10	36.26	22.82	8.33	5.11
1999	29,854.7	18,795.93	7,053.04	4,005.74	36.38	22.90	8.59	4.88
2000	32,917.7	20,536.26	7,785.62	4,595.85	36.82	22.97	8.71	5.14
1981–2000					30.35	19.79	7.59	2.97

Note: The investment rate of 1981–2000 is arithmetically averaged.

Source: China Statistical Yearbook (NBS, 2001).

It is interesting that, contrary to some East Asian economies, China's industrial share of GDP does not show a significantly increasing trend. For instance, Singapore, Korea and Thailand all experienced a rapid growth in the size of manufacturing sector, so that the share of manufacturing in GDP rose continuously from a very low level.

China's experience is, however, different from that of these East Asian NIEs because of its overindustrialized state under the pre-1978 centrally planned system. China's pre-1978 economy was dominated by a Soviet type of catch-up strategy, which very much emphasizes the development of heavy and military industries. After the opening-up and market-orientated reform policies were implemented, China entered a new industrialization phase that was typified by the rapid emergence and proliferation of millions of rural and small-sized industrial enterprises (so-called township and village enterprises, or TVEs). These TVEs have entered almost all the manufacturing industries and mining sectors that were formerly dominated by large-sized state enterprises (Otsuka, Liu and Murakami, 1998). The importance of large and heavy industrial enterprises has continuously declined as a result of this rural industrialization process.

In order to understand the manufacturing expansion, in Table 15.3 I further calculate and show the investment growth in Chinese manufacturing industries in 1981, 1998 and 2000. For simplicity, I classify the manufacturing sector into 11 industries. The calculations show that since the 1980s, except for textiles, ordinary machinery and manufacturing which were defined as 'other' in Table 15.3 (categories whose relative investment shares have shrunk), all manufacturing industries have experienced a rapidly growing share of investment. Such growth clearly benefited from widening markets, both in China and in abroad, in which China had a comparative advantage.

Investment in housing construction

Toh and Ng (2002) emphasized the accountability of housing construction when they explained the investment peak in the rapid development phase of Singapore. According to them, housing construction – both private and public residential housing construction – accounted for a major proportion of the investment boom between 1981 and 1985.[4]

China does not directly disclose annual data of investment in housing construction completed, but we can derive some data by indirect means from information on China's capital construction investment. These data are: floor space of housing construction completed annually; floor space of individual housing completed in urban and rural areas; and floor space of residential housing completed. Table 15.4 provides the total floor space of housing construction completed annually in China between 1985 and 2000.

As Table 15.5 indicates, the total floor space of housing construction includes the relevant figures for both urban (cities/towns) and rural com-

Table 15.3 Sectoral shares of investment in China's manufacturing industries (1981–2000)

		2000				1998				1981	
		Investment in capital construction	Investment in renovation and renewals	Total	Share (%)	Investment in capital construction	Investment in renovation and renewals	Total	Share %	Investment in capital construction	Share %
Manufacturing		1,175.11	2,104.15	3,279.26	100.00	1,484.08	1,797.3	3,281.38	100.00	216.01	100.00
Electrical and electronic products	Electrical equipments and machinery	29.19	79.09			34.62	71.37				
	Electronic and telecommunications equipment	214.80	147.52			178.05	76.60				
	Instruments, metals, cultural and office machinery	9.21	10.55			7.39	8.02				
	Total	253.20	237.16	490.36	14.95	220.06	155.99	376.05	11.46	5.06	2.34
Chemistry and chemical products	Raw chemical materials and chemical products	172.18	274.67			201.91	280.32				
	Medical and pharmaceutical products	42.42	91.20			30.22	52.01				
	Chemical fibres	11.79	34.94			53.02	20.01				
	Total	226.39	400.81	627.20	19.13	285.15	352.34	637.49	19.43	16.34	7.56

Table 15.3 Sectoral shares of investment in China's manufacturing industries (1981–2000) – *continued*

		2000				1998				1981	
		Investment in capital construction	Investment in renovation and renewals	Total	Share (%)	Investment in capital construction	Investment in renovation and renewals	Total	Share %	Investment in capital construction	Share %
Transportation equipment	Transportation equipment	107.56	178.90	286.46	8.74	186.66	150.05	336.71	10.26	2.60	1.20
Machinery and equipment	Ordinary machinery	31.18	61.08			27.83	67.45				
	Equipment for special purposes	29.93	43.10			23.42	47.10				
	Total	61.11	104.17	165.28	5.04	51.25	114.55	165.80	5.05	15.53	7.19
Metal products	Metal products	17.28	29.20	46.48	1.42	19.18	21.62	40.80	1.24	1.20	0.56
Petroleum processing and coking	Petroleum processing and coking	32.79	129.91	162.70	4.96	137.84	105.03	242.87	7.40	8.21	3.80
Rubber and plastics	Rubber products	8.40	20.86			11.61	29.50				
	Plastic products	27.70	38.96			17.15	30.97				
	Non-metal mineral products	61.42	112.18			70.67	103.90				
	Total	97.52	172.00	269.52	8.22	99.43	164.37	263.80	8.04	2.68	1.24

Table 15.3 Sectoral shares of investment in China's manufacturing industries (1981–2000) – *continued*

		2000				1998				1981	
		Investment in capital construction	Investment in renovation and renewals	Total	Share (%)	Investment in capital construction	Investment in renovation and renewals	Total	Share %	Investment in capital construction	Share %
Metals	Smelting and processing of ferrous metals	50.85	269.11			155.95	242.99				
	Smelting and processing of non-ferrous metals	39.76	82.00			24.35	61.30				
	Total	90.61	351.11	441.72	13.47	180.3	304.29	484.59	14.77	21.51	9.96
Food, beverage and tobacco	Food processing	32.43	43.95			33.09	49.93				
	food production	37.57	47.75			26.99	28.09				
	beverages	26.27	82.52			25.23	84.14				
	tobacco	18.23	45.24			8.95	69.23				
	Total	114.50	219.47	333.97	10.18	94.26	231.39	325.65	9.92	9.26	4.27
Textiles	Textiles	29.57	107.86			23.13	61.97				
	garments and other fibre products	17.67	17.28			10.00	12.27				
	Total	47.25	125.14	172.39	5.26	33.13	74.24	107.37	3.27	19.86	9.19

Table 15.3 Sectoral shares of investment in China's manufacturing industries (1981–2000) – *continued*

		2000				1998				1981	
		Investment in capital construction	Investment in renovation and renewals	Total	Share (%)	Investment in capital construction	Investment in renovation and renewals	Total	Share %	Investment in capital construction	Share %
Others	Leather, furs, down and related products	12.18	4.54			8.89	4.58				
	Timber processing, bamboo, cane, palm fibre and straw products	8.22	15.15			9.58	13.96				
	Furniture manufacturing	7.15	5.55			8.07	4.05				
	papermaking and paper products	39.54	79.91			117.02	58.44				
	Printing and recording media reproduction	13.05	22.85			15.47	18.05				
	Cultural, education and sports goods	2.66	3.66			0.97	2.53				
	Other manufacturing	44.11	24.60			16.84	22.64				
	Total	126.92	156.27	285.89	8.72	176.84	124.25	301.09	9.18	113.76	52.66

Note: The unit is 100 million RMB yuan. The unit of share is given as a percentage.

Sources: Author's caculation. The basic data for estimation are from *China Statistical Yearbook* (NBS, 2002, 1999 and 1982). The data for manufacturing industries come from *China Statistical Yearbook of Investment* (NBS, 2001), p. 529.

Table 15.4 Total floor space of housing construction completed annually in China (1985–2000)

Year	Total floor space of housing construction completed (10,000 sq.m)		Floor space of individual housing completed in rural areas (10,000 sq.m)		% of individual floor space completed in rural areas to total floor space of housing completed		% of floor space completed in cities/towns to total floor space of housing completed		Floor space of newly-built houses in rural areas (100 million Sq.m) 9
	Total 1	Residential housing 2	Total 3	Residential housing 4	Total 5 3/1	Residential housing 6 4/2	Total 7 1-5	Residential housing 8 1-6	
1985	122,084.00	90,972.00	78,973	69,542	0.65	0.76	0.35	0.24	7.22
1986	151,184.00	117,667.00	103,225	94,468	0.68	0.80	0.32	0.20	9.84
1987	141,963.00	107,697.00	96,477	85,524	0.68	0.79	0.32	0.21	8.84
1988	135,943.00	104,801.00	89,092	80,799	0.66	0.77	0.34	0.23	8.45
1989	105,749.00	83,197.00	71,026	66,134	0.67	0.79	0.33	0.21	6.76
1990	107,793.00	86,289.00	71,136	67,812	0.66	0.79	0.34	0.21	6.91
1991	119,107.00	94,002.00	79,501	74,193	0.67	0.79	0.33	0.21	7.54
1992	114,800.00	85,017.00	65,338	60,442	0.57	0.71	0.43	0.29	6.19
1993	122,021.00	76,779.00	56,012	46,129	0.46	0.60	0.54	0.40	4.81
1994	136,550.00	97,510.00	65,390	57,646	0.48	0.59	0.52	0.41	6.18
1995	145,600.00	107,433.00	73,522	66,230	0.50	0.62	0.50	0.38	6.99
1996	161,988.98	121,932.92	87,277	79,531	0.54	0.65	0.46	0.35	8.28
1997	166,057.13	121,100.96	85,888	77,287	0.52	0.64	0.48	0.36	8.06
1998	170,904.75	127,571.61	83,864	77,031	0.49	0.60	0.51	0.40	7.99
1999	187,357.07	139,305.93	83,244	76,758	0.44	0.55	0.56	0.45	8.34
2000	181,974.44	134,528.83	81,270	75,515	0.45	0.56	0.55	0.44	7.97

Sources: The data of column 1 and column 2 are based on *China Statistical Yearbook* (NBS, 2001), section 6-1; 1999, p183, section 6-1; 1998, p. 185, section 6-1; 1997, p. 149, section 5-1; 1996, p. 139, section 5-1; 1995, p. 137, section 5-1; 1993, p. 145, section 5-1; 1991, p. 143, section 5-1; 1989, p. 447, section 10-1; 1988, p. 559, section 10-1. Data of column 3 and column 4 are quoted from *China Statistical Yearbook* (NBS, 2001), section 6-34. Data of column 5 to column 8 are calculated by the author. Data of column 9 are quoted from *China Statistical Yearbook* (NBS, 2002), section 10-27.

Table 15.5 Estimated unit cost of housing construction and of private residential housing

| Year | Housing built for individuals in cities/towns and in industrial and mining areas | | | | | | Housing built for individuals in rural areas | |
| | Floor space of housing construction completed 10,000 sq.m | | Value of housing construction completed 10,000 RMB yuan | | Costs of housing construction completed RMB yuan/sq.m | | Costs of housing construction completed (RMB yuan/sq.m) | |
	Total 1	Residential housing 2	Total 3	Residential housing 4	Total 5 3/1	Residential housing 6 4/2	Total 7	Residential housing 8
1985	7,081.36	6,306.80	567,917	493,872	80.20	78.31	44	45
1986	8,115.37	7,234.80	745,623	654,192	91.88	90.42	49	41
1987	9,120.19	8,294.36	1,005,133	899,614	110.21	108.46	63	57
1988	10,526.83	9,433.15	1,568,475	1,401,141	149.00	148.53	83	72
1989	8,565.38	7,822.55	1,402,278	1,260,234	163.71	161.10	112	97
1990	7,180.55	6,492.93	1,247,034	1,103,317	173.67	169.93	109	96
1991	7,554.40	6,808.24	1,403,230	1,250,861	185.75	183.73	115	102
1992	9,673.43	8,586.22	2,164,663	1,897,651	223.77	221.01	143	112
1993	11,463.44	9,812.95	3,385,002	2,804,212	295.29	285.77	181	165
1994	14,098.18	12,268.36	4,513,203	3,870,038	320.13	315.45	201	174
1995	15,194.84	13,333.90	5,523,894	4,770,290	363.54	357.76	233	204
1996	16,556.86	14,518.78	6,552,198	5,629,097	395.74	387.71	258	222
1997	17,570.24	15,165.03	7,041,112	5,938,633	400.74	391.60	280	245
1998	20,781.49	18,227.39	8,485,630	7,272,165	408.33	398.97	286	248
1999	21,830.37	19,246.43	9,175,357	7,818,281	420.3	406.22	229	234
2000	21,763.53	18,929.01	9,529,931	8,120,255	437.89	428.98	242	245

Sources: The data of columns 1–4 are quoted from China Statistical Yearbook (NBS, 2001), section 6-33. The data of columns 5 and 6 are obtained by author's estimation. The data of column 7 and column 8 are quoted from China Statistical Yearbook (NBS, 2001), section 6-34.

munities. The rural share is greater than that of the urban sector. The average cost of housing construction per square metre in China is estimated here by averaging the costs of cities/towns and of rural areas, weighted by their respective shares in total floor space. Since there is no information released in statistical publications about the estimated costs per square metre of housing construction, either in cities/towns or in rural areas, I have instead used the estimated costs of private residential housing construction, both in cities/towns and in rural areas. This is acceptable,

Table 15.6 Total investment in housing construction in China (including residential and non-residential housing)

Year	Average unit cost of total housing construction (RMB yuan/sq.m) 1	Average unit cost of residential housing RMB yuan/sq.m 2	Investments in housing construction 100 million RMB yuan 3	Investment in residential housing 100 million RMB yuan 4	Investment in non-residential housing 100 million RMB yuan 5
1985	56.67	52.99	691.85	482.06	209.79
1986	62.72	50.88	948.23	598.69	349.54
1987	78.11	67.81	1,108.87	730.29	378.58
1988	105.44	89.60	1,433.38	939.02	494.37
1989	129.06	110.46	1,364.80	918.99	445.80
1990	130.99	111.53	1,411.98	962.38	449.60
1991	138.35	119.16	1,647.85	1,120.13	527.72
1992	177.73	143.61	2,040.34	1,220.93	819.41
1993	242.72	213.31	2,961.69	1,637.77	1,323.92
1994	262.95	231.99	3,590.58	2,262.13	1,328.45
1995	298.27	262.43	4,342.81	2,819.36	1,523.45
1996	321.36	280.00	5,205.68	3,414.12	1,791.56
1997	337.96	297.78	5,612.07	3,606.14	2,005.92
1998	348.39	308.39	5,954.15	3,934.18	2,019.97
1999	336.13	311.50	6,297.63	4,339.38	1,958.25
2000	349.74	325.95	6,364.37	4,384.97	1,979.41

Note: Column 1 Table 5 5 × Table 4 7 + Table 5 7 × Table 4 5 Column 2 Table 5 6 × Table 4 8 + Table 5 8 × Table 4 6 Column 3 1 × Table 4 (1) ÷ 10000 Column 4 2 × Table 4 2 ÷ 10000 Column 5 3–4

Sources: Author's own calculations based on Table 15.4 and Table 15.5.

since the difference between costs per square metre of general housing and private residential housing construction should not be great.

Thus, the estimated annual investment in China's housing construction is obtained by multiplying the average unit cost of total housing construction per square metre by the total floor space of housing construction per annum. Annual investment of non-residential housing equals the total investment in housing construction minus the investment in residential housing per annum. This is presented in Table 15.6.

From the estimates of gross fixed investment set out in Table 15.3 and those of total investment in housing (Table 15.6), it is inferred that investment in housing accounted for about 30 per cent of total investment in the 1980s, although in and after the 1990s, this percentage declined. In the late 1990s investment in housing was about 20 per cent of gross investment in fixed assets, or about 7 per cent of Chinese GDP (much less than the 14.4 per cent recorded in Singapore between 1966 and 1998).[5]

The share of public investment

In current statistical practice in China, data on fixed investment are broken down and classified by 'who owns', 'who manages', 'where the money comes from', and 'on what the money is spent'. Since the outset of China's economic reforms, there has undoubtedly been an increase in the share of non-state investment (the sum of 'individual investment', 'private investment' and 'investment by other type of ownership'[6]) in total social fixed investment. Furthermore, the share of in-budget investment by the state in total fixed investment has also declined sharply.[7]

Table 15.7 calculates and breaks down gross investment rates by different ownership of investments. In making the calculations, we have summed 'individual investors' and so-called 'investment by other type of ownership'. As Table 15.7 indicates, the proportion of investment by state and collective sectors does not drop, but the share of private investment has really increased. After about 1993, with a swelling inflow of foreign investment into China, the private investment rate almost doubled. During 1980–2000 the state sector's investment rate still accounted, on average, for 61.25 per cent of total fixed investment; the corresponding figure for the collective sector was about 14 per cent. Of all private investment, individual investment accounted, on average, for 40 per cent; FDIs were only about 10 per cent or so. For example, in the peak year of 1996, RMB 274.7 billion *yuan* of FDI (including that from Hong Kong, Macau and Taiwan) accounted for only 12 per cent of total fixed investment in China, which was less than 40 per cent of private investment.

Thus, as a whole, real private investment accounted for no more than a quarter of total fixed investment in China. Considering that the average investment rate in China in 1980–2000 was about 30 per cent, the share of public investment (mainly consisting of state and collective investments)

Table 15.7 Investment shares of state-owned, collectively-owned and private sectors (1980–2000)

Year	State sector investment	Collective sector investment	Individual investment	Investment by other type of ownership	Private investment	Total social investment rate	Accounted for by		
							State investment	Collective investment	Private investment
1980	745.9	46.0	119.0		119.0	20.16	16.51	1.02	2.63
1981	667.5	115.2	178.3		178.3	19.76	13.73	2.37	3.66
1982	845.3	174.3	210.8		210.8	23.24	15.97	3.29	3.98
1983	952.0	156.3	321.8		321.8	24.10	16.04	2.63	5.42
1984	1,185.2	238.7	409.0		409.0	25.56	16.53	3.33	5.70
1985	1,680.5	327.5	535.2		535.2	28.37	18.75	3.65	5.97
1986	2,079.4	391.8	649.4		649.4	30.59	20.38	3.84	6.37
1987	2,448.8	547.0	795.9		795.9	31.70	20.47	4.57	6.65
1988	3,020.0	711.7	1,022.1		1,022.1	31.84	20.23	4.77	6.85
1989	2,808.2	570.0	1,032.2		1,032.2	26.08	16.61	3.37	6.10
1990	2,986.3	529.5	1,001.2		1,001.2	24.35	16.10	2.85	5.40
1991	3,713.8	697.8	1,182.9		1,182.9	25.88	17.18	3.23	5.47
1992	5,498.7	1,359.4	1,222.0		1,222.0	30.33	20.64	5.10	4.59
1993	7,925.9	2,317.3	1,476.2	1,352.9	2,829.1	37.74	22.88	6.69	8.17
1994	9615.0	2,758.9	1,970.6	2,697.6	4,668.2	36.45	20.56	5.90	9.98
1995	10,898.2	3,289.4	2,560.2	3,271.5	5,831.7	34.23	18.64	5.63	9.97
1996	12,006.2	3,651.5	3,211.2	4,044.6	7,255.8	33.75	17.69	5.38	10.69
1997	13,091.7	3,850.9	3,429.4	4,569.1	7,998.5	33.49	17.58	5.17	10.74
1998	15,369.3	4,192.2	3,744.4	5,100.3	8,844.7	36.26	19.62	5.35	11.29
1999	15,947.8	4,338.6	4,195.7	5,372.7	9,568.4	36.38	19.43	5.29	11.66
2000	16,504.4	4,801.5	4,709.4	6,902.5	11,611.9	36.82	18.46	5.37	12.99
1980–2000						29.86	18.29	4.23	7.34
Share						100.00%	61.25%	14.17%	24.58%

Note: The unit of investment is 100 million RMB yuan; investment rates are given as percentages.

Source: China Statistical Yearbook (NBS, 2001).

in GDP was therefore about 23 per cent, much higher than in Singapore and Taiwan in 1966–98 (9.1 per cent and 10.6 per cent, respectively).[8]

Has China over-invested?

Growing attention has been paid to the growth/investment pattern in recent literature (e.g., Sun, 1998; Young, 2000; Song, Liu and Jiang, 2001; Qin and Song, 2002; Zhang, 2002), but the purpose of most recent studies has been either to carry out growth accounting analysis or to estimate investment functions of China. In this section I shall not repeat that exercise; rather, I examine carefully and directly the time pattern of investment with respect to total output, or GDP, in China in the past two decades by:

(a) converting nominal investment rates to real rates;
(b) calculating the real ICORs, which are a direct measurement of the change of investment efficiency over time at aggregate level.

Investment to GDP ratios in real terms

In his article reviewing the growth pattern of East Asian economies, Young (1994, p. 7) mentioned that:

> with the exception of Hong Kong, during the 1960–85 period each of the NICs experienced an extraordinary rise in its investment to GDP ratio [I/GDP]. Between 1960 and 1980 the I/GDP ratio doubled in Taiwan, tripled in Korea and quadrupled in Singapore ... this increase is not typical of the world economy where, with the exception of high-performing Asia, I/GDP ratios were constant or declining.

Initially, the annual investment rates presented in Table 15.1 exhibit an upward pattern, indicating that China experienced a slow but increasing investment/GDP ratio. This pattern, however, may partially reflect the relative price change between output and capital goods, since the investment rates in Table 15.1 are calculated in nominal terms. Since the output price and price of capital goods are unlikely to change at the same pace, it it necessary to convert these ratios into real terms in order to see how China's investment–output ratio has changed over time.

The *China Statistical Yearbook* does not provide a GDP deflator, and we must therefore estimate the implicit deflator of China's GDP, using information about both the current value of GDP and the GDP index, as shown in Table 15.8.

For the price index of capital goods, we use the price index of investment in fixed assets as representative. The *China Statistical Yearbook*, however, began to provide such an index only after 1993, and the starting year of

Table 15.8 China's implicit GDP deflators (1978–2000)

Year	Current GDP 100 million RMB yuan (1)	GDP index at comparable price previous year 100 (2)	GDP index at current price previous year 100 (3)	Implicit GDP deflator estimated by (3)/(2)*100 previous year 100 (4)	GDP deflator converted into 1990 price (5)
1978	3,624.1	111.7	113.19	101.33	55.07
1979	4,038.2	107.6	111.43	103.56	57.03
1980	4,517.8	107.8	111.88	103.78	59.19
1981	4,862.4	105.2	107.63	102.31	60.56
1982	5,294.7	109.1	108.89	99.81	60.44
1983	5,934.5	110.9	112.08	101.07	61.09
1984	7,171.0	115.2	120.84	104.89	64.08
1985	8,964.4	113.5	125.01	110.14	70.57
1986	10,202.2	108.8	113.81	104.60	73.82
1987	11,962.5	111.6	117.25	105.07	77.56
1988	14,928.3	111.3	124.79	112.12	86.96
1989	16,909.2	104.1	113.27	108.81	94.63
1990	18,547.9	103.8	109.69	105.68	100.00
1991	21,617.8	109.2	116.55	106.73	106.73
1992	26,638.1	114.2	123.22	107.90	115.16
1993	34,634.4	113.5	130.02	114.55	131.92
1994	46,759.4	112.6	135.01	119.90	158.17
1995	58,478.1	110.5	125.06	113.18	179.02
1996	67,884.6	109.6	116.09	105.92	189.61
1997	74,462.6	108.8	109.69	100.82	191.17
1998	78,345.2	107.8	105.21	97.60	186.58
1999	82,067.5	107.1	104.75	97.81	182.49
2000	89,403.6	108.0	108.94	100.87	184.08

Note: Columns (1)–(3) are based on *China Statistical Yearbook*; columns (4) and (5) are calculated by the author.

Source: *China Statistical Yearbook* (NBS, 2001).

this index is 1991 (1990=100). Fortunately, Jefferson, Rawski and Zheng (1996, p. 175) estimated China's price index of investment in fixed assets between 1979 and 1992. Since both Jefferson, Rawski and Zheng (1996) and the *China Statistical Yearbook* estimated their indices similarly by averaging the deflators of construction/installation and machinery/equipment purchases, we think that of Jefferson, Rawski and Zheng is generally consistent with the *China Statistical Yearbook*'s. Therefore, for 1978–89, I insert Jefferson, Rawski and Zheng's price index of investment in fixed assets to provide a complete picture, as shown in Table 15.9.

Figure 15.4 exhibits the patterns of relative price changes of the deflator for investment in fixed assets and the implicit GDP deflator during 1978–2000. The relative price ratio curve shows that the price for capital

Table 15.9 China's price index of investment in fixed assets (1978–2000)

	Index 1990 = 100	Index previous year = 100	Adjusted index 1990 = 100
1978			
1979	41.3		41.3
1980	41.3		41.3
1981	43.8		43.8
1982	44.0		44.0
1983	47.6		47.6
1984	51.0		51.0
1985	58.2		58.2
1986	66.6		66.6
1987	73.9		73.9
1988	79.5		79.5
1989	98.3		98.3
1990	100.0		100.0
1991	111.9	109.5	109.5
1992	125.5	115.3	126.3
1993		126.6	159.8
1994		110.4	176.5
1995		105.9	186.9
1996		104.0	194.3
1997		101.7	197.6
1998		99.8	197.3
1999		99.6	196.5
2000		101.1	198.6

Sources: The figures in column 2 are quoted from Jefferson, Rawski and Zheng (1996); The figures in column 3 are taken from *China Statistical Yearbook* (NBS, 1993, p. 269; 1995, p. 250; 1996, p. 272; 1997, p. 283; 1998, p. 318; 1999, p. 310; 2000, e-version, section 9 14; 2001, e-version, section 9 14). The figures in column 4 are estimated by the author, based on both these sources.

Figure 15.4 Price of capital goods relative to GDP deflator (1990 = 1)

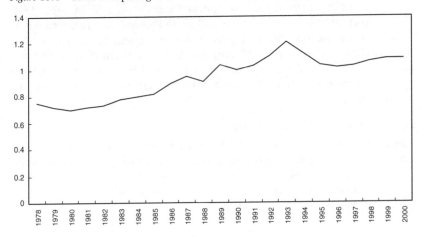

Figure 15.5   China's real investment/GDP ratios

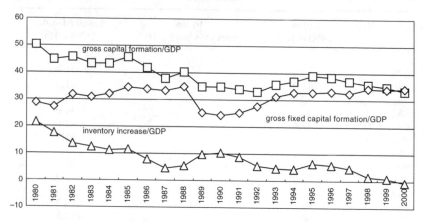

goods relative to the price for GDP increased by 61.3 per cent from 1978 to 1993, but then (1993–2000) fell by 10.7 per cent, so that there must have been a difference between nominal and real investment rates. This curve of relative price ratio in Figure 15.3 also tells us that the ratio was greater than 1 after 1990, and less than 1 before 1990, suggesting that before 1990, China's real investment rates (in constant 1990 prices) must have exceeded nominal rates, and vice versa after 1990.

With these relative price changes in mind, it is not reasonable to observe the pattern of investment/GDP ratios only in nominal terms. Rather, it is necessary to convert these nominal investment/GDP ratios into real values based on the relative price change between the price index for capital goods and the GDP deflator.

Figure 15.5 presents these adjusted investment rates in real terms in the expectation that, contrary to the nominal rates estimated in Table 15.1, China's real investment/GDP ratios will no longer follow a rising trend. As Figure 15.5 indicates, the real gross value of capital formation in fact increased less slowly than GDP, and thanks to the slight drop in the proportion of inventory increase, the growth of real fixed capital formation generally remained fairly constant relative to that of real GDP during the reform period.

Incremental capital–output ratio

Identifying the pattern of real investment/GDP ratios is important to understanding whether China has overinvested since the implementation of its economic development programme in the early 1980s. To some extent, this ratio can be used as a proxy measure of the efficiency of its use of capital throughout the economy.

A direct and simple measurement of investment efficiency at the aggregate level, however, may be carried out by calculating the so-called ICOR, which is the reciprocal of the marginal productivity of capital stock:

$$ICOR = I/\Delta GDP$$

Based on estimates of both GDP and gross values of capital formation, including their deflators, I have calculated China's real ICOR during 1979–2000 (see Figure 15.6). My calculations show that during this period China's average ICOR was 5.1, compared with 4 for Singapore, 6 for Hong Kong, and 3 for Taiwan (all during 1987–97).[9]

Between the 1970s and 1990s, three of the 'four little dragons' (Hong Kong is the exception) and the 'little tigers' (e.g., Malaysia, Thailand), as well as Japan itself, experienced a rising pattern of ICOR. But during 1979–2000, China underwent a decline in its ICOR. Apart from the exceptional fluctuation during the three years of retrenchment following Tiananmen in 1989, China's ICOR had moved downwards since 1979, suggesting a better performance than most East Asian NIEs and emerging economies at a similar stage of development. Only after 1992 did China's ICOR begin to increase slightly, primarily due to continuing large-scale investment in urban infrastructure and national transportation networks, which had previously long been underdeveloped areas of the economy.

Why, then, has China shown a better ICOR performance than most NIEs and emerging economies in East Asia? The main reason is that during most of the period of institutional transition and growth, China's success relied primarily on the rapid entry and expansion of rural and small industrial

Figure 15.6 China's real incremental capital–output ratio

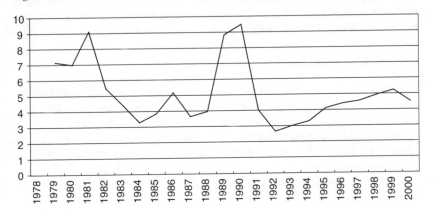

Figure 15.7 China's growth, real income and investment rate, 1978–2000

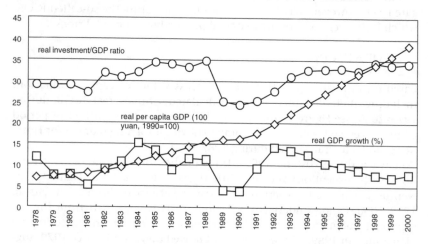

businesses, whose production technology was labour-intensive and market-orientated (Lin, Cai and Li, 1994; Liu, Yao and Zhang, 1999). Though China has maintained a higher percentage of public investment than NIEs, thanks to its huge supply of cheap labour and access to both domestic and foreign markets, the process of rural industrialization and the proliferation of non-state firms have shown remarkable development compared with other economies in East Asia.

Figure 15.7 shows the performance of Chinese economy in the context of the investment-growth nexus. It indicates that since the beginning of economic reform and opening-up, over a period of two decades China secured rapid and sustained growth, and generated a continuous rise in real per capita income. In the context of both China and the entire world, this has been a great achievement. At the same time, the proportion of investment to GDP has remained basically unchanged, a pattern that is different from those of many other NIEs and emerging economies in East Asia during their periods of high economic growth.

Concluding remarks

In this chapter we have analysed China's investment-growth nexus in the context of the high growth experiences of East Asian economies. Through an examination of the pattern of real investment/GDP ratio and the ICOR during the period of high growth, this chapter shows that China has performed better than most East Asian economies at similar stages of economic development.

China's economic growth was propelled largely by the rural industrialization, and thus was facilitated by the sectoral shift of rural labour from family farming to industrial manufacturing activities in township and village enterprises. This process of rural industrialization has been extremely beneficial to economic growth since China has an almost unlimited supply of cheap rural labour, enabling the sustained sectoral shift of labour to generate improved allocative efficiency that has, in turn, led to more rapid growth.

Theoretically speaking, as long as this proliferation of small-sized firms and rural industrialization can continue, China can continue to maintain high growth without facing a rise in its investment/GDP ratio or capital/labour ratio. In practice, a further requirement is that China should continue to liberalize its economy, and enable and encourage the private sector to play an overwhelming part in China's future sustained growth.

Notes

1   In his paper titled 'Lessons from the East Asian NICs: A Contrarian View', Young (1994) concludes that one of the most important characteristics of the East Asian NICs lies in their successful expansion of investment and employment in manufacturing rather than in their striking growth rate of productivity, and thus they deserve the title of 'industrialization'. In his elegant article, Krugman (1994) presents a critical comment on the Asia Miracle in a non-technical way. Felipe (1999) offers a majestic literature survey about East Asia's economic growth and efficiency change.

2   According to the definition given in *China Statistical Yearbook* (NBS, 2001), for example, total social investment in fixed assets covers: investment in capital construction, investment in renovation and renewals of existing facilities, investment in real estate development, investment in other fixed assets by state-owned units, investment in other fixed assets by collective-owned units (including those in cities and towns, and rural areas), and private investment in house construction (in cities and towns, industrial and mining areas and rural areas).

3   Between 1981 and 1985, the rate of investment in fixed assets in Singapore rose to 46 per cent, which probably reflected the high growth speed of its investment in capital construction. According to Toh and Ng (2002), more than half of investment was spent in residential housing and construction.

4   Ibid.

5   The proportion of investment in housing in China is lower than that in Hong Kong, but is similar to Taiwan's. The average proportion of investment in housing was 12.6 per cent in Hong Kong during 1966–98, and about 6.8 per cent in Taiwan. See Toh and Ng (2002, Table 1).

6   'Investment by other type of ownership' includes all investments made by such investors as joint ventures across ownerships, share-holding companies, FDI, and overseas Chinese from Hong Kong, Macau and Taiwan.

7   The investment financed through the state budget only accounted for about 10 per cent of total investment in capital construction during the year 1998. See *China Statistical Yearbook* (NBS, 2001, section 6–6).

8   According to Toh and Ng (2002), during the same period, Hong Kong's public investment rate was much lower, at only about 3.7 per cent.

9   The ICORs of Hong Kong, Taiwan and Singapore are mentioned and illustrated in Toh and Ng (2002, Fig. 5).

References

Felipe, J. (1999), 'Total Factor Productivity Growth in East Asia: A Critical Survey', *The Journal of Development Studies*, 35 (4), 1–41.

Jefferson, G., T. Rawski and Y. Zheng (1996), 'Chinese Industrial Productivity: Trends, Measurement and Recent Development', *Journal of Comparative Economics*, 23, 146–80.

Kim, J. and L. Lau. (1996), 'The Sources of Asian Pacific Economic Growth', *The Canadian Journal of Economics*, 29, Special Issue, part 2 (April), 448–54.

Krugman, P. (1994), 'The Myth of Asia's Miracle', *Foreign Affairs*, Nov./Dec., 62–78.

Lau, L. and J. Kim (1992), 'The Sources of Growth of the East Asian Newly Industrialized Countries', *Journal of the Japanese and International Economies*, unknown issue.

Lin, J., F. Cai and Z. Li (1994), *China's Miracle: Development Strategy and Economic Reform*, Shanghai: Shanghai SanLian Bookshop.

Liu, A., S. Yao and Z. Zhang (1999), 'Economic Growth and Structural Changes in Employment and Investments in China: 1985–1994', *Economic Planning*, 32, 171–90.

National Bureau of Statistics of China (NBS), various years, *China Statistical Yearbook*, Beijing: China Statistical Press.

National Bureau of Statistics of China (NBS) (2001), *China Statistical Yearbook of Investment*, Beijing: China Statistical Press.

Otsuka, K., D. Liu and N. Murakami (1998), *Industrial Reform in China*, Oxford: Clarendon Press.

Qin, D. and H. Song (2002), 'Excess Investment Demand and Efficiency Loss during Reforms: The Case of Provincial-level Fixed-Asset Investment in China', mimeo.

Song, H., Z. Liu and P. Jiang (2001), 'Analysing the Determinants of China's Aggregate Investment in the Reform Period', *China Economic Review*, 12, 227–42.

Sun, X (1998), 'Estimating Investment Function based on Cointegration: The Case of China', *Journal of Comparative Economics*, 26, 175–91.

Toh, M. and W. Ng (2002), 'Efficiency of Investment in Asian Economies: Has Singapore Over-Invested?', *Journal of Asian Economics*, 13, 52–71.

Young, A. (1994), 'Lessons from the East Asian NICs: A Contrarian View', *NBER Working Paper*, No. 4482.

Young, A. (2000), 'The Razor's Edge: Distortions and Incremental Reform in the People's Republic of China', *Quarterly Journal of Economics*, CXV (4), (November), 1091–1135.

Zhang J. (2002), 'Capital Formation, Industrialization and Economic Growth', *Economic Research Journal* (in Chinese), 7, 3–13.

16
Recent Developments in China's Agriculture and Prospects for Future Agricultural Trade: Observations from the Grain Sector*

Robert Ash

Since the end of the eighteenth century, when Thomas Malthus published his *Essay on Population*, there has been widespread concern that population growth would place unsustainable pressure on food supplies.[1] In terms of global food production capability, such fears have not been realized. Even so, hunger is a reality for more than 800 million people throughout the world.[2] Although most hungry people are concentrated in India and elsewhere in Asia, the problem is most acute in sub-Saharan African countries, where, despite a sharp fall in the annual rate of increase in the number of undernourished since the mid-1990s, the proportion of undernourished among the total population remains about 33 per cent.[3]

The persistence, on such a massive scale, of hunger and malnutrition, despite global food output having reached a level capable of feeding the world's population, highlights the critical importance of *distribution*. Producing food is one thing; ensuring that available supplies are shared equitably among the world's population is quite another. In the late 1970s and early 1980s, intense competition among major cereal exporters, such as the United States, Canada and the European Union, resulted in large rises in their grain stocks. Storing large amounts of cereals is costly; as a consequence, aid to poor countries increased sharply. But the gluts also caused international grain prices to fall, and encouraged exporting countries to reduce the sown area under cereals, either by cutting subsidies

*I am grateful to my co-editor, Lok Sang Ho (who incidentally has devoted more time and effort to preparing this book for publication than I), for encouraging me to write this chapter. It is the only chapter in the book that addresses China's agricultural problems. Given Y.Y. Kueh's significant writings on China's modern and contemporary agricultural development, I am especially glad to have had the opportunity to remind readers of the continuing significance of that old Chinese adage that 'agriculture is the foundation of the national economy'. Writing it has been a nostalgic experience, reviving memories of my agriculture-related joint ventures with Y.Y. Kueh years ago.

previously paid to farmers or by deliberately paying them not to plant cereals (so-called 'set-aside' policies). This longer-term response helped protect farmers in developed countries, but hurt developing countries which depended on imports of cheap food.

Generating sufficient food to keep its population healthy, productive and contented is the central economic issue that has faced China throughout virtually its entire history. For over 500 years after the founding of the Ming Dynasty, farmers produced enough 'basic' food – grain[4] – to provide China's population with sufficient energy to meet these requirements. But the cushion above subsistence was a narrow one, and not until the 1980s did grain output growth overtake population growth by a wide enough margin to guarantee China's basic food security. Meanwhile, natural disasters, especially floods and drought, frequently reduced output to levels resulting in local famines.[5]

To say that the 'great famine' between 1959 and 1961 marked a watershed for China's post-1949 agricultural development is a truism. With some 30 million peasants having died of starvation during these years, China renewed grain imports for the first time in more than a decade, and set out to restore food security to the centre of the policy agenda. Indeed, the food issue has remained a strategic preoccupation of the central government ever since, even though ever since the early 1980s grain output growth has generated a cushion well above mere subsistence requirements.[6] Increasing engagement in the world trading economy – part of the open-door strategy – has been a cornerstone of the Chinese government's reformist agenda since the beginning of the 1980s. The clearest recent expression of this policy stance was China's accession to the World Trade Organization (WTO). Implicit in such developments is, one assumes, a recognition of the power of orthodox economic principles, such as that of specialization in production based on comparative advantage. If the assumption is correct, the Chinese government's continuing commitment to maintaining 'basic' food self-sufficiency[7] reflects a deliberate choice to ignore orthodoxy. An intriguing question, not least against the background of widespread economic deprivation and social discontent among grain farmers, is how much longer this commitment can be sustained; and, if it *is* sustained, what kind of policy measures can the government find to obviate such problems in the grain sector?[8]

Through its foreign trade implications, the pursuit of grain self-sufficiency has a clear significance beyond China's own borders. China is so large that even quite small changes in its grain imports trade may have a *global* significance.[9] Much of the concern that was expressed in the second half of the 1990s about China's grain economy derived from a powerful international dimension to its perceived 'food problem'. If China could not feed itself, so the argument ran, it would have to turn to external sources of supply. One analyst suggested that an increasing propensity to purchase foreign grain in the wake of its inability, for reasons of both demand and supply, to maintain basic self-sufficiency would place a premium on higher-priced imports to the detriment of low-income, food-importing countries, especially in sub-Saharan Africa. From this derived the spectre of China squeezing out other countries competing for exportable supplies and 'starving the world'.[10]

Against the background of these general considerations, the rest of this chapter looks at some of the issues raised by the recent experience of China's grain sector. For reasons of time and space, the treatment is deliberately selective, and important determinants of the future trajectory of China's grain output and trade are ignored. The aim is merely to offer a critical review of the economic performance of the grain sector – in many ways, still the dominant agricultural activity – and to consider the implications of this record for China's foreign trade in food grains.

Agricultural and the rural development under the impact of reform

The economic reforms of the last 25 years have made China an increasingly urbanized society.[11] This is a process that will accelerate in the coming years, as China seeks to achieve an urbanization rate of 70 per cent by 2050. But for the time being, China remains a predominantly *rural* society. In 2004, almost 760 million people – 58 per cent of the total population – were officially registered as rural residents. Two-thirds of total employment takes place in the countryside; agriculture on its own accounts for 64 per cent of rural employment and, more remarkably, 44 per cent of *all* jobs in China. Well over 300 million people are currently still engaged in farming, forestry, animal husbandry and fisheries.[12]

China's reforms have generated a more diversified rural economy, in which high-return, non-farming activities have for some years accounted for more than half of rural GDP. In agriculture itself, diversification has also occurred. Since the 1980s, growing affluence – especially in eastern coastal provinces and among the urban population – has resulted in rapid rises in demand for non-staple foods. In turn, this has generated a steady expansion of non-cropping activities: animal husbandry, fishing, fruit farming, and so on. But despite a reduction of 19 million hectares between 1978 and 2004 – a fall of almost 16 per cent – grain cultivation still dominates farming. It accounts for two-thirds of the total sown area. An even higher proportion of farmers remained tied – not necessarily productively or full-time – to grain farming.[13]

Following the unambiguously positive impact (both in terms of agricultural growth and farmers' welfare) of early post-1978 reforms, the success of farm policy since the mid-1980s has been more mixed. In particular, the output growth of major crops, especially grain, has lagged behind that of non-cropping activities (above all, animal husbandry and fishing). The reasons for this are many and complex; not least, they reflect policy dilemmas whose scale and complexity would tax any government seeking to resolve them. But such dilemmas apart, the experience of recent years suggests that whereas the Chinese government deserves high marks for its ability to formulate rational farm policies, its record in *implementing* such policies has sometimes been disappointing. To a considerable extent, this disjunction reflects the dysfunctional nature of a system in which the interests of central and local governments often run in opposite directions. In particular, tensions between the central government's efforts on behalf of farmers and the farm sector, and the more self-serving activities of lower-level governments and local vested interests, have undermined the fulfilment of agricultural policy goals. The result has been to create widespread and increasing economic discontent and social dislocation in the rural sector, especially among grain farmers.[14]

The central government recognizes the potentially explosive consequences of recent trends towards the increasing polarization of Chinese society. It is no coincidence that since 2004 government leaders have placed increasing emphasis on the need to pursue a more sustainable and 'people-centred' development strategy. The notion of sustainability in a Chinese context should be understood not only in conventional terms of environmental protection and resource conservation, but also – critically – in terms of the need to halt and reverse potentially destabilizing forces associated with widening economic and social gaps between sectors and regions. In the past, the government's perception was that the greatest threat was that posed by urban discontent fuelled by large-scale lay-offs from state-owned enterprises. More recently, its concern seems to have shifted increasingly towards the dangers associated with the widespread social malaise among farmers.

Such conditions explain why agriculture has reverted to being a priority policy concern. The fact that for the first time since the second half of the 1980s the Central Committee of the Chinese Communist Party (CCP) saw fit – initially, in December 2003, and again in December 2004 – to issue guidelines on agricultural policy is the clearest expression of such concern.[15] Both documents make clear official perception of agriculture as a 'weak link' in the Chinese economy. As the more recent of the two puts it:

> agriculture remains a weak link in the development of the national economy; the situation regarding insufficient investment and fragile foundation has not changed; the mechanisms for increasing grain production and peasant income with lasting effectiveness have yet to be established; deep-structure conflicts that restrain the development of economic and social development in rural areas have not been eliminated; the obvious backwardness of economic and social development

in rural areas has not been fundamentally changed; rural reform and development are still ... going uphill against all odds and facing tough challenges; and the tasks for keeping the positive momentum of rural development remain very arduous.[16]

From this critique has emerged a package of measures, designed to improve economic and social conditions in the countryside. The essential policy thrust of these measures, as far as farmers are concerned, is summed up in a characteristic six-character Chinese phrase, translated as 'give more, take less, give free rein'.[17] The clear intent is to remove inhibitions that have previously undermined agricultural growth.

Such is the background to the Chinese government's implementation of important new agricultural policy initiatives during 2004 and 2005. These include efforts to improve land management and liberalize the grain market. More strikingly, they embrace the so-called 'two reductions' (the reduction and eventual elimination of the agricultural tax; and the removal of taxes on special farm products, except for tobacco) and "three subsidies" (the unprecedented provision of *direct* subsidies to grain farmers, and the use of subsidies in order to encourage the adoption of improved seed strains and to purchase modern agricultural tools and machinery). In 2004, lower taxes and the provision of direct subsidies benefited grain farmers to the tune of 45 billion yuan (around US$5.4 billion). Alongside a sharp rise in grain prices, such measures brought to a halt the previous four years' downward spiral of grain output and an even longer period of income stagnation. The Chinese government's understandable response was to hail this performance as marking a major turning point in economic and social conditions in the grain sector. Such official euphoria may, however, be premature. The 9 per cent rise in grain production in 2004 reflects recovery from the depressed output levels of previous recent years rather than renewed *net* growth. It remains to be seen whether grain production can attain a new trajectory of sustained growth that will enable the government in Beijing to reaffirm its adherence to basic self-sufficiency. If it cannot, China will have passed a watershed, characterized by much greater reliance on overseas markets to meet its nutritional aspirations.

Recent trends in grain output

The challenge of providing enough food to feed its population is dramatically captured in the finding that with about 7 per cent of the world's arable land, China needs to support about 21 per cent of the global population.

In terms of its implications for food security, the performance of the grain sector from the late 1950s to the end of the 1970s was disappointing. If anything, China's food security deteriorated during this 20-year period.

Since 1979, however, conditions have improved sharply under the impact of changes in both demand and supply conditions. On the one hand, economic reform has generated rapid rises in personal incomes, as a result of which rising prosperity – especially in eastern coastal provinces and among the urban population – has replaced population growth as the single most important determinant of food demand. On the supply side, output growth has been sufficiently buoyant to generate enough grain to meet subsistence requirements. Indeed, in many years since the early 1980s grain production levels have been high enough to meet the aspirations of a richer population seeking a more varied and nutritious diet, based on higher consumption of meat, poultry, fish and dairy produce. Overall, it is likely that demand for grain for direct consumption has now peaked in the countryside – it did so in cities a good many years ago – although regional differences in economic conditions in a country the size of China means that in

Table 16.1   Grain production in China, 1978–2004 (selected years)

	Total output of grain (million tons)	Average output of grain per head of total population (kg)
1978	304/8	316.6
1984	407.3	390.3
1985	379.1	358.1
1989	407.6	361.6
1990	446.2	390.3
1995	466.6	385.3
1996	504.5	412.2
1997	494.2	399.8
1998	512.3	410.5
1999	508.4	403.8
2000	462.2	365.1
2001	452.6	354.7
2002	457.1	355.8
2003	430.7	333.3
2004	469.5	361.2
Average annual output:		
1981–5	370.6	359.8
1986–90	408.8	368.4
1991–5	449.2	379.1
1996–2000	496.3	398.1
2001–4	452.5	351.2

Sources: NBS, *Zhongguo tongji nianjian* (China Statistical Yearbook) Beijing: Tongji chubanshe, (annual, various issues); *NBS* (2005), pp. 10 and 120; NBS, *Xin Zhongguo wushi nian nongye tongji ziliao* (*Fifty Years of Agricultural Statistical Materials on New China*) (Beijing: Tongji chubanshe, 2000), p. 37; NBS, *Xin Zhongguo wushi nian tongji ziliao huibian* (*Compendium of Statistical Materials for Fifty Years of New China*) (Beijing: Tongji chubanshe, 1999), p. 1.

poor areas the Engel ratio in respect to cereals for human consumption is still very high.

The apparent vagaries of grain production since the mid-1980s reflect a mix of factors, both climatic and policy-related. Table 16.1 presents estimates of total and average per capita production, as revealed by official statistics.

Table 16.1 reveals a pattern of varying fortunes in the output performance of the grain sector. Rapid growth in the wake of the early post-1978 reforms gave way to stagnation between 1984 and 1989, the effects of which were only mitigated by an outstanding harvest in 1990. In the first half of the 1990s, an upward trend was re-established. In 1996, total output for the first time exceeded 500 million tons, enabling per capita production to reach an unprecedented level of more than 400 kilograms. The late 1990s witnessed a series of record harvests, which took per capita output to about 400 kilograms, which was sufficient to maintain consumption at a level commensurate with prevailing urban and rural incomes. But far from this strong upward momentum being maintained, during 2000–3 production plummeted, precipitating a massive run on domestic grain stocks and eventually necessitating the reintroduction of large-scale cereal imports (see below).

Two inferences about food security may be drawn from these figures. The first is that China has enjoyed a comfortable cushion over mere *subsistence* requirements in every year since the early 1980s. Even in 2003 – the worst grain harvest since 1989 – Chinese farmers produced 43 million tons more than were required for subsistence purposes.[18] In this basic sense, I suggest that China's food situation remains very secure. However – the second inference – in terms of meeting consumer *expectations*, recent conditions offer a less optimistic interpretation. For example, in 2004, with grain output up by 39 million tons (9 per cent) from the low point of 2003, there was still a shortfall of some 50 million tons below what was required to meet such expectations.[19] The seriousness of the downturn in grain production after 1999 is captured in the finding that, between 2000 and 2004, China suffered a cumulative shortfall of almost 300 million tons of raw grain.

By any standards, excess demand on such a scale is formidable. An average annual shortfall of 60 million tons must surely have been reflected in rising grain imports. It is to the foreign trade impact of recent developments that I now turn.

China's grain trade

A decline of over 10 per cent in average annual grain output between the last four years of the 1990s and the first four years of the present decade would normally be reflected in increased imports. Remarkably, however, only in 2004 did China revert – for the first time since 1996 – to the status of being a net importer of cereals (rice, wheat and maize).[20] Relevant figures are shown in Table 16.2.

In every single year since the reforms were unveiled in 1979, China has met at least 95 per cent of its need for grain for consumption from domestic sources. As Table 16.2 shows, by the beginning of the 1990s the previous deficit on its grain trade account had been replaced by a surplus, which, except for 1995 and 1996, has persisted almost until the present day. The most remarkable aspect of this performance was that even after the sharp decline and subsequent stagnation of domestic production in and after 2000, China remained a net exporter of cereals. In 2003, for example, when grain production fell to a lower level than at any point since 1989, it still exported (net) more than 18 million tons of cereals and cereal flour, from which it earned US$2.2 billion.

Against the background of a decline in domestic cereal production by almost 78 million tons, how could China's net exports have risen by almost 12 million tons between 1999 and 2003? The answer lies in compensating adjustments that were made in domestic cereal stocks. Officially, the precise level of China's grain reserves is a state secret, but it is clear that in the wake of the bumper harvests of the late 1990s they had reached massive proportions.[21] By dipping into these reserves, the Chinese government was able to maintain its position as a net cereal exporter, even though by 2003 per capita supplies were lower than they had been since the 1980s.

Running down grain stocks cannot continue indefinitely, and by the beginning of 2004 China's grain reserves were seriously depleted. It is estimated that between the 1999–2000 and 2003–4 trade years, China's wheat stocks fell by almost 60 per cent, while coarse grain reserves contracted by almost two-thirds.[22] As Table 16.2 indicates, rice and maize have also come under pressure. Recourse to international markets for supplies of rice could pose a problem for China because of the small volume of rice, compared with the other cereals, that is traded in international markets. In 2004 China's overseas sales of rice had to be scaled down quite substantially, while imports rose.[23] According to an authoritative source, the overall impact of poor harvests after 1999 was to reduce China's total carryover stocks of grain from 326 million tons (1999) to 102 million tons in 2004.[24]

My calculations indicate that despite having risen by 9 per cent in 2004, domestic grain production was still some 50 million tons below what was required.[25] With reserves having meanwhile been run down to 'little more than pipeline supplies',[26] China was finally forced to import all three cereals (especially wheat). The outcome, as a variety of sources confirm, is that in 2004 China reverted, for the first time since 1996, to the status of a net cereal importer. Something of the significance and scale of this shift

Table 16.2 China's imports and exports of cereals, 1985–2004 (million tons)

	Wheat		Rice		Maize		All cereals		
	Exports	Imports	Exports	Imports	Exports	Imports	Exports	Imports	Balance
1985	0.00	5.41	1.02	0.00	6.34	0.09	7.36	5.50	1.86
1986	0.00	6.11	0.96	0.00	5.64	0.59	6.60	6.70	−0.10
1987	0.00	13.20	0.99	0.00	3.92	1.54	4.91	14.74	−9.84
1988	0.00	14.55	0.71	0.31	3.91	0.11	4.62	14.97	−10.35
1989	0.00	14.88	0.32	neg.	3.50	0.07	3.82	14.95	−11.13
1990	0.00	12.53	0.33	0.06	3.40	0.37	3.73	12.96	−9.23
1986–90 average	0.00	12.25	0.66	0.06	4.07	0.54	4.78	12.85	−8.12
1991	0.00	12.37	0.69	0.14	7.78	neg.	8.47	12.51	−4.04
1992	0.00	10.58	0.95	0.01	10.34	neg.	11.29	10.59	0.70
1993	0.29	6.45	1.44	0.10	11.10	neg.	12.83	6.55	6.28
1994	0.27	7.33	1.54	0.51	8.75	neg.	10.56	7.84	2.72
1995	0.23	11.63	0.06	1.65	0.12	5.26	0.41	18.54	−18.13
1991–5 average	0.16	9.67	0.94	0.48	7.62	1.05	8.72	11.20	−2.48
1996	0.57	8.30	0.28	0.77	0.24	0.45	1.09	9.52	−8.43
1997	0.46	1.92	0.95	0.36	6.67	neg.	8.08	2.28	5.80
1998	0.28	1.55	3.76	0.26	4.69	0.25	8.73	2.06	6.67
1999	0.16	0.51	2.72	0.19	4.33	0.08	7.21	0.78	6.43
2000	0.19	0.92	2.96	0.25	10.48	neg.	13.63	1.17	12.46
1996–2000 average	0.33	2.64	2.13	0.37	5.28	0.16	7.74	3.17	4.57

Table 16.2 China's imports and exports of cereals, 1985–2004 (million tons) – continued

	Wheat		Rice		Maize		All cereals		
	Exports	Imports	Exports	Imports	Exports	Imports	Exports	Imports	Balance
2001	0.71	0.74	1.87	0.29	6.00	0.04	8.58	1.07	7.51
2002	0.98	0.63	1.99	0.24	11.68	0.01	14.65	0.88	13.77
2003	neg.	0.45	2.62	0.26	16.39	neg.	19.01	0.71	18.30
2004	0.78	7.20	n.a.	0.67[a]	2.32	1.62[a]	3.10[b]	9.49[b]	–6.39[b]

neg. = negligible.

n.a. = not available.

[a] Estimates for Jan.–Nov. only.

[b] These are incomplete data and offer only an approximation.

Sources: 1985–2002: China Ministry of Agriculture, Zhongguo nongye fazhan baogao, 2003 (China Agricultural Development Report, 2003), Beijing: Zhongguo nongye chubanshe, 2004, pp. 127–9; 2003: Zhongguo tongji nianjian, 2004, pp. 723 and 726; 2004: Asia Pulse, 25 May 2005; Consulate General (Sydney, Australia), Economic and Commercial Section, 31 Jan. 2005; People's Daily online, 11 Jan. 2005.

is captured in a report which stated that China's imports of wheat and maize in the first eleven months of 2004 – totalling 6.61 million tons and 2.26 million tons respectively – represented year-on-year increases of 1,780 per cent and 2,160 per cent.[27] During the same period, imports of rice also rose by 236 per cent to 671,200 tons.[28] Such was the impact of shortfalls in output and stocks at home that in a single year (2004) China was transformed from being a quite minor player in international wheat markets to becoming the largest importer in the world.

The transformation of China's cereal trade account from surplus to deficit in 2004 no doubt defines a watershed, although it would be premature to argue that it marks a permanent structural shift in the pattern of China's agricultural trade.[29] That the deficit on the cereal account will persist through 2005 is in little doubt, given likely further increases in wheat and maize imports.[30] But erroneous predictions about the trajectory of China's grain output growth have been made in the past, and as of the time of writing, there is no certainty that China will find itself engaged in increasingly large overseas cereal purchases on a long-term basis.

If the foregoing analysis were conducted in terms of the Chinese definition of *grain*, recourse to large-scale imports of soybeans in recent years would show China to have run into deficit on its grain trade account several years before 2004. Relevant data are shown in Table 16.3.

The figures describe a dramatic story. Since the mid-1990s, alongside no significant decline in domestic production, imports of soybeans have surged.[31] In a single year – 1999–2000 – imports rose two-and-a-half-fold; and in the following three years (2000–3) they doubled again. The upshot was that by 2003 China had overtaken the European Union to become the largest soybean importer in the world.[32] Unlike cereals, the shift towards deficit status on the soya trade account was not the result of domestic production difficulties, but reflected deliberate policy adjustments. In particular, in anticipation of joining the WTO, in the mid-1990s the Chinese government liberalized soyabean trade (reducing tariffs and introducing tariff-rate quotas, or TRQs).[33] In any case, as a comparison of Tables 16.2 and 16.3 shows, the level of net imports of soybeans was sufficient to offset most of its cereal trade account surplus in 2002, and to remove it entirely in 2000, 2001 and 2003. Indeed, when all traded grain products[34] are taken into account, it is clear that China's grain trade account has been in deficit more often than not since the mid-1980s. This is illustrated in Table 16.4.

One final point deserves to be made: it is that because of their deliberate bias towards cereal producers, the farm policy initiatives taken by the Chinese government since 2004[35] are likely to strengthen further China's status as a major importer of soyabeans in coming years.[36]

The significance of the Chinese government's enforced large-scale overseas purchases of cereals in 2004, alongside the maintenance of high

Table 16.3   Domestic production, exports and imports of soyabeans

	Domestic output (million tons)	Exports (million tons)	Imports (million tons)	Imports as % of domestic output
1985	10.50	1.14	neg.	–
1986–9				
1990	11.00	0.94	neg.	–
1991	9.71	1.11	neg.	–
1992	10.30	0.66	0.12	1.20
1993	15.30	0.37	0.10	0.70
1994	15.60	0.83	0.05	0.30
1995	13.50	0.38	0.30	2.20
Average 1991–5	12.88	0.67	0.11	0.85
1996	13.22	0.19	1.11	8.40
1997	14.73	0.19	2.89	19.60
1998	15.15	0.17	3.20	21.10
1999	14.25	0.21	4.32	30.30
2000	15.41	0.22	10.42	67.60
Average 1996–2000	14.55	0.20	4.39	30.17
2001	15.41	0.26	13.94	90.50
2002	16.51	0.31	11.32	68.60
2003	15.39	0.27	20.74	134.70
2004	16.00	0.20	19.60	122.50

Sources: *Zhongguo nongye fazhan baogao* (2003), p. 130; NBS, *Zhongguo nongcun tongji nianjian* (*China Rural Statistical Yearbook*) Beijing: Tongji chubanshe, 2004, p. 155; *Zhongguo tongji nianjian*, 2004, pp. 723 and 726; USDA, Foreign Agricultural Service, *World Agricultural Production*, 'Modest world prices dampen oilseed expansion in 2005–06' (June 2005; see www.fas.usda.gov/wap/circular/2005/05–06/Wap%2006–05.pdf).

levels of soyabean imports, is most dramatically captured in movements in China's overall trade balance in farm products. Within just twelve months, the farm sector shifted from healthy surplus to sizeable deficit on its agricultural foreign trade account. In 2003 China recorded an annual surplus on its farm trade account of US$2.5 billion.[37] In 2004 this surplus was transformed into a deficit of US5.5 billion.[38] There is no doubt that the major shortfalls in domestic grain production since 2000 were mainly[39] to blame for this sudden and sharp deterioration in China's trade balance in farm goods, and there is not much doubt that the deficit will persist through 2005.

Table 16.4 China's foreign trade balance in all food grains

	Imports of grain and grain products (million tons)	Exports of grain and grain products (million tons)	Trade balance (+/–) (million tons)
1985	6.00	9.32	+ 3.32
1986	7.73	9.42	+ 1.69
1987	16.28	7.37	–8.91
1988	15.33	7.17	–8.16
1989	16.58	6.56	–10.02
1990	13.72	5.83	–7.89
1986–90 average	13.93	7.27	–6.66
1991	13.45	10.86	–2.59
1992	11.75	13.64	+ 1.89
1993	7.43	13.65	+ 6.22
1994	9.25	11.88	+ 2.63
1995	20.70	1.03	–19.67
1991–5 average	12.52	10.21	+ 2.31
1996	11.96	1.44	–10.52
1997	7.06	8.54	+ 1.48
1998	7.09	9.07	+ 1.98
1999	7.72	7.59	–0.13
2000	13.57	14.01	+ 0.44
1996–2000 average	9.48	8.13	+ 1.35
2001	17.38	9.03	–8.35
2002	14.17	15.14	+ 0.97
2003	22.82	22.21	–0.61

Sources: Zhongguo nongye fazhan baogao (2003), p. 131; *Zhongguo tongji nianjian* (2004), pp. 723 and 726.

Conclusion: China's food security, grain and cereal trade, and geo-strategic issues

China's agricultural resource endowment gives it a comparative advantage in the production of labour-intensive products, and a comparative disadvantage in that of land-intensive goods, such as cereals. In general, the imperative of maintaining food self-sufficiency has led the Chinese government to resist cereal imports, unless circumstances make such purchases absolutely necessary. Even so, under the impact of farm trade liberalization associated with WTO accession, there have been significant rises in China's exports of some labour-intensive goods, such as freshwater and seawater products, fruit, and fresh vegetables. Between 2001 and 2003, for example, the export value of mandarins, oranges and apples more than doubled, while that of fresh vegetables rose by 50 per cent; overseas sales of fish rose by almost 30 per cent in the same period. It is noteworthy that in terms of absolute value, the single biggest farm export category now comprises fresh-water and seawater products, which earned US$3.3 billion in 2003. Lower pro-duction costs could also make Chinese farmers internationally competitive in pigs and pork products, as long as improvements can be made in order to fulfil international sanitary and phyto-sanitary regulations. For the time being, however, it is likely that China's trade deficit will persist, with any rise in China's farm exports more than offset by growing imports of both land-intensive and labour-intensive agricultural products.

The Chinese government's stubborn[40] insistence on meeting at least 95 per cent of its grain requirements from domestic sources reflects geo-strategic concerns, not economic calculations. From an economic perspec-tive, the shift away from grain self-sufficiency has much to commend it. With arable land – water, too – in increasingly short supply and farm labour available in abundance, a contraction in land-intensive grain pro-duction and an expansion in labour-intensive cultivation farm activities promise to bring welfare gains to Chinese farmers, as well as incidentally helping to alleviate the problem of massive surplus labour in the grain sector. Foreign exchange earnings from the sale of non-grain farm products should easily be sufficient to finance grain imports. Meanwhile, the use of foreign grain to feed the coastal population would ease the high cost burden on China's overworked transport system.[41]

The geo-strategic reasoning that has underlined the government's demand for grain self-sufficiency is summed up in Chinese foreign policy analysts' belief that dependence on imported food could increase China's vulnerability *vis-à-vis* a foreign supplier – above all, the United States – whose strategic goals conflict with those of Beijing. If an exogenous shock, such as the suspension of American shipments of cereals or soya, were to deprive China of essential food supplies, the consequences (so the argu-ment runs) could be calamitous.

How real are such concerns? In an attempt to provide a preliminary answer to this question, I have used FAO data to review the Sino–US trade axis in relation to shipments of two cereals, wheat and maize, and also soyabeans. The relevant figures are shown in Table 16.5.

The estimates are quite instructive. They indicate that China's import dependence *vis-à-vis* the United States for wheat and soyabeans – and, in 1998 and 1999, for maize – has been significant. For wheat, it has ranged between 10 and 50 per cent; for soyabeans, between 40 per cent and 82 per cent (albeit around a falling trend); for maize, it averaged more than 70 per cent in the two relevant years.

These are formidable figures which suggest that the Chinese govern-ment's concern about potential vulnerability to trade sanctions has some basis in reality. Extrapolations from past experience are, however, notori-

Table 16.5 Chinese imports of wheat, maize and soyabeans from the United States, 1997–2003

	Wheat			Maize			Soyabeans		
	Total Chinese imports	Imports from the US	As %	Total Chinese imports	Imports from the US	As %	Total Chinese imports	Imports from the US	As %
1997	1.86	0.19	10.0	neg.	–	–	2.88	2.37	82.2
1998	1.49	0.32	21.4	0.25	0.19	75.3	3.19	1.75	54.8
1999	0.45	0.18	40.2	0.07	0.05	71.3	4.32	2.44	56.6
2000	0.88	0.15	17.5	neg.	–	–	10.42	5.41	51.9
2001	0.69	0.23	32.7	0.02	neg.	–	13.94	5.73	41.0
2002	0.60	0.16	26.7	neg.	–	–	11.31	4.62	40.8
2003	0.42	0.21	50.2	neg.	–	–	20.74	8.29	39.9

neg. = negligible.
Note: Unless otherwise indicated, all figures are given in million tons.
Source: UN Food and Agriculture Organization, Statistics Division, 2004.

ously hazardous. On the one hand, an opponent of China's adherence to food self-sufficiency would point out that even China's *global* cereal imports between 1997 and 2003 were tiny in relation to both domestic production and consumption requirements. By further inference, the contribution of shipments from the United States – and the potential impact on China's food security of their suspension – was even more marginal.[42] On the other hand, an apologist for the Chinese position would point out the exigencies of farming are such that adverse conditions may quite suddenly precipitate major changes in agricultural trade. In this respect, the events of 2004 are quite revealing. In this single year, not only did China's global imports of wheat increase precipitately, to a level that was about 7 per cent of domestic output, but dependence on the United States also rose sharply. For example, USDA estimates indicate that between 2003 and 2004 exports of American wheat to China grew from 0.24 million tons to 2.94 million tons (a rise of 1,225 per cent).[43] But dramatic though it was in percentage terms, the increased level of wheat shipments from the United States raised China's bilateral dependency ratio for this single product to no more than 4 per cent. In addition, maize imports from the United States have always been negligible, although this situation could change. Domestic shortfalls in maize could push China towards increasing dependence on the US, given the latter's role as by far the largest maize exporter in the world (as it is for rice).[44]

From the perspective of developments in China's agricultural sector during 2004–5, a few tentative conclusions may be drawn. First, with cereal exports slowing down and with China's export agents reluctant to sign new contracts, the government has shifted its focus towards meeting the needs of the domestic market, rather than supplying the international market. Second, in the face of continuing excess domestic demand for wheat, maize and rice, China will, at least for the time being, be a *net importer*. Third, pressure to undertake major purchases of soyabeans is unlikely to diminish, not least given the cereal-orientated thrust of recent policy initiatives in China's grain sector.

To what extent these trends will persist beyond the short term is, however, difficult to say. My hunch is that China *will* move towards greater import dependence, though I am reluctant to comment on the likelihood (according to some) that grain imports could reach 50 million tons within a relatively short period.[45] Interpreting the significance of such a rise, if it were to happen, depends on one's perspective. In 2003–4, some 242 million tons of grain – excluding soya – were traded *globally*. *Ceteris paribus*, imports of 50 million tons would result in China absorbing one-fifth of all traded grain within a comparatively short period, with potentially serious consequences, at least in the short run, for international prices.[46] From China's perspective, however, raising imports to 50 million tons would imply a reduction in its cereal self-sufficiency ratio from 95 per cent to about 90 per cent.

Notes

1 The famous quotation from Malthus reads: 'Population, when unchecked, increases in a geometrical ratio. Subsistence increases only in an arithmetical ratio' (*An Essay on the Principle of Population, as it Affects the Future Improvement of Society with Remarks on the Speculations of Mr. Godwin, M. Condorcet and Other Writers*, London, Printed for J. Johnson in St Paul's Church-yard, 1798), p. 14.

2 According to Food and Agriculture Organization (FAO) (2004), 852 million people were undernourished in 2000–2.

3 In such countries, calorie intake is only 70 per cent of the corresponding level in East Asia.

4 In China, the food issue has been dominated by grain, since the nutritional standards of the Chinese population have historically been determined by the direct consumption of grain: preferably cereals (rice, wheat and maize) and soybeans, but also 'inferior' grains, such as barley, millet, sorghum, potatoes, etc. Until as recently as the early 1980s, household budgets were dominated by spending on grain, and population growth was the chief determinant of increased food demand. Only in the last two decades have increases in income raised the dietary aspirations of a more affluent population – especially in cities and coastal provinces – and generated a more diversified food output mix, reflected in the rapid expansion of the consumption of meat, fish and dairy produce. Such structural changes have, however, intensified pressure on the grain sector by requiring farmers to produce increasing amounts of grain for *indirect* use (notably, to feed livestock. The use of grain for animal feed has more than doubled since the early 1980s and is projected to reach over 200 million tons – about a third of total grain requirements – by 2020.

5 It seems appropriate to remind readers here that the classic work for consideration of the impact of weather on China's agricultural production is Kueh (1995). Interestingly, since the publication of this book, evidence suggests that far from having been reduced, the impact of natural disasters on China's farm sector has, in fact, increased.

6 At times, however, the cushion above the level of production needed to meet the dietary aspirations of a richer population has remained narrow, and sometimes disappeared altogether. See below.

7 'Basic' in this context has meant ensuring that domestic output should meet at least 95 per cent of China's grain requirements.

8 Direct financial subsidies to farmers and abolition of the agricultural tax in China offer only short-term alleviation of the problems. A lasting solution will require profound structural changes, including further reform, the continuing large-scale transfer over a period of many years of farm labour, and the extension of agro-processing and agro-industries.

9 In his most recent book, Lester Brown points out that in 2004 China's domestic wheat production fell short of consumption requirements by 12 million tons, equivalent to Argentina's entire wheat harvest! See Brown (2005), p. 146.

10 See Brown (1995). Brown has maintained his pessimistic view of China's ability to generate sustained farm growth, although his more recent work recognizes that the apocalyptic scenario he drew in the mid-1990s was exaggerated (e.g., see Brown, 2005, p. 150).

11 Between 1979 and 2004, China's urban population increased, on average, by 4.5 per cent per annum; the corresponding figure for the rural population was –0.2 per cent: National Bureau of Statistics (NBS) (2005), p. 12.

12   The most recent source available to me shows that in 2002, some 324.87 million people were engaged in farming, forestry, animal husbandry and fisheries; in the rural sector alone, the corresponding figure was 312.6 million in 2003 (NBS and Ministry of Labour and Social Security (2005), pp. 8 and 29.

13   It is extremely hard to find estimates of the number of farmers engaged in grain cultivation. The First National Agricultural Census, however, reveals that in 1996, crop cultivation was the main economic activity of 95 per cent of all farmers. Given the dominance of grain farming within the cropping sector (in 1996 grain accounted for 74 per cent of the total sown area), a very high proportion of farmers must still have been tied to grain farming. See National Agricultural Census Office (1999), p. 59.

   Note that the bald statistics cited in the text conceal a picture of great complexity: for example, a regional analysis would reveal a much lower proportion of farmers engaged in cropping activities in eastern coastal China, compared with central and western areas (for evidence, see Mo (2004), p. 202). The same source cites sample survey evidence to the effect that in 2002, rural households worked on average for 9.83 months, of which farm work accounted for 6.7 months, and non-farm work 3.13 months (p. 204).

14   Grain farming has traditionally offered the lowest returns among all agricultural activities, a situation made worse in recent years (at least until autumn 2003) by depressed farm gate prices. Farmers' interests have been further damaged by illegal land seizures, and the imposition by local government officials of illegal fines, taxes and other levies. These are the factors that have generated farm protests, not infrequently accompanied by violence against local officials.

15   The titles of the two policy documents are: 'Opinions of the CCP Central Committee and State Council on a number of policies for promoting an increase in peasant incomes' (31 Dec. 2003), published by Xinhua News Agency (XHNA), 8 Feb. 2004; and 'Opinion of the CCP Central Committee and State Council on several policies for further strengthening rural work and enhancing overall production capacity of agriculture' (31 Dec. 2004), published by XHNA, 30 Jan. 2005.

16   Ibid.

17   *Duoyu, shaoqu, fanghuo.*

18   This statement assumes that 300 kg of raw grain per head of total population is sufficient to meet the subsistence needs of the population, as well as provide for seed and feed. Notice that in 1989, China's total population was smaller than in 2003 by 165 million people.

19   This finding is based on the assumption of a per capita grain consumption norm of 400 kg. In 2004 grain output was 8 per cent below the previous (1998) peak level, and per capita supplies were at about the level of 1989. The most important effect of grain sector improvements in 2004 was in terms of the income gain it brought to farmers. Average *rural* income rose by 12 per cent to reach 2,936 yuan, with income from farming up by 13.3 per cent to 1,746 yuan. Overall, farm income from grain sales increased by over 60 billion yuan.

20   Notice the emphasis on 'cereals': if the argument were couched in terms of all grains (which, following Chinese usage, includes soyabeans), China's emergence as a net *grain* importer pre-dates 2004.

21   In 2001, the US Department of Agriculture (USDA) released estimates which suggested that *commercial* reserves of rice, wheat and maize totalled 230 million tons, two-and-a-half times higher than was previously thought. In Nov. 2003, an article in *People's Daily* predicted that per capita 'grain reserves' for

2003 would fall below 350 kg, the lowest level for 20 years. FAO's *Food Outlook* (No. 4, Dec. 2004) was explicit in attributing most of the sharp decline in world cereal stocks in recent years to stock reductions in China ('major stock reduction in China has accounted for the bulk of the depletion of global inventories in the past few years').

22 A more recent estimate indicates a decline in wheat stocks from 92 million tons (marketing year [MY] 2000–1) to 38 million tons (MY 2004–5) (www.findarticles.com/p/articles/mi_m0HEE/is_41_61/ai_n6229970). The figure of 38 million tons is close to a USDA estimate, which indicated that wheat stocks totalled 42.4 million tons at the start of MY 2004–5 (i.e. July 2004). (see Lohmar (2004), p. 4). Lohmar predicted that these stocks would fall to 31.4 million tons by the end of MY 2004–5 [June 2005].

23 FAO, *Food Outlook* (No. 4, Dec. 2004).

24 Brown (2005), p. 147.

25 The adoption of a per capita grain consumption norm of 400 kg generates a total requirement of around 520 million tons in 2004.

26 Brown (2005), p. 147.

27 *China Daily*, 1 Mar. 2005.

28 Ibid.

29 Analysts inside and outside China have been caught out before. In 1984, following unprecedented grain output growth, there was a widespread feeling that the historical challenge of providing enough food for China's population had been resolved, but five years of output stagnation followed. In the mid-1990s, following alarmist reports suggesting that China's increasing cereal imports would 'starve the world', a series of record grain harvests turned China into a net grain exporter and enabled it to accumulate massive reserves.

30 Statistics published by China's Ministry of Commerce reveal that in the first four months of 2005, imports of cereals and cereal flour more than doubled, while exports of foodstuffs increased by less than 20 per cent (data available on Ministry of Commerce website, http://english.mofcom.gov.cn). USDA has also predicted that China will remain a net rice importer through 2005.

31 The exponential growth in soya imports since the late 1990s no doubt reflects rising demand for soya oil and meal and other soybean-related products associated with income growth, population expansion and urbanization. According to USDA, by MY 2003–4 China's soyabean consumption had reached 34.4 million tons, 4 times the level of 1980 (see Tuan *et al.* 2004, p. 2).

32 In 2003 Chinese soya imports accounted for about one-third of global trade shipments of soybeans. From a different perspective, the rise in the cost of soya imports (from US$2.5 to $7 billion) accounted for 30 per cent of the overall increase in China's farm imports during 2002–4 (see Gale, 2005, p. 3).

33 For more details, see Tuan *et al.* (2004).

34 Ranked by value, China's agricultural imports are dominated by soybeans, followed by edible and other vegetable oils, and cereals and cereal flour.

35 For example, see above, p. 299.

36 Tuan *et al.* make the point succinctly: 'China's reemphasised focus on food security for grains … is designed to spur food grain production and discourage soybean cultivation. Thus, this policy change suggests that China's growing demand for soybean and soybean products can only be satiated with continuing increases in imports' (2004, p. 12).

37 In 2002, the corresponding figure was US$5.7 billion. Thanks to rising prices, the cost of soybean imports more than doubled in 2003 to reach US$5.4 billion,

two-and-a-half times net earnings from China's trade in cereal and cereal flour (US$2.2 billion).

38 The USDA, which uses its own definition of agricultural trade, estimates that China's farm trade account shifted from a surplus of US$2.2 billion (2002) to a deficit of $2 billion (2003), which rose to $10.1 billion in 2004. See Gale (2005), p. 2.

39 But not solely: e.g., foreign raw cotton purchases by China grew more than ten-fold between 2002 and 2004 (from 0.17 million tons to 1.9 million tons).

40 'Stubborn' in the sense that it contradicts economic orthodoxy as captured in the notion of factor specialization based on the principle of comparative advantage.

41 Most of China's grain stocks are located in the north east. The burden on railways is suggested in the finding that in the first half of 2004 some 55.59 million tons of grain were transported by rail. In the same period, the railway system also carried 33.1 million tons of chemical fertilizers and other farm inputs.

42 By contrast, the implications for American farmers of suspending shipments of wheat to China would be serious, given that China is the fourth-largest market for American wheat. Since 2003 China has also become the largest market for US soybeans. Overall, China is the fifth-largest market for American agricultural goods.

43 Based on Department of Commerce, US Census Bureau, *Foreign Trade Statistics*.

44 As Table 16.5 shows, China's dependence on US soybeans has consistently been much higher than for wheat (let alone other cereals), although the degree of dependence has fallen as purchases from Brazil and Argentina have increased.

45 Imports of 50 million tons would be 150 per cent more than the previous peak (1995) level.

46 Such an argument is, however, fallacious to the extent that it ignores likely changes in the dynamics of grain farming in major producing countries that would result from China's increased involvement in international markets.

References

Brown, Lester (1995), *Who Will Feed China? Wake-Up Call for a Small Planet*, New York and London: W.W. Norton.

Brown, Lester (2005), *Outgrowing the Earth: The Food Security Challenge in an Age of Falling Water Tables and Rising Temperatures*, London and Sterling, VA: Earthscan.

FAO (2004), *The State of Food Insecurity in the World 2004*, Rome.

Gale, Fred (2005), 'China's Agricultural Imports Boomed During 2003–04', USDA, May.

Kueh, Y.Y. (1995), *Agricultural Instability in China, 1931–1991: Weather, Technology and Institutions*, Oxford: Clarendon Press.

Lohmar, B. (2004), 'China's Wheat Economy: Current Trends and Prospects for Imports', USDA, May.

Mo, Rong (ed.) (2004), *Zhongguo jiuye baogao, 2003–2004* (*China Employment Report, 2003–4*), Beijing: Zhongguo laodong shehui baozhang chubanshe.

National Agricultural Census Office (1999), *Abstract of the First National Agricultural Census in China*, 2nd edn, Beijing: China Statistics Press.

NBS (2005), *Zhongguo tongji zhaiyao, 2005* (*China Statistical Abstract, 2005*), Beijing: Zhongguo tongji chubanshe.

NBS and Ministry of Labour and Social Security (2005). *Zhongguo laodong tongji nianjian, 2004* (*China Labour Statistics Yearbook, 2004*), Beijing: Zhongguo tongji.

Tuan, Francis *et al.* (2004), 'China's Soybean Imports Expected to Grow Despite Short-term Disruptions', USDA, October.

17
Environmental Impact on the Manufacturing Sector of China's Accession to the World Trade Organization

Joseph C.H. Chai

Introduction

China was a member of GATT when it was established in 1947. After the Chinese Communist Party (CCP) came to power in 1949, China, in line with many Communist countries, considered GATT as a Western imperialist establishment. As a result, it cut its ties with GATT in 1950.

Almost 30 years later, China initiated the process of its re-integration with the world economy when, in the late 1970s, it introduced its 'open-door' policy. In 1986 China applied to re-join GATT. However, the negotiations for China's re-entry into GATT/WTO proved to be protracted and lasted for 13 years. During the negotiations China had to overcome several hurdles. One of the main obstacles was China's state trading system, under which trading rights had been mainly reserved for state-owned trading companies, and decision-making and trade barriers were non-transparent. Its western trading partners had great difficulty in gauging the precise extent of both tariff barriers (TBs) and non-tariff barriers (NTBs) that were in place, and in determining the 'price' China that should pay for its admission into GATT/WTO (Chai, 1989). Another major hurdle was whether China should be admitted as a developing or a developed country. China insisted that, in view of its relatively low income per capita, it should be admitted as a developing country (a status that would enable it to maintain relatively high TBs and NTBs to protect its domestic industries). By contrast, the US demanded that it should be admitted as a developed country because of its importance in world trade. One implication of having developed-country member status was that China would have to offer more substantial trade concessions to its trading partners as a 'price' for its entry into WTO. In the event, following extraction by the US of substantial market-opening concessions, China's 'long march' towards WTO accession finally ended on 15 November 1999 with the signing of the US–China bilateral WTO accord.

Accession to the WTO has committed China to significant reductions in TBs and NTBs in its industrial sector, to opening up its service sector to foreign investors, and the liberalization of its agricultural trade. At the same time, China is promised increased access to international markets for its manufactured exports. In particular, with the phasing-out of the Multi-Fibre Agreement (MFA), China's main manufactured export items, such as textiles and garments, will be free from quota restrictions in major Western markets. In short, accession to WTO is likely to result in profound changes in the output and trade pattern of the Chinese economy.

The focus of this chapter, however, is not the output and trade impact of China's accession to WTO, but rather its environmental impact. Specifically, it assesses the likely environmental effects of the changes in output and trade following Chinese accession to WTO. Owing to data limitations, the assessment is confined to the manufacturing sector alone. This focus can be readily justified by the fact that discharges by the manufacturing industry have been the main source of pollution in China. Manufacturing and power plants account for more than 70 per cent of national pollutant emissions in China (OECD, 2002, p. 595).

To date, there have been few studies on the environmental impact of China's WTO accession. Hu and Wanghua (2000) offer an optimistic assessment of this impact. Their findings suggest that if appropriate pollution control policies are put in place, favourable structural and technical effects associated with China's accession to WTO are capable of reducing water, air and soil pollution. However, they caution that increased automobile use caused by tariff reduction for imported cars may cause air quality in urban areas to worsen.

Luken and van der Tak (2002) also find that China's accession to WTO may have a favourable effect on China's environment. Their finding is grounded in the positive composition effect, as production shifts from polluting to less polluting industries and brings about a reduction in the pollution intensity of Chinese industry. However, they also predict that accelerated real GDP growth induced by WTO accession will increase some pollutant loads.

The remainder of this chapter is organized as follows. The second section presents the framework adopted to analyse the relationship between China's WTO accession and the environment, while the third section sets out the results and concluding remarks are given in fourth section.

Analytical framework

During the last two decades China has embraced trade liberalization (Zhang, Zhang and Wan, 1999; Chai, 2000), and its accession to WTO will further intensify this process. How will this impact on its environment? As some studies have demonstrated (Grossman and Krueger, 1993; Beghin and

Potier, 1997; Tisdell, 2000), the pollution impact of trade liberalization can be conceptually decomposed into three effects: the composition effect; the technical effect; and the scale effect. The *composition* effect reflects the freer post-WTO accession trade environment, which enables China to specialize in manufacturing activities in which it has a comparative advantage. The environmental impact of the resultant compositional change in manufacturing output may be positive or negative. It will be positive/negative if China has a comparative advantage in the production of less/more pollution-intensive industries. The *technical* effect is captured in China's ability to secure increased access to cleaner production technology as a result of two factors: first, greater post-accession openness to trade; and second, higher popular demand for a cleaner environment generated by rising per capita incomes associated with faster growth after China's WTO accession. In short, the technical effect is positive for the environment. The *scale* effect originates in the rise in China's manufacturing output as a result of its entry into WTO. Since higher output produces a larger emission of pollutants, its effect on the Chinese environment is negative. Thus, the net environmental impact of China's accession into WTO depends on whether the positive compositional and technical effects are, or are not, larger than the negative compositional and scale effects.

In order to quantify the various effects, the following procedure is adopted. The aggregate pollution of Chinese manufacturing activities, Y, may be described as:

$$Y = \sum_i s_i e_i Q \tag{17.1}$$

where s_i is sector i's share in total manufacturing output; e_i is the pollution intensity of sector I; and Q, is total output. Then the change in the aggregate pollution level resulting from China's accession into WTO is determined as follows:

$$\dot{Y} = \sum_i \dot{s}_i e_i Q + \sum_i s_i \dot{e}_i Q + \sum_i s_i e_i \dot{Q} \tag{17.2}$$

where a dotted variable represents that variable's time derivative. The first term on the right-hand side is the compositional effect, which represents the change in pollution level due to the change in China's manufacturing output composition. The second term is the technical effect, which indicates the change in pollution level caused by a change in China's manufacturing sectoral pollution intensity. The third term is the scale effect, which captures the change in pollution level induced by the change in total Chinese manufacturing output, in the absence of any change in output composition and sectoral pollution intensities.

The impact

Output effect

The output effect of China's accession into WTO can be assessed using either a partial or general equilibrium approach (see Laird and Yeats, 1990). Theoretically, the general equilibrium approach is preferable, since it takes into account not only the static, but also the dynamic – or growth – impacts, as well as sectoral interactions, following China's WTO accession. Others have tried to estimate the economic effects of China's WTO accession, using both partial and general equilibrium approaches (see OECD, 2002, annex ii for a summary). However, most of these studies focus on the *macro* impact of China's WTO accession on the Chinese economy. Of the few that assess the impact on Chinese manufacturing industries, the study by Zhai and Li (2000) uses a 41-sector computable general equilibrium (CGE) model of the Chinese economy, adapted from an OECD model (Beghin *et al.*, 1994). Like other CGE models, it assumes perfect competition and constant-returns-to-scale technology in all sectors. Zhai and Li's policy scenario is based on the market access commitment made by China in the 1999 US–China WTO accord. The policy package provides for (1) tariff reduction in industrial products; (2) the elimination of Chinese import quotas on industrial products by 2005; (3) the liberalization of agricultural trade via tariff-reduction for agricultural products and the introduction a TRQ system for agricultural products; and (4) the phasing-out of the MFA quota on Chinese exports of textiles and apparel under the WTO's Agreement on Textiles and Clothing.

Though Zhai and Li's study offers a reasonable guide to what would happen to China's industrial output after WTO accession, it suffers from some limitations. One is that they do not take account of the effects of other market access commitments made by China, such as liberalization of China's services market, reduction of barriers for foreign investment, protection of intellectual property rights, the agreement on general dispute settlements, and so on. Another limitation is that the assumption of constant return to scale technology and perfect competition may not be realistic for the current stage of Chinese economy.

The estimates made by Zhai and Li fall into two parts. One shows the predicted equilibrium in the benchmark year, 2010, in the absence of China's accession to WTO. The other suggests the counterfactual ('what if') equilibrium that would occur in 2010, with China having acceded to WTO. A comparison of the two parts allows the authors to estimate the output effect of China' s WTO accession. Their results reveal that China's WTO accession would boost China's 2010 GDP by 1.1 per cent (Table 17.1), while consumption and investment would increase by 1.05 and 0.81 per cent. China's trade balance would improve, with export growth outstripping that of imports. However, the income gain is not evenly distributed:

Table 17.1 Major macroeconomic variables under China's WTO accession in 2010 (% change relative to base case)

Variable	% change
GDP	1.10
Consumption	1.05
Investment	0.81
Exports	17.13
Imports	16.75
Government revenues	0.96
Urban household income	1.47
Rural household income	0.71
Terms of trade	−1.07
Real exchange rate	0.14

Source: Zhai and Li (2000).

Table 17.2 Impact of China's WTO accession on manufacturing sector output, 2010 (billlion yuan)

	Baseline output[a]	% share	Projected output[b]	% share	Output share change
Processed food[c]	1,839.3	9.4	1,855.1	8.9	−0.5
Textiles	2,101.3	10.7	2,593.0	12.5	1.8
Apparel	981.6	5.0	1,686.0	8.1	3.1
Leather	470.6	2.4	462.6	2.2	−0.2
Wood and furniture	750.0	3.8	748.5	3.6	−0.2
Paper and printing	950.0	4.8	946.2	4.6	−0.2
Petroleum refining	883.7	4.5	845.7	4.1	−0.4
Metallurgy	1,143.2	5.8	1,100.9	5.3	−0.5
Metal Products	1,291.7	6.6	1,276.2	6.2	−0.4
Chemical[d]	2,261.7	11.5	2,267.3	10.9	−0.6
Machinery[e]	5,455.0	27.7	5,420.2	26.1	−1.6
Building materials	1,100.0	5.6	1,098.9	5.3	−0.3
Other manufacturing	468.4	2.4	459.5	2.2	−0.2
Total	19,696.6	100.0	20,760.1	100.0	

[a] Without WTO accession.
[b] With WTO accession.
[c] Including beverages.
[d] Chemicals and chemical fibres.
[e] Including machinery, electric machinery, electronics, automobiles but excluding other transport equipment.

Source: Zhai and Li (2000).

urban household income is shown to rise, whereas that of the rural households is reduced.

Composition effect

In what follows, the impact of output change in 13 manufacturing sectors, as predicted by Zhai after China's WTO accession, is estimated for three main categories of pollutants (air, water and soil), following the analytical framework presented in the second section.

Table 17.2 presents the output change in China's manufacturing sector, as predicted by Zhai and Li for 2010, with and without China's WTO accession scenario. As shown in Table 17.2, the most significant change in the composition of Chinese manufacturing after WTO accession is highlighted in the expansion of labour-intensive light industries, such as textiles and apparel, and the contraction of capital and natural resource-intensive heavy industries, such as machinery, metallurgy, construction materials, petroleum processing, chemicals, and so on. Light industries, especially textiles and apparels, have relatively low pollution intensities, whereas heavy industries, except for machinery and metal products, are associated with relatively high pollution intensity (Table 17.3). Thus, the net impact of the higher share of the former and lower share of the latter significantly reduces Chinese manufacturing water, air and soil pollutants per million RMB of manufacturing output. The average water pollution intensity is predicted to drop from 5.2 to 5 tons per million RMB of manufacturing output, while that of air falls from 5.0 to 4.8 tons and that of soil from 42.8 to 40.5 tons per million RMB of manufacturing output. As a result, water, air and soil pollution for 2010 are projected to fall by 3.8, 3.3 and 5.4 per cent, respectively, below the levels suggested in the scenario without WTO accession (Table 17.4). In short, the composition effect of China's accession into WTO is largely positive.

Scale effect

The scale effect, as shown in equation (17.2), depends solely on the rate of manufactured output expansion. As a result of China's accession to WTO, Chinese manufacturing output is likely to expand by 5.4 per cent (Table 17.2). Thus, compared with the scenario in the absence of WTO accession, the emission of the three pollutants – water, air and soil – are likely to increase by 5.4 per cent (Table 17.4). The scale effect is therefore largely negative.

Technical effect

The technical effect of globalization of the Chinese economy during the last three decades has been positive (see Chai, 2000). The opening of China to the outside world has increased public awareness of industrial pollution problems in China. At the same time it has enabled China to secure greater

Table 17.3 Pollution intensity of the Chinese manufacturing sector, 1993 and 1997 (tons per million yuan)

	Water pollutant[a]			Air pollutant[b]			Soil pollutant[c]		
	1993	1997	% change	1993	1997	% change	1993	1997	% change
Processed food	10.1	5.4	−46.5	6.4	1.7	−73.4	40.1	15.4	−61.6
Textiles	2.0	1.5	−25.5	3.0	1.7	−43.3	23.7	14.1	−40.5
Apparel	0.8	0.8	0.0	0.9	0.9	0.0	7.4	7.4	0.0
Leather	4.6	2.3	−50.0	2.0	0.7	−65.0	15.4	5.7	−63
Wood and furniture	2.1	1.5	−28.6	4.0	1.8	−55.0	32.5	30.5	−6.2
Paper and printing	100.0	72.3	−27.7	17.0	9.3	−45.3	121.2	62.0	−48.8
Petroleum processing	1.5	1.0	−33.3	5.1	1.4	−72.5	102.7	23.9	−76.7
Metallurgy	3.4	2.9	−14.7	14.0	8.3	−40.7	467.3	307.0	−34.2
Metal products	1.2	0.2	−83.3	2.2	2.1	−4.5	15.5	8.8	−43.2
Chemical	7.3	4.5	−38.4	7.4	5.0	−32.4	127.9	87.8	−31.4
Machinery	0.3	0.2	−33.3	1.4	0.7	−50.0	14.7	7.2	−51.0
Building materials	1.5	1.3	−13.3	62.7	42.9	−31.6	82.5	51.6	−37.5
Other manufacturing	2.1	1.5	−28.6	4.0	1.8	−55.0	32.5	30.5	−6.2

[a] Sum of 11 types of water pollutants including Hg, Cd, Cr^{6+}, Pb, As, volatile phnol, cyanide, petroleum, COD, suspended substance and sulphide.
[b] Sum of three types of air pollutants including sulphur dioxide, industrial soot and dust.
[c] Sum of seven types of solid waste pollutants including dangerous wastes, metallurgical slag, coal ash, slag, coal gauges, tailing and radio active waste.

Sources: China Environment Yearbook (1994), p. 419 and (1998), pp. 580–1, 586 and 588.

Table 17.4   Environmental effects of China's accession to WTO (% of total 2005 emission without WTO accession)

	Composition effect	Scale effect	Technical effect	Aggregate effect
Water pollution	−3.8	5.4	−	+
Air pollution	−3.3	5.4	−	−
Soil pollution	−5.4	5.4	−	

Source: Author's own calculations.

access to advanced pollution abatement technology. These factors, alongside the government's increased efforts to control industrial pollution through its State Environmental Protection Agency (SEPA), have led to a significant drop in the sectoral pollution intensity of Chinese manufacturing output. SEPA survey data show that between 1993 and 1997, water pollution intensity declined by an unweighed average rate of 32.5 per cent, and air and soil pollution intensity fell by an unweighed average rate of 43.8 and 38.5 per cent respectively (Table 17.3).

China's accession to WTO is expected to intensify the globalization of the Chinese economy in the coming years. We may therefore suppose that, in addition to the positive technical impact, there will be a further reduction in Chinese manufactured sectoral pollution intensities. It is not, however, possible to predict the precise rate of decline.

Aggregate effect

As mentioned above, the net aggregate impact of China's WTO accession depends on whether the combined positive compositional and technical effects are larger or smaller than the negative scale effect. As Table 17.4 reveals, for water and air pollutants, the negative scale effect more than offsets the positive composition effect. In the absence of the technical effect, water and air pollution are therefore likely to worsen. For soil pollutants, however, the positive compositional effect offsets the negative scale effect. Thus, soil pollution may not worsen in the absence of the technical effect.

The future trajectory of the technical effect is difficult to predict, but experience indicates that the positive technical effect will be maintained, as long as appropriate pollution control policies are put in place. In short, there is reason for cautious optimism that China's accession to the WTO may not lead to a significant deterioration in the Chinese environment.

Conclusion

This chapter attempts to shed light on the environmental impact of China's accession to the WTO. It focuses on the manufacturing sector and considers the immediate impact of China's WTO accession on the emission of three main categories of pollutants: water, air and solid waste. The results show that the dismantling of import barriers in China's highly protected heavy industries and the phasing-out of MFA in China's export market after China's WTO accession will enable China to shift towards a pattern of specialization in line with its comparative advantage. As a result, China's resources will be redirected from capital, land, energy and other natural resource-intensive industries towards labour-intensive light industries. Since light industries are cleaner, this compositional change in Chinese manufacturing output is expected to reduce its water, air and soil pollution levels. At the same time, China's WTO accession promises to confer increased access to cleaner production technology and facilitate its use of such technology. This will lead to a significant decrease in the pollution intensity of its manufacturing sector. However, the expansion of China's manufacturing sector as a result of its accession to WTO is likely to *increase* the emission of all three pollutants. But because of the limited rate of expansion, this negative scale effect will not be large enough to offset the environmental gains from increased specialization in light industries and easier access to best international practice in pollution abatement technology. As a result, except for air pollution, China is expected to experience a fall in water and soil pollution levels after its accession to the WTO.

It is important to note the limitations of the above analysis. First, it only considers the pollutant emission of the manufacturing sector. Second, within the manufacturing sector, only the negative environmental impact associated with the direct scale effect of Chinese manufactured output expansion has been considered. The indirect scale effect, captured in the negative environmental impact of increased economic growth and consumption induced by higher manufacturing output, has not been considered. According to a report released by IMF on 8 April 2005, China is set to overtake the US and become the largest country in terms of car ownership in the near future. The report predicts that the number of cars in China will soar from 21 million in 2002 to 387 million in 2030, compared with 312 million cars in the US in the same year (*The Australian*, 4 August 2005). The pollution caused by the anticipated huge increase in car use in urban areas is likely to worsen urban air quality. Finally, it should be kept in mind that the validity of results presented here depends very much on acceptance of the output estimates of Zhai and Li.

References

Beghin, J. and M. Potier (1997), 'Effects of Trade Liberalization on the Environment in the Manufacturing Sector', *World Economy*, 20 (4), 435–56.

Beghin, J., D. Sebastien, D. Roland-Holst and D. van der Mensbrugghe (1994), *Prototype of CGE Model for the Trade and the Environment Program – Technical Specification*, Paris: OECD Development Centre.

Chai, J.C.H. (1989), 'China's GATT Membership: Impact on her Foreign Trade and Consequences for Her Trading Partners', in W. Klenner (ed.), *Trends in Economic Development in East Asia*, Berlin-Heidelberg: Springer Verlag, 75–92.

Chai, J.C.H (2000), 'Trade and Environment: Evidence from China's Manufacturing Sector', *Economics, Ecology and Environment Working Paper*, No. 42, Brisbane: The University of Queensland.

Grossman, G.M. and A.B. Krueger (1993), 'Environmental Impacts of a North American Free Trade Agreement', in P. Garber (ed.), *The Mexico-US Free Trade Agreement*, Cambridge, Mass: MIT Press.

Hu T. and Y. Wanghua (2000), 'Environmental and Trade Implication of China's WTO Accession – A Preliminary Analysis prepared for the Working Group on Trade and Environment', China Council for International Cooperation on Environment and Development.

Laird, S and A. Yeats (1990), *Quantitative Methods for Trade Barriers Analysis*, New York: New York University Press.

Luken, R.A. and C. van der Tak (2002), 'Industrial environmental management and the WTO rules: the case of China', in C.A. Magarinos, Y. Long and F.C. Servich (eds), *China in the WTO*, Basingstoke and New York: Palgrave Macmillan, 111–42.

OECD (2002), *China in the World Economy: The Domestic Challenges*, Paris: OECD.

Tisdell, C. (2000), 'Free Trade, Globalization, and Environment and Sustainability: Major Positions and the Position of WTO', *Economics, Ecology and the Environment Working Paper*, No. 39, Brisbane: The University of Queensland.

Zhai, F. and S. Li (2000), 'China's WTO Accession and Implications for its Regional Economies ", Development Research Center, Paper prepared for UNIDO project US/CPR/96/108, Beijing: The State Council of China.

Zhang Shuguang, Zhang Yansheng and Wan Zhongxin (1999), *Measuring the Costs of Protection in China*, Washington, DC: Institute of International Economics.

Part V

Corporate Governance and Management

18
The Supervisory Board in Chinese Corporate Governance

On Kit Tam and Helen Wei Hu

Introduction

China's joint stock limited companies are required to have a supervisory board by law (Company Law, 1994). Article 103 of the Company Law (1994) stipulates that both supervisors and directors are to be elected, appointed or replaced by shareholders' general meetings. Since the creation of supervisory boards for Chinese companies, their role and efficacy have been questioned. While Chinese corporate governance issues have attracted increasing interest from both regulators and researchers, the literature is primarily focused on the board of directors. The limited amount of research on supervisory boards is mostly descriptive and based on small samples of case studies.

This chapter attempts empirically to test some key propositions regarding the corporate governance role and functioning of the supervisory board. It provides a systematic investigation of the performance of China's supervisory boards based on a sample of 297 Chinese listed companies between 2001 and 2003. It will examine the structure and practices of supervisory boards and test how they may relate to firm performance. The interfacing monitoring and supervising roles of the two corporate boards in Chinese public companies will also be examined by a dual-board diagnostic model.

While China's supervisory boards are considered ineffective by most observers (Tenev, Zhang and Brefort, 2002; Tong, 2003), the conclusion is seldom substantiated by empirical evidence. Unlike studies of boards of directors, so far no empirical study has evaluated the effectiveness of the supervisory board and its impact on firm performance. This study will analyse the composition and characteristics of the Chinese supervisory board and its impact on firm performance. It also evaluates the monitoring efforts of supervisory boards and boards of directors in the context of their varying degrees of independence.

The findings suggest that the current Chinese supervisory boards are very much dominated by insiders with limited independence to challenge the board of directors or the Chief Executive Officer (CEO). Monitoring by the supervisory board is found to exert little influence on firm performance. In contrast, outside supervisors, although limited in number, have exhibited a positive impact on corporate governance and firm performance.

This chapter is organized as follows. The next section presents for empirical testing the proposition that the composition of a supervisory board will affect a firm's performance. The third section outlines the dual-board diagnostic model and its application to test the governance and performance effects of various types of dual board structures. It also outlines the methodology and data. The fourth section discusses the empirical results, while the final section provides some concluding remarks.

Role and composition of the supervisory board

Supervisory boards and boards of directors are ostensively parallel governance structures in China. According to China's Company Law, the main function of the supervisory board is to examine a company's financial affairs, and to check directors' and CEOs' legal and regulatory compliance, while corporate strategy (such as business or investment plans, or merger and acquisition decisions) are in the hands of the board of directors. Chinese supervisory boards play no role in determining the composition of the board of directors. It is the board of directors that convenes shareholders' meetings, and reports directly to the shareholders. The corporate governance reform initiated by China's regulatory authorities and the stock exchanges in recent years has focused primarily on the board of directors and the recent drive for independence is aimed at the board of directors, whereas supervisory board membership is mandated to include employee representatives so that independence is inherently constrained.

In continental Europe, the role and composition of the supervisory board have been quite extensively analysed.[1] However, the functioning of Chinese supervisory boards remains a largely unexplored subject. This study will investigate the composition of the supervisory board with a special focus on board independence, and find out what kind of impacts it has on firm performance.

Inside supervisors

Insiders are usually defined as board members who are also company employees (Hermalin and Weisbach, 1988). In this study, we define an *inside supervisor* as a member of the supervisory board who is a full-time employee of the company or of the company's controlling shareholder (in many cases the parent company).[2] Xu and Wang (1997) observed that it was rare to find a member of a supervisory board who was also an individual shareholder; the majority were company employees, or employees of the controlling shareholders.

Outside supervisors

Outside supervisor refers to a supervisory board member who is not an employee of the listed company or its controlling shareholder. A priori, outside supervisors can be expected to be more effective in performing their monitoring role as they have less conflict of interest compared to insiders, and a greater willingness to challenge other board members (Johnson, Daily and Ellstrand, 1996). The proportion of outsiders in a board is commonly used as a proxy of board independence (Baysinger and Hoskisson, 1990; Andres, Azofra and Lopez, 2005).

The supervisory board and firm performance

A widely accepted view in the corporate governance literature is that better-governed firms have superior market performance (Shleifer and Vishny, 1997). While the importance of having independent directors is almost universally recognized, academic studies on the relationship between director independence and firm performance are still mixed.[3] Studies on supervisory boards have mostly focused on Europe's various models but have produced no consensus view on the performance impact of independence. In a study of 94 Dutch public companies, Ees, Postma and Sterken (2003) found that the increased involvement of outsiders is negatively correlated to firm performance. On the other hand, Graziano and Luporini (2005) studied the two-tier board structure in continental Europe, where concentrated ownership in companies is common. They suggested that even if the supervisory board was controlled by the dominant shareholder, it was still possible for companies to achieve higher profits as long as the supervisory board did not interfere in operating decisions of the management board such as project selection. They argued that a two-tier board structure was indeed more appropriate than a one-tier board, where a strong ownership concentration was witnessed. In the context of China's corporate governance development, this study will examine empirically the proposition that the composition of supervisory board affects firm performance by testing the following hypothesis:

Hypothesis 1: Firm performance is affected by supervisory board composition

Analysis of the two-tier board structure

While the formal responsibilities of supervisors may appear quite comprehensive, an early study found that about one-quarter of supervisors did not regularly monitor company activities and financial affairs (Tam, 1999). Moreover, 78 per cent of supervisors were not prepared to investigate company affairs. Given this apparent weakness, in what circumstances may the supervisory board challenge the board of directors or the CEO?

To address the above question, this study proposes a *dual-board diagnostic model* to analyse the distribution of power between the three key governance groups in a firm: the board of directors, senior management, and the supervisory board. At the operational level, the power relationship among the groups is represented by its leader, that is, the Chairman of the board of directors (CM[BOD]), the CEO, and the Chairman of the supervisory board (CM[SUP]). To investigate the power distribution of group leaders, this study uses 'independence from the company CEO' as the criterion for the level of independence of its respective leader,[4] so that the relationship among them and the consequent capacity for independent monitoring can be defined and examined.

Dual-board diagnostic model

The dual-board diagnostic model (DBDM) differentiates the position of the three leaders to determine whether they are independent of each other by identifying their insider or outsider status. In all cases, the CEO of the company is definitely an insider, whereas board chairmen may come from a different background, and the combination of the three becomes important. For example, if all three are insiders, the monitoring function of the board of directors and the supervision role of the supervisory board are

Table 18.1 Dual-board diagnostic model of Chinese companies

DBDM	Chairman's outsider/ insider status[a]	Supervisory board independence	Conflicts of interest	Supervisory board monitoring role
Type 1	Outsider: OCMBOD Outsider: OCMSUP	Strong	Minimum at all levels	Effective at BOD and SUP
Type 2	Insider: ICMBOD Outsider: OCMSUP	Less strong	Some at BOD and management; Minimum at BOD and SUP	Ineffective at BOD and management; Effective at BOD and SUP
Type 3	Outsider: OCMBOD Insider: ICMSUP	Weak	Minimum at BOD and management; Some at BOD and SUP	Effective at BOD and management; Ineffective at BOD and SUP
Type 4	Insider: ICMBOD Insider: ICMSUP	Weakest	Maximum at BOD, SUP and management	Ineffective at BOD and SUP

[a] Definition: OCMBOD = Outsider Chairman of Board of Directors; OCMSUP = Outsider Chairman of Supervisory Board; ICMBOD = Insider Chairman of Board of Directors; ICMSUP = Insider Chairman of Supervisory Board; BOD = Board of Directors; SUP = Supervisory Board.

expected to be the weakest, since the influence of the CEO is potentially the greatest. On the other hand, if the chairmen of the two boards are out-siders, they will be more likely to have the capacity to challenge the CEO and act more independently. Based on the DBDM, any dual-board firm can be classified into one of the four types shown in Table 18.1.

In brief, DBDM-Type 1, with outsiders occupying the position of chair-man at both BOD and SUP, will have the highest level of independence among the four groups and the monitoring function played by the supervi-sory board can be expected to be the most effective. In contrast, Type 4 is all insiders, a combination that is set to compromise the independence of the supervisory board chairman who is likely to be a subordinate of the CEO and the chairman of the board. The capacity for independent moni-toring will therefore be greatly diminished. Type 2 and Type 3 are formed by an outside chairman in one of the boards. In the case of Type 2, where the supervisory board chairman is an outsider, there remains an opportu-nity for the supervisory board to exercise independent monitoring. However, for Type 3 companies, with an inside Chairman of the supervi-sory board, the capacity for effective monitoring can be expected to have greatly diminished. On the basis of the independence characteristics of these four DBDM types, this study will examine empirically whether they make any difference in terms of firm performance by testing the following:

Hypothesis 2: Firm performance varies according to DBDM type

Method and data

This study employs data from 337 companies listed on the Shanghai Stock Exchange (SHSE) and the Shenzhen Stock Exchange (SZSE) for the period 2001–3. Data on firms' financial performance are from company annual reports from 2001 to 2003. Data on ownership structure, board of directors and supervisory board is based on the year 2003. The rationale for the one-year data on ownership, board of directors and supervisory board is that ownership pat-terns are relatively stable (La Porta, Lopez-de-Silanes and Shleifer, 1999) while board structure changes slowly over time (Donaldson and Davis, 1991).

Firm performance in this study is measured by Tobin's Q, return on assets (ROA) and return on equity (ROE).[5] Two financial ratios, debt to asset (DAR) and earnings per share (EPS) are employed in this study as inde-pendent variables. These variables are generally considered as an important control mechanism to monitor the firm's survival capability and growth potential (Stickney and Weil, 1994; La Porta, Lopez-de-Silanes and Shleifer, 1999). To analyse the likely impact of the four types of DBDM companies, four dummy variables are added.

In studying the impact of various characteristics and practices of super-visory boards, such as the size of the board, some scholars consider a priori that a larger board will have more diversified and knowledgeable board members, which will in turn increase its problem-solving capabilities and enhance board efficiency (Haleblian and Finkelstein, 1993; Van den Berghe and Levrau, 2004). On the other hand, other empirical findings point out that the size of the supervisory board is negatively correlated to firm performance (Ees, Postma and Sterken, 2003), especially oversized boards (Andres, Azofra and Lopez, 2005). Likewise, the frequency of board meetings is treated as a useful indicator of directors' and supervisors' efforts, reflecting their preparation and engagement in effective communication and decision-making (Conger, Finegold and Lawler, 1998). The study of board meeting frequency by Vafeas (1999), however, finds that the frequency of meetings does not improve overall firm performance. Variables in this study includes indicators of independence such as the percentage of inside supervisors (IS) as a proportion of the supervisory board size; supervisory board size (SUPSIZE) and frequency of supervisory board meetings (SUPMTG). A ratio of SUP meetings over BOD meetings (SUPmtg/BODmtg) is employed to gauge supervisors' efforts (relative to board directors') devoted to completing their duties.

In addition, two more variables are included in the study; controlling shareholder ownership and firm size. These variables are important as ownership concentration has a direct effect on the composition of BOD and SUP, such as selecting board members and their chairmen, while firm size is usually found to have significant impact on board structure (Daily and Dollinger, 1993; Lang and Stulz, 1994). Detailed definitions of variables are given in Table 18.2.

Empirical results

First this study applies one-way univariate analysis of variance (ANOVA) and ordinary least squares (OLS) regression statistical models. After assessing the normality of 337 sample firms and eliminating outliers, 40 companies were eliminated so that the study had a final sample size of 297 companies. Descriptive statistics of the variables and test of normality are presented in Table 18.3.

Table 18.3 shows that Chinese listed companies are dominated by an insider-controlled supervisory board. On average, the supervisory board size is 4.5, quite similar in size to the supervisory board found in Dutch listed companies reported by Ees, Postma and Sterken (2003). More significantly, 80 per cent of the supervisors in Chinese companies are insiders. The frequency of supervisory board meetings is relatively low with a mean of 3.64 times per year, compared with an average of 6.7 meetings in OECD countries (Andres, Azofra and Lopez, 2005).

Impact of supervisory board composition

To investigate the relationships among inside and outside supervisors, board operation activities, ownership concentration and firm performance,

Table 18.2 Definition of variables

Variable	Definition
Tobin's Q	Ratio of the market value of equity and debt of a firm to the replacement cost of its assets.
ROA	Return on assets, a ratio that measures the efficiency with which assets are used.
ROE	Return on equity, a ratio that shows the amount of profit for the period available to the shareholders.
EPS	Earnings per share, a ratio that shows the earnings generated by the company and available to its shareholders.
DAR	Debt to total assets, a ratio that measures the contribution of long-term lenders to the long-term capital structure of a business.
1st Shareholder%	The percentage of company shares owned by the largest shareholder (this shareholder is also the controlling shareholder).
IS	Number of inside supervisors: supervisors who are full-time employees of the listed company or its controlling shareholder.
OS	Number of outside supervisors: supervisors who are neither employees of the listed company, nor of its controlling shareholder.
IS%	Percentage of inside supervisors over the total number of supervisors on a board.
OS%	Percentage of outside supervisors over the total number of supervisors on a board.
FIRMSIZE	Firm size measured by the natural logarithm of total assets.
SUPSIZE	Supervisory board size, measured by the total number of supervisors on a board.
SUPMTG	Frequency of supervisory board meetings, measured by the total number of supervisory board meetings in a year.
SUPmtg/BODmtg	Ratio of supervisory board meetings over board of directors meetings in a year.
DBDM Type[a]	Dummy variables represent the insider/outsider positions of two corporate boards' chairmen: DBDM Type 1 (OCMBOD–OCMSUP), the control group. DBDM Type 2 (ICMBOD–OCMSUP), equals 1 if DBDM is 2, otherwise 0. DBDM Type 3 (OCMBOD –ICMSUP), equals 1 if DBDM is 3, otherwise 0. DBDM Type 4 (ICMBOD–ICMSUP), equals 1 if DBDM is 4, otherwise 0.

[a]Detailed definition of the DBDM type can be found in Table 18.1.

Table 18.3 Descriptive statistics

	N Valid	Mean	Median	Standard Deviation	Skewness	Kurtosis	Minimum	Maximum
Tobin's Q	297	1.0553	1.0100	0.34994	0.955	1.636	0.32	2.44
ROA	297	0.0254	0.0200	0.03481	-0.142	1.294	-0.09	0.14
ROE	297	0.0476	0.0600	0.07553	-1.200	1.268	-0.31	0.25
EPS	297	0.1567	0.1500	0.19327	0.095	0.552	-0.43	0.69
DAR	297	0.4669	0.4700	0.16038	-0.120	-0.758	0.07	0.84
1st Shareholder%	297	40.1647	35.1200	17.88350	0.477	-0.699	7.02	84.98
IS	297	3.4200	3.0000	1.36400	0.687	0.618	1.00	9.00
OS	297	0.8800	0.0000	1.08400	1.157	0.847	0.00	5.00
IS%	297	80.4900	100.0000	22.51600	-0.742	-0.662	20.00	100.00
OS%	297	19.4900	0.0000	22.52700	0.750	-0.642	0.00	80.00
FIRMSIZE	297	21.3613	21.3527	0.88528	0.406	0.140	19.18	24.18
SUPSIZE	297	4.3000	5.0000	1.32300	0.712	0.133	3.00	9.00
SUPMTG	297	3.6400	3.0000	1.56400	0.708	0.320	1.00	9.00
SUPmtg/BODmtg	297	0.5379	0.5000	0.26550	0.778	-0.123	0.09	1.33

a Pearson's correlation test is employed. Time-series averages are measured, so as to minimize any huge fluctuation from a particular year (Anderson and Reeb, 2003). The correlations between variables are highlighted in Table 18.4.

First, the linear relationship is examined and a positive correlation between outside supervisors and firm performance is found, with Tobin's Q [r (297) = 0.118, $p < 0.05$] and ROE [r (297) = 0.117, $p < 0.05$]. This suggests that the independence of supervisory boards is important, since it enhances monitoring capacity and can contribute to a firm's profit maximization objective. This finding is consistent with Lee, Rosenstein, Rangan and Davidson (1992), who find that boards dominated by outsiders are associated with higher returns than those dominated by insiders.

Ownership concentration, as measured by the largest shareholder's ownership stake, is directly related to board composition, and is positively correlated to the proportion of inside supervisors (and negatively correlated to the proportion of outside supervisors). This affirms the expectation that concentrated ownership usually prefers an insider-dominated board. In terms of board characteristics, the size of supervisory board is affected by firm size, but size does not contribute to firm performance. It is interesting to note that board size is found to be positively correlated to the number of outside supervisors, which may suggest that more independent opinions are needed when the supervisory board gets bigger. The frequency of board meetings has no direct impact on firm performance.

To estimate the statistical relationship between firm performance and the set of independent variables including board composition, board size, board activity and so on, an OLS regression model is employed. Other than Tobin's Q, two more dependent variables (ROA and ROE) are examined as alternative measure of firm performance. This statistical technique is commonly used in the corporate governance literature (Tian, 2001; Andres, Azofra and Lopez, 2005). The following equations are estimated:

$$
\begin{aligned}
Tobin's\ Q = \ &\alpha + \beta 1EPS + \beta 2DAR + \beta 31stSH\% + \beta 4OS\% + \\
&\beta 5FIRMSIZE + \beta 6\ SUPSIZE + \beta 7\ SUPMTG + \\
&\beta 8\ SUPmtg/BODmtg + \varepsilon_I \qquad\qquad (18.1)
\end{aligned}
$$

$$
\begin{aligned}
ROA = \ &\alpha + \beta 1EPS + \beta 2DAR + \beta 31stSH\% + \beta 4OS\% + \beta 5FIRMSIZE + \\
&\beta 6\ SUPSIZE + \beta 7\ SUPMTG + \beta 8\ SUPmtg/BODmtg + \varepsilon_I \qquad (18.2)
\end{aligned}
$$

$$
\begin{aligned}
ROE = \ &\alpha + \beta 1EPS + \beta 2DAR + \beta 31stSH\% + \beta 4OS\% + \beta 5FIRMSIZE + \\
&\beta 6\ SUPSIZE + \beta 7\ SUPMTG + \beta 8\ SUPmtg/BODmtg + \varepsilon_I \qquad (18.3)
\end{aligned}
$$

Regression results are presented in Tables 18.5, 18.6 and 18.7. In each table, the first three columns display the annual cross-section performance for each year from 2001 to 2003, with the last column showing the pooled cross-section time-series regression. This provides a comparison of the sensitivity of the results as well as the trend of the results.

Table 18.4 Pearson correlations between variables

	Tobin's Q	ROA	ROE	DAR	EPS	1st Share-holder%	IS%	OS%	FIRM SIZE	SUP SIZE	SUPMTG	SUPmtg/BODmtg
Tobin's Q	–											
ROA	-0.051	–										
ROE	-0.011	0.906***	–									
DAR	0.198***	-0.403***	-0.171***	–								
EPS	-0.089	0.849***	0.870***	-0.224***	–							
1st Share-holder%	-0.429***	-0.140**	0.044	-0.204***	0.062	–						
IS%	-0.118**	-0.110	-0.116**	-0.008	-0.064	0.186***	–					
OS%	0.118**	0.111	0.117**	0.008	0.065	-0.186***	-0.1000***	–				
FIRMSIZE	-0.497***	-0.168***	-0.182***	0.077	0.322***	0.221***	0.006	-0.006	–			
SUPSIZE	-0.118**	0.125**	0.074	-0.092	0.081	0.040	-0.136**	0.138**	0.131**	–		
SUPMTG	-0.003	-0.097	-0.078	0.023	-0.091	-0.023	0.094	-0.094	-0.040	0.104	–	
SUPmtg/BODmtg	-0.061	0.065	0.040	-0.097	0.038	0.015	0.151**	-0.151***	0.018	0.073	0.614***	–
N	297	297	297	297	297	297	297	297	297	297	297	297

Notes: *** and ** denote two-tailed significance at the 1% and 5% level, respectively.

Table 18.5 Supervisory board and firm performance: OLS regression 1 – Tobin's Q as dependent variable

	2001	2002	2003	Pooled
Intercept	7.632	5.20***	3.018***	5.186***
	(12.956)	(12.332)	(8.276)	(12.661)
EPS	0.053	0.109**	0.133**	0.131**
	(1.225)	(2.247)	(2.287)	(2.597)
DAR	0.098**	0.205***	0.317***	0.203***
	(2.147)	(4.322)	(5.578)	(4.104)
1st Shareholder%	–0.256***	–0.214**	–0.277***	–0.275***
	(–5.738)	(–4.883)	(–5.011)	(–5.614)
OS%	0.088*	0.062	0.047	0.056
	(1.842)	(1.383)	(1.475)	(1.173)
FIRMSIZE	–0.513***	–0.472***	–0.326***	–0.487***
	(–11.753)	(–9.618)	(–5.711)	(–9.575)
SUPSIZE	–0.083*	–0.109*	0.027	–0.041
	(–1.005)	(–1.438)	(0.393)	(–0.878)
SUPMTG	0.052	0.016	0.076	0.002
	(0.947)	(0.270)	(1.226)	(0.037)
SUPmtg/BODmtg	–0.010	–0.022	–0.066	–0.023
	(–0.103)	(–0.358)	(–0.976)	(–0.389)
Adjusted R^2	0.422	0.395	0.301	0.385
F-Statistic	22.885	27.657	18.004	24.141
P-Value	0.000	0.000	0.000	0.000
N	306	305	304	300

Notes: ***, ** and * denote two-tailed significance at the 1%, 5% and 10% level, respectively. T-statistics based on corrected standard errors are in parenthesis.

Consistent results are found in all three regression models: that is, a positive correlation between outside supervisors and firm performance. Hence the results support the acceptance of Hypothesis 1. Although the result is not statistically significant in Tobin's Q, it is significant in ROA [β (297) = 0.071, p< 0.05] and ROE [β (297) = 0.065, p < 0.05]. The finding is consistent with the agency theory which considers outsiders to be more effective in their corporate governance role than insiders (Lee *et al.*, 1992; Pearce and Zahra, 1992).

Result on firm size shows a strong negative relationship between firm size and firm performance, with Tobin's Q [β (297) = –0.487, p < 0.01]. This implies large companies have higher agency costs and bureaucratic redundancy as highlighted by Sun, Tong and Tong (2002) and Qi, Wu and Zhang (2000). Ownership concentration is also found to be negatively correlated to firm performance, Tobin's Q [β (297) = –0.275, p < 0.01] and ROA [β (297) = –0.085, p < 0.01], indicating the existence of the agency problem between the controlling shareholders and minority shareholders. On the

Table 18.6   Supervisory board and firm performance: OLS regression 2 – ROA as dependent variable

	2001	2002	2003	Pooled
Intercept	0.177***	0.121***	0.065**	0.099***
	(7.008)	(5.387)	(2.183)	(4.097)
EPS	0.785***	0.784***	0.779***	0.823***
	(22.570)	(25.435)	(21.841)	(27.376)
DAR	−0.246***	−0.195***	−0.201***	−0.183***
	(−7.512)	(−6.508)	(−6.184)	(−6.221)
1st Shareholder%	−0.078**	−0.122***	−0.076**	−0.085***
	(−2.217)	(−4.089)	(−2.433)	(−2.904)
OS%	0.027	0.040	0.045	0.071**
	(0.859)	(1.363)	(1.448)	(2.513)
FIRMSIZE	−0.225***	−0.182***	−0.075**	−0.110***
	(−6.589)	(−5.548)	(−2.632)	(−3.620)
SUPSIZE	0.062	0.046	0.019	0.044
	(1.578)	(1.482)	(0.551)	(1.560)
SUPMTG	−0.029	−0.063*	−0.031	−0.052
	(−0.867)	(−2.158)	(−0.972)	(−1.477)
SUPmtg/BODmtg	0.026	0.041	0.013	0.056
	(0.633)	(1.152)	(0.328)	(1.578)
Adjusted R^2	0.513	0.553	0.437	0.484
F-Statistic	42.516	22.207	68.381	72.586
P-Value	0.000	0.000	0.000	0.000
N	305	307	306	300

Notes: ***, ** and * denote two-tailed significance at the 1%, 5% and 10% level, respectively. T-statistics based on corrected standard errors are in parenthesis.

other hand, the study has not discovered any significant contribution to firm performance by board operating activities such as board size, frequency of board meetings, or the meeting ratio of the two boards. This empirical finding supports the views of many previous studies that China's supervisory boards in the Chinese two-tier board system have been ineffective (Xu and Wang, 1997; Tam, 1999; Tenev, Zhang and Brefort, 2002).

Dual-board diagnostic model

To examine the difference that the four DBDM types may have on firm performance, one-way between-groups ANOVA is used in this study. Descriptive statistics table and ANOVA results are presented in Tables 18.8, 18.9 and 18.10.

Table 18.8 shows that Type 1 firms achieved the highest performance, with Tobin's Q [MD_{DBDM1} = 1.14] and ROA [MD_{DBDM1} = 0.03]. This is con-

Table 18.7 Supervisory board and firm performance: OLS regression 3 – ROE as dependent variable

	2001	2002	2003	Pooled
Intercept	0.287***	0.233***	0.220**	0.194***
	(5.924)	(4.057)	(2.314)	(3.578)
EPS	0.855***	0.887***	0.875***	0.913***
	(21.816)	(23.544)	(24.412)	(29.458)
DAR	0.157***	0.101**	0.009	0.054*
	(4.457)	(3.051)	(0.248)	(1.784)
1st Shareholder%	–0.062	–0.069**	–0.015	–0.037
	(–1.682)	(–2.483)	(–0.439)	(–1.23)
OS%	0.043	0.025	0.033	0.065**
	(1.185)	(0.786)	(1.024)	(2.229)
FIRMSIZE	–0.243***	–0.199***	–0.116**	–0.126***
	(–6.851)	(–5.753)	(–3.284)	(–4.033)
SUPSIZE	0.058	0.047	–0.014	0.010
	(1.083)	(0.951)	(–0.330)	(0.359)
SUPMTG	–0.074	–0.016	0.020	–0.013
	(–1.554)	(–0.382)	(0.458)	(–0.367)
SUPmtg/BODmtg	0.053	–0.007	0.012	0.029
	(1.843)	(–0.116)	(0.434)	(0.801)
Adjusted R^2	0.561	0.525	0.403	0.462
F-Statistic	59.513	32.577	55.254	57.365
P-Value	0.000	0.000	0.000	0.000
N	301	305	310	300

Notes: ***, ** and * denote two-tailed significance at the 1%, 5% and 10% level, respectively. T-statistics based on corrected standard errors are in parenthesis.

sistent with the expectation that outside board chairmen are more likely to enhance a firm's profit maximization objective. In contrast, when firms are controlled by insider chairmen, minority shareholders' interest are unlikely to be protected, and the lowest performance results are indeed witnessed [MD_{DBDM4} = 1.05] and ROA [MD_{DBDM4} = 0.02]. The same explanation also applies to ownership concentration. That is, DBDM Type 4 has the most serious ownership concentration problem, with the first shareholder owning 42 per cent company shares on average, reaching a maximum 1stSH% of 85 per cent.

In respect of supervisory board composition, the results reveal that the independence of a board is strongly affected by the independence of its chairman. Among the four types of DBDM companies, DBDM Type 1 experiences the highest board independence, with OS% [MD_{DBDM1} = 51.42], followed by DBDM Type 2, having OS% [MD_{DBDM2} = 45.85]. In comparison, DBDM Type 4 has the weakest board independence with the highest number of insiders, IS% [MD_{DBDM4} = 87.47]. Indeed, an insider-controlled

Table 18.8 Descriptive statistics on DBDM type

DBDM	Value	Tobin's Q	ROA	ROE	EPS	DAR	1st Share-holder%	IS	OS	IS%	OS%	FIRM SIZE	SUP SIZE	SUP MTG	SUPmtg/ BODmtg	N
DBDM 1[a]	Mean	1.14	0.03	0.04	0.12	0.42	32.68	2	2.16	48.61	51.42	21.19	4.16	3.21	0.50	19
	Std	0.48	0.05	0.10	0.19	0.23	18.57	0.94	1.12	17.38	17.49	0.91	1.30	1.40	0.26	
	Min.	0.39	−0.09	−0.31	−0.39	0.11	8.25	1	1	28.57	17	19.63	3	1	0.13	
	Max.	2.21	0.14	0.16	0.39	0.84	81.82	5	5	83.33	71	22.54	7	7	1	
DBDM 2[b]	Mean	1.10	0.02	0.05	0.13	0.49	36.42	2.44	2.09	54.15	45.85	21.35	4.53	3.88	0.48	34
	Std	0.39	0.02	0.05	0.14	0.15	17.72	1.16	1.11	18.94	19.04	0.88	1.48	1.75	0.23	
	Min.	0.39	−0.03	−0.04	−0.11	0.28	7.02	1	0	20	0	19.18	3	2	0.18	
	Max.	2.23	0.08	0.16	0.51	0.79	82.05	6	5	100	80	23.28	9	8	1	
DBDM 3[c]	Mean	1.13	0.03	0.06	0.18	0.47	31.35	2.75	1.15	72.88	27.10	21.20	3.90	3.65	0.57	20
	Std	0.36	0.04	0.08	0.21	0.14	14.04	0.85	0.99	21.46	21.51	0.72	1.33	1.35	0.28	
	Min.	0.57	−0.08	−0.19	−0.43	0.24	12.44	1	0	33.33	0	19.97	3	1	0.17	
	Max.	1.93	0.11	0.20	0.47	0.74	63.04	4	3	100	67	22.83	7	6	1.25	
DBDM 4[d]	Mean	1.05	0.02	0.04	0.16	0.47	41.79	3.73	0.57	87.47	12.25	21.39	4.30	3.65	0.55	230
	Std	0.34	0.04	0.12	0.21	0.16	17.79	1.30	0.85	18.20	17.63	0.91	1.29	1.57	0.27	
	Min.	0.32	−0.17	−1.25	−0.56	0.07	11.19	1	0	20	0	19.27	3	1	0.09	
	Max.	2.44	0.11	0.25	0.69	0.80	84.98	9	3	100	67	24.18	9	9	1.33	

[a] DBDM 1 (i.e., OCMBOD–OCMSUP)
[b] DBDM 2 (i.e., ICMBOD–OCMSUP)
[c] DBDM 3 (i.e., OCMBOD–ICMSUP)
[d] DBDM 4 (i.e., ICMBOD–ICMSUP)

Table 18.9   ANOVA results for accounting ratios according to DBDM types

	Tobin's Q	ROA	ROE	DAR	EPS	N
DBDM 1[a]	1.1374	0.0289	0.0363	0.4237	0.1211	19
DBDM 2[b]	1.0991	0.0235	0.0547	0.4897	0.1344	34
DBDM 3[c]	1.1289	0.0305	0.0653	0.4705	0.1858	19
DBDM 4[d]	1.0355	0.0249	0.0460	0.4668	0.1606	225
Total	1.0553	0.0254	0.0476	0.4669	0.1567	297
p-value	0.372	0.863	0.603	0.559	0.657	

[a] DBDM 1 (i.e., OCMBOD–OCMSUP)
[b] DBDM 2 (i.e., ICMBOD–OCMSUP)
[c] DBDM 3 (i.e., OCMBOD–ICMSUP)
[d] DBDM 4 (i.e., ICMBOD–ICMSUP)

Table 18.10   ANOVA results for supervisory board characteristics according to DBDM types

	1st Share-holder%	IS%	OS%	FIRM SIZE	SUP SIZE	SUPMTG	SUPmtg/ BODmtg	N
DBDM 1[a]	32.6832	48.61	51.42	21.1858	4.16	3.21	0.5005	19
DBDM 2[b]	36.4162	54.15	45.85	21.3507	4.53	3.88	0.4841	34
DBDM 3[c]	31.4705	71.45	28.53	21.2150	3.95	3.58	0.5663	19
DBDM 4[d]	42.0971	87.93	12.05	21.3901	4.31	3.65	0.5468	225
Total	40.1647	80.49	19.49	21.3613	4.30	3.64	0.5379	297
p-value	0.007	0.000	0.000	0.682	0.460	0.518	0.526	

[a] DBDM 1 (i.e., OCMBOD–OCMSUP)
[b] DBDM 2 (i.e., ICMBOD–OCMSUP)
[c] DBDM 3 (i.e., OCMBOD–ICMSUP)
[d] DBDM 4 (i.e., ICMBOD–ICMSUP)

supervisory board is the dominant form in China, with insiders constituting the majority of board members in all three DBDM firms except DBDM Type 1.

The ANOVA results from Tables 18.9 and 18.10 indicate that firm performance does not vary significantly according to DBDM type, rejecting Hypothesis 2. Part of the explanation for this finding is that the overwhelming majority of the DBDM Type 4 companies (that is, more than 75% of the sample of 225 companies) belongs to this category. Nevertheless, there are still some differences found in other variables, such as board composition – OS% [$F(3, 296)$ = 59.742, $p < 0.01$] – and ownership concentration – 1stSH% [$F(3, 296)$ = 4.104, $p < 0.01$]. Based on the above results, there are several aspects which suggest that the structure of the dual-board in DBDM Type 4 is not effective. First, it is an insider-dominated board with the lowest number of outside supervisors. Second, it has the highest percentage of ownership concentration. Most importantly, its financial performance as indicated by Tobin's Q and ROA is the worst among the four DBDM types.

Figure 18.1 shows the relationship between DBDM types and board composition, with DBDM Type 1 having the highest proportion of outside supervisors. A clear pattern demonstrating the independence of the supervisory board and the four types can be discerned. On the other hand, supervisory board size SUPSIZE and meeting times SUPMTG do not significantly differ according to DBDM type. This finding is not surprising and reinforces this study's earlier results that no such correlation has been detected.

Although the ANOVA test compares the performance differences among DBDM groups, it does not analyse how well the level of firm performance relates to each of the DBDM board characteristics. Consequently, an OLS regression is employed to examine the correlation between DBDM type and firm performance, and the equation is shown as follows:

Figure 18.1 DBDM types and proportion of insider/outside supervisors

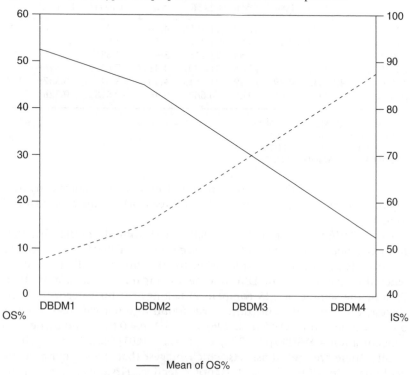

$$ROA = \alpha + \beta_1 EPS + \beta_2 DAR + \beta_3 1STSH\% + \beta_4 OS\% + \beta_5 FIRMSIZE + \beta_6 DBDM + $$
$$\beta_7 SUPSIZE + \beta_8 SUPMTG + \beta_9 SUPMTG/BODMTG + \varepsilon_I \qquad (18.4)$$

The result shows a sharp contrast between DBDM Type 1 and DBDM Type 4. It suggests that firms with all outsider chairmen in the two boards achieved the best performance among all DBDM types, while firms dominated by all insider chairmen achieved the worst performance. Results presented in Table 18.11 show that, in each individual year, there is a significant difference in firm performance between DBDM Type 1 and DBDM Type 4. The

Table 18.11   OLS regression of ROA on explanatory variables (four different types of DBDM: DBDM1, DBDM2, DBDM3, DBDM4) and control variables

	2001	2002	2003	Pooled
Intercept	0.210***	0.163***	0.088**	0.105***
	(8.352)	(7.135)	(2.746)	(4.249)
EPS	0.790***	0.819***	0.788***	0.828***
	(24.054)	(26.925)	(22.863)	(27.258)
DAR	−0.235***	−0.186***	−0.191***	−0.179***
	(−7.251)	(−6.258)	(−5.622)	(−6.029)
1st Shareholder%	−0.084**	−0.128***	−0.081**	−0.089***
	(−2.530)	(−4.265)	(−2.550)	(−3.007)
OS%	0.007	0.010	0.026	0.065*
	(0.191)	(0.264)	(0.679)	(1.818)
FIRMSIZE	−0.221***	−0.179***	−0.068*	−0.110***
	(−6.387)	(−5.995)	(−2.108)	(−3.625)
SUPSIZE	0.058	0.048	0.015	0.042
	(1.055)	(1.328)	(0.766)	(0.963)
SUPMTG	−0.019	−0.065*	−0.017	−0.051
	(−0.508)	(−1.783)	(−0.423)	(−1.478)
SUPmtg/BODmtg	0.020	0.038	0.006	0.053
	(0.492)	(1.048)	(0.257)	(1.508)
DBDM2[a]	−0.070	−0.049	−0.104**	−0.037
	(−1.339)	(−1.003)	(−2.016)	(−0.843)
DBDM3	−0.047	−0.024	−0.052	−0.029
	(−1.108)	(−0.600)	(−1.013)	(−0.759)
DBDM4	−0.122**	−0.092*	−0.114**	−0.078
	(−1.985)	(−1.418)	(−1.538)	(−1.407)
Adjusted R^2	0.419	0.361	0.334	0.379
F-Statistic	64.843	52.897	59.578	67.028
P-Value	0.000	0.000	0.000	0.000
N	305	307	306	300

Notes: [a] Dummy variables, DBDM2 = 1 if true, DBDM2 = 1 if true, DBDM3 = 1 if true, otherwise 0, DBDM1 as control group.
***, ** and * denote two-tailed significance at the 1%, 5% and 10% level, respectively. T-statistics based on corrected standard errors are in parenthesis.

pooled regression result, however, shows that the relationship between DBDM types and firm performance is not statistically significant,[6] which is consistent with the preceding results in ANOVA. Once again, the overwhelming sample size of DBDM Type 4 firms makes it problematic in discerning significant differences of firm performance among the four DBDM types. Nevertheless, comparing the overall financial performance of the four types of companies based on the pooled regression results does show that firms with all outsider chairmen (i.e., DBDM Type 1) achieved the best performance, while firms dominated by all insider chairmen (i.e., DBDM Type 4) achieved the worst performance. The regression is significant at the 1 per cent level, and the adjusted R^2 is 37.9 per cent, which is comparable to the acceptance level with other similar studies on Chinese boards of directors (Sun, Tong and Tong, 2002).

Conclusion

This study provides analysis and evidence to examine various perceptions and assertions regarding the functioning and effectiveness of the Chinese supervisory board, which is widely held to be of limited value to building corporate governance in Chinese companies. On the basis of the theoretical and empirical examination of board structure and board composition, this study has found that Chinese supervisory boards are controlled by insiders with a minimum level of independence. Test results show a significant positive relationship between the presence of outside supervisors and firm performance, suggesting outsiders are more effective in supervising company directors and CEOs than insiders.

Using the Dual-Board Diagnostic Model, the independence characteristics of supervisory boards and the possible differentiated impacts from the four types of groupings on firm performance are analysed. The results show that when the two boards of a firm both have outside chairmen (Type 1), ownership concentration tends to be low and firm performance superior. At the other extreme, when a company's two board chairmen are both insiders (Type 4), ownership concentration tends to be high, the percentage of outside supervisors will be low and the level of board independence will also be low, with some evidence of resultant inferior firm performance.

In summary, it has been empirically demonstrated that most Chinese supervisory boards are ineffective at the current stage. This is because the supervisory board is insider-dominated with limited independence to challenge the board of directors or the CEO. Internal governance mechanisms and board monitoring activities, such as the number of board members and the frequency of meeting times, have not contributed to improving firm performance. The majority of the Chinese listed companies are found to have insider chairmen on both corporate boards, and have led to below-average financial performance. Clearly, to improve the effectiveness of its governance role, the presence of more outsiders or independent supervisors will provide some immediate relief, although the improvement of China's corporate governance involves reform and development beyond changes to the supervisory board structure and its practices.

As investor protection in China is on the whole weak and as the country still lacks the full complement of institutions that facilitate the effective functioning of modern corporate governance arrangements, the independence of the supervisory board and of the board of directors is of particular significance. Until the Chinese government resolves the issue of divesting the massive state-owned shareholding in publicly listed companies, the ownership concentration problems in a context of insider control cannot be removed. As a result, the corporate governance role of the supervisory board as it is currently structured under Chinese law will not be effective. Thus, the study's examination of internal governance mechanisms (such as supervisory board size and board meetings) produces no evidence to indicate any significant contribution to firm performance, which agrees with many authors' views of ineffective Chinese supervisory boards. As Tam (1999) has argued, if the supervisory board were to remain, short of a redefinition of its function and responsibilities, its corporate governance role cannot be fulfilled.

Notes

1   See, for example, Andres, Azofra and Lopez (2005); Edwards and Weichenrieder (2004); Ees, Postma and Sterken (2003); Graziano and Luporini (2005); Maassen and Van den Bosch (1999).
2   This is consistent with the definition used by Xiao, Dahya and Lin (2004).
3   See, for example, Hermalin and Weisbach (1991), Bhagat and Black (2002) and Rosenstein and Wyatt (1990).
4   The proxy for independence is developed based on Hermalin and Weisbach's concept that 'Probably the most important factor determining a board's effectiveness is its independence from the CEO' (2003, p. 18).
5   Equation for the estimates for Tobin's Q value of Chinese firms is adopted from Chen (2001) and Wei and Varela (2003). For general discussion of problems of calculating this value, see, for example, Lang and Litzenberger (1989), Lindenberg and Ross (1981), Chung and Pruitt (1994) and Tenev, Zhang and Brefort (2002). ROA and ROE are frequently used as performance primary measures of firm's profitability. See Anderson and Reeb (2003) and Stickney and Weil (1994).
6   Similar results were found in Tobin's Q and ROE. Due to the insignificant relationship between firm performance and DBDM type, results were not shown here, but they can be obtained from the authors upon request.

References

Anderson, R.C. and Reeb, D.M. (2003), 'Founding-Family Ownership and Firm Performance: Evidence from the S&P 500', *Journal of Finance*, 58 (3), 1301–28.

Andres, Pablo de, V. Azofra and F. Lopez (2005), 'Corporate Boards in OECD Countries: Size, Composition, Functioning and Effectiveness', *Corporate Governance*, 13 (2), 197–210.

Baysinger, B.D. and R.R. Hoskisson (1990), 'The Composition of Boards of Directors and Strategic Control: Effects on Corporate Strategy', *Academy of Management Review*, 15 (2), 72–87.

Bhagat, S. and B. Black (2002), 'The Non-correlation between Board Independence and Long-term Firm Performance', *Journal of Corporation Law*, 27 (2), 231–74.

Chen, J. (2001), 'Ownership Structure as Corporate Governance Mechanism: Evidence from Chinese Listed Companies', *Economics of Planning*, 34 (1–2), 53–72.

Chung, K.H. and S.W. Pruitt (1994), 'A Simple Approximation of Tobin's Q, *Financial Management*, 23 (3), 70–4.

Company Law (1994), *The Company Law of the People's Republic of China*, Beijing.

Conger, J.A., D. Finegold and E.E. Lawler (1998), 'Appraising Boardroom Performance', *Harvard Business Review*, 76 (1), 136–48.

Daily, C.M. and M.J. Dollinger (1993), 'Alternative Methodologies for Identifying Family- versus Nonfamily-managed Businesses', *Journal of Small Business Management*, 31 (2), 79–88.

Donaldson, L. and J.H. Davis (1991), 'Stewardship Theory or Agency Theory: CEO Governance and Shareholder Returns', *Australian Journal of Management*, 16 (1), 49–64.

Edwards, J.S. and A.J. Weichenrieder (2004), 'Ownership Concentration and Share Valuation', *German Economic Review*, 5 (2), 143–71.

Ees, H. van, T.J.B.M. Postma and E. Sterken (2003), 'Board Characteristics and Corporate Performance in the Netherlands', *Eastern Economic Journal*, 29 (1), 41–58.

Graziano, C. and A. Luporini (2005), 'Ownership Concentration, Monitoring and Optimal Board Structure', *Working Paper*, http://papers.ssrn.com/so13/papers.cfm?abstract_id=657165.

Haleblian, J. and S. Finkelstein (1993), 'Top Management Team Size, CEO Dominance, and Firm Performance: The Moderating Roles of Environmental Turbulence and Discretion', *Academy of Management Journal*, 36, August, 844–63.

Hermalin, B. and M.S. Weisbach (1988), 'The Determinants of Board Composition', *Rand Journal of Economics*, 19, 589–606.

Hermalin, B. and M.S. Weisbach (1991), 'The Effects of Board Composition and Direct Incentives on Firm Performance', *Financial Management*, 20 (4), 101–12.

Hermalin, B. and M.S. Weisbach (2003), 'Boards of Directors as an Endogenously Determined Institution: A Survey of the Economic Literature', *Economic Policy Review – Federal Reserve Bank of New York*, 9 (1), 7–26.

Johnson, J.L., C. M. Daily and A.E. Ellstrand (1996), 'Board of Directors: A Review and Research Agenda', *Journal of Management*, 22 (3), 409–38.

La Porta, R., F. Lopez-de-Silanes and A. Shleifer (1999), 'Corporate Ownership around the World', *Journal of Finance*, LIV (2), 471–517.

Lang, L.H.P. and R.H. Litzenberger (1989), 'Dividend Announcements: Cash Flow Signalling vs. Free Cash Flow Hypothesis?', *Journal of Financial Economics*, 24 (1), 181–91.

Lang, L.H.P. and R. Stulz (1994), 'Tobin's Q, Corporate Diversification, and Firm Performance', *Journal of Political Economy*, 102 (6), 1248–80.

Lee, C.I., S. Rosenstein, N. Rangan and W.N. Davidson (1992), 'Board Composition and Shareholder Wealth: The Case of Management Buyouts', *Financial Management*, 21 (1), 58–72.

Lindenberg, E.B. and S.A. Ross (1981), 'Tobin's Q Ratio and Industrial Organization', *Journal of Business*, 54 (1), 1–32.

Maassen, G.F. and F.A. Van den Bosch (1999), 'On the Supposed Independence of Two-tier Boards: Formal Structure and Reality in the Netherlands', *Corporate Governance*, 7 (1), 31–7.

Pearce, J.A. and S.A. Zahra (1992), 'Board Composition from a Strategic Contingency Perspective', *Journal of Management Studies*, 29, 411–38.

Qi, D., W. Wu and H. Zhang (2000), 'Shareholding Structure and Corporate Performance of Partially Privatized Firms: Evidence from Listed Chinese Companies', *Pacific Basin Finance Journal*, 8, 587–610.

Rosenstein, S. and J. Wyatt (1990), 'Outside Directors: Board Independence and Shareholder Wealth', *Journal of Financial Economics*, 26 (2), 175–91.

Shleifer, A. and R.W. Vishny (1997), 'A Survey of Corporate Governance', *The Journal of Finance*, 52 (2), 737–83.

Stickney, C.P. and R.L. Weil (1994), *Financial Accounting: An Introduction to Concepts, Methods, and Uses*, Fort Worth, TX: Dryden Press.

Sun, Q., W.H.S. Tong and J. Tong (2002), 'How Does Government Ownership Affect Firm Performance? Evidence from China's Privatization Experience', *Journal of Business Finance and Accounting*, 29, 1–27.

Tam, O.K. (1999), *The Development of Corporate Governance in China*, Cheltenham: Edward Elgar.

Tenev, S., C. Zhang and L. Brefort (2002), *Corporate Governance and Enterprise Reform in China: Building the Institutions of Modern Markets*, Washington, DC: The World Bank.

Tian, G.L. (2001), 'State Shareholding and the Value of China's Firms', *Working Paper*, London Business School.

Tong, D. (2003), 'Current Conditions, Problems of Listed Companies and How to Exercise Regulation', *Working Paper*, www.iwep.org.cn.

Vafeas, N. (1999), 'Board Meeting Frequency and Firm Performance', *Journal of Financial Economics*, 53 (1), 113–42.

Van den Berghe, L. and A. Levrau (2004), 'Evaluating Boards of Directors: What Constitutes a Good Corporate Board?', *Corporate Governance*, 12 (4), 461–78.

Wei, Z. and O. Varela (2003), 'State Equity Ownership and Firm Market Performance: Evidence from China's Newly Privatized Firms', *Global Finance Journal*, 14, 65–82.

Xiao, J.Z., J. Dahya and Z. Lin (2004), 'A Grounded Theory Exposition of the Role of the Supervisory Board in China', *British Journal of Management*, 15, 39–55.

Xu, X.N. and Y. Wang (1997), 'Ownership Structure, Corporate Governance, and Corporate Performance: The Case of Chinese Stock Companies', *World Bank Policy Research Working Paper*, No. 1794.

19
Managerial Autonomy and Firm Performance in China's Listed Firms*

Eric C. Chang and Sonia M.L. Wong

Introduction

The relationship between managerial autonomy and firm performance is a much-studied topic in agency theory. Research on this issue dates back to Berle and Means (1932), who argue that while shareholders have a desire to maximize profits, managers' objectives often differ from shareholders' assumed profit maximization motive (Berle and Means, 1932; Jensen and Meckling, 1976). Managerial autonomy, defined as managers' decision-making latitude, allows managers to serve their own rather than shareholders' objectives and is therefore likely to be negatively associated with firm performance (Jensen and Meckling, 1976; Fama, 1980; Fama and Jensen, 1983a, 1983b; Jensen and Ruback, 1983). Such a negative relationship has been supported by a large body of empirical studies (for example, see Williamson, 1963b; Palmer, 1973; Berger *et al.*, 1997; Denis, Denis and Sarin, 1997).

Traditional agency theory assumes that only managers have incentive problems, and that controlling shareholders do not. If both managers and controlling parties are plagued by incentive problems, the relationship between managerial autonomy and firm performance depends on a comparison of managers' objectives and those of controlling parties. When controlling parties' objectives are better aligned with firm performance than those of managers, managerial autonomy is related negatively to firm performance, as traditional agency theory suggests. When, however, controlling parties' objectives are more poorly aligned with firm performance than those of managers, managerial autonomy is related positively to firm performance.

This study attempts to examine the relationship between managerial autonomy and firm performance in China's listed firms where managers

*This research is supported by Hong Kong Research Grants Council (RGC) Competitive Earmarked Research Grant Awards 2002-2003 (HKU7173/02H).

were monitored by state shareholders and grassroots organizations of the Chinese Communist Party (CCP; hereafter referred to as local party committees), who tend to give priority to social and political goals rather than to profit-maximization (Shleifer and Vishny, 1994; Qian, 1995; Boycko, Shleifer and Vishny, 1996; Shleifer and Vishny, 1998; Opper, Wong and Hu, 2002; Tenev, Zhang and Brefort, 2002). We test the performance implications of managerial autonomy among China's listed firms by employing data obtained from a survey (hereafter referred to as SSES) conducted by the Shanghai Stock Exchange and Integrity Management Consulting Firm.[1] We offer evidence that managerial autonomy among the listed firms has a positive effect on firm performance, suggesting that the managers' objectives might be more in line with profit maximization than those of state shareholders and party members.

We are not the first to examine the performance implications of managerial autonomy in situations in which controlling parties have incentive problems. In their analysis of political control of firms' decision-making in state-owned enterprises (SOEs), Boycko, Shleifer and Vishny (1996) argue that transferring control rights from politicians to managers (i.e., increasing managerial autonomy) can help improve firm performance, largely because managers are more concerned with firm performance than politicians. Their study, however, provides no systematic evidence to support this hypothesis. Groves *et al.* (1995), on the other hand, showed that when managers in China's SOEs were granted decision-making autonomy, they made increased use of bonus payments and hired more fixed-term contract workers. These two measures are positively correlated with higher productivity. Improved productivity does not, however, decrease government subsidies or increase profits. Groves *et al.* fail to explain why managerial autonomy does not lead to lower subsidies and higher profits. Our study attempts to provide evidence on the hypothesis of Boycko, Shleifer and Vishny (1996) and explicitly examines the financial performance implications of managerial autonomy within the context of China's listed firms.

This chapter is organized as follows. In the following section, we discuss the research background and state our hypothesis. The data and methods used to examine the performance implications of managerial autonomy are described in the next section. The fourth section reports the empirical results, and the final section provides a conclusion.

Research background and hypothesis

In this section, we examine the incentives of both the controlling parties and managers in China's listed firms and develop our hypothesis on the performance implication of managerial autonomy for these firms.

Incentives of state shareholders and party members

According to China's Company Law, which was promulgated in December 1993, China's listed firms are subject to two major types of control (Tenev, Zhang and Brefort, 2002). The most obvious and important type of control comes from shareholders. Theoretically, shareholders exercise their control over managers through the board of directors (BOD: see Opper, Wong and Hu, 2001). However, anecdotal evidence suggests that some firms' BODs are actually controlled by managers rather than by shareholders (Tam, 1999; Tenev, Zhang and Brefort; 2002). In order to assess more accurately the nature and the extent of shareholder control in the listed firms, we directly examine the incentives and the decision-making power of the largest share-holders, rather than of BODs.[2]

The largest shareholders in China's listed firms are likely to have non-profit-maximizing objectives. Such shareholders may, first of all, use firms to serve social and political objectives. For example, they may use the firms to provide excessive employment in order to maintain social stability (Xu and Wang, 1999; Bai *et al.*, 2000). By 1999, some 42 per cent of the largest shareholders in China's listed firms were holders of state shares, and 57 per cent were holders of legal person shares.[3] Among the largest shareholders holding legal person shares, SSES reveals that, at the end of 1999, more than 90 per cent were SOEs rather than private investors. In other words, nearly all of the largest shareholders are state entities who enjoy control rights but not cash flow rights, and thus tend to give priority to social and political goals rather than to firm performance (Shleifer and Vishny, 1994; Boycko, Shleifer and Vishny, 1996; Shleifer and Vishny, 1998; Tenev, Zhang and Brefort, 2002).

The second type of control over managers of China's listed firms comes from local party committees, which have exercised political control over the firms since the founding of the People's Republic of China. During the Cultural Revolution (1966–76), the operation and management of firms were entirely dictated by local party committees, and the position of manager was essentially eliminated (You, 1998). In late 1978, the leader-ship under Deng Xiaoping instituted a two-decades-long reform effort to transfer decision-making power from state and party bureaucrats to man-agers and shareholders. The promulgation of China's Company Law in 1993 constituted an important step in this process. The law specifies the rights and duties of shareholders, BODs, and managers in shareholding firms, and thus provides these decision-makers with a legal foundation from which to prevent state and party bureaucrats from interfering with their decision-making (World Bank, 1997). The law, however, did not entirely eradicate political control over managers. Concerning party activi-ties, Article 17 of the law states that 'the activities of the local party com-mittees of the CCP in a company shall be carried out in accordance with the Constitution of the CCP'. The constitution of the CCP, however, does little to clarify party responsibilities within enterprises, since Article 31 provides only a blanket statement that delegates the implementation of higher party decisions to local party committees at the firm level. What seems exceptionally important, however, is the fact that Article 31, section 7, explicitly assigns local party committees the right to 'supervise Party cadres and any other personnel'. This provision in effect gives local party committees the right to supervise personnel in shareholding firms. Since local party committees' primary duties are to promote political goals, it is likely that the committees also tend to give priority to social and political goals rather than to firm performance (Tam, 1999; McGregor, 2001; Opper, Wong and Hu, 2001, 2002).

Incentives of managers

SSES reveals that managers' main avenue of compensation is their salary. Since most managers aspire to a civil service rank, salaries for different categories of managers are usually low and undifferentiated. Furthermore, stock-based incentives are weak, because managers usually hold an insignificant numbers of employee shares, and stock options have not yet developed (Qian, 1995; Tenev, Zhang and Brefort, 2002). Externally, managers of most listed firms are still shielded from the competitive pressure for profits. Many listed firms continue to enjoy some degree of monopolistic power in the still highly regulated product markets. Moreover, an active market for corporate control does not yet exist. There have been only a few episodes of takeover battles since the two exchanges were established. Given the lack of appropriate compensation and external pressure, managers of listed firms have not only the incentive, but also the ability to entrench themselves at the expense of firm performance (Qian, 1995; Shanghai Stock Exchange, 2000; Tenev, Zhang and Brefort, 2002).

Salary, bonuses, and shares are only a few ways in which managers are rewarded. In a rent-seeking society such as China, on-the-job perks (e.g., better housing, use of cars, entertainment, restaurant meals, travel, diversion of assets, and business opportunities) associated with the position of manager in listed firms can be substantial (Qian, 1995). To capture these benefits, managers must keep their jobs. The criteria for assessing managers are therefore important determinants of managers' incentives. Groves *et al.* (1995) offers evidence that in China's early reform period even managers in traditional SOEs were fired because of poor enterprise performance. Chen and Wang (2005) and Chang and Wong (2005) further find that China's listed firms have an average CEO turnover rate as high as 25 per cent, and that CEO turnover is negatively related to corporate performance. The threat of dismissal because of poor performance will have a strong impact on managers' behaviour and limit their agency problems.

Hypothesis

The foregoing analysis of the incentives of the largest shareholders, local party committees and managers in China's listed firms indicates that that both managers and controlling parties have their own incentive problems. These problems can be partly reflected by the firms' poor performance. In 1999, China's overall economy grew at a rate of about 8 per cent. Under such favourable macroeconomic conditions, only 60.56 per cent of China's listed firms experienced a positive growth in profits, while the aggregation of profits for all the listed firms actually declined by 2 percentage points.

We expect managers' interests to rely more heavily on firm performance than those of the largest shareholders and local party committees. Managers whose firms perform poorly will be fired and so lose all the benefits and rents that they can capture. Poor firm performance may also have an adverse effect on their reputation and affect their future career. Large shareholders and local party committees, however, have multiple objectives, including their own interests, social and political objectives, and their parent groups' interests. Some of these objectives are in line with firm performance, but others may conflict with it.[4] Furthermore, given the absence of an active takeover market and the lack of outside competition for membership in local party committees, the controlling parties are unlikely to lose their control rights (and therefore the associated benefits), if their firm's performance declines. As a result, we expect that managers' incentives are better aligned with firm performance than are those of the controlling parties. We therefore offer the following hypothesis:

Hypothesis 1: Managerial autonomy in China's listed firms has a positive impact on the firm performance.

Data and econometric methodology

This section provides a detailed discussion of our data source and econometric methodology. First, we introduce our data source and explain how we attempt to measure managerial autonomy. Second, we describe the performance measures and the control variables included in our models. Finally, we specify the regression equation for estimation.

Data source of decision-making power

A question that arises from the testing of the impact of managerial autonomy is how we measure managerial autonomy. Most studies in the finance literature use proxy variables rather than direct measures. A frequently used approach is to adopt as proxies measures of certain conditions that either allow or restrict managerial autonomy. The most commonly adopted proxy variables are ownership variables; their use is based on the assumption that diffused ownership is a condition that affords managers the opportunity to pursue their own objectives (e.g., Demsetz and Lehn, 1985; Morck, Shleifer and Vishny, 1988). Others use different proxies, such as board composition and tenure of managers (e.g., Williamson, 1963b; Berger *et al.*, 1997; Denis, Denis and Sarin, 1997).

Although the use of proxy variables has the advantage of employing objective data, using proxy variables inevitably introduces noise, because the degree of managerial autonomy usually depends on a host of conditions including environmental, organizational and even psychological factors that cannot easily be captured by one or two proxy variables (Hambrick and Finkelstein, 1987; Hambrick and Abrahamson, 1995). Furthermore, conventional ownership variables may fail to portray the level of shareholder control over managers in China's listed firms because (1) small shareholders fail to exercise their control rights, and (2) managers are under the control of non-shareholders. In the first case, shareholders are likely to have control rights that exceed their rights as represented by their shareholding. In the second case, shareholders must share their control rights with local party committees, which tends to reduce shareholders' control rights relative to their shareholding. Where local party committees exist, managerial autonomy is the extent to which managers are free from both shareholder and party controls. Shareholding variables, which at best capture only shareholders' control, are unable to portray the level of managerial autonomy.

On the other hand, using a survey to obtain an assessment of the extent of managerial autonomy is intended to provide a direct measurement. This approach seeks to gather specific information available only to insiders in a firm's decision-making processes (Hellman and Schankerman, 2000). Studies based on survey respondents' assessment may therefore be able to offer insights and evidence that would be unobtainable had proxy variables been used. Nonetheless, respondents' assessments may suffer perception biases, and therefore caution must be used when data are employed and results are interpreted

In this study, we have employed survey data to assess the distribution of decision-making power in China's listed firms. Our survey includes a question that asked respondents (secretaries to BODs) to rate the level of decision-making power of managers, the largest shareholders, local party committees, and boards of supervisors in 63 decisions on a five-point scale. Responses ranged from no involvement at all (score 1) to complete control (score 5). We used distribution of decision-making-power data to construct a measure of managerial autonomy.

Sample size

Researchers distributed questionnaires to each of the 483 firms listed on the Shanghai Stock Exchange at the end of 1999. Of these firms, 257 returned the questionnaires (response rate: 53.54 per cent). As the first step in checking the survey data and ensuring their quality, we compared the data on basic firm characteristics, including listing age and industries, provided by respondents with those provided by annual reports. Of the 257 question-naires returned, we excluded one because of the existence of inconsistent data. We excluded six more because the firms were listed *only* by the B-share market and not by the main board A-share market. Among the remaining 250 respondents, 112, 113 and 113 provided a complete set of ratings on the decision-making power of the largest shareholders, local party committees and managers (respectively) in all decisions. When we limit our sample to only firms that provided complete data on decision-making power, the number of firms in our sample falls to 90, or about 19 per cent of the firms listed by the A-share market of the Shanghai Stock Exchange.

Table 19.1   Comparing the industrial distribution between sample firms and all China's listed firms (N=90)

Industries	SAMPLE$_{99}$	ALL$_{99}$
Agriculture	0	9
	(0.00%)	(1.91%)
Mining/quarrying	0	3
	(0.00%)	(0.64%)
Manufacturing	53	276
	(58.89%)	(58.60%)
Production and supply of	4	16
electric power, gas, and water	(4.44%)	(3.40%)
Construction	1	10
	(1.11%)	(2.12%)
Transportation, storage and postal	6	26
	(6.67%)	(5.52%)
Wholesale and retail	12	51
	(13.33%)	(10.83%)
Finance and insurance	0	4
	(0.00%)	(0.85%)
Real estate	3	14
	(3.33%)	(2.97%)
Social services	3	20
	(3.33%)	(4.25%)
Media	0	3
	(0.00%)	(0.64%)
Conglomerate	8	39
	(8.89%)	(8.28%)
No. of firms	90	471
	(100%)	(100%)

Validity and reliability of data

We evaluate non-response biases by comparing the industries represented in our samples with the corresponding industrial structure of all the firms listed by the A-share market of the Shanghai Stock Exchange. As shown in Table 19.1, the firms listed by the Exchange are unevenly distributed across industries. At the end of 1999, some 58.60 per cent of the firms belonged to the manufacturing industry, 10.83 per cent belonged to the wholesale and retail industry, and 8.28 per cent were conglomerates. The top three industries accounted for 77.71 per cent of all the listed firms. The distribution of firms in our sample is very similar to the distributions of population. Within our sample, 58.89 per cent of firms belonged to the manufacturing industry and 13.33 per cent were part of the wholesale and retail industry. Our sample includes observations for only eight of the 12 industries represented on the Exchange. The four unrepresented industries are agriculture, banking and insurance, mining and quarrying, and media. However, the number of firms belonging to these four industries is relatively small (with percentages in ALL_{99} at less than 1.91 per cent). Therefore, our sample appears to comprise a reasonably accurate representation of the overall industrial structure of the firms listed by the Shanghai Stock Exchange, suggesting that the sample may not suffer from non-response bias.

We attempted to use respondents' assessment of the power of the major decision-makers in 63 decisions to capture the decision autonomy of managers and local party committees. The list of the decisions and the average decision-making power of the major decision-makers in the firms (including managers, the largest shareholders, and local party committees) is provided in the Appendix. The decisions cover a wide range, including decisions on issues relating to finance and investment, the appointment and dismissal of key personnel, performance appraisal, organizational change, strategic planning, and external relationships, among others. The comprehensive coverage suggests that the lack of content validity might not be a problem for our measure.

We assess the reliability of our data by testing the internal consistency of the ratings for each decision-maker. Results indicate that our data is highly consistent, with Cronbach's alpha greater than 96 per cent (the results are presented in the Appendix).

Our data on decision-making power are provided by BOD secretaries. In the management structure of China's listed firms, the position of BOD secretary is similar to that of managing director; such an individual is expected to be the most knowledgeable about a listed firm. Although we cannot entirely rule out the possibility that respondent bias exists, systematic sources of bias that could affect our results are unlikely to be a problem. This is because respondents are unlikely to have perceived the specific linkage between managerial autonomy and firm performance on the questionnaire, which contains 74 questions covering nearly every aspect of the listed firms' corporate governance structure.

Measures of managerial autonomy

We attempt to capture the performance implications of managerial autonomy in two steps. First, on the basis of the survey data, we construct for each decision-maker an index of decision-making power, as rated by respondents. The average decision-making power of managers (MI), the largest shareholders (SI), and local party committees (PI) in 63 decisions are calculated as follows:

$$MI_i = \frac{\sum_{j=1}^{n} S_{ij}}{n} \qquad SI_i = \frac{\sum_{j=1}^{n} S_{ij}}{n} \qquad PI_i = \frac{\sum_{j=1}^{n} S_{ij}}{n}$$

where S_{ij} is the level of involvement of the decision-makers i in decision j, rated on a five-point scale ranging from no involvement at all (score 1) to complete control (score 5) in 63 decisions ($n = 63$). When MI, SI and PI are constructed, we treat all decisions as equally important and thus assign them equal weightings.

We use the ratio of managers' decision-making power to the total decision-making power of the largest shareholders and the local party committees as the measure of managerial autonomy (MD):

$$MD_i = \frac{MI_i}{SI_i + PI_i}$$

In essence, MD is a measure of the relative decision-making power of managers and controlling parties. A high value of MD implies a higher level of decision-making power on the part of managers relative to that of controlling parties and therefore implies greater latitude for managers to pursue their own objectives rather than the goals of the controlling parties.

Performance measurement

Performances of the listed companies are compared using three measures: return on assets (ROA), return on sales (ROS), and growth of sales (GOS). While ROA and ROS measures the firms' profitability, GOS measures the firms' growth.

Some researchers may be sceptical about the quality of Chinese firms' accounting data, given the embryonic state of China's accounting standards. The use of market-based performance measures may, however, generate other problems. China's stock market is no different from any other emerging market in that it is plagued by many speculative activities. To illustrate, at the end of 1999 more than 99 per cent of participants in the Shanghai Stock Market were small individual investors rather than institutional investors. In addition, the turnover velocity of stocks (defined as the total transaction volume/total number of tradable shares) reached as high as 421.55 per cent, indicating that, on average, each stock changed hands 4.2 times per year. Indeed, China's stock market has been described as a 'casino' because of the rampant speculative activities that take place within it (Wilhelm, 2001). For that reason, we chose not to use the market prices of stocks to construct performance measures. The accounting data we used for the construction of our performance measures was obtained from the Shanghai Wind Information Company Limited (WIND). To further ensure data accuracy and consistency, we have double-checked our data against the financial data published in the annual reports of the listed companies.

Other control variables

The main purpose of this study is to estimate the performance implications of managerial autonomy in China's listed firms. However, some factors can jointly affect the level of managerial autonomy and firm performance, and so may induce a spurious correlation between them. Based on various economic arguments, we introduce five sets of control variables in this study. Except for the industry code that is obtained from *China Securities and Futures Statistical Yearbook 2000,* data for all control variables come from WIND.

Market conditions

Firms in our sample come from various industries at various stages of the product life-cycle and are subject to different degrees of competition and regulation. Different market conditions provide firms with different opportunities to capture profit. Such differing conditions also leave different amounts of room for varying degrees of managerial autonomy (Hambrick and Finkelstein, 1987; Hambrick and Abrahamson, 1995). We therefore introduce the variable of industrial dummies (INDUSTRY$_i$) in our study.

Firm size

Firm size is another characteristic that may affect both level of managerial autonomy and firm performance of listed companies. On the one hand, large firms may have scale economies and better access to financial resources, which could improve firm performance (Fama and French, 1995). Xu and Wang (1999) and Qi, Woody and Hu (2000) document that the financial performance of China's listed firms is positively related to firm size. On the other hand, one might expect large firms to be associated with a higher degree of managerial autonomy because it is assumed that managers have incentives for empire-building (Baumol, 1959; Williamson, 1963a and b). In this study, we follow Qi, Woody and Hu (2000), using the logarithm of the book value of assets (hereafter ASSET) as a proxy to capture firm size.

Capital structure

We also take into account the possible effects of capital structure. Xu and Wang (1999) and Qi, Woody and Hu (2000) find that the debt-to-equity ratio of China's listed firms is negatively related to firm performance. Much of the capital structure research using the principal-agency approach also demonstrates that there is a relationship between managerial autonomy and capital structure (Fama, 1980; Stiglitz, 1985; Jensen, 1986). We have therefore introduced debt-to-equity ratio (hereafter DER) as a control variable.

State shareholding

The largest shareholders in China's listed firms are holders of either state shares or legal person shares. Qi, Woody and Hu (2000) and Xu and Wang (1999) find that the performance of China's listed firms is related negatively to state shares but positively to legal person shares.[5] As these two types of shareholders may have different incentives to monitor managers and may thereby be associated with different levels of managerial autonomy in the listed firms, we introduce a dummy variable indicating the presence of state shares to capture possible confounding effects.[6]

Lagged performance measures

We also include lagged performance measures as control variables to capture the possibility that managerial autonomy may be affected by previous firm performance. Managers in a poorly performing firm may experience a loss in decision-making latitude owing to an increase in supervision over them (Denis and Kruse, 2000). Furthermore, managerial autonomy and firm performance may be correlated for two reasons. The first is that a high level of managerial autonomy leads to improved performance; the second is that the level of managerial autonomy may be influenced by firm performance. The inclusion of lag performance can partially address this reverse-causality problem.

Regression models

We employ the following model to examine the performance implications of managerial autonomy:

$$P = \alpha + \sum_{t=1}^{7} \lambda_i INDUSTRY_i + \beta_1 ASSET + \beta_2 DER + \beta_3 DSTATE + \beta_4 P_L + \beta_5 MD + \varepsilon \quad (19.1)$$

where P denotes the performance measure proxy as either ROA, ROS or GOS; P_L is the corresponding performance measures lagged by one year; MD is the relative decision-making power between managers and controlling parties; α, λ_i, $\beta_1, \beta_2, \beta_3, \beta_4$ and β_5 are the coefficients for estimation. Our hypothesis suggests that β_5 is significantly positive.

Results

Descriptive statistics and sample data

Table 19.2 shows the descriptive statistics and Pearson correlation matrix. The ROA and ROS of our sample firms were 4.2 per cent and 9.1 per cent, respectively. Both of these percentages are lower than their corresponding levels in the preceding year (4.7 per cent and 14.2 per cent, respectively). The growth of sales was 9.1 per cent, which was higher than the growth of sales in 1998 (–9.7 per cent).

MD is 0.859, indicating that managers' decision-making power is, on average, less than that of controlling parties. MD is related negatively to ROA and ROS. No other simple correlation is found between managerial autonomy and other variables included in our model.

Regression results

Table 19.3 presents the estimated performance implications of managerial autonomy in China's listed firms. The coefficients are estimated by the ordinary least square (OLS) technique.[7] The coefficients of DER are negative in all regressions. Our results are consistent with those of Qi, Woody and Hu (2000), as well as those of Xu and Wang (1999). We, however, do not find a positive size effect in our model.

The focus of this model is the performance implications of managerial autonomy. Table 19.3 indicates that the coefficients of MD are positive in all regressions, with statistical significance at 1 per cent in ROA and ROS regressions and 5 per cent in GOS regression. This suggests that the performance of the listed firms tends to improve when managers have more latitude to pursue their own objectives. Our hypothesis that managerial autonomy is related positively to firm performance is therefore supported.[8]

Conclusion

Most existing studies of the relationship between managerial autonomy and firm performance focus mainly on private firms in mature market economies, in which shareholders have a desire to maximize profits, but managers' objectives often differ from shareholders' assumed profit maximization motive. In this study, we have conducted an empirical analysis of the relationship between managerial autonomy and firm performance in China's listed firms, in which managers were controlled by state shareholders and local Communist Party committees who are likely to have non-profit-maximizing objectives. We offer evidence that managerial autonomy has a positive effect on firm performance. Our results are in contrast to the predictions suggested by traditional agency theory and empirical evidence based on the investigations of private firms in mature market economies.

Table 19.2 Descriptive statistics and Pearson correlation matrix ($N = 90$)

Variables	Mean-Sample99	SD-Sample99	1	2	3	4	5	6	7	8	9
1 Return on Assets (ROA)	0.042	0.048									
2 Return on Sales (ROS)	0.091	0.240	0.648***								
3 Growth of Sales (GOS)	0.051	0.407	0.333***	0.395**							
4 Return on Asset$_{\text{Year}-1}$	0.047	0.051	0.640***	0.293**	0.260**						
5 Return on Sales$_{\text{Year}-1}$	0.142	0.219	0.247**	0.235**	0.089	0.646***					
6 Growth of Sales$_{\text{Year}-1}$	−0.097	0.592	0.282**	0.187	0.126	0.174	−0.272**				
7 Debt to Equity Ratio (DER)	1.288	1.879	−0.317***	−0.163	−0.203	−0.292***	−0.134	−0.025			
8 Logarithm of Asset (ASSET)	20.819	0.900	−0.133	0.058	0.073	−0.035	0.066	−0.035	0.430***		
9 Existence of State Shares (DSTATE)	0.722	0.450	0.095	0.051	0.047	0.001	−0.031	−0.069	0.127	0.063	
10 MI/ PI +SI (MD)	0.857	0.221	0.251**	0.211**	−0.004	0.029	−0.084	−0.001	0.002	−0.107	−0.057

PI = Decision-Making Power of Party Committee
MI = Decision-Making Power of Manager
SI = Decision-Making Power of Largest Shareholder
*** P*<0.01; ** P*<0.05

Table 19.3 OLS regression analysis of performance implications of managerial autonomy in China's listed firms

	ROA Model1	ROS Model2	GOS Model3
(Constant)	0.000	−0.658	−2.233*
	(0.103)	(0.652)	(1.271)
Industrial Dummy (INDUSTRY)	YES	YES	YES
Debt-to-Equity Ratio (DER)	−0.004*	−0.032**	−0.065**
	(0.002)	(0.015)	(0.027)
Logarithm of Asset (ASSET)	−0.002	0.026	0.099
	(0.005)	(0.031)	(0.059)
Existence of State Shares (PSTATE)	0.014	0.066	0.158
	(0.009)	(0.056)	(0.110)
MI / PI+SI (MD)	0.055***	0.290***	0.565**
	(0.018)	(0.111)	(0.230)
Return on Assets$_{Year-1}$	0.548***		
	(0.080)		
Return on Sales$_{Year-1}$		0.122	
		(0.121)	
Growth of Sales$_{Year-1}$			0.096
			(0.094)
No. of Firms	90	90	77
Adjusted R Square	0.449	0.132	0.119
F	7.041	2.125	1.859

The entries in the table are the standardized β with standard errors in parentheses.
ROA = Return on Assets
ROS = Return on Sales
GOS = Growth of Sales
PI = Decision-Making Power of Party Committee
MI = Decision-Making Power of Manager
SI = Decision-Making Power of Largest Shareholder
*** $P *< 0.01$; ** $P *<0.05$; * $P *<0.10$

Our results suggest that the incentives of managers in China's listed firms are better aligned with firm performance than the incentives of controlling parties, which are by and large state and political entities. This provides some empirical evidence to support the hypothesis of Boycko, Shleifer and Vishny (1996) that managers are more concerned than politicians with profits. Furthermore, our findings echo those of some other studies of managers' roles in transitional economies. Berglof (1995) found that managers in many transitional economies have not attempted to undertake large-scale asset stripping, even though they have gained substantial control over firms' decision-making. Rather, they have attempted to '[reduce] their work force substantially and closed down loss-making activities' (p. 64). Based on a review of case studies on the corporate governance of firms, Brada and Singh (1999) argue that:

the concern about increased managerial autonomy in transition economies seems ... to be somewhat misplaced ... [T]he type of shareholder activities proposed by many critics of corporate governance in transition economies would seem to replace the petty tutelage of managers by bureaucrats with petty tutelage by shareholders. The latter system is unlikely to yield results better than did the former. (p. 13)

This study not only has academic value, but also provides some practical policy implications for China's listed firms. These results imply that transferring decision-making rights from the largest shareholders and local party committees to managers could help improve firm performance. Nevertheless, this is only a second-best solution, given the existence of the distorted internal corporate governance structure in China and the weakness of legal protection for minority shareholders. In the long run, both controlling parties' and managers' incentives problems must be directly addressed. Fully privatizing listed firms and providing better protection for minority shareholders through reforms in corporate governance and legal systems are the ultimate keys to improving the performance of China's listed firms.

Appendix Table A17.1 Types of decision and reliability test

No.	Type	L. Shareholder	Manager	Party
1	Call of Shareholder Meeting	3.056	2.144	1.411
2	Agenda Setting in Shareholder Meeting	2.989	2.156	1.367
3	Call of Board Meeting	2.711	2.322	1.389
4	Agenda Setting in Board Meeting	2.578	2.400	1.422
5	Call of Supervisory Committee Meeting	2.133	1.689	1.511
6	Agenda Setting in Supervisory Committee Meeting	1.944	1.678	1.500
7	Call of Manager's Office Meeting	1.689	4.578	1.767
8	Agenda Setting in Manager's Office Meeting	1.678	4.589	1.767
9	Selection of Representatives Attending Manager's Office Meeting	1.489	4.567	1.656
10	Making Amendments to Company's Charter	2.600	2.167	1.433
11	Organizational Change	2.111	3.511	2.000
12	Creation and Abolition of Functional Departments	1.722	3.989	1.989
13	Selection of Functional Department Manager	1.633	4.389	2.144
14	Performance Appraisal of Functional Departments	1.511	4.411	2.022
15	Creation and Abolition of Business Departments	1.567	4.378	1.889
16	Selection of Business Department Managers	1.533	4.411	2.133
17	Performance Appraisal of Business Department	1.467	4.389	2.000
18	Creation and Abolition of Branch	1.811	3.789	1.767
19	Selection of Branch Manager	1.689	4.256	2.044
20	Performance Appraisal of Branch	1.600	4.300	1.878
21	Creation and Abolition of Subsidiaries	1.844	3.589	1.800
22	Selection of Subsidiary Manager	1.622	4.056	2.056
23	Performance Appraisal of Subsidiaries	1.544	4.167	1.911
24	Election and Dismissal of Chairman of Board of Directors	3.156	1.400	1.589
25	Performance Appraisal of and Remuneration Enjoyed by Board Chairman	2.711	1.444	1.589
26	Election and Dismissal of Board Members	2.944	1.433	1.544
27	Performance Appraisal of and Remuneration Enjoyed by Board Members	2.456	1.467	1.578
28	Election and Dismissal of Board Secretary	2.300	1.844	1.600

Appendix Table A17.1 Types of decision and reliability test – *continued*

No.	Type	L. Shareholder	Manager	Party
29	Performance Appraisal of and Remuneration Enjoyed by Board Secretary	2.056	2.067	1.622
30	Selection of Supervisory Committee Members	2.689	1.544	1.744
31	Performance Appraisal of and Remuneration Enjoyed by Supervisory Committee Members	2.400	1.600	1.689
32	Selection and Dismissal of Manager	2.533	1.856	1.844
33	Performance Appraisal of and Remuneration Enjoyed by Manager	2.211	1.967	1.767
34	Selection and Dismissal of Vice-Manager	2.111	3.267	1.978
35	Performance Appraisal of and Remuneration Enjoyed by Vice-Manager	1.944	3.156	1.889
36	Change in Shareholding Structure	2.878	2.211	1.356
37	Change in Debt/Equity Ratio	2.600	2.567	1.300
38	Dividend Plan	2.700	2.411	1.256
39	Share Placement and New Issue	2.722	2.500	1.278
40	New Investment in Technology	2.256	3.289	1.367
41	New Investment in Infrastructure	2.256	3.200	1.367
42	Financial Investment	2.078	3.067	1.322
43	Investment in Other Stock Companies	2.278	2.989	1.344
44	Sale of Assets	2.256	2.944	1.367
45	Loans for Fixed Asset Investment	1.967	3.400	1.344
46	Loans for Liquidity Fund	1.844	3.689	1.311
47	Loans through Mortgaging of Asset	2.111	3.011	1.356
48	Guarantee for Other Enterprises' Large-Scale Loans	2.122	2.889	1.333
49	Amount of External Donation	1.856	3.011	1.578
50	External Donation Plan	1.800	3.178	1.667
51	Contracting of Large-Scale Construction Projects	1.811	3.478	1.467
52	Merging with Other Enterprises	2.500	2.956	1.467
53	Being Merged By Other Enterprises	2.822	2.767	1.589
54	Formulation of Long-Term Development Plan	2.322	3.300	1.633
55	Formulation of Strategic Plan	2.289	3.333	1.611
56	Establishment of Long-Term Relationship with Other Enterprises	1.956	3.656	1.556

Appendix Table A17.1 Types of decision and reliability test – *continued*

No.	Type	L. Shareholder	Manager	Party
57	Change of Direction; Entry into New Industry and Market	2.367	3.333	1.567
58	Selection of Accounting (Auditing) Firm	1.933	2.589	1.322
59	Selection of Law Firm	1.856	2.833	1.333
60	Selection of Financial Consultant	1.722	3.033	1.344
61	Selection of Management Consultant	1.756	3.322	1.367
62	Training and Education for Board Members and Higher Management	1.778	2.933	1.678
63	Training and Education for Middle Management	1.567	4.233	1.822
	Average of Total Decision-Making Power	2.134	3.033	1.613
	Alpha	0.983	0.959	0.986

Notes

1   The survey is part of a three-year project conducted by the Shanghai Stock Exchange. The results of the project have been reported and published in *The Corporate Governance of China's Listed Firms* by the Shanghai Stock Exchange. The survey has also been used by Tenev, Zhang and Brefort (2002) and Opper, Wong and Hu (2002).

2   According to China's Company Law, each shareholding firm must establish a board of supervisors consisting of representatives of shareholders and employees in appropriate proportions to supervise the activities of managers. The board of supervisors enjoys control rights that are defined only vaguely. Furthermore, existing studies agree that boards of supervisors are not the key decision-makers in China's listed firms. They are 'more decorative than functional' and do not exert any real control over managers (Tenev, Zhang and Brefort, 2002, p. 100). Therefore, we do not treat boards of supervisors as controlling parties in this study.

3   There are four major types of share in China's listed companies: state shares, legal person shares, A-shares and B-shares. State shares are held mainly by state asset management agencies or SOEs. Legal person shares are held by domestic institutions or firms. While A-shares are held mainly by domestic individual investors, B-shares are held exclusively by foreign investors and are traded against foreign currency. National individual investors, however, have also been allowed to invest in B-shares since February 2001. Foreign investors have been allowed to invest in the A-share market through the Qualified Foreign Institutional Investors' Scheme since 2 December 2002.

4   Bai *et al.* (2000) developed a multitask theory of SOE reform whereby state shareholders are charged not only with the task of ensuring efficient production but also with the task of providing social welfare.

5   The finding that the proportion of legal person shares is positively associated with firm performance does not imply that the control rights of the legal person shareholders are related positively to firm performance. When there is a departure from the rule of one-share-one vote, Claessens *et al.* (1999) offer evidence that concentration of cash-flow rights in the hands of large-block holders is positively associated with corporate valuation, but concentration of these block holders' control rights is negatively associated with corporate valuation.

6   Similar results can be obtained when percentage of shareholding is used.

7   As our sample firms come from different industries, employing an OLS regression may be subject to a heteroscedasticity problem. We conducted a White test which suggests that the null hypothesis of a no heteroscedasticity problem cannot be rejected.

8   One may argue that the positive association between MD and performance reflects the utilization of a greater amount of managerial expertise rather than differences in incentives between managers and controlling parties. It is true that a higher level of MD implies a greater degree of involvement on the part of managers in decision-making and therefore possibly greater use of their professional knowledge. Nevertheless, they would not make productive use of their expertise to improve firm performance if their self-interest was not somehow tied to firm performance.

References

Bai, C.E., D.D. Li, Z.G. Tao and Y.J. Wang (2000), 'A Multitask Theory of State Enterprise Reform', *Journal of Comparative Economics*, 28 (4), 716–38.

Baumol, W.J. (1959), *Business Behaviour, Value and Growth*, New York: Macmillan.

Berger, P.G., O. Eli and L.Y. David (1997), 'Managerial Entrenchment and Capital Structure Decisions', *Journal of Finance*, 52 (4), 1411–38.

Berglof, E. (1995), 'Corporate Governance in Transition Economies: The Theory and its Policy Implications', in M. Aoki and H.K. Kim (eds), *Corporate Governance in Transitional Economies: Insider Control and the Role of Banks*, Washington, DC: The International Bank for Reconstruction and Development.

Berle, A.A. and G.C. Means (1932), *The Modern Corporation and Private Property*, New York: Macmillan.

Boycko, M., A. Shleifer and R.W. Vishny (1996), 'A Theory of Privatisation', *Economic Journal*. 106 (435), 309–19.

Brada, J.C. and I. Singh (1999), *Corporate Governance in Central and Eastern Europe: Case Studies of Firms in Transition*, New York: M.E. Sharpe.

Chang, Eric and S.M.L. Wong (2005), 'Chief Executive Officer Turnover and Performance of China's Listed Enterprises', *Working paper*, University of Hong Kong.

Chen, C.W. and J.W. Wang (2005), 'A Comparison of Shareholder Identity and Corporate Governance Mechanisms in the Monitoring of Listed Companies in China', *Working paper*, School of Business and Management, Hong Kong University of Science and Technology.

Claessens, S., S. Djankov, J. Fan and L. Lang (1999), 'Expropriation of Minority Shareholders: Evidence from East Asia', *The World Bank Policy Research Working Paper*, No. 2088, Washington, DC: The World Bank.

Demsetz, H. and K. Lehn (1985), 'The Structure of Corporate Ownership: Causes and Consequences', *Journal of Political Economy*, 93, 1155–77.

Denis, D.J., D.K. Denis and A. Sarin (1997), 'Agency Problems, Equity Ownership and Corporate Diversification', *Journal of Finance*, 52 (1), 135–60.

Denis, D.J. and T.A. Kruse (2000), 'Managerial Discipline and Corporate Restructuring Following Performance Declines', *Journal of Financial Economics*, 55 (3), 391–424.

Fama, E.F. (1980), 'Agency Problems and the Theory of the Firm', *Journal of Political Economy*, 88 (2), 288–307.

Fama, E.F. and K.R. French (1995), 'Size and Book-to-market Factors in Earnings and Returns', *Journal of Finance*, 50 (1), 131–55.

Fama, E.F. and M.C. Jensen (1983a), 'Separation of Ownership and Control', *Journal of Law and Economics*, 26 (2), 301–26.

Fama, E.F. and M.C. Jensen (1983b), 'Agency Problems and Residual Claims', *Journal of Law and Economics*, 26 (2), 327–49.

Groves, T., Y. Hong, J. McMillan and B. Naughton (1995), 'China's Evolving Managerial Labor Market', *Journal of Political Economy*, 103 (4), 873–92.

Hambrick, D.C. and E. Abrahamson (1995), 'Assessing Managerial Discretion across Industries: A Multi-method Approach', *Academy of Management Journal*, 38 (5), 1427–41.

Hambrick, D.C. and S. Finkelstein (1987), 'Managerial Discretion: A Bridge between Polar Views of Organizational Outcomes', in B.M. Staw and L.L. Cummings (eds), *Research in Organizational Behavior*, Greenwich, CT: JAL, 369–406.

Hellman, J.S. and M. Schankerman (2000), 'Intervention, Corruption and Capture: The Nexus between Enterprises and the State', *Economics of Transition*, 8 (3), 545–76.

Jensen, M.C. (1986), 'Agency Costs of Free Cash Flow, Corporate Finance, and Takeovers', *American Economic Review*, 76 (2), 323–39.

Jensen, M.C. and W.H. Meckling (1976), 'Theory and the Firm: Managerial Behavior, Agency Costs and Ownership Structure', *Journal of Financial Economics*, 3 (4), 305–60.

Jensen, M.C. and R.S. Ruback (1983), 'The Market for Corporate Control: The Scientific Evidence', *Journal of Financial Economics*, 11 (1), 5–50.

McGregor, R. (2001), 'The Little Red Book of Business in China', *Financial Times*, 2 July 2001.

Morck, R., A. Shleifer and R.W. Vishny (1988), 'Management Ownership and Market Valuation: An Empirical Analysis', *Journal of Financial Economics*, 20 (1/2), 293–315.

Opper, S., S.M.L. Wong and R. Hu (2001), 'The Power Structure in China's Listed Companies: The Company Law and its Enforcement', Hong Kong Institute of Economics and Business Strategy Working Paper, No. 1039, Hong Kong: The University of Hong Kong.

Opper, S., S.M.L. Wong and R. Hu (2002), 'Party Power, Market and Private Power: Evidence on Chinese Communist Party Persistence in China's Listed Companies', *Research in Social Stratification and Mobility (The Future of Market Transition)*, 19, 105–38.

Palmer, J.P. (1973), 'The Profit-performance Effects of the Separation of Ownership from Control in Large U.S. Industrial Corporations', *Bell Journal of Economic and Management Science*, 4 (1), 293–303.

Qi, D., W. Woody and Z. Hu (2000), 'Shareholding Structure and Corporate Performance of Partially Privatized Firms: Evidence from Listed Chinese Companies', *Pacific-Basin Financial Journal*, 8 (2), 587–610.

Qian, Y. (1995), 'Reforming Corporate Governance and Finance in China', in M. Aoki and H.K. Kim (eds), *Corporate Governance in Transitional Economies: Insider Control and the Role of Banks*, Washington, DC: The International Bank for Reconstruction and Development.

Shanghai Stock Exchange (2000), *The Corporate Governance of China's Listed Firms*, Shanghai: Shanghai Stock Exchange.

Shleifer, A. and R.W. Vishny (1994), 'Politicians and Firms', *Quarterly Journal of Economics*, 109 (4), 737–83.

Shleifer, A. and R.W. Vishny (1998), *The Grabbing Hand: Government Pathologies and their Cures*, Cambridge, MA: Harvard University Press.

Stiglitz, J.E. (1985), 'Credit Markets as a Control Mechanism', *Journal of Money, Credit and Banking*, 17 (2), 133–52.

Tam, O.K. (1999), *The Development of Corporate Governance in China*, Northampton, MA: Edward Elgar.

Tenev, S., C. Zhang and L. Brefort (2002), *Corporate Governance and Enterprise Reform in China: Building the Institutions of Modern Market*, Washington, DC: World Bank and the International Finance Corporation.

Wilhelm, K. (2001), 'Casinos by Another Name?', *Far Eastern Economics Review*, 164, 46–7.

Williamson, O. (1963a), *Behavioural Theory of the Firm*, Englewood Cliffs, NJ: Prentice Hall.

Williamson, O. (1963b), 'Managerial Discretion and Business Behavior', *American Economic Review*, 53, 1032–57.

World Bank (1997), *China's Management of Enterprise Assets: The State as Shareholder*, Washington, DC: World Bank.

Xu, X. and Y. Wang (1999), 'Ownership Structure and Corporate Governance in Chinese Stock Companies', *China Economic Review*, 10 (2), 75–98.

You, J. (1998), *China's Enterprise Reform: Changing State–Society Relations after Mao*, London: Routledge.

Y.Y. Kueh (Yak Yeow Kueh) Bibliography

Books and monographs

Was Mao Really Necessary? A Reassessment of the Chairman's Economic Legacy, Cheltenham, UK: Edward Elgar Publishing Ltd. (forthcoming).

China's Economic Reform: A Study with Documents (with Christopher Howe and Robert Ash), London and New York: Routledge Curzon Press, 2003, pp. i–xii and 1–404.

Globalization and Sino-American Economic Relations (in Chinese and English) (ed. with Zheng Weimin, with a contribution by Fred Bergsten), Beijing: Social Science Documentary Press, 2001, pp. i–v and 1–456.

Sustainable Economic Development in South China (ed. with Samuel P.S. Ho), London: MacMillan Press , and New York: St Martin's Press, January 2000, pp. i–xvi and 1–274.

Industrial Reform and Macroeconomic Instability in China (ed. with Joseph C.H. Chai and Gang Fan), Oxford: Oxford University (the Clarendon) Press, 1999, pp. i–x and 1–325.

China and the Asia Pacific Economy (ed. with Joseph C.H. Chai and Clem Tisdell), New York: Nova Science Publishers, 1997, pp. i–xx and 1–327.

The Political Economy of Sino-American Relations: A Greater China Perspective (ed.), Hong Kong: The University of Hong Kong Press, 1997, pp. i–ix and 1–299.

China Review 1997 (ed. with H.C. Kuan and M. Brosseau), Hong Kong: The Chinese University Press, 1997, pp. i–xxxii and 1–398.

The Chinese Economy under Deng Xiaoping (ed. with Robert Ash), Oxford Clarendon Press, 1996 (reprinted 1997), pp. i–viii and 1–288 (Updated version of *The Chinese Economy in the 1990s* co-edited with Robert Ash as a special issue for *The China Quarterly*, No.131, September 1992).

Agricultural Instability in China, 1931–1991: Weather, Technology, and Institutions, Oxford Clarendon Press, 1995, pp. i–xxv and 1–387. (reprinted 2002).

Economic Trends in Chinese Agriculture: The Impact of Post-Mao Reforms (ed. with Robert Ash), Oxford Clarendon Press, 1993, pp. i–xii and 1–405 (Updated version of *Food and Agriculture in China during the Post-Mao Era* co-edited with Kenneth R. Walker as a special issue for *The China Quarterly*, No. 116, December 1988).

Economic Planning and Local Mobilization in Post-Mao China, London: Contemporary China Institute, School of Oriental and African Studies, 1985, pp. i–xii and 1–57.

Foodgrain Production Instability in China and the World Grain Trade, Hong Kong: Institute of Social Studies, The Chinese University of Hong Kong, 1985, pp. i–vi and 1–65.

Local Level Planning in China, Geneva: International Labour Organization, 1982, pp. i–v and 1–85.

Articles and book chapters

'Mao and Agriculture in China's Industrialization: Three Antitheses in a Fifty-year Perspective, *The China Quarterly*, 2006 (forthcoming).

'China's New Industries and the East Asian Production Networks', in Ponciano S. Intal and Michael Angelo Cortez (eds), *Meeting the Challenges of Globalization: Production Networks, Industrial Adjustments, Institutions and Policies, and Regional Cooperation*, Manila: Cover and Pages Corporation, published for the International Development Research Center (Canada) and the Angelo King Institute for Economic and Business Studies, De La Salle University, Manila, 2006, pp. 1–73.

'The Full Convertibility of Renminbi: Sequencing and Influence', (with Shucheng Liu, Zhijun Zhao, Yue Ma, Mathew S. Yiu, and Shu-ki Tsang), in Shucheng Liu, Zhijun Zhao, and Yue Ma (eds), *Financial Opening and Macroeconomic Stability in China*, Beijing: Social Sciences Documentation Publishing House, August 2004, pp. 64–132 (reprinted from Hong Kong Institute of Monetary Research Working Paper No. 9/2002, April 2002).

'Banking Deregulation and Macroeconomic Impact in China: A Theoretical Analysis and Implications of WTO Accession for the Mainland and Hong Kong' (with Zhijun Zhao, Yue Ma, Shu-ki Tsang, Mathew S. Yiu, and Shucheng Liu), in Shucheng Liu, Zhijun Zhao, and Yue Ma (eds), *Financial Opening and Macroeconomic Stability in China*, op. cit. pp. 1–63 (reprinted from Hong Kong Institute of Monetary Research Working Paper No. 8/2002, April 2002).

'The Interplay of the "China Factor" and US Dollar Peg in the Hong Kong Economy' (with Raymond Ng), *The China Quarterly*, No. 170, June 2002, pp. 105–30.

'Coping with Globalization in China: Strategic Implications of WTO Accession', *Journal of World Investment*, Vol. 3, No. 1, February 2002, pp. 37–64.

'The Greater China Growth Triangle in the Asian Financial Crisis', in Shahid Jusuf, Simon Evenett, and Weiping Wu (eds), *Facets of Globalization: International and Local Dimensions of Development*, Washington, DC: The World Bank, 2001, pp. 57–77.

'Country of Origin, China's Value-Added Exports and Sino-US Trade Balance Reconciliation', (with Thomas J. Voon), *Journal of World Trade*, Vol. 34, No. 5, October 2000, pp. 123–36.

'Weathering the Asian Financial Storm in Hong Kong', in James C. Hsiung (ed.), *Hong Kong: the Super Paradox: Life After Return to China*, New York: St Martin's Press, 2000, pp. 235–64.

'Financial Restructuring for Economic Recovery in China and Hong Kong', in Fu-chen Lo and T. Palanivel (eds), *Financial Restructuring and Economic Perspectives in East Asia*, Tokyo: United Nations University Institute of Advanced Studies, 2000, pp. 127–44.

'Foreign Investment and Economic Change in China', in Joseph C.H. Chai (ed.), *The Economic Development of Modern China*, (Vol. III, Reforms and Opening Up Since 1979), Cheltenham: Edward Elgar Publishing), 2000, pp. 445–89 (reprinted from *The China Quarterly*, No. 132, September 1992).

'Economic Reform in Chinese Industry: Efficiency and Instability', in Kueh, Chai, and Fan (eds), *Industrial Reform and Macroeconomic Instability in China*, op. cit. pp. 3–20.

'Measuring the Changing Degree of Enterprise Autonomy and Constraints' (with Shuguang Zhang), ibid. pp. 46–86.

'Investment Financing and the Profitability Criterion', ibid. pp. 121–46.

'Prospects for a Transition to a Market Economy without Runaway Inflation', ibid. pp. 263–91.

'China and the Prospects for Economic Integration within APEC', in Chai, Kueh, and Tisdell (eds), *China and the Asia Pacific Economy*, op. cit. pp. 29–47.

'The Role of Hong Kong in Sino-American Economic Relations' (with Thomas Voon), in Kueh (ed.), *The Political Economy of Sino-American Relations*, op. cit. pp. 61–92.

'The Fifth Dragon: Economic Development' (with Robert Ash), in Brian Hook (ed.), *Guangdong: China's Promised Land*, Hong Kong: Oxford University Press, 1996, pp. 149–92.

'Industrial Deregulation and Economic Consequences for China: A GATT Perspective', in Dieter Cassel and Carsten Hermann-Pillath (eds), *The East, the West, and China's Growth: Challenge and Response*, Baden-Baden: Nomos Verlagsgesellschaft, 1995, pp. 309–34.

'Economic Integration within Greater China: Trade and Investment Flows between Hong Kong, Mainland China and Taiwan' (with Robert Ash), in David Shambaugh (ed.), *Greater China: The Next Superpower?* Oxford Clarendon Press, 1995, pp. 59–93 (reprinted from *The China Quarterly*, No. 136, December 1993).

'Whither Hong Kong in the Open-Door, Reforming Chinese Economy' (with Yin-ping Ho), in John Ravenhill (ed.), *The Political Economy of East Asia*, Cheltenham: Edward Elgar Publishing, 1995, pp.598–616 (reprinted from *The Pacific Review*, Vol. 6, No. 4, December 1993).

'The State of the Economy and Economic Reform', in Kuan Hsin-chi and Maurice Brosseau (eds), *China Review*, Hong Kong: The Chinese University Press, 1991, pp. 10: 1–25.

'Growth Imperatives, Economic Recentralization, and China's Open-Door Policy', *Australian Journal of Chinese Affairs* (renamed *China Journal*), No. 24, July 1990, pp. 93–119.

'China's Economic Reforms: Approach, Vision and Constraints', in Dieter Cassel (ed.), *Wirtschaftssysteme im Umbruch: Sowjetunion, China und industrialisierte Marktwirtschaften zwischen internationalem Anpassungszwang und nationalem Reformbedarf*, Munich: Verlag Franz Vahlen, 1990, pp. 255–75.

'Market-Oriented Transformation of China's Economic System as a Development Strategy' (with Zhao Renwei), in Dieter Cassel and Guenter Heiduk (eds), *China's Contemporary Economic Reforms as Development Strategy*, Baden-Baden: Nomos Verlagsgesellschaft, 1989, pp. 13–36.

'Bureaucratization and Economic Reform in Chinese Industry', in Wolfgang Klenner (ed.), *Trends of Economic Development in East Asia*, Heidelberg: Springer Verlag Berlin, 1989, pp. 381–92.

'The Maoist Legacy and China's New Industrialization Strategy', *The China Quarterly*, No. 119, December 1989, pp. 420–47.

'Where Will China Go From Here?' (Professorial Inaugural Lecture, Macquarie University, 28 August 1989), *The Australian Quarterly*, Spring 1989, pp. 358–69.

'Food Consumption and Peasant Incomes in Post-Mao Era', *The China Quarterly*, No. 116, December 1988, pp. 634–70.

'Weather Cycles and Agricultural Instability in China', *Journal of Agricultural Economics*, Vol. 37, No. 1, 1986, pp.101–4.

'Technology and Agricultural Development in China: Regional Spread and Inequality', *Development and Change*, Vol. 16, No. 14, October 1985, pp. 547–70.

'The Economics of the "Second Land Reform" in China', *The China Quarterly*, No. 101, March 1985, pp. 122–31.

'Economic Decentralization and Foreign Trade Expansion in China', in Joseph C.H. Chai and Chi-keung Leung (eds), *China's Economic Reforms*, Hong Kong: Centre for Asia Studies, Hong Kong University, 1985, pp. 444–81.

'China's New Agricultural-Policy Program: Major Economic Consequences, 1979–1983', *Journal of Comparative Economics*, Vol. 8, No. 4, December 1984, pp. 353–75.

'China's International Trade: Policy and Organizational Change and Their Place in the 'Economic Readjustment' (with Christopher Howe), *The China Quarterly*, No.100, December 1984, pp. 813–48.

'China's Food Balance and the World Grain Trade: Projection for 1985, 1990, and 2000', *Asian Survey*, Vol. 24, No. 12, December 1984, pp.1247–74.

'A Weather Index for Analyzing Grain Yield Instability in China, 1952–1981', *The China Quarterly*, No. 97, March 1984, pp.68–83.

'Population Growth and Economic Development in China', in Hermann Schubnell (ed.), *Population Policies in Asian Countries: Contemporary Targets, Measures, and Effects*, Hong Kong: Centre for Asian Studies, Hong Kong University, 1984, pp. 444–60.

'Fertilizer Supplies and Foodgrain Production in China, 1952–1982', *Food Policy*, Vol. 9, No. 3, 1984, pp. 219–31.

'China's Foodgrain Production, Consumption and Trade', *Rivista Internationale di Scienze Economiche e Commerciali* (International Review of Economics and Business), Vol. 31, No.9, September 1984, pp. 910–26.

'Weather, Technology, and Peasant Organization as Factors in China's Foodgrain Production, 1952–1981', *Economic Bulletin for Asia and the Pacific*, United Nations, Vol. 34, No. 1, June 1983, pp. 15–26.

'Economic Reform in China at the Xian Level', *The China Quarterly*, No. 96, December 1983, pp. 665–88.

Name Index

Notes: b = box; f = figure; n = note; t = table; **bold** = extended discussion or heading emphasized in main text.

Abe, S.   82, 85
Amiti, M.   47n, 62–3(n5), 63
Anderson, R.C.   347(n5), 347
Andres, P. de   347(n1), 347
Arize, A.C.   87, 99
Armington, P.S.   37, 63
Ash, R.   ii, xi, 4, 188, 198, 200n, 371–3
Ashenfelter, O.   191, 198
Azofra, V.   347(n1), 347

Bacchetta, P.   87, 99
Bai, C.E., *et al.* (2000)   368(n4), 368
   Li, D.D.   368
   Tao, Z.G.   368
   Wang, Y.J.   368
Barkoulas, J.T.   88, 89, 99
Barro, R.   117(n4)
Batteses, G.E.   255, 256, 268
Baum, C.F.   88, 89, 99
Becker, G.   198
Bennett, D., *et al.* (2000)   246, 252(n5), 253
   Liu, X.   253
   Parker, D.   253
   Steward, F.   253
   Vaidya, K.   253
Berger, P.G., *et al.* (1997)   350, 355, 369
   David, L.Y.   369
   Eli, O.   369
Berger, S.   236(n2), 237
Berglof, E.   363, 369
Bergsten, F.   371
Berle, A.A.   350, 369
Bhagat, S.   347(n3), 348
Bird, G.   102, 118
Black, B.   347(n3), 348
Blalock, G.   244, 253
Bleaney, M.   88, 96, 99
Bohara, A.K.   87, 100
Boisot, M.H.   226, 237(n9), 238
Borjas, G.   198
Boycko, M.   351, 363, 369
Brada, J.C.   363–4, 369
Brefort, L.   340, 347(n5), 349, 368(n1), 370

Brosseau, M.   371, 373
Brown, L.   2, 313(n9–10), 316

Caglayan, M.   88, 89, 99
Cassel, D.   373
Chai, J.C.H.   xi, 9, 317, 318, 322, 326, 371, 372, 373
Chan Hsiu-Yi   63(n12), 63
Chang, E.C.   xi, 10, 353, 369
Chang, M.   237(n12)
Chang Chun-Yen   237(n19), 238
Chen, C.W.   353, 369
Chen, E.K.Y.   203, 217
Chen, J.   347(n5), 348
Chen Liang-yu   12(n8)
Chen Shi-yi   273n
Chen Tain-Jy   82, 85
Chen Yu   xi, 8–9
Cheong, I.   82, 85
Cheung, K.Y.   243–4, 253
Cheung Kui-yin   xi, 3, 187, 198(n1), 199
Chiang, A.C.   207, 217
Chou, W.L.   87, 92, 93, 99–100, 203, 217
Chu, M.C.   252(n2), 253
Chu Chia-Shang, J.   173, 176, 177, 181, 185
Chuang, Y.C.   244, 253
Chung, K.H.   347(n5), 348
Cini, F.   147(n1), 149
Claessens, S., *et al.* (1999)   368(n5), 369
   Djankov, S.   369
   Fan, J.   369
   Lang, I.   369
Coats. W.L., Jr   104, 118
Coelli, T.J.   255, 256, 268(n3), 268
Cortez, M.A.   371
Cushman, D.O.   87, 100
Cyhn, J.W.   237(n24)   238

Dahya, J.   347(n2), 349
Darby, J., *et al.* (1999)   87, 92, 96–7, 99(n2, n4, n6), 100

Darby *et al. continued*
  Hallett, A.H.   100
  Ireland, J.   100
  Piscitelli, L.,   100
David, L.Y.   369
Davidson, W.N.   337, 348
Dellas, H.   100
Demsetz, H.   355, 369
Deng Xiaoping   101, 352, 371
  tour of southern China (1992)   152,
    156, 161, 171, 259
Denis, D.J.   350, 355, 369
Denis, D.K.   350, 355, 369
Djankov, S.   369
Dufey, G.   121, 149
Duffy, J.   42, 43n, 48n, 63

Edwards, J.S.   347(n1), 348
Edwards, S.   100
Ees, H. van   331, 334, 347(n1), 348
Eli, O.   369
Engel, C.   171, 185
Enright, M.   141, 149
Eucken, W.   viii
Evenett, S.   372

Fan, C.S.   xii, 3, 5, 171, 185, 187, 198(n1),
    199
Fan, J.   369
Fan, K.   182, 184(n1), 185
Fan Gang   371, 372
Färe, R., *et al.* (1994)   256, 257, 268
  Grosskopf, S.   268
  Norris, M.   268
  Zhang, Z.   268
Felipe, J.   295(n1), 296
Ferdinand, P.   ii
Fielding, D.   88, 99
Fischer, S.   66
Fisher, I.   7, 103, 104, 118
Frankel, J.   46n, 63, 258, 268

Gagnon, J.E.   87, 100
Gale, F.   315(n32), 316(n38), 316
Gali, J.   203, 217
Gertler, P.   244, 253
Giddy, I.H.   121, 149
Goh Chok Tong   65–6
Graziano, C.   331, 347(n1), 348
Greenaway, D.   96, 99
Greene, W.H.   92, 100
Grosskopf, S.   255, 268

Groves, T., *et al.* (1995)   351, 353, 369
  Hong, Y.   369
  McMillan, J.   369
  Naughton, B.   369
Guillaumont, P.   258, 268

Ha Jiming   182, 184(n1), 185
Hallett, A.H.   100
Ham, J.   191, 198
Heffernan, S.   148(n17), 149
Heiduk, G.   373
Hermalin, B.   347(n3–4), 348
Hermann-Pillath, C.   373
Hewson, J.R.   122, 149
Hicks, Sir John   154, 168
Hinke, L.E.   92, 99(n8), 100
Ho, S.P.S.   371
Ho, Y.K.   123, 149
Ho Lok-Sang   ii, xii, 7, 11, 12(n7), 102,
    104, 117(n2), 118, 200n, 203, 217,
    297n
Ho Yin-ping   373
Holbig, H.   ii
Hong, Y.   369
Hook, B.   ii, 372
Howe, C.   ii, xii, 9, 371, 373
Hsiung, J.C.   372
Hsu, P.F.   244, 253
Hu, A.   244, 253
Hu, R.   352, 368(n1), 370
Hu, T.   318, 326
Hu, Z.   359–60, 361, 370
Hu Wei, H.   xii, 10, 347(n6)
Hui, G.W.L.   123, 130, 149
Husserl, E.   viii

Intal, P.S.   371
Ireland, J.   100

Jackson, S.   xi
Jao, Y.C.   xii, 6, 123, 132, 136, 146,
    147, 148(n14), **149–50**, 203, 217
Javorcik, B.S.   244, 253
Jefferson, G.   244, 253, 290, 291n, 296
Jiang, P.   289, 296
Jiang, X.   251, 253
Johansen, S.   194, 199, 207, 208–9, 217
Johns, R.A.   121, 122, 150
Jones, J.   123, 150
Juselius, K.   194, 199
Just, R.E.   98(n1), 100

Kanas, A.   217
Kawai, M.   102, 118
Kawakami, M.   237(n13, n22), 238
Keller, W.W.   237(n21), 238
Keynes, J.M. (Lord Keynes)   26
Kim, J.   274, 296
Klein, L.   203
Klenner, W.   373
Knight, F.   98(n1), 100
Koray, F.   87, 100
Kosaka, H.   102, 118
Kraar, L.   12(n5)
Krause, L.   101n
Krugman, P.   8, 187, 199, 295(n1), 296
Kuan Hsin-chi   371, 373
Kueh Yak-Yeow   ii, 188, 198, 203, 217, 316
   bibliography   **371–4**
   impact of weather on agriculture 313(n5)
   pressed to continue research   x
   students   viii, x
   tributes   **viii–ix**, **x**, 121, 200n, 297n

Laird, S.   320, 326
Lall, S.   252(n3), 253
Lang, I.   369
Lang, L.H.P.   347(n5), 348
Lastrapes, W.D.   87, 100
Lau, L.   274, 296
Laurenceson, J.   xi
Leamer, E.E.   186, 199
Lee, C.I.   337, 348
Lee, J.   87, 100
Lehn, K.   355, 369
Lester, R.K.   237(n2–3), 237, 238
Leung Chi-keung   373
Levin, A.   173, 176, 177, 181, 185
Li, D.D.   368
Li, K.T.   237(n12)
Li, S.   320, 321n, 322, 325, 326
Li Guangzhong   xii, 7
Li Na   xii, 5
Lin, P.   xiii, 8–9, 101n, 243–4, 253
Lin, T.B.   203, 217
Lin, Z.   347(n2), 349
Lin Chien-Fu   173, 176, 177, 181, 185
Lindenberg, E.B.   347(n5), 348
Litzenberger, R.H.   347(n5), 348
Liu, X.   253
Liu, Z.   289, 296

Liu, Z.M.   244, 253
Liu Mingkang   128, 148(n7)
Liu Shucheng   372
Lo Fu-chen   372
Lohmar, B.   315(n22), 316
Long, G.Q.   242, 253
Lopez, F.   347(n1), 347
Lu, A.   236
Lucas, R.   168
   'externality of human capital'   155
Luken, R.A.   318, 326
Luporini, A.   331, 347(n1), 348

Ma Yue   xiii, 8, 101n, 202, 203, 209, 217, 218, 372
Maassen, G.F.   347(n1), 349
MacKinnon, J.G.   194, 199
Mahathir bin Mohamed, *Datuk* (later *Tun*) Dr   70
Malthus, T.R.   297, 313(n1)
Mao Zedong   viii, 1, 371, 373
Mathews, J.A.   237(n21), 238
McCallum, B.   101n
McKibbin, W.J.   79, 84, 84–5(n1), 85
McMillan, J.   369
Means, G.C.   350, 369
Meredith, G.   203, 217
Meyer, D.R.   123, 124, 150
Miller, M.   107, 118
Montiel, P.J.   92, 99(n8), 100
Moran, T.   252(n3), 253
Morck, R.   355, 370
Mundell, R.   117(n4)

Naughton, B.   369
Ng, F.   237(n6), 238
Ng, R.C.W.   xiii, 8, 203, 217, 372
Ng, W.   279, 295(n3–5, n8), 296(n9), 296
Ng Yew-Kwang   ii
Norris, M.   268

Okabe, M.   70, 85
Opper, S.   352, 368(n1), 370

Palanivel, T.   372
Palmer, J.P.   350, 370
Papageorgiou, C.   42, 43n, 48n, 63
Parker, D.   253
Parsley, D.   171, 181, 182, 185
Pauly, L.W.   237(n21), 238
Perkins, D.H.   81, 85

Piore, M.J.   237(n3), 238
Piscitelli, L.   100
Poon Shuk-Ching, T.   237(n23), 238
Porter, R.   ii
Postma, T.J.B.M.   331, 334, 347(n1),
    348
Pruitt, S.W.   347(n5), 348

Qi, D.   339, 349, 359–60, 361, 370
Qin, D.   289, 296
Qin, Julia Ya   67, 85

Rajan, R.   102, 118
Ramey, V.A.   198
Ran, J.   xiii, 7
Rangan, N.   337, 348
Rao, D.S.P.   255, 256, 268
Ravenhill, J.   373
Rawski, T.   290, 291n, 296
Rawski, T.G.   268(n5), 269
Reagan, R.W.   20
Reeb, D.M.   347(n5), 347
Reed, H.C.   123, 150
Richardson, J.D.   187, 199
Roberts, R.   121–2, 150
Rodriguez-Clare, A.   243, 253
Rogers, J.   171, 185, 203, 218
Romer, D.   258, 268
Rosen, S.   191, 199
Rosenstein, S.   337, 347(n3), 348, 349
Ross, S.A.   347(n5), 348

Sachs, J.D.   84, 85(n1), 85
Saggi, K.   243, 253
Samuelson, P.   19
Sarin, A.   350, 355, 369
Sauer, C.   87, 100
Saygili, M.   xiii, 3
Schenk, C.R.   123–4, 150–1
Schubnell, H.   374
Schuler, K.   105, 109, 117(n4), 118
Schumpeter, J.A.   223, 237(n5), 238
Sekkat, K.   96, 100
Servén, L.   87, 100
Shahid Jusuf   372
Shambaugh, D.   373
Shih, S.   225, 234, 235, 238
Shih, Y.C.   92, 93, 100
Shiller, R.   101n
Shin, K.   87, 100
Shleifer, A.   351, 355, 363, 369, 370

Singh, I.   363–4, 369
Siregar, R.Y.   203, 218
Smith, R.W.   237(n3), 238
Snow, J.   99(n10)
Song, H.   289, 296
Soros, G.   26, 103
Sterken, E.   331, 334, 347(n1), 348
Steward, F.   253
Stickney, C.P.   347(n5), 349
Stiglitz, J.E.   vii, xiii, 1, 2–3, 10, 11
    lecture at Chinese University of Hong
        Kong (16 March 2005)   vii, 17n,
        101, 106, 117(n1)
Su Ning   13(n10)
Suen, W.   191, 199
Sun, Q.   339, 349
Sun, X.   289, 296
Sung Yun-Wing   xii, 5, 154, 155, 159,
    161, 163, 168(n1), 169

Tam On-Kit   xiv, 10, 331, 340, 347,
    347(n6), 349, 370
Tang Shu-hung   203, 217
Tang Wing-Hin   200n
Tao, Z.G.   368
Taylor, A.   182, 185
Teece, D.J.   237(n25), 238
Tenev, S.   340, 347(n5), 349, 368(n1),
    370
Tisdell, C.A.   xi, 371, 372
Toh, M.   279, 295(n3–5, n8), 296(n9),
    296
Tong, J.   339, 349
Tong, W.H.S.   339, 349
Townsend, R.M.   153, 169
Tsang, J.   6
Tsang Shu-ki   202, 203, 209, 217, 218,
    372
Tuan, F., *et al.* (2004)   315(n31, n33,
    n36), 316
Tung Chee-Hwa   188

Vafeas, N.   334, 349
Vaidya, K.   253
Van den Bosch, F.A.   347(n1), 349
van der Tak, C.   318, 326
Varela, O.   347(n5), 349
Varoudakis, A.   96, 100
Vishny, R.W.   351, 355, 363, 369, 370
Voon, J.P.   xiv, 7
Voon, T.J.   372

Walker, K.R. 371
Walker, W.C. 203, 218
Wan, H. 101n
Wan Zhongxin 318, 326
Wang, J.W. 353, 369
Wang, Y. 330, 340, 349, 359–60, 361, 370
Wang, Y.J. 368
Wang Yuzhao 12(n3)
Wanghua, Y. 318, 326
Wei, Z. 347(n5), 349
Wei Shang-jin 171, 181, 182, 185, 258, 269
Wei Xiangdong xiv, 171, 185
Weichenrieder, A.J. 347(n1), 348
Weil, R.L. 347(n5), 349
Weisbach, M.S. 347(n3–4), 348
White, H. xi
Whittaker, D.H. 237(n11), 238
Wilcoxen, P. 84(n1), 85
Williamson, J. 101n, 107, 118
Williamson, O. 350, 355, 370
Wincoop, E.V. 87, 99
Wong, G. 12(n7), 203, 217
Wong, S.M.L. xiv, 10, 352, 353, 368(n1), 369, 370
Wong Kar-Yiu xiv, 3, 33, 62(n3, n5), 63(n12), 63, 64
Woo Wing-Thye xiv, 2–3, 74, 79, 81, 84, 85
Wood, A. 186, 198(n2), 199
Woody, W. 359–60, 361, 370
Wu, W. 339, 349

Wu Weiping 372
Wyatt, J. 347(n3), 349

Xiao, J.Z. 347(n2), 349
Xu, X.N. 330, 340, 349, 359–60, 361, 370

Yamamura, K. 154, 169
Yano, T. 102, 118
Yeats, Alexander 237(n6), 238, 320, 326
Yeh, J. 142, 151
Yiu, M.S. 203, 217, 372
You, J. 370
Young, A. 8, 274, 289, 295(n1), 296
Yu Po-Lung 237(n19), 238
Yue-Sai 250
Yuen Chi-Wa ii
Yusof Zainal Aznam 81 86

Zhai, F. 320, 321n, 322, 325, 326
Zhang, C. 340, 347(n5), 349, 368(n1), 370
Zhang, H. 339, 349
Zhang, Z. 87, 100
Zhang Jun xiv, 8, 273, 289, 294, 296
Zhang Shuguang 318, 326, 372
Zhang Yansheng 318, 326
Zhao Zhijun 372
Zheng, Y. 290, 291n, 296
Zheng He 1
Zheng Weimin 371
Zilberfarb, B. 100

Subject Index

Notes: b = box; f = figure; n = note; t = table; **bold** = extended discussion or heading emphasized in main text.

'abuse of dominant position'
(MNCs) **250–1**, 252(n8)
abuse of market power 240
Academica Sinica 228, 229f, 229t
accountability 111
Africa 27
African Development Bank 143n
agency problems 353
agency theory 339, 350, 361
agglomeration 155, 156
agglomeration economies 154, 164
aggregate demand 107–8, 116, 204–5, 215
Agreement on Trade-Related Investment Measures (TRIMs) 245
Agricultural Bank of China 128
agricultural instability (PRC) viii
agricultural tax 301, 313(n8)
agricultural tax-relief initiative (2004) 4
agricultural trade (liberalization) 320
agricultural trade (prospects) **297–316**
global significance **298–9**, 313(n9)
PRC 316(n38)
USDA's definition 316(n38)
see also grain trade
agriculture/farming ix, 20–1, 73, 80t, 174, 230t, 242, 295, 299, 314(n12), 356t, 357, 371, 373
CCP policy guidelines (2003, 2004) 300–1, 307, 314(n15)
development (reform era China) **299–301**, 302, 313–14(n11–17)
'foundation of national economy' (Chinese adage) 297n
'give more, take less, give free rein' (*duoyu, shaoqu, fanghuo*) policy 301, 314(n17)
grain: developments past and future (China) **297–316**
impact of weather (Kueh 1995) 313(n5)
'priority policy concern' (PRC) 300–1, 314(n15)
'two reductions' and 'three subsidies' 301
see also farm products; grain
agriculture (including service sector) 62(n4)
two-good, multivariety, three-country model 33, 34, 35, 38, 42, 44n, 46n, 47n, 48–56, 58t, 59–61
agro-industries 313(n8)
agro-processing 313(n8)
aid (to poor countries) 297
AIDS 84
air 318, 322–5
air cargo 154
air transportation 242
aircraft 243
Airport Authority (HKSAR) 142
Akaike Information Criterion (AIC) 94n, 113n, 114n
Anhui 268
animal feed 313(n4), 314(n18)
animal husbandry 299, 300, 314(n12)
annual reports 333, 356, 359
APEC 372
'Apple Clone' boom 234f
arbitrage 202, 205
Argentina 22, 102, 313(n9), 316(n44)
Argentine peso 107
depreciation (2001–2) 103, 109, 110, 117(n4)
'overvaluation' 103, 117(n4)
Armington assumptions 35, 37
Asia Pulse 306n
Asia-Pacific G-cubed (AP-GCUBED) model **73–5**, 84–5(n1)
baseline simulation **74**, 75f, 76–9, 80t
FDI-diversion with technological spillover simulation **72–3**, **74–5**, **77–9**, 79, 80t
'five conditions' 74–5
naive simulation 72, **74**, **75–7**
reduction in risk premium (FDI-diversion) simulation 72, **74**, 76f, **77**, **79**, 80t

Asia-Pacific region   121, 124, 127, 132, 137, 140, 141, 146, 148(n4), 229, 371
Asian bond fund initiative   27
Asian Development Bank   43–4n, 46n, 48n, 143n
Asian Dollar Market (Singapore, 1968–)   124, 138, 148(n15)
Asian Financial Crisis (AFC, 1997–8)   5, 20, 25, 68, 101, 102, 107, 110, 111, 113, 121, 128, 132, 136, 137, 145–7, 156, 161, 203, 215, 221, 372
Asian Miracle   8, 254, 273
Asian Monetary Fund (proposed)   25, 27
asset-stripping   363
assets   73, 85(n1), 116, 126, 127, 353, 359
   financial   73, 103
   fixed   274–6, 287, 290, 291t, 295(n2–3)
   liquid   25
   monetary   110
   net external   138, 139t, 139
   safe   24
   WCU-based   118(n11)
assets and liabilities   22, 106, 137
   external   138, 139t, 139
   foreign financial   136t, 147(n2)
assets under management (AUM)   141
Association of South-East Asian Nations (ASEAN)   33, 62(n2–3)
   'ASEAN-4' (Indonesia, Malaysia, Philippines, Thailand)   66, 68, 71t, 72, 75, **79–82**, 83
   ASEAN Secretariat website   47n, 48n
   doom-and-gloom projection 'not inevitable'   79
   economic impact of China's emergence as major trading nation   **79–82**
   see also China ASEAN FTA
Athens   18
Atomic Energy Council (Taiwan)   229f, 229t
AustraClear   145
Australia   34, 43n, 44–6n, 73, 75, 75f, 76, 77–8f, 104, 133t, 138t, 141, 148(n4, n13)
   stock exchange   135t

Authorized Institutions (AIs)   143t, 143n

backward linkages   243, 244, 252(n3)
Bahama Islands   144t, 148(n13)
balance of payments   126, 138
Balassa–Samuelson effect   92
Bank of China   128
bank deposits   110, 128t
   foreign currency   101
   real value protected   109
Bank of England   123, 125
bank headquarters   147(n2)
Bank for International Settlements (BIS)   25, 121, 135, 136t
   triennial central bank surveys   **132–4**
bank lending   125
bank runs (averted)   109
banking   viii, xiii, xiv, 123, 126–30, **135–8**, 146, 148(n13–16), 149(n21), 163, 189, 203, 216, 356t, 357, 372
   Japanese retrenchment in Hong Kong (1996–2003)   137, 137t
   see also 'international banking'
banking deregulation   372
banking licences   124, 127, 137t, 148(n5)
banknotes   105
bankruptcy   12, 84
banks   5, 21–2, 24, 105, 117(n8), 132, 139
   domestic   22, 122, 126, 127, 138
   foreign   23, 84, 122, 126–7, 138
   foreign   (intensity of activity) 123
   international   22, 147(n1)
   licensed   143n
   multinational (US)   148(n15)
   private   147(n2)
   smaller   128
   soundness   138, 138t
   US   148(n17)
Basel I Accord (1988)   128
Basel II Accord (for 2007)   148(n6)
baseline   *see* Asia-Pacific G-cubed model
Basic Law (HKSAR)   125, 126, 146
Beijing   13(n9), 170, 173, 177–8, 178t, 182, 183, 267
Beijing Second Daily Cosmetic Factory   250b
Belgium   136t, 137

Belgrade   67
Bermuda   144t
Board of Directors (BOD)   329–30, 333,
    347, 352
    meetings   334, 335–6t, 338–40t, 340,
    341–3t
Board of Directors: Chairman   332, 334
    insider/outsider   332t, 333, 335t,
    342–3t, 345, 346
Board of Directors: Secretaries   355
    'similar to managing director'
    357
board independence   330, 331
Bolivia   71t
bonds
    global indexed   106
    HKSAR (2004)   142
    WCU-denominated   104
bond-issuers   111
bonus payments   351, 353
borrowers   118(n11)
    non-MDB overseas   143t
    overseas   142
borrowing   26, 111
'Boss Island' phenomenon   228
brands   225, 226, 234–6, 248,
    249–50b, 250, 252(n7)
    'killing off'   240, 248
'brass-plate centres'   135, 148(n13)
Brazil   21, 27, 30, 102, 148(n13),
    316(n44)
'breakaway' employees   227
'Brunei' (Negara Brunei Darussalam)
    43–4n, 46n, 48n, 148(n4)
Brussels Stock Exchange   134n
budget balance   107f, 108, 109
budget constraints   73
building materials   321t, 323t
Bureau of Export Administration
    (USA)   252(n4)
bureaucracy   164, 364, 373
Bush Administration   (2001–) 20
business [academic discipline]   227t
business cycle   8, 191, 203
business environment   232, 235, 251
business institutional development
    (Taiwan)   233f
business linkages (Taiwan)   233
business networks   227–8
business opportunities   246, 252, 353
business practices/modes   234, 250–1

business services   164, 189, 192, 194–8,
    231
    relative wage rate   193t
business-licensing procedures   240

California   237(n18)
calorie intake   313(n3)
Cambodia   43n, 48n
Canada   34, 43–6n, 66, 93, 94t, 98f,
    104, 133t, 138t, 144t, 171, 297
capacity   *see* technological capacity
capital   1, 3, 10, 17, 32, 125, 130, 164,
    188, 203, 231, 244, 325
    cost   38–9
    domestic   47n, 48n
    effective   36–40, 43n, 47n
    endowed   40
    fixed   267, 268(n2)
    foreign   48n, 49, 156, 245, 248
    free flow   47n
    growth   262f, 262
    international movement   67
    non-Hong Kong   161
    physical   42, 43t, 268(n5)
    rental rate   35, 37, 39, 57, 63(n15)
    two-good, four-factor, three-country
       model (unilateral and regional
       trade liberalization)   34, 47–8n,
       49, 50t, 51, 52
capital: three types   34, 37, 40, 63(n7,
    n9–10)
    capital from ASEAN   35
    capital from PRC   35
    capital from ROW   35
capital adequacy ratio (CAR)   127–8, 137
    definition   48(n6)
capital construction   280–3t, 295(n2–3,
    n7)
capital controls   73, 129
capital deepening   264, 266, 267
capital disparity   19
capital equipment   226
capital flight/outflow   4, 109, 201
capital flows/movements   7, 22, 23, 34,
    35, 54t, 54, 59, 59t, 62, 62(n5), 102
    'costless'   36
    efficiency-enhancing   115
    international   33, 53, 63(n5)
    intra-industry   51, 55t, 55, 60, 60t,
       63(n12, n17)
    short-term   111

capital formation 293
  'fairly constant relative to real
    GDP' 292
  gross fixed 274, 275t
  gross value 274, 275t
capital formation deflator 293
capital funds 135
capital goods 77, 289–2
capital market 40–1, 63(n11), 111,
    116, 163, 223
capital mobility 129, 130, 132, 146
capital stock 43n, 48n, 70
  depreciation rate 267
  domestic 72
  estimation 259, **267**, 268(n2)
  fixed 47n
  marginal productivity 293
capital structure **360**, 360, 362t, 363t
capital use (efficiency) 292–3
capital utilization 266, 267
capital–labour ratio 42, 52, 264, 265t,
    266, 274, 295
carbon dioxide emission 29, 30
carbon sequestration **30**
career development 243
career prospects 354
Caribbean islands 153, 161, 162f,
    162
cars/automobiles 29, 243, 353, 321n,
    325
  'vehicles' 223
caution (buzzword) 10–11
Cayman Islands 148(n13)
Census and Statistics Department (CSD,
    HK/HKSAR) 138, 139, 140, 155,
    165n, 174, 190, 206
Central Asia 1
central banks xiii, 25, 106, 111,
    118(n11), 132
  Philippines 110
  PRC 125
  see also Bank of England; People's
    Bank of China
central government 98–9(n1),
    99(n10), 245, 300
  food security (PRC) 298
Central Moneymarkets Unit
    (CMU) 145
central planning x, 22, 171, 172, 254,
    276, 279
cereal exporters 297

cereal exports 312
cereal flour 315(n30, n34)
  export earnings (PRC) 315–16(n37)
cereal imports 303, 315(n29–30)
cereal output 315(n29)
cereal stocks 304, 315(n21), 315(n29)
cereals 310, 313(n4), 315(n34),
    316(n44)
  export earnings (PRC) 315–16(n37)
  geo-strategic issues **309–12**,
    316(n40–6)
  imports and exports (PRC,
    1985–2004) 305–6t
  net importer (PRC) 304, **312**,
    314(n20)
certificate of service provider 6
CGE models 85(n1), 230
chemicals 280t, 321t, 322, 323t
Chen Yuan
  'seven principles' (1996) **125–6**
Chengdu 67
cheque-clearing 145
Chiang Mai initiative 27
Chief Executive Officer (CEO) 330–2,
    346, 347(n4)
  turnover rate 353
child labour 10
China x–xiv, 69t, 71t, 73, 76–8f, 80t,
    121, 106, 122, 138t, 144t, 145,
    148(n4), 223, 236, 373
  backward regions 26
  cereals (imports and exports,
    1985–2004) 305–6t
  consumption of commodities 2
  domestic market (size) 148(n10)
  economic growth, real income, and
    investment rate
    (1978–2000) 294f
  economy ix, xi
  effect on developing world 3
  emergence as global economic
    giant **–2**
  enthusiasm for WTO
    membership 66–7
  fiscal position 84
  formally became member of WTO
    (11 November 2001) 62(n1)
  Hong Kong as fund-raising
    centre 130
  Hong Kong as OFC for **125–30**,
    131t, 148(n5–11)

China – *continued*
 Hong Kong's largest trading
   partner   170
 integration into global
   economy   **20–3**
 international trade expansion   255
 investment opportunities   66
 low-wage   82
 magnet for FDI   221
 'model and threat'   11
 'more service-oriented economy'
   9
 national income   37, 56, 57
 net exporter of cereals   304
 'net importer of agricultural
   products'   56
 net importer of cereals   304, **312**
 net importer of rice   315(n30)
 'not only producer, but also
   consumer'   53
 potential leader of Asian economic
   bloc   81
 price index of investment in fixed
   assets (1978–2000)   291t
 reliability as supplier   67, 70
 repercussions (international) of rapid
   rise   11
 reserves   26, 27
 responsibilities   31
 science parks   237(n18)
 sources of FDI   72
 stake in HKSAR's banking sector
   (1993–2003)   128t
 strains   31
 sustainable currency regime   **101–18**
 'swap market for technology'
   policy   8
 vendor finance   26
China: effects of RERV and RERM on
   commodity exports   **87–100**
 data and results   93–7
 empirical model   91–3, 99(n7–9)
 existing literature   87, 92, 96
 risk   90
 theoretical model   88–91, 99(n4–6)
China: emergence as major trading
   nation (economic impact)   **65–86**
 China's economic linkages to
   world   67–73
 economic impact on 'ASEAN-4'
   79–82

 economic impact on developed
   economies   82
 gorilla awakes   65–7
 levels of analysis   72–3
 quantifying the impact: AP-GCUBED
   model   73–5, 84–5(n1)
 questions addressed   66
 simulations   75–9
China: grain (developments past and
   future)   **297–316**
 agricultural and rural development
   (reform era)   299–301,
   313–14(n11–17)
 food security, grain and cereal trade,
   and geo-strategic issues   309–12,
   316(n40–6)
 grain output (trends,
   1978–2004)   301–3, 314(n18–19)
 grain trade (China)   303–9,
   314–16(n20–39)
 policy implementation
   'disappointing'   300
 reliance of overseas markets   301
 watershed (2004)   307, 315(n29)
China: Ministry of Agriculture   306n
China: Ministry of
   Commerce   252(n1), 253,
   315(n30)
China: Ministry of Foreign Trade and
   Economic Cooperation   251
China: Ministry of Labour and Social
   Security   314(n12), 316
China: open-door policy (1978/9–)   1,
   101, 126–7, 152–3, 156–7, 170, 172,
   190, 192–3, 198(n4), 240, 242, 259,
   294, 304, 317, 373
 virtue (empirical confirmation)   267
 see also economic reform
China: provinces/regions
 general: 6, 13(n9); impact of trade
   policy on TFP, efficiency and
   technology   **254–69;** TFP
   growth   **259–63, 267–8,**
   268(n1–5)
 geographical location: central
   provinces   260–1, 268; coastal
   provinces   259, 263, 263t, 267,
   299, 302, 310; eastern
   provinces   173, 260–1, 267, 299;
   inland/interior provinces   259,
   265, 267; north-east   316(n41);

northern 173; western provinces 260–2, 268
China: spillover effects of FDI and technology transfer (before and after WTO accession) **239–53**
abuse of dominant position 250–1, 252(n8)
DVD patent royalties (case study) 247–8b, 252(n7)
end of free-riding 246–8
FDI: competition concerns 248–51, 252(n7–8)
FDI: 'dancing with wolf' 248–51, 252(n7–8)
FDI in China: overview 240–2
literature survey 243–4
local brand acquisitions by Unilever and P&G (case study) 249–50b
no more forced technology transfer 245–6
ratio of foreign-invested enterprises' sales to industry total 241t, 241–2
quantifying FDI spillover effects in China 243–4
'swap market for technology' 242–4, 252(n1–3)
WTO membership and technology transfer 245–8, 252(n4–6)
China: WTO accession (2002–) 3, 8, 9, 17, 32–3, 42, 65, 66–7, 68, 77, 83, 84, 127, 152, 156, 166, 172, 173, 298, 307, 309, 372
admission as developed or developing country 317
impact on ASEAN and ROW ('scenario 1') **51–7**, 62, 63(n13–15)
managing China's integration into global economy **20–3**
new geo-politics **20–3**
new opportunities **23**
Sino–US agreement (1999) 161, 245, 317, 320
spillover effects (FDI and technology transfer) **239–53**
China: WTO accession (environmental impact on manufacturing sector) **317–26**
aggregate effect 324t, 324
manufacturing output 321t

China Banking Regulatory Commission (CBRC) 128, 148(n7)
China Construction Bank 128
'China as economic giant' 2
course taught by Y.Y. Kueh 12(n1)
China Electronic Acoustic Equipment Association 247b
China Environment Yearbook (1994) 323n
China factor 203, 372
China and global economy: challenges, opportunities, responsibilities **17–31**
challenge for US and other nations 18–20
environmental concerns and sustainable development 28–30
geopolitics following PRC's accession to WTO 20–3
managing PRC's integration into global economy 20–3
new opportunities 23
positive sum world 17–18
PRC's new role in global leadership 27–8
PRC's role in reforming international reserve system 23–7
re-defining PRC's role in global economy 30–1
strains on US and European economies 19–20
China and globalization **15–118**
China: effects of RERV and RERM on commodity exports **87–100**
China and global economy: challenges, opportunities, responsibilities **17–31**
China's emergence as major trading nation: economic impact **65–86**
China's WTO accession and FTA with ASEAN **32–64**
sustainable currency regime for HKSAR and PRC **101–18**
unilateral and regional trade liberalization **32–64**
China Government Securities Trust and Clearing Company 145
China, Hong Kong, and World Economy x, **1–13**
China and globalization **15–118**

China, Hong Kong, and World
    Economy – *continued*
  corporate governance and firm-level
      performance **10**
  corporate governance and
      management **327–70**
  course taught by Kueh Yak-Yeow
      viii
  distributional issues **2–4**, 12(n2–4)
  economic history (1979
      watershed) 1–2, 12(n1)
  environmental concerns **9–10**,
      13(n13)
  foreign direct investment, technology
      transfer, economic
      restructuring **219–69**
  future **10–12**
  Hong Kong (China's city and global
      city) **119–218**
  Hong Kong (unique and evolving
      roles) **4–6**, 12–13(n5–9)
  Hong Kong dollar and RMB **6–8**,
      13(n10)
  technology, investment,
      efficiency **8–9**, 13(n11–12)
  trade, investment, and implications
      for key economic
      sectors **271–326**
  zero sum versus positive sum **2–4**,
      12(n2–4)
China Poverty Relief Fund 12(n3)
*China Securities and Futures Statistical
    Yearbook 2000* 359
China-Affiliated Corporations Index
    (Red Chips Index) 162–3
China-ASEAN Free-Trade Agreement
    (FTA) 3, 42
  China's enthusiasm 81
  prior to ratification 35
  signed (November 2002) 33
  South-East Asia's welcome 81–2
China's investment pattern in context
    of East Asia **274–89**, 295(n2–8)
  industrial share of GDP 276–9,
      280–3t
  investment in housing
      construction 279, 284–5t,
      286–7, 295(n5)
  investment rates 274–6, 295(n2–3)
  share of public investment 287–9,
      295(n6–8)

structural change (manufacturing
    sector) 276–9, 280–3t
China's trade
  Hong Kong's role **155–60**, 168(n1)
Chinese Communist Party (CCP) 10,
    317
  constitution 352–3
  local party committees 351–8,
      361–4, 365–7t
  local party committees
      (incentives) **352–3**
Chinese Communist Party: Central
    Committee
  agricultural policy (guidelines,
      2003–4) 300–1, 307, 314(n15)
Chinese Customs 174
'Chinese model of development' 2
Chinese University of Hong Kong
  New Asia College x
  seminar (2005) 117(n4)
  Stiglitz lecture (16 March 2005) vii,
      17n, 101, 106, 117(n1)
Chinese wines 174, 175t, 178–81t,
    183–4t
Chongqing 268
CIA Factbook Online 46n
cigarettes 174, 175t, 178–81t, 183–4t
citation indices 225, 235
cities 3–4, 5, 6, 13(n9), 23, 140, 179,
    184(n1), 279, 295(n2), 302
  'urban areas' 172
  'urban discontent' 300
  'urbanization' 299, 313(n11)
civil service rank 353
civil war (PRC) 130
Claremont McKenna College 32n
Clearstream 145
Closer Economics Partnership
    Arrangement (Mainland and Hong
    Kong) 6, 129, 132, 163, 166, 170
clothing/apparel 2, 172, 318, 320, 322
Coca Cola 22
cointegration analysis 94t, 114t, 114,
    117(n9), **193–7**, 198(n5), 217(n1)
  Johansen's procedure 93, 113, 194,
      207, 208–9, 209t
Cold War era 153
collective sector 287, 295(n2)
colonialism/imperialism 232, 235–6,
    317
command economy 152

commercial property   12(n6)
Commercial Radio Hong Kong   6
commodities   18, 35, 52, 59, 106, 172, 177
  domestic prices   61
  non-tradable   175
  primary   66, 79, 81
commodity chain configurations   226
commodity market   172
commodity prices   2, 33, 39, 41, 170, 182
  state-fixed   171
communication costs   155
communications   140, 223
communism   1
companies/firms   34–8, 40, 85(n1), 159, 224t, 226, 227
  best practice   256
  Chinese   171, 173, 239, 244, 246, 248, 252, 347(n5)
  domestic   70, 241, 243, 246, 250, 251, 252
  EU   245, 246
  foreign   45n, 242, 243, 250, 251, 274
  'glass-ceilings'   236
  Hong Kong   162
  Hong Kong (relocation to southern China)   172–3, 188
  import-competing   81
  'incubated' high technology   230–1
  large/r   22, 235
  learning and personal development   227
  listed   xiv, 10, 129, 161–3, **350–70**
  local   266
  Mainland   161, 162, 163
  manufacturing   188, 248b
  non-state   294
  oligopolistic   63(n12)
  overseas registration   161
  private   130, 135, 361
  public (Dutch)   331
  publicly-listed (Malaysia)   81
  share-holding   295(n6), 353
  small   8, 22, 230, 235
  'spin-off'   231
  start-up   230, 231, 232
  survival capability and growth potential   333

Taiwanese   81, 161, 162, 227–8, 230–4, 235, 236
  technical efficiency   256
  wholly foreign-owned   240–1
company employees   330, 331
Company Law (PRC 1993/4)   330, 348, 368(n2)
  (Article 17)   352–3
  (Article 103)   10, 329
company performance   **10**, 329, 330, 346, 347(n5–6)
  data   333
  managerial autonomy and   **350–70**
  supervisory board and (hypothesis 1)   **331,** 339t, 339, 340t, 340, 341t
  varies according to DBDM type (hypothesis 2)   **333,** 341, 343, 346
company size   334, 335–6t, 338–9t, 339, 340–3t, 345t, **359**
  ASSET   359, 362t, 363t
comparative advantage   153, 154, 166, 226, 279, 298, 309, 316(n40), 319, 325
  'comparative disadvantage'   309
competencies   234f, 234
competition   xiii, 22–3, 156, 243, 354, 255
  FDI: 'dancing with wolf'   **248–51,** 252(n7–8)
  incentive for technology transfer   246, 252
  monopolistic   35, 40, 62(n5), 63(n12)
  unfair methods   242–3, 251
competition concerns   240
competition process   240
Competition-Restricting Behaviour of Multinational Companies in China and Countermeasures (SAIC, 2004)   251
competitive pressures   223
competitiveness   33, 53, 82, 148(n16), 172, 189, 202, 259
  global   9
  PRC's exports   67
competitors   226, 233f, 242, 243
'composite good standard'   104
Computer and Communications Laboratory (CCL, Taiwan)   233

conflict of interest   129, 331, 332t
conglomerates   356t, 357
  vertically-integrated   81
constant-returns-to-scale   320
construction   276, 277f, 295(n3–4),
    322, 356t
construction and installation works
    (C&I)   276, 277f, 277, 278t, 290
consumer expectation   **303**, 314(n19)
  rational   89
consumer goods   12, 172
consumer loans   23
consumer price index (CPI)   99(n7),
    105, 111, 174, 204, 206, 209t, 210f
  foreign   92
  variance decomposition   211–15
consumers   35, 37, 56, 63(n14)
consumption   21, 26, 36, 37, 38, 73,
    320, 321t
contacts (formal and informal)   242
contracts
    (multilateral/specialized)   155
controlling shareholder
    ownership/ownership
    concentration   334–47, 350, 361,
    363, 368(n8)
  employees   330, 331
Convertibility Undertaking
    (HKMA)   117(n8)
corporate governance (CG)   xiv, **10**,
    148(n16), 358, 363–4
  supervisory board (Chinese)   **329–49**
  surveys   128–9
corporate governance and
    management   **327–70**
  managerial autonomy and firm
    performance   **350–70**
  supervisory board in Chinese
    corporate governance   **329–49**
corporate social responsibility   12
corporate strategy   330
corporate valuation   368(n5)
corruption   5, 164
cost advantage   189, 246
cost-minimization   256
costs   155, 164, 228, 255
  fixed   154
  marginal   154
cotton   2, 21, 316(n39)
Council of Agriculture (Taiwan)   229f,
    229t

Council of Europe Social Development
    Fund   143n
counterfeiting   244
country characteristics   91, 97
country size   259, 263
Court of Final Appeal
    (HKSAR)   149(n20)
credibility   26, 103, 246
  sustainable currency regime   **110–11**
credit   22
Cronbach's alpha   357
Cultural Revolution (1966–76)   352
cultural and sports products   241t, 242,
    283t
culture and history   224, 224t
currency/currencies   24, 25, 116, 124,
    125, 202
  'anchoring'   7
  Asian   11
  domestic   91, 97, 104, 105, 109, 110,
    203
  foreign   90, 91, 92, 101, 203
  Hong Kong dollars and the
    RMB   **6–8**, 13(n10)
  importing country   88–9
  local   110
  local (price in US dollars)   117
  tied to US dollar   112–13
  WCU-based   116
  see also reserve currencies
currency appreciation   109, 112f
currency basket links   102–3
currency board   105, 106
  rule-based   116
  traditional   115
  WCU-based   **115–16**
currency board arrangement
    (CBA)   202, 203, 204
Currency Board System (CBS)   7, 203,
    208
currency convertibility   101, 105, 106,
    116, 117(n7), 126, 129, 130, 132,
    135, 146
  capital account   163
  real   109, 110
currency depreciation   103–4, 106,
    109, 115
currency devaluation   110
currency integration   115–16
currency overvaluation   103, 116,
    117(n4, n6)

currency regime *see* 'sustainable currency regime'
currency stability 126
currency substitution 203, 216
currency undervaluation 88, 90, 91, 97, 117(n6)

dairy produce 302, 313(n4)
Dalian 101
data deficiencies 43–4n, 46–8n, 91, 93, 99(n7–8), 130, 132, 138, 139, 148(n14), 155, 158, 166, 268(n1–2, n4), 279, 286, 289, 318
Data Envelopment Analysis (DEA) 254–5, 256
DEA programming 259, 268(n3)
Datastream 93
Davidson-MacKinnon test 265n
Dayak tribes (Sarawak) viii
Dayawan nuclear power station 174
de-industrialization 83
debt 123, 149(n21)
ease of selling 26
foreign 73
governmental (risk-free bond-rate borrowing) 85(n1)
WCU-denominated 116, 118(n11)
debt-to-assets ratio (DAR) 335t, 336t, 338–43t, 345t
debt-to-equity ratio (DER) 360, 362–3t, 366t
debt-issuers 106
decentralization (PRC economy) **153–4**, 164, 373
decision-making 99(n1), 364
decision-making power **354–5**, 356, 357, 362–3t
index 358
decomposition *see* variance decomposition analysis
defence 224t, 231
deflation 105
deforestation 30
Delivery versus Payment (DvP) settlement 145
Democratic Progressive Party (DPP, Taiwan) 228
demographic trends 223
Denmark 148(n13)
deposit-taking companies (DTCs) 143n

deposits 137t, 206
cross-border 135, 136t, 138, 148(n13)
renminbi-denominated 129
depreciation *see* currency depreciation
derivatives xi, 123, 132, 149(n21)
detergents 240, 250b, 252(n7)
developed economies 24, 31, 72, 81, 83, 186, 198, 298
'advanced countries/economies' 187, 223, 225
'advanced industrial countries' 18, 19
economic impact of China's emergence as major trading nation **82**
'high-income economies' 67
'industrial world' 4, 11, 27
'industrialized countries' 138, 141, 142
'OECD countries' 73, 113, 144, 171
developing countries 18, 21, 25, 27, 30, 65, 72, 87, 186, 187, 191, 198, 239, 243, 256, 297–8
China 'role model' 17, 29, 31
'emerging economies' 293
'least-developed countries' 28
'less-developed countries' 19, 24
development paths (NIEs) 222
development rounds 27–8
see also Uruguay Round
dietary aspirations 302, 313(n4, n6)
diffusion *see* technological diffusion
directors 329, 331
distance functions
input-oriented 256
output-oriented 256, 257
distribution (finished products) 190, 198(n5)
distribution channels 250
distributional issues **2–4**, 12(n2–4)
division of
labour/specialization 154–5, 224t, 259, 298, 325
global 65, 82, 83
international 79
domestic financial centre (DFC) 130
'dotcom' boom and bust 223
drugs (generic) 28

dual-board diagnostic model
  (DBDM)   329, **332–3**, **340–6**,
  347(n6)
  descriptive statistics   342t
  distribution of corporate power   332
  firm performance varies according to
    DBDM type (hypothesis 2)   **333**,
    341, 343, 346
  hypothesis 2 rejected   343
  proportion of insider/outsider
    supervisors   344f
duoyu, shaoqu, fanghuo ('give more, take
  less, give free rein')
DVD royalties   240, 246, **247–8b**, 252
  'feeding fish before eating it'   248b

Earth Policy Institute   2
East Asia/'Far East'   xii, 20, 24, 27, 66,
  70, 72, 130, 132, 137, 140, 146,
  147(n1), 234, 274, 276, 279, 293,
  294, 313(n3)
  economic impact of China's
    emergence as major trading
    nation   **82**
  production networks   371
East Asian Miracle   274, 295(n1)
Eastern Europe and FSU (EEFSU)   73
Eastman Kodak   251
econometrics   xi, xii, 256
  impulse response and variance
    decomposition analysis   201,
    204
  IS-LM model (structural VAR
    process)   **205**, 206
  managerial autonomy and firm
    performance   **358–60**
economic agents   73, 89, 99(n1), 255
Economic Creativity Index   71n
economic cycles/business cycles   201,
  215
economic development   viii, x, xiii,
  374
economic downturn/recessions   25,
  197, 203
economic fundamentals   102, 105,
  106, 115, 116
economic growth   xiv, 4, 18, 27, 29,
  79, 84, 190, 208, 239, 257, 325
  attributable to TFP growth (China,
    1990s)   **262–3**, 268(n5)
  effect of trade volume   255

environmental concerns   **9–10**,
  13(n13)
  PRC   8, **273–96**
  sources   254
  sustainable   102
economic integration, regional   ix
economic reform (China,
    1978/9–)   viii, ix, 32, 84, 156, 170,
    172, 198(n4), 274, 279, 287, 292,
    294, 352, 371–3
  agricultural and rural
    development   **299–301**,
    313–14(n11–17)
  grain output   **301–3**, 314(n18–19)
  grain trade   304
  investment rates (1978–2000)   275t,
    276
  'should be continued'   295
  'Xian level'   374
  see also China: open-door policy
economic security   67
economies of scale   34, 36, 62, 81, 154,
  164, 228, 359
Economist Intelligence Unit   182
economists   19, 32, 66, 103, 117(n4),
  186–7, 254
Ecuador   71t
edible oils   174, 175t, 177–82, 183–4t
education   21, 222, 224, 224t, 229,
  230t, 235, 266
  Taiwan   227
  wage premium   186
efficiency   **8–9**, 11, 13(n11–12), 111,
  116, 156, 242, 254
efficiency improvement   **254–69**
eggs   174, 175t, 178–81t, 182, 183–4t
electrical/electronics sector   2, 65, 225,
  237(n6), 233f, 235, 244, 280t
electricity   174, 175t, 178–81t, 183–4t,
  231, 237(n18), 242
  electric power, gas and water
    (production and supply)   356t
electronic commercial business   172
electronic and telecommunication
  equipment   241t, 242
electronics   223, 321n
Electronics and Semi-Conductors
  (ERSO) laboratory (Taiwan,
  1973–)   230, 233
Eleventh of September (2001)   156
emission trading   10, 29–30

empiricism
  currency substitution   203, 216
  dynamic general equilibrium
      framework   73
  economic growth (sources)   267
  economic growth attributable to TFP
      growth   255, 266
  effects of RERV and RERM on
      commodity exports   87, **91–3**,
      97, 99(n7–9)
  effects of trade on earnings
      inequality   187, 190, 198,
      198(n1)
  firm performance affected by
      supervisory board
      composition   **331**
  growth of TFP and of its components
      in Chinese provinces   **259–63**,
      267–8, 268(n1–5)
  HKSAR's 'middleman role'   5, 152,
      153
  impact of trade policy on growth of
      TFP, efficiency, and
      technology   **264–6**, 268(n6)
  macroeconomic instability (structural
      VAR approach)   **206–16**,
      217(n1–2)
  managerial autonomy and firm
      performance   350, 361, 363
  price convergence and market
      integration (HK and
      Mainland)   **177–83**, 184(n1)
  'revealed' trade policy   **263–4**
  risk   88
  size of supervisory board versus firm
      performance   334
  spillover effects of FDI in
      China   239, **243–4**, 252
  supervisory board in corporate
      governance (empirical
      confirmation of
      ineffectiveness)   329, 340, 346–7
  vertical effects of FDI   244
employment   18, 65, 124, 197, 239,
    264, 295(n1), 352
  growth   262f, 262
  manufacturing sector   79
  lost by HK to southern
      China   188–90
  rural   299, 314(n12)
employment-creation   158

energy/power   23, 73, 80t, 237(n18),
    318, 325
energy (emissions) efficiency   29
energy saving   242
Engel ratio   303
engineering/engineers   191, 227, 227t,
    230t
entrepôt trade   153, 154, **156–7**, 158f,
    164, 166
environment   2, **9–10**, 11, 13(n13), 17,
    28–30, 31, 300
  composition effect   9, 318, 319,
      321t, 322, 323t, 324t
  demonstration effect   10
  impact on manufacturing sector of
      China's accession to
      WTO   **317–26**
  output effect   320–2
  scale effect   321t, 322, 329t
  technical effect   322–4
Environmental Protection
    Administration (Taiwan)   229f,
    229t
equipment and instruments purchase
    (E&I)   277f, 277, 278t
equity   12(n5), 123, 142
equity market   149(n21)
  access   138, 138t
  HKSAR   **134–5**, 148(n12)
  world's top eleven (2002–4)   134t
Essay on Principle of Population
    (1798)   297, 313(n1)
euro/euro zone   26, 104, 106
  price differentials   179, 184(n1)
Euroclear   145
euromarket   122
Euronext Stock Exchange
    (2000–)   134t, 135t
Europe   2–4, 18, 26, 30, 67, 75–6,
    77–8f, 96, 141, 227, 234, 236
  strains on economy   **19**
  supervisory boards   330, 347(n1)
European Bank for Reconstruction and
    Development   143n
European Company for Financing of
    Railroad Rolling Stock
    (Eurofima)   143n
European Investment Bank   143n
European monetary mechanism   104
European Union   21, 27, 81, 145, 221,
    307

exchange control
   liberalization   148(n11)
exchange rate appreciation
   two-year real   112f, 112–13
exchange rate controls
   capital account   126, 139, 163
   current account   126
exchange rate fluctuations   26, 106, 200
exchange rate index
   effective   102–3, 212–13t
   nominal effective   204, 209t
exchange rate policy   10
exchange rate regimes   xii
   crawling peg   115
   fixed   87, 97
   floating   102, 202, 203
   managed float   102
   nominal peg   115
exchange rate stability   20, 115
exchange rate system
   target zone arrangement   217
exchange rate variations   205
exchange rates   11, 21, 24, 104, 107,
   110, 111, 202–3, 205
   effective   208, 211, 215
   losses   116
   new arrangement   101
   nominal   xii, 93, 109, 115, 117(n3),
   118(n10)
   pegged   87, 97, 99(n10), 203
   right   **107–10**
   risks   116
   trade-weighted effective   206
   USD-HKD   103
   see also real exchange rate
exclusive dealing   251
Executive Yuan (Taiwan)   228, 229f
expectations   107
expertise   160, 164
   foreign   266, 267
   managerial   368(n8)
export data   88
export promotion   273
export taxes   258
export-demand   91
export-deviation   76–7
export-supply function   91
exports   7, 21, 23, 48, 49t, 51, 52,
   53–4t, 58t, 59, 60, 66–8, 72, 76–82,
   84, 155, 166, 168(n2), 173, 202, 235,
   242, 247b, 258, 264, 320, 321t, 372

cereals   297
   effects of RERV and RERM   **87–100**
   FDI with technological spillovers
      case   78f
   income-elastic   96
   manufactured   318
   USA   99(n10)
external balance   107, 108, 109
external economy   154
external relationships   357, 366t
'externality of human capital'
   (Lucas)   155

F-statistic   339t, 340t, 341t, 345t
factor accumulation   262, 263t
factor cost   193t, 195t
factor endowments   42
factor mobility   179
factor movements
   perfect and costless   63(n6, n15)
factor price equalization   186
Factor Price Equalization Theorem
   (Samuelson)   19, 190, 191
factor prices   33, 39, 41, 45
factor specialization   316(n40)
factor substitution   36
factors of production   190
FAO   310, 311n, 313(n2), 315(n21), 316
farm inputs   316(n41)
farm products   309–10
farmers   3–4, 298, 310, 314(n19)
FDI   3, 4, 11, 23, 33, 48n, 48, 49, 51–4,
   60, 82–4, 127, 148(n10), 221, 225,
   259, 265t, 287, 295(n6)
   annual value (China inward,
      1979–2003)   240f
   in China   65, 164
   in China (Hong Kong's role)   **160–2**
   in China (overview)   **240–2**
   competition concerns   **248–51**,
      252(n7–8)
   contracted   160, 161, 162f, 162
   crowding out effect   243
   'dancing with wolf'   **248–51**,
      252(n7–8)
   demonstration effect   242, **243**, 244
   entry mode   240–1
   global distribution   68
   Hong Kong in Mainland China   190
   Hong Kong 'largest source of inward
      investment to PRC'   173

host economy **74**
link with technological diffusion 70, 71t
manufacturing 68, 69t
most-promising locations 68–70
primary goal (China's policies) 242
role 264
spillover effects (China) 239
by Taiwan in PRC 9
utilized 160, 161, 162
see also investment
FDI flows (to ASEAN countries) 47n
FDI inflow 273
FDI spillovers 234f
cross-section data 244
horizontal 242–3, 244, 246, 248
panel data 244
pooled time-series data 244
quantification **243–4**
vertical 242, 243, 244, 246, 252(n3)
FDI, technology transfer, economic restructuring **219–69**
China: spillover effects of FDI **239–53**
Chinese provinces: impact of trade policy on TFP **254–69**
Taiwan: scientific and technological development **221–38**
FDI-diversion 68, 70, **72**, **74**, 75, 76f, **77**, 79, 80t
manufacturing sector 70
with technological spillovers **72–3**, **74–5**, **77–9**
fertilizers 316(n41), 374
finance ix, xi, 166, 189, 223, 231, 356t, 357, 366–7t
Finance Index 71n
finance industry 190
financial centres 122
capital-exporting 139
financial crises 5, 23
financial entrepôt 125, 139
financial 'free' zones 122
financial institutions 123, 124, 126, 127, 164
financial intermediaries 139
financial markets 22–3, 102, 103, 111, 113, 123, 126, 129, **141–5**
sophistication 138, 138t
financial
regulation/supervision **127–9**

financial repression 126, 130
financial restructuring 372
financial sector xiv, 21, 73, 127, 146, 147
financial services 20, **22–3**, 126, 139, 145, 164, 173, 192, 194–8, 236, 242
relative wage rate 193t
WTO agreement 22
financial system 122, 123, 235
global 17, 23, 24, 27, 31
instability 27
relative efficiency 71n
Finland 71t
First Basic Law for Science and Technology (Taiwan, 1997) 237(n15)
First National Agricultural Census (PRC 1999) 314(n13)
first-difference form 206, 217(n1)
fiscal deficit (HKSAR, 2002–) 142
fiscal policy xii, 109, 200
fiscal surplus (HK) 142
fish/fishing 299, 300, 302, 310, 313(n4), 314(n12)
freshwater and seawater products 309
food 172, 282t, 298, 315(n30), 373, 374
global production capability 297
processed 321t, 323t
food distribution **297**
Food Outlook (FAO) 315(n21)
food security/self-sufficiency 4, **309–12**, 315(n36), 316(n40–6)
basic 298, 299, 301–2, 313(n7)
cushion above subsistence 298, 303, 313(n6), 314(n18)
'ninety-five per cent' rule 310, 312, 313(n7), 316(n40)
footwear 235
foreign direct investment *see* FDI
foreign exchange xiv, 101, 123, 126, 149(n21)
Herstatt losses (1974) 148(n17)
market conditions 108f
volatility 200
Foreign Exchange Adjustment Centre (Shenzhen, 1985–) 101
foreign exchange certificates (1980–) 101

foreign exchange control   7, 102
foreign exchange market   8, 109, 123
  government intervention   202
  Hong Kong   **132–4**
  turnover (global, 2001–4)   133t
foreign exchange policy   20
foreign exchange reserves   23,
    148(n11)
foreign investment   57, 152, 372
  in China (Hong Kong's role)   **160–3**
  not allowed in ports (PRC)   156
Foreign Trade Statistics (USA)   316(n43)
foreign-funded enterprises (FFEs)   242,
    244, 264, 265t, 266
foreign-invested enterprises (FIEs)   241,
    273
Fortune magazine   5
four little dragons   276, 293
France   xi, 34, 43–6n, 93, 94–5t, 98f,
    133t, 136t, 137, 138t, 141, 144t,
    225
free trade   19, 83, 125
Free Trade Area of Americas (FTAA)   81
free trade areas   33, 61, 82, 163
  see also CEPA
free-riding   **246–8**
fruit farming   299, 309–10
Fujian   13(n9), 267
full employment   104, 107f, 108–10,
    116, 117(n6)
functional form   255–6
fund management   103, 141, 141t
Fundamental Equilibrium Exchange
    Rate (FEER)   107, 109
funding   231, 273n
furniture   2, 283t

Gansu   268
GARCH procedure   92, 93
GATT (1947–)   127, 317, 373
GCUBED model   84(n1)
GDP   28, 29, 44–6n, 75–7, 82, 84, 91,
    96, 109, 110, 139, 142, 160, 164,
    165t, 171, 173, 186, 191, 195t, 216,
    254, 263, 264, 273, 287, 320, 321t
  annual nominal   93
  China   8, 111
  cyclical components (Hong
      Kong)   170
  growth   262f, 262, 263t, 318
  growth rate (HK)   200, 201f, 215

industrial share   **276–9, 280–3t**
  nominal   104, 259
  OECD countries   113
  real   108, 206, 210f, 211, 259, 262f,
      262, 263t, 292, 318
  real (FDI diversion case)   76f
  real (FDI with technological spillovers
      case)   78f
  real (variance decomposition)   215
  rural   299
  variance decomposition   212t
GDP deflator   92, 93, 105, 111, 259,
    289–93
Georgia Tech: Technology Policy and
    Assessment Centre   9, 13(n12)
Germany   2, 9, 34, 43n–6n, 71t, 93,
    94–5t, 98f, 133t, 136t, 137, 138t,
    144t, 190, 223, 225
  stock exchange   134t
Germany: Federal Government   222
Germany: *Länder* (states)   222
Giant (company)   235
Gini coefficient   187
global economy   2, 32, 73, 83
  China's (re-)integration into   **20–3**,
      152, 173, 317
  China's linkages   **67–73**
  impact of China   18
  new landscape   **17–18**
  re-defining PRC's role   **30–1**
  strains   **20**, 30–1
global financial centres (GFCs)   124,
    129, 137
global leadership (PRC's role)   **27–8**
global trading system   17, 31
Global Value Chains   223
global warming   29, 30
globalism   11
globalization   10, 11, 19, 22, 31, 83,
    123, 142, 246, 322, 324, 371, 372
  modern (1979–)   1
gold   24, 111, 124
goods   10, 32, 35, 37, 40, 48, 63(n8),
    166, 174, 188
  capital-intensive   47n, 72, 82
  cheap, good-quality   66
  final   221
  foreign   127
  intermediate (imported)   243
  international movement   67
  labour-intensive   47n, 67

manufactured   12, 81, 129
non-tradable   68, 180t, 180
primary   117(n7)
goods and services
  imported (deflator)   206
gorilla (PRC) awakes   **65–7**
government (economic agent)   73
government revenues   321t
governments   2–3, 24, 81, 83–4, 87, 88,
    118(n11), 174, 226
  China   171, 172, 241, 242, 245, 248,
    250–2, 266, 267, 300, 301, 307,
    309, 312, 324, 347
  depreciation of debts (halted)   111
  Hong Kong/HKSAR   7, 124,
    148(n15), 155, 188, 200
  interest payments   107
  leadership and expenditure (science
    and technology,
    Taiwan)   **228–31**, 237(n14–20)
  provincial   258
  Taiwan   222, 236
grain   2, 298, 313(n4), 371
  competition for exportable supplies
    ('starving the world')   299,
    313(n10), 315(n29)
  foreign (propensity of PRC to
    purchase)   298–9
  'includes soyabeans' (Chinese
    usage)   **307**, **314(n20)**
  net importer (PRC)   314(n20)
  output growth (1978–)   299–300
  trade balance (PRC)   308, 309t
  'two-thirds of total sown area'   299,
    314(n13)
  yield instability   374
grain: developments past and future
    (China)   **297–316**
grain consumption
  per capita   314(n19)
  per capita norm   315(n25)
grain farmers
  deprivation, discontent   298, 300,
    314(n14)
  number   314(n13)
grain farming
  dynamics   316(n46)
grain market
  liberalization   301
grain output/production   298–304,
    315(n29, n36)

per capita (1978–2004)   302t, 303,
    304
requirement   304, 315(n25)
shortfalls   308
total (1978–2004)   302t, 303
trends (PRC, 1978–2004)   **301–3**,
    314(n18–19)
grain prices   172, 301
grain reserves/stocks   297, 303,
    314–15(n21), 316(n41)
  commercial   **314(n21)**
  'seriously depleted'   304
  'state secret'   304
grain sales   314(n19)
grain trade (China)   **303–9**,
    314–16(n20–39), 374
  geo-strategic issues   **309–12**,
    316(n40–6)
  implications of China economic
    performance   299
Granger causality test   196, 196t, 198
'great famine' (PRC, 1959–61)   viii
  'thirty million deaths'   298
Greater China   140, 188, 371, 372, 373
gross margin   166
  Hong Kong's Mainland-related
    trade   **158–60**
growth accounting analysis   254, 289
Growth Competitiveness Index   71n
growth poles/hubs   3, 146–7
growth of sales (GOS)   358, 360, 361,
    362t, 363t
GTAP 4 database   74
Guangdong   9, 13(n9, n13), 145, 188,
    190, 267, 372
Guangxi   267
Guangzhou   101, 170, 173, 177, 178t,
    182, 183
Guernsey   144t
Guiding Catalogue of Foreign Investment
    (1995)   242
  subsequent revisions (2002
    latest)   242
Guizhou   268

H-shares   130, 131t, 162–3
Hainan   267
hair-dressing   174, 175t, 178–81t,
    183–4t
half-life   176, 177, 180t, 181–4
Hang Seng Bank   162

head-hunting   viii
health   11, 21, 84
heavy industry   279, 322, 325
Hebei   267
Heckscher–Ohlin model   190, 197
hedging   23, 155
Heilongjiang   268
Henan   268
Herstatt risk   145, 148(n17)
heteroscedasticity problem   368(n7)
high-school tuition fees   174, 175t,
    177–82, 183–4t
high-technology goods   235
Himalayas   29
history   221
    economic (1979 watershed)   **1–2**, 3,
        5
Hitachi   247b, 237(n11)
'homeland security'   222
Hong Kong/HKSAR   viii, xi–xiv, 11, 34,
    43n–6n, 66, 71t, 72, 73, 82, 221,
    236(n2), 254, 276, 287, 289, 293,
    295(n5–6), 296(n9), 372, 373
    budget (2003–04)   142
    'certainly not an OFC'   122
    China's most important trade
        partner   173
    China's OFC   **125–30**, 131t,
        148(n5–11)
    comparative advantage in
        trading   153
    development contrasted to that of
        Taiwan   235–6
    dominant supplier of FDI to
        PRC   186
    economic performance 'volatile'
        (1983–)   200
    economic rebound/recovery
        (2003–)   5–6, 12(n6), 132, 134,
        138–9, 146
    economic restructuring   188–9
    emergence as IFC (dating)   123–4,
        147(n2)
    external bank loans and deposits
        (2002–4)   136t, 136
    free port   125, 127
    functions performed for PRC   6
    GDP   6
    handover to PRC sovereignty
        (1997–)   ix, 5, 121, 125, 126,
        127, 146, 161, 172

international hub (commercial and
    financial)   5–6
    metamorphosis into knowledge-based
        economy   146
    middleman role   5
    monetary conditions 'totally
        dependent on US policy'   215
    'negative economic growth'
        (1998)   5, 12(n7)
    'new creditor to world'   139
    'not a tax haven'   124
    offshore exports of Mainland
        goods   166
    offshore imports for Mainland
        166
    onshore and offshore activities
        'completely fused'   122, 124
    public investment rate   295(n8)
    'regional/international financial
        centre'   163
    structural problems   146–7, 191
    sustainable currency regime
        101–18
    total trade   188, 192t
    trade statistics   190–1
    unique and evolving roles   **4–6**,
        12–13(n5–9)
    US dollar market   124
    water   13(n13)
    world ranking (as IFC)   122–3
    world's busiest container port   154
Hong Kong: Exchange Fund   126
Hong Kong: macroeconomic instability
    (internal and external
    factors)   **200–18**
    conditions for macroeconomic
        stability under dollar peg   202–3
    econometric techniques   205
    empirical evidence (structural VAR
        approach)   206–16, 217(n1–2)
    HKD peg to USD (exacerbation of
        macroeconomic volatility)   201
    IS-LM model   204–6
    open economy theoretical
        model   203–4
Hong Kong: Trade and Industry
    Department   140
*Hong Kong Annual Digest of
    Statistics*   192
Hong Kong as China's city and as global
    city   **119–218**

Hong Kong as China's middleman
  (evolving role) **152–69**
  challenges 164
  Hong Kong: gross margin of
    Mainland-related trade 158–60
  Hong Kong: Mainland trade handled
    by 168t
  Hong Kong: Mainland-related
    entrepôt trade and offshore
    trade 156–7, 158f
  Hong Kong: offshore merchandising
    of mainland related trade 167t
  Hong Kong: offshore trade
    (estimation) 166, 167–8t
  Hong Kong: role in China's
    trade 155–60, 168(n1)
  Hong Kong: role in foreign
    investment in China 160–3
  Hong Kong: service hub 163–4,
    168(n2)
  intermediation (theory) 153–5
  intermediation and
    decentralization 153–4
  large trading centres
    (efficiency) 154–5
  'smaller share of bigger pie' 152
Hong Kong customs 127, 155
Hong Kong dollar 102–3, 114, 115,
  125, 126, 145
  and the RMB **6–8**, 13(n10)
  debt instruments 142, 143t
  effective exchange rate 202f
  official and market rates (parity) 202
  tied/pegged to US dollar (1983–) 7,
    200–1, **202–3**, 205, 215, 216, 372
Hong Kong Economic Journal
  Daily 148(n19)
Hong Kong Exchanges and Clearing Ltd
  (HKEX) 130
Hong Kong as a financial centre of
  China and the world **121–51**
  banking 135–8, 148(n13–16)
  chapter purpose 121, 146
  conceptual and historical issues
    (literature review) 121–4,
    147(n1–2)
  conclusions 146–7, 149(n21–2)
  equity market 134–5, 148(n12)
  foreign exchange market 132–4
  Hong Kong (China's OFC) 125–30,
    131t, 146, 148(n5–11)

Hong Kong ('regional financial
  centre') 124–5, 147–8(n3–4)
Hong Kong (world IFC) **130**, **132–5**,
  148(n12)
  international investment
    position 138–45
  market infrastructure 145–6,
    148–9(n17–20)
  'one country, two currencies' 126
Hong Kong Interbank Offer Rate
  (HIBOR) 206
  variance decomposition 213t
Hong Kong and Mainland: economic
  integration (effect on Hong Kong's
  unskilled workers) **186–99**
  background information 187–90
  chapter purpose 186
  cointegration analysis 193–7,
    198(n5)
  data 187, 191–3
  econometric method (causality
    test) 187
  empiricism (effects of trade on
    earnings inequality) 187, 198,
    198(n1)
  hypothesis confirmed 196, 198
  literature on trade and
    inequality 186, 198
  one-way causal effect
    confirmed 196, 198
  policy implications 186, 187
  summary 197–8
  theoretical background 190–1,
    198(n2–4)
Hong Kong and Mainland: market
  integration **170–85**
  chapter purpose 170
  data 173–5
  descriptive statistics of prices
    178t
  development of market economy in
    China 171–2
  econometric method (Levin, Lin, and
    Chu) 176–7, 180t, 181, 183t,
    184t
  economic integration (HK and
    Mainland) 172–3
  empirical results and
    implications 177–83, 184(n1)
  methodology 175–7
  noteworthy observations 183–4

Hong Kong and Mainland: market
    integration – *continued*
  pitfalls of using low-frequency
      data   182
  price convergence and market
      integration (HK and
      Mainland)   173–83, 184(n1)
  regression analysis   181
  variability of price differential   178t,
      179t
Hong Kong Monetary Authority
    (HKMA)   105, 117(n8), 125–6, 127,
    145, 148(n5)
  data source   133n, 148(n18)
  policy objective   202
  repurchase agreement with PBC   126
Hong Kong Monetary Authority:
    Exchange Fund   142
Hong Kong Mortgage Corporation   142
Hong Kong Research Grants Council
    (RGC)   170n, 200n, 350n
Hong Kong Stock Market   5, 12(n5),
    130, 132, 162–3
  funds raised by H-shares and Red
      Chips (1993–2004)   131t
  world ranking as equity
      market   134t, 135
  world ranking as new issue
      market   135, 135t
Hong Kong Total Exports Volume Index
    (HKEXI)   113, 113t, 114t, 117
  actual/forecasted   114–15
Hong Kong Trade Development Council
    (HKTDC)
  surveys   155, 166, 168n, 168
Hongkong and Shanghai Banking
    Corporation Limited   x
Hook, B.   ii, 372
host currency   104, 117(n3)
  real value   115
  single   106
hours worked   268(n4)
household budgets   313(n4)
household income (HK/HKSAR
    1981–2001)   187, 188t
households   36, 37, 38, 73, 85(n1),
    116
housing   6, 12(n6), 29, 203, 295(n2–3),
    353
Housing Authority (HKSAR)   145,
    148–9(n20)

housing construction
  floor space   279, 284–5t, 286, 287
  investment   **279, 284–5t, 286–7,**
      295(n5)
  non-residential   286t, 287
  residential   279, 284–5t, 286, 286t,
      287
  rural areas   279, 284–5t, 286
  unit costs   285t, 286, 286t, 287
  urban areas   279, 284–5t, 286
Hsinchu Park (1980–)   230–1, 232,
    237(n19)
Hubble telescope   222
Hubei   268
human capital   42, 43t, 83, 155
  general   191
  specific   191
human resources/personnel   222, 224,
    224t, 235
  appointment and dismissal   357,
      365–7t
  Taiwan   **227–8,** 237(n12–13)
Hunan   268
hunger/malnutrition   297, 313(n2)
Hutchison Whampoa   156
hypergrowth (Chen)   8, 9, 10, 13(n11)

IBM   22
IC (integrated circuits)   227, 234
  local design houses (Taiwan)   **231**
ideology   152
import barriers   325
import duties   258
import quotas   320
import-competing sectors   52
import-demand function   91
importing country   87, 91
imports   18, 35, 48, 49t, 51, 53t, 54t, 58t,
    59, 60, 66, 68, 72, 82, 127, 158, 166,
    168(n2), 202, 245, 259, 320, 321t
  agricultural (PRC)   315(n34)
  cheap   11
  grain   298, 299, 303, 310, 312,
      316(n45)
  prices   212–13t, 216
impulse response   201, 204, 205, 209,
    210f, 211, 215, 217(n2)
incentives   264, 351, 354, 368(n8)
  controlling shareholders   350
  managers   350
  systemic reforms   26

income   124, 158, 179, 302, 320
  agricultural (efforts to raise)   4
  China   190
  disposable   107
  national   60, 61
  per capita   190, 294, 317, 319
  real   294f, 294
  rural   303, 314(n19), 321t, 322
  urban   303, 321t, 322
income distribution   57, 57t, 62, 186
  impact (in HK) of investment by HK
    in PRC   198(n1)
income inequality   4, 81, 184, 190
  HK/HKSAR (1981–2001)   187–8, 188t
income tax   35, 37
incremental capital–output ratio
    (ICOR)   274, 289, **292–4**, 296(n9)
  real   293f
  reciprocal of marginal productivity of
    capital stock   293
independence of board   *see* board
    independence
indexed unit of account (Ho, 2000)   7,
    104
India   11, 19, 20, 27, 66, 69t, 71t, 73,
    84, 144t, 297
  economic deregulation   79
'Indicators of Technology-Based
    Competitiveness'   9
indigenous innovation   81
indigenous innovation index   71t,
    71n, 72
Indonesia   xiv, 25, 30, 43n, 45–6n,
    48n, 62(n3), 66, 68–79, 80t, 102,
    110, 148(n4), 244
  see also 'ASEAN-4'
Industrial and Commercial Bank of
    China   128
industrial reform   372
industrial sectors   191–2, 241t, 273,
    276, 318
industrial share of GDP   **276–9**, **280–3t**
Industrial Technology Research Institute
    (ITRI, Taiwan)   230, 231, 233,
    233f, 236
industrial-bureaucratic complex   84
industrial-military complex   84
industrialization   66, 295(n1), 371
  rural   8, 274, 279, 294–5
industries/industry   viii, ix, 82, 87, 91,
    359

Chinese   248, 373
  export-oriented   68
  import-competing   77
  labour-intensive (relocation to
    China)   65
  non-competitive   83
  prohibited (China)   242
inflation   25–6, 88, 103, 105, 117(n6),
    201f, 203, 208, 372
  cause (HK)   200, 201
  domestic   216
  foreign   215
inflationary pressure   116, 204, 205,
    215
information   223
information technology (IT)   227, 233,
    234
  three-stage approach (Taiwan)   233,
    233f
information technology (IT) firms   234
information technology (IT)
    products   225, 231
  Taiwan's share of world markets
    (2003)   226t
infrastructure   9, 231, 242, 259
  urban   293
initial public offerings (IPO)   135,
    145–6, 148–9(n20)
Inner Mongolia   264, 265, 268,
    268(n6)
innovation   224, 228, 252(n3)
  financial needs   223
  French system   222
  technological   83
innovation systems   232
innovativeness   148(n16)
input–output   40, 254, 256, 257, 259
inputs   8, 159
  freedom to import   240
  imported   158
inside supervisors (IS)   334, 335–6t,
    338t, 339, 341–3, 344f, 346, 347
insider dealing   10
institutional evolution
    (Taiwan)   **221–38**
insurance   23, 139, **142**, **144–5**, 155,
    156, 166, 192–8, 356t, 357
  relative wage rate   193t
insurance companies   144t, 191
Integrity Management Consulting
    Firm   351

intellectual property (IP)   224, 224t,
    233f
intellectual property rights (IPR)   8,
    239, 244, 252, 320
    IPR laws: enforcement
        (China)   245–6
    IPR protection   246, 248b
Inter-American Development
    Bank   143n
interest payments, real   111
interest rate arbitrage   202, 205
interest rates   8, 24, 25, 102, 103, 110,
    111, 203
    domestic   109, 211
    HK   201f, 201
    nominal   118(n10), 206
    nominal (HK)   204, 205, 211,
        212–13t, 215, 216
    nominal (USA)   204, 205, 208, 209t,
        211, 212–13t, 215, 216
    real   108, 108f, 109, 215, 216f
    USA   201f, 201, 206, 208, 211
interest withholding tax   148(n15)
intermediation   164
    theory   **153–5**
internal balance   107, 107f, 109
international accounting
    standards   162
'international banking'   122
'international banking centre'
    (IBC)   122
    'subtle difference' from an IFC   123
International Centre for Study of East
    Asian Development   32n
International Economic Data Bank
    (IEDB), Canberra   93
international finance   xi, xiii, xiv
    vicissitudes (1812–2006)   139
International Finance
    Corporation   143n
international financial centres (IFCs)
    classification   **124–5**, 147–8(n3–4)
    conceptual review   **121–3**, 147(n1)
    global   122
    historical review   **123–4**, 125,
        147(n2)
    'integrated'   124, 125146
    regional   122
    'subtle difference' from an IBC   123
    'traditional centre'   125
    variables (Reed, 1981)   147(n2)

International Index (degree of
    integration into international
    economy)   71n
international investment position (IIP,
    HKSAR)   **138–45**
    'other financial markets and
        industries'   141–5
    regional headquarters   139–41
International Labour Organization
    website   43n
International Monetary Fund
    (IMF)   25, 27, 66, 325
    statistics   111, 148(n14)
international settlement
    vehicle   **106–7**
inventory increase   275n
    ratio to GDP (China,
        1978–2000)   276, 276f
investment   ix, 2, 6, **8–9**, 13(n11–12),
    21, 24, 31, 73, 81, 99(n1–2, n4, n6),
    153, 164, 170, 221, 231, 268(n2),
    320, 321t, 357, 358, 366t, 372, 373
    aggregate   **274**
    agriculture   300
    collective sector   287, 288t
    domestic   171
    fixed   287
    foreign   171, 287, 320
    gross   276, 287
    price indices   267
    private   287, 288t, 295(n2)
    public   **287–9**, 294, 295(n6–8)
    social   274, 275t
    state   287, 288t
    see also FDI
investment (by HK in PRC)
    impact on income distribution of
        Hong Kong   198(n1)
investment banking   132, 135
investment barriers   246
investment deflator   267
investment diversion   54–5
investment efficiency   274, 289
investment funds   134n
investment, investment efficiency and
    economic growth in
    China   **273–96**
    introduction   273–4
    China's investment pattern in context
        of East Asia   274–89, 295(n2–8)
    literature   274, 289, 295(n1)

'over-investment'
    (discussion) 289–94, 296(n9)
    policy requirement 295
    sectoral shift (rural labour) 294–5
investment rates 278t, 294f
    nominal/real 289, 292
investment-GDP ratio (China) 8,
    274–6, 295, 295(n2–3)
    gross fixed capital formation 274,
        275t
    gross value of capital formation 274,
        275t
    nominal 274, 292
    real 294
total social investment in fixed
    assets 274, 275t, 277, 278t, 287,
        288t, 295(n2)
real (China 1980–2000) 292f, 292
investment-growth model/nexus 273,
    274, 294
investment–output ratio 289
investor protection 10, 347
investors 26, 116, 129, 139, 142,
    147(n1), 161
    Americans and Japanese 227
    foreign 8, 228, 239, 240, 244, 250,
        252, 368(n3)
    individual 358, 368(n3)
    institutional 358–9
    private 352
    risk premium 68, **72**, **74**, 76f, **77**
Ireland 71t, 136t, 137, 144t
IS-LM open economy model 201
    estimation results **208–16**, 217(n2)
    Hong Kong **203–4**, **204–6**
    identification of shocks **206–8**,
        217(n1)
    modifications 204
islands 122
Isle of Man 144t
Italy 34, 43–6n, 93, 94–5t, 98f, 136t,
    137, 144t
    stock exchange 134–5t

Jakarta 46n
Japan xii, 2, 9, 20, 25, 33, 34, 43–6n, 62,
    66, 67, 71t, 72, 73, 75–6, 77–8f, 82,
    93–7, 98f, 104, 129, 133t, 136t, 138t,
    141, 142, 144t, 148(n4), 160, 170,
    190, 234f, 237(n15), 250, 274, 293
    banking crisis (1991–2003) 136, 146

bubble economy 12(n6)
business restructuring 223
economic stagnation (1991–) 103,
    221
industrial policy 232
savings 116
scientific performance
    (factors) 224t, 225
stagnation of growth rate 221
Japan Bank for International
    Cooperation (JBIC) 68
Japanese yen 103, 106
Jersey 148(n13)
jewellery 174, 175t, 177, 178–81t, 182,
    183–4t
Jiangsu 13(n9), 267
Jiangxi 268
Jilin 264, 265, 268, 268(n6)
Jing Hua Shi Bao (*Jinghua Times*) 247b
job fairs 12–13(n8)
job losses 11, 300
Joint Declaration 126, 146
joint ventures 240, 241, 242, 245, 251,
    295(n6)
JVC 247b

knowledge 19, 226, 228
Korea, Republic of 33, 66, 69t, 71t, 72,
    73, 75f, 76, 77–8f, 82, 102, 106,
    148(n4), 221, 254, 276, 279, 289
Korea Securities Depository 145
Korean 'model' 230, 234, 237(n24)
    Taiwanese contrast 235
Kuala Lumpur 141
Kuomintang (KMT) 228
Kyoto Protocol 11, **29–30**
Kyungpook National University
    (Korea) 273n

L'Oréal 250
laboratories (public sector) 228
labour 1, 72, 244
    agricultural 310, 313(n8)
    cheap/inexpensive 172, 247b, 294,
        295
    effective 42, 43t
    migrant 3–4
    physical 42
    rural 274, 294–5
    skilled 186, 189–92, 194, 196–7,
        198(n2)

labour – *continued*
  supply and demand   3
  two-good, four-factor, three-country
    model (unilateral and regional
    trade liberalization)   34, 36, 38,
    39, 40, 42, 43t, 47n, 63(n5)
  unskilled   186, 190–2, 194, 196,
    196t, 197, 198(n2, n4)
labour costs   172
labour force/workforce   83, 240, 363
  ageing   223
  better-educated   189
  global   79
labour input   221, 259, 268(n4)
labour market   11, 40
  institutions   73, 85(n1)
labour mobility   243, 252(n2)
labour turnover   242
laissez-faire   123, 235
land   156, 164, 172, 314(n14), 325
  arable   301, 310
language   84
Laos   43n, 44n, 48n
large trading centres
    (efficiency)   **154–5**
Latin America   102, 112
law   126
  corporate (reform required)   364
  environmental protection   10
  international   67
  PRC   252(n8)
law of one price (LOP)   171, 175
Law against Unfair Methods of
    Competition (PRC, 1993)   251
lawsuits   242
lawyers   163
leasing enterprises   172
leather   241t, 242, 321t, 323t
legal frameworks   229
legislation   122
  anti-monopoly   251
Levin–Lin–Chu test (price
    differentials)   180t, 181, 183–4t
liabilities
  convertibility   116
  short-term, foreign-denominated   24
Liaoning   267
liberalization   223, 295, 318
  economic   259
  financial   22–3
link coefficient   105, 116

LINK project   203
Link REIT   145–6, 148–9(n20)
liquefied petroleum gas   174, 175t,
    178–81t, 183–4t
Lisbon Stock Exchange   134n
Lithuania   244
litigation   146, 148–9(n20)
little tigers   293
living standards   175, 179
LM curve   204
loans   127, 128t, 137, 137t
  cross-border   135, 136t, 138, 148(n13)
lobbying   27, 232
local content requirements   237(n22),
    243, 245
'local corporates'   142, 143t
local governments   245, 300, 314(n14)
local office (LO)   **140**
log likelihood   195t
logging   30
logistics   6, 234, 226
London   122, 123, 139, 140, 141, 164
  'global financial centre' (GFC)   124,
    129, 137
London Stock Exchange   134t, 135t
long run PPP   92–3
loss function   99(n5)
loss-making activities   363
Lucky Film   251
lumber certification   30
Luxembourg   71t, 144t, 148(n13)

Macau   4, 287, 295(n6)
machinery   279, 281t, 290, 301, 321t,
    323t, 322
macroeconomic adjustments   147, 204
macroeconomic instability   371
  Hong Kong (internal and external
    factors)   **200–18**
macroeconomic stability   7, 202, 216,
    372
  conditions (under US dollar
    peg)   201, **202–3**
  'could not be fulfilled'   215
  WCU link   **103–6**, 117(n4–8)
macroeconomics   xiii
maize   304, 313(n4), 314(n21)
  imports and exports (China)   305–6t,
    307
  Sino–US trade (1997–2003)   310,
    311t, 312

Making Globalization Work (Stiglitz) 27
Malaysia xiv, 25, 43–5n, 48n, 62(n3), 65–6, 68–81, 102, 148(n4), 276, 293
  national taboos 81
  see also 'ASEAN-4'
Malmquist TFP index 255, **256–8**, 266
  definition 256
management 252(n3)
  senior 332
management board 331
management control 140
managerial autonomy and firm performance (China's listed firms) **350–70**
  control variables 359–60, 368(n5–6)
  data and econometric methodology 354–60, 365–7t, 368(n5–6)
  data (validity and reliability) 357–8, 365–7
  hypothesis (managerial autonomy has positive impact on firm performance) 354, 360
  incentives: managers 353
  incentives: state shareholders and party members 352–3, 368(n2–3)
  performance measurement 358–9, 360
  proxy variables (disadvantages) 355
  results 361, 362–3t
  reverse-causality problem 360
  social and political goals 351
  types of decisions and reliability test 365–7t
managerial autonomy: measure (MD) 358, 360, 361, 368(n8)
managerial skills 266, 267
managers 10, 83, 352, 354, 355, 356, 368(n2)
  incentives **353**, 363
  'more concerned than politicians with profits' 363
  see also managerial autonomy
Mandatory Provident Fund (MPF, HKSAR, 2000–) 141
manufacturers 6
  brand-owning 225
  foreign 225, 247b
  Indian 66
  USA 99(n10)

manufacturing 79–83, 172–3, 192, 194–8, 198(n4–5), 229–31, 234, 241, **273**, 295, 295(n1), 357
  decline (HK/HKSAR) 188–90
  durable/non-durable goods 73, 74–5, 80t
  environmental impact (China's accession to WTO) **317–26**
  investment (sectoral shares, China, 1981–2000) 280–3t
  labour-intensive 82, 196
  output (impact of China's WTO accession) 321t
  output (rate of expansion) 322
  relative wage rate 193t
  SITC (5–8) 95–6t, 96
  structural change (China) **276–9**
  two-good, multivariety, three-country model 33–5, 38, 42, 46n, 47t, 47n, 48–56, 58t, 59–61
manufacturing output 319, 324, 325
maquiladoras 65
market access 20, 23, 67, 70, 72, 81–2, 245, 246, 318, 320
market capitalization 134, 134t
  H-shares and Red Chips 162–3
market-clearing 73, 85(n1)
market conditions **359**, 363t
market economies 17, 21–2, 23, 276, 361
  development in PRC **171–2**
  global 172
market equilibrium **40–1**, 63(n10–11)
market forces 171
market information 154, 242
market infrastructure **145–6**, 148–9(n17–20)
market integration (HK and Mainland) **173–83**, 183–4, 184(n1)
market mechanism 172, 221
market orientation 294
market prices 37
market rigidity 216
market share 33, 137, 137t, 225, 243, 248
market size 240
market structures 224, 224t, 225
marketing 82, 156, 159, 190, 198(n5), 226, 232, 234

markets   2, 221, 226, 279
  competitive   203, 224t, 256
  domestic   203, 235, 236, 243, 294,
    312
  export   23, 325
  foreign   243, 294
  human resources   224, 224t
  international   243, 312, 316(n46),
    318
  world   223, 234, 255
  see also financial markets
Marxism   152
Mass Transit Railway Corporation   142
Mathematica   45
mathematics   227t
matrix of polynomials   206
Maxam (toothpaste)   249b, 252(n7)
maximum likelihood estimation   194
measurement errors   76
meat   2, 302, 313(n4)
media   242, 356t, 357
medical services (hospital in-patient
    fees)   174, 175t, 178–81t, 182,
    183–4t
medicine   227t, 230t
merchandising   155, 165t, **166**, 168n
  commission rate   166
  gross margin   166
merchanting   155, 165t, **166**, 168n
merchants   154
mergers and acquisitions (M&A)   241,
    250, 251, 330
metallurgy   321t, 322, 323t
metals/metal products   281t, 282t,
    321t, 323t
methodology   171
  black market premium   99(n8)
  'flawed'   123
  Malmquist TFP index   **256–8**, 259,
    266
  measuring policy component of
    trade   **258–9**
  measuring TFP growth   **255–6**
  non-parametric   254, 255–6
  parametric   254, 255–6
  supervisory board in Chinese
    corporate governance   **333–4**,
    335t, 347(n5)
Mexico   22, 65, 66
Microsoft   251, 252(n8)
Midwest (USA)   22

migration (rural–urban)   3–4
military industry   279
millet   313(n4)
minerals   79, 81
Ming Dynasty   1, 298
Mingpao   6
minimum wage   11, 12, 18
mining   73, 80t, 356t, 357
Mininurse (skin-care brand)   250
ministries (Taiwan)   228
  science and technology budget   229t
minority shareholders   10, 339, 341,
    364
Mitsubishi   247b
model-based methodology   99(n8)
models
  two-differentiated product,
    multifactor/four-factor, three-
    country (Saygili and Wong)   3,
    33, 34, **34–41**, 61–2, 62–3(n4–11)
monetary anchor
  nominal   104, 117(n3)
  real   102, 104, 109, 115
monetary authority   105, 106
monetary conditions   108, 109
Monetary Conditions Index   **108–9**,
    118(n10)
monetary instability   215
monetary policy   xii, 10, 179
  flexibility   203
monetary stability   **103–6**, 117(n4–8)
  WCU link   **103–6**, 117(n4–8)
monetary systems   125
money
  'nominal'   105
  nominal demand   204
money demand function   209
money market equilibrium   204
money supply   205, 212–13t, 216
  M1   206
  M2   206
  nominal   204, 210f, 211, 212t, 215
  variance decomposition   212t, 214f
monitoring   329, 331, 332, 332t, 333,
    337, 346, 360
monopolies   353
Monthly Digest of Statistics (Hong
    Kong)   206
Morocco   28
mortgage markets   23
most-favoured nation (MFN)   67, 127

motor fuel   174, 175t, 178–81t, 183–4t
MSG2 model   84–5(n1) 85
Multi-Fibre Agreement (MFA)   318, 325
   quota system   320
multilateral development banks
      (MDBs)   142, 143t
multinational corporations
      (MNCs)   12, 19, 123, 160, 163,
      235, 236, 243, 248, 252
   'abuse of dominant position'   **250–1**,
      252(n8)
   'corporations'   2
   Hong Kong subsidiaries   161
   superiority (technological and
      managerial)   239–40
   technology transfer   242, 252(n3)
   'transnational corporations
      (TNCs)'   68, 69t
Mumbai Stock Exchange   135t
Myanmar   43n, 44n, 46n, 48n

National Agricultural Census Office
      (PRC)   314(n13), 316
National Association of Securities
      Dealers Automated Quotations
      (NASDAQ)   134, 134–5t, 148(n12)
National Bureau of Statistics (NBS,
      PRC)   296, 302n, 308n,
      313–14(n11–12), 316
National Development and Reform
      Centre (PRC): China Price
      Information Centre   174
national financial centre (NFC)   130
National Science Council (NSC),
      Taiwan   231, 236, 237(n15), 238
   budget   229t, 229
   grants   230t
   range of activities 'unique'
      (international perspective)   230
   role   228–30
   Science News   237(n19)
*National Science Council
   Review*   237(n19)
National Social Sciences Foundation
      (China)   273n
'national treatment' principle   127,
      173
nationalism (economic)   79
nationalization   161
natural disasters   298, 313(n5)
natural resources   17, 259

natural sciences   230t
Negotiable Certificates of Deposits   206
negotiation   156
Netherlands   136t, 137, 144t
network cards   9
networks   237(n26)
new issue market   135, 135t
New York   22, 123, 139, 140, 141, 164
   'global financial centre' (GFC)   124,
      129, 137
New York Stock Exchange   134t, 135,
      135t
New Zealand   73, 75–6, 77f, 78f, 148(n4),
newly-industrializing countries
      (NICs)   289
newly-industrializing economies
      (NIEs)   8, 273, 274, 279, 293, 294,
      295(n1)
   differences   222
   institutional evolution
      (Taiwan)   **221–38**
   literature   221
niches   81, 82, 83
Ningxia   268
non-bank financial institutions
      (NBFIs)   126–7, 130, 139
non-performing loans (NPLs)   84,
      128
non-tariff barriers   74, 317, 318
Nordic Investment Bank   143n
normalized cointegrating
      coefficients   113, 114t, 117(n9)
North America   **82**, 141
North Korea   84
North–South agreements (global)   28
Notebook PC Consortium   233
null hypothesis   93, 114t, 181, 177,
      194, 208, 368(n7)
numéraire   41

Office of President (Taiwan)   228
Office of Strategic Industries and
      Economic Security (USA)   252(n4)
offshore banking centres   121, 125
   definition (Johns)   22
offshore financial centres   146
   definition (Roberts)   121–2
offshore funding centres   160, 162
offshore trade (Hong Kong)   155–6,
      156–7, 158f, 165t
   estimation   **166**, 167–8t

on-the-job learning 224t
'one country, two systems' 126, 146
one-standard-error criterion (Shapiro and Watson) 211
one-tier board 331
OPEC 73
Open Lab Business Incubator (OLBI) programme (Taiwan) 230–1
'open standards' 225
Organisation for Economic Co-operation and Development (OECD) 144, 171, 326
  OECD model 320
  OECD statistics 111
  OECD GDP Volume Index (OGDP) 113, 113t, 114t, 117
  Rest of OECD (ROECD) 73
ordinary least squares (OLS) 263, 337, 339–40t, 361t, 368(n7)
  DBDM-type versus firm performance 344–5, 345t
  pooled data 244
organizational change 357, 365t
original design manufacturer (ODM) 233–4f, 234
original equipment manufacturer (OEM) 233, 233–4f, 234
  OEM-ODM contracts 225
  OEM-type contracts 234
output 21, 37, 88, 108, 189–91, 197, 235, 289
  contribution to GDP 193, 193t, 194, 196
  domestic 215, 216, 313(n7)
  global 7
  multiple-currency-denominated 110
  potential 204, 209t, 212–13t
  total 319
  variance decomposition 214f
output effect (PRC's WTO accession) 320–2
  partial and general equilibrium approaches 320
output price 289
outside supervisors 335–6t, 338–9t, 339–46
outsourcing 11, 223, 226, 228
'over-investment' (discussion) 289–94
  ICOR 292–4, 296(n9)
  investment to GDP ratios 289–92
  literature 289

over-the-counter (OTC) derivatives 134
overheating 104, 147, 200
  investment and consumer expenditures 201
overnight lending rates 110
overseas Chinese 295(n6)
overvaluation *see* currency overvaluation
ownership concentration 331

P-value 265n, 339–41t, 345t
Panasonic 247b
Panda detergent 250b
panel data 175, 182, 244
  prices 5, 170, 173, 176–7
panel unit root tests 175, 177
panic 105, 109, 116
paper and printing 321t, 323t
Papua New Guinea 30
'paradox of value' (Boisot) 226, 237(n9)
parent company **140**, 330
parent groups 354
Paris 141, 147(n1), 222
Paris Stock Exchange 134n
patents 225, 244, 246, 247b, 248
Payment versus Payment (PvP) settlement 145
Pearl River Delta 12, 173
Pearson correlation matrix 337, 338t, 361, 362t
peasant income 300, 314(n15), 373
peasant organization 374
Penang (Malaysia) 65
People's Bank of China (PBC) 7, 13(n10), 125–6
  repurchase agreement with HKMA 126
People's Daily 314–15(n21)
perception 102, 110, 355
perfect competition 230, 254
performance appraisal xi, 357, 365–6t
performance factors
science and technology 224t, 226
performance measures, lagged **360**
Permanent Normal Trade Relations (PNTR) Act (USA, 2000) 67
perpetual inventory (assumption) 259, 267

personal services 190
petroleum/oil 2, 23, 106, 241t, 281t, 321t, 322, 323t
  oil crises 5
  oil fields 81
  oil prices 18
pharmaceuticals 27, 248
phenomenology viii
Philippines 43–5n, 48n, 62(n3), 66, 68–79, 80t, 110, 144t, 148(n4)
  see also 'ASEAN-4'
Philips (corporation) 231, 247b
Phillips curve 88, 203, 205, 208
Phillips–Perron (PP) statistics/test 94t, 193, 193t
Pioneer 247b
planning
  failure (China) 237(n18)
  local-level (PRC) 371
polar ice cap 29
policy-makers 236(n2), 256
political connections 5
political reform 164
political will 83
pollution
  air, soil, water 318, 322–5
  impact of trade liberalization 318, **319**, 321t, **322–4**
  public awareness 322
pollution abatement technology 324, 325
pollution intensity 319, 322, 323t, 324
pooled cross-section time-series regression 337
pooled regression results 345n
population xii, 3, 43n, 46n, 263, 263t, 273, 301, 314(n18)
  'geometrical ratio' (Malthus) 297, 313(n1)
  urban 302
population growth 313(n4), 374
pork 174, 175t, 178–81t, 183–4t, 310
ports/container ports 5, 125, 127, 140, 154, 156, 173
portfolio diversification 25
portfolio investment 148(n10), 160, **162–3**
positive sum world **17–18**
post-war era (1945–) 32, 61, 124, 172, 223
pound sterling 103–4, 124

poverty 3, 4, 11, 27, 188
predatory pricing 251
preferences **36–7**, 44, 46t, 61
preferential policies 258
price adjustments 216
price convergence (HK and Mainland) **173–83**, 183–4, 184(n1)
  city-specific fixed effects 182–3
  convergence tendency 177
  half-life 177, 181–2
  test 175–6
price differentials 177, 179, 180
  half-life 176, 182
  regional (sub-national) 63(n6)
price discrepancies 177
price dispersion 179–80
price indices 268(n2)
  investment 267
price level 109, 117(n3)
  aggregate 205
  domestic 117, 117(n6)
price reform 172
price rigidity 117(n6)
price stability 84, 102
prices 18, 81, 89, 290t
  categories (PRC) 172
  domestic 55, 105, 202, 215, 216
  export 88
  farm gate 314(n14)
  grain 297
  import 204, 205, 208, 209t, 209, 211, 214f
  international 216, 312
  relative 92, 93, 94t, 292
  relative change 289, 290
  unit root tests 93, 94t
  variance decomposition 214f
  world system 203
PricewaterhouseCoopers website 45n
principal–agency approach 360
private sector 222, 224t, 230, **231–4**, 236, 237(n21–5), 295
  failure (California) 237(n18)
private sector savings deficiency 107
privatization 10, 364
processes, new 243
processing 159
  labour-intensive 264
Procter & Gamble (P&G) 250b
product cycles 82, 226, 359

product design 159
product markets, highly regulated 353
product quality 243, 252(n3)
production 36, 47n, 68, 154, 171, 255,
  257, 368(n4)
  gross domestic 258
  industrial 170, 235
  labour-intensive 294
  non-stochastic quadratic cost 89
  South China 158
production capacities 252(n3)
production chain 81, 82, 83, 159, 164
production costs 310
production fragmentation 1
production frontier 256
production growth
  decomposition 257, 258f
production processes 225, 266
production sector 73
production technology 189, 319
  definition 256
productivity 3, 8, 12, 31, 57, 61, 189,
  223, 243, 244, 254, 266, 267, 351
  growth rate 295(n1)
productivity gap 184
products 38, 176, 259
  agricultural 174
  differentiated 34, 35
  foreign 243
  industrial 84, 320
  labour-intensive 84, 309, 310
  land-intensive 309, 310
  new 226, 236, 242, 243
products and services
  semi-tradable goods 174, 175t,
    177–82, 182, 183t, 184t
  services 174, 175t, 177–84
  tradable goods 174, 175t, 175,
    177–84
profit-maximization 10, 11, **37–40**,
  254–5, 256, 337, 341, 350, 351,
  361
profitability 226, 233f, 347(n5), 372
profits 2, 198(n4), 246, 331, 353, 354,
  359
  Hitachi 237(n11)
profits tax 142, 143n
project selection 331
property prices 24
protectionism 2–3, 4, 19, 20, 67
public ownership 171

public sector viii, 222, 224t, 226, 231,
  236, 256, 264–5, 267
  research budgets 228
public sector deficits 223
purchasing power 7, 12, 26, 103, 105,
  110
  constant 111
  real 105, 106
Purchasing Power of Money (Fisher,
  1911) 7
purchasing power parity (PPP) 92, 93,
  97, 171, 175

Qinghai 268
Qualified Debt Instruments
  (QDIs) 142
Qualified Foreign Institutional
  Investors' Scheme (PRC,
  2002–) 368(n3)
quality control 227
quan shehui guding zichan touzi e (total
  social investment in fixed
  assets) 274, 275t, 295(n2)
questionnaires 355–8
  non-response bias 357
  respondent bias 357
  response rate 355
  types of decisions and reliability
    test 365–7t
quota restrictions 318

railways 316(n41)
rainforests 30, 31
random effects 244
ratios
  government expenditure to
    GDP 264, 265t, 266
  investment to GDP **289–92**
raw materials 242, 247b, 225
re-exports (entrepôt trade) 155, 156,
  159, 166, 173
  HK/HKSAR (1991–2004) 168t
re-insurance 142, 145
real economy 104
Real Effective Exchange Rate
  index 108f, 117
real estate 47n, 142, 189, 192, 194–8,
  295(n2), 356t
  relative wage rate 193t
real estate investment trusts
  (REITs) 145

real exchange rate (RER) 88–92, 96, 98–9(n1), 99(n8), 102–8, 116, 117, 203, 204, 321t
  effective 105
  PPP 97
  unintended change 117(n3)
  WCU/HKD 113
real exchange rate anchors 103
real exchange rate fluctuations 103
real exchange rate targeting 103
real exchange rate misalignment (RERM): effects on commodity exports (China) **87–100**
  absolute form 92
real exchange rate volatility (RERV) **87–100**
real monetary anchor *see* monetary anchor
real monetary unit standard 115
real money balance 102
real property market (HKSAR) 132
Real Time Gross Settlement (RTGS) 145
reciprocity 127
Red Chips 130, 131t
reform, organizational 203
regional (supra-national) financial centres (RFCs) 124, 147(n3)
regional headquarters (RHQs) **139–41**, 163, 168(n2)
  definition **140**
regional office (RO) **140**
regions
  sub-national 63(n6), 300
  supra-national 124, 140, 147(n3)
regulation failure (California) 237(n18)
regulations 127, 252, 252(n8)
regulatory authorities 122, 330
regulatory environment 164
remittance 129
renminbi (RMB) 11, 26, 89, 92, 115, 125–7, 129, 130, 163
  appreciation against US dollar (21 July 2005) 7
  convertibility (prospective) 110, 372
  exchange rate 'controlled by central government' 98–9(n1)
  Hong Kong dollars and **6–8**, 13(n10)
  liberalization 101
  managed float system (2005–) 7, 102

misalignment against foreign currencies 98f, 99(n3)
  'no timetable for full convertibility' 126
  overvaluation 103
  re-pegged to basket of currencies 97
  real exchange rate 91
  revaluation 88, 99(n10), 102, 103
  undervaluation 88, 97
  USD exchange rate 87
renovation and renewals 280–3t
rent-seeking society (PRC) 353
Report on Hong Kong Trade in Services for 2003 165n
representative offices 163, 168(n2)
research 228
  integration (public and private sectors, Taiwan) 229
  material sciences 235
  private sector 228, 230
  'pure' 223, 224t
research consortia 232
research and development 222, 224, 224t, 234f, 235, 236, 245
  budget 225
  expenditures 231
  industrial application 223
  R&D/GDP ratio 229
  R&D personnel 243
research grants (Taiwan) 229, 231
reserve assets 103, 105
  diversification 25
  new 101, **106–7**, 111
  US dollar 106
reserve currencies 126
  alternatives to US dollar 25, 26–7
reserve system (international) PRC's role in reform **23–7**
resource allocation 53, 56, 203, 266
restaurants 192–8, 353
  relative wage rate 193t
restricted licence banks (RLBs) 143n
retail sector/systems 6, 171–2, 192–8, 356t, 357
  relative wage rate 193t
retail price index (RPI) 92, 93
return on assets (ROA) 333, 335–6t, 337, 338t, 339, 340t, 342–3t, 344, 345t, 347(n5), 358, 360, 361, 362t, 363t

return on equity (ROE) 333, 335t, 336t, 337, 338t, 339, 341t, 342–3t, 347(n5–6)

return on sales (ROS) 358, 360, 361, 362–3t

reverse engineering 242

reverse-causality problem 360

rice 174, 175t, 178t–81t, 183–4t, 312, 313(n4), 314(n21)
  imports (into PRC) 304
  imports and exports (China) 305–6t, 307, 315(n30)

rising tide 'raises all ships' (concept) 81

risk 23, 24, 25, 87, 102, 106, 110, 118(n11), 128, 145, 155, 163, 164, 226
  empirical analysis 88
  financial and technological 228
  industry's attitude 88

risk premium (for investors) 68, **72**, **74**, 76f, **77**

risk-aversion 87, 88, 89, **90**, 91, 96, 97

risk-loving **90**

risk-neutrality **90**

risk-taking 224

RMB *see* renminbi

rule of law 5, 146
  international 20

rules of game 23, 31, 239, 245, 251

rules and regulations 258

rural areas 172, 273, 295(n2)
  economic diversification 299
  underemployment 3

rural development (reform era China) **299–301**, 313–14(n11–17)

rural population (PRC) 313(n11)

rural society **299**

Russia 81

sanctions, international 67

Sarawak viii

SARS epidemic (2003) 121, 132, 134, 136, 137, 141, 146

savers 25, 116, 139

savings 23, 206

scale effect (pollution impact of trade liberalization) 9, **319**, 321t, **322**, 324t, 325

Schumpeterian model 224t

Schwarz Criterion 94n

science parks 227, 229, 231, 236, 237(n18)

science and technology 148(n16), 229, 237(n15)
  policy problems 225

Science and Technology Plan (Taiwan, 2005–8) 237(n16)

scientific base 75

scientific research (publicly-funded) 222, 237(n3)

scientists/scientific workers 83, 222

Second Land Reform (PRC) 373

securities 124, 125, 128–9, 142

Securities and Futures Commission (SFC, HK, 1989–) 129, 141, 141n, 145

Securities and Futures Ordinance 129

seed 301, 314(n18)

Seemingly Unrelated Regression (SUR) methodology 88, 95–6t

seigniorage 111, 106

semi-conductors 237(n11)

serial correlation 176

service exports
  HK's Mainland-related 164, 165t, 166

service hub (HKSAR) **163–4**, 168(n2)

service sector 155, 166, 190, 318
  HK/HKSAR 189
  included under 'agriculture' 62(n4)
  labour-intensive 189
  under-development (PRC) 152

services 73, 75, 80t, 174, 197
  managerial 236
  neither land-intensive nor labour-intensive 164
  professional 163, 166
  pure 166
  value-adding 77, 82, 164
  see also agriculture

services market (China) 320

set-aside policies 298

Shaanxi 268

Shandong 267

Shanghai xiv, 12–13(n8–9), 101, 126, 141, 147, 152, 164, 170, 173, 177, 178t, 182, 183, 267
  advantage of location 163
  'domestic financial centre of China' 163

Shanghai: New Pudong Area 130

Shanghai Stock Exchange (SHSE) 333, 355–9, 368(n1)
Shanghai Stock Exchange survey (SSES) 351, 352, 353
Corporate Governance of China's Listed Firms 368(n1), 370
Shanghai Toothpaste Factory (STF) 249b
Shanxi 264, 265, 268, 268(n6)
Shapiro 218
one-standard-error criterion 211
shareholders 141, 350, 354, 361, 364, 368(n2)
dominant shareholder 331
largest 355–8, 360, 362t, 363t, 365–7t
rights and duties (PRC) 352
shareholders' meetings 10, 329, 330
shareholding, state-owned 347
shares 353
one-share, one vote rule (departures) 368(n5)
turnover velocity 358–9
shares: types (PRC listed companies) 368(n3)
A-shares 356, 357, 368(n3)
B-shares 356, 368(n3)
legal person shares 352, 360, 368(n3, n5)
state shares 360, 368(n3, n5)
Shenzhen 101, 130, 152, 156–7, 170, 173, 174, 178t, 182, 183
benchmark city 177, 179, 181
Shenzhen: Bao An District 247b
Shenzhen Stock Exchange (SZSE) 333
shipping 18, 154, 156
shocks 32, 34, 81, 83, 84, 121, 310
CPI 215
demand 215
domestic demand 215
domestic price 216
effective exchange, effective 215
foreign inflation 215
identification in IS-LM model **206–8**, 209, 210f, 211, 217(n1)
import price 215
interest rate 215
monetary 205
money supply 215, 216
stochastic 205

structural 203–4, 205, 207
US interest rate 215
short-term random events 107
Sichuan 268
Silk Road 1
simulation 74–80
Singapore 43n, 45n, 48n, 62(n3), 69t, 71t, 72, 73, 82, 124, 132, 133t, 136t, 137, 138, 138t, 140, 141, 144t, 145, 146, 148(n4, n16), 149(n22), 155, 221, 254, 276, 279, 287, 289, 293, 295(n3–4), 296(n9)
'constrained by mini-size status' 255
development contrasted from that of Taiwan 235
search for niche 66
single currency links 103, 116
Sino–US economic relations 371
SITC 93, 95–6t, 96, 237(n6)
6Cs (Hitachi, Panasonic, Mitsubishi, Time Warner, Toshiba, JVC) 247b
skills 189, 197, 226, 233, 234f
dissemination 228
upgraded 190
skyscrapers 156
'social networks of capital' (Meyer) 124
social polarization 300
social safety net 2, 11, 17
social services 21, 356t
social stability 352
social welfare 368(n4)
socialist economy 22
socialist market economy x, 172
'society' 221
sociology 124
soft budget constraints 264
soil 318, 322–5
Sony 247b
sorghum 313(n4)
sources of growth (debate) 221
South Africa 135t, 144t
South China/southern China 158, 159, 259, 371
relocation by HK firms 172–3, 188–9, 198(n4)
South China Sea 67, 84
South-East Asia 3, 25, 66, 72, 81, 82, 140, 141
South–South agreements 28

Southern (Tainan) Science Park
　(1995–)　231
soybeans　307, 310, 312, 313(n4),
　314(n20)
　cost of imports (PRC)　315–16(n37)
　cultivation discouraged　315(n36)
　imports (PRC)　307, 308t, 315(n34)
　'largest importer in world' (China,
　　2003–)　307, 315(n32)
　prices　315–16(n37)
　production, exports, imports (PRC
　　1985–2004)　308t
　Sino–US trade (1997–2003)　310,
　　311t, 316(n41, 44)
Spain　12(n5), 134–6t, 137
Special Economic Zones　240
specialization　*see* division of labour
speculation/speculators　105, 145, 358–9
spillovers　74, 78f, 79, 80t, 239–52
spot price data (HKSAR)　174
Spring Festival　4
stability (*wending*)　10
　trade-off versus restructuring　83–5
staff recruitment　231
Stalinists　84
standardization　234
Stanford　231
Startup Index　71n
State Administration for Foreign
　Exchange (SAFE, PRC)　102
State Administration for Industry and
　Commerce (SAIC, PRC)　250–1, 253
state asset management
　agencies　368(n3)
state budget (China)　287, 295(n7)
State Development and Planning
　Commission (PRC)　251
State Economic and Trade Commission
　(PRC)　251
State Environmental Protection Agency
　(SEPA, PRC)　324
state-owned banks (SOBs)　84, 128, 129
state-owned enterprises (SOEs)　10, 84,
　241, 264–7, 295(n2), 317, 352, 353,
　368(n3)
　decision-making　351
　lay-offs　300
　'low efficiency' finding
　　confirmed　266
　multi-task theory (Bai *et al.*,
　　2000)　368(n4)

PRC　130, 135
　reform　368(n4)
state shareholders　351, 361, 368(n4)
　incentives　**352–3**
state shareholding　**360**, 362t, 363t,
　368(n5–6)
state trading system　317
statistical bias　153
statistical data　123
Statistical Yearbook (China)　244
statutory bodies　142, 143t
steady state　85(n1)
　neo-classical growth equilibrium
　　73
steel　2, 12(n2), 18, 20, 67
stochastic maximization process　88
stochastic trend　194
stock markets　5, 123, 134, 134t, 135t,
　330
　PRC　130
　Thailand　110
stock options　353
stock prices　2
Stolper–Samuelson theorem　19, 186,
　190, 191, 198
Straits Times　66, 70
strategic planning　357, 366–7t
structural adjustment　83
structural change
　manufacturing sector
　　(China)　**276–9**, **280–3t**
sub-contracting　227, 228, 232,
　233f
Sub-Saharan Africa　21, 297, 299
subsidies　223, 297–8, 313(n8), 351
　agricultural　21
　direct to grain farmers (PRC)　**301**
　export　21
　non-trade-distorting　21
　production　21
subsistence　12, 302, 314(n18)
　'increases in arithmetical ratio'
　　(Malthus)　297, 313(n1)
substitution　*see* currency substitution
sugar　174, 175t, 178–81t, 183–4t
'super disintegration' (Shih)　225–6,
　234
supervisors　329
　formal responsibilities　331
　insider　**330**, 332, 337, 347(n2)
　outsider　**331**, 332, 337

supervisory board   332, 333
  and firm performance (hypothesis
      1)   **331**, 339t, 339, 340t, 340,
      341t
Supervisory Board: Chairman   332
  insider/outsider   332t, 333, 335t,
      341, 342–3t, 345–6
supervisory board in Chinese corporate
      governance   **329–49**
  descriptive statistics   336t, 342t
  domination by insiders with limited
      independence   329–30
  dual-board diagnostic model   332–3,
      340–6, 347(n6)
  empirical results   334, 336t, 337–40,
      341t
  employee representatives   330
  existing literature   329, 331
  findings   329
  hypothesis   1 (firm performance
      affected by supervisory board
      composition)   **331**, 339t, 339, 346
  hypothesis   2 (firm performance
      varies according to DBDM
      type)   **333**, 341, 343, 346
  insiders   329–30
  introduction   329–30
  outsiders   330
  regressions   337, 339t, 340t, 341t
  supervisory board (role and
      composition)   330–1, 347(n1–3)
  two-tier board structure   331–4, 335t,
      347(n4–5)
  variables   334, 335t, 338t
supervisory boards   10, 355
  composition   337, 341, 343, 346
  efficiency   334
  independence   332t, 337, 341, 344,
      346, 347, 347(n4)
  frequency of meetings   334–46
  monitoring role   332t, 333, 337
  'more decorative than functional'
      (Tenev, Zhang, Brefort)   368(n2)
  problem-solving capabilities   333
  size   334–46
  structure   346, 347
suppliers (local)   243, 252(n3)
supply and demand   12, 18, 154, 299,
      302
  currency   107
  labour   3

surveys   166
sustainability (buzzword)   10–11
sustainable currency regime for HKSAR
      and PRC   **101–18**
  chapter thesis   102, 103
  credibility   110–11
  data sources   116–17
  existing literature   107
  implications for world   111–16,
      117–18(n9–11)
  new reserve assets and international
      settlement vehicle   106–7
  right exchange rate   107–10
  search for efficient managed
      adjustment mechanism   102
  simulation exercise   113–15
  variables (listed)   117
  WCU link for macroeconomic and
      monetary stability   103–6,
      117(n4–8)
sustainable development   **28–30**, 371
'swap market for technology'   239,
      242–4, 252(n1–3)
Swiss Stock Exchange   134t
Switzerland   71t, 122, 133t, 136t, 137,
      138t, 141, 144t

taboos   81
Taipei   141
Taiwan   9, 66, 69t, 71t, 72–3, 75f, 76,
      77–8f, 82, 84, 127, 130, 138t, 147,
      148(n4), 188, 254, 276, 287, 289,
      293, 295(n5–6), 296(n9), 373
  multi-party era   228
  returnees   231, 237(n12)
Taiwan: Department of Health   229f, 229t
Taiwan: Ministry of Economic Affairs
      (MOEA)   229f, 229t, 229, 231, 232
Taiwan: Ministry of Education   229f,
      229t
Taiwan: Ministry of Transport and
      Communications   229f, 229t
Taiwan: scientific and technological
      development   **221–38**
  background   221–3, 236–7(n1–5)
  central government budget   228, 229t
  company histories   237(n21)
  contrasted from other NIEs   222,
      235–6, 237(n21)
  direct government leadership and
      expenditure   228–31

Taiwan: scientific and technological
    development – *continued*
  divergence (public versus private
    interests)   233f, 236
  framework   224–6, 237(n6–11)
  human resource development   227–8
  'limits reached to most recent
    phase'   222
  literature   221
  performance factors   224t, 224–5,
    226
  private sector   231–4, 237(n21–5)
  public sector administration   228,
    229f
  share of world markets (2003)   226t
  stress and strain   236
  trends   221
  vision, strategy, tactics   228–9, 232,
    233f
Taiwan Electronic and Electrical
    Manufacturers' Association
    (TEEMA)   232
Taiwan Semi-Conductor Manufacturing
    Company (TSMC)   231–2,
    237(n12)
Taiwan Stock Exchange   135t
takeovers   353, 354
tariff barriers (TBs)   74, 317, 318
tariff rates   34, 42, 58
  unilateral reduction   72
tariff-rate quotas (TRQs)   307,
    315(n33), 320
tariff-reduction   52, 68, 72, 320
tariffs   258, 129 35, 37, 44t, 67
  lost revenues   56
tax concessions   122, 143n, 240, 242
tax havens   135, 148(n13), 153, 162f
  'second-largest investor in
    Mainland'   161
taxi fares   174, 175t, 178–81t, 183–4t
tax policy   179
tax rates   37, 41, 58
  effective   43, 57
tax revenue   37, 55
tax system, progressivity   19
tax treatment   142
taxation   124
  corporate   42, 43, 45t, 47n, 53, 56, 58
  effective   52
taxes   29, 107, 122, 127, 301
  illegal   314(n14)

tea production   252(n7)
technical assistance   252(n3)
technical effect (pollution impact of
    trade liberalization)   9, **319**, **322–4**
technical know-how   2
technological capacity (overall)   70,
    71t, 71n, 72
technological change
  four phases   233, 234f, 234
technological diffusion   75, 79, 83,
    84
  link with FDI   70, 71t
technological frontier economy   225
technological progress   **254–69**
'technological standing' (PRC)   9
technological versatility   81
technology   2, **8–9**, 13(n11–12), 17, 19,
    23, 31, **36–7**, 44, 47t, 61, 197, 254,
    256, 373, 374
  advanced   242, 246, 251–2, 267
  constant-returns-to-scale   320
  foreign   244, 248, 267
  labour-intensive   274
  new/state-of-the-art   75, 145, 242,
    255
technology gap learning theory   244
technology gaps   19
technology institutions   227
technology licensing   243, 246
technology targeting/targets   229, 230
technology transfer   8, 19, 70, 73, 234f,
    235, 236, 266
  competition effect   246
  forced   **245–6**, 252
  spillover effects (China)   239, **242–4**,
    252(n1–3)
  'swap market for technology'   239,
    242–4, 251–2, 252(n1–3)
  voluntary   245
technology transfer index   71t, 71n, 72
telecommunications   6, 132
televisions   237(n22), 248
tenants   149(n20)
terms of trade   56, 56t, 57, 61, 321t
test statistics   114t, 193–4
  maximal-eigenvalue   194, 195t
  trace   194, 195t
Texas Instruments   237(n12)
textiles   23, 191, 235, 241t, 244, 279,
    282t, 318, 320, 321t, 322, 323t
Thai baht   110

Thailand   25, 43–5n, 48n, 62(n3), 66,
    68–79, 80t, 102, 110, 148(n4), 276,
    279, 293
  see also 'ASEAN-4'
theory
  effects of RERV and RERM on
      commodity exports   87, **88–91**,
      97, 99(n4–6)
  effects of trade on wage
      inequality   **190–1**, 198(n2–4)
  HKSAR's role as China's
      middleman   152
  impact of trade policy on growth of
      TFP, efficiency and
      technology   264
  impulse response analysis   217(n2)
  intermediation   **153–5**
  investment and economic
      growth   295
  LOP   171
  partial and general equilibrium
      approaches   320
  PPP   171
  trade   28
  trade diversion   156
Thomson (company)   247b
3Cs (Philips, Pioneer, Sony)   247b
three-country model (unilateral and
      regional trade
      liberalization)   **34–41**,
      62–3(n4–11)
  ASEAN   33–5, 37, 40, 42–62
  China   33–5, 36, 37, 40, 42–62
  factor endowments   42, 43t, 51,
      61
  rest of world (ROW)   33–5, 37, 40,
      42–62
Tiananmen (1989)   259, 293
Tianjin   267
Tibet   84, 268(n1)
Tide (P&G detergent)   250b
tied sales   251
Time Warner   247b
time-series data   175, 194, 208, 337
  pooled   244
  univariate trend   193
Tobin's Q   333, 335–6t, 337–40,
    342–3t, 344, 347(n5–6)
Tokyo   124, 132, 137, 139, 140, 141,
    146, 147(n1)
  'global financial centre' (GFC)   124

Tokyo Stock Exchange   134t, 135t
toothpaste   240, 248, 249b
Toronto Stock Exchange   134t, 135t
Toshiba   247b
total factor productivity (TFP)   70,
    254–69
  growth   **255–6**
  growth (Chinese
      provinces)   **259–63**, **267–8**,
      268(n1–5)
  growth (impact of trade
      policy)   **264–6**, 268(n6)
  Malmquist index   **256–8**, 259, 266
total factor productivity growth
  primary source   261
  'residual'   256
total factor productivity growth
    rate   **74–5**
tourism   6, 132, 140, 165t, 166, 236
township and village enterprises
    (TVEs)   279, 293–4, 295
trade   xiii, xiv, 7, 8, 31, 48, 53t, 59, 62,
    115, 140, 152, 154, 186, 236, 255,
    373
  agricultural   318
  bilateral   82
  bilateral (Hong Kong–China)   170,
      173, 188, 191–6, 198
  direct   153
  East Asia   225, 237(n6)
  foreign   ix, 51, 153, 164
  import/export   192–8
  indirect   153
  inter-industry   34, 35, 50t, 51, 221
  international   33, 82, 160, 259, 273
  intra-industry   33–5, 50t, 51, 55t, 55,
      60, 60t, 62, 63(n12, n16)
  intra-regional   3, 33–5, 50t, 51, 55t,
      55, 60, 60t, 62, 63(n12, n16), 221
  measuring policy component
      258–9
  merchandise   2, 163
  multilateral system   81
  North–South (global)   191
  'positive factor for productivity
      growth' (Chen)   8–9
  relative wage rate   193t
  Sino–US   310, 372
  structural factors influencing   258–9
  USA–Mexico   188
trade associations (TAs)   232, 233f

trade balance 48, 49t, 63(n16), 202, 320
  farm products (PRC) 308
  Sino–US 372
trade barriers 74, 246
trade decentralization 153
trade diversion 59–60, 158
trade financing 156, 203
trade imbalance 51, 73
trade, investment, and implications for
    key economic sectors **271–326**
  China: investment, investment
    efficiency and economic
    growth **273–96**
  China: WTO accession
    (environmental impact on
    manufacturing sector) **317–26**
  grain: developments past and future
    (China) **297–316**
trade issues 11
trade liberalization 66–7, 318
  China's WTO accession and FTA with
    ASEAN **32–64**
  multilateral 61
trade liberalization: unilateral and
    regional **32–64**
  assumption that no capital flows from
    PRC or ASEAN to ROW 35, 37,
    63(n7, n10, n17)
  assumptions 42
  benchmark (before PRC's accession to
    WTO) 34, 45, 48–51, 63(n12)
  'best guess' **62**
  data sources 42
  first-order conditions 38
  further research required **62**
  'important point' 51
  market equilibrium 40–1,
    63(n10–11)
  maximization problems 37, 38
  preferences and technologies 36–7, 61
  scenario 1 (PRC member of WTO but
    before PRC-ASEAN FTA) 34,
    51–7, 63(n13–15)
  scenario 2 (PRC member of WTO and
    after PRC-ASEAN FTA) 34,
    58–61, 63(n16–17)
  simulation and the
    benchmark 41–51
  solving the system 41–5, 46–8t
  three-country model 34–41,
    62–3(n4–11)

reduced-form equations 41
two-good, multivariety/four-factor,
    three-country model 3, 33, 34,
    61–2
utility and profit-
    maximization 37–40, 63(n9)
values of parameters 42
trade negotiations
  bilateral 28
  fair agreement 27–8, 31
  'hand-up', not handout 28
  multilateral 27–8
trade openness 132, 198(n2), 258
trade orientation 221
trade policy
  'revealed' 258–9, **263–4**
trade policy: impact on TFP, efficiency,
    and technology **254–69**
  empirical results 259–66
  estimating capital stock 267
  existing literature 254–5, 266
  'flying geese' hypothesis
    supported 261
  list of regions and provinces
    267–8
  'low efficiency' finding (SOEs)
    confirmed 266
  methodological and conceptual
    issues 255–9
  TRAPOL residual 263–5, 266–7
trade restrictions 63(n14)
trade sanctions 310
trade secrets 245
trade volume 48, 49t
  observed **255**, 258, 263–4, 265–6
trading 156, 164
trading centres/hubs 154, 171
trading companies 153, 154
trading services 154, 158
training 83, 227, 232, 236, 243,
    252(n3)
transaction costs 153, 155, 182
transistor screens 234f
transitional economies 22, 256, 266,
    273, 363–4
transparency 111, 116, 127, 128, 164,
    317
transport/transportation 6, 140,
    163, 165t, 166, 172, 232, 310,
    316(n41)
  national networks 293

transportation costs   35–6, 44, 46t,
    63(n8, n14), 155, 176, 177, 259
transportation equipment   241t, 281t
transportation hubs   154
transportation services (sector)   192,
    194–8
  relative wage rate   193t
transportation, storage, and postal
    (sector)   356t
transshipment   154
travel   6, 13(n9), 155, 353
tropical countries   30
trucking   156
Turkey   xiii
two-good, multivariety, three-country
    model (unilateral and regional trade
    liberalization)   3, 33, 61–2
  benchmark (before PRC's accession to
      WTO)   34, 42, 44–5t, **45**, **48–51**,
      53–4n, 55, 56–7t, 63(n12)
  scenario 1 (PRC member of WTO but
      before PRC-ASEAN FTA)   34,
      41–3, 44–5t, **51–7**, 58n–60n, 62,
      63(n13–15)
  scenario 2 (PRC member of WTO and
      after PRC-ASEAN FTA)   34, 41,
      42, 44–5t, 56–7t, **58–61**, 62,
      63(n16–17)
two-tier board structure   **331–4**, 335t,
    347(n4–5)

UN statistics   188
uncertainty   67, 87, 98–9(n1), 99(n2),
    121, 146, 256
uncovered interest parity (UIP)
    condition   204, 205, 209
unemployment   18, 73, 116, 117(n6),
    132, 191–4, 195t, 197
  avoided (HK, 1980s, early
      1990s)   189
  manufacturing sector   83
  UK   103, 117(n5)
  urban   84
  USA   99(n10)
Unilever   249b, 252(n7)
Unilever (China) Limited   249b
unit root   175, 181, 182, 194
  nominal exchange rates   93, 94t
United Kingdom   69t, 93, 94t, 103–4,
    117(n5), 121, 124, 133t, 134, 136t,
    138, 138t, 139, 141, 144t, 225

United Microelectronics Corporation
    (UMC)   231, 232
United States of America   xi–xiv, 2, 4,
    6, 9, 24, 27, 30, 33, 34, 43–8n, 62,
    68, 71t, 73, 75–7, 77f, 78f, 93, 94t,
    96t, 96, 98f, 104, 133t, 134, 136t,
    138–9, 141, 144t, 160, 170, 171,
    186, 187, 190, 201, 208, 221–3, 227,
    232, 234, 236, 239, 274, 297, 310,
    325
  banking regulation (nineteenth-
      century)   22
  bilateral trade agreements   28
  'built-in incentive to depreciate its
      currency'   106
  challenged   **18–20**
  declining global dependence   3
  dependence of farmers on Chinese
      market   316(n41)
  exports of maize/wheat to
      China   312
  fiscal and trade deficits   20, 26
  free trade agreement with
      Morocco   28
  GDP   19
  'makes enemies'   28
  PRC's biggest export market   67
  real income (median household)   19
  scientific performance
      (factors)   224t, 225
  shrinking weight in HKSAR's foreign
      trade 8
  strains on economy   **19–20**
  theory of mutual inter-dependence
      (with PRC)   26
  world's 'consumer of last resort'   25
  'world's richest country'   20
universities   xi–xiv, 81, 228, 235, 236
  Harvard   viii
  research-funding   237(n3)
university enrolment   227
University of Macau   200n
urban areas   *see* cities
Uruguay Round   20–1, 28
US: Census Bureau   316(n43)
US: Department of
    Commerce   316(n43)
'US Commercial Technology Transfers
    to PRC'   252(n4)
US cities   182
  price differentials   179, 184(n1)

US Congress   65n, 67
US Department of Commerce
   website   47n
US Department of Agriculture
   (USDA)   308n, 312, 314(n21),
   315(n30), 316(n38)
   website   308n
US dollar   7–8, 24, 25, 93, 104–6,
   110–15, 117, 117(n8), 124, 148(n17)
   appreciation against WCU   111,
   112f, 112–13
   Hong Kong dollar pegged (1983–)   to
   7, 200–1, **202–3**, 205, 215, 216,
   372
   reserve asset   106
   RMB exchange rate   87, 88
US Federal Reserve Bank   200, 206
US Treasury   99(n10), 127, 151
   bills   24
   obligations   126
utility   **37–40**
utility function   88, 89, 99(n5)

value-added   158, 159, 244
value chains   226, 233, 233f, 234, 236,
   237(n25)
variance decomposition analysis   201,
   204, 205, 209, 211–15
vector auto-regression (VAR)   8, 94n,
   114n, 194
   linear   217
   non-linear   217
   reduced form   208, 209
   standard structural   217(n1)
   structural   201, 204, 205, 206, 211
vegetable oils   315(n34)
vegetables   309–10
vendor finance   26
vested interests   221, 300
Vietnam   11, 43n, 45n, 48n, 69t
violence   314(n14)

wage equalization   19
wage gap (skilled versus unskilled
   labour)   **186–99**
wage levels/rates   41, 117(n6)
wage–rental ratio   57, 61, 63(n15)
wages   2, 11–12, 164
   downward pressure   18, 19
   rigidity   85(n1), 117(n6)
   stickiness   73

Walras's law/model   41, 63(n11), 153
warehousing   154, 156
Washington Consensus   27
Washington Council on International
   Trade   252(n6), 253
water   9, 13(n13), 231, 310, 318, 322–5
Watson   211, 218
weather/climate   303, 313(n5), 373,
   374
   drought/flood   298
websites   13(n12), 43n–48n
   AP–GCUBED model   84–5(n1)
   Bank of Canada   118(n10)
   China: Ministry of Commerce   253,
   315(n30)
   'findarticles'   315(n22)
   GCUBED model   85
   HKTDC   168
   US Federal Reserve Bank   206
   US–China Business Council   253
   USDA   308n
   Washington Council on International
   Trade   252(n6), 253
   World Federation of
   Exchanges   134n
welfare   33, 51, 62
   PRC–ASEAN FTA   60, 60t, 61
   WTO–accession (PRC)   55, 56t, 56,
   61(n13)
welfare gains   223, 310
wending yadao yice (stability dominates
   everything)   10
West Germany   viii
Western Europe   **82**
wheat   304, 310, 313(n4), 314(n21)
   Argentina's harvest versus PRC's
   shortfall (2004)   313(n9)
   imports and exports (China)   305–6t,
   307, 312
   'largest importer in world' (China,
   2004)   307
   Sino–US trade (1997–2003)   310,
   311t, 316(n41, 44)
wheat stocks   304, 315(n22)
White test   368(n7)
wholesale sector   171–2, 192–8, 356t,
   357
   relative wage rate   193t
Wind Information Company Limited
   (Shanghai)   359
women   11–12, 117(n5)

wood and furniture 321t, 323t
workers 42, 57, 61, 79, 190
  displaced 83
  fixed-term contract 351
  'lack incentives' 254
  skilled 242, 243
  unskilled 1–2, 3, 4, 18–19, 190
workers (Hong Kong unskilled): effect of
    economic integration between
    Hong Kong and Mainland
    China **186–99**
working poor 12
World Bank (International Bank for
    Reconstruction and
    Development) xiii, 43n, 143n, 151
World Competitiveness Report 70
World Currency Unit (Ho's
    proposal) 7, 11, 107, 109–14, 116,
    117
  bonds 104
  composition of basket 111
  economic zones 104, 117(n7)
  exchange ratios 111
  nominal value 104
  output basket 104–5
World Currency Unit link 114
  macroeconomic and monetary
    stability **103–6**, 117(n4–8)
World Economic Forum 70, 71n,
    86
  qualitative indicators of banking and
    finance 138, 138t, 148(n16),
    151
world economy *see* global economy

World Federation of Exchanges
    (WFE) 134, 134n
World Penn Tables 43n, 48n
world trade 155, 317
World Trade Organization
  dispute-settlement mechanism 246,
    320
  website 44n
  see also China: WTO accession
World Trade Organization: Agreement
    on Textiles and Clothing 320
World Trade Organization: Agreement
    on Trade-Related Investment
    Measures (TRIMs) 245
World War II 130, 222

Xiamen 101
Xi'an Jiaotong University (Xi'an)
    32n
Xinhua News Agency
    (XHNA) 314(n15)
Xinjiang 268

Yangzi Delta 163
youth 224t
Yue-Sai 250
Yunnan 268

zero-sum game/mentality 17, 18
zero sum versus positive sum **2–4**,
    12(n2–4)
Zhejiang 13(n9), 267
Zhonghua toothpaste 249b, 252(n7)
Zhuhai 101